MW01025526

CORPORATE LAW

THIRD EDITION

by

STEPHEN M. BAINBRIDGE
William D. Warren Distinguished Professor of Law
UCLA School of Law

CONCEPTS AND INSIGHTS SERIES®

Concepts and Insights Series is a trademark registered in the U.S. Patent and Trademark Office.

© 2002 FOUNDATION PRESS
© 2009 By THOMSON REUTERS/FOUNDATION PRESS
© 2015 LEG, Inc. d/b/a West Academic

    444 Cedar Street, Suite 700
    St. Paul, MN 55101
    1-877-888-1330

Printed in the United States of America

ISBN: 978-1-60930-471-3

SUMMARY OF CONTENTS

TABLE OF CONTENTS

CORPORATE LAW

THIRD EDITION

Chapter 1

AN INTRODUCTION TO THE CORPORATION

§ 1.1   What Is a Corporation?

A leading legal dictionary defines the corporation as "an artificial person or legal entity created by or under the authority of the laws of a state or nation. . . ."[1] Although technically correct, this definition is not especially enlightening. It's more helpful to think of the corporation as a legal fiction characterized by six attributes: formal creation as prescribed by state law; legal personality; separation of ownership and control; freely alienable ownership interests; indefinite duration; and limited liability.[2] Taken together, these six attributes give the corporate form considerable advantages for large businesses as compared to the other forms of business organizations available under U.S. law. Each of these attributes will be discussed in far greater detail during the course of this text, but an overview at the outset may prove helpful.

A.   Formal Creation

One creates a corporation by filing a document called the articles of incorporation (a.k.a. charter) with the appropriate government office of the chosen state of incorporation. The articles are the most important of the corporation's organic documents. They set out the corporation's essential rules of the road—the basic terms under which it will operate. Each state corporate statute sets forth the minimum provisions the articles must contain. Model Business Corporation Act (MBCA) § 2.02, for example, requires the articles to include the corporation's name, the number of shares the corporation is authorized to issue, the name and address of the corporation's registered agent, and the name and address of the incorporator. In addition, § 2.02 lists numerous optional provisions that must be included in the articles if the corporation wishes to avail itself of them. Among the more important of these are provisions relating to division of shares into classes and series and liability of directors.

Once prepared, the articles are filed with the appropriate state agency, which in most states is the Secretary of State's office. In

---

[1] Black's Law Dictionary 307 (5th ed. 1979).

[2] Note that the latter four of these attributes are default rules. Some corporations opt out of one or more of them. In particular, close corporations often unify ownership and control to one degree or another and/or restrict transfer of ownership interests.

1

some states, the Secretary of State's office then issues a document called the certificate of incorporation. In other states, the Secretary of State will simply return a copy of the articles of incorporation, along with a receipt, to the incorporator. At this point, the corporation comes into existence. The initial board of directors thereupon holds an organizational meeting at which corporate bylaws are adopted, officers are appointed, and other loose ends are tied up.

The bylaws adopted at that meeting are the corporation's basic internal operating rules. Other than certain provisions that must be contained in the articles of incorporation, most of the corporation's internal affairs will be governed by the bylaws. Virtually anything may be contained in the bylaws. MBCA § 2.06, for example, allows the bylaws to "contain any provision for managing the business and regulating the affairs of the corporation that is not inconsistent with law or the articles of incorporation."

Although the formal steps necessary to create a corporation are quite straightforward, glitches sometimes occur. In some of these cases, the founders begin doing business in the belief that they properly formed a corporation, but the company in fact remains unincorporated due to some technical defect in the filing process. This "defective incorporation" problem embroils one in a complex body of doctrine all too likely leading to undesirable results. The competent lawyer and well-counseled client take pains to ensure compliance with the requisite formalities.

B. Legal Personality

The law generally treats a corporation as though it were a legal person, having most of the rights and obligations of real people, and having an identity wholly apart from its constituents. Corporate law statutes, for example, typically give a corporation "the same powers as an individual to do all things necessary or convenient to carry out its business and affairs."[3]

---

[3] MBCA § 3.02. As a legal person, a corporation has most of the constitutional rights possessed by natural persons. See, e.g., Citizens United v. FEC, 558 U.S. 310 (2010) (corporation has First Amendment right to spend money on supporting political candidates or causes); First Nat'l Bank of Boston v. Bellotti, 435 U.S. 765, 784 (1978) (corporation has First Amendment right of free speech); Hale v. Henkel, 201 U.S. 43 (1906) (corporation gets Fourth Amendment protection against unreasonable searches and seizures but not protected by Fifth Amendment privilege against self-incrimination); Blake v. McClung, 172 U.S. 239 (1898) (corporation not covered by the privileges and immunities clause of the Fourteenth Amendment or of the comity clause of Article IV); Minneapolis & St. Louis Ry. Co. v. Beckwith, 129 U.S. 26, 28 (1889) (corporation entitled to due process of law under the Fifth and Fourteenth Amendments); Santa Clara County v. Southern Pacific Railroad Co., 118 U.S. 394, 416 (1886) (corporation entitled to equal protection of the law under the Fourteenth Amendment).

Although the corporation's legal personality obviously is a fiction, it is a very useful one. Consider a large forestry company, owning forest land in many states. If the company were required to list all of its owners—i.e., every shareholder—on every deed recorded in every county in which it owned property, and also had to amend those filings every time a shareholder sold stock, there would be an intolerable burden not only on the firm but also on government agencies that deal with the firm.

An even more useful feature of the corporation's legal personality, however, is that it allows partitioning of business assets from the personal assets of shareholders, managers, and other corporate constituents.[4] This partitioning has two important aspects. On the one hand, asset partitioning creates a distinct pool of assets belonging to the firm on which the firm's creditors have a claim that is prior to the claims of personal creditors of the corporation's constituencies. By eliminating the risk that the firm will be affected by the financial difficulties of its constituencies, asset partitioning reduces the risks borne by creditors and thus enables the firm to raise capital at a lower cost. On the other hand, asset partitioning also protects the personal assets of the corporation's constituencies from the vicissitudes of corporate life. The doctrine of limited liability means that creditors of the firm may not reach the personal assets of shareholders or other corporate constituents.

Despite the utility of the fiction of corporate legal personhood, it is critical to remember that treating the corporation as an entity separate from the people making it up bears no relation to economic reality. The corporation is not an entity but an aggregate of various stakeholders acting together to produce goods or services.

C.   Separation of Ownership and Control

Corporations differ from most other forms of business organizations in that ownership of the firm is formally separated from its control. Although shareholders nominally "own" the corporation, they have virtually no decisionmaking powers—just the right to elect the firm's directors and to vote on an exceedingly limited—albeit not unimportant—number of corporate actions. Rather, management of the firm is vested by statute in the hands of the board of directors, who in turn delegate the day-to-day running of the firm to its officers, who in turn delegate some responsibilities to the company's employees.[5] The conflicts of interest created by

---

[4] See Henry Hansmann and Reinier Kraakman, The Essential Role of Organizational Law, 110 Yale L.J. 387 (2000), on which the following discussion draws.

[5] Close corporations may differ. To be sure, the statutory separation of ownership and control applies to closely held corporations. Vesting formal

this separation of ownership and control drive much of corporate law, especially the fiduciary obligations of officers and directors.

Although the separation of ownership and control is one of the corporation's essential attributes, it is also one of its most controversial ones. This controversy began taking its modern shape in what still may be the most influential book ever written about corporations, Berle and Means' *The Modern Corporation and Private Property*.[6] They identified three types of public corporations, classified according to the nature of share ownership within the firm:

- *Majority control*: a corporation having a dominant shareholder (or group of shareholders acting together) who owns more than 50% of the outstanding voting shares. Majority controlled corporations exhibit a partial separation of ownership and control: minority shareholders share in the corporation's ownership, but not in its control.

- *Minority control*: a corporation having a dominant shareholder (or group of shareholders acting together) who owns less than 50% of the outstanding voting shares, but is nevertheless able to exercise effective voting control. Minority controlled corporations also exhibit partial separation of ownership and control.

- *Managerial control*: a corporation in which no one shareholder (or group of shareholders acting together) owns sufficient stock to give him working control of the firm. Managerial controlled corporations exhibit complete separation of ownership and control.

The growth of managerial control occurred, according to Berle and Means, because stock ownership was dispersed amongst many shareholders, no one of whom owned enough shares to affect materially the corporation's management. In turn, Berle and Means believed that dispersed ownership was inherent in the corporate system. Important technological changes during the decades preceding publication of their work, especially the development of modern mass production techniques, gave great advantages to firms large enough to achieve economies of scale, which gave rise to giant

---

decisionmaking power in the board of directors of a close corporation, however, is often unacceptable to the shareholders of such a firm. In this respect, a close corporation often closely resembles a partnership that for some business reason has been organized as a corporation. Under special statutory provisions, close corporations can be set up to give shareholders extensive management powers resembling those of partners.

[6] Adolf A. Berle, Jr. and Gardiner C. Means, The Modern Corporation and Private Property (1932).

industrial corporations. These firms required enormous amounts of capital, far exceeding the resources of most individuals or families. They were financed by aggregating many small investments, which was accomplished by selling shares to many investors, each of whom owned only a tiny fraction of the firm's stock. Vesting decisionmaking power in the corporation's board of directors and managers allowed these investors to remain passive, while preventing the chaos that would have resulted from seeking to involve so many people in day-to-day decisionmaking.

While separation of ownership and control facilitated the growth of large industrial corporations, Berle and Means recognized that that separation created the potential for shareholder and managerial interests to diverge. As the residual claimants on the corporation's assets and earnings, the shareholders are entitled to the corporation's profits. But it is the firm's management, not the shareholders, which decides how the firm's earnings are to be spent. Thus, there is a risk that management will expend firm earnings on projects which benefit management, rather than shareholders. Suppose the President of Acme, Inc., is musing over the following question: "I can either spend $100 million on a new corporate jet or I can distribute the $100 million to the shareholders by increasing the size of the dividend." Can you doubt that some (most?) managers will buy the jet?

Corporate law has tried three policy responses to the potential divergence of shareholder and managerial interests created by the separation of ownership and control: (1) Some corporate laws try to reunite ownership and control, giving shareholders more control over the firm. The federal proxy rules are an example of such rules. (2) Corporate governance uses both legal and market mechanisms for disciplining managers who abuse their positions, such as judicial review under the duties of care and loyalty and hostile corporate takeovers. (3) Some laws try to align management and shareholder interests. Examples of this approach include tax provisions encouraging management to own a larger percentage of the firm's shares.

D. Indefinite Duration

A corporation commonly is said to have a perpetual duration. In actuality, the corporation has an indefinite legal existence terminable only in rare circumstances: voluntary dissolution, which requires a recommendation of the board of directors that is approved by a vote of a majority of the shareholders; a merger or consolidation with another corporation; an insolvency liquidation in bankruptcy; or involuntary dissolution by judicial decree, which typically requires proof of deadlock or oppressive behavior by controlling shareholders.

E.   Transferability

One of the great advantages of the corporate form is that shares of stock are freely transferable. Absent special contractual restrictions, shareholders are free to sell their shares to anybody at any price. A transfer of stock has no effect on the corporation, except that there is now a new voter of those shares. For public corporations, this process is facilitated greatly by the secondary trading markets.

Although shares of stock in a closely held corporation are freely transferable in theory, the lack of a readily available secondary trading market for such shares means they seldom are easily transferable in practice. Moreover, investors in a closely held corporation often prefer to restrict transferability. Like any other personal relationship, the success or failure of a small business often depends upon maintaining a rather delicate balance between the owners. Free transferability of ownership interests threatens that balance. In closely held corporations, shareholders therefore often agree to special contractual restrictions on the alienability of shares.

F.   Limited Liability

The limited liability doctrine holds that shareholders of a corporation are not personally liable for corporate obligations and thus put at risk only the amount of money that they invested in buying their shares. Suppose, for example, an employee of Acme, Inc., commits a tort against Paula Plaintiff. Under the tort and agency law doctrine of vicarious liability, Acme is held liable to Plaintiff for $10 million in damages resulting from the employee's tortious conduct. Acme has only $1 million in assets. The limited liability doctrine bars Plaintiff from seeking to recover the unsatisfied $9 million remainder of her claim from Acme's shareholders. The shareholders' investment in Acme stock may be worthless if Acme becomes bankrupt as a result of Plaintiff's lawsuit, but the shareholders will have lost only that portion of their wealth they invested in Acme.[7]

---

[7] In rare circumstances, courts may invoke an equitable exception to the limited liability rule called "piercing the corporate veil." If invoked, the veil piercing remedy allows shareholders to be held personally liable for the corporation's obligations. In the preceding example, if Paula Plaintiff successfully invokes the veil piercing doctrine, the court will allow her to recover the unsatisfied portion of her claim from Acme's shareholders. See Chapter 4.

G.   Some Fundamental Distinctions

Corporations come in a wide variety of flavors: business corporations, municipal corporations, and ecclesiastical corporations, to name a few. In this text, we are concerned solely with business corporations. In particular, we omit both nonprofit and quasi-governmental corporations.[8]

Business corporations generally are divided into two main categories: close corporations (a.k.a. closely held corporations) and public corporations (a.k.a. publicly held corporations). As a general rule of thumb, close corporations tend to be smaller than public corporations, but size is not what distinguishes the two categories. Instead, they are distinguished by the presence or absence of a secondary trading market for their shares of stock. Public corporations are those whose stock is listed for trading on a secondary market, such as the New York Stock Exchange or the NASDAQ system. Close corporations are those whose stock is not listed on such a market.

Corporate securities, like all commodities, are traded in markets. Corporate lawyers distinguish between two basic types of markets in which a corporation's securities (such as stocks or bonds) are traded: the primary market and the secondary market. The primary market is the one in which the corporation sells its shares to investors. An initial public offering (IPO), for example, takes place on the primary market.

The secondary market is a trading market: the one in which investors trade stocks among themselves without any significant participation by the original corporate issuer of the shares. The New York Stock Exchange and the American Stock Exchange are well-known, highly organized, and thoroughly regulated examples of secondary markets. Market professionals working on these exchanges facilitate the trading process by matching buy and sell orders from investors.

Having a corporation's securities listed for trading on a secondary market is significant because it makes the securities

---

[8] Many charitable organizations are organized as corporations, even though they do not carry on for profit business activities. Special "nonprofit" corporation statutes govern these organizations. Not for profit corporations can also qualify for special tax treatment under both state and federal law. As the name implies, the profit motive is what distinguishes business corporations from nonprofit corporations.

Quasi-governmental corporations refer to corporations created by the government (be it federal, state, or local) to carry out some public function. In contrast, private corporations are created by and owned by private individuals to carry out private functions. Sometimes the term "public corporation" is used by an author who is really referring to a quasi-governmental corporation. Because our focus is solely on private business corporations, we shall use the term "public corporation" solely in the sense described in the text.

liquid. In other words, investors can freely sell their securities without involving the firm. Liquidity, in turn, makes it easier and cheaper for the company subsequently to raise capital in the primary market, because investors generally prefer (and are willing to pay more) for liquid securities. The difference in liquidity of publicly held corporate stock and that of close corporation stock has important theoretical and doctrinal consequences.

§ 1.2   Sources of Corporate Law

Corporate law differs in two important respects from the common law courses taken by most law students during the first year of law school. First, statutes are far more important in corporate law than is the case in most of the so-called common law courses. When faced with a corporate law issue, the first place one always looks is the corporation statute of the state of incorporation.[9] Second, as far as public corporations are concerned, federal law is much more important in corporate law than is the case in common law subjects. Indeed, publicly held corporations can be said to function in a dual regulatory scheme consisting of federal securities law and state corporate law.

A.   State Corporate Law

Virtually all U.S. corporations are formed ("incorporated") under the laws of a single state by filing articles of incorporation with the appropriate state official.[10] The state in which the articles of incorporation are filed is known as the "state of incorporation." Selecting a state of incorporation has important consequences, because of the so-called "internal affairs doctrine"—a conflicts of law rule holding that corporate governance matters are controlled by the law of the state of incorporation. Virtually all U.S. jurisdictions follow the internal affairs doctrine, even if the corporation in question has virtually no ties to the state of incorporation other than the mere fact of incorporation.

Suppose, for example, that Acme, Inc., is incorporated in Delaware, but all of Acme's assets are located in Illinois. All of Acme's shareholders, directors, and employees reside in Illinois.

---

[9] Although one must pay careful attention to the applicable state corporation statute, judicial opinions remain quite important in corporate law. Corporation statutes almost never rise to the level of detail found in, say, the federal tax code. Many provisions of corporation statutes are quite vague. Worse yet, corporation statutes often fail to address important issues. Courts have filled the resulting gaps through a process far more closely resembling common law adjudication than statutory interpretation. The fiduciary duties of directors and officers are especially prominent examples of this process, but they are hardly the only ones.

[10] A very few exceptions are formed under federal law, most of which are actually quasi-governmental entities, such as the Federal Deposit Insurance Corporation, or part of an industry that is heavily regulated by the federal government, such as credit unions and banks.

Acme's sole place of business is located in Illinois. An Acme shareholder brings suit against the board of directors, alleging that its members violated their fiduciary duty of care. The law suit is filed in an Illinois court. Despite all these Illinois ties, the Illinois court usually nevertheless will apply Delaware law.[11] There are a few exceptions to this rule, most notably with respect to security for expenses statutes in derivative actions and shareholder inspection rights, which we'll take up later in the text.

A few states make a more general exception to the internal affairs doctrine for so-called pseudo-foreign corporations. A foreign corporation is one incorporated either by a state or nation other than the state in question. A pseudo-foreign corporation that has most of its ties to the state in question rather than to the state of incorporation. Many Delaware corporations are pseudo-foreign corporations. They are incorporated in Delaware, but most of their operations are located in one or more other states. In most states, there is no significant legal difference between a foreign and a pseudo-foreign corporation, and the internal affairs doctrine will be applied to invoke the law of the state of the incorporation with respect to both. California and New York are the principal exceptions to this rule. Both states purport to apply parts of their corporate laws to pseudo-foreign corporations formed in other states but having substantial contacts with California or New York.[12] In 2005, the Delaware supreme court held that the California statute was unconstitutional under the Due Process and Commerce Clauses of the U.S. Constitution.[13] Ultimately, however, the U.S. Supreme Court will have to decide the issue.

The internal affairs doctrine takes on particular transactional significance when considered in conjunction with the constitutional restrictions on a state's ability to exclude foreign corporations. With rare exceptions, states have always allowed foreign and pseudo-foreign corporations to do business within their borders. As early as 1839, for example, the U.S. Supreme Court held that federal courts should presume a state would recognize foreign corporations in the absence of an express statement to the contrary by the legislature.[14] A subsequent Supreme Court decision implied that states could not exclude foreign corporations from doing business within the state provided that the business constituted interstate commerce under

---

[11] See, e.g., Paulman v. Kritzer, 219 N.E.2d 541, 543 (Ill.App.1966), aff'd, 230 N.E.2d 262 (Ill.1967) (applying Delaware fiduciary duties to the directors of a Delaware corporation).

[12] See, e.g., Cal. Corp. Code § 2115; N.Y. Bus. Corp. L. §§ 1317–20.

[13] VantagePoint Venture Partners 1996 v. Examen, Inc., 871 A.2d 1108 (Del. 2005).

[14] Bank of Augusta v. Earle, 38 U.S. 519, 597 (1839).

the Commerce Clause of the U.S. Constitution.[15] These decisions effectively created a common market for corporate charters. If Illinois, for example, adopts a restrictive corporation law, its businesses are free to incorporate in a less restrictive state, such as Delaware, while continuing to conduct business within Illinois.

Speaking of Delaware, it is far and away the dominant source of state corporation law. This is so because more than half of the corporations listed for trading on the New York Stock Exchange and nearly 60% of the Fortune 500 corporations are incorporated in Delaware. Delaware's dominance can be ascribed to a number of factors: There is a considerable body of case law interpreting the Delaware General Corporation Law (DGCL), which allows legal questions to be answered with confidence. Delaware has a separate court, the Court of Chancery, devoted largely to corporate law cases. The Chancellors have great expertise in corporate law matters, making their court a highly sophisticated forum for resolving disputes. They also tend to render decisions quite quickly, facilitating transactions that are often time sensitive.

The most important alternative to Delaware law is the American Bar Association's Model Business Corporation Act (MBCA). The 1969 MBCA was adopted in whole or in large part by about 35 states. The 1984 MBCA has been adopted in whole by 24 states and in part by many others. Delaware, California, and New York remain the commercially most important holdouts. Each has preserved a largely unique corporate statute, although each also has adopted some elements of the MBCA.

An important nonstatutory source of corporate law is the American Law Institute's *Principles of Corporate Governance*, promulgated in 1992 after over ten years of work and considerable controversy. The ALI PRINCIPLES resemble the ALI's well-known restatements of the law; each section sets forth some black letter rule of law, followed by explanatory comments and notes. Critics argue that the ALI PRINCIPLES do not restate existing law, but rather propose important changes in the law. In fairness, however, while initial drafts of the ALI PRINCIPLES frequently proposed quite radical reforms, most sections of the ALI PRINCIPLES, as finally adopted, ended up quite close to existing law.

B.   Federal Law

The issuance and trading of stocks and other corporate securities was largely unregulated until the passage of the first state "blue sky law" by Kansas in 1911. These laws were a response to widespread fraud in the sale of securities. Indeed, the name

---

[15] Paul v. Virginia, 75 U.S. 168 (1868).

supposedly refers to unscrupulous promoters who would sell building lots in the clear blue sky. State regulation proved largely ineffective, however, because the statutes had a limited jurisdictional reach, many statutes contained numerous special interest exemptions, and states had limited enforcement resources.

In the aftermath of the Great Stock Market Crash of 1929 and the subsequent Great Depression, there was widespread agreement that the time had come for federal regulation of the securities markets. Between 1933 and 1940 Congress passed 7 statutes regulating various aspects of the industry, which have been amended on various subsequent occasions and joined by a few other highly specialized statutes.

The most important of these statutes for our purposes are the Securities Act of 1933 and the Securities Exchange Act of 1934. The Securities Act regulates primary market sales of securities by issuing corporations. The Securities Exchange Act regulates a host of matters, but is generally concerned with trading of corporate securities on securities exchanges and other secondary markets.[16]

Although the two statutes are concerned with different transactions, they have the same basic purposes. The first is requiring corporations and other issuers of securities to provide full disclosure to ensure that investors have all the information they need to make informed decisions about buying, selling, or voting securities. The second is to punish fraud committed in connection with securities transactions.

The Securities Act follows a transactional disclosure model; i.e., it focuses attention on getting information concerning certain transactions from the issuer to investors. Accordingly, that act applies only when an issuer is actually selling securities. As long as a company can raise funds by other means, the Securities Act does not require it to provide any disclosures whatsoever. Obviously, this leaves a significant gap in the disclosure requirements. The Securities Exchange Act addresses this problem by imposing a periodic disclosure system on certain issuers. It focuses attention on regularly and routinely getting information from the issuer to the market. In addition, the Securities Exchange Act includes a hodge-podge of other provisions, concerned with regulating secondary market trading and preventing fraud.

---

[16] Subject to certain exemptions, all corporations that sell securities to the public are subject to the Securities Act. In contrast, the Securities Exchange Act applies to a narrower range of businesses. Although the Act has a complex set of rules for deciding which provisions apply to which corporations, as a general rule of thumb it applies only to publicly held corporations.

The Securities Exchange Act is also notable because it created the Securities and Exchange Commission (SEC), the primary federal agency charged with administering the various securities laws. The agency is headed by five Commissioners, who must be confirmed by the Senate. No more than three can belong to the same political party. Most of the agency's work, of course, is done not by the Commissioners but by the professional staff. The agency staff is organized into Divisions and Offices having various specialized responsibilities. The professional staff is comprised mainly of lawyers, although it also includes a number of accountants and economists. The staff has three primary functions: it provides interpretative guidance to private parties raising questions about the application of the securities laws to a particular transaction; it advises the Commission as to new rules or revisions of existing rules; and it investigates and prosecutes violations of the securities laws.

The U.S. Supreme Court has held repeatedly that the federal securities laws do not preempt state corporate law, but instead place only a limited gloss on the broader body of state law.[17] A fair rule of thumb is that state law is concerned with the substance of corporate governance, while federal law is concerned with disclosure and a limited number of procedural aspects of corporate governance (such as the solicitation of proxies and the conduct of a tender offer). In certain areas, the dividing line between the federal and state role remains controversial. As we'll see, the two most important disputes concern shareholder voting rights and state regulation of takeovers.

---

[17] See, e.g., CTS Corp. v. Dynamics Corp. of Am., 481 U.S. 69 (1987); Burks v. Lasker, 441 U.S. 471 (1979); Santa Fe Indus. v. Green, 430 U.S. 462 (1977).

Chapter 2

FORMING THE CORPORATION

§ 2.1   Introduction

Until the middle of the nineteenth century, incorporating a business required one to persuade the state legislature to pass a special law granting the company a corporate charter. The steadily increasing number of corporations caused an increase in applications for a charter and for amendments to existing charters, which constituted a considerable legislative burden. The process also invited corruption, because influential legislators frequently received under the table payments for their support.

As the nineteenth century progressed, states began adopting so-called enabling corporate laws. These statutes created the modern process of incorporating a business. Under the enabling laws, a corporation was formed simply by jumping through certain statutory hoops, the most important of which were preparing articles of incorporation conforming to the statute's requirements and filing them with the appropriate state official. Today, all states have enabling statutes and creating a corporation has become a straightforward process.

§ 2.2   Forming the Corporation

Incorporating a business is an astonishingly simple process. Articles of incorporation meeting certain minimal statutory requirements are drafted. One or more incorporators sign the articles and deliver them to the state of incorporation's secretary of state's office, along with a check for any applicable fees or taxes. The secretary of state retains the original articles and returns a copy to the incorporator with a receipt for the fee. Unless the articles provide to the contrary, the corporation comes into existence at the moment the secretary of state's office accepts the articles for filing.

Some states impose additional requirements, usually additional filings. Some require filing of the articles with the county in which the corporation's registered office or principal place of business is located. A few require newspaper publication of the articles or a notice of incorporation. Several require newly formed corporations to receive payment for shares meeting some minimum amount of capital (typically $1,000) before transacting business or incurring debt.

After the articles of incorporation are filed with the secretary of state, an organizational meeting is held. If the articles name the initial directors, the incorporator's role is finished and the directors will run the organizational meeting. At the organizational meeting, the directors appoint officers, adopt bylaws, and carry out any other business necessary to complete the organization of the corporation. If the articles do not name the initial directors, the incorporator runs the organizational meeting. The incorporator may elect a board of directors, appoint officers, adopt bylaws, and otherwise complete the corporation's organization. Alternatively, the incorporator may simply elect a board of directors and leave those tasks to the new board. The option of using the incorporator to conduct the organizational meeting permits one to avoid naming the initial directors in the articles in cases where confidentiality is important.

Minutes of the organizational meeting and, indeed, of all board and shareholder meetings should be kept. The minutes serve three purposes: (1) they are one of the formalities relevant to ensuring that the corporation's shareholders will get the benefit of limited liability; (2) the minutes provide a record of actions authorized by the board of directors (such a record is sometimes needed as proof that a corporate agent is authorized to enter into a contract); and (3) a director who disagrees with some proposed corporate action, and causes his dissent to be recorded in the minutes, may not be held personally liable in connection with the action.[1]

§ 2.3　Drafting the Organic Documents

A corporation's articles and bylaws set out the firm's basic internal organization and governance rules.

A.　Articles of Incorporation

Modern articles of incorporation usually are bare-bones documents, containing little more than the statutorily mandated terms. MBCA § 2.02(a), for example, only requires the articles to contain four items:

- *Name.* A corporation's name may not be the same or confusingly similar to that of another corporation incorporated or qualified to do business in the state of incorporation. The name must also include some word or abbreviation indicating that the business is incorporated, such as corporation, company, "Inc." or the like.

---

[1] MBCA § 8.24(d).

- *Authorized shares.* The articles must state the maximum number of shares the corporation is authorized to issue.

- *Registered agent.* The articles must state the name of the corporation's registered agent and the address of its registered office. The registered office must be located within the state of incorporation. The registered agent receives service of process when the corporation is sued.

- *Incorporators.* The articles must state the name and address of each incorporator.

Under MBCA § 2.02(b), the articles of incorporation also may contain any of several optional provisions. Some of these options alternatively may be included in the bylaws, but many must be included in the articles of incorporation in order to be effective. Some of the more common and important optional provisions include:

- *Statement of purpose.* The articles may state the nature of the corporation's business or the purposes for which it was formed. At one time purpose and power clauses had considerable importance because of the ultra vires doctrine, but the erosion of that doctrine has rendered such clauses mere formalities. A number of states, prominently including Delaware, nevertheless still require that the articles contain a statement of corporate purpose. It is sufficient, however, to state that "the purpose of the corporation is to engage in any lawful act or activity. . . ."[2]

- *Classes and series of shares.* Corporate stock may be separated into multiple classes and series. If the corporation wishes to do so, the articles must identify the different classes and state the number of shares of each class the corporation is authorized to issue. Where one or more classes of shares have certain preferential rights over other classes, those rights must be spelled out in this part of the articles.

- *Director and officer indemnification and liability limitation.* We will see many situations throughout this text in which directors or officers of a corporation may be held liable for misconduct. Most corporate statutes now permit the articles to include provisions

---

[2] DGCL § 102(a)(3).

limiting the scope of a director's liability and/or permitting indemnification of directors.

The articles of incorporation may be amended at any time. A three-step process is normally involved. First, the board of directors must recommend the amendment to the shareholders. Second, the shareholders must approve the amendment.[3] Finally, the amendment must be filed with the secretary of state's office.[4]

The vote necessary to approve an amendment is the principal state-by-state variation on these basic themes. Under the MBCA, an amendment is approved if more shares are voted affirmatively than voted negatively.[5] In Delaware, by contrast, amendments to the articles must be approved by a majority of the shares eligible to vote.[6]

Suppose, for example, that Acme, Inc. has 1,000 voting shares outstanding. Shareholders owning 600 shares are present at the annual meeting of the shareholders. At that meeting, the board of directors recommends an amendment to the articles changing the firm's name to "Ajax, Inc." 250 shares are voted yes, 100 are voted no, and the remainder abstain. If Acme is incorporated in a MBCA state, the amendment passes. In Delaware, however, because the amendment was not approved by a majority of the outstanding shares entitled to vote (i.e., at least 501 affirmative votes), it failed.

B. Bylaws

Bylaws are the rules a corporation adopts to govern its internal affairs. Bylaws tend to be far more detailed than the articles of incorporation, for three reasons: (1) bylaws need not be filed with the state government, which means they are not part of the public record; (2) bylaws are more easily amended than articles of incorporation (see below); and (3) officers and directors tend to be more familiar with bylaws than with the articles, which makes them a ready repository of organizational rules. In the event of a conflict between a bylaw and the articles, the latter controls.

The bylaws typically deal with such matters as number and qualifications of directors, board vacancies, board committees, quorum and notice requirement for shareholder and board meetings, procedures for calling special shareholder and board meetings, any special voting procedures, any limits on the transferability of shares, and titles and duties of the corporation's officers.

---

[3] MBCA § 10.03(b).

[4] MBCA § 10.06.

[5] MBCA § 10.03(e).

[6] DGCL § 242(b)(1).

1. Adoption and Amendment

The corporation's initial bylaws are adopted by the incorporator or the initial directors at the corporation's organizational meeting. At early common law, only shareholders had the power to amend the bylaws. Many states thereafter adopted statutes allowing shareholders to delegate the power to amend the bylaws to the board of directors. DGCL § 109(a) typifies this approach: It provides that only shareholders have the power to amend bylaws, unless the articles of incorporation expressly confer that power on the board of directors. An article provision authorizing the board to amend the bylaws, moreover, does not divest the shareholders of their residual power to amend the bylaws.

In contrast, the MBCA reflects a modern trend of vesting the power to amend the bylaws in both the directors and the shareholders. MBCA § 10.20(b) allows the directors to amend the bylaws unless (1) the articles of incorporation give that power solely to the shareholders or (2) the shareholders amend the bylaw in question and provide that the directors cannot thereafter further amend the bylaw. By implication, MBCA § 10.20(a) authorizes the shareholders to amend the bylaws even though the directors also have that power. Notice that amendment of the bylaws is one of the few corporate actions the shareholders are entitled to initiate. Unlike the articles of incorporation, where an amendment must first be recommended by the board, no prior board action is required on a bylaw amendment.

The concurrent power of both shareholders and boards to amend the bylaws raises the prospect of cycling amendments and counter-amendments. Suppose the shareholders adopted a bylaw limiting the number of terms a board member can serve. Disliking that limitation, the board repeals the new bylaw provision using its concurrent power to amend the bylaws. The MBCA allows the shareholders to forestall such an event. As noted, MBCA § 10.20(b)(2) authorizes the board to adopt, amend, and repeal bylaws unless "the shareholders in amending, repealing, or adopting a bylaw expressly provide that the board of directors may not amend, repeal, or reinstate that bylaw." In the absence of such a restriction, however, the board apparently retains its power to amend or even repeal the bylaw. If the board does so, the shareholders' remedies presumably are limited to readopting the term limit amendment, this time incorporating the necessary restriction, and/or electing a more compliant board.

Delaware § 109 is more problematic, as it lacks any comparable grant of power to the shareholders. Worse yet, because the board only has power to adopt or amend bylaws if that power is granted to it in the articles of incorporation, a bylaw prohibiting board amendment would be inconsistent with the articles and, therefore, invalid. As a result, there is "significant legal uncertainty" as to whether "a stockholder-adopted bylaw can be made immune from repeal or modification by the board of directors."[7]

2. Legality

DGCL § 109(b) imposes an important limitation on the otherwise sweeping scope of permissible bylaws:

> The bylaws may contain any provision, *not inconsistent with law or with the certificate of incorporation*, relating to the business of the corporation, the conduct of its affairs, and its rights or powers or the rights or powers of its stockholders, directors, officers or employees.

MBCA § 2.06(b) contains a comparable limitation.

Clear conflicts between the statute or articles and the bylaws present little difficulty. What if the bylaw nominally complies with the letter of the law, but conflicts with its spirit, however?

A critical issue here is whether shareholder-adopted bylaws may limit the board of directors' discretionary power to manage the corporation. There is an odd circularity in the Delaware code with respect to this issue. On the one hand, DGCL § 141(a) provides that "[t]he business and affairs of every corporation organized under this chapter shall be managed by or under the direction of a board of directors." A bylaw that restricts the board's managerial authority thus seems to run afoul of DGCL § 109(b)'s prohibition of bylaws that are "inconsistent with law." On the other hand, DGCL § 141(a) also provides that the board's management powers are plenary "except as may be otherwise provided in this chapter." Does an otherwise valid bylaw adopted pursuant to § 109 squeeze through that loophole?

In *Teamsters v. Fleming Companies*,[8] the Oklahoma supreme court upheld a bylaw limiting the board of directors' power to adopt a poison pill (a type of corporate takeover defense). The bylaw provided:

> The Corporation *shall* not adopt or maintain a poison pill, shareholder rights plan, rights agreement or any other form of "poison pill" which is designed to or has the effect

---

[7] General DataComm Industries, Inc. v. State of Wisconsin Investment Board, 731 A.2d 818, 821 n. 1 (Del.Ch.1999).

[8] International Broth. of Teamsters General Fund v. Fleming Companies, Inc., 975 P.2d 907 (Okla.1999).

of making acquisition of large holdings of the Corporation's shares of stock more difficult or expensive . . . unless such plan is first approved by a majority shareholder vote. The Company *shall* redeem any such rights now in effect.

The board argued that shareholders could not adopt a bylaw imposing such mandatory limitations on the board's discretion. The court rejected that argument. Absent a contrary provision in the articles of incorporation, it held, shareholders may use the bylaws to limit the board's managerial discretion.

In *CA, Inc. v. AFSCME Employees Pension Plan*,[9] the Delaware supreme court took a different approach. First, the decision reaffirmed the bedrock principle of Delaware corporate law that it is the board of directors of a corporation, not the corporation's shareholders, that is empowered to manage the corporation's business and affairs. Second, shareholder-adopted bylaws may not prevent the directors from fulfilling their fiduciary duties. Third, bylaws may not "mandate how the board should decide specific substantive business decisions," but may "define the process and procedures by which those decisions are made." Again, the implication seems to be that Delaware would reject *Fleming*. Where the line will be drawn between impermissible bylaws that mandate substantive decisions and permissible bylaws that are merely procedural, however, likely will be decided by the Delaware courts on a case-by-case basis in the future.

As for the conflict between sections 109 and 141, the court stated that: "Because the board's managerial authority under Section 141(a) is a cardinal precept of the DGCL, we do not construe Section 109 as an 'except[ion] . . . otherwise specified in th[e] [DGCL]' to Section 141(a). Rather, the shareholders' statutory power to adopt, amend or repeal bylaws under Section 109 cannot be 'inconsistent with the law,' including Section 141(a)." Although that passage appears to hold that § 141 trumps § 109, later in the opinion the court seemingly back tracked on that issue, stating: "What we do hold is case specific; that is, wherever may be the location of the bright line that separates the shareholders' bylaw-making power under Section 109 from the directors' exclusive managerial authority under Section 141(a), the proposed Bylaw at issue here does not invade the territory demarcated by Section 141(a)." As with the substance/procedure divide, accordingly, the precise relationship between §§ 109 and 141 apparently remains subject to future case-by-case analysis.

[9] 453 A.2d 227 (Del.2008).

Note that all of these problems would go away if state corporation codes treated bylaws the same way as articles of incorporation or, for that matter, virtually every other corporate action. The shareholder power to initiate bylaw amendments without prior board action is unique. It is also an historical anachronism states unthinkingly codified from old common law principles lacking either rhyme or reason. There simply is no good reason to treat bylaws differently than articles of incorporation.

§ 2.4   Preincorporation Transactions by Promoters

A corporation does not exist until its articles of incorporation are filed with the secretary of state's office. As a practical matter, however, the company's promoter often begins planning and preparing for the business long before undertaking the formal step of filing the articles.[10] If the promoter enters into contracts on behalf of the corporation before the articles are filed, three legal questions may arise: (1) Once the articles are filed, does the corporation become a party to the contract? (2) Once the articles are filed, is the promoter liable if the corporation breaches the contract? (3) If the articles are not filed, is the promoter liable on the contract?

A.   Corporation as Party

In agency law, a principal is not bound by contracts entered into by his agent unless the agent had authority to make the contract. If the principal ratifies an unauthorized contract, however, the principal is bound just as though the contract had been authorized from the outset. How do these rules apply when the principal is a newly formed corporation and the agent is a promoter who transacted business on the firm's behalf before it was formed?

The prevailing corporate law doctrine is that a corporation may not ratify acts that took place before it came into existence. The corporation may, however, adopt them. The difference is largely semantic, but may be important for purposes of the statute of frauds.[11]

---

[10] In the broadest sense, the promoters are those individuals actively involved in organizing the corporation. In the present context, the term is used in a narrower sense to refer to persons who purport to act as agents of the business prior to its incorporation. Passive investors who do not act on the business' behalf during the pre-incorporation phase generally are not regarded as promoters. Instead, their potential liability is taken up under the defective incorporation doctrine discussed below.

[11] See, e.g., McArthur v. Times Printing Co., 51 N.W. 216 (Minn.1892) (corporation may adopt pre-incorporation contract; if the corporation does so, the contract is deemed made as of the date of its adoption for purposes of the statute of frauds).

If the board adopts the contract, the corporation may enforce the contract, but is also liable if it subsequently breaches the contract.[12] The trouble in many cases is deciding whether or not the corporation in fact adopted the contract.

When the board of directors passes a resolution expressly adopting the contract, of course, there is no difficulty in holding the corporation to the contract. In the absence of an express action by the board, the court has to infer from the corporation's conduct whether an adoption was effected. In *McArthur v. Times Printing Co.,*[13] for example, plaintiff was given a one-year employment contract by the promoter of a publishing corporation. After the corporation was formed, the directors failed to formally adopt the contract. All of the directors knew of the contract, however, and allowed the corporation to accept the benefits of plaintiff's employment. The court held that the corporation had implicitly adopted the contract by acquiescence. The knowing receipt of the benefits of the contract constituted an implied adoption. In addition, the other party to the contract may be able to assert quasi-contract or estoppel claims against the corporation even if the board of directors fails to adopt the contract.[14]

B. Promoter's Liability After the Corporation Is Formed

Absent an agreement to the contrary, the promoter remains liable on the contract even after the corporation comes into existence. This is true even if the corporation adopts the contract. In order for the promoter to avoid liability on the contract, the other party must agree to excuse the promoter once the corporation comes into existence. If the contract explicitly releases the promoter, there is no difficulty, but many contracts are either ambiguous or silent with respect to the promoter's post-incorporation liability. If so, the court must infer whether the parties intended to release the promoter from liability on the contract. In doing so, the court will consider a number of factors, including:

- *Form of signature:* Did the promoter sign the corporation in his individual capacity or as an agent of the corporation? If the form of signature explicitly designates the promoter as an agent of the corporation, this may demonstrate an intent that only the corporation would be bound by the contract.

---

[12] Jacobson v. Stern, 605 P.2d 198 (Nev.1980).

[13] 51 N.W. 216 (Minn.1892).

[14] See, e.g., Clifton v. Tomb, 21 F.2d 893 (4th Cir.1927).

- *Partial performance:* Has the promoter partially performed on the contract? Partial performance is deemed evidence of an intent to be personally bound by the contract.

- *Other party's knowledge and conduct:* Did the other party know that the business was to be incorporated? Did the other party do anything else that indicates an intent to look solely to the corporation for performance? If so, that may indicate an intent to release the promoter.

In *Quaker Hill, Inc. v. Parr*,[15] for example, plaintiff sold a large quantity of nursery stock (plants) to Denver Memorial Nursery, Inc. The contract was signed by "E.D. Parr, Pres." An accompanying promissory note was signed: "Denver Memorial Nursery, Inc./E.D. Parr, Pres./James P. Presba, Sc'y.-Treas." Plaintiff knew that the corporation had not been formed at the time the contract was made, but one of plaintiff's agents nevertheless urged defendants to make the contract in the corporation's name. Defendants eventually formed a corporation under a different name, but the corporation failed to perform. Plaintiff therefore sued defendants, seeking to hold them personally liable on the contract. The court acknowledged that, as general rule, promoters are personally liable on contracts made on behalf of a corporation before its incorporation. An exception to the general rule, however, is made for cases in which the contract is made on behalf of the corporation and the other party intended to look to the corporation and not to the promoters for payment. On these facts, the court held, the exception applied, and the defendant promoters were not personally liable. The key fact was that plaintiff's agent actually urged defendant to make the contract in the corporation's name, from which the court inferred that plaintiff intended to look solely to the corporation for payment.

The exception carved out in *Quaker Hill* is best understood as being grounded in the estoppel doctrine. In a subsequent case, *Goodman v. Darden, Doman & Stafford Assoc.*,[16] for example, DDS entered into a contract with Goodman to repair an apartment building. The named parties were DDS and "Building Design and Development, Inc. (In Formation)/John A. Goodman, President." DDS knew Building Design and Development did not exist when the contract was made. DDS also knew that Goodman intended to form a corporation for the very purpose of limiting his liability. Finally, DDS made some payments in Building Design and Development's name. The court nonetheless held the promoter

---

[15] 364 P.2d 1056 (Colo.1961).

[16] 670 P.2d 648 (Wash.1983).

personally liable on the contract. In doing so, it distinguished *Quaker Hill* on grounds that DDS did not urge Goodman to make the contract in the corporation's name or even suggest incorporation to him. Accordingly, the requisite grounds for estoppel were not present. This result suggests that, absent the unusual facts of *Quaker Hill*, promoters normally will be held liable for breach of pre-incorporation contracts.

MBCA § 2.04 provides that "[a]ll persons purporting to act as or on behalf of a corporation, knowing there was no incorporation under [the MBCA], are jointly and severally liable for all liabilities created while so acting." On its face, this statutory language is inconsistent with the holding in *Quaker Hill*. The official comment to § 2.04, however, opines that the statute does not foreclose application of an estoppel doctrine to appropriate facts. Under this formulation, someone who knows the corporation does not exist, but nevertheless urges the defendants to transact business in the corporation's name, may be estopped from seeking to hold the defendants personally liable. The MBCA approach thus can be squared with the common law.

C. Promoter's Liability in the Event the Corporation Never Comes into Existence

Absent an agreement to the contrary, the promoter remains liable on the contract if the corporation never comes into existence. The rules of contract interpretation for determining the parties' intent discussed in the preceding section apply to this situation, as well.

D. Policy

If all of this strikes the reader as dry and formalistic, that is because it is dry and formalistic. A modest degree of ex ante planning and attention to contract language will solve a multitude of problems. A competently drafted preincorporation contract will specify the status of the enterprise, the intentions of the parties with respect to formation of the business, and the rights of the various parties.

Unfortunately, many small start-up businesses try to wing it without legal advice. In such cases, the estoppel-based interpretation of Quaker Hill gets it about right. In general, the promoter is the cheapest cost avoider—the promoter controls the incorporation process and ought to have an incentive to ensure that that process is carried through promptly and with due regard to creditor interests. The incorporation process has become so simple that promoters ought not to get the benefit of limited liability until the corporation is validly formed. A general presumption that promoters are liable on preincorporation contrasts, such as that provided by MBCA § 2.04, gives the promoter an incentive to carry through the incorporation process and, moreover, to ensure that the contract is carried out. On the other hand, where the creditor knew the corporation did not yet exist, but nevertheless urged the promoter to transact business in the corporation's name, allowing the creditor to hold the promoter personally liable would give the former a windfall and encourage creditors to mislead promoters as to the latter's rights.

§ 2.5   Defective Incorporation

The preceding section dealt with pre-incorporation transactions in which the promoter and, perhaps, the third party knew the corporation had not been formed as of the date of the transaction. This section deals with a slightly different variant of the problem: pre-incorporation transactions by a promoter who erroneously believes that the corporation exists as of the date of the transaction.

Defective incorporation was a fairly serious problem decades ago when incorporating a business involved far more technicalities than it does today. Older corporation statutes required compliance with substantial procedural formalities as a condition of incorporation, such as multiple local filings, notice by publication, minimum capital requirements, and the like. It was easy for some minor glitch in the incorporation process, such as failing to file all the requisite documents or failing to do so in all the requisite offices, to prevent the corporation from coming into existence as a legal entity.

Defective incorporation was a concern for promoters and other investors because limited liability attached only to validly formed corporations. A defectively incorporated business could be viewed as a partnership or sole proprietorship, neither of which confer limited liability on their owners, rather than a corporation. Common law courts worked out two responses to the defective incorporation problem: the de facto corporation and the corporation by estoppel.

A.   De Facto Corporation

If the promoter failed to form a legal corporation because of some technical defect in the incorporation process, a court may nevertheless treat the business as a de facto corporation. A de jure corporation is a true corporation: A legal entity that has been validly formed by complying with all statutory requirements. The term is also sometimes used for corporations that substantially complied with the statutory requirements for incorporation, but failed to comply with some very minor technical requirement. In the latter case, neither the state nor nonstate parties may contest the corporation's existence. If a defect in the incorporation process prevents the business from being treated as a de jure corporation, but the promoter made a good faith effort to incorporate the business, and carried on the business as though it were a corporation, some courts treat the firm as a de facto corporation. The state may contest the existence of the corporation, but nonstate parties who transact business with a de facto corporation may not hold the firm's promoters or investors personally liable for the firm's obligations.

The rationale seems to be a concern that imposing full personal liability on the promoter may amount to a windfall for the other party to the transaction, which probably believed it was dealing with a corporation having limited liability. As long as the creditor thought it was dealing with a de jure corporation, the firm's defective incorporation is irrelevant. Personal liability would constitute a windfall the creditor did not expect and has done nothing to earn.

The most widely used standard for invoking the de facto corporation doctrine is whether (1) there was a good faith effort to incorporate the business and (2) the putative shareholders carried on the business as though it were a corporation, especially with respect to the transaction in question. In *Cantor v. Sunshine Greenery, Inc.*,[17] for example, the promoter mailed articles of incorporation to the secretary of state's office. The articles were officially filed only after some unexplained delay. In the meanwhile, assuming that the articles had been filed and that the corporation existed, the promoter entered into a lease on the corporation's behalf. The lessor had considerable business experience, but did not require the promoter to guarantee the lease personally. Instead, the lessor knew and expected that the corporation would be responsible for the lease. When the corporation failed to perform, lessor sought to hold the promoter personally liable. The court held that, because of the delay in filing the articles, the business was not a legal corporation at the time the lease was made. The promoter's execution of articles of incorporation, the good faith effort to file them, and the carrying on of business in the corporation's name, however, justified treating the firm as a de facto corporation. The promoter therefore could not be held personally liable.[18]

Some jurisdictions use an alternative three-part test: (1) a statute must exist under which incorporation was legally possible;

---

[17] 398 A.2d 571 (N.J.App.Div.1979).

[18] Inactive investors present an even stronger case for invoking the de facto corporation doctrine and are rarely held personally liable for the firm's obligations. See, e.g., Flanagan v. Jackson Wholesale Bldg. Supply Co., 461 So.2d 761, 765 (Miss.1984) (declining to hold inactive investor personally liable).

(2) there was a "colorable" (a.k.a. "bona fide") attempt to incorporate the business; and (3) there was an actual use or exercise of corporate powers and privileges. The difference between the two tests is largely semantic. Both tend to collapse into the question of whether there was a good faith effort to incorporate the business.

B. Corporation by Estoppel

Cases occasionally arise in which the promoter made no good faith effort to incorporate the business. This failure precludes one from invoking the de facto corporation doctrine. As noted, however, imposing full personal liability on the firm's would-be shareholders gives the other party to the transaction a windfall. Courts developed the corporation by estoppel doctrine to deal with such cases. The corporation by estoppel doctrine differs from the more familiar concept of equitable estoppel. There is no requirement of a misrepresentation, of reasonable reliance, or of a change in position. Instead, someone who deals with the firm as though it were a corporation is estopped later to deny the corporation's existence.

A leading example of the doctrine in action is *Cranson v. International Business Machines Corp.*,[19] in which the defendant was asked to invest in a corporation that was about to be created. Defendant was advised by an attorney that the business had been incorporated. Defendant bought shares, received a stock certificate, and was shown the corporation's seal and minute book. Defendant was elected an officer and director of the corporation. The firm operated as though it were a corporation and conducted business in its corporate name. Due to an oversight by the attorney, of which defendant was unaware, the firm was not incorporated until about seven months after Defendant invested in the firm. During that period the corporation entered into a contract to purchase typewriters from a supplier. The supplier dealt with the firm as though it were a corporation, and dealt with Defendant as an agent of the firm. When the corporation defaulted, the supplier sought to hold Defendant personally liable. The court held that the supplier was estopped to deny the corporation's existence and, accordingly, could not hold Defendant personally liable.

In *Cranson*, the Maryland Court of Appeals distinguished the corporation by estoppel doctrine from the de facto corporation doctrine by holding that the latter could be invoked only if articles of incorporation were filed. A corporation by estoppel, however, could be found because the third party had dealt with the firm as though it were a corporation and relied on the firm, not the individual defendant, for performance. While there is general

---

[19] 200 A.2d 33 (Md.1964).

agreement that the de facto corporation doctrine requires a good faith effort to incorporate, opinion is divided as to whether *Cranson* correctly held that a failure to file articles of incorporation—standing alone—precludes application of the de facto corporation doctrine.

C. Statutory Efforts to Abolish the Common Law Doctrines

Over the years, the MBCA's drafters have repeatedly tried to dispose of the common law rules on defective incorporation. Section 50 of the 1950 MBCA provided that a corporation comes into existence when the secretary of state issues a certificate of incorporation and that the certificate constituted conclusive evidence thereof. Section 139 stated: "All persons who assume to act as a corporation without authority so to do shall be jointly and severally liable for all" obligations of the firm. Nothing in the 1950 statute appeared to contemplate either common law doctrine; to the contrary, § 139 appeared to impose full personal liability unless a de jure corporation existed, while § 50 appeared to require a certificate of incorporation be issued in order for a de jure corporation to exist. A good faith effort to comply with the statute was simply irrelevant. The 1969 MBCA explicitly embraced this interpretation, stating in the drafters' comments that § 50 was intended to abolish the de facto corporation doctrine.

Even in MBCA states, however, some courts nevertheless persisted in using the common law defective incorporation doctrines. Some continued to apply the corporation by estoppel doctrine when there was no attempt to incorporate.[20] Others held that the phrase "assume to act" in MBCA § 139 limited liability to active participants in the business—inactive investors of a defectively incorporated business would not be held personally liable.[21]

The 1984 MBCA's drafters recognized that courts were resisting their predecessors' attempt to abolish the de facto corporation and corporation by estoppel doctrines. Accordingly, the drafters chose to relax the statutory standard slightly. MBCA § 2.04 now provides: "All persons purporting to act as or on behalf of a corporation, knowing there was no incorporation under [the MBCA], are jointly and severally liable for all liabilities created while so acting." By negative inference, neither inactive investors nor active investors who are unaware of the defective incorporation may be held personally liable. The MBCA approach thus should lead to the

---

[20] See, e.g., Sherwood & Roberts-Oregon, Inc. v. Alexander, 525 P.2d 135 (Or.1974).

[21] Timberline Equip. Co. v. Davenport, 514 P.2d 1109 (Or.1973).

same result as the common law doctrines in most cases, but (arguably) provides a clearer rule allowing for greater predictability.

D. Policy

The policy issue posed by defective incorporation cases is essentially the same as those posed in cases involving preincorporation contracts. Do we want to maximize the incentive for promoters promptly and accurately to complete the incorporation process? Or do we want to give creditors who deal with a corporation (or what they think is a corporation) an incentive to protect themselves through devices such as personal guarantees? The MBCA's drafters tried to split that baby by (1) limiting liability to active participants—persons who act on the purported firm's behalf—who know no corporation exists and (2) admitting the possibility of estoppel for preincorporation contracts in which the creditor urged the promoter to use the putative corporation's name despite the creditor's knowledge that no corporation had been formed. If the MBCA's solution is not exactly Solomonic in its wisdom, the statute does seem get it about right. In case (1), the risk of liability gives the parties who control the incorporation process an incentive to carry out that process promptly, validly, and with due regard to creditor interests. In case (2), however, the MBCA denies a windfall to creditors who not only fail to protect themselves but affirmatively go out of their way to induce a contract from those who may be reluctant to transact business in their own names.

§ 2.6   Promoter's Fiduciary Duties

A corporation's promoter often controls assets that would be useful to the business. This is especially likely where a promoter incorporates a pre-existing business previously operated as a partnership or sole proprietorship. In such cases, the promoter is on both sides of the transaction, representing both himself and the corporation. The resulting conflict of interest should be readily apparent: On the one hand, the promoter is an agent of the corporation, charged with a fiduciary duty to get the best possible deal for the corporation. On the other hand, the promoter has a natural selfish interest to get the best possible deal for himself.

In this situation, courts impose a fiduciary duty of loyalty on promoters analogous to that imposed in connection with interested director transactions: If the transaction is later challenged, the promoter has the burden of proving that he dealt fairly with the corporation. If the promoter fails to do so, the corporation may void the transaction and/or recover any secret profits earned by the promoter.

Two issues are critical in determining whether the promoter breached his fiduciary duty to the corporation. First, was the promoter on both sides of the transaction or was the corporation represented by independent parties? In negotiations with the promoter, the corporation should be represented by independent directors who are neither dominated nor controlled by the promoter. Second, did the promoter provide full disclosure of the conflict and of the facts of the transaction?

In *Frick v. Howard*,[22] for example, the promoter bought a parcel of land for $240,000. Shortly thereafter the promoter transferred the property to the corporation for $350,000, taking a mortgage. At the time of the transaction, the promoter was the sole stockholder and dominated the board of directors. The promoter also signed the mortgage on the corporation's behalf. The corporation later defaulted on the mortgage and the promoter attempted to foreclose on the mortgage. Because the promoter dominated the board at the time the sale took place, he had a fiduciary duty to give the corporation the benefit of his bargain. In other words, he could not earn a profit on the transaction without violating his fiduciary duty to the corporation. The mortgage was void for lack of consideration and foreclosure was not allowed.[23]

Courts disagree as to whether promoters owe fiduciary duties to persons who become shareholders of the corporation after the transaction between the promoter and the corporation took place. The majority view (the so-called "Massachusetts rule") is that such a duty exists if, at the time of the transaction between the promoter and the corporation, the promoter planned to bring in additional shareholders.[24] The minority view is that the promoter owes no fiduciary duty to subsequent investors.[25]

---

[22] 126 N.W.2d 619 (Wis.1964). In *Frick*, the promoter's fiduciary duty ran to the corporation. The promoter also owes fiduciary duties to his co-promoters. See, e.g., Glassell v. Prentiss, 346 P.2d 895 (Cal.App.1959).

[23] The *Frick* decision can be criticized as resting on a highly formalistic understanding of the corporation's separate legal personhood. At the time the transaction occurred, the promoter and the corporation were economically one and the same. If the promoter wanted to move an asset from his personal account to his corporate account, that is no different than if he had shifted his change between his pants pockets. The law ought to be concerned only if the transaction somehow injured investors who became shareholders between the time the transaction occurred and the time promoter sought to foreclose on the mortgage.

[24] See, e.g., Old Dominion Copper Mining & Smelting Co. v. Bigelow, 89 N.E. 193 (Mass.1909); Northridge Co-op. Section No. 1, Inc. v. 32nd Ave. Constr. Corp., 141 N.E.2d 802 (N.Y.1957).

[25] See, e.g., Old Dominion Copper Mining & Smelting Co. v. Lewisohn, 210 U.S. 206 (1908).

Suppose, for example, that Acme Mining Corporation is formed in December, at which time Promoter and Co-promoter are the sole shareholders. In return for 2,500 shares of Acme stock, Promoter sells 49 acres of land to Acme. In early January, the sale is approved by Promoter and Co-promoter in their capacity as shareholders of the company. The following April, Plaintiff buys 1000 Acme shares. Plaintiff later sues, alleging that Acme paid too high a price for Promoter's land. Under the minority view, Plaintiff may not prevail because he owned no shares at the time of the challenged transaction. Under the majority view, Plaintiff may not prevail because there was no plan, at the time of the challenged transaction, to sell stock to additional shareholders.[26]

§ 2.7   Corporate Powers and Purposes

During the 19th century, state corporation codes typically required that the articles of incorporation set forth the purposes for which the corporation was organized. At that time, this requirement had considerable substantive importance because of the ultra vires doctrine. Most states have sharply emasculated this doctrine in recent years, however, so that ultra vires now is largely a dead letter.

The ultra vires doctrine grew out of suspicion by some early 19th Century legislatures and courts that corporations were a source of potential mischief and evil. As a result, governments closely regulated corporations. As this suspicion faded in the middle of the 19th Century, states started adopting general enabling corporate laws. Under these statutes, all one had to do to form a corporation was to jump correctly through the statutory hoops described above. Traces of the traditional suspicion of corporations lingered for some time thereafter, however, taking the form of restrictions on the purposes for which corporations could be organized and the powers corporations were authorized to exercise. In addition, these statutes required that the articles of incorporation specify which of the permissible purposes the corporation was organized to achieve and which of the statutory powers it would exercise.

---

[26] The majority rule is almost as problematic as the *Frick* ruling. The relevant consideration ought not to be the existence of a plan to bring in additional investors, but whether such investors got full disclosure of relevant facts before investing. In *Frick*, if subsequent investors were told the material facts of the property sale and mortgage, they should have no claim against the promoter. The same should be true in the example in the text. In both cases, provided there was disclosure, the price investors should pay for the corporation's shares ought to reflect the effect of the self-dealing transaction on the firm's value. Allowing them subsequently to sue for breach of fiduciary duty gives them a windfall. In any case, investing in a corporation is voluntary. Investors who make an informed decision to buy shares following a self-dealing transaction by a promoter have made their bed and ought to lie in it—even if that turns out to be uncomfortable or even unwise.

If a corporation exceeded the powers and purposes set forth in the statutes or the firm's articles, it was said to be acting "ultra vires." Suppose that neither the corporate statute nor the firm's articles gave it the power to make loans. If the firm lent money, no matter how small an amount, that action was ultra vires. An ultra vires act was illegal and, accordingly, null and void.

The ultra vires doctrine was frequently asserted as a defense in contract suits involving corporations. On the one hand, if the other party breached the contract, the corporation could not enforce an ultra vires contract against it. On the other hand, if the corporation breached the contract, it could assert the ultra vires doctrine as a defense against a breach of contract suit brought by the other party. The ultra vires doctrine also could be asserted affirmatively in a shareholder suit against officers and directors who caused the firm to commit an ultra vires act. The responsible officers and directors could be held personally liable for any losses resulting from the action.

In the leading case of *Jacksonville, M., P. Railway & Navigation Co. v. Hooper*,[27] for example, the plaintiffs leased a resort hotel to the defendant railroad corporation. The hotel was located near the railroad's seaside terminal. The lease required the railroad corporation to insure the hotel, but the corporation failed to do so. The hotel burnt down during the lease term. When plaintiffs sued the railroad for breach of the lease, the railroad defended on grounds that the lease was ultra vires. The railroad's powers included the right to "erect and maintain all convenient buildings . . . for the accommodation and use of [its] passengers." The railroad argued that operating a resort hotel was not within the scope of this grant of power. The court held that the corporate powers clause was sufficiently broad to encompass operation of a resort hotel located near one of its terminals. As a result, the action was not ultra vires, and the corporation was liable for breaching the lease.

The ultra vires doctrine frequently had inefficient (not to mention harsh and unfair) results. If one of the parties to an ultra vires contract later regretted its bargain, it could breach the agreement with impunity, even if the transaction had been completed. The doctrine was even less attractive in tort cases, where it was sometimes invoked as a defense against tort suits brought by those injured by corporate agents committing an ultra vires act.

To avoid such outcomes, courts began eviscerating the doctrine. Some courts limited the doctrine's impact by broadly construing the corporation's purpose and powers clause to encompass the

---

[27] 160 U.S. 514 (1896).

transaction in question.[28] Other courts enforced completed transactions by invoking such equitable doctrines as estoppel, quasi-contract, and waiver.

Moving the story forward towards the present, recall that state corporation laws gradually became more liberal, making the incorporation process much simpler. At about the same time, states began abandoning any effort to regulate the substantive conduct of corporations through the incorporation process. Several statutory reforms had a direct impact on the importance of the ultra vires doctrine, reducing it to its present non-issue status.

First, states have abandoned the effort to limit corporate powers and purposes. MBCA § 3.01(a) provides that every corporation shall have the purpose of engaging in any lawful business,[29] unless the articles set forth a more limited purpose. Section 3.02 says that every corporation shall have "the same powers as an individual to do all things necessary or convenient to carry out its business and affairs," including a list of specified powers. Section 2.02(b)(2) makes optional the inclusion of a purpose clause in the articles. Taken together, these provisions make it essentially impossible for an act to be ultra vires: if the corporation can pursue any lawful purpose and use any lawful power in so doing, no action can be said to be ultra vires, because no corporate act can involve an impermissible power or purpose.[30]

Second, states have enacted statutory limits on standing to challenge ultra vires acts. It is difficult to imagine a situation in which a transaction planner would choose to put limits on a corporation's purposes or powers in the articles of incorporation. But even if the articles include some such limitation, MBCA § 3.04(a) provides that the validity of a corporation's act may not be challenged on the ground that it lacks the power to so act. In one fell swoop, this provision de facto eliminates the ultra vires doctrine. Because the validity of the act cannot be challenged, neither the corporation nor the other party to the transaction can raise the ultra vires doctrine as a defense to a breach of contract or tort claim.

----

[28] See, e.g., Jacksonville M., P. Ry. & Nav. Co. v. Hooper, 160 U.S. 514 (1896).

[29] The MBCA position that a corporation may engage in any lawful activity and exercise any lawful power implicitly suggests that a corporation exceeds its lawful powers, and thus commits an ultra vires act, by engaging in illegal conduct. Although courts sometimes refer to illegal corporate acts as ultra vires, corporate law scholars disfavor this usage. As with natural persons, corporations have the power to break the law, but not the right to do so.

[30] DGCL § 102(a)(3) retains a requirement that the articles include a purpose clause, but allows the drafter simply to state that the corporation's purpose is to engage in any lawful business. The substantive effect is the same as the MBCA approach.

MBCA § 3.04(b) contains three limited exceptions under which the ultra vires doctrine has some lingering validity: (1) a shareholder may bring suit to enjoin an ultra vires act; (2) the corporation may bring suit against an officer or director who commits an ultra vires act; and (3) the state may bring an involuntary dissolution suit against the corporation for abusing its authority. An interesting example of these provisions at work is provided by *Inter-Continental Corp. v. Moody.*[31] The corporation guaranteed a note given by its president to a lender. When the lender brought suit against the corporation to enforce the guarantee, the corporation raised the ultra vires defense. In addition, a shareholder intervened to enjoin performance of the guarantee on ultra vires grounds. The court held that Texas' ultra vires statute, comparable to MBCA § 3.04, barred the corporation from raising the ultra vires defense even if the other party knew the transaction exceeded the corporation's powers or purposes. The court further held that the statute permits a shareholder to intervene to enjoin the contract, however, even if the corporation solicited him to do so. Only if the shareholder was acting as the corporation's agent would the shareholder be denied standing. Interestingly, the shareholder would not become the corporation's agent even where the corporation notified the shareholder of the suit and suggested the shareholder intervene. If the corporation paid the shareholder's attorney's fees, however, an agency could be found. Perhaps surprisingly, uncompensated collusion between the defendant corporation and one of its shareholders thus seems possible.

---

[31] 411 S.W.2d 578 (Tex.Civ.App.1966).

Chapter 3

FINANCING THE CORPORATION

§ 3.1 Introduction

The numerous technological changes wrought by the Industrial Revolution, especially the development of modern mass production techniques in the nineteenth century, gave great advantages to firms large enough to achieve economies of scale. In turn, those advantages gave rise to giant industrial corporations. These firms required enormous amounts of capital, far exceeding the resources of any single individual or family. They could be financed only by aggregating many small investments, which was accomplished by selling stock or bonds to many investors—each of whom held only a tiny fraction of the firm's total capital.

Capital markets facilitated this process in at least two respects. First, the primary market gave issuers access to a large and ever-growing pool of potential investors. Second, the secondary markets for corporate stocks and bonds gave investors essential liquidity and, accordingly, encouraged investment. In a liquid market, investors can freely sell their securities without involving the firm. Liquidity, in turn, makes it easier and cheaper for the company subsequently to raise capital in the primary market, because investors generally prefer (and will be willing to pay more for) liquid securities.

A. Corporate Capital Structure

A corporation's capital structure consists of the permanent and long-term contingent claims on the corporation's assets and future earnings issued pursuant to formal contractual instruments called securities. There are two basic types of securities: debt and equity. In most cases, of course, the funds needed to finance the corporation will largely come from bank loans or retained earnings, not through selling debt or equity securities. Bank loans and retained earnings are not regarded as being part of the corporation's capital structure, however, because neither involves a securitized investment in the firm.

Equity securities are issued in the form of shares, which represent "the units into which the proprietary interests in a corporation are divided."[1] As this statutory definition suggests, the law traditionally regards a corporation as being owned by the holders of its equity securities. Holders of debt securities are not in

---

[1] MBCA § 1.40(22).

any sense owners of the corporation; rather, they are creditors of the corporation.

The law's conception of equity security holders as the corporation's owners has the important consequence that corporate officers and directors owe fiduciary duties to the equity security holders. In contrast, the relationship between the corporation and its debt security holders is essentially contractual. Directors and officers normally owe no fiduciary duties to debt security holders.[2]

Another important distinction between debt and equity securities is their respective risk exposure. All else being equal, equity securities are riskier than debt securities issued by the same corporation. Equity securities represent the "residual claim," which means their holders are entitled to whatever funds are left after all other claims on the corporation's assets and earnings have been satisfied. In contrast, debt securities represent a fixed claim on the corporation's assets and earnings superior to that of the equity. Because debt securityholders are entitled to be paid before the equity securityholders, they are less likely to be hurt by sub-par corporate performance.

A third important difference between debt and equity is their respective duration. Although equity securities often change hands, the securities themselves represent permanent claims on the corporation. In contrast, debt securities usually are limited in duration. At some contractually specified date, the debt security will mature and the corporation will pay off the principal.

B. Equity Securities

Many corporations divide their equity securities into multiple classes of stock, of which common and preferred stock are the basic forms. As with other corporation statutes, the MBCA requires the articles of incorporation to authorize one or more classes of stock together having unlimited voting rights and one or more classes that together are entitled to receive the assets of the corporation upon dissolution.[3] They need not be the same class, however, which gives transaction planners considerable flexibility.

1. Common Stock

Common stock carries two basic rights, voting and economic, both of which are subject to being unbundled and sold separately. As to voting rights, holders of common stock have a limited right to participate in corporate decisionmaking by electing directors and

---

[2] See, e.g., Metropolitan Life Ins. Co. v. RJR Nabisco, Inc., 716 F.Supp. 1504 (S.D.N.Y.1989); Simons v. Cogan, 549 A.2d 300 (Del.1988); Katz v. Oak Indus., 508 A.2d 873 (Del.Ch.1986).

[3] MBCA § 6.01(b).

voting on major corporate decisions. The number of votes which can be cast by any one shareholder are determined by the number of shares owned, usually on a one-vote per share basis.

As to economic rights, holders of common stock possess the residual claim on the corporation's assets. In other words, each share of common stock has an equal right to participate in distributions of the firm's earnings in the form of dividends and, in the event the corporation is liquidated, to share equally in the firm's assets remaining after all prior claims have been satisfied.

2. *Preferred Stock*

Preferred stock is an odd beast, neither wholly fish nor wholly fowl, which lies on the boundary between debt and equity. As the name implies, preferred stock is given certain rights superior to those of common stock. (Remember that the claims of creditors always come before the claims of shareholders, regardless of the type of stock in question.) Specifically, preferred stock may have a preference over common stock with respect to dividends and/or liquidation. If the corporation is liquidated, preferred stock with a liquidation preference has a right to be paid a specified portion of the corporation's assets before any portion thereof is distributed to the common shareholders.

Preferred stock with a dividend preference will receive dividends before any are paid to the common stock. Dividends differ significantly from interest payable on a bond. The corporation must pay the required interest on its debt securities or it will be deemed to be in default. In the event of a default, creditors have various rights under the bankruptcy laws to force a liquidation or reorganization of the firm. In contrast, the corporation is not required to pay dividends to the preferred stock. Its obligation merely is to pay the stated dividend to the preferred shareholders before any dividend is paid to the common stock. Most corporations, however, voluntarily assume certain additional obligations to give the preferred shareholders some assurance they will receive the stated dividend.

The preferred stock's right to dividends is usually cumulative; i.e., if the corporation fails to pay a dividend, the missed dividends accumulate and all missed dividends must be paid before any dividend is paid to the common. Suppose the preferred shares are entitled to a $1 dividend in each calendar quarter and the corporation has failed to pay any dividends for the four preceding quarters. In this situation, the corporation would have to pay the dividend for the current quarter ($1) plus the four missed dividends ($4, for a total payment of $5 per share) before it could pay dividends to the common stock. Alternatively, although preferred stock usually has no voting rights, many corporations give preferred shareholders the right to elect some or all directors in the event a specified number of dividends are missed.

The preferences and other rights of preferred stock are spelled out in the articles of incorporation. MBCA § 6.02, however, allows the corporation to create so-called "blank check" preferred stock. If blank check preferred is authorized, the rights and preferences of the preferred stock will not be contained in the articles. Instead, the articles will empower the board of directors to specify those rights and preferences at the time the shares are issued. An amendment to the articles, creating the shares and detailing their rights and preferences, must be filed with the secretary of state's office before the shares are issued, but this amendment does not require shareholder approval.

Blank check preferred has obvious advantages. If the articles authorize blank check preferred, the board can respond quickly and flexibly to changing market conditions. The ability to precisely tailor dividend rates and other provisions for prevailing market conditions lowers the corporation's cost of capital and thus benefits the shareholders.

On the other hand, blank check preferred has even more obvious disadvantages. The name says it all: would you give someone a blank check? There is some risk that the board of directors will abuse their power to set the terms of the blank check preferred. Early defenses against hostile takeovers, for example, often involved the use of blank check preferred.

C. Debt Securities

Debt securities come in three basic forms: (1) bonds, which are secured long-term instruments; (2) debentures, which are unsecured long-term instruments; and (3) notes, which are short-term instruments that usually are unsecured. Although the dividing line between bonds and debentures on the one hand and notes on the other is not always precise, a good rule of thumb is that notes are obligations having a maturity of nine months or less. For purposes of semantic convenience, all debt securities are referred to as bonds in this text unless the context requires otherwise.

Bonds typically consist of two distinct rights. First, the bondholder is entitled to receive a stream of payments in the form of interest over a period of years. Second, at the end of the bond's prescribed term (i.e., at maturity), the bondholder is entitled to the return of the principal—the amount paid to purchase the bond. (There are certain other types of bonds, such as zero-coupon bonds and asset-backed securities, having somewhat different characteristics, but we will ignore them.)

1. Bond Value and Interest Rates

Bonds are typically issued in $1,000 denominations with a coupon rate expressed as some percentage of the face value of the bond. A $1,000 bond with an 8% coupon rate, for example, pays $80 per year in interest. The value of a bond at any time prior to maturity is not determined by its denomination (or face value), but by the price the bond would command if sold in the market. A bond's secondary market price is a function of the bond's coupon rate and current market interest rates for bonds with similar risks. The relationship between current price and yield is an inverse one: if market rates have risen since the bond was issued, its current price will fall. In converse, if market rates have fallen, the bond's current price will rise.

The current value of a bond varies inversely with market interest rates because the coupon rate does not change when market rates do. If you bought a ten year $1,000 bond with a coupon rate equal to prevailing market rates of 6%, you purchased (among other things) the right to receive $60 per year in interest for ten years. If market rates fall to 5%, a newly issued $1,000 bond with a coupon rate equal to the market rate carries only the right to get $50 per year in interest. All other things being equal, it should be obvious that the previously-issued bond paying $60 per year is worth more than the subsequently-issued bond paying $50: if you would rather receive $60 per year than $50 per year, you would be willing to pay more for a bond that pays $60 per year.

2. The Indenture

Bonds are issued pursuant to complex contracts called indentures. In general, however, all of the indenture's myriad terms are designed to accomplish a single task: protecting the bondholder's right to interest and return of principal.

One of the more important parts of the indenture is the statement of what actions will constitute a default by the issuer. If a default occurs, the bondholders are entitled to accelerate the maturity of the bonds: they become immediately due and payable. Thus, if the bond is scheduled to mature on January 1, 2030, the issuer normally would not be required to pay back the principal until that date. If a default occurs today, however, the bondholders will be entitled to immediate return of their investment. Failure to pay interest when owed is the most obvious event of default, but many indentures will specify certain other violations of the indenture to be events of default.

The indenture typically contains a variety of restrictions, whose violation will either constitute an event of default or which may mature into an event of default if not cured. Restrictions on the corporation's ability to pay dividends are common. While most indentures permit the payment of some reasonable level of dividends, indentures by particularly risky companies may prohibit the payment of any dividends during the life of the bonds. The goal of such provisions is to retain earnings within the firm, so they are available to the bondholders in the event of a default. Another common restriction is the negative pledge covenant, which restricts the corporation's ability to issue debt senior to the bonds covered by the indenture.

Call provisions allow the issuer to repay the principal before maturity. A related provision is the sinking fund, which requires the issuer to pay back the principal in installments throughout the life of the bond.

In a corporation having hundreds or thousands of bondholders, it obviously would be very difficult for the issuer to bargain with all of the bondholders or for the bondholders to effectively enforce the indenture agreement. Instead, two intermediaries act on behalf of the bondholders. One is the underwriter: the investment banking firm that sells the bonds to the public. The underwriter negotiates the terms of the indenture with the issuer. The other intermediary is the indenture trustee. The indenture trustee's job is an enforcer: if the issuer defaults, it is the indenture trustee who takes action (such as bringing suit) on behalf of the bondholders to enforce their rights under the indenture.

D. Convertible Securities

A corporation may issue securities that are convertible into another form of the corporation's securities. Convertible bonds and convertible preferred stock are the most common types of convertibles. Solely for purposes of convenience, the following discussion refers only to convertible bonds. In general, the principles discussed apply equally to convertible preferred.

A convertible bond essentially combines two different types of securities into a single instrument. One half of the package is a traditional bond, with the usual right to periodic interest and ultimate repayment of principal. The other half is a warrant, which is a type of option issued by the corporation. The warrant's holder receives a right to purchase securities of the corporation (usually common stock) at the price and on those conditions specified by the warrant.

In order to exercise the conversion feature, the holder of a convertible bond surrenders it to the corporation, which thereupon issues the number of shares of common stock specified in the indenture. The so-called "conversion ratio" is the number of shares the bondholder will receive when the bond is surrendered. The conversion price is the per share cost of those shares to the shareholder. If the conversion ratio is known, the conversion price may be determined by dividing the face value of the bond by the conversion ratio. Conversely, if the conversion price is known, the conversion ratio may be determined by dividing the face value of the bond by the conversion price. The indenture typically states the conversion price, rather than the conversion ratio.

As an example, assume Acme, Inc., issues convertible bonds having a face value of $1,000 and a coupon rate of 8%. The indenture states that upon surrender of the bond the holder will receive 1 share for every $25 of the bond's face value. The conversion price thus is $25, which gives us a conversion ratio of 40 shares per bond ($1,000 divided by $25).

The conversion price tells us the minimum price the corporation's stock must reach before it makes economic sense for the holder to convert the bond into stock. The issuer will normally set the conversion price 10–30% above the stock market price prevailing when the bonds are issued. Only if the stock's market price subsequently rises towards and past the conversion price, will the holder profit by converting. Suppose that in the preceding example the market price of the corporation's stock was $20 when the bond was sold. If the holder bought the bond for $1,000 (face value) and immediately exercised the conversion right, he would receive 40 shares worth $20 on the market. The holder would lose money on the deal, because he would surrender a bond worth $1,000 to receive shares worth $800. If the stock price subsequently rises to $30, however, the holder could profit by exercising the conversion feature. Now he would surrender a bond with a face value of $1,000 to receive stock worth $1,200.

Until quite recently, most corporate law statutes permitted only down-stream conversion. In other words, a security could be convertible only into junior securities. Bonds could be converted into common stock, but stock could not be converted into bonds. MBCA § 6.01(c)(2) permits up-stream conversion, but few companies appear to have availed themselves of this option.

E.   Asset Backed Securities

In an asset securitization transaction, a company sells some assets (typically accounts receivable) to a so-called "bankruptcy remote vehicle" (BRV), which pays for those assets with the proceeds of an offering of fixed income securities. Like traditional factoring, which it somewhat resembles, asset securitization creates value in several ways.

The type of debt issued by a firm affects its debt capacity. Most mature firms issue claims on their general cash flows and assets. These claims depend on the firm's going-concern value. Determining this value for growth firms is difficult, due to information asymmetries and valuation discrepancies. Consequently, capital providers apply a significant uncertainty discount when they advance funds to such firms. One way for growth firms to access the debt market is through asset securitization, which does not rely on the value of the firm as a going concern. They are instead tied to specific, easier-to-measure asset values. Growth firms thus can use asset-based borrowings to enhance an otherwise constrained balance sheet.

Securitization also creates value by increasing liquidity. It turns illiquid raw assets into securities that can be bought and sold much more easily.

Finally, securitization creates value by dividing the risks associated with a particular lending arrangement and selling the risks off to the investors most able (or willing) to bear that particular type of risk. Put another way, securitization generally takes the different characteristics of the raw asset and puts them into separate classes, which can be sold separately rather than bundled. Accordingly, each risk characteristic can be sold to the buyer who is best able to bear that risk. Credit risk can be sold to those who best understand credit risk or who are hedged against credit risk, for example, without obliging the buyer to bear other risks they understand less well or for which they are not the best bearer.

§ 3.2   Issuance of Securities: The Business Context

The vast majority of U.S. corporations are closely-held. These corporations rarely sell securities. Any sales they do make are effected through private placements to small numbers of investors. No public secondary market exists on which their shares are traded. If such a corporation decides to "go public," it does so by conducting an initial public offering of its securities.

Going public has a number of significant advantages. It necessarily creates a public secondary market when the initial shareholders (or bondholders) begin trading the corporation's securities with other investors. The availability of a secondary market makes the corporation's securities liquid, which means investors can freely sell their securities without involving the firm. Liquidity, in turn, makes it easier and cheaper to subsequently raise capital in the primary market, because investors generally prefer (and will be willing to pay more) for liquid securities. A secondary market also permits the firm to utilize stock-based forms of management compensation. Finally, banks may charge lower interest rates to public firms, because changes in stock prices are a good barometer of the firm's condition. This same factor also means that the issuer can often offer a lower interest rate in subsequent private placements of debt securities with institutional investors.

On the other hand, there are some significant disadvantages associated with going public. A public corporation is subject to unsolicited changes of control through hostile tender offers and proxy contests. A public corporation also must provide far greater disclosure to investors, which results in reduced privacy on sensitive issues like executive compensation and research.

Once a corporation decides to raise funds through a primary market offering, it next must decide whether to utilize the services of an underwriter or to sell the securities itself in a direct offering. Direct offerings by issuers are very rare. Typically, only well-established firms making a private placement of debt securities to institutional investors use direct offerings.

Once they go public, established corporations rarely return to the primary market for further public offerings. If an established corporation needs primary market financing, it normally relies on private placements of debt securities. Because the regulatory burden faced by issuers is significantly reduced in the private placement context, private placements are faster and much less expensive than underwritten public offerings.

After going public, and listing their shares for trading on a stock market, such as the NYSE or NASDAQ, the listed company is bound not only by the corporation law code of their state of incorporation and the federal securities laws, but also by the contract they sign with the stock exchange on which they have their principal listing. For New York Stock Exchange-listed companies, the NYSE's Listed Company Manual governs. For NASDAQ-listed companies, the Listing Qualifications set out the relevant rules.

§ 3.3   Issuance of Securities: Corporate Law Aspects

Most regulatory burdens on issuing securities today are imposed by federal law. Several state corporate law doctrines, however, continue to affect the issuance process. Three seem especially worthy of note: (1) the respective roles of the board of directors and the shareholders; (2) the law governing subscription agreements; and (3) preemptive rights. The legal capital rules governing issuance of stock are taken up separately in Chapter 13.

A. The Respective Roles of the Board and Shareholders

State law empowers the board of directors to cause the corporation to issue debt securities, at any time and for any valid purpose, without shareholder action or approval. The board thus essentially has unfettered discretion to issue debt, subject to its fiduciary duties and any pre-existing contractual restrictions on the issuance of additional debt.

The board's authority with respect to issuing additional stock is slightly less sweeping. In general, the board has wide discretion to issue additional shares of stock, so long as there is a valid purpose for doing so and the corporation receives adequate consideration for the shares. In three situations, however, the board must obtain shareholder approval before issuing additional stock.

If the corporation wishes to issue additional shares in excess of the number of authorized shares, shareholder approval of an amendment increasing the number of authorized shares is required. Suppose, for example, that Acme Corporation's articles of incorporation authorize 30,000 shares of common stock, 10,000 of which are already outstanding. The board could authorize the sale of up to 20,000 shares without shareholder approval, but the board wishes to sell 40,000 shares. Because Acme's articles presently authorize only 30,000 shares, the board must ask the shareholders to approve an amendment increasing the number of authorized shares of common stock from 30,000 to at least 50,000. In real life, this is fairly rare. The articles normally set an authorized number of shares exceeding the number of shares the corporation would expect to issue in the near term.

If the board of directors wishes to issue a new class of shares not authorized in the articles, it must ask the shareholders to approve an amendment authorizing the new class. In the preceding example, the articles authorized only common stock. If the board wishes to sell preferred stock, it must first ask the shareholders to approve an amendment creating a class of preferred stock and setting the number of authorized shares of the new class.

Finally, the Model Act requires shareholder approval of an issuance of shares (or convertible securities) if (1) the shares are issued for noncash consideration and (2) the issued shares represent more than 20 percent of the voting power of the shares outstanding prior to the issuance.[4] The major stock exchanges and NASDAQ have similar requirements in their listing standards.

B. Subscription Agreements

A subscription agreement is a contract pursuant to which an investor agrees to buy corporate stock. If the subscription agreement is entered into by an investor and an existing corporation, ordinary contract law rules govern. If the subscription agreement is signed before the business is incorporated, however, a more complex body of corporate law applies.

At one time, promoters commonly used subscription agreements to measure investor interest in the proposed corporate venture. The promoter solicited investors to subscribe for shares. If enough investors agreed to buy stock in the venture, the promoter went forward with the incorporation. After incorporation, the firm made "calls" for payment on the investors. A number of legal problems arose in connection with subscription agreements, the most important of which was the question of whether the subscription agreement constituted a binding contract.

Recall that a corporation cannot make contracts until it comes into de jure existence. The majority common law view therefore treated subscription agreements as a continuing offer, rather than a binding contract. An investor therefore could revoke the subscription agreement at any time before the firm was incorporated or, in some states, before the corporation issued the call for payment.[5]

Most modern corporation statutes reject the common law approach. MBCA § 6.20(a) is typical. It provides that a subscription agreement is irrevocable for six months after it is signed, unless the agreement states to the contrary or all subscribers agree to a revocation.

C. Preemptive Rights

When a corporation issues additional shares, the proportional financial interests and voting rights of existing shareholders are reduced. Preemptive rights were developed to provide a mechanism for preserving the proportional interests of existing shareholders. Preemptive rights give the shareholder the right to purchase a pro rata share of any new issues at the new issue price.

---

[4] MBCA § 6.21(f).

[5] See, e.g., Hudson Real Estate Co. v. Tower, 30 N.E. 465 (Mass.1892); cf. Minneapolis Threshing Machine Co. v. Davis, 41 N.W. 1026 (Minn.1889) (pre-incorporation subscription agreement constituted a continuing offer to the corporation, but also constituted a binding contract among the subscribers).

Suppose Susan Shareholder owns 200 of Acme, Inc.'s 1,000 outstanding shares. Assume the corporation's book value is $12,000—or $12 per share. Acme plans to issue 400 additional shares at $10 per share. Before that dilutive transaction, Susan's stock gave her 20% of the corporation's voting power. Afterwards, Susan will only have about 14% of the voting power. Worse yet, after the dilutive transaction, the book value of Susan's stock will have declined to $11.42 (the corporation received an additional $4,000 in assets, raising its value to $16,000, but that value is now divided by 1,400 shares).

If Acme's stock is subject to preemptive rights, Shareholder is entitled to buy enough new shares to maintain her proportional interest in the corporation. Before any additional shares are issued, Susan owns 20% of the outstanding shares. She is therefore entitled to buy 80 of the 400 additional shares when they are issued. If she does so, she will still own a 20% interest in the corporation (she will own 280 out of 1,400 shares, which is 20%). Shareholder must pay the price asked by the corporation, which is $10 on these facts.

Under MBCA § 6.30, shareholders of a corporation are entitled to preemptive rights only if the articles of incorporation explicitly provide for them. About two-thirds of the states follow the MBCA's "opt in" approach, most notably including Delaware. Most of the rest follow an "opt out" approach, under which shareholders are entitled to preemptive rights unless the articles of incorporation provide to the contrary. Virtually all public corporations have chosen to eliminate preemptive rights, because of the complications they create when the corporation wishes to issue new stock. In any event, because shareholders must make an additional investment in order to exercise their preemptive rights, those rights provide only limited protection for shareholders who wish to maintain their existing proportional interest in the corporation.

§ 3.4   Issuance of Shares: Federal Law

State corporate law imposes few meaningful restrictions on a corporation's ability to issue equity or debt securities. A corporation proposing to issue securities, however, does face significant regulatory hurdles from federal securities law. The Securities Act of 1933 is the main federal statute regulating primary market transactions.[6] The Securities Act has two principal goals: assuring adequate disclosure of material information to investors and preventing fraud.[7] As to the former, the Act follows a transactional

---

[6] 15 U.S.C. §§ 77a–77z–3.

[7] See, e.g., Rubin v. U. S., 449 U.S. 424, 431 (1981) ("these provisions were enacted to protect against fraud and promote the free flow of information in the public dissemination of securities").

disclosure model; i.e., the Act focuses on getting information concerning certain transactions from the issuer to investors. As to the latter, the Act imposes both civil and criminal liability on those who use fraud in the sale of securities.

A. The Registration Process

Securities Act § 5(a) makes it unlawful to sell a security unless a registration statement is in effect with respect to the securities. In other words, unless an exemption is available, the prospective issuer must file a registration statement with the SEC and wait for the registration statement to become effective before selling securities. The registration statement contains extensive disclosures and includes a subsidiary disclosure document called a prospectus that must be delivered to investors.

As originally adopted, the Securities Act and the Securities Exchange Act established two separate disclosure systems. The Securities Act imposed transactional disclosure obligations, requiring disclosure in connection with particular transactions. In contrast, the Securities Exchange Act imposed a system of periodic disclosures on certain companies. This created a certain amount of overlap and duplication. In the early 1980s, the SEC adopted a program of integrated disclosure, which partially combined the two systems. Under the integrated disclosure system, an issuer planning a registered offering first looks to the various registration statement forms to determine which form it is eligible to use. The issuer then looks to Regulation S–K for the substantive disclosure requirements. Regulation S–K adopted uniform disclosure standards for both Acts, so that virtually all filings are now prepared under identical instructions. As a result, the style and content of disclosure documents under both Acts are now essentially identical.

The registration statement forms and Regulation S–K spell out in great detail the information that must be contained in the registration statement. But their requirements do not tell the complete story. The registration statement must not only contain the information specifically required by the forms, but also must contain any additional material information which is necessary to give investors a clear picture of the company and the securities it is offering.[8]

B. Exemptions from Registration

Issuers have several good reasons to avoid registration when selling securities. First, a registered public offering is a very

---

[8] See, e.g., In re Universal Camera Corp., 19 S.E.C. 648 (1945).

expensive proposition. Lawyers, accountants, and printers are required, none of whom come cheap. Underwriters and dealers take substantial commissions. Second, a registered public offering subjects the issuer to on-going disclosure obligations under the Securities Exchange Act. Third, a registered public offering easily can take months to complete. Finally, some important liability provisions attach only to registered public offerings.

On the other hand, the consequences of failing to register securities before selling them are severe. The SEC may seek civil fines and other sanctions. In egregious cases, such as where the failure to register is coupled with fraudulent practices, the SEC may refer the matter to the Justice Department for criminal prosecution. Purchasers of unlawfully unregistered securities may seek rescission of the sale under Securities Act § 12(a)(1).[9]

Many issuers therefore seek to structure the transaction so as to qualify for one of the several exemptions that permit unregistered sales.[10] In this context, the exemption's provisions drive the planning process. Exemptions from registration are also important where the issuer and its counsel (if any) fail to realize that registration is required or deliberately ignore the registration requirements. In this context, the availability of an exemption determines the outcome of the resulting litigation.

The party claiming an exemption always has the burden of proving that the exemption was available in connection with the transaction in question. In other words, exemptions are an affirmative defense to a $5 charge. As a planning matter, it is critical that the issuer's lawyers create a full paper trail of the transaction so that every element of the exemption may be proved.

There are a number of exemptions available, including:

- *Private placements:* Securities Act § 4(2) exempts "transactions by an issuer not involving any public offering." Although the tests used to distinguish exempt private placements from public offerings that

---

[9] Securities Act § 12(a)(1) imposes strict liability for offers or sales made in violation of Section 5. Under Section 12(a)(1), only the seller of a security can be held liable. The principal remedy is rescission: the buyer can recover the consideration paid for the security, plus interest, less income received on the security. If the buyer no longer owns the securities, he can recover damages comparable to those which would be provided by rescission.

[10] We are mainly concerned here with transactional exemptions. If A sells a nonexempt security to B in an exempt transaction, B is not automatically free to resell that security. B must either register it or utilize another exempt transaction. In contrast, exempt securities are always exempt from the registration requirements. Thus, the initial sale need not be registered. Nor is the registration requirement applicable to subsequent transactions. Both types of exemptions relieve only the issuer from the registration requirements. Most civil liability provisions continue to apply, even if one of the exemptions is available.

must be registered vary somewhat from court to court, most look at some or all of the following factors: (1) A small number of offerees should be involved. (2) The issuer should not use mass solicitations or general advertising. (3) Investors should be knowledgeable, sophisticated, and experienced. (4) Investors should be given access to the same kind of information as would be provided by a registration statement. (5) The issuer should take steps to prevent resales by the purchasers.[11]

- *Reg D:* Securities Act § 3(b) authorizes the SEC to adopt rules exempting transactions where registration is not necessary in light of the relatively small amount of money involved. Regulations A and D thereunder offer a number of exemptions from registration for smaller offerings made to a limited number of people. In effect, these exemptions function as regulatory safe harbors providing greater certainty to issuers than the vaguer standards applicable to private placements.

- *Intrastate Offerings:* The Securities Act applies only to sales or purchases of securities made by the "use of any means or instruments of transportation or communication in interstate commerce or of the mails."[12] Because of the sweeping modern definition given interstate commerce, very few transactions escape capture by this jurisdictional nexus. When the Act was adopted Congress believed there should be a specific exemption for offerings that satisfy the jurisdictional nexus, but nevertheless are made by issuers with localized operations as part of a plan to raise local financing. Section 3(a)(11), the intrastate offering exemption, resulted. Section 3(a)(11) exempts from registration "any security which is part of an issue offered and sold only to persons resident within a single State or Territory, where the issuer of such security is a person resident and doing business within or, if a corporation, incorporated by and doing

[11] See, e.g., Doran v. Petroleum Management Corp., 545 F.2d 893 (5th Cir.1977) (setting forth four factors: number of offerees and their relationship to each other and the issuer; number of units offered; size of the offering; manner of the offering); see also American Bar Association, Section 4(2) and Statutory Law—A Position Paper of the Federal Regulation of Securities Committee, 31 Bus. Law. 485 (1975) (setting out four attributes of an exempt offering: offeree qualification as a knowledgeable and sophisticated investor; access to information; manner of offering; and absence of resales).

[12] Securities Act § 5(a)(1).

business within, such State or Territory." So long as these requirements are met, the issuer may use selling devices falling within the sphere of interstate commerce, such as telephone contacts, general advertisements, airline travel, and out-of-state dealers or underwriters.

C. Civil Liabilities for Securities Fraud and Other Violations

Before the Securities Act's adoption, securities fraud was solely the province of state common law—under which it was treated just like any other kind of fraud. Plaintiff had to prove that the defendant had misrepresented a material fact. Plaintiff also had to prove all of the other elements of common law fraud: reliance, causation, scienter, and injury. Finally, plaintiff's recovery was limited to the amount of loss: the difference between what he paid and what the securities were truly worth. In light of these limitations, the common law was almost incapable of dealing with securities fraud. Many securities cases, for example, involve omissions—i.e., failures to speak. How does a plaintiff show reliance on silence? As a result, prior to the Securities Act, securities fraud cases were rare and even more rarely successful. To achieve its goal of attacking fraud in securities transactions Congress therefore adopted civil and criminal liability provisions far more liberal than those available at common law.

A person who violates the securities laws faces three possible antagonists. First, the SEC. Securities Act § 20(a) gives the SEC broad power to investigate violations of the Act or the SEC rules adopted under the Act. Section 20(b) gives the SEC the power to bring a civil action in US District Court seeking an injunction against on-going or future violations. A number of other sanctions are potentially available under other statutes. For example, the SEC can suspend or bar a professional underwriter, broker or dealer from working in the securities industry. The SEC may also impose a variety of administrative penalties on violators.

Second, the Justice Department. Section 20(b) authorizes the SEC to refer securities violations to the Attorney General who may then institute criminal proceedings against the violator. We shall largely ignore criminal liabilities herein.

Finally, the plaintiff's bar. Many plaintiffs' lawyers handle securities cases on an occasional basis. In addition, however, there is a small, but active and very capable, group of plaintiffs' lawyers who specialize in securities litigation under the civil liability provisions discussed below. Our focus herein will be on the civil liability provisions available in private party securities fraud litigation.

The Securities Act contains two express private causes of action for securities law violations. Section 11 imposes civil liability for fraudulent registration statements. Not only is § 11 restricted to securities sold through the use of a registration statement, but the misrepresentation or omission must be in the registration statement. In contrast, § 12(a)(2) is the general civil liability under the Securities Act for fraud and misrepresentation. Although it overlaps somewhat with § 11, § 12(a)(2) is a broader remedy. Liability under § 12(a)(2) arises not only in connection with material misrepresentations or omissions in a registration statement, but also in connection with misrepresentations or omissions made in other writings or oral statements used in connection with any public offering.

For our purposes, however, SEC Rule 10b–5, adopted under the Securities Exchange Act, is far more important. Because Rule 10b–5's significance for the study of corporate law is mainly bound up with the law of insider trading, however, we'll defer consideration of the rule until Chapter 11.

D. Becoming a Reporting Company: Registration Under the Securities Exchange Act

If a corporation is required to register under the Securities Exchange Act,[13] it becomes subject to the Act's periodic disclosure rules. In addition, the corporation also becomes subject to the proxy rules under § 14, the tender offer rules under §§ 13 and 14, and certain of the Act's anti-fraud provisions. Finally, the company becomes subject to the extensive rules under the Sarbanes-Oxley Act of 2002 and the Dodd-Frank Act of 2010.

There are three basic categories of companies subject to the Securities Exchange Act's requirements. The first two are identified by §§ 12 and 13(a) of the Act. Section 13(a) requires periodic reports from any company registered with the SEC under Section 12 of the Act. In turn, § 12(a) requires that any class of securities listed and traded on a national securities exchange (such as the New York or American Stock Exchanges) must be registered under the Securities Exchange Act. In addition, as amended by the Jumpstart Our Business Startups Act (the "JOBS Act"), § 12(g) and the rules there under require all other companies with assets exceeding $10 million

---

[13] It is sometimes said that the Securities Exchange Act registers companies, while the Securities Act registers securities. In fact, the former registers classes of securities, but the point is otherwise well-taken. A corporation that has registered a class of securities under the Securities Exchange Act must nevertheless register a particular offering of securities of that class under the Securities Act.

and a class of equity securities held by either (1) 2,000 or more persons or (2) 500 or more persons who are not accredited investors to register that class of equity securities with the SEC. The third and final group of companies subject to the Securities Exchange Act is identified by § 15(d), which picks up any issuer that made a public offering of securities under the Securities Act. Issuers with less than 1,200 record shareholders, however, are not subject to this requirement except during the fiscal year in which they made the offering.

The periodic reports required by the Securities Exchange Act include: (1) Form 10, the initial Securities Exchange Act registration statement. It is only filed once with respect to a particular class of securities. It closely resembles a Securities Act registration statement. (2) Form 10–K, an annual report containing full audited financial statements and management's report of the previous year's activities. It usually incorporates the annual report sent to shareholders. (3) Form 10–Q, filed for each of first three quarters of the year. The issuer does not file a Form 10–Q for the last quarter of the year, which is covered by the Form 10–K. Form 10–Q contains unaudited financial statements and management's report of material recent developments. (4) Form 8–K, which must be filed within 4 business days after certain important events affecting the corporation's operations or financial condition, such as bankruptcy, sales of significant assets, or a change in control of the company.

Chapter 4

LIMITED LIABILITY AND PIERCING
THE CORPORATE VEIL

§ 4.1   Introduction

Limited liability means that shareholders of a corporation are not personally liable for debts incurred or torts committed by the firm. If the firm fails, shareholders' losses thus are limited to the amount the shareholders invested in the firm—i.e., the amount the shareholders initially paid to purchase their stock.

MBCA § 6.22(b) offers a typical statutory formulation of the doctrine: "Unless otherwise provided in the articles of incorporation, a shareholder of a corporation is not personally liable for the acts or debts of the corporation except that he may become personally liable by reason of his own acts or conduct." Notice that § 6.22(b) contains two provisos. First, the articles of incorporation may provide for personal liability. This is nothing more than an example of the familiar principle that most corporate law rules are default rules—i.e., off-the-rack principles that may be modified by contract. Second, personal "liability may be assumed voluntarily or otherwise."[1] A shareholder, for example, voluntarily may assume liability through a personal guaranty. A guaranty is a contract by which the guarantor is bound to perform in the event of a breach of contract by the party whose performance is guaranteed. Contract creditors of close corporations often require controlling shareholders to personally guarantee the firm's debts.

Alternatively, personal liability may be involuntarily thrust upon a shareholder under the equitable remedy known as "piercing the corporate veil."[2] Limited liability entails negative

---

[1] MBCA § 6.22 cmt.

[2] There is substantial disagreement in the literature as to whether veil piercing is an equitable remedy. The significance of the issue, of course, is that equitable remedies need not be tried before a jury but parties subject to legal remedies generally are entitled to trial by jury. Compare International Fin. Serv. Corp. v. Chromas Tech. Canada, Inc., 356 F.3d 731 (7th Cir.2004) (veil piercing is equitable remedy and affords no right to jury trial); Schultz v. General Elec. Healthcare Financial Services Inc., 360 S.W.3d 171 (Ky.2012) (holding "that the doctrine of piercing the corporate veil arises in equity") with Bower v. Bunker Hill Co., 675 F.Supp. 1254, 1261–62 (E.D.Wash.1986) (veil piercing is a legal remedy because it seeks a money judgment and thus a right to jury trial exists). See also Wm. Passalacqua Builders, Inc. v. Resnick Developers South, Inc., 933 F.2d 131 (2d Cir.1991) (holding that "it was entirely proper for the district court to submit the corporate disregard issue to the jury" because, inter alia, whether the corporate form should be pierced "is the sort of determination usually made by a jury because it is so fact specific"); American Protein Corp. v. AB Volvo, 844 F.2d 56, 59 (2d Cir.1988) (veil piercing is an equitable remedy but issue is normally submitted to a jury).

externalities—it allows shareholders to externalize part of the costs of their investment onto other corporate constituencies and, in a sense, to society at large. In appropriate cases, the veil piercing rules allow those injured by the corporation to force the corporation's shareholders to internalize the harm committed by the firm. As a seminal 1912 law review article put it, "When the conception of corporate entity is employed to defraud creditors, to evade an existing obligation, to circumvent a statute, to achieve or perpetuate monopoly, or to protect knavery or crime, the courts will draw aside the web [i.e., veil] of entity, will regard the corporate company as an association of live, up-and-doing, men and women shareholders, and will do justice between real persons."[3]

Obviously, veil piercing is where much of the action is for lawyers. From a litigation standpoint, veil piercing allows creditors to satisfy their claims out of the personal assets of shareholders. From a transactional planning perspective, the risk of veil piercing requires lawyers to exercise some care in forming the corporation and advising the client as to its conduct.

Having said that, it is critical to stress that veil piercing is the exception, not the rule. The law permits incorporation of a business for the very purpose of avoiding personal liability.[4] The equitable exception obviously could easily swallow the legal rule unless courts are careful to permit veil piercing only in certain egregious cases. Accordingly, many decisions in this area state that courts will pierce the veil only reluctantly.[5]

Note: Our analysis of veil piercing will focus on cases in which a creditor seeks to pierce the veil of a close corporation to hold liable for the corporation's acts or debts the natural person who is the

---

[3] I. Maurice Wormser, Piercing the Veil of Corporate Entity, 12 Colum. L. Rev. 496, 517 (1912). Shareholders may also face personal liability in connection with watered stock or unlawful dividends. In some states, special statutory provisions impose personal liability on shareholders with respect to certain corporate debts. New York and Wisconsin, for example, do so with respect to employee wages. See, e.g., N.Y. Bus. Corp. L. § 630.

[4] "Because society recognizes the benefits of allowing persons and organizations to limit their business risks through incorporation, sound public policy dictates that imposition of alter ego liability be approached with caution." Las Palmas Associates v. Las Palmas Center Associates, 235 Cal.App.3d 1220, 1249 (1991). The *Las Palmas* court approvingly cited Cascade Energy & Metals Corp. v. Banks, 896 F.2d 1557, 1576 (10th Cir.1990), in which the 9th Circuit held (applying Utah law) that "corporate veils exist for a reason and should be pierced only reluctantly and cautiously. The law permits the incorporation of businesses for the very purpose of isolating liabilities among separate entities." See also Bartle v. Home Owners Co-op., 127 N.E.2d 832, 833 (N.Y.1955) ("The law permits the incorporation of a business for the very purpose of escaping personal liability").

[5] See, e.g., Cascade Energy & Metals Corp. v. Banks, 896 F.2d 1557, 1576 (10th Cir.), cert. denied sub nom. Weston v. Banks, 498 U.S. 849 (1990); McCulloch Gas Transmission Co. v. Kansas-Nebraska Natural Gas Co., 768 F.2d 1199, 1200 (10th Cir.1985); DeWitt Truck Brokers v. W. Ray Flemming Fruit Co., 540 F.2d 681, 683 (4th Cir.1976); Cherry Creek Card & Party Shop, Inc. v. Hallmark Marketing Corp., 176 F.Supp.2d 1091, 1096 (D.Colo.2001).

controlling shareholder. Unfortunately, veil piercing terminology often is also used to allocate liabilities within corporate groups. Suppose Ajax Corporation is a wholly owned subsidiary of Parent Inc., which is a public corporation. Agents of Ajax cause a mass tort. The resulting plaintiff class brings claims that far exceed Ajax's value and, accordingly, seeks to reach Parent's assets and those of its shareholders. The claim against Parent's shareholders will fail. Shareholders of public corporations are effectively immune from veil piercing claims. Insofar as the liability of natural persons is concerned, veil piercing is really an issue only for the very smallest close corporations.

But what of Parent itself? In many cases nominally characterized as veil piercing, the defendant is not an individual but rather a second corporation. Where a plaintiff seeks to hold a parent or other affiliated corporation liable for the acts of another member of a corporate group, courts generally apply the same standards applicable to individual defendants. Holding a parent corporation liable for the acts of a subsidiary nevertheless presents a conceptually different problem than holding an individual shareholder liable. One useful reform of veil piercing law would be to stop thinking of the parent-subsidiary problem in veil piercing terms. Instead, parent-subsidiary liability is more appropriately treated as a variant of the related doctrine of enterprise liability.

§ 4.2   Thinking About Limited Liability

An example is always helpful, so we begin with one of corporate law's hoariest chestnuts—*Walkovszky v. Carlton*.[6] Plaintiff Walkovszky was a pedestrian struck by a New York City taxi cab operated by the Seon Cab Corp. In turn, Seon was one of 10 taxi cab corporations controlled by defendant-shareholder Carlton. Each corporation carried only the minimum liability insurance required by law ($10,000). Each corporation also owned two taxis, doubtless beat-up hacks worth little, but was otherwise judgment proof. Seon's assets, accordingly, were hopelessly inadequate to satisfy Walkovszky's claimed $500,000 damages. Indeed, the combined assets of all 10 cab companies probably would not have sufficed, even if Walkovszky had been able to reach them.

If Walkovszky could have held Carlton personally liable, Carlton's individual assets might well have satisfied his claim. Unfortunately for Walkovszky, Seon's corporate status meant that the limited liability doctrine insulated Carlton from personal liability for a tort committed by one of Seon's agents. In order to

---

[6] 223 N.E.2d 6 (N.Y.1966).

circumvent that obstacle, Walkovszky invoked the equitable doctrine of piercing the corporate veil.

Walkovszky first complained that none of the ten corporations had a separate identity; instead, each was part of a single enterprise through which Carlton operated the taxi cab business. The court rejected this theory. The mere fact that a corporation is part of a larger enterprise is insufficient to justify veil piercing, or so the court opined. Splitting a single business up into many different corporate components thus will not result in the controlling shareholder being held personally liable for the obligations of one of the corporate entities. At most, only the larger corporate combine, taken as a whole, could be held liable.

Alternatively, Walkovszky contended that Carlton's multiple corporate structure constituted an unlawful fraud on the public. The court rejected this theory, as well. Fraud can justify veil piercing in appropriate cases, suggested the court, but Carlton committed no fraud. There is nothing intrinsically fraudulent about deciding to incorporate or about dividing a single enterprise into multiple corporations, even when done solely to get the benefit of limited liability. Both possibilities are an unavoidable consequence of the statutory grant of limited liability to all corporations.

Although the Court of Appeals affirmed the lower court's dismissal of Walkovszky's complaint, the court did not deprive Walkovszky of all hope of reaching Carlton's personal assets. The court not only remanded the case with leave for Walkovszky to file an amended complaint, it went so far as to suggest a theory under which it believed the corporate veil could be pierced on the facts of the case: the alter ego doctrine.

According to the *Walkovszky* court, a shareholder may be held personally liable for the corporation's acts and debts on a principal-agent theory if the shareholder uses his control of the corporation to further his own, rather than the corporation's, interests. The corporation is treated as the agent of the shareholder-principal and liability is imposed on the shareholder under the familiar tort/agency law doctrine of vicarious liability. On remand, Walkovszky (not surprisingly) amended his complaint to allege that Carlton was conducting the business in his individual capacity. The amended complaint was held to state a cause of action,[7] after which the parties reportedly settled.

Walkovszky's version of the alter ego doctrine treats limited liability as an expression of agency principles. As the story goes, the

---

[7] Walkovszky v. Carlton, 287 N.Y.S.2d 546 (N.Y.App.Div.), aff'd, 244 N.E.2d 55 (N.Y.1968).

corporation is the principal of its employee-agents and, accordingly, incurs contractual or tort obligations because of its agents' actions. As with any other principal, the corporation may be held vicariously liable for the actions of its agents. Because the law generally does not regard a corporation as the agent of its shareholders, however, those shareholders may not be held vicariously liable for the firm's torts or debts. Why not? The answer one usually gets is quite formalistic, treating limited liability as a corollary of the corporation's status as a separate legal person. In the eyes of the law, it is the corporation that incurs the debt or commits the tort and the corporation which must bear the responsibility for its actions. Where the shareholders treat the corporation as their "alter ego," however, the firm is treated as their agent and the shareholders may be held vicariously liable for the corporation's actions. As we shall see, this formulation introduces a number of unfortunate doctrinal complications and, indeed, errors into limited liability law.

§ 4.3   Veil Piercing and Related Doctrines

Courts have given various names to the veil piercing rule set out in *Walkovszky*. Some veil pierce when the corporation is the controlling shareholder's "alter ego," others when the firm is the controlling shareholder's "corporate dummy," and still others when it is his "instrumentality." No matter which of these names the court chooses, you will not find a bright-line standard. As then-New York Court of Appeals Judge Benjamin Cardozo observed over six decades ago, veil piercing is a doctrine "enveloped in the mists of metaphor,"[8] a complaint that remains true today. Veil piercing cases are highly fact-specific. Successful veil piercing claims differ only in degree, but not in kind, from unsuccessful claims. It is therefore very hard to make sweeping generalizations in this area. What follows is thus somewhat of an exercise in futility—an attempt to impose doctrinal coherence and clarity on an area all too often characterized by ambiguity, unpredictability, and even a seeming degree of randomness. Having said that, however, we can at least identify those factors that point towards veil piercing and those that point against it.

A. Standards

Control is the common (if sometimes implicit) feature of all the concepts used to describe cases in which veil piercing is appropriate. Minority shareholders who do not actively participate in the corporation's business or management are rarely held liable on a

---

[8] Berkey v. Third Ave. Ry. Co., 155 N.E. 58, 61 (N.Y.1926).

veil piercing theory. Hence, it seems clear that control is an essential prerequisite for holding a shareholder liable.

The more difficult question is whether control, standing alone, suffices. It is at this point in the analysis that thinking about the limited liability in agency terms can lead one astray. In setting out its alter ego theory, the *Walkovszky* court embraced an agency-based approach to the problem. How does one show that the corporation was the defendant shareholder's agent? Recall that the agency relationship is defined as one in which (1) the principal consents that the agent act on the principal's behalf and subject to the principal's control and (2) the agent consents so to act. Consensual control over someone acting on your behalf thus suffices to establish an agency relationship.

Given its agency-based approach to the problem, accordingly, the *Walkovszky* court implied that Carlton faced personal liability merely upon a showing that he dominated and controlled Seon. But that cannot be right. If domination and control suffices, courts would be obliged to veil pierce far more often than they in fact do.

The problem is that, as is true of most veil piercing cases, *Walkovszky* involved a close corporation with a single dominant shareholder. Such a shareholder's ability to elect the board of directors by definition gives him control of the corporation. In exercising that control, such a shareholder's decisions naturally are based on his own best interests. The corporation thus has no interests other than the interests of the dominant shareholder. Hence, it begs the question to describe a corporation, as the *Walkovszky* court did, as "a 'dummy' for its individual stockholders who are in reality carrying on the business in their personal capacities for purely personal rather than corporate ends."[9] The close corporation with a single dominant shareholder has no "corporate ends" separate from those of its owner. In apparent recognition of this fact, courts generally require plaintiff to show something more than mere control.[10]

Interpreting New York law, the Second Circuit has rejected the conjunctive phrasing of these tests, holding that the veil may be pierced either "to prevent a fraud or other wrong, or where a parent [corporation] dominates and controls a subsidiary [corporation]."[11] At first blush, the disjunctive phrasing of this standard appears to

---

[9] Walkovszky v. Carlton, 223 N.E.2d 6, 8 (N.Y.1966).

[10] Luis v. Orcutt Town Water Co., 22 Cal. Rptr. 389 (Cal.App.1962) ("It is not true that any whollyowned subsidiary is necessarily the alter ego of the parent corporation."); Shafford v. Otto Sales Co., 260 P.2d 269, 277 (Cal.App.1953) ("complete stock ownership and actual one-man control will not alone be sufficient").

[11] Carte Blanche (Singapore) Pte., Ltd. v. Diners Club Int'l, Inc., 2 F.3d 24, 26 (2d Cir.1993).

endorse a reading of *Walkovszky* that permits veil piercing simply by a showing of control. In fact, however, the Second Circuit requires something more than a mere showing of control. Instead, in order to show domination by the controlling shareholder, plaintiff must prove some misuse of the corporate form, typically by invoking the same sort of factors described in the next section.[12]

Courts applying the so-called instrumentality rule require plaintiffs to show: (1) control of the corporation by defendant that is so complete as to amount to total domination of finances, policy, and business practices such that the controlled corporation has no separate mind, will or existence; (2) such control is used to commit a fraud, wrong or other violation of plaintiff's rights; and (3) the control and breach of duty owed to plaintiff was a proximate cause of the injury.[13] Note that this standard clearly rejects any implication that control, standing alone, suffices.

While the instrumentality rule on its face requires something more than control and domination, courts have sometimes been rather sloppy in applying it. In *Zaist v. Olson*,[14] for example, defendant owned and controlled two corporations, East Haven and Olson, Inc. Acting for East Haven, Olson hired plaintiff to do construction work. Before full payment could be made, East Haven went bankrupt. Plaintiff sought to recover from Olson personally. Applying the instrumentality rule, the court found Olson personally liable. The majority opinion emphasized that the firms had the same office, all of the work went to benefit Olson—not East Haven, corporate formalities were ignored, and East Haven was undercapitalized and had no separate financial identity. But so what? Many of these facts seem irrelevant to the applicable standard. Who cares if the firms had the same office, after all? At most, some of these facts tend to establish that Olson controlled East Haven and, accordingly, that the first prong of the instrumentality test might be satisfied. Unfortunately, as one of the dissenting judges pointed out, plaintiff failed to show—and the majority did not require it to show—that the other two elements of the instrumentality standard were met: "I do not agree that the facts found by the referee support a conclusion that the control which [Olson] undoubtedly did exercise over The East Haven Homes, Inc., was used by [Olson] 'to commit fraud or wrong, to

---

[12] See, e.g., Wm. Passalacqua Builders, Inc. v. Resnick Developers South, Inc., 933 F.2d 131, 139 (2d Cir.1991) ("control must be used to commit a fraud or other wrong that causes plaintiff's loss"); American Protein Corp. v. AB Volvo, 844 F.2d 56, 60 (2d Cir.1988) (a claim of domination requires a showing that "such domination must have been used to 'commit fraud or wrong' against plaintiff").

[13] See, e.g., Zaist v. Olson, 227 A.2d 552, 558 (Conn.1967); Collet v. American Nat'l Stores, Inc., 708 S.W.2d 273, 284 (Mo.App.1986).

[14] 227 A.2d 552 (Conn.1967).

perpetrate the violation of a statutory or other positive legal duty, or a dishonest and unjust act in contravention of' the plaintiffs' legal rights."[15] To which the dissent fairly could have had added that the majority also failed to require plaintiff to show that Olson's misconduct was the proximate cause of plaintiff's injury. If the requirement that plaintiff must show something more than mere control is to have teeth, the dissent's position seems unassailable.

Other states, perhaps most notably California and Illinois, use a slightly different test, which requires plaintiff to meet two requirements: (1) the corporation was the controlling shareholder's alter ego; and (2) adherence to the limited liability rule would "sanction a fraud or promote injustice."[16] Under this standard, the prospect of an unsatisfied claim is not enough to meet the latter prong of the test.[17] After all, why would a plaintiff invoke the doctrine if the corporation had enough assets to satisfy the claim? If an unsatisfied claim sufficed, the veil would be pierced in every case. As in *Walkovszky*, accordingly, incorporating a business to avoid personal liability neither promotes injustice nor sanctions a fraud. Instead, there must be some element of unjust enrichment.[18] Of course, unjust enrichment itself is a pretty ambiguous standard, which further illustrates the broad discretion courts have in veil piercing cases.

A third set of courts uses a test superficially similar to, but subtly different than, the California/Illinois standard. Under Virginia law, for example, a court must find (1) undue domination and control of the corporation by the defendant and (2) that the corporation was a device or sham used to disguise wrongs, perpetuate fraud, or conceal crime.[19] Again, the mere existence of

---

[15] Zaist v. Olson, 227 A.2d 552, 560 (Conn.1967) (House, J., dissenting). The other dissenting judge agreed that the majority's conclusion was "not warranted by the record," but dissented mainly on the grounds that contract creditors who choose to deal with a close corporation without demanding a personal guarantee from the dominant shareholder do so at their own risk. Id. at 561 (Cotter, J., dissenting).

[16] Van Dorn Co. v. Future Chemical and Oil Corp., 753 F.2d 565, 570 (7th Cir.1985); Minifie v. Rowley, 202 P. 673, 676 (Cal.1921).

[17] Associated Vendors, Inc. v. Oakland Meat Co., 26 Cal. Rptr. 806, 816 (Cal.App.1962) ("it is not sufficient to merely show that a creditor will remain unsatisfied if the corporate veil is not pierced"). The same is true under the other tests discussed in this section. In Connecticut, for example, which uses the instrumentality standard, the supreme court has held that courts should decline "to apply the instrumentality rule where the corporations were formed for legitimate purposes and the parties engaging in transactions with those corporations were fully aware of the type of business with which they were dealing. In the absence of a claim that the corporation was formed for an improper purpose, or that the plaintiffs were improperly induced to enter into a contract with the corporation, the mere breach of a corporate contract cannot of itself establish the basis for application of the instrumentality rule." Campisano v. Nardi, 562 A.2d 1, 7 (Conn.1989) (footnote omitted).

[18] Sea-Land Services, Inc. v. Pepper Source, 941 F.2d 519 (7th Cir.1991).

[19] See, e.g., Perpetual Real Estate Services, Inc. v. Michaelson Properties, Inc., 974 F.2d 545, 548 (4th Cir.1992) (applying Virginia law).

an unsatisfied claim should not suffice; nor should the mere fact of control.

The first prong of both the California/Illinois and Virginia standards resembles the *Walkovszky* standard—both initially look to whether the shareholder treated the corporation as his alter ego. Both, however, reject the notion that control, standing alone, suffices. Both add a second factor asking for something beyond mere control. As between the two, the Virginia standard appears to contemplate more egregious misconduct by the defendant shareholder; in particular, the Virginia standard appears to look for some element of active and intentional misconduct by the shareholder-defendant.[20] Yet, neither seems any more useful than *Walkovszky* as an *ex ante* guide to planning the capital structure and operation of a newly-formed corporation. As the leading treatise on California corporate law opines of its standard, "it merely measures the rule by the length of the Chancellor's foot. The generalized phrases, 'sanction a fraud or promote injustice,' are useless in predicting the outcome of a particular case."[21]

B. Critical Factors in Any Veil Piercing Case

As is readily apparent from the nature of the tests just outlined, none provide a bright-line standard. One can identify a number of factors, however, which courts applying those tests commonly cite to justify veil piercing.

1. Nature of the Claim

Contract v. Tort. Courts ought to be far less willing to pierce the corporate veil in contract cases than in tort cases. Contract creditors can protect their interests by demanding a personal guaranty from the firm's controlling shareholders. If contract creditors fail to protect themselves, there is no reason for the law to do so.[22]

Although the contract/tort distinction makes so much sense as to seem unassailable, it has received a surprisingly mixed reception from courts. On the one hand, a substantial number of courts

---

[20] On the one hand, "by this second requirement, Virginia, unlike some jurisdictions, mandates proof of fraud or a legal 'wrong' as a requisite to recovery." C.F. Trust, Inc. v. First Flight Ltd. Partnership, 306 F.3d 126, 135 (4th Cir.2002). On the other hand, the Virginia supreme court has also stated that the second requirement is satisfied "although the acts of the parties amount to constructive fraud only, the rule not being limited to cases where they have been guilty of actual fraud and criminal intent." Lewis Trucking Corp. v. Commonwealth, 147 S.E.2d 747, 753 (Va.1966) (citation omitted).

[21] Harold Marsh, Jr. and R. Roy Finkle, Marsh's California Corporation Law § 16.16 at 1392 (3d ed. 1990).

[22] See, e.g., Perpetual Real Estate Services, Inc. v. Michaelson Properties, Inc., 974 F.2d 545 (4th Cir.1992); Brunswick Corp. v. Waxman, 459 F.Supp. 1222 (E.D.N.Y.1978), aff'd, 599 F.2d 34 (2d Cir.1979).

correctly have accepted the proposition that they ought not pierce on behalf of contract creditors in the absence of fraud or other unusual circumstances.[23] Indeed, at least one state (Texas), has even enshrined the distinction in statute.[24] On the other hand, an older but still widely cited opinion by the D.C. Circuit expressly rejected the "position of some commentators" that contract creditors should not be allowed to pierce the veil.[25]

In any case, even courts that disfavor veil piercing in contract cases recognize that the logic behind doing so does not hold in cases in which the shareholder caused the creditor's failure to protect itself. Hence, for example, the veil should be pierced in contract cases if the corporation or the controlling shareholder misrepresented the firm's financial condition to a prospective creditor.[26] Indeed, if it was the controlling shareholder who misled the creditor, it may be unnecessary to invoke the veil piercing doctrine. Recall that the MBCA's section on limited liability contains a proviso under which a shareholder "may become personally liable by reason of his own acts or conduct." MBCA § 6.22(b). Misleading a prospective creditor seems like just the sort of conduct this provision was intended to capture.

Note on statutory claims. We are concerned here solely with the equitable veil piercing remedy available under state law. In a growing category of cases nominally categorized as veil piercing, however, both the liability and/or the remedy arise out of some specific statute. Environmental liabilities under CERCLA, for example, have become a common source of veil piercing-like claims. Although veil piercing principles are sometimes invoked in these cases, they are more properly regarded as *sui generis.* Most such statutes contain language that creates a separate basis for imposing personal liability on shareholders.

2. The Nature of the Defendant

To this point, our analysis of veil piercing has focused on cases like *Walkovszky*—i.e., those in which a creditor seeks to pierce the veil of a close corporation to hold a natural person, such as Carlton, who is the controlling shareholder, liable for the corporation's acts or debts. Our analysis will continue to focus on cases of that ilk, but

---

[23] See, e.g., Secon Serv. System, Inc. v. St. Joseph Bank and Trust Co., 855 F.2d 406, 415–16 (7th Cir.1988); Perpetual Real Estate Services, Inc. v. Michaelson Properties, Inc., 974 F.2d 545 (4th Cir.1992); U.S. v. Jon-T Chemicals, Inc., 768 F.2d 686, 693 (5th Cir.1985); Laya v. Erin Homes, Inc., 352 S.E.2d 93, 100 (W.Va.1986).

[24] Tex. Bus. Corp. Act § 2.21A(2).

[25] Labadie Coal Co. v. Black, 672 F.2d 92, 100 (D.C.Cir.1982).

[26] Browning-Ferris Indus. of Ill., Inc. v. Ter Maat, 195 F.3d 953, 959–60 (7th Cir.1999); Perpetual Real Estate Services, Inc. v. Michaelson Properties, Inc., 974 F.2d 545, 550 (4th Cir.1992); United States v. Jon-T Chemicals, Inc., 768 F.2d 686, 693 (5th Cir.1985).

it is important to note three alternative settings in which veil piercing is potentially at issue. As we shall see, none is an appropriate case in which to invoke the veil piercing remedy.

Passive shareholders of a close corporation. Shareholders who neither control the corporation nor are actively involved in its management are unlikely to be held liable on a veil piercing theory. Instead, it is shareholders like Carlton—the dominant controlling investor—who are most at risk. This result follows naturally from the phrasing of the relevant standards, all of which require some element of control before the veil will be pierced.

Shareholders of a public corporation. Consistent with the theoretical justification for treating close and public corporations differently for veil piercing purposes, shareholders of the latter are almost never subjected to a veil piercing claim. Indeed, about two-thirds of such suits brought against individual defendants involved corporations having three or fewer shareholders.[27] Hence, veil piercing is really an issue only for the very smallest close corporations.

Parent-subsidiary or sibling corporations. In many cases nominally characterized as veil piercing, the defendant is not an individual but rather a second corporation. Where a plaintiff seeks to hold a parent or other affiliated corporation liable for the acts of another member of a corporate group, courts generally apply the same standards applicable to individual defendants. Some scholars argue that courts should be more willing to pierce the corporate veil in the parent-subsidiary context than with respect to an individual shareholder, but there seems to be little support in the case law for that proposition.[28]

3.   The Laundry List

At some point in most veil piercing opinions, the court will set out a long list of factors against which the facts of the case at bar are then compared. The precise content of the list varies considerably across jurisdictions, but the following example from a California decision exhaustively canvasses the factors likely to be cited as relevant to veil piercing:

> A review of the cases which have discussed the problem discloses the consideration of a variety of factors which were pertinent to the trial court's determination under the

---

[27] Robert B. Thompson, The Limits of Liability in the New Limited Liability Entities, 32 Wake Forest L. Rev. 1, 9 n.48 (1997) ("Piercing occurs only within corporate groups or in close corporations with fewer than ten shareholders.").

[28] See U.S. v. Bestfoods, 524 U.S. 51, 61–62 (1998) (citing numerous authorities for the "bedrock" proposition that parents generally are not liable for a subsidiary's acts or debts).

particular circumstances of each case. Among these are the following: [1] Commingling of funds and other assets, failure to segregate funds of the separate entities, and the unauthorized diversion of corporate funds or assets to other than corporate uses; [2] the treatment by an individual of the assets of the corporation as his own; [3] the failure to obtain authority to issue stock or to subscribe to or issue the same; [4] the holding out by an individual that he is personally liable for the debts of the corporation; [5] the failure to maintain minutes or adequate corporate records, and the confusion of the records of the separate entities; [6] the identical equitable ownership in the two entities; [7] the identification of the equitable owners thereof with the domination and control of the two entities; [8] identification of the directors and officers of the two entities in the responsible supervision and management; [9] sole ownership of all of the stock in a corporation by one individual or the members of a family; [10] the use of the same office or business location; [11] the employment of the same employees and/or attorney; [12] the failure to adequately capitalize a corporation; [13] the total absence of corporate assets and undercapitalization; [14] the use of a corporation as a mere shell, instrumentality or conduit for a single venture or the business of an individual or another corporation; [15] the concealment and misrepresentation of the identity of the responsible ownership, management and financial interest, or concealment of personal business activities; [16] the disregard of legal formalities and the failure to maintain arm's length relationships among related entities; [17] the use of the corporate entity to procure labor, services or merchandise for another person or entity; [18] the diversion of assets from a corporation by or to a stockholder or other person or entity, to the detriment of creditors, or the manipulation of assets and liabilities between entities so as to concentrate the assets in one and the liabilities in another; [19] the contracting with another with intent to avoid performance by use of a corporate entity as a shield against personal liability, or the use of a corporation as a subterfuge of illegal transactions; [20] and the formation and use of a corporation to transfer to it the existing liability of another person or entity.[29]

---

[29] Associated Vendors, Inc. v. Oakland Meat Co., 26 Cal.Rptr. 806, 813–15 (Cal.App.1962) (citations omitted).

No fewer than 20 separate (albeit overlapping) factors, many of which have multiple sub-factors! Most of which, moreover, are wholly unrelated to the policy concerns presented by limited liability. Worse yet, the court fails to give any guidance as to how the factors should be weighted or balanced. It contented itself with merely observing that in all prior California cases in which the veil had been pierced "several of the factors mentioned were present."

As an example of the laundry list in action, consider the Seventh Circuit Court of Appeals' opinion *Sea-Land Services, Inc. v. Pepper Source*:

> The first and most striking feature that emerges from our examination of the record is that these corporate defendants are, indeed, little but Marchese's playthings. [Gerald J.] Marchese is the sole shareholder of [Pepper Source], Caribe Crown, Jamar, and Salescaster. He is one of the two shareholders of Tie-Net. Except for Tie-Net, none of the corporations ever held a single corporate meeting. (At the handful of Tie-Net meetings held . . ., no minutes were taken.) During his deposition, Marchese did not remember any of these corporations ever passing articles of incorporation, bylaws, or other agreements. As for physical facilities, Marchese runs all of these corporations (including Tie-Net) out of the same, single office, with the same phone line, the same expense accounts, and the like. And how he does "run" the expense accounts! When he fancies to, Marchese "borrows" substantial sums of money from these corporations interest free, of course. The corporations also "borrow" money from each other when need be, which left at least [Pepper Source] completely out of capital when the Sea Land bills came due. What's more, Marchese has used the bank accounts of these corporations to pay all kinds of personal expenses, including alimony and child support payments to his ex-wife, education expenses for his children, maintenance of his personal automobiles, health care for his pet—the list goes on and on. Marchese did not even have a personal bank account! (With "corporate" accounts like these, who needs one?)[30]

All of which makes for unusually entertaining reading, but so what? What should we learn to guide clients or even to litigate future

---

[30] Sea-Land Services, Inc. v. Pepper Source, 941 F.2d 519, 521 (7th Cir.1991). Pepper Source was the debtor corporation, having defaulted on debts owed Sea-Land. The other named entities were nominally separate corporations also controlled by Marchese. Sea-Land sought to pierce the corporate veil in order to hold Marchese liable.

cases? Perhaps the clearest lesson is that controlling shareholders should maintain some distance between their personal life and their business. Yet, are we really surprised that the single shareholder of a corporate enterprise fails to draw a sharp distinction between his personal and business life?[31]

The court's criticism of Marchese's disregard for corporate formalities seems especially puzzling. Disregard for corporate formalities typically is said to include such significant blunders as: (a) failure to keep separate corporate books and records; (b) failure to hold periodic meetings of the board of directors and of the shareholders; (c) failure to appoint a board of directors; or (d) failure to formally issue stock to the shareholders in the form of share certificates. Although it will strike many clients as unduly picayune, the competent transactional lawyer will encourage the client to carefully comply with these seemingly technical formalities. But while a controlling shareholder's failure to observe these and similar corporate formalities is often cited with great fanfare in opinions ordering veil piercing, it fairly might be asked why this fact is considered relevant. Recall that we worry about limited liability mainly because it permits shareholders to externalize risk. If so, what on earth does Marchese's failure to hold corporate meetings have to do with anything? Setting aside the rare cases in which failure to observe corporate formalities misleads a creditor into believing it is dealing with an individual rather than a corporation, there simply is no causal link between the creditor's injury and the shareholder's misconduct. Perhaps courts believe a failure to observe the requisite corporate formalities inferentially indicates a potential disregard for creditors' interests—if you play fast and loose with formalities, maybe courts suspect that you are likely to play fast and loose with your bills, as well. But even that explanation seems tenuous, at best.

Relying on the shareholder's disregard for corporate formalities as a justification for veil piercing seems especially problematic on *Sea-Land*'s facts because this was a contract case. As we have seen, contract creditors like Sea Land generally should not get relief. As another court explained in a case focusing on the undercapitalization factor:

> When, under the circumstances, it would be reasonable for
> [a creditor] entering into a contract with the corporation

---

[31] In the court's defense, it went on to hold that Marchese's cited misconduct only established his domination and control of Pepper Source and the affiliated enterprises. Sea-Land was also obliged to show that "honoring the separate corporate existences of the defendants 'would sanction a fraud or promote injustice.'" Sea-Land Services, Inc. v. Pepper Source, 941 F.2d 519, 522 (7th Cir.1991) (quoting Van Dorn Co. v. Future Chemical and Oil Corp., 753 F.2d 565, 570 (7th Cir.1985)). In other words, the court (correctly) held that control is not enough to justify piercing the veil.

> . . . to conduct an investigation of the credit of the
> corporation prior to entering into the contract, such party
> will be charged with the knowledge that a reasonable
> credit investigation would disclose. If such an
> investigation would disclose that the corporation is grossly
> undercapitalized, based upon the nature and the
> magnitude of the corporate undertaking, such party will
> be deemed to have assumed the risk of the gross
> undercapitalization and will not be permitted to pierce the
> corporate veil.[32]

It is hard to see why the same logic should not apply to nonfinancial factors, such as disregard for corporate formalities. Yet, the corporate formalities clearly matter. Disregard of corporate formalities does not always lead to veil piercing, but the empirical data shows that courts do pierce in two-thirds of those cases in which they explicitly state that the defendant had failed to comply with those formalities. Conversely, courts decline to pierce in over 90% of cases in which they explicitly note that the defendant complied with the corporate formalities.[33]

In sum, the laundry list approach found in many opinions seems wholly nonexplanatory. The laundry list is simply an *ex post* rationalization of a conclusion reached on grounds that are often unarticulated. Not surprisingly, the most commonly cited judicial justifications for veil piercing are mere conclusory statements, such as "domination or control," "alter ego," and the like.

4.   Is Undercapitalization, Standing Alone, Enough?

In *Walkovszky v. Carlton*, Judge Keating dissented on grounds that Carlton's corporations were undercapitalized. When forming his corporations, Carlton put into each only the minimum amount of capital required to purchase the taxis. The corporations carried the minimum amount of liability insurance permitted by statute. Carlton drained all income out of the corporations. These actions, taken together, meant that Carlton's taxi cab companies lacked sufficient assets to meet their potential personal injury liability. According to Keating's dissent, the attempt to carry on a business in corporate form without providing a sufficient financial base was an abuse of the corporate process justifying a piercing of the corporate veil:

> What I would merely hold is that a participating
> shareholder of a corporation vested with a public interest,

---

[32] Laya v. Erin Homes, Inc., 352 S.E.2d 93, 100 (W.Va.1986).

[33] Robert B. Thompson, Piercing the Corporate Veil: An Empirical Study, 76 Cornell L. Rev. 1036, 1064–65 n.141 and 1067 (1991).

organized with capital insufficient to meet liabilities which are certain to arise in the ordinary course of the corporation's business, may be held personally responsible for such liabilities. Where corporate income is not sufficient to cover the cost of insurance premiums above the statutory minimum or where initially adequate finances dwindle under the pressure of competition, bad times or extraordinary and unexpected liability, obviously the shareholder will not be held liable.[34]

As Keating's dissent implies, undercapitalization can be understood in either of two senses: (a) the funds put into the corporation at the outset were clearly insufficient to satisfy existing contractual and likely tort obligations; or (b) all profits are drained out of the firm in the form of dividends or salaries paid to the controlling shareholders, leaving it with insufficient reserves to meet its likely obligations. In some cases, such as *Walkovszky*, the firm may be undercapitalized in both senses of the word.

Keating's proposed rule sounds sensible enough at first blush, but quickly crumbles once one begins to think about operationalizing it. Suppose prospective shareholders of a close corporation come to you for advice in setting up their corporation. Consider the questions you have to answer in order to ensure that they will get the benefit of limited liability under Keating's standard. Is their corporation "vested with a public interest"? How do you decide? What liabilities are "certain" to arise in the ordinary course of their business? And how much capital/insurance is necessary to safeguard against them? What are "extraordinary and unexpected liabilities"? Would jurors, operating with the benefit of hindsight, be tempted to use the plaintiff's damages as a rough guide to the amount of necessary capital? The jurors might well look at the damage claim, compare it to the amount of capital, and if damages exceed capital, conclude the firm was undercapitalized. Keating's standard thus makes ex ante transaction planning less certain, while increasing litigation costs by introducing some inherently ambiguous considerations into the analysis.

It also seems noteworthy that there is no statutory basis for treating either form of undercapitalization as grounds for piercing the veil. In most states, the corporation statute neither requires any initial capital contribution nor mandates the maintenance of any minimum capital. In the few states with minimum capital requirements, the amounts involved are nominal typically $1,000.

---

[34] Walkovszky v. Carlton, 223 N.E.2d 6, 13 (N.Y.1966) (Keating, J., dissenting).

Perhaps these sort of concerns have motivated the courts' well-nigh universal refusal to treat undercapitalization, standing alone, as dispositive. To be sure, undercapitalization is one of the factor courts commonly consider, which may result in personal liability, when taken in conjunction with the factors we discussed earlier, but it is not enough standing alone to pierce the corporate veil.[35] Put another way, "some 'wrong' beyond a creditor's inability to collect" must be shown before the veil will be pierced.[36]

The case usually cited for the proposition that undercapitalization alone suffices, *Minton v. Cavaney*,[37] arguably does not in fact stand for that proposition and, in any event, probably is no longer good law even in its home jurisdiction. In *Minton*, plaintiffs' child drowned in a swimming pool operated by the Seminole Hot Springs Corporation. Plaintiffs won a judgment of $10,000 against the corporation, but could not collect because the corporation had no assets. Plaintiffs then brought a veil piercing suit against Cavaney, who was the corporation's lawyer, a shareholder, and a director. In the course of his opinion for the California Supreme Court, Chief Justice Traynor stated that a shareholder can be held liable if the firm is undercapitalized and the shareholder was actively involved in the business. At first blush, *Minton* thus appears to be consistent with Judge Keating's *Walkovszky* dissent. Both purport to regard undercapitalization standing alone as sufficient to pierce the corporate veil. On closer examination, however, *Minton* proves more complicated than Traynor acknowledged.

Cavaney admittedly served in various corporate capacities, but only temporarily and as an accommodation to his client. Cavaney was to receive one of three shares but no shares were ever issued. Indeed, the state commissioner of corporations refused to allow the corporation to issue stock. The corporation never had any substantial assets and "never functioned as a corporation." Arguably, the pool business never was a proper corporation at all. If so, Cavaney was the co-owner of a business for profit—in other words, a partnership. Under partnership law, Cavaney would be fully and personally liable for firm obligations. Hence, the real issue in *Minton* is not whether the business was undercapitalized but rather what legal form the business took.

---

[35] See, e.g., Browning-Ferris Indus. of Ill., Inc. v. Ter Maat, 195 F.3d 953, 959–60 (7th Cir.1999); Gartner v. Snyder, 607 F.2d 582, 588 (2d Cir.1979) ("Although Enterprises was thinly capitalized, that alone is not a sufficient ground for disregarding the corporate form. We know of no New York authority that disregards corporate form solely because of inadequate capitalization.").

[36] Sea-Land Services, Inc. v. Pepper Source, 941 F.2d 519, 524 (7th Cir.1991).

[37] 364 P.2d 473 (Cal.1961).

In any event, *Minton*'s importance is often over-stated. Justice Traynor was an activist judge who viewed the tort system primarily as a compensation scheme.[38] *Minton*, arguably, is just another example of his pro-plaintiff stance. If so, it can be dismissed as a sport. Tellingly, subsequent California cases have not followed *Minton*. Instead, they follow the mainstream in treating undercapitalization as merely a relevant, but not dispositive, factor.[39] At least one subsequent California decision thus squarely refused to hold "that, per se, inadequate capitalization renders the shareholders . . . liable for the obligations of the corporation."[40]

5.   The Take-Home Lesson: Operationalizing Veil Piercing

Those who like tidy doctrines that admit of easy application will not care for veil piercing law. Judicial opinions in this area tend to open with vague generalities and close with conclusory statements, with little or no concrete analysis in between. There simply are no bright-line rules for deciding when courts will pierce the corporate veil. This makes life hard for litigators, of course, but it also makes life hard on those of us who work as transactional lawyers. Our job is to keep our client out of court in the first place. In this context, that means our job is to help our clients set up their business so as to insure that they will get the benefit of limited liability.

Once again, let's use *Walkovszky v. Carlton* as our model. Suppose you were Carlton's lawyer. Carlton comes by your office and asks, "how do I avoid losing these cases in the future?" What do you tell him? Telling him not to use the corporation as his alter ego, dummy or instrumentality will not be very helpful, even though those are the precise things the court said he should avoid. You need to operationalize those vague standards.

Assuming Carlton wants to stay in charge, you can't do much about the control-based aspects of the relevant standards. Instead, it is the second prong of those standards that give you some flexibility. Yet, those standards don't provide much in the way of guidance either. Telling Carlton to avoid disguising wrongs, perpetuating frauds, or concealing crimes isn't going to get you very far.

---

[38] See G. Edward White, Tort Law in America: An Intellectual History 181 (1980).

[39] See, e.g., Arnold v. Browne, 103 Cal.Rptr. 775, 783 (Cal.App.1972).

[40] Harris v. Curtis, 87 Cal.Rptr. 614, 617 (Cal.App.1970). Courts in other jurisdictions "have unanimously rejected [*Minton*'s] approach." Waste Management, Inc. v. Danis Industries Corp., 2004 WL 5345389 at *16 (S.D.Ohio2004). See, e.g., Poyner v. Lear Siegler, Inc., 542 F.2d 955 (6th Cir.1976) (rejecting *Minton* and concluding that, under the law of Kentucky, undercapitalization alone does not justify piercing a corporation's veil).

Here then is where the laundry list of factors comes into play. From a transactional planning perspective, you want to set up the business so as few of the relevant factors are present. Hence, using the *Associated Vendors* list as a template, one might advise Carlton as follows: Do not commingle personal and corporate funds. Issue stock certificates. Adopt and comply with articles of incorporation and bylaws. Appoint a board of directors. Hold regular board and shareholder meetings. Keep minutes of those meetings. Keep corporate financial books and records, which are kept separate from personal effects. Comply with any statutory capital and/or insurance requirements. Take funds out of the corporation in the form of salary and/or dividends paid on a regular basis, being careful not to draw funds out haphazardly or as needed for personal matters.

None of these precautionary actions have very much to do with the real policy concerns at issue in this area. Which of them, if any, would make Walkovszky feel better about his uncompensated injuries? Which of them would help sort out risks that ought to be internalized from those that appropriately may be externalized? Which of them promote capital formation? Which of them promote populist notions of economic democracy? None. Yet, if Carlton had taken such precautions, on what principled basis could the court have pierced the veil under the relevant standards?

C.   What Law Applies?

A number of federal decisions applying New York choice of law rules have held that the state of incorporation (of the corporation whose veil is to be pierced) has the paramount interest with respect to veil piercing claims and, accordingly, applied that state's law.[41] The state of incorporation's interest derives from the fact that it is that state whose law confers limited liability on the enterprise in the first place.[42]

---

[41] See, e.g., Fletcher v. Atex, Inc., 68 F.3d 1451, 1456 (2d Cir.1995); Soviet Pan Am Travel Effort v. Travel Committee, Inc., 756 F.Supp. 126, 131 (S.D.N.Y.1991). New York relies on a choice of law rule known as the paramount interest test, under which "the law of the jurisdiction having the greatest interest in the litigation will be applied and . . . the facts or contacts which obtain significance are those which relate to the purpose of the particular law in conflict." Intercontinental Planning, Ltd. v. Daystrom, 248 N.E.2d 576, 582 (N.Y.1969) (internal quotation marks omitted).

An interesting wrinkle on the choice of law problem is presented when the veil piercing claim arises under a federal statute. In U.S. v. Bestfoods, 524 U.S. 51 (1998), the Supreme Court noted the "significant disagreement among courts and commentators over whether, in enforcing CERCLA's indirect liability, courts should borrow state law, or instead apply a federal common law of veil piercing." Id. at 63 n.9. Unfortunately for those who like doctrinal closure, the court declined to resolve that disagreement. Id.

[42] Soviet Pan Am Travel Effort v. Travel Committee, Inc., 756 F.Supp. 126, 131 (S.D.N.Y.1991).

Surprisingly, Delaware courts do not always apply the law of the state of incorporation. Where a Delaware parent corporation is to be held liable for the acts of a non-Delaware subsidiary (i.e., the subsidiary's corporate veil is to be pierced), Delaware courts have applied Delaware law.[43] On the other hand, where it is a Delaware corporation whose veil is to be pierced, Delaware courts do apply their state's law.[44]

D. Related Doctrines

1. Reverse Veil Piercing

Reverse piercing of the corporate veil is a rare and somewhat controversial variant of the basic doctrine.[45] If invoked, it permits a shareholder to disregard the corporation's separate identity, just as "forward" veil piercing permits a creditor to do so. Suppose, for example, that Frank Farmer is the controlling shareholder of Family Farms, Inc. In addition to 800 acres of prime Minnesota farmland, Family Farms owns a farmhouse that Frank uses as his personal residence. All of Family Farms' profits are paid out to Frank as salary or dividends. Although separate corporate books are maintained and both director and shareholder meetings are held, other corporate formalities are ignored. Two years ago Family Farms borrowed $1 million from the First National Bank of St. Paul, giving the bank a mortgage on the land and farmhouse. Family Farms defaulted on the loan last month. First National is now seeking to foreclose on the farm and the house. Under Minnesota's Farm Homestead Act, up to 80 acres of farmland owned by an individual is exempt from foreclosure. The Act does not preclude foreclosure on corporate-owned property. Frank seeks reverse veil piercing, so that the farmhouse and 80 acres of land will be deemed his personal assets and thus a homestead exempt from foreclosure. On facts very much like these, Minnesota courts have allowed reverse veil piercing. They concluded that the farm corporation was the farmer's alter ego and that allowing reverse veil piercing would work no injustice against the farm's creditors.[46]

The precedents are roughly evenly divided between those that accept reverse veil piercing and those that reject the doctrine.[47] In

---

[43] Japan Petroleum Co. (Nigeria) Ltd. v. Ashland Oil, Inc., 456 F.Supp. 831, 840 n. 17 (D.Del.1978).

[44] Mobil Oil Corp. v. Linear Films, Inc., 718 F.Supp. 260, 267 (D.Del.1989).

[45] See Messick v. PHD Trucking Service, Inc., 678 P.2d 791, 793 (Utah 1984) (calling reverse piercing a "little recognized" theory).

[46] See, e.g., Cargill, Inc. v. Hedge, 375 N.W.2d 477 (Minn.1985); State Bank v. Euerle Farms, Inc., 441 N.W.2d 121 (Minn.App.1989).

[47] Compare, e.g., Hogan v. Mayor & Aldermen of Savannah, 320 S.E.2d 555 (Ga.App.1984) (rejecting reverse veil piercing) and Kiehl v. Action Manufacturing Co., 535 A.2d 571 (Pa.1987) (same) with Crum v. Krol, 425 N.E.2d 1081

jurisdictions where it is accepted, a shareholder seeking reverse veil piercing must make the same sort of factual showing required of creditors in a forward veil piercing case. In other words, one way of determining whether a court should allow reverse veil piercing in the preceding hypothetical is to flip the situation around, asking: If First National had sought to hold Frank personally liable on the mortgage, would a court permit forward veil piercing on the facts of this case? On the one hand, a number of our laundry list of factors are present: (1) use of corporate assets for personal purposes (the farmhouse); (2) draining of funds; and (3) disregard of some corporate formalities. On the other hand, a strong argument could be made against forward veil piercing in this case, because First National's claim sounds in contract.

So-called "outsider reverse piercing" presents yet another wrinkle on limited liability. In this situation, a personal creditor of the shareholder seeks to disregard the corporation's separate legal existence. Unlike regular veil piercing, in which a creditor of the corporation is trying to reach the personal assets of a shareholder, in this situation a creditor of the shareholder wants to reach the assets of the corporation in order to satisfy the creditor's claims against the shareholder.[48] A number of courts have recognized such a cause of action.[49] Consistent with the proposition that judicial recognition of reverse veil piercing is closely related to policy questions are a number of cases involving outsider reverse piercing in which federal courts invoked the theory to permit the U.S. government recover a taxpayer's delinquent taxes from the taxpayer's business enterprise.[50] (Of course, these cases are

---

(Ill.App.1981) (accepting doctrine) and State Bank v. Euerle Farms, Inc., 441 N.W.2d 121 (Minn.App.1989) (same).

[48] See, e.g., Shamrock Oil & Gas Co. v. Ethridge, 159 F.Supp. 693 (D.Colo.1958); Minich v. Gem State Developers, Inc., 591 P.2d 1078 (Idaho 1979); Central National Bank & Trust Co. of Des Moines v. Wagener, 183 N.W.2d 678 (Iowa 1971).

[49] See, e.g., McCall Stock Farms, Inc. v. U.S., 14 F.3d 1562, 1568 (Fed.Cir.1993) (appellant's "unidirectional theory" of veil piercing is "contrary to an overwhelming weight of authority"); FDIC v. Martinez Almodovar, 671 F.Supp. 851, 877 (D. Puerto Rico 1987) ("Although the usual situation is for a creditor to attempt to pierce a corporate veil in order to impose liability on the shareholders, the corporate veil may also be pierced 'in reverse', that is, to impose liability on the corporation for the obligations of its shareholders."); Towers v. Titus, 5 B.R. 786, 795 (N.D.Cal.1979) ("despite defendants' protestations to the contrary, the doctrine may be used both in its classic sense, to pierce the corporate veil to impress the debts of a corporation upon an individual, or in a 'reverse' sense, to disregard the corporation form to reach the assets of a corporation for the debts of an individual."). But see, e.g., Cascade Energy & Metals Corp. v. Banks, 896 F.2d 1557 (10th Cir.), cert. denied sub nom. Weston v. Banks, 498 U.S. 849 (1990) (rejecting doctrine).

[50] See, e.g., Towe Antique Ford Foundation v. Internal Revenue Service, 999 F.2d 1387, 1390 (9th Cir.1993); Shades Ridge Holding Co. v. United States, 888 F.2d 725, 728 (11th Cir.1989), cert. denied sub nom. Fiorella v. United States, 494 U.S. 1027 (1990); Valley Finance, Inc. v. United States, 629 F.2d 162, 171–72 (D.C.Cir.1980), cert. denied sub nom. Pacific Development, Inc. v. United States, 451 U.S. 1018 (1981).

consistent with our hypothesis only if one assumes that the government always wins tax cases.)

In *C.F. Trust, Inc. v. First Flight L.P.*,[51] the Virginia supreme court recognized outsider reverse piercing as valid under Virginia law. In doing so, the court opined "that there is no logical basis upon which to distinguish between a traditional veil piercing action and an outsider reverse piercing action. In both instances, a claimant requests that a court disregard the normal protections accorded a corporate structure to prevent abuses of that structure." In fact, however, the two situations are quite different and any similarities are wholly superficial.

The problem presented by outsider reverse veil piercing is reminiscent of the issues raised by the old "jingle rule" of partnership law. Section 40 of the UPA (1914) provides that personal creditors of a partner have priority with respect to the partner's personal assets and creditors of the partnership have priority with respect to partnership assets. The "jingle rule," however, has been superseded for all practical purposes by section 723 of the federal Bankruptcy Code. That section provides that the firm's creditors will be paid out of firm assets and then have equal rights to participate with personal creditors in dividing up personal assets. The rationale for this change seems to have been that prospective creditors of the partnership rely on the creditworthiness of the individual partners in making lending and contracting decisions. In response to the federal law, UPA (1997) § 807 de facto repealed the jingle rule.

To the extent that outsider reverse veil piercing effectively gives priority to personal creditors in the corporate setting, it seems just as problematic as the old jingle rule, albeit for slightly different reasons. As with the jingle rule question, the issue is whose creditors shall have priority with respect to which assets? Outsider reverse veil piercing allows the creditor to avoid the more demanding proof required by traditional theories of conversion or fraudulent transfer. Outsider reverse veil piercing also effectively bypasses the standard approach to collecting a judgment against a corporate shareholder, in which the creditor attaches the debtor's shares in the corporation rather than the assets of the corporation itself. Unsecured creditors who relied on firm assets in lending to the corporation are thus disadvantaged. Similarly, if there are other shareholders, their interests are adversely affected if the corporation's assets can be directly attached by the personal creditor of one shareholder. In contrast, in ordinary (i.e., forward) veil piercing cases, a creditor may reach only the assets of the

---

[51] 580 S.E.2d 806 (Va.2003).

controlling shareholder who is determined to be the corporation's alter ego.[52]

2.   Enterprise Liability

In *Walkovszky v. Carlton*, plaintiff Walkovszky complained that Seon and its sister corporations had no separate existence, but rather were components of Carlton's single business enterprise. Recall that the court rejected this theory, holding that the corporate veil may not pierced simply because the defendant corporation is part of a larger enterprise. The mere fact that a corporation is part of a larger enterprise is insufficient to justify veil piercing. Splitting a single business up into many different corporate components thus will not result in the controlling shareholder being held personally liable for the obligations of one of the corporate entities. At most, only the larger corporate combine as a whole could be held liable.

The distinction between veil piercing and enterprise liability is subtle, especially when one is dealing solely with corporate groups rather than individual shareholders. Properly understood, veil piercing is a vertical form of liability—it provides a mechanism for holding a shareholder personally liable for the corporation's obligations. Enterprise liability provides a horizontal form of liability—it offers a vehicle for holding the entire business enterprise liable.

While the single business enterprise theory thus will not allow one to reach a shareholder's personal assets, enterprise liability can be a useful remedy in some settings. If correctly (and successfully) invoked, enterprise liability does permit a creditor to reach the collective assets of all of the corporations making up the enterprise. Suppose, for example, that one of Carlton's other corporations was better capitalized than Seon, having sufficient assets to satisfy Walkovszky's claim. Enterprise liability would allow Walkovszky to reach the assets of that other corporation. In fact, an enterprise liability theory would permit plaintiff to recover from all ten of Carlton's corporations (although not from Carlton individually). Obviously, this theory is most useful when the responsible corporation is insolvent, but the enterprise as a whole has sufficient assets to satisfy the creditor's claim.

Gartner v. Snyder is a useful real world example of enterprise liability in action. A real estate developer used three corporate entities to develop a housing project in New York. The three corporations acted as one: all documents were kept in a single file; all financial records were kept in a single account book; letters

---

[52] See Cascade Energy & Metals Corp. v. Banks, 896 F.2d 1557, 1577 (10th Cir.1990) (rejecting reverse veil piercing on these grounds); Acree v. McMahan, 585 S.E.2d 873 (Ga.2003) (same).

purportedly being sent on behalf of one entity were typed on another's letterhead; offices were shared; no separate corporate formalities were observed. On these facts, the Second Circuit opined that enterprise liability would be appropriate, but that the controlling shareholder could not be held personally liable.[53]

A California appellate court similarly imposed enterprise liability in *Pan Pacific Sash & Door Co. v. Greendale Park, Inc.*,[54] in which the promoters of a real estate venture split the business into two corporations: one that owned the land and one that was to provide construction services. The land corporation had all the assets, while the construction company incurred all the debts. Plaintiff was a supplier who sold building materials to the construction corporation. When the debt was not paid, he attempted to reach the assets of the land corporation. The court allowed plaintiff to do so, holding that the land corporation was the alter ego of the construction company. Hence, the court used a *Walkovszky*-like alter ego doctrine to achieve an enterprise liability result. Among the grounds cited for imposing liability in this case were: (1) both corporations were half of a single venture; (2) they had the same shareholders, directors, and officers; (3) they occupied the same premises; (4) they had common employees; and (5) neither was adequately capitalized.

Under *Pan Pacific*, the basic standard for invoking enterprise liability requires a two-pronged showing: (1) such a high degree of unity of interest between the two entities that their separate existence had de facto ceased and (2) that treating the two entities as separate would promote injustice.[55] The observant reader will note substantial overlap between the factors considered in enterprise liability cases, such as *Gartner* and *Pan Pacific*, and the veil piercing cases. Indeed, while the remedies are conceptually distinct, in practice the line between them tends to blur. In many cases, much the same set of facts could be invoked to justify either or both remedies. Yet, comparing cases like *Pan Pacific* to, say, *Walkovszky* is like comparing apples to oranges. As we shall see, one useful reform in this area would be to more clearly distinguish the two remedies. Veil piercing ought to be limited to holding natural persons liable for the debts and obligations of the corporations of which they are shareholders. Enterprise liability

---

[53] Gartner v. Snyder, 607 F.2d 582, 588 (2d Cir.1979) (dictum). Hence, if plaintiff Walkovszky had wished to invoke enterprise liability, he would have been obliged to show that Carlton did not respect the separate identities of the corporations, as, for example, in the assignment of drivers, in the use of bank accounts, in the ordering of supplies, etc.

[54] 333 P.2d 802 (Cal.App.1958).

[55] See Las Palmas Assoc. v. Las Palmas Center Assoc., 235 Cal.App.3d 1220, 1250 (1991) (adopting *Pan Pacific* standard in an explicitly enterprise liability theory case).

ought to be invoked whenever one is attempting to hold an entire corporate group liable, whether one is nominally dealing with affiliated corporations or a parent and subsidiary. The current practice of trying to use the same doctrine—i.e., veil piercing—to deal both with the liability of natural persons (such as that of Carlton in *Walkovszky*) and that of parent corporations for the acts of their subsidiaries has been the source of much doctrinal and theoretical confusion.

As to the first prong of the *Pan Pacific* test, common ownership is an important—if not essential—consideration.[56] Yet, at the same time, common ownership, standing alone, is not enough. In *Macrodyne Indus., Inc. v. State Board of Equalization*, the court held that (albeit for tax purposes) a parent corporation's ownership all of the stock of the subsidiary corporation did not "establish the identity of the corporations."[57] Neither did the fact that the two had common management and direction. As long as the two behaved "as separate entities," the court would treat them as such. Because the principals had respected the separate corporate existence of the two entities and they had independent business purposes, the court treated the two as separate entities.

Merely showing control, moreover, in the absence of an intent to defraud or promote injustice, is insufficient to overcome the presumption in favor of respecting the separate corporate existence of the various enterprises. As we have seen, there must be some injustice that would result from respecting the separate corporate existence of the various entities. What sorts of misconduct would or would not meet that standard? The prospect of an unsatisfied claim is not enough to meet the latter prong of the test.[58] After all, why would a plaintiff invoke the doctrine if the corporation had enough assets to satisfy the claim?

Conversely, at least by negative implication, where the assets of the corporation whose alleged misconduct purportedly was the proximate cause of plaintiff's injury suffice to satisfy the plaintiff's claims, the court should not disregard the separate existence of any affiliated corporations.[59] If the court will not treat the affiliated

---

[56] See, e.g., Associated Vendors, Inc. v. Oakland Meat Co., 210 Cal. App.2d 825, 839 (1962).

[57] 192 Cal.App.3d 579, 581 (1987).

[58] Cf. Associated Vendors, Inc. v. Oakland Meat Co., 210 Cal.App.2d 825, 842 (1962) ("it is not sufficient to merely show that a creditor will remain unsatisfied if the corporate veil is not pierced").

[59] In California, plaintiffs frequently invoke enterprise liability where the principal defendant is solvent so as to expand the size of the enterprise so as to support a larger punitive damage claim. In Walker v. Signal Cos., Inc., 84 Cal.App.3d 982 (1978), the court held that: "the sole basis for holding [the parent] liable would be to enable the plaintiffs to obtain an increased award of punitive damages because

corporations as a single business enterprise (or pierce the corporate veil, for that matter) to ensure that a tort or contract creditor's claims will be satisfied, the court certainly should not do so where those claims can be satisfied out of the assets of the principal defendant.

The mere fact that one divided one's business activities into multiple corporations likewise fails to satisfy the second prong. As the New York court held in *Walkovszky*, incorporating a business to avoid personal liability neither promotes injustice nor sanctions a fraud. Walkovszky contended that Carlton's multiple corporate structure constituted an unlawful fraud on the public. The court rejected this theory. There is nothing intrinsically fraudulent about deciding to incorporate or about dividing a single enterprise into multiple corporations, even when done solely to get the benefit of limited liability. Both possibilities are an unavoidable consequence of the statutory grant of limited liability to all corporations. As a California court observed: "It is well recognized that the law permits the incorporation of businesses for the very purpose of isolating liabilities among several entities."[60] Instead, presumably, there must be some element of unjust enrichment.[61]

---

of the substantial net worth of the parent. There is no factual justification to do so." Id. at 1001.

[60] Pacific Landmark Hotel, Ltd. v. Marriott Hotels, Inc., 19 Cal.App.4th 615, 628 (1993).

[61] Cf. Sea-Land Services, Inc. v. Pepper Source, 941 F.2d 519 (7th Cir.1991) (Illinois law).

Chapter 5

MANAGING THE CORPORATION

§ 5.1   The Allocation of Corporate Decisionmaking Power

Most public corporations are marked by a separation of ownership and control. Shareholders, who are said to own the firm, have virtually no power to control either its day-to-day operation or its long-term policies. In contrast, the board of directors and senior management, whose equity stake often is small, effectively controls both. As a doctrinal matter, moreover, corporate law essentially carves this separation into stone.

As the Delaware code puts it, for example, the corporation's business and affairs "shall be managed by or under the direction of a board of directors."[1] In contrast, under the Delaware code, shareholder voting rights are essentially limited to the election of directors and approval of charter or bylaw amendments, mergers, sales of substantially all of the corporation's assets, and voluntary dissolution. As a formal matter, only the election of directors and amending the bylaws do not require board approval before shareholder action is possible. In practice, of course, even the election of directors (absent a proxy contest) is predetermined by the existing board nominating the next year's board.

The statutory decisionmaking model thus is one in which the board acts and shareholders, at most, react. To be sure, the shareholders' right to elect the board of directors can give the former de facto control even though the statute assigns de jure control to the latter. Consequently, we can speak of a "control block," i.e., shares held by one or more shareholders whose stock ownership gives them effective control. Firms having such a shareholder exhibit a partial separation of ownership and control. The dominant shareholder controls the firm, despite owning less than 50% of the outstanding voting shares, leaving the minority shareholders without significant control power. Majority controlled firms, in which a dominant shareholder (or group of shareholders acting together) owns more than 50% of the outstanding voting shares, likewise exhibit a partial separation of ownership and

---

[1] DGCL § 141(a). Herein, we will use "decision" as a shorthand for a process that often is much less discrete in practice. Most board of director activity "does not consist of taking affirmative action on individual matters; it is instead a continuing flow of supervisory process, punctuated only occasionally by a discrete transactional decision." Bayless Manning, The Business Judgment Rule and the Director's Duty of Attention: Time for Reality, 39 Bus. Law. 1477, 1494 (1984).

control. Where no such control block exists, however, control passes from the firm's shareholders to its directors. Although shareholders of such firms retain the right to elect directors, the incumbent board controls the election process, and thus the firm. The board of directors is the key player in the formal corporate decisionmaking structure.

How well does this statutory model match up to the real world? In practice, most corporate actions are actually taken by corporate officers and subordinate employees pursuant to delegated authority. Yet, even a board that has been thoroughly captured by senior management typically retains at least some formal functions. The board, moreover, retains the power to hire and fire firm employees and to define the limits of their authority. In addition, certain extraordinary acts may not be delegated, but are instead reserved for the board's exclusive determination.

In practice, it thus is possible to identify several roles that most boards perform most of the time. First, and foremost, the board monitors and disciplines senior management. Second, while boards almost never get involved in making day-to-day operational decisionmaking, most boards have some managerial functions. Broad policymaking is commonly a board prerogative, for example. Even more commonly, however, individual board members provide advice and guidance to senior managers with respect to operational and/or policy decisions. Finally, the board provides access to a network of contacts useful in gathering resources and/or obtaining business.

Among these functions, however, the board's monitoring role reigns supreme. To be sure, at one time, corporation statutes affirmatively required the board to manage the corporation. Delaware's statute, for example, formerly provided: "The business and affairs of every corporation organized under this chapter shall be managed by a board of directors."[2] It was only when the legislature added the phrase "or under the direction of" that the statute expressly contemplated the delegation of managerial functions to corporate officers.

Query, however, whether boards of large public corporations ever really managed firms in the sense of day-to-day operational decisionmaking? To the contrary, that they have never done so is suggested by the very antiquity of complaints that boards fail to actively manage their firms.[3] Instead, the emergence of large public

---

[2] Delaware General Corporation Law § 141(a), quoted in Ernest L. Folk III, The Delaware General Corporation Law: A Commentary and Analysis 50 (1972).

[3] See, e.g., William O. Douglas, Directors Who Do Not Direct, 47 Harv. L. Rev. 1305 (1934).

corporations in the 19th century (such as the railroads) both necessitated and facilitated the concomitant emergence of a class of professional managers. Oversight of such managers long has been the board's primary function.

In fact, the old statutory formulation did not preclude the board from delegating management responsibility. Indeed, as early as 1922, the Delaware Chancery Court held that the directors' role was one of supervision and control, with the detailed conduct of the business being a matter that properly could be delegated to subordinate employees.[4] The modern statutory formulation that the firm shall be "managed by or under the direction of" the board of directors simply codifies this understanding.

§ 5.2   The Problem of Managerialism

An early New York decision opined that the board of directors' powers are "original and undelegated."[5] Yet, in the real world, senior "managers dominate their boards by using their de facto power to select and compensate directors and by exploiting personal ties with them."[6]

Although board capture remains a serious problem, it's worth noting that several trends have coalesced in recent decades to encourage more active and effective board oversight. Much director compensation is now paid in stock, for example, which helps align director and shareholder interests.[7] Courts have made clear that effective board processes and oversight are essential if board decisions are to receive the deference traditionally accorded them under the business judgment rule, especially insofar as structural decisions are concerned (such as those relating to corporate acquisitions).[8] Third, director conduct is constrained by an active market for corporate control, ever-rising rates of shareholder litigation, and, some say, activist shareholders.[9] In sum, modern boards of directors are smaller than their antecedents, meet more

---

[4] Cahall v. Lofland, 114 A. 224, 229 (Del.Ch.1921), aff'd, 118 A. 1 (Del.1922).

[5] Manson v. Curtis, 119 N.E. 559, 562 (N.Y.1918).

[6] Barry Baysinger & Robert E. Hoskisson, The Composition of Boards of Directors and Strategic Control: Effects on Corporate Strategy, 15 Acad. Mgmt. Rev. 72, 72–73 (1990).

[7] See Charles M. Elson, Director Compensation and the Management-Captured Board: The History of a Symptom and a Cure, 50 SMU L. Rev. 127 (1996).

[8] See Stephen M. Bainbridge, Independent Directors and the ALI Corporate Governance Project, 61 Geo. Wash. L. Rev. 1034, 1068–81 (1993) (describing how judicial review of management buyouts and other conflict of interest transactions focuses on role of independent directors).

[9] Daniel P. Forbes & Frances J. Milliken, Cognition and Corporate Governance: Understanding Boards of Directors as Strategic Decision-making Groups, 24 Acad. Mgmt. Rev. 489 (1999).

often, are more independent from management, own more stock, and have better access to information.

In any event, the institutional structure created by corporate law allows but does not contemplate one-man rule. If it comes to overt conflict between board and top management, the former's authority prevails as a matter of law, if not always in practice. Indeed, it is the necessity for retaining dismissal of senior management as a potential sanction that explains why the board is at the apex of the corporate hierarchy rather than functioning as an advisory committee off to the side of the corporate organizational chart. One can imagine a structure of corporate authority identical to current norms except that the board acts as a mere advisory body to a single autocratic CEO. On the face of it, such a structure seemingly would preserve most advantages of the current structure. Consequently, it is the board's power to hire and fire senior management that explains their position at the apex of the corporate hierarchy.

§ 5.3   Consequences of the Separation of Ownership and Control

"The separation of ownership from control produces a condition where the interests of owner and of ultimate manager may, and often do, diverge."[10] Will the board of directors use its control of the corporation to further the selfish interest of the board members rather than the best interests of the corporation's shareholders and other constituencies? To ask the question is to answer it. Given human nature, it would be surprising indeed if directors did not sometimes shirk or self-deal. Economists refer to this phenomenon as the principal-agent problem or as agency costs. Much of corporate law is best understood as a mechanism for constraining these costs.

Agency costs are defined as the sum of the monitoring and bonding costs, plus any residual loss, incurred to prevent shirking by agents.[11] In turn, shirking is defined to include any action by a member of a production team that diverges from the interests of the team as a whole. As such, shirking includes not only culpable cheating, but also negligence, oversight, incapacity, and even honest mistakes. In other words, shirking is simply the inevitable

---

[10] Adolf A. Berle & Gardiner C. Means, The Modern Corporation and Private Property 6 (1932).

[11] Michael C. Jensen & William H. Meckling, Theory of the Firm: Managerial Behavior, Agency Costs and Ownership Structure, 3 J. Fin. Econ. 305 (1976).

consequence of bounded rationality and opportunism within agency relationships.[12]

A sole proprietorship with no agents will internalize all costs of shirking, because the proprietor's optimal trade-off between labor and leisure is, by definition, the same as the firm's optimal trade-off. Agents of a firm, however, will not internalize all of the costs of shirking: the principal reaps part of the value of hard work by the agent, but the agent receives all of the value of shirking. In a classic article, Professors Alchian and Demsetz offered the useful example of two workers who jointly lift heavy boxes into a truck.[13] The marginal productivity of each worker is difficult to measure and their joint output cannot be separated easily into individual components. In such situations, obtaining information about a team member's productivity and appropriately rewarding each team member are very difficult and costly. In the absence of such information, however, the disutility of labor gives each team member an incentive to shirk because the individual's reward is unlikely to be closely related to conscientiousness.

Although agents ex post have strong incentives to shirk, ex ante they have equally strong incentives to agree to a corporate contract containing terms designed to prevent shirking. Bounded rationality, however, precludes firms and agents from entering into the complete contract necessary to prevent shirking by the latter. Instead, there must be some system of ex post governance: some mechanism for detecting and punishing shirking. Accordingly, an essential economic function of management is monitoring the various inputs into the team effort: management meters the marginal productivity of each team member and then takes steps to reduce shirking. (No implication is intended that ex post governance structures are noncontractual.)

---

[12] A simple example of the agency cost problem is provided by the bail upon which alleged criminals are released from jail while they await trial. The defendant promises to appear for trial. But that promise is not very credible: The defendant will be tempted to flee the country. The court could keep track of the defendant—monitor him—by keeping him in jail or perhaps by means of some electronic device permanently attached to the defendant's person. Yet, such monitoring efforts are not free—indeed, keeping someone in jail is quite expensive (food, guards, building the jail, etc.). Alternatively, the defendant could give his promise credibility by bonding it, which is exactly what bail does. The defendant puts up a sum of money that he will forfeit if he fails to appear for trial. (Notice that the common use of bail bonds and the employment of bounty hunters to track fugitives further enhances the credibility of bail as a deterrent against flight.) Of course, despite these precautions, some defendants will escape jail and/or jump bail. Hence, there will always be some residual loss in the form of defendants who escape punishment. Notice, by the way, that this example illustrates how the economic analysis can be extended beyond the traditional agency relationship.

[13] Armen A. Alchian & Harold Demsetz, Production, Information Costs, and Economic Organization, 62 Am. Econ. Rev. 777 (1972).

The process just described, of course, raises a new question: who will monitor the monitors? In any organization, one must have some ultimate monitor who has sufficient incentives to ensure firm productivity without himself having to be monitored. Otherwise, one ends up with a never ending series of monitors monitoring lower level monitors. Alchian and Demsetz solved this dilemma by consolidating the roles of ultimate monitor and residual claimant. According to Alchian and Demsetz, if the constituent entitled to the firm's residual income is given final monitoring authority, he is encouraged to detect and punish shirking by the firm's other inputs because his reward will vary exactly with his success as a monitor.

Unfortunately, this elegant theory breaks down precisely where it would be most useful. Because of the separation of ownership and control, it simply does not describe the modern publicly held corporation. As the corporation's residual claimants, the shareholders should act as the firm's ultimate monitors. But while the law provides shareholders with some enforcement and electoral rights, these are reserved for fairly extraordinary situations. In general, shareholders of public corporation have neither the legal right, the practical ability, nor the desire to exercise the kind of control necessary for meaningful monitoring of the corporation's agents.

The apparent lack of managerial accountability inherent in the modern corporate structure has troubled legal commentators since at least Adolf Berle's time.[14] And, to be sure, agency costs are an important component of any viable theory of the firm. A narrow focus on agency costs, however, easily can distort one's understanding. In the first instance, corporate managers operate within a pervasive web of accountability mechanisms that substitute for monitoring by residual claimants. The capital and product markets, the internal and external employment markets, and the market for corporate control all constrain shirking by firm agents.

In the second, agency costs are the inescapable result of placing ultimate decisionmaking authority in the hands of someone other than the residual claimant. Because we could substantially reduce agency costs by eliminating discretion, but do not do so, one infers that discretion has substantial virtues. In a complete theory of the firm, neither discretion nor accountability can be ignored, because both promote values essential to the survival of business

---

[14] Adolf A. Berle, Jr. and Gardiner C. Means, The Modern Corporation and Private Property 6 (1932) ("The separation of ownership from control produces a condition where the interests of owner and of ultimate manager may, and often do, diverge, and where many of the checks which formerly operated to limit the use of power disappear.").

organizations.[15] At the same time, however, the power to hold to account is ultimately the power to decide.[16] Directors cannot be made more accountable without undermining their discretionary authority. Establishing the proper mix of discretion and accountability thus emerges as the central corporate governance question.

§ 5.4   The Board of Directors

A.   Why a Board?

At the apex of the corporate hierarchy stands not a single individual but a collective—the board of directors. Why? Put another way, why not vest the ultimate power of fiat in an individual autocrat rather than a collegial group?

The commentary to the MBCA's provisions on board meetings provides a well-accepted answer:

> A well-established principle of corporate common law accepted by implication in the Model Act is that directors may act only at a meeting unless otherwise expressly authorized by statute. The underlying theory is that the consultation and exchange of views is an integral part of the functioning of the board.[17]

Granted, the drafters' argument runs afoul of the old joke that a camel is a horse designed by a committee, yet their "underlying theory" is pervasively reflected in the statutory rules governing corporate boards.

B.   Board of Directors Housekeeping Rules

1.   *The Requirement That Boards Act Collectively by Meeting*

The board of directors is a collegial body that, for the most part, is expected to make decisions by consensus. The legal rules governing the board of directors thus put considerable emphasis on the need for collective rather than individual action. As the Restatement (Second) of Agency puts it, for example, a director "has no power of his own to act on the corporation's behalf, but only as one of a body of directors acting as a board."[18] Accordingly, an individual director acting alone generally has neither rights nor

---

[15] Michael P. Dooley, Two Models of Corporate Governance, 47 Bus. Law. 461 (1992).

[16] Kenneth J. Arrow, The Limits of Organization 78 (1974).

[17] MBCA § 8.20 cmt.

[18] Restatement (Second) of Agency § 14 C cmt.

powers.[19] Instead, unless otherwise authorized by statute, only collective decisions taken at a meeting of the board at which a quorum is present are binding on the corporation.[20] This common law principle is reflected, albeit by negative implication, in DGCL § 141(b)'s statement that "[t]he vote of the majority of the directors present at a meeting at which a quorum is present *shall be the act of the board of directors. . . .*"[21]

2.   Board Size

Corporate statutes historically required that boards consist of at least three members, who had to be shareholders of the corporation and, under some statutes, residents of the state of incorporation.[22] Today these requirements have largely disappeared. DGCL § 141(b) authorizes boards to have one or more members and mandates no qualifications for board membership. MBCA §§ 8.02 and 8.03 are comparable.[23] As a default rule, allowing single member boards probably makes sense. It gives promoters maximum flexibility, while allowing the creation of multi-member boards at low cost. In practice, however, multi-member boards are the norm for corporations of any significant size.[24]

In theory, larger boards may facilitate the board's resource-gathering function by providing interlocking relationships with potential customers, suppliers, and other strategic partners. Large boards also provide more opportunities to create insurgent coalitions that constrain agency costs with respect to senior management. On the other hand, however, large boards likely will be contentious and fragmented, which reduces their ability to collectively monitor and discipline senior management. In such

---

[19] This general statement is subject to the caveat that individual directors do have rights to inspect corporate books and records. See, e.g., Cohen v. Cocoline Products, Inc., 150 N.Y.S.2d 815 (1956).

[20] See e.g., Greenberg v. Harrison, 124 A.2d 216 (Conn.1956) (directors cannot vote by proxy); Baldwin v. Canfield, 1 N.W. 261 (Minn.1879) (corporation not bound by a sale of land where the board never met to vote, even though all directors individually executed the deed). But see, e.g., Myhre v. Myhre, 554 P.2d 276 (Mont.1976) (board could act informally in a close corporation in which all shareholders were also directors).

[21] DGCL § 141(b) (emphasis supplied). MBCA § 8.21 and DGCL § 141(f) authorize boards to act without a meeting by means of written consents, but require unanimity.

[22] MBCA § 8.03(a) cmt.

[23] Under current law, only natural persons may serve as directors. For an argument that one or more should be allowed to serve as a corporation's board of directors, see Stephen M. Bainbridge & M. Todd Henderson, Boards-R-Us: Reconceptualizing Corporate Boards, 66 Stanford L. Rev. 1051 (2014).

[24] Board sizes vary widely. A 1999 survey found that slightly less than half of had 7 to 9 members, with the remaining boards scattered evenly on either side of that range. National Association of Corporate Directors, Public Company Governance Survey 1999–2000 7 (Oct. 2000) (44 percent between 7 and 9).

cases, the senior managers can affirmatively take advantage of the board through coalition building, selective channeling of information, and dividing and conquering. In sum, the question of whether there is an optimum board size lacks a parsimonious answer. As is so often the case, one size likely will not fit all.

3.   Electronic Participation in Board Meetings

Modern statutes typically provide that directors may participate in board meetings by conference call or speakerphone, provided that all participants can hear one another.[25] The requirement that members be able to "hear" one another seems quaint in an era of electronic mail, instant messaging, and so forth. Interestingly, however, research on decisionmaking has found that groups linked by computer make fewer remarks and take longer to reach decisions than do groups meeting face to face.[26]

As with other aspects of the rules governing board meetings, accordingly, there seems to be a legitimate basis for otherwise formalistic rules. Electronic communication takes place mostly through text-based mediums. Reading and typing, for many people, are slower and require greater effort than verbal communication. Text-based communication also deprives participants of social cues, such as body language and tone of voice, that may be important signals. Social norms constraining behavior apparently function less well in text-based communication, as demonstrated by the flaming phenomenon in Usenet discussion groups.

4.   Notice of Board Meetings

Unless the articles of incorporation require otherwise, no notice of regularly scheduled board meetings is required.[27] Special meetings require at least two days' notice.[28] As a matter of statutory law, the requisite notice need not announce the purpose of the meeting. Because the directors' duty of care requires them to make an informed decision, however, it is advisable to provide directors of advance notice of the reason for calling a meeting and any relevant documentation.[29] Notice may be waived in writing, either before or

---

[25] See, e.g., DGCL § 141(i); MBCA § 8.20(b).

[26] Starr Roxanne Hiltz et al., Experiments in Group Decision Making: Communication Process and Outcome in Face-to-Face versus Computerized Conferences, 13 Human Communication Research 225, 243–44 (1986); Jane Siegel et al., Group Processes in Computer-Mediated Communication, 37 Org. Behavior & Human Decision Processes 157 (1986).

[27] MBCA § 8.22(a).

[28] MBCA § 8.22(b).

[29] See, e.g., Smith v. Van Gorkom, 488 A.2d 858 (Del.1985), in which the court held that the board breached its fiduciary duty of care by "approving the 'sale' of the Company upon two hours' consideration, without prior notice, and without the exigency of a crisis or emergency." Id. at 874. The court went on to note: "None of the directors, other than Van Gorkom and Chelberg [two insiders], had any prior

after the meeting.[30] Attendance at a meeting also constitutes waiver of notice, unless the director objects to the lack of notice at the beginning of the meeting and thereafter refrains from voting.[31] Any party may challenge the adequacy of notice in any context in which the validity of the board's actions are challenged.[32] As with other requirements relating to board meetings, the notice rules are intended to ensure that the board functions as a collegial body, all of whose members participate and get the benefit of the participation by all other members.

5.   *Quorum and Voting*

The statutory default for a quorum is a majority of the directors, although the articles or bylaws may provide for either a greater or lesser number.[33] As for voting, the statute further provides: "If a quorum is present when a vote is taken, the affirmative vote of a majority of directors present is the act of the board of directors unless the articles of incorporation or bylaws require the vote of a greater number of directors."[34] Note that the statute effectively treats abstentions as no votes, because abstaining directors are "present." By negative implication, this provision also ensures "that the board of directors may act only when a quorum is present."[35] If the quorum is broken by departing directors, the board may not act. Directors who are present at the meeting are deemed to assent to any actions taken unless they, inter alia, ensure that their dissent is noted on the minutes of the meeting.[36] This provision reinforces the notion of the board as a collegial body, "forcefully bringing the position of the dissenting member to the attention of the balance of the board of directors."[37]

6.   *Board Term Limits*

Corporate law statutes generally limit directors to one year terms of office, although the Delaware code provides that directors shall serve until their successor is elected and qualified.[38] Where

---

knowledge that the purpose of the meeting was to propose a cash-out merger of Trans Union. . . . Without any documents before them concerning the proposed transaction, the members of the Board were required to rely entirely upon Van Gorkom's 20-minute oral presentation of the proposal." Id.

[30] MBCA § 8.23(a).

[31] MBCA § 8.23(b).

[32] Schroder v. Scotten, Dillon Co., 299 A.2d 431 (Del.Ch.1972).

[33] See, e.g., DGCL § 141(b) (providing a minimum quorum of 1/3 of the directors); MBCA § 8.24(b) (same).

[34] MBCA § 8.24(c).

[35] MBCA § 8.24 cmt.

[36] MBCA § 8.24(d).

[37] MBCA § 8.24 cmt.

[38] DGCL § 141(b).

the corporation has adopted a classified board, the directors' term of office is either two or three years, depending on whether the board was divided into two or three classes respectively. In any case, the statutes are silent as to the number of terms a director may serve. Because corporation statutes broadly authorize corporations to adopt articles of incorporation specifying director qualifications, however, corporations may adopt charter provisions limiting the number of times someone may serve as a director.

Director term limits remain rare, but are becoming more common. On the one hand, a high degree of turnover among board members may be healthy because a skeptical outsider perspective helps prevent groupthink. On the other hand, however, high turnover discourages individual board members from investing in firm-specific human capital. As such, high turnover rates undermine both the board's ability to effectively monitor and its role as a source of institutional memory. High turnover rates also interfere with group cohesiveness, with potentially adverse effects on the role of social norms as a mechanism of team governance. The prescriptive lesson is that one size will not fit all and firms should be allowed to determine whether director term limits are in their individual interest.

§ 5.5   Board Composition

A.   Board Qualifications

Corporate statutes historically required that directors be shareholders of the corporation and, under some statutes, residents of the state of incorporation. Today these requirements have largely disappeared. DGCL § 141(b) mandates no qualifications for board membership, nor does MBCA § 8.02. Interestingly, however, requiring directors to own stock in the corporation has come back into vogue in recent years. Although neither the MBCA nor the DGCL require corporations to impose any qualifications on board membership, both permit corporations to do so in their articles of incorporation. Many public corporations now require directors to own stock and, moreover, compensate directors in stock rather than cash.

B.   Independence

In recent decades, however, there has been growing acceptance of the idea that a substantial number of a corporation's directors should be outsiders who are not beholden to the corporation's CEO or other top managers. State corporation law statutes, however, generally have remained silent on the subject. Instead, insofar as public corporations are concerned, the principal rules governing the composition of the board of directors are provided by stock exchange listing standards.

This trend accelerated following the Enron scandal. In passing the Sarbanes-Oxley Act, Congress and the SEC left board reform mainly to the stock exchanges. In response, all three major exchanges—the NYSE, NASDAQ, and the American Stock Exchange (AMEX)—amended their corporate governance listing requirements to:

- Require that a majority of the members of the board of directors of most listed companies must be independent of management.

- Define independence using very strict bright-line rules.

- Expand the duties and powers of the independent directors.

- Expand the duties and powers of the audit committee of the board of directors.

Although these changes apply only to publicly traded companies having stock listed on one of the three major exchanges, this is one of the areas in which large privately held corporations and nonprofits have been under particular pressure to become SOX compliant. Auditors, creditors, and other key stakeholders expect larger firms to, at the very least, create an audit committee composed of outside directors and ensure that at least one member of the audit committee is a financial expert.

1.   *The Majority Independent Board*

The NYSE mandates that all listed companies "must have a majority of independent directors."[39] In addition, as we'll see below, the NYSE has mandated the use of several board committees comprised of outsiders. Finally, the NYSE's Listed Company Manual provides that: "To empower non-management directors to serve as a more effective check on management, the non-management directors of each listed company must meet at regularly scheduled executive sessions without management."[40] Although the rule does not indicate how many times per year the outside directors must meet to satisfy this requirement, emerging best practice suggests that there should be such a meeting held in conjunction with every regularly scheduled meeting of the entire board of directors.

---

[39] NYSE Listed Company Manual § 303A.01.

[40] Id., § 303A.03.

The NASDAQ and AMEX standards are substantially similar. One wrinkle is that NASDAQ expressly states an expectation that executive sessions of the outside directors will be held at least twice a year.

Note that both the NYSE and NASDAQ exempt controlled companies—i.e., those in which a shareholder or group of shareholders acting together control 50% or more of the voting power of the company's stock—from the obligation to have a majority independent board.

2. Who Is Independent?

State corporation law traditionally used a rather vague standard to decide whether a given director was independent of management. As one Delaware judicial opinion put it, the question is whether "through personal or other relationships the directors are beholden to" management.[41] In *Beam ex rel. Martha Stewart Living Omnimedia, Inc. v. Stewart*,[42] the Delaware supreme court further explained that:

The primary basis upon which a director's independence must be measured is whether the director's decision is based on the corporate merits of the subject before the board, rather than extraneous considerations or influences. . . . Independence is a fact-specific determination made in the context of a particular case. The court must make that determination by answering the inquiries: independent from whom and independent for what purpose? . . . In order to show lack of independence, the complaint of a stockholder-plaintiff must create a reasonable doubt that a director is not so "beholden" to an interested director (in this case Stewart) that his or her "discretion would be sterilized."

The inquiry into a director's independence usually focuses on economic considerations: "A director is considered interested where he or she will receive a personal financial benefit from a transaction that is not equally shared by the stockholders. Directorial interest also exists where a corporate decision will have a materially detrimental impact on a director, but not on the corporation and the stockholders."[43] In *Stewart*, however, the court opined that:

A variety of motivations, including friendship, may influence the demand futility inquiry. But, to render a director unable to consider demand, a relationship must be of a bias-producing nature. Allegations of mere personal friendship or a mere outside business

---

[41] Aronson v. Lewis, 473 A.2d 805, 815 (Del.1984).
[42] 845 A.2d 1040 (Del.2004).
[43] Rales v. Blasband, 634 A.2d 927, 936 (Del.1993).

relationship, standing alone, are insufficient to raise a reasonable doubt about a director's independence.

The court further cautioned that: "Not all friendships, or even most of them, rise to this level and the Court cannot make a reasonable inference that a particular friendship does so without specific factual allegations to support such a conclusion."

In contrast to these vague state law standards, the new NYSE and NASDAQ listing requirements adopt strict bright-line rules for deciding whether a director is adequately independent to count towards the requisite majority.

NYSE Listed Company Manual § 303A.02, for example, sets out the following tests for determining whether a director is independent:

> (a)(i) No director qualifies as "independent" unless the board of directors affirmatively determines that the director has no material relationship with the listed company (either directly or as a partner, shareholder or officer of an organization that has a relationship with the company).
>
> (ii) In addition, in affirmatively determining the independence of any director who will serve on the compensation committee of the listed company's board of directors, the board of directors must consider all factors specifically relevant to determining whether a director has a relationship to the listed company which is material to that director's ability to be independent from management in connection with the duties of a compensation committee member, including, but not limited to: (A) the source of compensation of such director, including any consulting, advisory or other compensatory fee paid by the listed company to such director; and (B) whether such director is affiliated with the listed company, a subsidiary of the listed company or an affiliate of a subsidiary of the listed company.
>
> (b) In addition, a director is not independent if:
>
> (i) The director is, or has been within the last three years, an employee of the listed company, or an immediate family member is, or has been within the last three years, an executive officer, of the listed company.
>
> (ii) The director has received, or has an immediate family member who has received, during any twelve-month period within the last three years, more than $120,000 in direct compensation from the listed company, other than

director and committee fees and pension or other forms of deferred compensation for prior service (provided such compensation is not contingent in any way on continued service).

(iii)(A) The director or an immediate family member is a current partner of a firm that is the company's internal or external auditor; (B) the director is a current employee of such a firm; (C) the director has an immediate family member who is a current employee of such a firm and who participates in the firm's audit, assurance or tax compliance (but not tax planning) practice; or (D) the director or an immediate family member was within the last three years (but is no longer) a partner or employee of such a firm and personally worked on the listed company's audit within that time.

(iv) The director or an immediate family member is, or has been within the last three years, employed as an executive officer of another company where any of the listed company's present executive officers at the same time serves or served on that company's compensation committee.

(v) The director is a current employee, or an immediate family member is a current executive officer, of a company that has made payments to, or received payments from, the listed company for property or services in an amount which, in any of the last three fiscal years, exceeds the greater of $1 million, or 2% of such other company's consolidated gross revenues.

In effect, the rule requires that the board of directors determine that a nominee has no material direct or indirect relationship with the listed company. The NYSE cautions that "it is best that boards making 'independence' determinations broadly consider all relevant facts and circumstances. In particular, when assessing the materiality of a director's relationship with the listed company, the board should consider the issue not merely from the standpoint of the director, but also from that of persons or organizations with which the director has an affiliation."

The rule further specifies that certain individuals cannot be deemed independent. An employee of the listed company cannot be deemed independent until at least five years after the employment ended. A former affiliate or employee of the listed company's present or former auditor likewise cannot be deemed independent until at least five years after the affiliation or auditing relationship terminated. A director may not be deemed independent if he is employed (or has been employed in the last five years) by a company in which an executive officer of the listed company serves as a member of the board of directors' compensation committee. Directors with immediate family members in any of the foregoing categories are likewise subject to a five-year "cooling off period."

§ 5.6   Removal and Vacancies

Modern statutes generally allow the shareholders to remove directors with or without cause, unless the articles of incorporation specify that directors may be removed only for cause.[44] Removal is accomplished by the affirmative vote of a majority of the shares cast at a meeting at which a quorum is present. The board has no right to remove one of its members,[45] although the board obviously could recommend that shareholders remove one of its members and call a special meeting of the shareholders for that purpose. Grounds to remove a director for cause include "fraud, criminal conduct, gross abuse of office amounting to a breach of trust, or similar conduct."[46]

At early common law, the reservation to shareholders of the power to elect directors was interpreted to mean that the board could not fill vacancies. In contrast, modern statutes typically provide that vacancies in the board, whether the result of removal, resignation, death, expansion of the board, or what have you, may be filled either by the board or by the shareholders.[47]

§ 5.7   Board Committees

A.   State Law

Virtually all states allow the board to establish committees to which some board powers may be delegated, although a number do so only on an opt-in basis pursuant to which committee formation must be authorized by the articles of incorporation or bylaws. Section 141(c)(2) of the Delaware General Corporation Law, for example, provides that the board may set up one or more committees consisting of one or more members. The jurisdiction and powers of the committee must be specified either in the bylaws or in the board resolution creating the committee. All of the powers and authority of the board may be delegated to such committees, except that board committees are barred from acting on matters requiring shareholder approval or changes to the bylaws. In order to accommodate new stock exchange listing standards governing director nomination, which call for corporations to use a separate

---

[44] See, e.g., MBCA § 8.08(a).

[45] Dillon v. Berg, 326 F.Supp. 1214 (D.Del.), aff'd, 453 F.2d 876 (3d Cir.1971); Bruch v. National Guarantee Credit Corp., 116 A. 738 (Del.Ch.1922).

[46] MBCA § 8.08 cmt.

[47] See, e.g., MBCA § 8.10(a).

nominating committee composed solely of independent directors, the relevant provisions were amended in 2004 to allow a committee to make recommendations for shareholder action (with respect to the election or removal of directors).

B. Stock Exchange Standards

The NYSE Listed Company Manual mandates the establishment of three committees, consisting of a Nominating and Corporate Governance Committee (§ 303A.04), a Compensation Committee (§ 303A.05), and an Audit Committee (§ 303A.06).

1. *The Nominating and Corporate Governance Committee*

NYSE Listed Company Manual § 303A.04 requires that listed companies set up "a nominating/corporate governance committee composed entirely of independent directors." The Committee must have a written charter specifying how it will go about identifying candidates for board membership and selecting those candidates to be nominated. The Committee should have sole power to select headhunters and negotiate their fees. Companies in which a shareholder or group of shareholders acting together control 50% or more of the voting power of the company's stock are exempt from the nominating committee requirement.

In addition to nominating director candidates, many companies assign responsibility for selecting new CEOs to the nominating committee. In cooperation with the compensation committee, the nominating committee may take the lead in negotiating the terms of a newly appointed CEO's employment agreement. Finally, the nominating committee may be tasked with setting director compensation, although many firms assign that job to the compensation committee.

Note that the NYSE listing requirement includes "corporate governance" as part of the nominating committee's job. This aspect of the committee's duties remains relatively poorly defined. In general, however, the intent seems to be that the nominating committee should serve as the board of directors' principal point of contact with shareholders. As a practical matter, one common task given this committee is assigning directors to other board committees (typically subject to approval by the entire board).

2. *The Compensation Committee*

As the name suggests, the compensation committee reviews and approves (or recommends to the full board) the compensation of senior executives and generally oversees the corporation's compensation policies. Proponents of having a separate compensation committee deal with such matters, rather than the board as a whole, argue that inside directors, even if recused from considering their own compensation, cannot objectively evaluate the compensation of other senior executives in light of the close relationship between one executive's compensation and that of another.

Under NYSE Listed Company Manual § 303A.05, the board of directors of all listed companies must have a compensation committee. The committee must be comprised solely of independent directors.[48] Only listed companies in which a shareholder or group of shareholders acting together own 50% or more of the stock are exempt from this requirement.

The NYSE also requires that the compensation committee adopt a written charter setting out the committee's purpose, responsibilities, and powers. At a minimum, the compensation committee must have power to:

- Set performance goals for the CEO to meet, evaluate the CEO's performance in light of those goals, and set the CEO's pay. If the board wishes, the compensation committee may simply recommend a pay figure for the CEO, on which all the independent directors would then act. Notice that, in either case, only independent directors are involved in setting the CEO's salary.

- Make recommendations to the board of directors with respect to the pay of other executive officers and any incentive or stock-based compensation plans that are subject to board approval.

- Produce a compensation committee report on executive officer compensation to be included in the listed company's annual proxy statement or annual report on Form 10–K.

The NYSE expects that the charter will vest the power to hire, fire, and compensate such consultants in the compensation committee rather than the CEO.

3. The Audit Committee

To ensure that financial statements are accurate and complete, the SEC requires corporations to have those statements audited by an independent firm of certified public accountants. In order to

---

[48] The NYSE definition of "independent director" includes the following provision: "The director or an immediate family member is, or has been within the last three years, employed as an executive officer of another company where any of the listed company's present executive officers at the same time serves or served on that company's compensation committee."

prevent management and the outside auditor from getting too cozy with one another, it's long been good practice for the corporation's board of directors to have an audit committee. Ideally, the audit committee provides a forum for independent directors to discuss the firm's financial results outside of management's presence and ensures that the audited financial statements fairly and accurately represent the company's financial picture.

Enron, WorldCom, and the various other scandals of 2000–2002, especially those involving former Big 6 accounting firm Arthur Andersen, demonstrated that there were serious problems with all of the key players: management, the outside auditor, and the board of directors and its audit committee. The wave of restated financials in 2001–2002 confirmed that there were basic, widespread problems with the financial disclosures provided by many companies. Congress, the SEC, and the stock exchanges struck back in various ways.

For decades, the NYSE required listed companies to have an audit committee comprised solely of independent directors. The committee had to have at least three members, all of whom were "financially literate." At least one committee member had to have expertise in accounting or financial management.[49]

When Sarbanes-Oxley was under consideration by Congress, a consensus quickly formed in favor of imposing a tougher version of the NYSE requirements on all public corporations. SOX § 301 therefore ordered the SEC to adopt rules requiring that the stock exchanges and NASDAQ adopt listing requirements mandating the creation by listed companies of audit committees satisfying the following specifications:

1. *Committee Responsibilities*: The audit committee is responsible for appointing, compensating, and supervising the company's outside auditor. The outside auditor "shall report directly to the audit committee." The committee also must resolve "disagreements between management and the auditor regarding financial reporting."

2. *Independence*: All members of the audit committee must be independent, which § 301 defines as precluding the committee member from being an "affiliated person" of the company and from accepting

---

[49] SOX § 2(3) defines the term "audit committee" as "a committee (or equivalent body) established by and amongst the board of directors of an issuer for the purpose of overseeing the accounting and financial reporting processes of the issuer and audits of the financial statements of the issuer."

any "consulting, advisory, or other compensatory fee" from the company except for directors' fees.

3.   *Whistleblowers*: The audit committee must establish procedures for handling complaints about the way the company conducts its accounting, internal audit controls, and outside audits. The procedure must include a mechanism for "the confidential, anonymous submission by employees . . . of concerns regarding questionable accounting or auditing matters."

4.   *Hiring Advisors*: In addition to empowering the audit committee to hire and pay the outside auditor, the company also must empower the committee to hire "independent counsel and other advisors, as it determines necessary to carry out its duties," with the outside advisor's fees paid by the company.

NYSE Listed Company Manual § 303A.06, for example, thus now provides that each listed company must have an audit committee. Unlike the nominating and compensation committee requirements, even companies with a controlling shareholder must comply with the audit committee rules.

In § 303A.07, the NYSE sets out additional committee requirements:

- The Committee must have at least three members. (Note that a growing number of firms are appointing as many as five individuals to the audit committee so as to help share the high workload imposed on this committee's members.)

- All committee members must be independent, both as defined in SOX § 301 and the NYSE Listed Company Manual.

- All committee members must be "financially literate" and at least one member "must have accounting or related financial management expertise." It's left up to the company's board of directors to decide what that means and whether the members qualify.

- The audit committee must have a written charter specifying its duties, role, and powers.

- The committee is charged with oversight of "(1) the integrity of the listed company's financial statements, (2) the listed company's compliance with legal and regulatory requirements, (3) the independent auditor's qualifications and independence, and (4) the performance of the listed company's internal audit function and independent auditors."

- The committee must prepare an annual report on the audit process to be included in the company's annual proxy statement.

- The audit committee must establish procedures for receiving and dealing with complaints "regarding accounting, internal accounting controls, or auditing matters" and set up a process for confidential, anonymous submission by employees "of concerns regarding questionable accounting or auditing matters." (Because of this requirement, many companies assign responsibility for oversight of the business' compliance programs generally to the audit committee. Firms that chose not to do so, typically so as to avoid overloading the audit committee's members with work, commonly assign this task to the Nominating and Corporate Governance committee.)

- The audit committee must have the power to engage independent counsel and other advisors and to pay such advisors.

- The committee must have the power to set the compensation of the outside auditor.

- At least once a year, the committee must receive a report from the outside auditor on the adequacy of the company's internal controls.

- The committee is to review the company's annual and quarterly disclosure reports, specifically including the MD & A section, as well as the financial statements.

- The committee is to review earnings announcements and other guidance provided analysts.

- The committee must meet periodically in executive session with both the company's internal and outside auditors.

- The committee must review any disagreements between management and the auditors.

§ 5.8   Officers

A.   Delegation of Corporate Powers to Officers

Assume a public corporation incorporated in a Model Business Corporation Act state. The Company's Chief Executive Officer just retired. Who will select the CEO's replacement? In all probability, the board of directors will make that decision. Recall that under MBCA § 8.01(b) all corporate powers are exercised by or under the board's authority—which includes the power to hire and fire. A significant personnel decision, such as the one in question, almost certainly would be made by the board. On the other hand, one would scarcely expect the board of directors of a public corporation to make minor personnel decisions, such as hiring a shop foreman.

Put bluntly, the modern public corporation is just too big for the directors to manage on anything resembling a day-to-day basis. Many directors of large corporations are outsiders, moreover, who have full time jobs elsewhere and therefore can devote relatively little time to the running of the business for which they act as directors. MBCA § 8.01(b) reflects these basic truisms in two respects. First, the statute provides that the "business and affairs of the corporation" shall be "managed by or under the direction of" the board. This formulation is intended to make clear that the board's role is to formulate broad policy and oversee the subordinates who actually conduct the business day-to-day. Second, the statute also provides that corporate powers may be exercised "under the [board's] authority," which allows (but does not require) the board to delegate decisionmaking authority to corporate officers.[50] In turn, corporate officers may delegate some of their responsibilities to less senior employees, and so forth down the organizational chart.

B. Officers as Agents

Suppose a newly appointed CEO wishes to hire an Administrative Assistant. If the CEO signs an employment contract with a prospective assistant, purporting to act on behalf of the corporation, will that contract be binding on the firm? The answer to that question depends on whether the CEO has authority as that term of art is used in agency law. Accordingly, we must (briefly) digress into agency law and the authority of agents.

1. *The Agency Relationship Defined*

The agency relationship, in its broadest sense, includes any relationship in which one person (the agent) is authorized to act on behalf of another person (the principal). More specifically, an

---

[50] Older corporation statutes required corporations to have specified officers. MBCA (1969) § 50 required a president, one or more vice presidents, a secretary, and a treasurer. Modern statutes allow the corporation to designate in its bylaws such officers as it wishes to have and allow officers to hold multiple offices. See, e.g., MBCA § 8.40. Being an officer, as opposed to a nonofficer employee, has legal significance for a couple of limited purposes. First, the scope of an officer's implied or apparent authority is probably broader than that of a nonofficer employee. Second, officers are subject to the short-swing profit liability provision in Securities Act Section 16(b).

agency relationship arises when there is a manifestation of consent by the principal that the agent act on the principal's behalf and subject to the principal's control, and the agent consents to so act.[51] The requisite manifestation of consent can be implied from the circumstances, which makes it possible for the parties to have formed a legally effective agency relationship without realizing they had done so. Corporate employees, especially officers, are generally regarded as agents of the corporation.[52]

Curiously, neither an individual director nor even the board as a whole are regarded as agents of the corporation.[53] In a sense, when the board acts collectively, it functions as a principal in agency law terms. Unless shareholder approval is required, after all, the act of the board is the act of the corporation. As to the individual director, recall that he "has no power of his own to act on the corporation's behalf, but only as one of the body of directors acting as a board."[54]

2. Authority of Agents

An agent may have either actual or apparent authority to enter into contracts on behalf of the corporate principal.[55] Likewise, in some settings, the corporation may be estopped from denying the authority of its employees. Determining whether an agent had the requisite authority in any given situation can be challenging. The differences between the various categories of authority are complex and subtle. In addition, many of the categories overlap—it is not at all uncommon for more than one type of authority to be present in a single transaction. Finally, the courts are not always precise when using labels. For example, estoppel and inherent authority are often called apparent authority. For our purposes, however, it is critical for you to understand that the legal consequences of an agent's actions do not depend on the type of authority at hand. For purposes of determining whether or not the corporate principal is bound by the contract vis-à-vis the third party to the transaction, authority is authority and the different types of authority are essentially irrelevant.

---

[51] Restatement (Second) of Agency § 1.

[52] Restatement (Second) of Agency § 14 C cmt. a.

[53] Restatement (Second) of Agency § 14 C.

[54] Restatement (Second) of Agency § 14 C cmt. b.

[55] The Restatement (Second) of Agency also recognized a concept called "inherent agency power," which it defined as "a term used in the Restatement of this subject to indicate the power of an agent which is derived not from authority, apparent authority or estoppel, but solely from the agency relation and exists for the protection of persons harmed by or dealing with a servant or other agent." The Restatement (Third) of Agency has abandoned this concept. See generally Stephen M. Bainbridge, Agency, Partnership, & LLCs (2d ed. 2014).

Why then does the law distinguish between different categories of authority? It will be helpful to focus for a moment on the two basic types of authority: "actual authority" and "apparent authority." Consider the following hypothetical: Pam owns Whiteacre. Alan is her real estate broker and, indisputably, her agent. Ted is an outsider who claims that Alan entered into a contract on Pam's behalf to sell Whiteacre. Suppose Ted seeks to prove the existence of authority by evidence relating to communications between Pam and Alan, such as a letter from Pam to Allen in which Pam directed Alan to sell Whiteacre. In this instance, Ted is attempting to establish the existence of actual authority. In contrast, suppose Ted seeks to establish authority by evidence relating to communications from Pam to Ted. Suppose Pam sent Ted a letter in which she said that she had ordered Alan to sell Whiteacre. In this case, Ted is trying to establish apparent authority. Importantly, the contract will be no less binding if Ted proves apparent authority rather than actual. The difference between actual and apparent authority thus arises out of the way in which Ted seeks to prove that Alan was authorized to enter into the contract. In other words, the different categories of authority really are ways of classifying the proof the plaintiff must offer to bind the principal to the contract.

Actual authority exists when the agent reasonably believes the principal has consented to a particular course of conduct.[56] Actual authority can be express, as where the principal instructs the agent to "sell Whiteacre on my behalf." In the corporate context, express actual authority is usually vested in officers by a resolution of the board and/or a description of the officer's duties set forth in the bylaws.[57] Actual authority can also be implied, however, if the principal's acts or conduct are such the agent can reasonably infer the requisite consent. An agent has incidental actual authority, for example, to use all means reasonably necessary to carry out a particular result expressly mandated by the principal. A pattern of acquiescence by the board in a course of conduct may also give rise to implied actual authority to enter into similar contracts in the future.[58]

A contract entered into by an agent, purportedly on the principal's behalf, can be binding even if the agent lacks actual

<hr>

[56] Restatement (Second) of Agency §§ 7 & 26.

[57] Compare Musulin v. Woodtek, Inc., 491 P.2d 1173 (Or.1971) (unless authorized by the bylaws or board resolution, corporate officers lacked authority to execute a promissory note on the corporation's behalf) with King World Prod., Inc. v. Financial News Network, Inc., 660 F.Supp. 1381 (S.D.N.Y.1987) (corporate officer had actual authority to execute a lease based, *inter alia*, on the job description in his employee contract).

[58] Restatement (Second) of Agency § 7 cmt. c & § 26 cmt. d.

authority. Apparent authority exists where words or conduct of the principal lead the third party to reasonably believe that the agent has authority to make the contract.[59] Of particular importance with respect to the authority of corporate officers is the concept of apparent authority implied by custom. Suppose the board of directors instructed the CEO not to hire an assistant. The CEO thus lacked actual authority. The CEO nonetheless signs a prospective assistant to an employment contract that purports to be binding on the corporation. Is it binding? If the assistant (the third party) knew that the corporation had placed the CEO in that position and it was customary for CEOs to have authority to hire assistants, the CEO will have apparent authority by virtue of that custom and the contract will be binding.[60]

3.   Authority of Corporate Officers

Most of the case law on the apparent authority of corporate officers relates to the powers of presidents. Corporate presidents are regarded as general agents of the corporation vested with considerable managerial powers. Accordingly, contracts that are executed by the president on the corporation's behalf and arise out of the ordinary course of business matters are binding on the corporation.[61]

Cases dealing with the authority of subordinate officers are much rarer. As to vice presidents, a number of (mostly older) cases hold they have little or no implied or apparent authority to bind the corporation. Accordingly, they have only such authority as is expressly conferred on them in the bylaws or by board resolution.[62] The corporate secretary is assumed to be the custodian of the corporation's books and records. Accordingly, the secretary has actual authority to certify those records. Otherwise, however, the secretary has no authority other than that conferred on him by the bylaws or board resolutions.[63]

---

[59] Restatement (Second) of Agency § 27.

[60] Restatement (Second) of Agency § 27 cmt. d.

[61] See, e.g., Evanston Bank v. Conticommodity Servs., Inc., 623 F.Supp. 1014 (N.D.Ill.1985) (president's inherent authority extended only to ordinary matters); Belcher v. Birmingham Trust Nat'l Bank, 348 F.Supp. 61 (N.D.Ala.1968) (president has power to bind corporation in ordinary course of business); Quigley v. W. N. Macqueen & Co., 151 N.E. 487 (Ill.1926) (by virtue of his office, president has power to bind the corporation to contracts made in the ordinary course of business).

[62] See, e.g., Interstate Nat'l Bank v. Koster, 292 P. 805 (Kan.1930); James F. Monaghan, Inc. v. M. Lowenstein & Sons, 195 N.E. 101 (Mass.1935); Musulin v. Woodtek, 491 P.2d 1173 (Or.1971).

[63] See, e.g., In re Drive-In Development Corp., 371 F.2d 215 (7th Cir.1966) (corporation estopped to deny validity of board resolutions certified by corporate secretary); Meyer v. Glenmoor Homes, Inc., 54 Cal.Rptr. 786 (Cal.App.1966) (secretary had power to affix corporate seal to documents but no authority re contracts of indebtedness); Blair v. Brownstone Oil & Refining Co., 120 P. 41 (Cal.App.1911) (no authority to execute release); Ideal Foods, Inc. v. Action Leasing

An important line of cases limits the implied and apparent authority of corporate officers—of whatever rank—to matters arising in the ordinary course of business. In the leading decision of *Lee v. Jenkins Bros.*, the Second Circuit held:

> The rule most widely cited is that the president only has authority to bind his company by acts arising in the usual and regular course of business but not for contracts of an "extraordinary" nature. . . .

> Apparent authority is essentially a question of fact. It depends not only on the nature of the contract involved, but the officer negotiating it, the corporation's usual manner of conducting business, the size of the corporation and the number of its stockholders, the circumstances that give rise to the contract, the reasonableness of the contract, the amounts involved, and who the contracting third party is, to list a few but not all of the relevant factors. In certain instances a given contract may be so important to the welfare of the corporation that outsiders would naturally suppose that only the board of directors (or even the shareholders) could properly handle it. It is in this light that the "ordinary course of business" rule should be given its content.[64]

As *Lee* suggests, there is no bright line between ordinary and extraordinary acts. It seems reasonable to assume, however, that acts consigned by statute to the board of directors will be deemed extraordinary.[65] Consequently, for example, extraordinary acts doubtless include the various acts specified in MBCA § 8.25(e) that a board of directors may not delegate to a committee.[66] (Of course, once the board has made its decision with respect to an

Corp., 413 So.2d 416 (Fla.App.1982) (secretary is a ministerial position with no authority to conduct business); Shunga Plaza, Inc. v. American Employers' Ins. Co., 465 P.2d 987 (Kan.1970) (corporate secretary has no power to bind the corporation unless the board has entrusted him with management of the business); Easter Oil Corp. v. Strauss, 52 S.W.2d 336 (Tex.Civ.App.1932) (secretary had no authority to execute promissory note).

[64] Lee v. Jenkins Bros., 268 F.2d 357, 365–70 (2d Cir.), cert. denied, 361 U.S. 913 (1959). See also In re Mulco Products, Inc., 123 A.2d 95 (Del.Super.Ct.1956); Lucey v. Hero Int'l Corp., 281 N.E.2d 266 (Mass.1972).

[65] See, e.g., Plant v. White River Lumber Co., 76 F.2d 155 (8th Cir.1935) (sale of all or substantially all corporate assets).

[66] The Model Business Corporation Act provides that the following decisions may not be delegated to a committee of the board, but rather must be made by the board as a whole: (1) Authorize dividends or other distributions, except according to a formula or method, or within limits, prescribed by the board of directors. (2) Approve or propose to shareholders action that the statute requires be approved by shareholders. (3) Fill vacancies on the board of directors or, in general, on any of its committees. (4) Adopt, amend, or repeal bylaws. Model Bus. Corp. Act Ann. § 8.25(e) (2001).

extraordinary matter, implementation of that decision can be delegated to officers.)

In general, when one must decide a particular action is ordinary or extraordinary, the following factors seem especially pertinent:[67] How much of the firm's assets or earnings are involved? Suppose a corporation running an auto parts store has $100,000 in cash available. A decision to spend $500 to buy a cash register would be ordinary, while a decision to spend $50,000 to expand the business into a neighboring location probably would be regarded as extraordinary. How much risk is involved? A decision to buy one cash register is not very risky and would be an ordinary action, while a decision to open a new store might be very risky and therefore extraordinary. A decision to buy inventory on installment where the purchase price is paid off in three months probably would be seen as ordinary. A decision to take out a thirty-year loan probably would be seen as extraordinary. How long will the action have an effect on the corporation? How much would it cost to reverse the decision? A decision to open a new store might be very expensive to reverse, as the corporation might not be able to get out of the lease if things went bad. Such a decision thus would be extraordinary.

As to most matters falling in the gray area between ordinary and extraordinary, a small host of decisions could be cited on either side. There is relatively little consistency of outcome in this area. Courts are divided, for example, as to whether such basic matters as filing a lawsuit[68] or executing a guarantee of another corporation's debts are ordinary or extraordinary.[69] One is tempted to remind the courts that Emerson's famous dictum against a fetish for consistency holds only that a *"foolish* consistency is the hobgoblin of little minds."

How should cases falling between the extremes be resolved? Put bluntly, the authority of corporate officers should be regarded as virtually plenary. Only matters expressly reserved to the board by statute, the articles of incorporation, or the bylaws should be

---

[67] ALI PRINCIPLES § 3.01 rptr. note.

[68] Compare Custer Channel Wing Corp. v. Frazer, 181 F.Supp. 197 (S.D.N.Y.1959) (president had authority to do so) with Lloydona Peters Enter., Inc. v. Dorius, 658 P.2d 1209 (Utah 1983) (no authority to do so); Ney v. Eastern Iowa Tel. Co., 144 N.W. 383 (Iowa 1913) (no authority to do so with respect to the corporation's largest shareholder). See also Youell v. Grimes, 217 F. Supp. 2d 1167, 1177 (D. Kan. 2002) (holding that "officers have the authority to hire counsel on behalf of a corporation without board approval"); Steiner v. Meyerson, 1995 WL 441999, at *10 (Del. Ch. July 19, 1995) ("As Meyerson is Telxon's chief executive officer, he undoubtedly possesses the authority to hire and fire the corporation's legal counsel.").

[69] Compare Sperti Products, Inc. v. Container Corp. of Am., 481 S.W.2d 43 (Ky.App.1972) (president had authority) with First Nat'l Bank v. Cement Products Co., 227 N.W. 908 (Iowa 1929) (no authority to do so).

deemed "extraordinary" and, consequently, beyond the scope of senior officers' authority.

One rationale for this position is suggested by simple statutory interpretation. Recall that both the MBCA and Delaware law provide that the business of the corporation "shall be managed by or under the direction of a board of directors."[70] The use of the disjunctive prior to the phrase "under the direction of" suggests that the statute's drafters anticipated that the corporation would be managed by its officers with the board mainly exercising oversight authority. Unless a decision is expressly reserved to the board, the statutory language thus contemplates that a corporation may act through its officers subject to review by the board.

This reading of the statute comports with modern board practice. The de facto role of the board in most large public corporations consists of providing informal advice to senior management (especially the CEO) and episodic oversight. An extensive definition of extraordinary acts thus seems a needless formality.

An alternative justification for the proposed rule rests on the costs the existing rule imposes on third parties. Persons who do business with a corporation do so at some peril of discovering that their transaction will be deemed to implicate an extraordinary act and, accordingly, required express board action. An expansive definition of extraordinary matters increases this risk. Transaction costs thus increase in several respects. An expansive variant of the rule creates uncertainty, obliging third parties to take costly precautions. They may insist, for example, on seeing an express authorization from the board. Uncertainty about the outer perimeters of the rule also encourages opportunism by the corporation. If contracts dealing with extraordinary matters are voidable, the corporation effectively has a put with respect to the transaction. Uncertainty as to the enforceability of a contract gives the board leverage to extract a favorable settlement of the third party's claims.

---

[70] DGCL § 141(a); see also MBCA § 8.01.

Chapter 6

THE DUTY OF CARE AND THE BUSINESS JUDGMENT RULE

§ 6.1 Introduction

The duty of care requires corporate directors to exercise "that amount of care which ordinarily careful and prudent men would use in similar circumstances."[1] Because the corporate duty of care thus resembles the tort law concept of reasonable care, one might assume the duty of care is violated when directors act negligently. At this point, however, one encounters the business judgment rule and the one thing about the business judgment rule on which everyone agrees is that it insulates directors from liability for negligence. "While it is often stated that corporate directors and officers will be liable for negligence in carrying out their corporate duties, all seem agreed that such a statement is misleading. . . . Whatever the terminology, the fact is that liability is rarely imposed upon corporate directors or officers simply for bad judgment and this reluctance to impose liability for unsuccessful business decisions has been doctrinally labeled the business judgment rule."[2]

Beyond this point, however, agreement ceases. Two basic ways of reconciling the duty of care and the business judgment rule compete in the case law. One treats the rule as a standard of review. Hence, for example, some courts and commentators argue that the business judgment rule shields directors from liability so long as they act in good faith. Others contend that the rule simply raises the liability bar from mere negligence to, say, gross negligence or recklessness.

The other conception one sees in the case law treats the rule as an abstention doctrine that creates a presumption against judicial review of duty of care claims. The court will abstain from reviewing the substantive merits of the directors' conduct unless the plaintiff can rebut the business judgment rule by showing that one or more of its preconditions are lacking.[3]

---

[1] See, e.g., Graham v. Allis-Chalmers Mfg. Co., 188 A.2d 125, 130 (Del.1963).

[2] Joy v. North, 692 F.2d 880, 885 (2d Cir.), cert. denied, 460 U.S. 1051 (1983).

[3] See, e.g., Brehm v. Eisner, 746 A.2d 244, 264 n.66 (Del.2000) (stating that "directors' decisions will be respected by courts unless the directors are interested or lack independence relative to the decision, do not act in good faith, act in a manner that cannot be attributed to a rational business purpose or reach their decision by a grossly negligent process that includes the failure to consider all material facts reasonably available").

A. *Shlensky* and Abstention

In *Shlensky v. Wrigley*, plaintiff-shareholder Shlensky challenged Philip K. Wrigley's famous refusal to install lights in Wrigley Field.[4] Shlensky was a minority shareholder in the corporation that owned the Chicago Cubs and operated Wrigley Field. Wrigley was the majority stockholder (owning 80% of the stock) and president of the company. In the relevant period, 1961–1965, the Cubs consistently lost money. Shlensky alleged that the losses were attributable to their poor home attendance. In turn, Shlensky alleged that the low attendance was attributable to Wrigley's refusal to permit installation of lights and night baseball. Shlensky contended Wrigley refused to institute night baseball because the latter believed (1) that baseball was a day-time sport and (2) that night baseball might have a negative impact on the neighborhood surrounding Wrigley Field. The other defendant directors allegedly were so dominated by Wrigley that they acquiesced in his policy of day-only baseball, which allegedly violated their duty of care.

The defendants moved to dismiss for failure to state a claim, asserting a strong abstention version of the business judgment rule: "defendants argue that the courts will not step in and interfere with honest business judgment of the directors unless there is a showing of fraud, illegality or conflict of interest." The court's analysis of that claim opened by extracting "certain ground rules" from prior precedents:

- "[C]ourts of equity will not undertake to control the policy or business methods of a corporation although it may be seen that a wiser policy might be adopted and the business more successful if other methods were pursued."

- "We have then a conflict in view between the responsible managers of a corporation and an overwhelming majority of its stockholders on the one hand and a dissenting minority on the other a conflict touching matters of business policy, such as has occasioned innumerable applications to courts to intervene and determine which of the two conflicting views should prevail. The response which courts make

---

[4] Shlensky v. Wrigley, 237 N.E.2d 776, 777–78 (Ill.App.1968). The court also found Shlensky's claim defective for failure to allege damages. This is mainly an issue of causation. To be sure, the Cubs' poor attendance probably contributed to the firm's losses, but was poor home attendance attributable to the lack of night baseball or to the Cubs' performance? During the relevant time period, the Cubs were pretty consistent losers. In any event, this portion of the court's opinion is dicta. Once the court decided the business judgment rule was applicable, the inquiry could have (and should have) ended.

to such applications is that it is not their function to resolve for corporations questions of policy and business management. The directors are chosen to pass upon such questions and their judgment unless shown to be tainted with fraud is accepted as final."

- "In a purely business corporation . . . the authority of the directors in the conduct of the business of the corporation must be regarded as absolute when they act within the law, and the court is without authority to substitute its judgment for that of the directors."

Collectively, these "ground rules" describe the business judgment rule in action. From them, moreover, we can distill a basic statement of that rule: absent a showing of fraud, illegality, or conflict of interest, the court must abstain from reviewing the directors' decision.

The *Shlensky* court thus could have (and, perhaps, should have) dismissed plaintiff's claim without touching on the substantive merits of the defendants' decision or the motivation behind that decision. Curiously, however, the court took some pains to posit legitimate business reasons for that decision. The court opined, for example, that "the effect on the surrounding neighborhood might well be considered by a director." Likewise, the court asserted that "the long run interest" of the firm "might demand" consideration of the effect night baseball would have on the neighborhood. Does this mean that courts will examine the substantive merits of a board decision? No. The court did not require defendants to show either that such considerations motivated their decisions or that the decision in fact benefited the corporation. To the contrary, the court acknowledged that its speculations in this regard were irrelevant dicta:

> By these thoughts we do not mean to say that we have decided that the decision of the directors was a correct one. That is beyond our jurisdiction and ability. We are merely saying that the decision is one properly before directors and the motives alleged in the amended complaint showed no fraud, illegality or conflict of interest in their making of that decision.[5]

In sum, if we may invoke an appropriate metaphor, the Illinois court did not even allow Shlensky to get up to bat.

---

[5] The principle so announced is a very old one, indeed. See, e.g., Leslie v. Lorillard, 18 N.E. 363, 365 (N.Y.1888) (opining that "courts will not interfere unless the [directors'] powers have been illegally or unconscientiously executed; or unless it be made to appear that the acts were fraudulent or collusive, and destructive of the rights of the stockholders. Mere errors of judgment are not sufficient. . . .").

Although *Shlensky* is a particularly explicit example of the abstention version of the business judgment rule, it is far from unique. In *Kamin v. American Express Co.*,[6] for example, plaintiff challenged the board's decision to declare an in-kind dividend of shares in a second corporation. The court dismissed for failure to state a claim, opining: "The directors' room rather than the courtroom is the appropriate forum for thrashing out purely business questions which will have an impact on profits, market prices, competitive situations, or tax advantages." Hence, absent "fraud, dishonesty, or nonfeasance," the court would not substitute its judgment for that of the directors.

Abstention does not mean courts simply rubberstamp the board's decision. Both *Shlensky* and *Kamin* make clear that the business judgment rule has no application when fraud and/or self-dealing are present. Both cases also imply various prerequisites must be satisfied before the rule may be invoked. *Kamin*'s reference to "non-feasance" suggests, for example, that the business judgment rule may only be invoked where the board has made a conscious business decision—a point that becomes especially significant with respect to the burgeoning class of board oversight cases.[7] The good faith and disinterested independence of the directors also are often identified as conditions on which the rule is predicated.[8] The board's decision must be an informed one.[9] Finally, albeit controversially, some courts and commentators contend that the business judgment rule does not protect an irrational decision.[10] If these preconditions are satisfied, however, the abstention cases hold that the inquiry must end. There will be no judicial review of the substantive merits of the board's decision—whether those merits are measured in terms of fairness, reasonableness, wisdom, care, or what have you.

B. *Technicolor* and Substantive Review

In sharp contrast to *Shlensky* and its ilk, the Delaware supreme court's decision in *Cede & Co. v. Technicolor, Inc.*[11] embraced a conception of the business judgment potentially

---

[6] 383 N.Y.S.2d 807 (Sup.Ct.1976), aff'd, 387 N.Y.S.2d 993 (App.Div.1976).

[7] See, e.g., Aronson v. Lewis, 473 A.2d 805, 813 (Del.1984) (stating that the business judgment rule is inapplicable "where directors have either abdicated their functions, or absent a conscious decision, failed to act").

[8] See, e.g., Auerbach v. Bennett, 393 N.E.2d 994, 999 (N.Y.1979) (so long as directors were disinterested and acted in good faith, the business judgment rule required court to defer to board committee's recommendation to dismiss a shareholder derivative suit).

[9] See, e.g., Smith v. Van Gorkom, 488 A.2d 858, 873 (Del.1985).

[10] See, e.g., Brehm v. Eisner, 746 A.2d 244, 264 (Del.2000) ("Irrationality is the outer limit of the business judgment rule."); cf. ALI PRINCIPLES § 4.01(c)(3) (director must rationally believe action to be in corporation's best interest).

[11] 634 A.2d 345 (Del.1993).

allowing far more intrusive judicial review. In late 1982, the board of Technicolor approved a merger of the company into a subsidiary of MacAndrews and Forbes Group, Inc. (MAF), for a cash consideration of $23 per share. Plaintiff Cinerama, Inc., the beneficial owner of 4.4% of Technicolor stock, dissented from the merger and brought suit. As the unusually convoluted litigation evolved, Cinerama eventually settled on a theory of the case positing that Technicolor's board violated its duty of care when it approved the merger.

Cinerama's claim requires a brief digression on the Delaware Supreme Court's earlier decision in *Smith v. Van Gorkom*.[12] As with *Technicolor*, the *Van Gorkom* decision arose out of a shareholder's duty of care-based challenge to a board of directors' decision to approve a merger. In concluding that the business judgment rule did not entitle the directors to protection in that case, the court focused on the process by which the board made its decision, exhaustively detailing its many purported process failures. *Van Gorkom* thus established a requirement of what might be called procedural or process due care as a prerequisite for invoking the business judgment rule: Directors who fail "to act in an informed and deliberate manner" may not assert the business judgment rule as a defense to care claims.[13]

In assessing Cinerama's breach of fiduciary duty claim, Chancellor Allen expressed "grave doubts" that Technicolor's board had discharged its *Van Gorkom* duties.[14] He found it unnecessary to resolve those doubts, however, because he believed Cinerama could not prove damages: Allen had already determined the fair value of Technicolor at the time of the merger to be $21.60 per share, but the merger paid them $23.

On appeal, Justice Horsey's opinion for the supreme court began with a fairly standard statement of the board of directors' authority to manage the business and affairs of the corporation. The justice immediately went off the rails, however, by describing the business judgment rule as being intended "to preclude a court from imposing itself *unreasonably* on the business and affairs of a corporation." Compare that formulation to *Van Gorkom*'s statement that the rule's purpose is to "protect and promote the full and free exercise of the managerial power granted to Delaware directors." The striking contrast between these formulations strongly implies that the board's decision will no longer get much in the way of

---

[12] 488 A.2d 858 (Del.1985).

[13] Smith v. Van Gorkom, 488 A.2d 858, 873 (Del.1985).

[14] Cinerama, Inc. v. Technicolor, Inc., 17 Del. J. Corp. L. 551, 560 (Del.Ch.1991), available at 1991 WL 111134, rev'd, 634 A.2d 345 (Del.1993).

deference. Instead of preserving the board's decisionmaking authority, the *Technicolor* version of the business judgment rule apparently allows courts to second-guess board decisions if it is "reasonable" to do so.

Justice Horsey's willingness to second-guess board decisions is further suggested by his treatment of Chancellor Allen's duty of care analysis. Recall that Allen expressed "grave doubts" as to whether Technicolor's board satisfied its *Van Gorkom* duties. On appeal, Justice Horsey transformed the Chancellor's "grave doubts" into five "presumed findings" of gross negligence on the board's part: (1) the board had failed to make a "prudent search for alternatives" before approving the agreement; (2) once the merger agreement was signed, the board had no reasonable basis for believing that competing bids might be made; (3) most directors had little information about the merger and its terms before the meeting at which they approved it; (4) MAF locked up the transaction through stock options granted by the corporation and the two principal shareholders; and (5) the board was not "adequately informed" before approving the agreement. In sum, he concluded, that Cinerama had proven that the directors of Technicolor failed to inform themselves fully concerning all material information reasonably available prior to approving the merger agreement.

Yet, it gets worse. To be sure, Justice Horsey described the business judgment rule as "a powerful presumption" against judicial interference with board decisionmaking. But he then proceeded to gut the rule:

> Thus, a shareholder plaintiff challenging a board decision has the burden at the outset to rebut the rule's presumption. To rebut the rule, a shareholder plaintiff assumes the burden of providing evidence that directors, in reaching their challenged decision, breached any one of the triads of their fiduciary duty—good faith, loyalty or due care. If a shareholder plaintiff fails to meet this evidentiary burden, the business judgment rule attaches to protect corporate officers and directors and the decisions they make, and our courts will not second-guess these business judgments. If the rule is rebutted, the burden shifts to the defendant directors, the proponents of the challenged transaction, to prove to the trier of fact the "entire fairness" of the transaction to the shareholder plaintiff.[15]

---

[15] Cede & Co. v. Technicolor, Inc., 634 A.2d 345, 361 (Del.1993) (emphasis supplied).

Notice how the justice puts the cart before the horse. Directors who violate their duty of care do not get the protections of the business judgment rule; indeed, the rule is rebutted by a showing that the directors violated their fiduciary duty of "due care." But this is exactly backwards. Under the abstention theory of the business judgment rule, the rule's core purpose is to prevent precisely what *Technicolor* requires. Recall that the rule prevented Shlensky from even getting up to bat with his care claims. The business judgment rule thus precludes courts from asking the question of—let alone deciding—whether the directors violated their duty of care. In contrast, under *Technicolor* the business judgment rule's primary function is the procedural task of assigning burdens of proof. In that limited guise, moreover, the rule merely assigns to plaintiff the burden of establishing a prima facie case—the same burden plaintiff bears in all civil litigation. If plaintiff fails to carry that burden, the business judgment rule requires the court to dismiss the lawsuit without inquiry into the merits of the decision. But so what? Under this conception, the business judgment rule is nothing more than a restatement of the basic principle that the defendant is entitled to summary judgment whenever plaintiff fails to state a prima facie case. At best, *Technicolor* thus trivializes the rule.

By opening the courthouse door to care questions at the outset of the litigation, however, *Technicolor* went beyond merely trivializing the rule to gutting it. Arguably, *Technicolor* broadened the scope of judicial review of board decisionmaking to reach not just the process by which the decision was made but also the substance of the directors' decision. Significant consequences follow from this distortion of the business judgment rule. It is commonly held, for example, that mere allegations of director impropriety do not entitle plaintiff to discovery.[16] Yet, one can plausibly read *Technicolor* as authorizing precisely the sort of fishing expeditions the business judgment rule was intended to prevent.

Technicolor can be reconciled with the mainstream of business judgment rule analysis only by interpreting the duty of "due care" as being limited to the adequacy of the decisionmaking process. At several points in the opinion, Justice Horsey in fact so characterized that duty.[17] In addition, numerous Delaware precedents interpret the requirement of due care as being limited to questions of process.[18] Yet, nothing in *Technicolor* explicitly limits its references

---

[16] See, e.g., Stoner v. Walsh, 772 F.Supp. 790, 800 (S.D.N.Y.1991).

[17] See, e.g., Cede & Co. v. Technicolor, Inc., 634 A.2d 345, 367 (Del.1993) (duty of care requires that directors "act on an informed basis").

[18] See, e.g., Brehm v. Eisner, 746 A.2d 244, 264 (Del.2000) ("Due care in the decisionmaking context is *process* due care only."; emphasis in original); Citron v. Fairchild Camera & Instrument Corp., 569 A.2d 53, 66 (Del.1989) ("our due care examination has focused on a board's decision-making process").

to the duty of care to the decisionmaking process. Arguably, the cart remains before the horse.

C. Where Is Delaware Now?

In view of Delaware's prominence in corporate jurisprudence, the importance of knowing where Delaware stands on such a fundamental question should be apparent. Unfortunately, Delaware law on this score remains ambiguous. In *Brehm v. Eisner*,[19] for example, the Delaware supreme court failed even to cite *Technicolor*. More significantly, Chief Justice Veasey's opinion for the court explicitly rejected, as "foreign to the business judgment rule," plaintiffs' argument that the rule could be rebutted by a showing that the directors failed to exercise "substantive due care":

> Courts do not measure, weigh or quantify directors' judgments. We do not even decide if they are reasonable in this context. Due care in the decisionmaking context is *process* due care only. . . .
>
> . . . Thus, directors' decisions will be respected by courts unless the directors are interested or lack independence relative to the decision, do not act in good faith, act in a manner that cannot be attributed to a rational business purpose or reach their decision by a grossly negligent process that includes the failure to consider all material facts reasonably available.

If *Brehm* is not as pure an abstention decision as was *Shlensky*, it is close enough for government work. None of the preconditions to the rule's application stated by *Brehm* contemplate substantive review of the merits of the decision. Even the chief justice's reference to a rational business purpose requires only the possibility that the decision was actuated by a legitimate business reason, not that directors must prove the existence of such a reason. As long as the board satisfies the preconditions laid out by *Brehm*, the court will abstain from reviewing the substantive merits of the decision.

On the other hand, in *McMullin v. Beran*, the Delaware supreme court reaffirmed the *Technicolor* approach. Per Justice Holland, the court explained that:

> The business judgment rule "operates as both a procedural guide for litigants and a substantive rule of law." Procedurally, the initial burden is on the shareholder plaintiff to rebut the presumption of the business judgment rule. To meet that burden, the shareholder plaintiff must effectively provide evidence that the

---

[19] 746 A.2d 244 (Del.2000).

defendant board of directors, in reaching its challenged decision, breached any *one* of its "triad of fiduciary duties, loyalty, good faith or due care." Substantively, "if the shareholder plaintiff fails to meet that evidentiary burden, the business judgment rule attaches" and operates to protect the individual director-defendants from personal liability for making the board decision at issue.[20]

Once again, the business judgment rule is treated as a standard of review rather than an abstention doctrine. Unlike poor old Shlensky, who was not even allowed up to bat, litigants suing under *McMullin* get to present evidence that the board failed to exercise due care. This distinction has important procedural consequences. In *Shlensky*, plaintiff could not survive a motion to dismiss, while plaintiff in *McMullin* was able to do so. As the probability increases that a cause of action will survive a motion to dismiss, both the probability that more such actions will be brought and the settlement value of such actions also increase.

About all one can say with confidence, therefore, is that we probably have not heard the last word on this subject.[21]

§ 6.2   Why a Business Judgment Rule?

The business judgment rule's traditional justification is that courts are not business experts.[22] But so what? Business law is not the only context in which judges are called upon to review complex issues arising under conditions of uncertainty. Reviewing a baseball team's board of directors' refusal to play games at night, for example, seems no more technically demanding than reviewing medical or product design decisions. Yet, no "medical judgment" or "design judgment" rule precludes judicial review of malpractice or product liability cases.

One explanation for the business judgment rule focuses on decisionmaker incentives. Justice Jackson famously observed of the U.S. Supreme Court: "We are not final because we are infallible, but we are infallible only because we are final."[23] Neither courts nor boards of directors are infallible, but someone must be final.

---

[20] McMullin v. Beran, 765 A.2d 910, 916–17 (Del.2000) (footnotes omitted).

[21] See, e.g., McPadden v. Sidhu, 964 A.2d 1262, 1275 (Del. Ch. 2008) (explaining that the plaintiff had "alleged with particularity that the Director Defendants breached their duties of care so as to rebut the business judgment rule"); E. Norman Veasey & Christine T. Di Gugliemo, What Happened in Delaware Corporate Law and Governance From 1992–2004? A Retrospective on Some Key Developments, 153 U. PA. L. REV. 1399, 1421–28 (2005) (stating that the abstention "approach is consistent with the Delaware doctrine that the [business judgment] rule is a presumption that courts will not interfere with, or second-guess, decision making by directors.").

[22] See, e.g., Dodge v. Ford Motor Co., 170 N.W. 668, 684 (Mich.1919).

[23] Brown v. Allen, 344 U.S. 443, 540 (1953) (Jackson, J., concurring).

Otherwise we end up with a never ending process of appellate review. The question then is a simple one: Who is better suited to be vested with the mantle of infallibility that comes by virtue of being final—directors or judges?

Judges necessarily have less information about the needs of a particular firm than do that firm's directors. A fortiori, judges will make poorer decisions than the firm's board:

> [C]ourts recognize that after-the-fact litigation is a most imperfect device to evaluate corporate business decisions. The circumstances surrounding a corporate decision are not easily reconstructed in a courtroom years later, since business imperatives often call for quick decisions, inevitably based on less than perfect information. The entrepreneur's function is to encounter risks and to confront uncertainty, and a reasoned decision at the time made may seem a wild hunch viewed years later against a background of perfect knowledge.[24]

Put another way, judges are no less subject to bounded rationality than any other decisionmakers. Just as the limits on cognitive competence impede the ability of market actors to write complete contracts, those same limits necessarily impede judicial review. Only with the benefit of hindsight will judges be able to make better decisions than boards, but we have already seen that hindsight review is problematic. While market forces work a sort of Darwinian selection on corporate decisionmakers, moreover, no such forces constrain erring judges.[25] As such, rational shareholders might prefer the risk of managerial error to that of judicial error.

The posited preference for managerial error, however, only extends to decisions motivated by a desire to maximize shareholder wealth. Given that market forces encourage directors to make such decisions carefully, such a preference makes sense. Where the directors' decision was motivated by considerations other than shareholder wealth, as where the directors engaged in self-dealing or sought to defraud the shareholders, however, the question is no longer one of honest error but of intentional misconduct. Despite the limitations of judicial review, rational shareholders would prefer judicial intervention with respect to board decisions so tainted. As former Delaware Chief Justice Veasey observed, "investors do not want self-dealing directors or those bent on entrenchment in office. . . . Trust of directors is the key because of the self-governing

---

[24] Joy v. North, 692 F.2d 880, 886 (2d Cir.1982), cert. denied, 460 U.S. 1051 (1983).

[25] Frank H. Easterbrook & Daniel R. Fischel, The Economic Structure of Corporate Law 100 (1991).

nature of corporate law. Yet the law is strong enough to rein in directors who would flirt with an abuse of that trust."[26] The affirmative case for disregarding honest errors thus simply does not apply to intentional misconduct. To the contrary, given the heightened potential for self-dealing in an organization characterized by a separation of ownership and control, the risk of legal liability may be a necessary deterrent against such misconduct.

A second justification for the business judgment rule is that it encourages directors to take risks. According to the ALI PRINCIPLES, for example, the rule protects "directors and officers from the risks inherent in hindsight reviews of their unsuccessful decisions" and avoids "the risk of stifling innovation and venturesome business activity."[27] The ALI's explanation is valid but incomplete. The prospect of duty of care litigation, after all, probably does far less to stifle innovation and business risk-taking than does product liability and securities fraud litigation.

At the outset, we therefore need a story explaining why hindsight review of business decisions is inconsistent with shareholder interests. One lies readily to hand. As the firm's residual claimants, shareholders do not get a return on their investment until all other claims on the corporation have been satisfied. All else equal, shareholders therefore prefer high return projects. Because risk and return are directly proportional, however, implementing that preference necessarily entails choosing risky projects. All of which should be familiar concepts by now.

Rational shareholders will have a high tolerance for such risks, however. First, the doctrine of limited liability substantially insulates shareholders from the downside risks of corporate activity. Limited liability, of course, means that shareholders of a corporation are not personally liable for debts incurred or torts committed by the firm. If the firm fails, a shareholder's losses thus are limited to the amount the shareholder has invested in the firm—i.e., the amount the shareholder initially paid to purchase his stock. Put another way, because shareholders do not put their personal assets at jeopardy, they effectively externalize some portion of the business' total risk exposure to creditors.

Second, portfolio theory teaches that shareholders can eliminate firm-specific risk by holding a diversified portfolio. Investors, on average, are risk averse. Accordingly, they must be compensated—paid a higher return—for bearing risk. Hence, we

---

[26] E. Norman Veasey, An Economic Rationale for Judicial Decisionmaking in Corporate Law, 53 Bus. Law. 681, 694 (1998).

[27] ALI PRINCIPLES § 4.01 cmt. d at 141.

speak of a risk premium, which is the difference in the rate of return paid on a risky investment and the rate of return on a risk-free investment. The risk premium, however, will only reflect certain risks. Investors can eliminate unsystematic risk by diversifying their portfolio, but diversification cannot eliminate systematic risk. Ergo, portfolio theory claims, investors must be compensated for bearing systematic risk but need not be compensated for bearing unsystematic risk.

Given limited liability and diversification, shareholders will be indifferent to corporate policies that affect unsystematic risks, but will prefer policies that portend a higher return by increasing the firm's beta. In contrast, management will be risk averse with respect to such policies. Corporate managers frequently have substantial firm-specific human capital, which constitutes an investment upon which the managers can earn a return only so long as they remain with that firm. Managers obviously cannot diversify their human capital among a number of different firms and thus commit their principal source of wealth to the fortunes of a single firm. If pursuing a risky course of action fails to pay off, management may suffer far greater losses than do their diversified shareholders. As such, managers will be averse to risks shareholders are perfectly happy to tolerate.

The diversion of interests as between shareholders and managers will be compounded if managers face the risk of legal liability, on top of economic loss, in the event a risky decision turns out badly. Board decisions rarely involve black-and-white issues, instead they typically involve prudential judgments among a number of plausible alternatives. Given the vagaries of business, moreover, even carefully made choices among such alternatives may turn out badly.

At this point, the well-known hindsight bias comes into play. Decisionmakers tend to assign an erroneously high probability of occurrence to a probabilistic event simply because it ended up occurring.[28] Knowledge that an injury occurred, for example, biases jurors to impose negligence liability even though there was a very low probability of such an injury and, if viewed ex ante, precautions against such an injury were not cost effective. Knowing with the benefit of hindsight that a business decision turned out badly likewise could bias judges or juries towards finding a breach of the duty of care.[29]

---

[28] Christine Jolls et al., A Behavioral Approach to Law and Economics, 50 Stan L. Rev. 1471, 1523–27 (1998).

[29] As the Delaware Chancery Court explained in In re Citigroup Inc. Shareholder Derivative Litigation:

In other words, both shareholders and judges will find it difficult to distinguish between competent and negligent management. By virtue of the hindsight bias, bad outcomes are often regarded, ex post, as foreseeable ex ante. If bad outcomes result in liability, however, managers will be discouraged from taking risks:

> Corporate directors of public companies typically have a very small proportionate ownership interest in their corporations and little or no incentive compensation. Thus, they enjoy (as residual owners) only a very small proportion of any "upside" gains earned by the corporation on risky investment projects. If, however, corporate directors were to be found liable for a corporate loss from a risky project on the ground that the investment was too risky . . . their liability would be joint and several for the whole loss (with I suppose a right of contribution). Given the scale of operation of modern public corporations, this stupefying disjunction between risk and reward for corporate directors threatens undesirable effects. Given this disjunction, only a very small probability of director liability based on "negligence", "inattention," "waste," etc., could induce a board to avoid authorizing risky investment projects to any extent! Obviously, it is in the shareholders' economic interest to offer sufficient protection to directors from liability for negligence, etc., to allow directors to conclude that, as a practical matter, there is no risk that, if they act in good faith and meet minimal proceduralist standards of attention, they can face liability as a result of a business loss.[30]

Rational shareholders therefore should prefer a regime that encourages managerial risk-taking by, inter alia, pre-committing to a policy of not litigating the reasonableness of managerial business decisions. Obviously, however, the practicalities of running a large

---

It is almost impossible for a court, in hindsight, to determine whether the directors of a company properly evaluated risk and thus made the "right" business decision. In any investment there is a chance that returns will turn out lower than expected, and generally a smaller chance that they will be far lower than expected. When investments turn out poorly, it is possible that the decision-maker evaluated the deal correctly but got "unlucky" in that a huge loss—the probability of which was very small—actually happened. It is also possible that the decision-maker improperly evaluated the risk posed by an investment and that the company suffered large losses as a result.

Business decision-makers must operate in the real world, with imperfect information, limited resources, and an uncertain future. To impose liability on directors for making a "wrong" business decision would cripple their ability to earn returns for investors by taking business risks. Indeed, this kind of judicial second guessing is what the business judgment rule was designed to prevent. . . .

In re Citigroup Inc. S'holder Derivative Litig., 964 A.2d 106, 126 (Del. Ch. 2009).

[30] Gagliardi v. TriFoods Int'l, Inc., 683 A.2d 1049, 1052 (Del.Ch.1996).

corporation with fluid stock ownership preclude effecting such a policy by contract. The business judgment rule thus can be seen as providing a default (off the rack) rule that both shareholders and managers would prefer, as Judge Ralph Winter opined in *Joy v. North*:

> Although the rule has suffered under academic criticism, it is not without rational basis. . . . [S]hareholders to a very real degree voluntarily undertake the risk of bad business judgment. Investors need not buy stock, for investment markets offer an array of opportunities less vulnerable to mistakes in judgment by corporate officers. Nor need investors buy stock in particular corporations. In the exercise of what is genuinely a free choice, the quality of a firm's management is often decisive and information is available from professional advisors. Since shareholders can and do select among investments partly on the basis of management, the business judgment rule merely recognizes a certain voluntariness in undertaking the risk of bad business decisions.[31]

Judge Winter further explained:

> [B]ecause potential profit often corresponds to the potential risk, it is very much in the interest of shareholders that the law not create incentives for overly cautious corporate decisions. Some opportunities offer great profits at the risk of very substantial losses, while the alternatives offer less risk of loss but also less potential profit. Shareholders can reduce the volatility of risk by diversifying their holdings. In the case of the diversified shareholder, the seemingly more risky alternatives may well be the best choice since great losses in some stocks will over time be offset by even greater gains in others. Given mutual funds and similar forms of diversified investment, courts need not bend over backwards to give special protection to shareholders who refuse to reduce the volatility of risk by not diversifying. A rule which penalizes the choice of seemingly riskier alternatives thus may not be in the interest of shareholders generally.

Note that Winter's portfolio theory-based justification for the business judgment rule implicitly identifies an important distinction between the function of liability rules in tort and corporate law. A basic function of tort liability is loss spreading. By encouraging potential tortfeasors (such as automobile drivers) to

---

[31] 692 F.2d 880, 885 (2d Cir.1982), cert. denied, 460 U.S. 1051 (1983).

purchase insurance, the tort system encourages the process by which the risk of loss is shifted from specific victims to a larger pool.[32] In contrast, if directors were routinely held liable, losses would be shifted from the larger pool of residual claimants to a small group of specific individuals. Because that larger pool can reduce the risk of loss by holding a diversified pool of investments, however, the insulation provided directors by the business judgment rule can be seen as a form of corporate self-insurance. Hence, the analogy between tort and corporate liability fails because the imposition of liability in those contexts has differing effects with respect to an important social policy.

Taken together, these considerations argue for treating the business judgment rule as an abstention doctrine rather than a standard of review. If the business judgment rule is treated as a substantive standard of review, judicial intervention all too easily could become the norm rather than the exception. How one frames the question matters a lot. In polling, for example, both the order in which questions are asked and the way in which they are phrased can affect the outcome.[33] The same is true of legal standards. This is why *Technicolor* is so troubling. Under the decision's cart before the horse formulation, the business judgment rule does not preclude judicial review of cases in which the board failed to exercise reasonable care. Yet, if the business judgment rule is to have teeth, it is precisely those cases in which it is especially important for courts to abstain.[34] No matter how gingerly courts apply a substantive standard, trying to measure the "quantity" of negligence is a task best left untried.[35] Courts will find it difficult to resist the temptation to tweak the standard so as to sanction honest decisions that, with the benefit of hindsight, proved unfortunate and/or appear inept. All of the adverse effects of judicial review outlined above are implicated, however, whether or not the board exercised reasonable care. Unfortunately, *Technicolor* and its ilk threaten to nullify this essential aspect of the business judgment rule.

If the business judgment rule is framed as an abstention doctrine, however, judicial review is more likely to be the exception rather than the rule. Starting from an abstention perspective, the court will begin with a presumption against review. It will then

---

[32] Kenneth B. Davis, Jr., Once More, the Business Judgment Rule, 2000 Wis. L. Rev. 573, 575.

[33] See, e.g., Brad Edmondson, How to Spot a Bogus Poll, Am. Demographics, Oct. 1996, at 10.

[34] Lyman Johnson, The Modest Business Judgment Rule, 55 Bus. Law. 625, 633 (2000).

[35] Henry G. Manne, Our Two Corporation Systems: Law and Economics, 53 Va. L. Rev. 259, 271 (1967).

review the facts to determine not the quality of the decision, but rather whether the decisionmaking process was tainted by self-dealing and the like. The requisite questions to be asked are objective and straightforward: Did the board commit fraud? Did the board commit an illegal act? Did the board self-deal? Did the board make an informed decision (i.e., exercise what *Brehm* called process due care)? The merits of the board's decision are irrelevant, as well they should be. The business judgment rule thus builds a prophylactic barrier by which courts pre-commit to resisting the temptation to review the substance of the board's decision.

§ 6.3   The Law of Business Judgment

To review, the duty of care requires directors to exercise the same care that "ordinarily careful and prudent men would use in similar circumstances."[36] The business judgment rule, however, provides that courts will abstain from reviewing board decisions unless those decisions are tainted by fraud, illegality, or self-dealing. Operationalizing those vague statements requires some heavy lifting. Because the order in which one takes up questions matters, we focus on the business judgment rule in this section. Since courts should only reach duty of care questions after determining that the business judgment rule does not apply to the case at bar, analysis of that duty is deferred to the following section.

A.   The Nature of the Rule

Courts often refer to the business judgment rule as "a presumption" that the directors or officers of a corporation acted on an informed basis, in good faith, and in the honest belief that the action taken was in the best interests of the company.[37] This phraseology is unfortunate, at best. The business judgment rule is not a presumption "in the strict evidentiary sense of the term."[38] Instead, it is more in the nature of an assumption; namely, courts assume they should not review director decisions absent fraud, illegality, or self-dealing. In any event, these disputes over terminology are largely inconsequential. The bottom line is that even clear mistakes of judgment rarely result in personal liability on the part of corporate directors.

---

[36] See, e.g., Graham v. Allis-Chalmers Mfg. Co., 188 A.2d 125, 130 (Del.1963).

[37] See, e.g., Panter v. Marshall Field & Co., 646 F.2d 271, 293 (7th Cir.), cert. denied, 454 U.S. 1092 (1981); Treadway Cos., Inc. v. Care Corp., 638 F.2d 357, 382 (2d Cir.1980); Johnson v. Trueblood, 629 F.2d 287, 292 (3d Cir.1980), cert. denied, 450 U.S. 999 (1981); Unocal Corp. v. Mesa Petroleum Co., 493 A.2d 946, 954 (Del.1985); Aronson v. Lewis, 473 A.2d 805, 812 (Del.1984); Auerbach v. Bennett, 393 N.E.2d 994 (N.Y.1979).

[38] R. Franklin Balotti & James J. Hanks, Jr., Rejudging the Business Judgment Rule, 48 Bus. Law. 1337, 1345 (1993).

B. Preconditions

The business judgment rule reflects a balance pursuant to which directors are given substantial discretion, but are not allowed to put their own interests ahead of those of the shareholders. In other words, we give them carte blanche to make decisions that might turn out badly, but no discretion to make selfish decisions. This balance is reflected in the various preconditions courts have identified that must be satisfied before directors may avail themselves of the rule's protection.

1. An Exercise of Judgment

The business judgment rule is relevant only where directors have actually exercised business judgment. A decision to refrain from action is protected just as much as a decision to act, but there is no protection where directors have made no decision at all.[39] Instead, the consequences of inaction are subject to review under the duty of care.[40]

2. Disinterested and Independent Decisionmakers

The business judgment rule "presupposes that the directors have no conflict of interest."[41] "A director is interested if he will be materially affected, either to his benefit or detriment, by a decision of the board, in a manner not shared by the corporation and the shareholders."[42] Consequently, for example, a director who sells or leases property to or from the corporation is interested in that transaction. Similarly, a director who contracts to provide services to the corporation is interested in that transaction.

Directors also can be interested in a transaction by virtue of indirect connections. In *Bayer v. Beran*,[43] for example, the corporation hired the wife of its president. Their spousal relationship gave the president an indirect interest in the transaction. Similarly, in *Globe Woolen Co. v. Utica Gas & Electric Co.*,[44] a director of the defendant was also the president and chief stockholder of the plaintiff. By virtue of those business

---

[39] See, e.g., Aronson v. Lewis, 473 A.2d 805, 813 (Del.1984) ("the business judgment rule operates only in the context of director action").

[40] See, e.g., Graham v. Allis-Chalmers Mfg. Co., 188 A.2d 125 (Del.1963). In certain cases, however, inaction by a board of directors with respect to its oversight responsibilities will be reviewed under the good faith standard. See, e.g., In re Caremark Int'l Inc. Deriv. Litig., 698 A.2d 959 (Del.Ch.1996); see generally § 7.5 infra.

[41] Lewis v. S.L. & E., Inc., 629 F.2d 764, 769 (2d Cir.1980).

[42] Seminaris v. Landa, 662 A.2d 1350, 1354 (Del.Ch.1995).

[43] 49 N.Y.S.2d 2 (Sup.Ct.1944).

[44] 121 N.E. 378 (N.Y.1918).

relationships, he was deemed interested in the transaction even though he was not a party to the contract.

In addition to lacking a personal interest in the transaction in question, a director must be independent.[45] "A director is independent if he can base his decision 'on the corporate merits of the subject before the board rather than extraneous considerations or influences.' "[46] In particular, a director who is beholden to, or under the influence of an interested party, lacks the requisite independence.

Where the board has acted collectively, it is not enough to show that a single director was interested or lacked independence. The business judgment rule will still insulate the board's decision from judicial review unless plaintiff can show that a majority of the board was interested and/or lacked independence.[47] In order to prove that the directors were not independent, plaintiff must establish personal or business relationships by which the directors are either beholden to or controlled by the interested party.

3. Absence of Fraud or Illegality

The business judgment rule will not insulate from judicial review decisions tainted by fraud or illegality.[48] The key issue in this context is whether the board has a duty to act lawfully.[49] In the oft-cited *Miller v. American Telephone & Telegraph Co.* decision,[50] the Third Circuit held that directors have such a duty. AT & T failed to collect a debt owed it by the Democratic National Committee for telecommunications services provided during the 1968 Democrat Party's convention. Several AT & T shareholders brought a derivative suit against AT & T's directors, alleging that the failure to collect the debt violated both federal telecommunications and campaign finance laws. Ordinarily, a board decision not to collect a debt would be protected by the business judgment rule. Citing a 1909 New York precedent,[51] however, the

---

[45] See, e.g., Rales v. Blasband, 634 A.2d 927, 935 (Del.1993) ("the board must be able to act free of personal financial interest and improper extraneous influences").

[46] Seminaris v. Landa, 662 A.2d 1350, 1354 (Del.1995) (quoting Aronson v. Lewis, 473 A.2d 805, 816 (Del.1984)).

[47] See Odyssey Partners, L.P. v. Fleming Cos., Inc., 735 A.2d 386, 407 (Del.Ch.1999).

[48] See, e.g., Shlensky v. Wrigley, 237 N.E.2d 776, 778 (Ill.App.1968).

[49] Note that the issue here is distinct from the problem of board oversight discussed below. In oversight cases, corporate employees have committed some criminal act and the board is charged with having failed to prevent those acts. Here we ask a different question; namely, what happens when the board affirmatively instructs its subordinates to violate the law?

[50] 507 F.2d 759, 762 (3d Cir.1974) (diversity case arising under New York corporation law).

[51] Roth v. Robertson, 118 N.Y.S. 351 (Sup.Ct.1909).

Third Circuit held that the business judgment rule did not insulate defendant directors from liability for illegal acts "even though committed to benefit the corporation."[52]

Assuming a duty to act lawfully exists, operationalizing it is a nontrivial task. Should there be a de minimis exception?[53] If a package delivery firm told its drivers to illegally double-park, so as to speed up the delivery process, for example, it is hardly clear that liability should follow. Should the business judgment rule be set aside only where the board ordered violations of criminal statutes or should it also be set aside where the board authorized violation of some civil regulation? The criminal law long has distinguished between crimes that are malum in se and those that are merely malum prohibitum. The latter are acts that are criminal merely because they are prohibited by statute, not because they violate natural law. It is said that "misdemeanors such as jaywalking and running a stoplight are mala prohibita, as are most *securities-law* violations."[54] Individuals routinely make cost-benefit analyses before deciding to comply with some malum prohibitum law, such as when deciding to violate the speed limit. Is it self-evident that directors of a corporation should be barred from engaging in similar cost-benefit analyses?[55]

And, yet, still more questions must be answered if a duty to act lawfully is to be imposed. If neither the corporation nor the board was convicted or even indicted, for example, should plaintiff have to make out the elements of the criminal charge?[56] If so, to what extent does the criminal law concept of reasonable doubt come into play? Is a knowing violation of criminal law a per se violation of the duty of care unprotected by the business judgment rule?[57] How are damages to be measured and is causation an issue?[58] And so on.

---

[52] Miller v. AT & T Co., 507 F.2d 759, 762 (3d Cir.1974). See also Abrams v. Allen, 74 N.E.2d 305 (N.Y.1947) (directors can be sued where they used corporate property to commit "an unlawful or immoral act"); Di Tomasso v. Loverro, 12 N.E.2d 570 (N.Y.App.1937) (directors liable for entering into a contract that was an illegal restraint of trade).

[53] Cf. ALI PRINCIPLES § 2.01 cmt. g (acknowledging that the "de minimis principle" applies to corporate law compliance "as elsewhere in the law").

[54] Black's Law Dictionary 401 (pocket ed. 1996) (emphasis supplied).

[55] But cf. ALI PRINCIPLES § 2.01 cmt. g ("With few exceptions, dollar liability is not a 'price' that can properly be paid for the privilege of engaging in legally wrongful conduct.").

[56] *Miller* answered that question in the affirmative. Miller v. American Telephone & Telegraph Co., 507 F.2d 759, 763–64 (3d Cir.1974). Accord ALI PRINCIPLES § 4.01(a) cmt. d.

[57] That question is answered in the negative by ALI PRINCIPLES § 4.01(a) cmt. d.

[58] Under the so-called net loss rule, directors cannot be held monetarily liable if the overall gains to the corporation from the violation exceed the losses directly attributable thereto, such as fines or legal expenses. See James D. Cox,

The point is not that corporations should be allowed to break the law. They should not. If a corporation breaks the law, criminal sanctions should follow for the entity and/or the responsible individuals. The point is only that fiduciary obligation and the duty to act lawfully make a bad fit. If the question is one of reconciling authority and accountability, it is not self-evident that corporate law should hold directors accountable simply for deciding that the corporation's interests are served by violating a particular statute. After all, "[a] business corporation is organized and carried on primarily for the profit of the stockholders. The powers of the directors are to be employed for that end."[59]

Put another way, the point of the business judgment rule is that shareholders should not be allowed to recover monetary damages simply because the directors made the wrong decision. Allowing shareholders to sue over a decision made with the intent of maximizing corporate profits is nothing less than double-dipping, even if the decision proves misguided. This claim is further supported by the realities of shareholder litigation. Shareholder lawsuits alleging that directors violated the purported duty to act lawfully will be brought as derivative actions. The real party in interest in derivative litigation is the plaintiff's attorney, not the nominal shareholder-plaintiff. In most cases, the bulk of any monetary benefits go to the plaintiffs' lawyers rather than the corporation or its shareholders. In practice, such litigation is more likely to be a mere wealth transfer from corporations and their managers to the plaintiff bar than a significant deterrent to corporate criminality. Accordingly, the illegality of a board decision—standing alone—should not result in automatic director liability. Indeed, one could make the case that illegality should not constitute a basis—again, standing alone—for rebutting the business judgment rule. At the very least, however, courts should carefully consider whether the decision to cause an illegal act was in fact so grossly negligent as to violate the director's duty of care.[60]

4. Absence of Waste

The business judgment rule will not protect board of director actions amounting to waste. A showing of waste requires proof that the consideration received is so clearly inadequate that the transaction effectively amounts to a gift of corporate assets serving

---

Compensation, Deterrence, and the Market as Boundaries for Derivative Suit Procedures, 52 Geo. Wash. L. Rev. 745, 765 (1984).

[59] Dodge v. Ford Motor Co., 170 N.W. 668, 684 (Mich.1919).

[60] In Delaware, however, the issue has been dealt with in recent years under the good faith standard. See § 7.4 infra

no corporate purpose.[61] In other words, the court will dismiss a waste claim so long as any reasonable person might conclude that the deal made sense. Because courts correctly regard the waste doctrine as setting out a very stringent standard of review, successful waste claims are quite rare.[62]

5. Rationality

In *Sinclair Oil Corp. v. Levien,* the Delaware supreme court held that so long as the board's decision could be attributed to any rational business purpose the business judgment rule precluded the court from substituting its judgment as to the merits of the decision for those of the board.[63] Similarly, in *Brehm v. Eisner,* the court held that the business judgment rule does not apply when the board has "act[ed] in a manner that cannot be attributed to a rational business purpose."[64]

The reference to a "rational business purpose," properly understood, does not contemplate substantive review of the decision's merits. "*Sinclair*'s use of [the word] rational is to be equated with conceivable or imaginable and means only that the court will not even look at the board's judgment if there is any possibility that it was actuated by a legitimate business reason. It clearly does not mean, and cannot legitimately be cited for the proposition, that individual directors must have, and be prepared to put forth, proof of rational reasons for their decisions."[65]

> [W]hether a judge or jury considering the matter after the fact, believes a decision substantively wrong, or degrees of wrong extending through "stupid" to "egregious" or "irrational", provides no ground for director liability, so long as the court determines that the process employed was either rational or employed in a *good faith* effort to advance corporate interests. To employ a different rule— one that permitted an "objective" evaluation of the decision—would expose directors to substantive second

---

[61] See, e.g., Grobow v. Perot, 539 A.2d 180, 189 (Del.1988) ("what the corporation has received is so inadequate in value that no person of ordinary, sound business judgment would deem it worth that which the corporation has paid"); Michelson v. Duncan, 407 A.2d 211, 224 (Del.1979) ("no person of ordinary, sound business judgment would say that the consideration received for the options was a fair exchange for the options granted").

[62] See Steiner v. Meyerson, 1995 WL 441999 at *5 (Del.Ch.1995) ("rarest of all—and indeed, like Nessie, possibly non-existent—would be the case of disinterested business people making non-fraudulent deals (non-negligently) that meet the legal standard of waste!").

[63] 280 A.2d 717, 720 (Del.1971).

[64] 746 A.2d 244, 264 n.66 (Del.2000).

[65] Michael P. Dooley, Two Models of Corporate Governance, 47 Bus. Law. 461, 478–79 n.58 (1992).

guessing by ill-equipped judges or juries, which would, in the long-run, be injurious to investor interests.[66]

Instead, "such limited substantive review as the rule contemplates (i.e., is the judgment under review 'egregious' or 'irrational' or 'so beyond reason,' etc.) really is a way of inferring bad faith."[67]

Put another way, inquiry into the rationality of a decision is a proxy for an inquiry into whether the decision was tainted by self-interest. In *Parnes v. Bally Entertainment Corp.*, for example, the Delaware supreme court stated that: "The presumptive validity of a business judgment is rebutted in those rare cases where the decision under attack is 'so far beyond the bounds of reasonable judgment that it seems essentially inexplicable on any ground other than bad faith.' "[68] In that case, Bally's CEO allegedly demanded bribes from prospective takeover bidders and, moreover, allegedly received such a bribe from the successful bidder. In holding that the plaintiff shareholder had stated a cause of action, the court observed that "it is inexplicable that independent directors, acting in good faith, could approve the deal" when it was so tainted.

Litwin v. Allen is often cited as an exception to the foregoing proposition.[69] Put another way, *Litwin* supposedly creates an "incredible stupidity" exception to the business judgment rule. Under this reading of the opinion, it stands as an example of a board decision so irrational as to not deserve the protection of the business judgment rule. One problem with this analysis is that *Litwin* involved the directors of a bank, who are typically held to a higher standard of accountability than directors of other corporations. Another is that *Litwin* is a sport—a case that falls well outside the norm. It is cited so often, because it stands alone as plausible precedential support for the irrationality exception to the business judgment rule. Finally, consistent with our hypothesis that courts use rationality as a code word for self-dealing, the *Litwin* court found the transaction in question to be "so improvident, so risky, so unusual, and unnecessary as to be contrary to fundamental conceptions of prudent banking practice." Although the court expressly declined to find a violation of the duty of loyalty, it seems fair to ask whether "we have reason to disbelieve the

---

[66] In re Caremark International Inc. Derivative Litig., 698 A.2d 959, 967 (Del.Ch.1996) (emphasis in original).

[67] In re RJR Nabisco, Inc. Shareholders Litig., 1989 WL 7036 at *13 n.13 (Del.Ch.1989).

[68] 722 A.2d 1243, 1246 (Del.1999) (quoting In re J.P. Stevens & Co., Inc., 542 A.2d 770, 780–81 (Del.Ch.1988)).

[69] 25 N.Y.S.2d 667 (Sup.Ct.1940).

protestations of good faith by directors who reach 'irrational' conclusions?"[70]

In sum, it may be that there are some board decisions that are so dumb that the business judgment rule will not insulate them from judicial review.[71] Even if the set of such decisions is not an empty one, however, the tail ought not wag the dog. Because a prerequisite of rationality easily can erode into a prerequisite of reasonableness, courts must tread warily here. If they want to persist in requiring that there be a rational business purpose, at least they can ensure that that requirement lacks teeth.

> 6.   *An Informed Decision (a.k.a. Process Due Care)*

It is frequently said that the exercise of "reasonable diligence and care" is a precondition for the business judgment rule's application.[72] This phraseology is most unfortunate. It implies the necessity to inquire into the care exercised by the board, which in turn easily slides into the *Technicolor* error of treating compliance with the duty of care as an essential prerequisite for invoking the rule. The problem reduces to one of mere semantics, however, if we understand the requirement of "reasonable diligence and care" as being limited to the process by which the decision was made. Numerous Delaware decisions confirm that judicial references to a requirement of due care really go to the adequacy of the decisionmaking process—what the court has begun calling "process due care."[73] It would be better to follow the lead of those decisions and simply stop talking about whether the board exercised "reasonable diligence and care." Instead, the requisite precondition would be better stated as a rational and good faith decisionmaking process.

Smith v. Van Gorkom[74] was the seminal process case. In 1980, Trans Union's CEO and chairman, Van Gorkom, negotiated a merger between Trans Union and an entity controlled by financier

---

[70] Michael P. Dooley, Fundamentals of Corporation Law 263 (1995).

[71] See Gagliardi v. TriFoods Int'l, Inc., 683 A.2d 1049, 1051–52 (Del.Ch.1996) ("There is a *theoretical* exception . . . that holds that some decisions may be so 'egregious' that liability for losses they cause may follow even in the absence of proof of conflict of interest or improper motivation. The exception, however, has resulted in no awards of money judgments. . . ."; emphasis supplied).

[72] See, e.g., S. Samuel Arsht, The Business Judgment Rule Revisited, 8 Hofstra L. Rev. 93, 100 (1979).

[73] Brehm v. Eisner, 746 A.2d 244, 264 (Del.2000) ("Due care in the decisionmaking context is *process* due care only."; emphasis in original); Citron v. Fairchild Camera & Instrument Corp., 569 A.2d 53, 66 (Del.1989) ("our due care examination has focused on a board's decision-making process"); In re Caremark Int'l Inc. Deriv. Litig., 698 A.2d 959, 967 (Del.Ch.1996) ("compliance with a director's duty of care can never appropriately be judicially determined by reference to *the content of the board decision* that leads to a corporate loss, apart from consideration of the good faith *or* rationality of the process employed"; emphasis in original).

[74] 488 A.2d 858 (Del.1985).

Pritzker. Trans Union's board and shareholders approved the deal. Plaintiff-shareholder Smith sued, alleging that the board's approval of the deal merger violated the Trans Union directors' duty of care. The defendant directors contended that their decision to sell the company should be protected by the business judgment rule.

The court began its analysis by noting that the business judgment rule provides a presumption that in making a decision the directors acted on an informed basis, in good faith and in the honest belief that the decision was in the firm's best interests. None of the usual triad of exceptions to the rule i.e., fraud, illegality, or self-dealing—were present in this case, as the court acknowledged.[75] The protection provided by the business judgment rule is unavailable, however, if the directors failed to inform themselves of all material information reasonably available to them. In the course of its opinion, the court focused closely on issues of board process. Indeed, one can plausibly read *Van Gorkom* as providing a procedural roadmap by which corporate decisions, at least of this magnitude, ought to be made. Accordingly, it seems appropriate to identify those aspects of the Trans Union board's conduct by which the court was troubled.

Consultations. During his negotiations with Pritzker, Van Gorkom consulted only with Trans Union's controller (Peterson). Worse yet, once he told other senior managers about the impending deal, their initial reaction was strongly negative. In particular, Romans (Trans Union's CFO) objected that the price was too low, the transaction would have adverse tax consequences for some shareholders, and an option given Pritzker to buy Trans Union shares amounted to a "lock-up" that would inhibit competing offers. Such evidence likely proved quite damning in the court's own decisionmaking process. Having evidence in the record of these types of internal disagreements obviously raised questions about the fairness of the transaction. The take-away lesson is that deal-makers should, early in the process, consult with senior management and get them "on board." In addition, Van Gorkom would have been well-advised to consult in advance with the board of directors and kept them informed as to the progress of the negotiations.

---

[75] One could perhaps construct a self-dealing argument by focusing on the fact that Van Gorkom was very close to the mandatory retirement age and owned 75,000 shares of Trans Union stock. At $55 per share, those shares would be worth over $4 million; on the stock market, the shares had recently traded in a range of $30 to $39 per share. Even at the high end of that range, those shares were worth less than $3 million. One thus could argue that Van Gorkom's large stockholdings and his imminent mandatory retirement meant that he had an incentive to sell the company. If so, however, his incentive clearly is to get the best possible price. The more money for which Trans Union was sold, the more money Van Gorkom would have in retirement. Consequently, his self-interest was directly in-line with the interests of the shareholders, who presumably also would want the best possible price.

Setting the price. When selling an entire business, whether the sale is nominally structured as a merger or not, the board of directors "must focus on one primary objective—to secure the transaction offering the best value reasonably available for all stockholders."[76] In his negotiations with Pritzker, it was Van Gorkom who proposed the price of $55. In evaluating the potential for a management-sponsored leveraged buyout, Romans had earlier determined that such a buyout would be easy at a price of $50 but very difficult at a price of $60. Van Gorkom then seemingly split the difference, picking $55 out of the air as a price he would accept for his shares.

The court emphasized that the price thus was based on an evaluation of the feasibility with which a leveraged deal could be financed, rather than the Trans Union's value.[77] To the extent the court's analysis rests on the idea that a company has some intrinsic value, the decision is seriously flawed. As with any other asset, a company is worth only what somebody is willing to pay for it. Although the company's only value thus is its market value, an asset can have different values in different markets. (Otherwise, arbitrage would never be profitable.) Two distinct markets are implicated in this setting. On the one hand, there is the ordinary stock market in which Trans Union's shares trade. On the other, however, there is the market for corporate control. Prices in the latter market typically exceed those in the former. Hence, we speak of a "control premium" that is paid when someone buys all of the shares of a company's stock.

Trans Union's board made no effort to determine what control was worth to Pritzker, such as by ordering a valuation study, and in the absence of such a determination had no basis for deciding whether the price was a fair one. Put another way, the real issue, which is not well-framed in the majority opinion, is what the firm was worth to Pritzker and, accordingly, whether the board of directors did a good job in capturing that value on behalf of their shareholders. Trans Union's own estimate suggested that a price of up to $60 per share feasibly could be financed, albeit with some difficulty. The feasibility study, moreover, was prepared internally by an officer who presumably did not do such studies for a living. Although the court explicitly stated that boards are not obliged to hire outside financial experts, investment bankers in fact do valuation and feasibility studies for a living. The well-advised board thus obtains a fairness opinion that, at least in theory, gives them some basis for evaluating what the prospective buyer could afford,

---

[76] McMullin v. Beran, 765 A.2d 910, 918 (Del.2000).

[77] See, e.g., Smith v. Van Gorkom, 488 A.2d 858, 874 (Del.1985) (noting that the directors "were uninformed as to the intrinsic value of the Company").

and would be willing, to pay. Not surprisingly, *Van Gorkom* is sometimes referred to as the "Investment Bankers' Full Employment Act."

Negotiations. Van Gorkom's negotiations with Pritzker appear to have been less than demanding. Van Gorkom asked for a meeting, at which he basically said "if you'll pay $55, here's how you can finance the deal." Pritzker counter-offered with $50 per share, which Van Gorkom rejected. Pritzker then agreed to $55. Pritzker's quick acceptance of the price suggests that he thought he was getting a bargain, which enhances our questions about the adequacy of the price.

Time pressures. Pritzker imposed a tight time deadline in order to prevent leaks and the increased stock price that usually follows such leaks. As a result, the process went quite quickly and many decisions were made under significant time constraints. All of which evidently troubled the court, as it several times noted that there was no crisis or emergency justifying such speed. Does *Van Gorkom* thus imply that the board can never make quick decisions? Probably not. The speed with which the decision was made likely would have been unobjectionable if the process was otherwise adequate. A cautionary note is sounded, however, by the Delaware supreme court's recent observation that: "History has demonstrated boards 'that have failed to exercise due care are frequently boards that have been rushed.' "[78]

Information and process. The central issue in *Van Gorkom* was the board's failure to make an informed decision. The legal standard that emerges from the decision is straightforward—directors must inform themselves of all material information reasonably available to them.[79] This standard seemingly requires an in-depth study of the problem. The board must be informed of the company's value to the bidder, the course of the negotiations, the terms of the offer and their fairness, and the like.

This standard is too demanding. Information is costly and shareholders will only want managers to invest an additional dollar in gathering information where there is an additional dollar generated from better decision making. By requiring directors to have all information "reasonably available" to them the *Van Gorkom* court required the directors to over-invest in information.[80]

---

[78] McMullin v. Beran, 765 A.2d 910, 922 (Del.2000).

[79] The Delaware supreme court subsequently defined the term "material" in this context as "relevant and of a magnitude to be important to directors in carrying out their fiduciary duty of care in decisionmaking." Brehm v. Eisner, 746 A.2d 244, 259 n.49 (Del.2000).

[80] Cf. In re RJR Nabisco, Inc. Shareholders Litig., 1989 WL 7036 (Del.Ch.1989), in which Chancellor Allen observed that "information has costs." Id at *19. He further opined "that the amount of information that it is prudent to have

In contrast, the ALI PRINCIPLES only require directors to be informed to the extent that they reasonably believe to be appropriate under the circumstances.[81] Unlike the Delaware standard, at least as read literally, the ALI standard permits directors to make decisions on less than all reasonable available information, provided they reasonably believe doing so is appropriate given the situation. The time available to make the decision may require that the directors take risks to secure what appears to be a good outcome, which includes the risk that they do not have all of the relevant facts. A decision to accept that risk in order to secure the benefits of a proposed transaction will be appropriate under some circumstances.

In practice, of course, there are significant limitations on the board's ability to gather primary sources of information. Nobody seriously expects boards to read merger agreements cover to cover— not even the *Van Gorkom* court.[82] Reading long and boring legal documents is what boards pay their lawyers and subordinates to do. Under the circumstances, however, Trans Union's directors had a duty of inquiry. Considering the haste and other circumstances surrounding the decision, they should have pressed Van Gorkom with regard to the details of the deal. Instead, the board blindly relied on Van Gorkom's assertion that the price was fair. Van Gorkom failed to disclose, and the board failed to make sufficient inquiry to discover, key facts suggesting that the deal was not as attractive as it might seem on first blush.[83]

Qualitative studies of board processes have found wide variances. Some boards simply go through the motions of showing up and voting, without having done their homework. The Delaware supreme court concluded that the Trans Union directors were just such a board—the board was "grossly negligent in approving the 'sale' of the Company upon two hours' consideration, without prior notice, and without the exigency of a crisis or emergency." Other boards, however, exhibit far greater diligence. Such boards research issues, participate actively in discussion, and exercise critical judgment.

---

before a decision is made is itself a business judgment of the very type that courts are institutionally poorly equipped to make." Id.

[81] ALI PRINCIPLES § 4.01(c)(2).

[82] Smith v. Van Gorkom, 488 A.2d 858, 883 n.25 (Del.1985) ("We do not suggest that a board must read *in haec verba* every contract or legal document which it approves. . . .").

[83] In other words, the formal structure of the corporate governance system vests most decisionmaking power in the board of directors, especially with regard to major corporate changes such as a merger. Facts tending to suggest that senior officers are trying to railroad a decision through the board therefore are inconsistent with that model. Unfortunately for Trans Union's directors, the *Van Gorkom* record was rife with such facts.

How should corporate law encourage boards to exercise due diligence in the decisionmaking process? Should the corporate statute specify board procedures, for example? In general, corporation codes do not mandate detailed rules of board process or procedure. How the board sets its agenda, whether formal voting rules are observed, and other matters of parliamentary procedure are left to the board's discretion. Yet, there are lots of theoretical reasons—such as Arrow's Impossibility Theorem[84]—to think that the procedural rules for aggregating individual preferences have outcome determinative effects. Laboratory experiments on group decisionmaking, such as studies of mock juries, confirm that procedural matters such as the taking of straw votes and the setting of agendas do affect outcomes.[85] To be sure, it is doubtful whether ex ante legislative solutions would be viable given the complexities and uncertainties of life. Ex post judicial review of board process may be beneficial, however.

Consistent with that hypothesis, *Van Gorkom* rests not on failure to comply with some judicially imposed decisionmaking model but on the absence of a sufficient record of any deliberative process. Put differently, if the decisionmaking process is adequate, the court will continue to defer to the decision that emerges from that process. The basic thrust of the opinion then is that the board must provide some credible, contemporary evidence that it knew what it was doing. If such evidence exists, the court will not impose liability—even if the decision proves to have been the wrong one.

Summation. While the substantial criticism to which *Van Gorkom* has been subjected is not wholly unmerited, the more exaggerated fears of judicial intervention into board decisionmaking processes were clearly overstated. Strict adherence to the court's decisionmaking model likely is not a prerequisite for the business judgment rule to be applicable. On the facts of the case before it, however, the court concluded that the board had abdicated its responsibility and allowed itself to be railroaded by management to so great an extent that deference became inappropriate. In addition, the decision at issue related to a major transaction having final period consequences. Accountability thus appropriately trumped authority.

---

[84] According to Arrow's Theorem, there is no consistent method of making a fair choice among three or more options. As a result, when individual preferences differ, the outcome of a decisionmaking process will be determined by the process itself.

[85] Mock juries reviewing the same evidence, for example, regularly reach differing verdicts. See James H. Davis, Some Compelling Intuitions about Group Consensus Decisions, Theoretical and Empirical Research, and Interpersonal Aggregation Phenomena: Selected Examples, 1950–1990, 52 Org. Behav. & Human Decision Processes 3, 23–33 (1992) (summarizing studies).

In closing, however, it should be noted that *Van Gorkom* probably has resulted in many board decisions being over-processed. In many cases, even relatively minor board decisions are subjected to exhaustive review, with detailed presentations by experts. Why? The answer lies in the incentive structures of the relevant players. Who pays the bill if the director is found liable for breaching the duty of care? The director.[86] Who pays the bill for hiring lawyers and investment bankers to advise the board? The corporation and, ultimately, the shareholders. Suppose you were faced with potentially catastrophic losses, for which somebody offered to sell you an insurance policy. Better still, you don't have to pay the premiums, someone else will do so. Buying the policy therefore doesn't cost you anything. Would not you buy it?

It's also important to consider the incentives of the lawyers who advise corporations. Deciding how much time and effort to spend on making decisions is itself a business decision. Because that decision is driven by liability concerns, however, legal advice is usually critical to the making of the decision. Why might lawyers have an incentive to encourage boards to over-invest in the decisionmaking process? The cynical answer is that a more complicated decisionmaking process, which is driven by liability concerns, is likely to result in higher fees. A less cynical explanation is that the law is full of sports, mutants, and mistakes. Clients often lack the information or willingness to recognize that their situation was one of the exceptions that proves the rule. Instead, clients tend to blame the lawyer for an adverse outcome even if the lawyer did nothing wrong. Because the lawyers will be blamed even if losing the case was an act of god equivalent to a 100 year flood, lawyers are often conservative in giving advice. (The term conservative here is not used in its political sense, but rather in the sense of being cautious.) In economic terms, lawyers are risk averse. In a risky situation, the best thing for the lawyer to do is to point the client towards strategies whose outcome is certain.

In sum, the incentives of both sellers and buyers of legal advice are congruent. Lawyers have strong incentives to encourage clients to expend a lot of time, energy, and money on the decisionmaking process, while corporate boards of directors have strong incentives to take that advice. All of which goes to show that otherwise puzzling things become readily explicable if one understands the economic incentives at play.

---

[86] Note that this assumes that neither indemnification nor insurance is available. Given the ready availability of indemnification under Delaware law and the reasonable availability of D & O insurance, the caution often seen in board decisionmaking is truly puzzling.

C. The Contextual Business Judgment Rule

The business judgment rule is badly misnamed. In the legal literature, it is conventional to distinguish between standards and rules. Rules say "drive 55 mph," while standards say "drive reasonably." So defined, the business judgment rule is not a rule but a standard. The question is not whether the directors violated some bright-line precept, but whether their conduct satisfied some standard for judicial abstention.

The greater flexibility inherent in standards frequently comes into play in business judgment rule jurisprudence, as courts fine tune the doctrine's application to the facts at bar.[87] Delaware courts thus view the fiduciary responsibilities of directors, and thus the appropriate degree of judicial review, as depending "upon the specific context that gives occasion to the board's exercise of its business judgment."[88] Although the partition admittedly is somewhat artificial, a useful first cut at striking the necessary balance between authority and accountability is provided by the distinction between operational issues, such as whether to install lighting in a baseball park, and structural choices, especially those creating a final period situation, such as takeovers.[89] This chapter focuses on the business judgment rule as it relates to operational decisions. Omitted from this chapter thus are such matters as:

- The role of the business judgment rule in conflict of interest transactions, which is discussed in Chapter 7.

- The extent to which the business judgment rule controls board efforts to terminate shareholder derivative litigation, which is discussed in Chapter 8.

- The relationship between the business judgment rule and the shareholder wealth maximization norm, which is discussed in Chapter 9.

- The conditional business judgment rule governing management resistance to takeover bids, which is discussed in Chapter 12.

Taken together with the cases discussed in this chapter, these omitted applications suggest that three distinct versions of the business judgment rule can be identified. One is the traditional business judgment rule under which courts essentially decline to

---

[87] Cf. Stahl v. Apple Bancorp, Inc., 579 A.2d 1115, 1125 (Del.Ch.1990) (Chancellor Allen opined that "inquiries concerning fiduciary duties are inherently particularized and contextual").

[88] McMullin v. Beran, 765 A.2d 910, 918 (Del.2000).

[89] See E. Norman Veasey, The Defining Tension in Corporate Governance inAmerica, 52 Bus. Law. 393, 394 (1997) (drawing a similar distinction between "enterprise" and "ownership" decisions).

review decisions made by the board. A second, arguably more intrusive, variant of the business judgment rule is applied in cases such as *Van Gorkom* or *Technicolor*, which involve the sale of the business. The third variant, which might be called a conditional business judgment rule, is applied to takeover defenses per *Unocal* and its progeny.

As illustrated by the dichotomy between *Shlensky* and *Technicolor*, operational decisions typically (and appropriately) receive much less probing review than do the structural ones covered by the latter two variants of the rule. The principle is sufficiently well-established that a few examples will suffice. In *Shlensky*, the court declined to overrule the board's decision not to install lights in Wrigley Field.[90] In *Dodge v. Ford Motor Co.*,[91] the court refused to enjoin the board's decision to expand its factories, despite evidence that the decision was motivated by concerns other than shareholder wealth maximization. In *Theodora Holding Corp. v. Henderson*,[92] and *Ella M. Kelly & Wyndham, Inc. v. Bell*,[93] the business judgment rule insulated corporate charitable giving from judicial review. In *Kamin v. American Express Co.*,[94] the business judgment rule precluded review of a spin-off transaction. In *Weiss v. Samsonite Corp.*,[95] Vice Chancellor Jacobs held that the rule protected a board's decision to take on considerable additional debt as part of a leveraged recapitalization. And the beat goes on.

Such results are tolerable because most operational decisions do not pose much of a conflict between the interests of directors and shareholders. Granting, for example, that Wrigley appears to have preferred the neighborhood's interests to those of his shareholders, what selfish interests was he advancing? Perhaps he was simply trying to comply with what he saw as appropriate business ethics. Or, as we have already suggested, maybe he had eccentric ideas about how baseball was to be played. At worst, he might have reaped some psychological benefits from implementing his attitudes. Even assuming arguendo that these sort of psychological benefits implicate the kinds of self-dealing concerns that justify setting aside the business judgment rule, it is not clear that Wrigley's "self-interest" conflicted with the interests of their shareholders. With their theoretically perpetual duration,

---

[90] Shlensky v. Wrigley, 237 N.E.2d 776 (Ill.App.1968).

[91] 170 N.W. 668 (Mich.1919).

[92] 257 A.2d 398 (Del.Ch.1969).

[93] 266 A.2d 878 (Del.1970).

[94] 383 N.Y.S.2d 807 (Sup.Ct.), aff'd, 387 N.Y.S.2d 993 (1976).

[95] 741 A.2d 366 (Del.Ch.), aff'd, 746 A.2d 277 (Del.1999).

corporations must plan for the long-term.[96] As the *Shlensky* court's dictum suggested, it is plausible that Wrigley's opposition to lights was in the shareholders' best long-term interest. Drunken fans reveling in the darkness might have a deleterious effect on the neighborhood. If so, attendance might decline as the neighborhood declined.

We doubt whether Wrigley made the right decision. But so what? Operational decisions are a species of what economists refer to as repeat transactions. Where parties expect to have repeated transactions, the risk of self-dealing by one party is constrained by the threat that the other party will punish the cheating party in future transactions. To be sure, shareholder discipline is not a very important check on directorial self-dealing. Yet, as we have seen, it is just one of an array of extra-judicial constraints that, in totality, give directors incentives to exercise reasonable care in decisionmaking. True, these constraining forces do not eliminate the possibility of director error. The directors will still err from time to time. That is precisely the sort of error, however, that the courts traditionally—and appropriately—eschew reviewing.

D. Application to Officers

It is reasonably well-settled that officers owe a duty of care to the corporation.[97] It is less well-settled that officers get the benefit of the business judgment rule. Under the ALI PRINCIPLES, the rule applies to both directors and officers.[98] Judicial precedents are divided, however.[99]

What should the rule be? The theoretical justifications for the business judgment rule extend from the boardroom to corporate officers. Many corporate decisions are made by officers, for example,

---

[96] Accordingly, directors may pursue plans that are in the corporation's "best interests without regard to a fixed investment horizon." Paramount Communications, Inc. v. Time Inc., 571 A.2d 1140, 1150 (Del.1989). See also In re Reading Co., 711 F.2d 509 (3d Cir.1983) (corporate pricing and dividend policies that failed to maximize short-term profits nevertheless could rationally be seen as in corporation's long-term interest).

[97] See ALI PRINCIPLES § 4.01 cmt. a; see, e.g., MBCA § 8.42(a)(2) (requiring that officers exercise the "care that a person in a like position would reasonably exercise under similar circumstances").

[98] ALI PRINCIPLES § 4.01.

[99] Compare Galef v. Alexander, 615 F.2d 51, 57 n.13 (2d Cir.1980) (holding that the business judgment rule "generally applies to decisions of executive officers as well as those of directors"); FDIC v. Stahl, 854 F.Supp. 1565, 1570 n.8 (S.D.Fla.1994) (holding that the rule "applies equally to both officers and directors") with Platt v. Richardson, 1989 WL 159584 at *2 (M.D.Pa.1989) (holding that the rule "applies only to directors of a corporation and not to officers."). At least one court claims that the former view is the majority position, rejecting argument that "the business judgment rule applies only to the conduct of corporate directors and not to the conduct of corporate officers" on grounds that it was "clearly contrary to the substantial body of corporate case law which has developed on this issue." Selcke v. Bove, 629 N.E.2d 747, 750 (Ill.App.1994).

who are likely to be even more risk averse than directors. Accordingly, insulation from liability may be necessary to encourage optimal levels of risk-taking by officers.

§ 6.4   The Duty of Care

Because the business judgment rule is so pervasive, the underlying duty of care remains poorly developed. Recent statutory developments, however, shed important new light both on the duty of care and its sometimes tenuous relationship with the business judgment rule.

A.   Is the Duty of Care a Negligence Standard?

As we have seen, Delaware law requires directors to exercise "that amount of care which ordinarily careful and prudent men would use in similar circumstances."[100] The ALI PRINCIPLES similarly require directors to use "the care that an ordinarily prudent person would reasonably be expected to exercise in a like position and under similar circumstances."[101] Until recently, the MBCA likewise required that directors discharge their duties "with the care an ordinarily prudent person would exercise under similar circumstances."[102] All of these statements sound like negligence standards.[103] Yet, as Professor Bishop famously observed: "The search for cases in which directors of industrial corporations have been held liable in derivative suits for negligence uncomplicated by self-dealing is a search for a very small number of needles in a very large haystack."[104] A more recent survey found only twelve cases imposing liability on directors for negligence in the absence of a concurrent breach of the duty of loyalty or other conflict of interest.[105]

The paucity of such cases doubtless owes much to the business judgment rule. Yet, it also reflects a fundamental disagreement as to whether negligence is the appropriate standard of review in the corporate context. Precedents in several jurisdictions adopt ordinary negligence as the relevant standard of review in duty of care cases.[106] In contrast, the Delaware courts have adopted gross

---

[100] See, e.g., Graham v. Allis-Chalmers Mfg. Co., 188 A.2d 125, 130 (Del.1963).

[101] ALI PRINCIPLES § 4.01(a).

[102] MBCA § 8.30 cmt.

[103] Delaware tort law defines negligence as "the want of due care or want of such care as a reasonably prudent and careful person would exercise under similar circumstances." Orsini v. K-Mart Corp., 1997 WL 528034 at *3 (Del.Super.1997).

[104] Joseph W. Bishop, Jr., Sitting Ducks and Decoy Ducks: New Trends in the Indemnification of Corporate Directors and Officers, 77 Yale L.J. 1078, 1099 (1968).

[105] 1 Dennis J. Block et al., The Business Judgment Rule: Fiduciary Duties of Corporate Directors 167–72 (5th ed. 1998).

[106] See, e.g., FDIC v. Stahl, 89 F.3d 1510 (11th Cir.1996) (Florida law); Theriot v. Bourg, 691 So.2d 213 (La.App.1997) (rejecting gross negligence standard in favor

negligence as the relevant standard,[107] which they define as "reckless indifference to or a deliberate disregard of the stockholders" or conduct outside the "bounds of reason."[108]

B. Causation

Whether the standard of review is one of gross negligence or just ordinary negligence, the negligence-like phrasing of the duty of care might reasonably lead one to assume that liability should be imposed only where all the elements of the negligence cause of action are made out. In tort law, liability for negligence requires not just a breach of the duty of care but also a showing of causation and damages. An early opinion by famed jurist Learned Hand confirmed that just such a showing is required in the corporate duty of care context. In *Barnes v. Andrews*,[109] one Maynard set up a corporation to make starters for Ford Motors. Defendant Andrews purchased shares and agreed to serve as a director. The business was unable to get production going due to the incompetence of the factory manager and interpersonal conflicts between key employees. Andrews resigned in June 1920. In the spring of 1921, the company went bankrupt. The bankruptcy receiver sued Andrews for breaching the duty of care, charging that Andrews failed to give adequate attention to the company's business.

Judge Hand concluded that Andrews had breached his duty of care. Having accepted the post as director, Andrews had a duty to be informed as to whether the company was moving towards production and, if not, whether anything could be done to resolve the problem.[110] Consequently three of the key elements of a negligence cause of action were satisfied: there was a duty, a breach of that duty, and an injury (the company went under). Yet, Andrews escaped liability. Judge Hand held that plaintiff must show not only a breach, but also that the performance of the director's duties would have avoided a loss. In other words, plaintiff must prove causation. On these facts, plaintiff could not do so. Andrews was

---

of a "reasonable care" standard); Litwin v. Allen, 25 N.Y.S.2d 667, 699 (Sup.Ct.1940) (stating that liability must be imposed on facts of that case if "the doctrine that directors of a bank are liable for negligence" is to be preserved).

[107] See, e.g., McMullin v. Beran, 765 A.2d 910 (Del.2000) ("Director liability for breaching the duty of care 'is predicated upon concepts of gross negligence.' "); Smith v. Van Gorkom, 488 A.2d 858, 873 (Del.1985) (gross negligence is the proper standard for determining whether a business judgment was an informed one).

[108] Rabkin v. Philip A. Hunt Chemical Corp., 547 A.2d 963, 970 (Del.Ch.1986). The *Rabkin* court further suggested that that standard created a higher threshold of liability than the usual tort concept of gross negligence. Id.

[109] 298 F. 614 (S.D.N.Y.1924).

[110] Judge Hand acknowledged that Andrews was not obliged to single-handedly solve the problem. An individual director can only counsel and advise the officers, but Andrews did have a duty to keep himself informed and to offer such advice.

only one person and there was nothing a single director could have done to make the company successful.[111]

All of which seemed reasonably well-settled until *Technicolor* got into the act.[112] At one point in that long-running saga, Chancellor Allen ruled that plaintiff Cinerama could not prevail on its duty of care claims because it had failed to prove a financial injury caused by the Technicolor board's alleged misfeasances. In so holding, Allen relied on *Barnes*. The supreme court reversed, opining it to be "a 'mystery' how the [chancery] court discovered the *Barnes* case and then based its decision on *Barnes*."[113] Perhaps Chancellor Allen found the *Barnes* case by glancing at virtually any major corporate law text. If so, such a glance would have demonstrated that *Barnes* was (and still is) routinely cited as the leading authority for the well-accepted proposition that "the undoubted negligence of directors may not result in liability if the plaintiff cannot show that the negligence proximately caused damages to the corporation."[114] Even the Emanuel's law outline in print at the time cited *Barnes* for the proposition that "the traditional tort notions of cause in fact and proximate cause apply in [the duty of care] context."[115] Ditto the corporation law nutshell in print at the time *Technicolor* was decided, which likewise cited Barnes as "the leading case" for this proposition.[116] The true mystery thus is how the Delaware supreme court failed to discover *Barnes*' well-established status in corporate law jurisprudence. To be sure, the *Barnes* issue does not come up very often, but that is only because duty of care cases that reach the damages phase of litigation are so few and far between.

Technicolor's rejection of *Barnes* has troubling systemic implications. Under *Technicolor*, once plaintiff rebuts the business judgment rule by proving a breach of the duty of care (which you will recall itself puts the cart before the horse), the defendants have

---

[111] Part of the problem is that the receiver sued only Andrews. If he had sued all the directors, as was done in *Van Gorkom*, he might have been more successful. If all of the directors had acted as Andrews did, the receiver could have argued that, acting collectively, the board could have stepped in and required that the incompetent employees be fired. On the other hand, Judge Hand opined that it was not clear that the company would have been successful even if a substitute had been brought in for the incompetents. Consequently, plaintiff still might not have been able to prove the amount of loss that could have been avoided.

[112] For post-*Barnes* precedents assuming that plaintiff must prove causation, see Miller v. AT & T Co., 507 F.2d 759, 763 n.5 (3d Cir.1974) (New York law); Pierce v. Lyman, 3 Cal.Rptr.2d 236, 240 (Cal.App.1991); Rabkin v. Philip A. Hunt Chemical Corp., 1987 WL 28436 at *4 (Del.Ch.1987); Shlensky v. Wrigley, 237 N.E.2d 776, 780–81 (Ill.App.1968); Francis v. United Jersey Bank, 432 A.2d 814, 829 (N.J.1981).

[113] Cede & Co. v. Technicolor, Inc., 634 A.2d 345, 370 (Del.1993).

[114] Robert C. Clark, Corporate Law 126 (1986).

[115] Steven Emanuel, Corporations 128 (1989).

[116] Robert W. Hamilton, The Law of Corporations (3d ed. 1991).

the burden of establishing "entire fairness." The court thus conflated the duties of loyalty and of care, which Delaware courts previously had been careful to keep separate.[117] Corporate law's "sweeping grant of authority to the board is, of course, subject to the overarching normative constraint that the directors exercise their authority with the intention of benefiting the shareholders and not themselves."[118] Where directors have conflicted interests, accountability necessarily trumps the principle of deference to board decisions. Consequently, courts review loyalty claims under a most exacting standard. In the classic case of *Weinberger v. UOP, Inc.*,[119] for example, the court described the entire fairness standard as placing on the defendant directors the burden of proving, subject to "careful scrutiny by the courts," "their utmost good faith and the most scrupulous inherent fairness of the bargain." This exacting burden is justified, inter alia, because knowledge of facts necessary to prove the nature and extent of self-dealing typically are peculiarly within the possession of the defendants.

The concept of entire fairness, however, has little relevance to a duty of care case like *Van Gorkom* or *Technicolor*. In the first place, the relevant factual issues go not to fairness but to negligence and errors of judgment, which are precisely the sorts of issues the business judgment rule was intended to prevent courts from addressing. In the second place, invocation of entire fairness carries with it important remedial implications. In *Weinberger*, the court had authorized the use of "any form of equitable or monetary relief as may be appropriate, including rescissory damages" in loyalty cases. By conflating the loyalty and care analyses, *Technicolor* extends this broad grant of remedial authority to care claims, with potentially catastrophic consequences. Rescissory damages make sense in a loyalty case like *Weinberger*, because the wrongdoer was also the beneficiary of the wrongdoing.[120] In a care case like *Technicolor*, however, an award of rescissory damages would have the effect of ordering the defendant directors to return a benefit that they never received. As a practical matter, moreover, rescissory damages threaten to be so astronomical as to substantially chill the decisionmaking process. The threat of substantial liability is appropriate in loyalty cases. It ensures that the wrongdoer retains neither its ill-gotten gains nor their tainted fruits. By increasing the

---

[117] See generally Michael P. Dooley, Fundamentals of Corporation Law 249–54 (1995). For a careful demonstration that *Technicolor*'s importation of entire fairness into the duty of care was a doctrinal novelty, see Lyman Johnson, Rethinking Judicial Review of Director Care, 24 Del. J. Corp. L. 787, 799–801 (1999). Johnson correctly concludes there is "no clear and reasoned prior authority" supporting *Technicolor* in this respect. Id. at 801.

[118] Michael P. Dooley, Fundamentals of Corporation Law 250 (1995).

[119] 457 A.2d 701 (Del.1983).

[120] Michael P. Dooley, Fundamentals of Corporation Law 256 (1995).

size of the nominal sanction, it also enhances the deterrent effect of loyalty litigation. But such enormous liability makes no sense in care litigation. By definition there are no ill-gotten gains to be recouped. More important, by increasing the deterrent effect of judicial review, coupled with its expansion of the scope of review, *Technicolor* substantially undermines the board's decisionmaking authority. Where legal standards are vague and the potential liability exposure is substantial, rational actors will not pursue a course of action that takes them into legal gray areas. Sensible directors thus will focus on making a defensible decision, rather than on making the best decision.

C. Reliance on Officers

Wholly separate from the business judgment rule, both the Delaware code and the MBCA provide statutory safe harbors for directors who rely in good faith on information and reports from their subordinates. DGCL § 141(e) provides:

> A member of the board of directors, or a member of any committee designated by the board of directors, shall, in the performance of such member's duties, be fully protected in relying in good faith upon the records of the corporation and upon such information, opinions, reports or statements presented to the corporation by any of the corporation's officers or employees, or committees of the board of directors, or by any other person as to matters the member reasonably believes are within such other person's professional or expert competence and who has been selected with reasonable care by or on behalf of the corporation.

MBCA § 8.30(e) is similar.

In *Smith v. Van Gorkom*,[121] Trans Union's directors sought the safe harbor provided by § 141(e), but were denied admittance. To be sure, Van Gorkom had made a presentation to the board, albeit of only 20 minutes duration. Van Gorkom's oral presentation was based principally on his understanding of the relevant documents, but he had neither seen nor been briefed on the terms of the documents. His oral presentation thus did not qualify as a "report" for purposes of § 141(e) because Van Gorkom himself was uninformed as to the details of the plan.

It is unlikely, of course, that the chairman and directors of a major corporation are going to parse through lengthy merger agreements with a fine tooth comb. Doing so is what they pay lawyers and investment bankers to do. If Van Gorkom had been

---

[121] 488 A.2d 858, 875 (Del.1985).

briefed by the company's legal counsel, such that Van Gorkom could accurately relate the details to the board, that should have sufficed to qualify his presentation as a "report."

That the board receives a report is not enough, of course. The board's reliance on such a report must be in good faith, which on these facts imposed a duty of inquiry. Considering the haste and other circumstances surrounding the decision, the board should have pressed Van Gorkom with regard to the details on which his presentation was based. Instead, the board blindly relied on Van Gorkom's assertion that the price was fair.[122]

D. Oversight Cases

Monitoring management is one of the board's three principal functions, of course, and, arguably, *prima inter pares.* Oddly, however, the business judgment rule rarely will insulate the directors from liability in connection with that function. The rule applies only where the board has exercised business judgment, while most oversight cases arise precisely because the board has failed to act.

It is well-settled that the duty of care requires directors to pay on-going attention to the business and affairs of the corporation. In the leading case of *Francis v. United Jersey Bank,*[123] defendant Pritchard was the widow of the company's former president. She was also the company's largest shareholder and a director. Her sons Charles and William were also shareholders, officers, and directors of the company. Despite her husband's warning that Charles "would take the shirt off my back," Pritchard paid no attention to the business. Meanwhile, her nefarious sons had systematically robbed the company by causing the corporation to make purported loans to themselves in excess of any reasonable salary or dividends.[124]

As the court bluntly put it, Pritchard "was old, was grief-stricken at the loss of her husband, sometimes consumed too much alcohol, and was psychologically overborne by her sons." None of which excused her failure to pay attention to the corporation's business:

---

[122] Smith v. Van Gorkom, 488 A.2d 858, 875 (Del.1985). See also Hanson Trust PLC v. ML SCM Acquisition, Inc., 781 F.2d 264 (2d Cir.1986) (directors have a duty of inquiry with respect to conclusory statements of advisers).

[123] 432 A.2d 814 (N.J.1981). Pritchard had died before case was brought and, technically, the defendant was her estate. We shall ignore that complication, which is irrelevant to the analysis.

[124] Structuring their scheme as loans was actually quite clever. From a tax perspective, salary and dividends are taxable to the recipient, but the proceeds of a loan is not taxable income. From an accounting perspective, loans are corporate assets, so the money in a sense stays on the books, making it appear that the firm is solvent, while salary and dividends must be deducted from assets, which would have made it obvious that the company was in the red.

> Directors are under a continuing obligation to keep informed about the activities of the corporation. . . . Directors may not shut their eyes to corporate misconduct and then claim that because they did not see the misconduct, they did not have a duty to look. The sentinel asleep at his post contributes nothing to the enterprise he is charged to protect.[125]

Maybe she never should have become a director, but having done so she had a duty to be informed and to take action to prevent the loss.[126]

Courts do not expect super-human performance. Directors are not expected to know, in minute detail, everything that happens on a day-to-day basis.[127] At the very least, however, a director should have a rudimentary understanding of the firm's business and how it works, keep informed about the firm's activities, engage in a general monitoring of corporate affairs, attend board meetings regularly, and routinely review financial statements. In doing so, if the director's suspicions are aroused, she should make inquiries into doubtful matters, raise objections to apparently illegal or questionable behavior, and resign if corrections aren't made. All of which Pritchard failed to do.

Pritchard's conduct was actionable because she failed over an extended period of time to pay attention to misconduct occurring right under her nose. *Francis* thus leaves open the extent to which the duty of care requires directors to proactively monitor the conduct of corporate subordinates. This question is especially controversial with respect to the board's duty, if any, affirmatively to ensure that the corporation complies with the law. Oddly, however, the Delaware supreme court has chosen to treat this issue as one arising under the duty of loyalty rather than the duty of care. Accordingly, we defer consideration of it to the next chapter.[128]

---

[125] Francis v. United Jersey Bank, 432 A.2d 814 (N.J.1981). Accord Theriot v. Bourg, 691 So.2d 213, 224 (La.App.1997) (holding that "advanced age" does not lessen "the standard of care required of a director of a corporation").

[126] It might be asked how one reconciles *Francis* with Barnes v. Andrews, 298 F. 614 (S.D.N.Y.1924). The two cases are similar in that both Pritchard and Andrews were charged with not keeping themselves informed about the business. In *Francis*, however, Pritchard could have taken effective action. Simply by reading the financial statements she could have determined that there was wrongdoing and, probably, put a stop to it by telling her sons to cease and desist. Moreover, the loss can be quantified by the amount of the illegal loans the sons took from the company.

[127] Rabkin v. Philip A. Hunt Chemical Corp., 1987 WL 28436 *2 (Del.Ch.1987).

[128] See § 7.5 infra.

E. Shareholder Ratification

In *Smith v. Van Gorkom*,[129] the Trans Union director defendants argued that shareholder approval of the challenged merger cured their alleged duty of care violations. Even the plaintiffs conceded that a transaction tainted by director care violations was merely voidable, rather than void. As with other voidable corporate actions, such a transaction therefore could be ratified by majority vote of the shareholders. On the facts of *Van Gorkom*, however, shareholder approval was unavailing. Only a fully informed vote of the shareholders could protect the directors from liability. Because they had failed to disclose various material facts, notably including the "fact that the Board had no reasonably adequate information indicative of the intrinsic value of the Company," the shareholder vote was uninformed.

A fully informed shareholder vote thus extinguishes duty of care claims.[130] Because litigated care claims frequently involve transactions requiring shareholder approval, such as mergers and the like, this is a significant additional protection for directors. The sticking point, of course, will be the adequacy of disclosure. It is hard to imagine a board disclosure along the lines of: "we're very sorry but we violated the duty of care in the following particulars, which we shall now describe at great length." As in *Van Gorkom*, if the court believes the directors violated their duty of care, it likely will find material nondisclosures as well.

F. The MBCA

Some scholars have sought to reconcile the duty of care and the business judgment rule by distinguishing between standards of conduct and standards of review.[131] According to this conception, the duty of care is a standard of conduct, which specifies how directors should conduct themselves. In contrast, the business judgment rule is a standard of review, which sets forth the test courts will use in determining whether the directors' conduct gives rise to liability.[132] Unlike typical negligence tort cases, in which the standard of review and the standard of conduct are identical, in

---

[129] 488 A.2d 858, 889–90 (Del.1985).

[130] In re Wheelabrator Technologies Shareholders Litig., 663 A.2d 1194, 1200 (Del.Ch.1995).

[131] See, e.g., Melvin Aron Eisenberg, The Divergence of Standards of Conduct and Standards of Review in Corporate Law, 62 Fordham L. Rev. 437 (1993).

[132] A somewhat similar conception of the rule is captured by the purported distinction between the business judgment rule, which is said to shield corporate officers and directors from personal liability in connection with business decisions, and the business judgment doctrine, which shields the decision itself from review. See Revlon, Inc. v. MacAndrews & Forbes Holdings, Inc., 506 A.2d 173, 180 n.10 (Del.1985). The Delaware Supreme Court has recognized, but not adopted, that distinction. Id.

corporate law they purportedly diverge. The function of the business judgment rule thus is to create a less demanding standard of review than the (largely aspirational) standard of conduct created by the duty of care. But what is the standard? It may be mere subjective good faith, it may be a requirement of rationality, it may be gross negligence. No one seems to know for sure, although some argue that the business judgment rule entails "some objective review of the quality of the [board's] decision, however limited."[133]

The MBCA recently adopted a different version of the dual standards approach. MBCA § 8.30 sets forth the standards of conduct for directors. Analogously to those Delaware decisions describing the duty of care as process oriented, § 8.30 focuses on the manner in which the board carried out its duties, not the correctness or reasonableness of its decisions.[134] Under § 8.30(a) the director must act in good faith and in a manner the director reasonably believes to be in the corporation's best interest. Note the absence of any reference to due or reasonable care. Those references appear only in § 8.30(b), which relates solely to the directors' duty to make informed decisions. When "becoming informed" the board is to exercise "the care that a person in a like position would reasonably believe appropriate under similar circumstances." There is a striking contrast with the *Van Gorkom* obligation to gather all materially information reasonably available to the board. Under the MBCA, directors can act on less than all available information, provided doing so satisfies the reasonable person standard.

Conduct that satisfies the requirements of § 8.30 cannot result in liability. Conduct falling short of those aspirational goals can only result in liability if it violates the standards of director liability set forth in MBCA § 8.31.[135] Specifically, under § 8.31(a)(2), liability can be imposed where the director acted in bad faith, did not reasonably believe the action to be in the corporation's best interest, was not informed to the extent the director reasonably believed appropriate under the circumstances, was interested in the transaction, was not independent, engaged in self-dealing, or failed to exercise oversight over a sustained period.[136] Although the

---

[133] William L. Cary and Melvin Aron Eisenberg, Corporations 603 (7th ed. 1995).

[134] MBCA § 8.30 cmt.

[135] As implied by the basic dichotomy between standards of conduct and review, the statute thus contemplates a level of director conduct that falls short of the statutory ideal but for which the directors will not be liable. Courts will need to be vigilant to preserve a reasonable breadth for the resulting no man's land.

[136] MBCA § 8.31(b). Unlike *Technicolor*, there is no hint in § 8.31 that courts can review the merits of board decisions. Also unlike *Technicolor*, § 8.31(b) treats causation as an element of the care claim. In order to recover monetary damages, plaintiff must prove both that harm resulted to the corporation and that that harm was proximately caused by the defendant director's misconduct.

drafters deny any intent to codify the business judgment rule,[137] it's readily apparent that MBCA § 8.31(a)(2) effectively codifies a fairly aggressive version of the abstention approach to judicial review advocated by our interpretation of the business judgment rule.[138] Unlike *Van Gorkom*, for example, under which a court asks whether the director gathered all material information reasonably available, a court under § 8.31 asks only whether the director was informed to the extent the director reasonably believed appropriate under the circumstances, a much more deferential standard.

§ 6.5   Statutory Responses to *Van Gorkom* and the "D & O Liability Crisis"

It is often said that, absent the protections of the business judgment rule, no rational person would agree to serve as a director. Especially with respect to large public corporations, the potential liability of directors takes on catastrophic dimensions.[139] After *Smith v. Van Gorkom*, director and officer liability insurance became very hard to get.[140] Delaware and many other states responded to this purported crisis by adopting limitations on director liability and/or amending their existing indemnification statutes.

A.   Liability Limitation Statutes

DGCL § 102(b)(7) provides that a corporation's articles of incorporation may (but need not) contain:

> A provision eliminating or limiting the personal liability of a director to the corporation or its stockholders for monetary damages for breach of fiduciary duty as a director, provided that such provision shall not eliminate or limit the liability of a director: (i) For any breach of the director's duty of loyalty to the corporation or its

---

[137] Neither § 8.30 nor 8.31 attempts to codify the business judgment rule. Nor do they purport to displace it. Courts in MBCA states apparently remain free to continue common law development of the rule. At the same time, however, the statute establishes a floor for director liability. Courts cannot reinterpret the rule so as to bypass the statute and impose liability.

[138] MBCA § 8.31(a) provides that the standard of review applies to both affirmative decisions (whether it be a decision to act or refrain from acting) *and* a failure to act. Note the contrast with the business judgment rule, which gives no protection to directors who fail to exercise business judgment.

[139] No less a jurist than Learned Hand endorsed this concern. See Barnes v. Andrews, 298 F. 614, 617 (S.D.N.Y.1924) ("No men of sense would take the office, if the law imposed upon them a guaranty of the general success of their companies as a penalty for any negligence."); see also Solimine v. Hollander, 19 A.2d 344, 348 (N.J.Ch.1941) (indemnification of expenses required so as to encourage responsible persons to serve). This view, however, seems inconsistent with the notion that a sufficiently high return will induce even risk averse persons to take on a risky job.

[140] See generally Roberta Romano, What Went Wrong with Directors' and Officers' Liability Insurance?, 14 Del. J. Corp. L. 1 (1989).

stockholders; (ii) for acts or omissions not in good faith or which involve intentional misconduct or a knowing violation of law; (iii) under § 174 of this title [relating to liability for unlawful dividends]; or (iv) for any transaction from which the director derived an improper personal benefit.

MBCA § 2.02(b)(4) is similar. Virtually all states now have some such statute. Most public corporations have amended their charters to include such provisions.

Several aspects of the Delaware statute seem especially noteworthy. First, it applies only to directors. Although officers also are subject to a duty of care, they are denied exculpation by charter provision. In *Arnold v. Society for Savings Bancorp, Inc.*,[141] the supreme court held that, as to a defendant who is both a director and an officer, an exculpatory § 102(b)(7) provision applies only to actions taken solely in his capacity as a director.

Second, the statute limits only the monetary liability of directors. Equitable remedies are still available. Because the real party in interest in many shareholder suits is the plaintiff's attorney rather than the shareholders, and because attorneys' fees can be recovered in connection with equitable remedies, § 102(b)(7) does not eliminate the incentive to bring shareholder litigation.

Third, the Delaware supreme court held in *Emerald Partners* that a § 102(b)(7) provision is an affirmative defense.[142] Defendant directors thus have the burden of proving that they are entitled to exculpation under the statute. If aggressively applied, *Emerald Partners* could mean that a § 102(b)(7) provision rarely will entitle directors to a dismissal on grounds that plaintiff's complaint fails to state a cause of action. Consequently, plaintiffs will be entitled to discovery, which some might call a fishing expedition, and the settlement value of such claims will go up. Thus far, however, the chancery court has continued to hold a § 102(b)(7)-based motion to dismiss is appropriate pre-discovery where plaintiff solely alleged violations of the duty of care.[143]

Most importantly, however, notice that the statute apparently distinguishes self-dealing ("improper personal benefit") from the

---

[141] 650 A.2d 1270 (Del.1994).

[142] Emerald Partners v. Berlin, 726 A.2d 1215, 1223–24 (Del.1999). See also McMullin v. Beran, 765 A.2d 910, 926 (Del.2000).

[143] See, e.g., McMillan v. Intercargo Corp., 768 A.2d 492 (Del.Ch.2000); In re Lukens Inc. Shareholders Litig., 757 A.2d 720 (Del.Ch.1999). A subsequent Delaware supreme court decision in the *Emerald Partners* litigation confirmed this approach, while emphasizing that limited discovery is available where plaintiff has adequately alleged a violation of the duty of loyalty or of good faith. Emerald Partners v. Berlin, 787 A.2d 85 (Del.2001).

duty of care. Given *Technicolor*'s conflation of loyalty and care causes of action, plaintiffs can end-run § 102(b)(7) provisions by characterizing their claim as a loyalty violation. Interestingly, Chancellor Allen has suggested that *Van Gorkom* itself can be interpreted as a loyalty case.[144] Similarly, the Delaware supreme court has opined that *Van Gorkom* included a disclosure violation and implied that such violations have a loyalty component.[145] Ironically, a § 102(b)(7) provision thus might not have insulated the directors from liability in the very transaction that motivated the statute's adoption.

B. Indemnification Statutes

At common law, corporate employees were entitled to indemnification for expenses incurred on the job, including certain legal liabilities, but directors were not.[146] Today, however, all states have statutory provisions authorizing director indemnification to some degree.[147] As usual, we will focus on the Delaware statute.

DGCL § 145 distinguishes in the first instance between direct suits against a director or officer by a shareholder or other third party and derivative suits brought against a director or officer "by or in the right of the corporation." As to the former, § 145(a) authorizes the corporation to indemnify the director or officer for expenses plus "judgments, fines, and amounts paid in settlement" of both civil and criminal proceedings. In contrast, as to derivative litigation, § 145(b) authorizes indemnification only for expenses, albeit including attorney's expenses. If the director or officer was held liable to the corporation, moreover, he may only be indemnified with court approval.

Section 145 also distinguishes between mandatory and permissive indemnification. Under § 145(c), the corporation must indemnify a director or officer who "has been successful on the merits or otherwise." As for directors and officers who are

---

[144] Gagliardi v. TriFoods Int'l, Inc., 683 A.2d 1049, 1052 n.4 (Del.Ch.1996) ("I see it as reflecting a concern with the Trans Union board's independence and loyalty to the company's shareholders").

[145] Cinerama, Inc. v. Technicolor, Inc., 663 A.2d 1156, 1166 n.18 (Del.1995) ("In *Van Gorkom*, it was unnecessary for this Court to state whether the disclosure violation constituted a breach of the duty of care or loyalty or was a combined breach of both since 8 Del.C. § 102(b)(7) had not yet been enacted."). In addition, according to the Sixth Circuit, a § 102(b)(7) liability limitation provision may not insulate directors from duty of care claims based on intentional or reckless misconduct. McCall v. Scott, 250 F.3d 997, 1000–01 (6th Cir.2001).

[146] See, e.g., New York Dock Co. v. McCollom, 16 N.Y.S.2d 844 (Sup.Ct.1939).

[147] See generally James J. Hanks, Jr. & Larry P. Scriggins, Protecting Directors and Officers From Liability—The Influence of the Model Business Corporation Act, 56 Bus. Law. 3 (2000); Mae Kuykendall, A Neglected Policy Option: Indemnification of Directors for Amounts Paid to Settle Derivative Suits—Looking Past "Circularity" to Context and Reform, 32 San Diego L. Rev. 1063 (1995).

unsuccessful, indemnification is permissive, so long as it is not precluded by statute.

Because of the long delays inherent in litigation, indemnification may be of little assistance to a director or officer who has been bankrupted by legal or other costs in the meanwhile. Under § 145(e), the corporation may advance expenses to the officer or director provided the latter undertakes to repay any such amount if it turns out he is not entitled to indemnification.

Section 145(f) authorizes the corporation to enter into written indemnification agreements with officers and directors that go beyond the statute. Unfortunately, the plain text of the statute is, at best, ambiguous. Section 145(f) merely provides that statutory indemnification rights "shall not be deemed exclusive of any other rights" to indemnification created by "bylaw, agreement, vote of the stockholders or disinterested directors or otherwise." It seems clear that the statute authorizes indemnification agreements mandating payment of expenses that the statute merely permits. Indeed, most "public corporations have extended indemnification guarantees via bylaw to cases where indemnification is typically only permissive [by statute]."[148] In addition, an indemnification agreement properly may mandate advancement of expenses even though such advancement is merely permissive under § 145(e).[149]

Does § 145(f), however, allow the corporation to indemnify directors or officers where statutory indemnification is not permitted? In *Waltuch v. Conticommodity Services*,[150] the Second Circuit answered that question in the negative. Along the way, the court proffered several other noteworthy interpretations of open issues under § 145.

Waltuch was the silver trader for Conticommodity, a commodities trading firm. In 1979, the silver market famously went nuts after the Hunt brothers tried to corner the market. Silver prices spiked upwards but then crashed. Waltuch and Conticommodity were sued for fraud and market manipulation by their clients and, in a separate enforcement proceeding, the Commodity Futures Trading Commission (CFTC). Conticommodity paid $35 million to settle the private party litigation. Waltuch was dismissed from that litigation without having to make any monetary payment. He incurred $1.2 million in legal expenses in connection the private party litigation. Waltuch settled the CFTC litigation. To do so, he paid a $100,000 fine and agreed to a six

---

[148] VonFeldt v. Stifel Fin. Corp., 714 A.2d 79, 81, n.5 (Del.1998).

[149] See, e.g., Citadel Holding Corp. v. Roven, 603 A.2d 818 (Del.1992).

[150] Waltuch v. Conticommodity Services, Inc., 88 F.3d 87 (2d Cir.1996).

month ban on trading. He spent an additional $1 million in legal fees in that proceeding.

Waltuch sued Conticommodity under § 145 and the indemnification provisions of Conticommodity's articles on incorporation. Article Nine thereof provided:

> The Corporation shall indemnify and hold harmless each of its incumbent or former directors, officers, employees and agents . . . against expenses actually and necessarily incurred by him in connection with the defense of any action, suit or proceeding threatened, pending or completed, in which he is made a party, by reason of his serving in or having held such position or capacity, except in relation to matters as to which he shall be adjudged in such action, suit or proceeding to be liable for negligence or misconduct in the performance of duty.

Section 145(a) only authorizes indemnification of expenses incurred by a director or officer who "acted in good faith." Conticommodity claimed that Article Nine therefore was invalid, because it implicitly mandated indemnification of bad faith actions. Waltuch claimed that § 145(f) authorized the article without the need for any good faith limitation.

The court more or less split the baby down the middle. The standard adopted charitably can be described as elusive, although slippery probably fits the bill even better: "indemnification rights may be broader than those set out in the statute, but they cannot be inconsistent with the 'scope' of the corporation's power to indemnify, as delineated in the statute's substantive provisions." Where the statute requires good faith, as it does in both subsections (a) and (b), an agreement that purports even by implication to authorize indemnification for non-good faith conduct is inconsistent with the scope of the statute and therefore invalid. Accordingly, Conticommodity need not (indeed, may not) indemnify Waltuch for his legal expenses in connection with the CFTC proceeding. Because Waltuch had stipulated in the lower court that he would not seek to demonstrate his good faith, Waltuch cannot even go back and litigate that issue.[151]

As to the private litigation, however, Waltuch arguably had been "successful." Recall that § 145(c) mandates indemnification where the defendant was "successful on the merits *or otherwise*." Waltuch claimed he was "successful" because he was dismissed from

---

[151] Interpreting California law, the federal Fourth Circuit has held that a director or officer who intentionally participates in illegal activity cannot be deemed to have acted in good faith even if the conduct benefits the corporation. In re Landmark Land Co., 76 F.3d 553 (4th Cir.1996).

the private party cases without having to contribute to the settlement. Conticommodity claimed Waltuch was dismissed as a direct result of its $35 million settlement. The court adopts a no questions asked approach to § 145(c): "the only question a court may ask is what the result [of the underlying litigation] was, not why it was."[152] Unlike subsections (a) and (b), there is no good faith limitation under § 145(c). Accordingly, opined the Second Circuit, success for purposes of subsection (c) does not require "moral exoneration."[153] It only requires escape. Waltuch satisfied that standard and thus was entitled to mandatory indemnification for his expenses in the private party litigation.[154]

Why did the legislature omit a requirement of good faith from the mandatory indemnification provision in Section 145(c)? The omission may have been intended to avoid collateral litigation. Suppose a director succeeds on the merits, but in a way that does not resolve the issue of his good faith—e.g., avoiding conviction in a criminal case. In seeking indemnification, the issue of good faith thus would not be subject to any form of collateral estoppel and would have to be litigated. Not only does this add collateral litigation, it also raises the specter of suits for "fees for fees," as Vice Chancellor Jacobs so aptly put it. Omitting a requirement of good faith forecloses these risks.

Second, the legislature may have intended to permit indemnification of directors who act in bad faith but nonetheless prevail. Why? Here are some possibilities: (1) Do not chill directors from taking risks. The good faith clause of § 145(a) includes a requirement that the party seeking indemnification had no "reasonable cause to believe that [his] conduct was illegal." Perhaps the director thought the conduct was illegal, but thought it was worth taking the risk (e.g., bribes to get a contract). Perhaps the legislature thought such a director should be indemnified if taking that risk was vindicated by an acquittal at trial. (Note that such an acquittal would not constitute an adjudication of the director's good faith.) Suppose he had gone ahead in the face of a warning from

---

[152] Waltuch v. Conticommodity Services, Inc., 88 F.3d 87, 96 (2d Cir.1996). Where a case was dismissed without prejudice because the same issues were being litigated in a different proceeding, however, the Delaware federal district court has denied mandatory indemnification under § 145(c). Galdi v. Berg, 359 F.Supp. 698 (D.Del.1973).

[153] Avoiding indictment or successfully plea bargaining away criminal charges, for example, constitutes "success on the merits or otherwise." See, e.g., Merritt-Chapman & Scott Corp. v. Wolfson, 321 A.2d 138 (Del.Super.1974) (indictment dismissed pursuant to plea bargain); Stewart v. Continental Copper & Steel Indus., Inc., 414 N.Y.S.2d 910 (App.Div.1979) (indictment avoided; interpreting Delaware law).

[154] Interpreting a California statute limiting mandatory indemnification to situations in which the defendant prevailed "on the merits," a California appeals court held that a judicial determination of the merits of the defense was required. American Nat'l Bank & Trust Co. v. Schigur, 148 Cal.Rptr. 116 (Cal.App.1978).

corporate counsel that there was a "strong possibility" the conduct would violate a criminal statute? (2) Encourage people to serve as directors of Delaware corporations, and thereby also encourage incorporators to incorporate in Delaware, by providing them with maximum protection.

Finally, if an officer or director is obliged to sue the corporation seeking indemnification, is a prevailing officer or director entitled not only to indemnification of attorney's fees incurred in the underlying litigation but also those fees incurred in the indemnification suit?[155] In *Mayer v. Executive Telecard*,[156] the plaintiff sought indemnification for expenses incurred in successfully defending federal securities antifraud claims. Mayer prevailed in his initial lawsuit seeking indemnification. Mayer then sued again, claiming he was entitled to reimbursement for his legal expenses in the first lawsuit. Vice Chancellor Jacobs referred to this as seeking "fees for fees," which Jacobs held § 145(a) did not allow. The statute authorizes only "the indemnification of fees incurred in the underlying action, not fees for fees." In dictum, however, Jacobs went on to opine that § 145(f) "arguably" authorizes indemnification agreements covering fees for fees.

In *Baker v. Health Management Systems, Inc.*,[157] the New York court of appeals interpreted the comparable New York indemnification statute as likewise barring recovery of "fees on fees," as that court called them. As Jacobs had done in *Mayer*, moreover, the court stated in dicta that the New York statute authorized corporations "to provide indemnification of fees on fees in by-laws, employment contracts or through insurance." A strong dissent argued that the statute's plain text mandated indemnification of expenses that are " 'reasonable,' and 'actually and necessarily incurred as a result of the underlying action.' " As the majority pointed out, however, departures from the standard American Rule that each party pays its own attorney's fees required explicit statutory authorization. In addition, the majority contended that nothing in the legislative history indicated an intent to authorize fees for fees.

In *Stifel Financial Corp. v. Cochran*,[158] however, the Delaware supreme court overruled *Mayer* and several other chancery court precedents rejecting fees for fees. Noting that DGCL § 145 is a remedial statute, the court observed: "An attorney representing a

---

[155] Suits brought under DGCL § 145 seeking indemnification are subject to a three year statute of limitations. Stifel Fin. Corp. v. Cochran, 809 A.2d 555 (Del.2002).

[156] 705 A.2d 220 (Del.Ch.1997).

[157] 772 N.E.2d 1099 (N.Y.2002).

[158] 809 A.2d 555 (Del.2002).

former director who is being denied statutorily authorized indemnification must seek compensation from his client or remain uncompensated, a result 'inimical to the interests' of the former director and contrary to the express purpose of § 145 to protect directors from personal liability for corporate expenses." In contrast to *Baker*'s view that indemnification statutes should be narrowly construed, the Delaware supreme court argued that "the indemnification statute should be broadly interpreted to further the goals it was enacted to achieve."[159]

Law professor and legal realist Karl Llewellyn famously observed that "there are two opposing cannons [of statutory construction] on almost any point."[160] The issue raised by Cochran and *Baker* is just such a point. On the one hand lies the canon that rules in derogation of the common law should be strictly and narrowly construed. On the other lies the canon that remedial statutes should be liberally construed so as to effect their purposes. Although the question is a close one, my own view is that *Cochran* was correctly decided. The indemnification statute is, in fact, a remedial statute intended to encourage directors and officers to resist frivolous lawsuits by ensuring that their reasonable expenses will be reimbursed borne by the corporation if they prevail. Accordingly, it encourages capable persons "to serve as corporate directors, secure in the knowledge that expenses incurred by them in upholding their honesty and integrity as directors will be borne by the corporation they serve."[161] When a court refuses to award fees for fees, it frustrates these purposes by encouraging corporations routinely to oppose indemnification claims, which in turn may lead directors and officers to settle for less than their full expenses. In addition, as the dissent in *Baker* pointed out, the

---

[159] Curiously, the Delaware supreme court in *Cochran* indicated that a corporation could adopt indemnification provisions disallowing fees for fees. Stifel Financial Corp. v. Cochran, 809 A.2d 555, 562 (Del.2002) (opining that corporations "remain free to tailor their indemnification bylaws to exclude 'fees on fees,' if that is a desirable goal"). At first blush, this dicta seems to be the simple obverse of Vice Chancellor Jacobs' dicta in *Mayer* that § 145(f) authorized a corporation to adopt indemnification provisions allowing payment of fees for fees. Upon reflection, however, there is a big difference between corporate indemnification provisions that extend indemnification rights to areas not covered by statute and indemnification provisions that deny rights authorized by statute. DGCL § 145(c), for example, states that the director or officer "shall be indemnified" to the extent he "has been successful on the merits." Nothing in that section contemplates corporate indemnification rights restricting the scope of mandatory indemnification. Section 145(f) authorizes the corporation to create more expansive indemnification rights than authorized by the statute, but nowhere authorizes the corporation to restrict rights granted by statute. Hence, as least as to cases in which the director or officer is entitled to mandatory indemnification under § 145(c), the *Cochran* court's off-hand dicta seems clearly erroneous.

[160] Karl Llewllyn, Remarks on the Theory of Appellate Decision & The Rules of Canons About How Statutes are to be Construed, 3 Vand.L.Rev. 395 (1950).

[161] Rodman Ward, Jr., et al., Folk on the Delaware General Corporation Law § 145 (2001).

plaint text of the New York statute clearly seems to embrace not just the initial suit but also any other expenses "actually and necessarily incurred as a result of the underlying action." Delaware § 145(a) similarly refers to "any action." Where the director is obliged to file a second proceeding to enforce his right to indemnification, that proceeding obviously is an "action" that is a "result" of the underlying lawsuit.[162]

---

[162] MBCA § 8.54(b) mandates fees for fees incurred in suits to enforce mandatory indemnification and grants the court discretion to award fees for fees in suits brought to enforce permissive indemnification.

Chapter 7

THE DUTY OF LOYALTY

§ 7.1 Distinguishing Care and Loyalty

It is well-settled that directors have a duty to maximize shareholder wealth. As the Michigan supreme court famously observed in *Dodge v. Ford Motor Co.*: "A business corporation is organized and carried on primarily for the profit of the stockholders."[1] To be sure, in many settings, the business judgment rule will preclude judges from evaluating the shareholder wealth effects of board decisions. It is also well-settled, however, that the business judgment rule does not preclude judicial review of self-dealing transactions.

At first blush, the differing legal treatment of care and loyalty seems puzzling. Because both reduce shareholder wealth, negligence and self-dealing arguably differ more in degree than in kind.

On closer examination, however, loyalty does differ in kind, not just in degree, from care. Few of the arguments for insulating negligent board of director carry over to self-dealing. For example, decisions implicating the duty of care typically are collective actions of the board as a whole. In making such decisions, the board is constrained to exercise reasonable care in decisionmaking by a combination of external market forces and internal team governance structures. Judicial review thus is at best redundant and may, in fact, have deleterious consequences for the efficiency of decisionmaking.

In contrast, self-dealing typically is more difficult to detect than is negligence. Self-dealing transactions rarely implicate the entire board. To the contrary, they often involve misconduct by a single director. Those who intentionally self-deal, moreover, likely will also actively seek to conceal their defalcations. Given the potential gains of self-dealing in an organization characterized by a separation of ownership and control, legal liability thus may be a necessary deterrent against such misconduct. When an individual director engages in self-dealing, moreover, he has already betrayed the internal team relationships that characterize boards. Courts appropriately are less concerned about destroying internal team relationships in such cases.

---

[1] 170 N.W. 668, 684 (Mich.1919). See generally Chapter 9.

Yet, the intensity of judicial rhetoric in loyalty cases suggests something else is going on as well. Judge Cardozo's famous dictum on the duties of a partner, holding them to "something stricter than the morals of the market place,"[2] has provided a model for countless decisions excoriating those who self-deal. In part, this rhetoric likely rests on an assessment of self-dealing as reflecting greater moral culpability than does mere negligence. In part, however, judicial rhetoric in this area also likely reflects an attempt by judges to inculcate desirable social norms of honesty and trustworthiness.

As we review the material that follows, pay especially close attention to one question that frequently recurs; namely, to what extent does approval of a conflicted interest transaction by the board of directors or shareholders insulate that transaction from the exacting scrutiny usually applied to self-dealing?

§ 7.2 Conflicted Interest Transactions

Directors and officers frequently contract with or otherwise transact business with their corporations. Such transactions range from routine and pervasive, such as employment and compensation agreements, to unusual one-time events, such as a sale of real property. In either case, the director has an obvious conflict of interest.[3] On the one hand, the director is acting in his own self-interest, with an incentive to get the best possible deal. On the other hand, the director is a fiduciary with an obligation to maximize shareholder wealth.

Conflicted interest transactions take two forms. In a direct transaction, the director is dealing directly with the firm, such as where a director sells property to the firm. In an indirect transaction, a person or entity in which the director has an interest is dealing with the firm. Both types potentially create a conflict of interest. Indirect conflicted interest transactions, however, present greater problems in several respects. On the one hand, they are more likely to escape ex ante notice, whether because of deliberate concealment or mere inadvertence. On the other hand, as the director's interest becomes more attenuated, an indirect transaction may not rise to the level of a legitimate conflict of interest.[4]

---

[2] Meinhard v. Salmon, 164 N.E. 545, 546 (N.Y.1928).

[3] For semantic convenience, we shall refer solely to directors in this section. Unless otherwise indicated, however, the same legal principles also apply to conflicted interest transactions between an officer and the corporation.

[4] Absent classic self-dealing, in which the director stands on both sides of the transaction, the requisite benefit must be material or even "substantial." See Cinerama, Inc. v. Technicolor, Inc., 663 A.2d 1156, 1169 (Del.1995).

At early common law, conflicted interest transactions were voidable by the corporation without regard to whether they were fair to the corporation or had been approved by the board or shareholders.[5] At an abstract level, prohibiting conflicted interest transactions fails to give due deference to the principles of party autonomy and freedom of contract, which are important values both in themselves and because they promote efficient transactions. At a practical level, many transactions between the corporation and a director prove beneficial to both sides. If a director owns a valuable piece of property, which would be useful to the corporation, should not the director be allowed to sell it to the firm? Yet, what rational director would do so under the early common law rule? A rule that makes conflicted interest contracts voidable at the corporation's option in effect gives the firm a put option in the underlying transaction. If the deal goes sour, the corporation can walk away from it, which will deter directors from making such contracts in the first place. Accordingly, consistent with the general modern corporate law trend of policing conflicts of interest rather than prohibiting them, the law gradually moved towards permitting interested director transactions subject to judicial review. Modern statutes have even further liberalized this area.[6]

A.   Common Law Evolution

In 1918, the New York court of appeals decided the oft-cited case of *Globe Woolen Co. v. Utica Gas & Electric Co.*[7] John F. Maynard was the major shareholder, president, and a board member of Globe, a textile manufacturer. Maynard also was a director of Utica, a utility. Globe had long considered converting its mills to electrical power; but Maynard had insisted on a guaranty that electricity would be cheaper than the plants' existing steam-generated power. A Utica employee, Greenidge, presented to Maynard the results of a study claiming such a conversion would

---

[5] See, e.g., Cuthbert v. McNeill, 142 A. 819, 820 (N.J.Ch.1928) ("a director of a corporation cannot deal with the corporation which he represents. It does not matter how much good faith may have been exercised on his part, his contracts with his corporation are voidable at the instance of the corporation—they will not stand if repudiated as contracts" by the corporation).

[6] Sarbanes-Oxley Act § 402 bars publicly held corporations registered with the SEC from directly or indirectly lending or arranging for the extension of credit to their own officers or directors. Prior to § 402, such loans were permitted by state corporate law so long as the firm complied with the rules discussed in this section. The state law rules, of course, still apply to related party transactions in close corporations.

In addition, Sarbanes-Oxley § 406 requires a corporation to adopt a code of ethics applicable to its CEO, CFO, controller, and chief accountant. If the company fails to do so, it must disclose that failure and explain its reasons for not adopting the required code. In order to pass muster, the ethics code must provide for "the ethical handling of actual or apparent conflicts of interest between personal and professional relationships."

[7] 121 N.E. 378 (N.Y.1918).

generate considerable savings for Globe. Based on that study, Maynard and Greenidge prepared a contract for Utica to supply power to Globe, which included a guarantee that Globe would realize savings of $300 per month. The contract was brought before the Utica board of directors' executive committee for approval. At the meeting, one director asked whether the deal was a profitable contract for Utica, to which Greenidge responded affirmatively. A resolution was then moved and carried that the directors approve the contract. A subsequent contract further obligated Utica with respect to any expansion of the mills. It also provided that, in the case of a shortage of power, Globe would get preference over every other customer except the city. These changes were not disclosed to the board, which was told that the second contract was practically identical to the first. Again the contract was ratified by the board.

As to both contracts, Maynard presided over the meeting, but did not vote. The contracts proved unprofitable for Utica. It is not clear why. The problems may have resulted from a change in the mills' operations, which required additional power, or because steam may have been more efficient since excess steam was used for heating. In any event, by the time things came to a head, Utica never had been paid a dime for the power it supplied. To the contrary, Utica owed Globe about $12,000 under the guaranty. Utica sought to void the contract.

In an opinion by Judge Cardozo, the court first held that the transaction would have been voidable if Maynard had voted for it. Because Maynard did not vote, however, the transaction received a presumption of propriety. Yet, even so, the director remains subject to "the duty of constant and unqualified fidelity." In order for a conflicted interest transaction to stand as valid, it must be ratified by a fully informed and disinterested majority of the board and be fair to the corporation. "There must be candor and equity in the transaction, and some reasonable proportion between benefits and burdens." The contract at bar failed both prongs of this conjunctive standard. Maynard failed to disclose material facts about planned changes in Globe's business that rendered the contract a loser for Utica. As to fairness, no matter what changes Globe made in the mills' operations, Utica was still held to its guarantee. As a result, Utica supplied power for free—indeed, it had to pay for the privilege.

Because *Globe Woolen* phrased the disclosure and fairness standards in the conjunctive, and per se voided the contract if the director failed to abstain from voting, entering into conflicted interest transactions remained a risky proposition. As the 20th Century wore on, however, the law continued to liberalize. In the New York supreme court's subsequent *Bayer v. Beran* decision, for example, the court evaluated an indirect interested director transaction implicating the president of Celanese Corporation.[8] The firm sold a type of rayon fabric under the trade name "Celanese." In order to appeal to an up-scale clientele, the firm invested a good deal of effort in convincing consumers that Celanese was not really rayon, a project that eventually ran afoul of Federal Trade Commission fair advertising rules. After the FTC in 1937 required that the firm's product be marketed under the name "celanese rayon," the corporation began a new advertising campaign directed at up-scale consumers. As part of that campaign, the corporation in 1941 started sponsoring a classical music radio program.

A conflict of interest arose when Jean Tennyson, wife of the corporation's president, Camille Dreyfus, was hired to sing on the program. The board of directors did not formally vote to approve Tennyson's contract and, in fact, were unaware of her participation in the project until after the project as a whole had been approved. Indeed, the project itself had been approved only informally.

Failure to obtain formal approval by a disinterested majority following full disclosure would have damned the contract under *Globe Woolen*. Yet, the court declined to impose liability on Dreyfus or his fellow directors. Because of the conflict of interest, the business judgment rule did not apply. Instead, Dreyfus and the other directors bore the burden of proving the fairness of the transaction. After "careful scrutiny," however, the court deemed the contract to be fair. Tennyson's compensation was reasonable, the program was not designed to further her career, and the company got its money's worth from the radio campaign.[9] As a result, a fair transaction would be upheld even if it was not approved by the board, which made transacting business with one's corporation a much less risky proposition.

B.   Interested Director Statutes

Conflicted interest transactions today are governed by so-called interested director statutes, of which DGCL § 144 is typical. Section 144(a) states that an conflicted interest transaction shall not be "void or voidable solely" because of the director's conflict or "solely because the director or officer is present at or participates in the meeting of the board or committee which authorizes the contract or transaction, or solely because any such director's or officer's votes are counted for such purpose," provided at least one of three conditions are satisfied. Subsection (a)(1) shields transactions

---

[8] 49 N.Y.S.2d 2 (Sup.Ct.1944).

[9] ALI PRINCIPLES § 5.08 adopts a new rule prohibiting directors from knowingly advancing the pecuniary interests of their associates, a term that includes spouses.

approved by "a majority of the disinterested directors" provided there has been full disclosure of the material facts relating both to the transaction and to the director's conflict of interest. Subsection (a)(2) shields transactions "specifically approved in good faith by vote of the shareholders," again following full disclosure. Subsection (a)(3) shields a transaction that is "fair as to the corporation as of the time it is authorized, approved or ratified, by the board of directors, a committee or the shareholders."[10] The three subsections are in the disjunctive, so satisfying any one will invoke the statute's protection for the challenged transaction.

1. Approval of Conflicted Interest Transactions by a Disinterested Board Majority

Under DGCL § 144(b), an interested director may be counted towards the quorum necessary for board action.[11] Subsection (a) rejects common law cases like *Globe Woolen* that invalidate a conflicted interest transaction solely because the interested director voted on the transaction. Subsection (a) also rejects common law cases invalidating transactions in which a majority of the board is interested. So long as the transaction is approved by a majority of disinterested directors, even if they be less than a quorum, the transaction is not void or voidable solely on any of those grounds.

Because the statute does not fully validate related party transactions, but only shields them from per se invalidation, a critical question is whether valid action under the statute precludes judicial review of a properly approved transaction. Unfortunately, there is surprisingly little case law on the effect of approval by the

---

[10] In Marciano v. Nakash, 535 A.2d 400 (Del.1987), the Delaware supreme court rejected a claim that § 144 is the sole means of validating conflicted interest transactions under Delaware law. Section 144 did not preempt the common law, but instead simply overturned those common law cases deeming conflicted interest transactions voidable per se. Modern Delaware common law does not purport to invalidate conflicted interest transactions solely by virtue of the director's interest. Instead, such a transaction will be upheld, so long as the director proves it was fair to the corporation. Id. at 404.

[11] There is an interesting distinction between the general director voting rule set out in DGCL § 141(b) and that of § 144(a)(1). The former looks to whether the proposed action was approved by a "majority of the directors present at a meeting at which a quorum is present." The latter requires the "affirmative votes of a majority of the disinterested directors." Note the absence of the qualifying word "present" in the latter. Suppose the corporation has 5 directors, one of whom is interested in the transaction. Two of the four disinterested directors attend the board meeting at which the transaction is to be approved. Because the interested director counts towards a quorum, they can proceed to vote. Assume both disinterested directors vote to approve the transaction, while the interested director abstains. A majority of the directors present at the meeting voted for the transaction, so it is properly approved for purposes of § 141(b). Yet, two out of four disinterested directors is not a majority and, as such, the transaction seemingly has not been approved for purposes of § 144(a)(1). Cf. Beneville v. York, 769 A.2d 80, 82 (Del.Ch.2000) (noting that under "traditional rules of board governance" a motion on which the board is evenly divided fails). Presumably the transaction therefore would have to pass muster under § 144(a)(3).

disinterested directors. The leading Delaware case remains *Puma v. Marriott*,[12] in which a disgruntled Marriott Corporation shareholder challenged the corporation's purchase of six other companies from the Marriott family. At the time of the transaction, the Marriott family collectively owned 44% of Marriott Corporation's stock. Four of the nine directors were Marriott family members. The acquisition was unanimously approved by the five disinterested directors. Without reference to § 144, the court held that on those facts the business judgment rule was the applicable standard of review.

Some commentators contend the same rule applies to transactions reviewed under § 144(a)(1).[13] Dicta in at least one Delaware supreme court decision seemingly supports this view.[14] It also is supported by a few decisions from other jurisdictions interpreting comparable statutes.[15]

2. Approval of Conflicted Interest Transactions by Shareholders

In *Fliegler v. Lawrence*,[16] defendant John C. Lawrence was president of Agau Mines, Inc., a gold and silver mining corporation. Lawrence had individually acquired some antimony properties, which he offered to Agau. In consultation with Lawrence, the Agau board declined on grounds that the corporation's legal and financial position did not allow it to undertake the venture. Lawrence then formed the United States Antimony Co. (USAC), to which the properties were transferred. USAC granted Agau an option to acquire USAC in exchange for Agau stock, which Agau eventually exercised. The decision to exercise the option was approved by the shareholders. Dissenting Agau shareholders then sued.

Defendants relied on DGCL § 144(a)(2) in arguing that shareholder approval relieved defendants of the common law obligation to prove the transaction's fairness. The court agreed that shareholder ratification of a conflicted interest transaction shifted

---

[12] 283 A.2d 693 (Del.Ch.1971).

[13] See, e.g., Michael P. Dooley, Two Models of Corporate Governance, 47 Bus. Law. 461, 490 (1992); Charles Hansen et al., The Role of Disinterested Directors in "Conflict" Transactions: The ALI Corporate Governance Project and Existing Law, 45 Bus. Law. 2083, 2093–94 (1990). But see Melvin Aron Eisenberg, Self-Interested Transactions in Corporate Law, 13 J. Corp. L. 997, 1005 (1988) (contending that "approval by disinterested directors should not insulate a self-interested transaction from judicial review for fairness").

[14] Marciano v. Nakash, 535 A.2d 400, 405 n. 3 (Del.1987) (opining that "approval by fully-informed disinterested directors under section 144(a)(1) . . . permits invocation of the business judgment rule and limits judicial review to issues of gift or waste with the burden of proof upon the party attacking the transaction").

[15] See, e.g., Cohen v. Ayers, 596 F.2d 733, 740 (7th Cir.1979) (under New York law, after approval by the disinterested directors, "the business judgment rule is again applicable [to an interested director transaction] and the plaintiff can succeed only by meeting the burden applicable to challenges of any corporate transaction").

[16] 361 A.2d 218 (Del.1976).

the burden of proof from the defendants to the objecting shareholders. On the facts of this case, however, the burden would not shift. A majority of the shares voted in favor of the transaction had been cast by the interested defendants in their capacities as Agau shareholders. In the court's view, those votes should not count. Instead, only the votes cast by disinterested shareholders count and only the vote of a majority of such disinterested shareholders has the desired burden-shifting effect.

The court's reading of § 144 is inconsistent with a plain-meaning approach to statutory construction. Section 144(a)(1) requires approval by "a majority of the disinterested directors," but § 144(a)(2) requires only approval by a "vote of the shareholders." The statute's drafters thus inserted a requirement of disinterest in (a)(1) but not in (a)(2). Accordingly, on the face of the statute, shareholder approval ought to be effective even if the shareholders are not disinterested.

Although the court was not faithful to the statutory language, its interpretation does appeal to common sense. Cases arising under these statutes confront courts with issues of ethics and morality, principles of fiduciary obligation, and situations in which the facts are all important. Consequently, the courts tend to treat the precise language of these provisions somewhat cavalierly.

Assuming disinterested shareholder approval were to be obtained, what effect would such approval have on judicial review of the transaction? In broad dicta, the Delaware supreme court rejected a defense argument that shareholder approval precluded judicial review of the transaction:

> We do not read the statute as providing the broad immunity for which defendants contend. It merely removes an "interested director" cloud when its terms are met and provides against invalidation of an agreement "solely" because such a director or officer is involved. Nothing in the statute sanctions unfairness to Agau or removes the transaction from judicial scrutiny.[17]

After an extended analysis of the transaction's history and terms, the court concluded the deal was fair to Agau and held for defendants.

---

[17] Fliegler v. Lawrence, 361 A.2d 218, 222 (Del.1976). See also Lewis v. S.L. & E., Inc., 629 F.2d 764, 769 (2d Cir.1980) (interpreting New York's conflicted interest statute as allowing judicial scrutiny of the transaction's fairness); Remillard v. Remillard-Dandini Co., 241 P.2d 66, 73 (Cal.App.1952) ("Even though the requirements of § 820 [California's conflicted interest transaction statute] are technically met, transactions that are unfair and unreasonable to the corporation may be avoided.").

Under *Fliegler*, disinterested shareholder approval thus does not preclude judicial review. Shareholder approval or ratification of a conflicted interest transaction, however, does not simply shift the burden of proof with respect to the fairness of a transaction. An objecting shareholder cannot prevail simply by showing that a properly approved transaction is unfair. Fairness was the standard of review in *Fliegler* because § 144(a)(2), as interpreted by the court, had not been satisfied. If § 144(a)(2) had been satisfied, the burden of proof would have shifted to the objecting shareholders to 'demonstrate that the terms are so unequal as to amount to a gift or waste of corporate assets." Put another way: "Approval by fully informed, disinterested shareholders pursuant to § 144(a)(2) invokes 'the business judgment rule and limits judicial review to issues of gift or waste with the burden of proof upon the party attacking the transaction.' "[18]

3.   Fairness Absent Valid Approval or Ratification

DGCL § 144(a)(3) shields from voidability those transactions that are fair to the corporation "as of the time" they are approved or ratified by the board or shareholders. Section 144(a)(3) thus covers situations in which board or shareholder approval was obtained but in a manner inadequate for purposes of subsections (a)(1) or (a)(2). Subsection (a)(3) applies, for example, where the interested director failed to disclose material facts.[19] Alternatively, it would also apply where the approval was effected by the vote of interested parties.

The interested director bears the burden of proving the transaction's fairness.[20] What are the hallmarks of a fair transaction? One might plausibly determine fairness by asking whether the terms of the transaction are within the range of terms to which disinterested parties bargaining at arms-length might have agreed. In *HMG/Courtland Properties v. Gray*,[21] however, Vice Chancellor Strine rejected that interpretation on the grounds that failure to disclose material facts is highly relevant to a determination of fairness. If undisclosed facts had been known to the corporation, it might have insisted on terms at the low end of the range of fair value or refused to transact at all.

---

[18] In re Wheelabrator Tech., Inc., Shareholders Litig., 663 A.2d 1194, 1203 (Del.Ch.1995) (quoting Marciano v. Nakash, 535 A.2d 400, 405 n. 3 (Del.1987)).

[19] Cede & Co. v. Technicolor, Inc., 634 A.2d 345, 366 n. 34 (Del.1993) ("a nondisclosing interested director can remove the taint of interestedness by proving the entire fairness of the challenged transaction").

[20] Marciano v. Nakash, 535 A.2d 400, 405 n. 3 (Del.1987).

[21] 749 A.2d 94 (Del.Ch.1999). See also U.S. v. Lemire, 720 F.2d 1327, 1336 n. 10 (D.C.Cir.1983) ("where an official of the corporation does not disclose his personal interest in a transaction, the transaction is merely voidable and the company may choose to go ahead with the transaction . . . as long as the transaction is fair to the corporation").

Under *HMG/Courtland Properties*, a transaction is not unfair solely because there are undisclosed material facts. Such an interpretation would be inconsistent with the clear thrust of § 144(a)(3), which contemplates that transactions may be deemed fair even though the requisite board or shareholder approval was tainted by nondisclosures. Indeed, such an interpretation would essentially negate subsection (a)(3) as to the class of transactions as to which it is most likely to apply. Instead, *HMG/Courtland Properties* simply requires nondisclosing defendants to show that (1) the terms of the deal were within the range of fair value and (2) the corporation would not have gotten a materially better deal if the defendants had "come clean."

Finally, suppose the corporation's CEO approved a contract with a director without referring the transaction to the board or shareholders. Absent the director's conflict of interest, such a transaction normally would be binding. As an agent of the corporation, its CEO has expansive actual and apparent authority to enter into contracts on behalf of the corporation. As for the conflict of interest issue, however, DGCL § 144(a)(3) is inapplicable, because the transaction received neither board nor shareholder approval. Recall, however, that § 144 is not the only means of validating conflicted interest transactions under Delaware law. If the director proves the transaction was fair to the corporation, no liability will result.[22]

4.   MBCA Subchapter F

Former MBCA 8.31 largely tracked DGCL § 144, although there were a few key differences. MBCA § 8.31(a)(1) allowed directors to approve or ratify a conflicted interest transaction, while DGCL § 144(a)(1) speaks only of authorization. MBCA § 8.31(a)(3) ambiguously referred to transactions that are "fair to the corporation," while DGCL § 144(a)(3) is limited to transactions that are fair to the corporation "as of the time" they are approved or ratified by the board of shareholders. Note how this distinction implicated not only timing issues, but also the validity of transactions that are unapproved by either board or shareholders. Although former MBCA § 8.31 remains on the books in many states, in the Model Act it has been superseded by new subchapter F.

A striking difference between subchapter F and its predecessor—or DGCL § 144, for that matter—is the sheer level of

---

[22] Marciano v. Nakash, 535 A.2d 400, 403 (Del.1987).

complexity.[23] Section 8.60 opens with a purportedly bright-line definition of "conflicted interest" transactions. Such transactions include not those effected or proposed to be effected by the corporation, but also those by a subsidiary of the corporation or any other entity which the corporation controls. In order for the transaction to be a conflicted one, however, the director must know when the deals is made that the director or "a related person" is a party to the transaction.[24] The director also must know that he or a related person has a beneficial financial interest in the transaction or is so closely linked to the transaction that the interest would reasonably be expected to exert an influence on the director's judgment if the director were called upon to vote on the transaction.[25] Note that the foregoing definition encompasses mainly classic self-dealing of the sort defined as direct interests. MBCA § 8.60(1)(ii) addresses indirect interests, deeming such interests conflicting when the director knows that the other party is an entity of which the director is an owner, employee, or an affiliate of such an entity.

Subsection 8.61(a) then preempts the field of conflicted interest transactions. Unlike DGCL § 144, which does not preempt the common law, MBCA subchapter F is intended to do so. If a transaction does not satisfy the statutory definition of a conflicted interest transaction, no liability or equitable relief may be granted on grounds that the director had an interest in the transaction. Suppose a corporation enters into a contract with the cousin of a director. Cousins are not related persons as defined by the statute. The contract thus is not a conflicted interest transaction, as defined by the statute, and a court has no authority to set it aside or otherwise grant relief. Similarly, where the director's allegedly conflicted interest arises out of nonfinancial considerations, such as the desire to join a country club, the court lacks authority to intervene.

As to transactions falling within the statutory definition of a conflicted interest transaction, subsection 8.61(b) creates three safe harbors. If any of the three is satisfied, a court may neither enjoin or set aside the transaction nor impose liability in connection with it on grounds that the director had an interest in the transaction. Approval by a fully informed majority of disinterested directors

---

[23] Another difference is that subchapter F applies only to directors, not officers. Conflicts of interest on the part of officers, as well as nonofficer employees, are left to agency law.

[24] Related person is defined by § 8.60(3) to include "the spouse (or a parent or sibling thereof) of the director, or a child, grandchild, sibling, parent (or spouse of any thereof) of the director, or an individual having the same home as the director," plus specified trusts and estates.

[25] MBCA § 8.60(1)(i).

(who must number at least two) suffices.[26] So does approval by fully informed shareholders.[27] Alternatively, absent the requisite approvals, a transaction is validated if fair to the corporation.[28]

The third safe harbor obviously contemplates judicial review of the transaction's merits. As with Delaware law, moreover, the concept of fairness embraces both the terms of the deal and the course of dealing by the interested party. If the interested director failed to disclose material information, for example, the court may treat the transaction as voidable or even impose monetary damages.[29]

C. Executive Compensation

Although executive compensation long has been a subject of intense controversy in both the popular and academic literature, it presents few doctrinal complexities. A compensation contract between the corporation and one of its officers does not differ in kind from any other conflicted interest transaction covered by the statutes considered in this section. If the disinterested directors, following full disclosure, approve the contract in good faith, the transaction will receive the protection of the business judgment rule.[30] Accordingly, many public corporations have established compensation committees staffed by independent directors to review and approve executive compensation.

As a result, successful shareholder challenges to executive compensation typically involve close corporations in which disinterested director approval was not (or could not) be obtained. In such cases, the burden of proof remains on the defendant executive to prove that the compensation was fair to the corporation. In *Wilderman v. Wilderman*,[31] for example, the Delaware chancery court identified a number of factors to be considered: (1) whether the Internal Revenue Service allowed the

---

[26] MBCA §§ 8.61(b)(1) and 8.62.

[27] MBCA §§ 8.61(b)(2) and 8.63. MBCA § 8.60(7) specifies the disclosure required by the interested director to include the existence and nature of the conflict and all facts known to the director "that a director free of such conflicting interest would reasonably believe to be material in deciding whether to proceed with the transaction."

[28] MBCA § 8.61(b)(3).

[29] MBCA 8 8.61 cmt.

[30] See, e.g., Zupnick v. Goizueta, 698 A.2d 384 (Del.Ch.1997) (after holding that approval of a stock option-based compensation plan by the disinterested directors shifted the burden of proof to plaintiff to show waste, the court further held: "To state a cognizable claim for waste where there is no contention that the directors were interested or that shareholder ratification was improperly obtained, the well-pleaded allegations of the complaint must support the conclusion that 'no person of ordinary, sound business judgment would say that the consideration received for the options was a fair exchange for the options granted.' ").

[31] 315 A.2d 610 (Del.Ch.1974).

corporation to take a deduction for the challenged compensation (unreasonable compensation may not be deducted); (2) the value of the challenged compensation relative to that paid other employees; (3) the ability of the executive; (4) the executive's salary history; (5) and whether the salary is reasonable in relation to the corporation's success.

§ 7.3   Corporate Opportunities

The doctrine generically known as "organizational opportunities" deals with situations in which an agent usurps a business opportunity that rightfully belongs to the principal. In doing so, the agent has violated his fiduciary duty to the principal by usurping this opportunity for his own gain. This prohibition of against usurping organizational opportunities is found in agency law, partnership law, and, in its most developed form, corporate law.

A.   Delaware's Standard

Guth v. Loft, Inc. remains Delaware's classic statement of the corporate opportunity doctrine.[32] Loft was a manufacturer and retailer of candy, syrups, drinks and food. It did not manufacture a cola syrup, instead selling Coke in its retail outlets. Charles Guth was the president and a director of Loft. To greatly simplify a complex set of facts, Guth obtained effective control of the then-struggling Pepsi-Cola Corporation. Guth then began a clandestine program of using Loft funds, facilities, and employees to get Pepsi off the ground. Loft later sued Guth on the grounds that the chance to acquire Pepsi was a corporate opportunity. In other words, Loft alleged that Guth had a duty to give Loft an informed chance to acquire Pepsi before doing so himself. Put yet another way, Loft essentially claimed that Guth had to give Loft a right of first refusal to acquire Pepsi.

At that time, there were three common law tests used by the courts to determine whether or not something was a corporate opportunity. The *Guth* court invoked all three: First, it identified what is now known as the line of business test. Is the business venture in question intimately or closely associated with the existing or prospective businesses of the corporation? On that score, the court held Pepsi was squarely within Loft's lines of business. As noted, Loft was both a manufacturer and purchaser of soft drink syrups. Although it was not presently in the business of making cola syrups, the court held that the line of business test had to allow for future development or expansion of the firm. Making cola syrups was within Loft's reasonable future business. Loft had a continuing

---

[32]   5 A.2d 503 (Del.1939).

business need for cola syrups to supply its retail outlets. Then, as now, cola-flavored syrups were the major soft drink product. Indeed, because Guth had used the powers of his position as president to terminate Loft's contract with Coca-Cola, that on-going need had been greatly exacerbated.[33] Loft also had the knowledge, experience and resources necessary to exploit the Pepsi opportunity. The combination of the need and the ability brought the Pepsi opportunity within Loft's line of business.[34]

Second, the court asked whether Loft had a prior interest or expectancy in the opportunity. Arguably, one could distinguish between an interest and an expectancy. A director or officer takes the corporation's "interest" if he takes something to which the firm has a better right. The director or officer takes an "expectancy" if he takes something which, in the ordinary course of things, would come to the corporation—i.e., something the corporation could expect to receive. If an officer bought land to which the corporation had a contractual right, for example, the officer took an "interest." If the officer took the renewal rights to a lease the corporation had, the officer took an "expectancy."

As a practical matter, however, courts do not make such fine distinctions.[35] When Guth discontinued Loft's contract with Coca Cola, for example, it became a matter of business necessity that Loft acquire an alternative source of cola syrups. Because Guth's actions created the need, the court opined, Loft had an equitable interest in the opportunity to buy Pepsi. Loft also had an equitable interest in Pepsi because of the way in which Guth handled the transaction. Guth's use of corporate funds and facilities to operate Pepsi for his own personal profit amounted to stealing from the company, giving the company an equitable right to the fruits of his theft.

---

[33] In his capacity as Loft's president, Guth terminated the supply contract with Coca-Cola. Guth then caused Loft to enter into a supply contract with Pepsi. Note that Guth's conduct thus also implicated the conflict of interest transaction doctrine discussed in the preceding section. A corporate officer or director may only compete with the corporation if the competition involves no breach of duty. Here there was a clear cut breach of duty because of Guth's self-dealing. He controlled Loft and thus could force it to buy syrup from Pepsi; he controlled Pepsi and thus could set the terms on which the syrup would be supplied. By being on both sides of the transaction he had a rather pronounced conflict of interest.

[34] In Beam ex rel. Martha Stewart Living Omnimedia, Inc. v. Stewart, 833 A.2d 961 (Del.Ch.2003), aff'd, 845 A.2d 1040 (Del.2004), the court said a venture is within the corporation's line of business if it is "an activity as to which [the corporation] has fundamental knowledge, practical experience and ability to pursue."

[35] See, e.g., Southeast Consultants, Inc. v. McCrary Engineering Corp., 273 S.E.2d 112, 117 (Ga.1980) (asking whether the corporation had a " 'beachhead' in the sense of an equitable expectancy growing out of a pre-existing relationship"); Shapiro v. Greenfield, 764 A.2d 270, 278 (Md.App.2000) (noting that Maryland uses the interest or expectancy standard, which it said is focused "on whether the corporation could realistically expect to seize and develop the opportunity").

Finally, the court looked to the capacity in which Guth discovered the opportunity. Pepsi's prior owner had not approached Guth in his personal capacity, but rather as Loft's president. If it had been the other way around, however, Guth might have been allowed to take the opportunity. The capacity standard is highly problematic. Every director or officer will claim that the opportunity was presented to him in his individual capacity. Courts therefore should ignore the form of the transaction, on the assumption that the deal was structured to create an appearance of individual capacity, and put a heavy burden of proof on the director to show that it was presented to him as an individual. Where the sole evidence is the director's word, the court should presume that the opportunity was presented to him in his capacity as a director or officer.

Guth, of course, is an easy case. Not only did Guth appropriate an opportunity that Loft could have exploited, but he also engaged in a massive campaign of self-dealing and outright theft. Analysis by platitude more than sufficed. Subsequent cases involving less egregious conduct therefore have helped flesh out the doctrine.

In *Broz v. Cellular Information Systems, Inc.*,[36] Robert Broz was the sole shareholder and President of RFB Cellular, Inc., a small cell phone company. Broz was also a member of the board of Cellular Information Systems, Inc., which also provided cell phone service. David Rhodes, a broker, informed Broz of an opportunity to acquire a cellular telephone service license called Michigan–2, which would entitle the buyer to provide cell phone service to an area in rural Michigan. RFB Cellular already owned and operated a similar license known as Michigan–4.

Broz bought Michigan–2 for RFB Cellular without formally offering it to Cellular Information Systems. Before doing so, Broz did mention the opportunity informally to Richard Treibick, Cellular Information Systems' CEO and to Peter Schiff, a Cellular Information Systems board member, both of whom expressed a lack of interest on Cellular Information Systems' behalf. During the relevant time period, Cellular Information Systems was in financial difficulty and was in the process of being acquired by PriCellular, Inc., yet another cell phone operator. PriCellular was bidding on the Michigan–2 license, a fact of which Treibick was well aware. Broz outbid ProCellular. Because of financing difficulties, PriCellular's acquisition of Cellular Information Systems was not completed until shortly after RFB Cellular's successful bid for the license. Once PriCellular completed its acquisition of Cellular Information Systems, it caused Cellular Information Systems to sue Broz for

---

[36] 673 A.2d 148 (Del.1996).

breach of fiduciary duty, claiming that Broz had usurped the Michigan–2 opportunity.

The Delaware supreme court held Broz had not violated his fiduciary obligation to Cellular Information Systems by failing to formally offer the Michigan–2 license to Cellular Information Systems. The court identified four relevant considerations: (1) Is the corporation financially able to take the opportunity? (2) Is the opportunity in the corporation's line of business? (3) Does the corporation have an interest or expectancy in the opportunity? (4) Does an officer or director create a conflict between his self-interest and that of the corporation by taking the opportunity for himself?

The line of business factor obviously was satisfied. Cellular Information Systems was in the business of operating cellular phone franchises. Michigan–2 was a cellular phone franchise. Yet, Cellular Information Systems' stated business plans did not contemplate further expansion of its cellular phone business. To the contrary, Cellular Information Systems was divesting some of its existing licenses. Accordingly, Cellular Information Systems had no interest or expectancy in the license. The court further emphasized that Cellular Information Systems lacked the financial capacity to acquire the Michigan–2 license. Cellular Information Systems had only recently emerged from a bankruptcy reorganization and remained in a precarious financial position. Finally, just as Guth was clearly a bad guy, Broz was a good guy. The court took pains to stress that formal processes were not required. Broz did not have to formally present the opportunity to Cellular Information Systems' board, not did that board have to formally reject the opportunity, before Broz was free to take it. Formal processes may create a safe harbor, but they are not required.

The standard that emerges from cases like *Guth* and *Broz* is not very precise. The lists of relevant considerations differ not just in number but also in substantive content. In *Guth*, the capacity in which the director or officer learned of the opportunity is one of the relevant factors. In *Broz*, the court merely "note[s] at the outset" that Broz learned of the Michigan–2 opportunity in his individual capacity and, moreover, emphasizes that this fact is not dispositive.

The listed considerations also seems somewhat arbitrary. One could readily construct a longer laundry list of factors that seem at least as relevant as those on which the *Guth* and *Broz* courts relied. For example, one might readily consider such facts as: (1) Were there prior negotiations with the firm about the opportunity? (2) Did the director conceal the opportunity from the firm? (3) Did the director make use of corporate funds or property in exploiting the opportunity? (4) Will the opportunity involve competition with the firm or otherwise thwart firm policy? (5) Did the corporation have a substantial need that the opportunity would have filled? (6) Did the corporation have the necessary technical resources to exploit the opportunity? (7) Is the director an insider?

Additional imprecision follows from the court's insistence that the listed considerations are factors not elements. Put another way, the court evaluates the director or officer's conduct under the totality of the circumstances.[37]

From a transactional planning standpoint, the lack of clear guidance places considerable value on obtaining a safe harbor. Formal presentment of the opportunity to the board may not be required by Delaware law, but it is surely the prudent course of action.

B.   The ALI Approach

ALI PRINCIPLES § 5.05 bifurcates the definitional and conduct inquiries, requiring the court to ask two distinct questions: (1) Was the business venture was a corporate opportunity within the definition of § 5.05(b)? (2) If so, was the venture properly rejected by the appropriate decisionmaker per § 5.05(a). The ALI PRINCIPLES thus focus on disclosure and rejection by the corporation.

ALI PRINCIPLES § 5.05(b) identifies four distinct ways in which a venture might be deemed a corporate opportunity. Note that the four definitions are phrased in the disjunctive, such that the venture will be deemed a corporate opportunity if any of the four is satisfied:

- A business venture of which a director or senior executive becomes aware in connection with the performance of his functions as a director or senior executive. (§ 5.05(b)(1)(A))

- A business venture of which a director or senior executive becomes aware under circumstances that should reasonably lead the director or senior executive to believe that the person offering the opportunity expects it to be offered to the corporation. (§ 5.05(b)(1)(A))

- A business venture of which a director or senior executive becomes aware through the use of corporation information or property and which the

---

[37] See Broz v. Cellular Information Systems, Inc., 673 A.2d 148 (Del.1996) ("the totality of the circumstances indicates that Broz did not usurp an opportunity that properly belonged to CIS").

director or senior executive reasonably should be
expected to believe would be of interest to the
corporation. (§ 5.05(b)(1)(B))

- Any business venture of which a senior executive
becomes aware and knows is closely related to a
business in which the corporation is engaged or
expects to engage. (§ 5.05(b)(2))

Note that the fourth definition, which resembles the common law
line of business standard, applies only to senior executives. Outside
directors thus have greater freedom to engage in business ventures
that fall within the firm's line of business.

Suppose the Delaware supreme court had adopted this
approach. Would *Broz* have been decided any differently? Probably
not. Michigan–2 likely would be deemed a corporate opportunity
under § 5.05(b)(2), but that section applies only to senior executives.
As for the other three categories, the *Broz* facts do not fall within
any of them. Broz learned of the opportunity in his individual
capacity, not while performing corporate functions. The broker who
brought the venture to Broz's attention specifically avoided offering
it to the firm. Broz made no use of corporate property or assets.

If a venture is deemed a corporate opportunity, § 5.05(a)
generally requires disclosure and rejection by a proper corporate
decisionmaker. As for the disclosure prong of the standard, there
must be full disclosure of both the venture and the resulting conflict
of interest. Per ALI PRINCIPLES § 5.05(d), good faith but defective
disclosure may be cured by corrective disclosure followed by
ratification of the decision by the corporate decisionmaker who
initially made the decision to reject it.

As for the rejection prong, a post-disclosure rejection of the
opportunity by an appropriate corporate decisionmaker does not
foreclose judicial review but does affect the standard of review. The
disinterested shareholders may either reject the venture before the
director or senior executive takes it or ratify a prior taking. If there
is valid shareholder action, judicial review is limited to determining
whether the decision amounts to a waste of corporate assets, with
the burden of proof on the plaintiff.[38] The disinterested directors
may reject a venture before it is taken by a director, but may not
ratify a taking ex post.[39] In the case of a senior executive who is not
a director, the venture may be rejected in advance—but not
ratified—by a disinterested superior. In either of the latter cases,
the business judgment rule provides the standard of review.

---

[38] ALI PRINCIPLES § 5.05(a)(3)(C).
[39] ALI PRINCIPLES § 5.05(a)(3)(B).

Finally, if none of those conditions are satisfied, a director or senior executive can also avoid liability by showing that the transaction was fair to the corporation.[40]

Note that all of these provisions require an affirmative rejection of the opportunity by some decisionmaker acting on the corporation's behalf. Is a director or officer per se liable for taking an opportunity without first presenting it to the board? Not per se, but the odds of escaping liability are slim. If the only reason the officer or director did not offer the opportunity to the corporation was a good faith belief that the business venture was not a corporate opportunity, § 5.05(e) is applicable. This section permits ex post ratification under those circumstances. When § 5.05(e) is read together with § 5.05(a), however, it appears that only ex post ratification by the disinterested shareholders will be availing. Consequently, the fairness of the defendant's conduct standing alone is not a defense under § 5.05. This seemingly harsh rule is justified by the need for certainty and the need to encourage directors and senior executives to resolve close cases in favor of disclosure.

C. Defenses

1. Capacity

Those charged with usurping a corporate opportunity frequently defend their conduct by claiming they learned of the opportunity in their individual—rather than corporate—capacity. Under Delaware law, the capacity in which the defendant learned of the opportunity is a relevant, but not dispositive, consideration.[41] Under the ALI approach, capacity is relevant to determining whether the business venture meets the definition of a corporate opportunity. On the one hand, if the director or senior executive learns of the venture while performing corporate functions, the venture is a corporate opportunity.[42] On the other hand, where a senior executive is concerned, a venture that falls within the corporation's line of business will be deemed a corporate opportunity without regard to the capacity in which the executive learned of the venture. Capacity thus is not a complete defense under either Delaware law or ALI approach.

2. Financial or Technical Inability

In many cases, the defendant will argue that the corporation lacked the money and/or the technical ability to exploit the

---

[40] ALI PRINCIPLES § 5.05(a)(3)(A).

[41] Broz v. Cellular Information Systems, Inc., 673 A.2d 148, 155 (Del.1996).

[42] ALI PRINCIPLES § 5.05(b)(1)(A).

opportunity. In *General Automotive Manufacturing Co. v. Singer*,[43] for example, defendant Singer was a key managerial employee of General Automotive, a small firm engaged in the business of machine shop jobbing. Singer's employment contract called for him to devote his "entire time, skill, labor and attention" to the job, and to work 5 1/2 days per week. When customers sent business to Singer that he believed General Automotive could not handle, Singer sent the work out to other shops, taking a finder's fee from the customer. Singer took the position that he was running a separate brokering business with respect to orders that General Automotive could not handle. Singer made a profit of $64,088 on his side business, which General Automotive sued to recover. Applying agency law principles analogous to the corporate opportunity doctrine, the court held that Singer had a duty to "exercise good faith by disclosing to Automotive all the facts regarding this matter."

Assume Singer sincerely believed that General Automotive could not handle the work. Assume Singer also sincerely believed that his own reputation might be impaired if General Automotive tried and failed. Even so, Singer should not make this decision on his own in light of his conflicting interest. Put another way, what is the harm in disclosure? On questions of an agent's duty to disclose, it is almost always decisive to ask: "Why didn't you tell me?"

The financial inability defense is even more problematic than the technical incapacity defense proffered by Singer. A director or officer frequently is involved in raising funds for the firm. Consequently, the financial inability defense creates an incentive for directors and officers to fail to use their best efforts to help the firm raise the necessary funds. Put another way, if the defendant director or officer could finance the venture, why should we not assume that the firm likely could have done so?[44] Conversely, if the defendant director or officer could finance the venture, but the corporation could not, why should we not encourage the director or officer to make his resources available to the corporation at a fair rate of return?[45]

---

[43] 120 N.W.2d 659 (Wis.1963).

[44] A showing that the director or officer failed to use his best efforts to raise the necessary funds will vitiate a financial ability defense. See, e.g., Banks v. Bryant, 497 So.2d 460, 462 (Ala.1986).

[45] At least one court has implied the existence of a duty for officers and directors of a solvent corporation to do so. See Irving Trust Co. v. Deutsch, 73 F.2d 121, 124 (2d Cir. 1934) (noting "the wisdom of a rigid rule forbidding directors of a solvent corporation to take over for their own profit a corporate contract on the plea of the corporation's financial inability to perform. If the directors are uncertain whether the corporation can make the necessary outlays, they need not embark it upon the venture; if they do, they may not substitute themselves for the corporation any place along the line and divert possible benefits into their own pockets."). But see Anderson v. Clemens Mobile Homes, Inc., 333 N.W.2d 900, 905 (Neb.1983)

Curiously, however, the Delaware supreme court allowed a variant of the financial inability defense in *Broz.* More precisely, the court identified the corporation's financial ability to effectively exploit the business venture as one of the considerations relevant in deciding whether the venture is a corporate opportunity.[46] Worse yet, a number of courts have held that financial and/or technical inability properly can be raised as affirmative defenses.[47]

If the corporation's financial or technical inability to exploit the venture must be considered either as a relevant consideration or an affirmative defense, a position we deplore in light of the perverse incentives it creates, courts still should be sensitive to the conflicted interests at issue in this setting. Consequently, courts should apply a stringent standard to determining financial or technical inability. Delaware Chancellor Chandler, for example, suggests the corporation must be practically defunct before the financial incapacity defense will be given weight. Technical insolvency, such as inability to pay current bills when due or inability to secure credit, is not enough—the corporation must be on the way down the tubes.[48]

3. Refusal to Deal

In *Energy Resources Corp. v. Porter*,[49] defendant James Porter was a vice-president and head scientist of plaintiff ERCO. Before joining ERCO, Porter had taught chemical engineering at MIT, where he apparently developed professional relationships with two Howard University professors named Cannon and Jackson. The three scientists developed a joint proposal to the Department of Energy for a research grant. Howard University was designated the lead applicant, with ERCO acting as a subcontractor. Porter, Cannon, and Jackson are all African-Americans. Howard University is a historically black college. Jackson subsequently decided that he did not want to serve as a front "for white firms getting minority money." Accordingly, Jackson persuaded Porter to leave ERCO and start his own firm (called EEE in the opinion). Jackson and Porter eliminated ERCO from the application,

---

(director has no duty "to use or pledge his personal funds to enable the corporation to take advantage of a business opportunity").

[46] Broz v. Cellular Information Sys., Inc., 673 A.2d 148, 155–56 (Del.1996).

[47] See, e.g., Katz Corp. v. T.H. Canty & Co., 362 A.2d 975, 980 (Conn.1975); CST, Inc. v. Mark, 520 A.2d 469, 471 (Pa.Super.1987). Cases rejecting financial inability as a defense include: W.H. Elliott & Sons Co. v. Gotthardt, 305 F.2d 544, 546–47 (1st Cir.1962); Irving Trust Co. v. Deutsch, 73 F.2d 121, 124 (2d Cir.1934); Electronic Dev. Co. v. Robson, 28 N.W.2d 130, 138 (Neb.1947).

[48] Stephanis v. Yiannatsis, 1993 WL 437487 at *4 (Del.Ch.1993) (quoting 18B Am. Jur. 2d Corporations § 1790 at 642–43 (1985)), aff'd on other grounds, 653 A.2d 275 (Del.1995).

[49] 438 N.E.2d 391 (Mass.App.1982).

substituting EEE as the subcontractor. Porter misled ERCO management as to both the status of the application and his reasons for quitting. After Jackson and Porter won the government grant, ERCO sued Porter for usurping a corporate opportunity.

Porter relied on the so-called "refusal to deal" defense. Porter argued—and the trial court agreed—that Jackson's refusal to deal with ERCO relieved Porter of his obligations to ERCO. The appeals court reversed, holding that a refusal to deal must be disclosed to the corporation before an officer or director may take the opportunity for personal gain. The result should be noncontroversial. A contrary result would encourage officers or directors to avoid the corporate opportunity doctrine simply by finding an intransigent partner willing to make the requisite objections. At the very least, Porter owed ERCO the chance to call Jackson's bluff—and perhaps to submit a rival application if Jackson was adamant in his refusal to deal.

§ 7.4   Good Faith

The notion that directors ought to act in good faith pervades Delaware's corporate governance jurisprudence. Only directors who, *inter alia*, act in good faith are entitled to indemnification of legal expenses.[50] Only directors who, *inter alia*, rely in good faith on corporate books and records or reports from corporate officers or certain advisors are "fully protected" against shareholder claims.[51] Related party transactions are partially insulated from judicial review, *inter alia*, only if they are approved by the disinterested directors or shareholders in good faith.[52] The business judgment rule presumes that directors acted, *inter alia*, in good faith.[53] And so on.

Despite these longstanding references to good faith, however, it is fair to say that the concept remained essentially undefined until quite recently. Instead, a director's obligation to act in good faith traditionally was subsumed into the duties of care and loyalty. If there was no breach of either of those duties, courts did not perform a separate inquiry on the issue of good faith.

---

[50] DGCL § 145.

[51] DGCL § 141(e).

[52] DGCL § 144(a)(1)–(2).

[53] See, e.g., Aronson v. Lewis, 473 A.2d 805, 812 (Del.1984) (defining the business judgment rule as "a presumption that in making a business decision the directors of a corporation acted on an informed basis, in good faith and in the honest belief that the action taken was in the best interests of the company").

The process of giving content to good faith began with the Delaware supreme court's decision in *Cede & Co. v. Technicolor, Inc.*:[54]

> [A] shareholder plaintiff challenging a board decision has the burden at the outset to rebut the rule's presumption. To rebut the rule, a shareholder plaintiff assumes the burden of providing evidence that directors, in reaching their challenged decision, breached any one of *the triads of their fiduciary duty-good faith, loyalty or due care.* If a shareholder plaintiff fails to meet this evidentiary burden, the business judgment rule attaches to protect corporate officers and directors and the decisions they make, and our courts will not second-guess these business judgments. If the rule is rebutted, the burden shifts to the defendant directors, the proponents of the challenged transaction, to prove to the trier of fact the "entire fairness" of the transaction to the shareholder plaintiff.[55]

The court's use of the term "triad" signaled the then-novel proposition that good faith was a freestanding fiduciary obligation having equal dignity with the traditional concepts of care and loyalty.

In *Walt Disney Co. Deriv. Litig.*,[56] the Delaware supreme court began to clarify the meaning of the triad formulation by defining good faith as encompassing "all actions required by a true faithfulness and devotion to the interests of the corporation and its shareholders. A failure to act in good faith may be shown, for instance, where the fiduciary intentionally acts with a purpose other than that of advancing the best interests of the corporation, where the fiduciary acts with the intent to violate applicable positive law, or where the fiduciary intentionally fails to act in the face of a known duty to act, demonstrating conscious disregard for his duties." The court held that a plaintiff could rebut the business judgment rule by showing that the board of directors acted in bad faith. The court declined to decide whether good faith was an independent fiduciary duty whose breach would give rise to liability absent a breach of the duty of care or loyalty, however.

In *Stone v. Ritter*,[57] the court resolved the issue left open in *Disney*. In doing so, the court oddly recast the triad formulation, as a mere "colloquialism," explaining that "the obligation to act in good faith does not establish an independent fiduciary duty that stands

---

[54] 634 A.2d 345 (Del.1993).
[55] Id. at 361 (emphasis supplied; citations omitted).
[56] 906 A.2d 27 (Del.2006).
[57] 911 A.2d 362 (Del.2006).

on the same footing as the duties of care and loyalty." Instead, the obligation to act in good faith is now subsumed wholly within the duty of loyalty:

> [T]he fiduciary duty of loyalty is not limited to cases involving a financial or other cognizable fiduciary conflict of interest. It also encompasses cases where the fiduciary fails to act in good faith. As the Court of Chancery aptly put it . . ., "[a] director cannot act loyally towards the corporation unless she acts in the good faith belief that her actions are in the corporation's best interest."

This formulation appears to be a compromise between those who wanted to elevate good faith to being part of a triad of duties and those who did not, with the former losing as a matter of form, and the latter losing as a matter of substance.

On close examination, this formulation makes little sense. First, the court took some pains to emphasize that a failure to act in good faith was "a 'necessary precondition to liability.'" Are there other conditions that must be satisfied in order for a bad faith act to constitute a breach of the duty of loyalty?

Second, and more important, the doctrinal consequences of subsuming good faith into loyalty are quite odd. The duty of loyalty traditionally focused on cases in which the defendant fiduciary received an improper financial benefit. Accordingly, the traditional remedy was to strip that benefit away from the defendant. In related party transactions whose terms are unfair to the corporation, for example, the transaction may be voided. Where a defendant usurps a corporate opportunity, the corporation gets a constructive trust on the opportunity.

By subsuming good faith into the duty of loyalty, however, *Stone* extends the domain of the duty of loyalty to cases in which the defendant received no financial benefit. In such cases, the traditional remedy is inapt. There is neither a transaction to be voided nor a res to be seized.

Liability for acts in bad faith thus will look a lot more like that imposed in cases involving a breach of the duty of care than the duty of loyalty. If someone "intentionally acts with a purpose other than that of advancing the best interests of the corporation," for example, it makes no sense to ask whether the action was fair to the corporation. Instead, the relevant question is whether the corporation was harmed and, if so, by what amount.

Good faith thus raises the issue of causation in a way that traditional loyalty concerns do not. After all, if we're setting out to recover the amount by which the defendant harmed the corporation, presumably we need to show that the defendant's conduct in fact harmed the corporation. Indeed, it would be unfair to impose liability without a showing of causation. To be sure, in *Technicolor*, the Delaware supreme court held that causation was not an element of the duty of care claim, a ruling that the court presumably will extend to the good faith context, but we saw in Chapter 6 that that decision made no sense. In sum, by subsuming good faith into the duty of loyalty, *Stone* makes it doctrinally even more difficult to require causation, while simultaneously creating a conceptually difficult task of crafting appropriate remedies.

§ 7.5   Oversight and Loyalty

Famed corporate lawyer Bayless Manning observed that most of what boards do "does not consist of taking affirmative action on individual matters" but rather of "a continuing flow of supervisory process, punctuated only occasionally by a discrete transactional decision."[58] It thus has long been settled that the duty of care requires directors to pay on-going attention to the business and affairs of the corporation.[59]

Directors are not expected to know, in minute detail, everything that happens on a day-to-day basis. Instead, a director is expected to have a rudimentary understanding of the firm's business and how it works, keep informed about the firm's activities, engage in a general monitoring of corporate affairs, attend board meetings regularly, and routinely review financial statements.[60] Beyond these obligations, the question remained as to whether boards have an obligation to monitor proactively the conduct of corporate subordinates.

In *Caremark Int'l Inc. Deriv. Litig.*,[61] Delaware Chancellor Allen opined that a board of directors in fact has an obligation proactively to take affirmative compliance measures:

> [I]t would, in my opinion, be a mistake to conclude that our Supreme Court's statement in *Graham* concerning

---

[58] Bayless Manning, *The Business Judgment Rule and the Director's Duty of Attention: Time for Reality*, 39 BUS. LAW. 1477, 1494 (1984).

[59] See, e.g., American Bar Ass'n, *Corporate Director's Guidebook Third Edition*, 56 BUS. LAW. 1571, 1582 (2001) (stating that the duty of care expresses "the need to pay attention, to ask questions and to act diligently and reasonably to become and remain generally informed").

[60] See Grimes v. Donald, 1995 WL 54441 at *8 n.6 (Del.Ch.1995) (stating that a board meets "its management responsibilities by appropriately appointing and monitoring, corporate officers and exercising informed business judgment with respect to corporate goals and performance"), aff'd on other grounds, 673 A.2d 1207 (Del.1996); *see also* American Bar Ass'n, *supra* note 2, at 1582 (stating that the duty of care requires directors "to become and remain generally informed, including doing the 'homework' of reading materials and other preparation in advance of meetings in order to participate effectively in board deliberations").

[61] 698 A.2d 959 (Del.Ch.1996).

"espionage" means that corporate boards may satisfy their obligation to be reasonably informed concerning the corporation, without assuring themselves that information and reporting systems exist in the organization that are reasonably designed to provide to senior management and to the board itself timely, accurate information sufficient to allow management and the board, each within its scope, to reach informed judgments concerning both the corporation's compliance with law and its business performance. . . .

Thus, I am of the view that a director's obligation includes a duty to attempt in good faith to assure that a corporate information and reporting system, which the board concludes is adequate, exists, and that failure to do so under some circumstances may, in theory at least, render a director liable for losses caused by non-compliance with applicable legal standards.

Even though *Caremark* was dicta and arguably inconsistent with supreme court precedent, it quickly became well accepted by the chancery court as good law.[62] Yet, for over a decade, the Delaware supreme court found no occasion on which to address squarely *Caremark*'s validity.

In *Stone v. Ritter*,[63] shareholders of AmSouth Bancorporation brought a derivative suit against AmSouth's directors alleging a "classic Caremark claim." In 2004, AmSouth had paid $50 million in fines and penalties to the federal government to settle criminal and civil charges that the bank had failed to file reports of suspicious activity required by the federal anti-money-laundering regulations. The plaintiffs thereafter brought a derivative claim, seeking to recover the $50 million from the directors. Plaintiffs alleged that "defendants had utterly failed to implement any sort of statutorily required monitoring, reporting or information controls that would have enabled them to learn of problems requiring their attention."

As we saw in the preceding section, in *Stone*, the Delaware supreme court established that a director's obligation to act in good faith was subsumed by the duty of loyalty. *Stone* also became the Delaware supreme court's first opinion addressing the status of *Caremark*.

In *Stone*, the Delaware supreme court confirmed that "*Caremark* articulates the necessary conditions for assessing

---

[62] See, e.g., Guttman v. Huang, 823 A.2d 492, 506 (Del.Ch.2003) (opining that "the *Caremark* decision is rightly seen as a prod towards the greater exercise of care by directors in monitoring their corporations' compliance with legal standards").

[63] 911 A.2d 362 (Del.2006).

director oversight liability." In doing so, however, the court described *Caremark* as a case in which the operative standards are good faith and loyalty rather than care, stating that:

> [T]he *Caremark* standard for so-called "oversight" liability draws heavily upon the concept of director failure to act in good faith. That is consistent with the definition(s) of bad faith recently approved by this Court in its recent *Disney* decision, where we held that a failure to act in good faith requires conduct that is qualitatively different from, and more culpable than, the conduct giving rise to a violation of the fiduciary duty of care (i.e., gross negligence). In *Disney*, we identified the following examples of conduct that would establish a failure to act in good faith: ... where the fiduciary intentionally fails to act in the face of a known duty to act, demonstrating a conscious disregard for his duties.

The Court further explained that such an intentional failure "describes, and is fully consistent with, the lack of good faith conduct that the *Caremark* court held was a 'necessary condition' for director oversight liability, i.e., a sustained or systematic failure of the board to exercise oversight—such as an utter failure to attempt to assure a reasonable information and reporting system exists."

In doing so, the Delaware supreme court radically reinterpreted *Caremark*, turning the oversight issue into one of loyalty rather than care. To be sure, there are several references to good faith in *Caremark*, the most notable of which is Allen's statement that "only a sustained or systematic failure of the board to exercise oversight—such as an utter failure to attempt to assure a reasonable information and reporting system exists—will establish the lack of good faith that is a necessary condition to liability." Nevertheless, even the most cursory reading of *Caremark* demonstrates that Allen viewed oversight liability as a species of the duty of care. Indeed, Allen explicitly distinguished a board's failure to monitor proactively corporate performance from charges of self-dealing and "loyalty type problems arising from cases of suspect director motivation."

Why did the Delaware supreme court so brazenly misinterpret *Caremark*? One possibility is that the Court was seeking to limit the potential liability exposure of corporate directors. By focusing on the duty of care, *Caremark* permits imposition of liability where directors are grossly negligent in exercising their oversight responsibilities. In contrast, *Stone* imposes a higher state of mind requirement by holding that "imposition of liability requires a showing that the directors knew that they were not discharging their fiduciary obligations."

On the other hand, by subsuming *Caremark* into good faith, the court makes a violation of the *Caremark* duties non-exculpable. Hence, there is the potential for *Stone* to expand the scope of director liability.

The process of common law adjudication is one of creative destruction. Courts constantly rethink and rework the law. Where a court changes the law by overturning prior precedent, however, it ought to do so clearly and for a good reason that is well stated. Unfortunately, *Stone*'s reinterpretation of *Caremark* failed both to advance a convincing explanation for why seemingly well-settled doctrine should be overturned and to set forth clearly the new rules of the game.

§ 7.6   Fiduciary Duties of Controlling Shareholders

A.   Introduction

At early common law, it was well-settled that a shareholder acting as a shareholder was entitled to vote his shares without regard to the interests of other shareholders.[64] As a general matter, it remains the law that shareholders are allowed to act selfishly in deciding how to vote their shares. Conversely, where a shareholder is elected to the board of directors, and acts in his capacity as a director, the shareholder-director naturally assumes fiduciary obligations towards the other shareholders.[65]

Falling between those two extremes is the case of a shareholder with voting control. Absent cumulative voting, such a shareholder's voting power will suffice to elect the entire board of directors. Recognizing that such a board may not act independently of the controlling shareholder, courts early began to extend the board's fiduciary duties to the controlling shareholder.[66] Agency concepts provide a useful way of looking at the problem. Under familiar principles of vicarious liability, the controlling shareholder can be held liable (as principal) for the acts of the directors (as its agents). In other words, it is not necessary to disturb the notion that shareholders as such are independent of the corporation and of each other. Instead, the controlling shareholder is derivatively liable for the misconduct of its agents. To be sure, courts do not require proof of an agency relationship between the controlling

---

[64] See, e.g., Haldeman v. Haldeman, 197 S.W. 376, 381 (Ky.1917).

[65] Zahn v. Transamerica Corp., 162 F.2d 36, 45 (3d Cir.1947).

[66] See, e.g., Pepper v. Litton, 308 U.S. 295, 306 (1939) ("A director is a fiduciary. So is a dominant or controlling stockholder or group of stockholders.").

shareholder and the board. Instead, they ask whether the shareholder controlled the corporation and whether the board lacked independence.

B. Identifying Controlling Shareholders

In the federal securities laws, there is a presumption that a shareholder who owns ten percent or more of the voting stock has control.[67] ALI PRINCIPLES § 1.10(b) likewise presumes a shareholder who owns more than 25 percent of the voting stock has control. It is certainly true that a shareholder who owns relatively small amounts of stock nevertheless can exercise effective control. John D. Rockefeller, for example, succeeded in his famous struggle to oust the chairman of the board of Standard Oil of Indiana despite controlling only 14.9 percent of Standard Oil's stock. A bright-line presumption of control, however, is inappropriate in this setting. The basis for imposing fiduciary obligations on a controlling shareholder is not mere ownership of a specified amount of stock, but rather the creation of a de facto agency relationship between the shareholder and the board of directors. In other words, the question is whether a majority of the board lacks independence from the allegedly controlling shareholder. Determining whether such a relationship exists necessarily must be done on a case by case basis. Any bright-line rule inevitably will be set arbitrarily and therefore prove simultaneously over-and under-inclusive.

Under Delaware law, a shareholder is deemed to have control if the shareholder either owns a majority of the voting stock or exercises control over corporate decisionmaking.[68] If the shareholder owns less than 50 percent of the voting stock, plaintiff must show evidence of actual control of corporate conduct.[69] Consequently, for example, the Delaware supreme court in *Kahn v. Lynch Communication Systems, Inc.*,[70] held that a 43.3 percent shareholder exercised control, not based on the number of shares it owned, but because the board of directors deferred to the shareholder's wishes.

---

[67] A.A. Sommer, Jr., Who's "In Control"?—SEC, 21 Bus. Law. 559, 568 (1966).

[68] See, e.g., Solomon v. Armstrong, 747 A.2d 1098, 1116 n. 53 (Del.Ch.1999) ("Under Delaware law, the notion of a 'controlling' stockholder includes both *de jure* control and *de facto* control.").

[69] See, e.g., Emerald Partners v. Berlin, 726 A.2d 1215, 1221 n. 8 (Del.1999). Similar standards have been adopted in other jurisdictions, as well. See, e.g., Locati v. Johnson, 980 P.2d 173, 176 (Or.App.1999) ("In order to be a controlling shareholder who owes fiduciary duties a shareholder must either be (1) an individual who owns a majority of the shares or who, for other reasons, has domination or control of the corporation or (2) a member of a small group of shareholders who collectively own a majority of shares or otherwise have that domination or control.").

[70] 638 A.2d 1110 (Del.1994).

C. Parent-Subsidiary Transactions

One of corporation law's central legal fictions is the idea that a corporation is a legal person possessing most of the rights and powers of a natural person. One of the resulting powers with which corporations are endowed is that of owning stock in another corporation. Consequently, one corporation may own all or part of the stock of a second corporation. If Corporation A owns 100 percent of the stock of Corporation B, for example, we refer to Corporation A as the parent and Corporation B as a wholly-owned subsidiary. If Corporation A owns only 51 percent of Corporation B's voting stock, Corporation A still would be called the parent, but Corporation B now would be called a majority-owned subsidiary. This nomenclature change reflects an important change in the ownership structure of Corporation B. Corporation A is still the principal stockholder, but now there are outsiders who own a minority interest in the firm. Logically enough, these outsiders are termed minority shareholders. (If Corporation A controls Corporation B, while owning less than a majority of the stock, Corporation B would be referred to as a minority-controlled subsidiary.)

Transactions between parent companies and wholly-owned subsidiaries rarely raise corporate law concerns, beyond whatever ministerial requirements the statutes may impose. In contrast, transactions between parent corporations and their majority-owned or minority-controlled subsidiaries have been a fertile field for litigation. Understandably, minority shareholders often feel that the parent company is using its voting control of the subsidiary to benefit itself at their expense. In such cases, the minority asserts that the parent company should owe them a duty of loyalty comparable to that owed by directors.

1. *The Canonical* Sinclair Oil *Opinion*

The canonical parent-subsidiary case remains the Delaware supreme court's opinion in *Sinclair Oil v. Levien*.[71] Sinclair Oil owned 97 percent of the stock of a subsidiary, the Sinclair Venezuelan Oil Company (Sinven), with the remaining 3 percent being held by minority shareholders. A minority shareholder challenged three transactions between Sinclair Oil and Sinven: (1) Payment of large cash dividends by Sinven; (2) Sinclair Oil's use of other (wholly-owned) subsidiaries to develop oil fields located outside of Venezuela; and (3) Sinclair Oil's actions with respect to a contract between Sinven and another Sinclair Oil subsidiary.

---

[71] 280 A.2d 717 (Del.1971).

What standard of review should a court apply to such disputes? The Delaware supreme court identified two standards potentially applicable in such situations: the business judgment rule and the intrinsic fairness rule. Under the business judgment rule, the directors of Sinven get the benefit of a rebuttable presumption of good faith. Under the intrinsic fairness test, the burden of proof is on the directors to show, subject to close scrutiny, that the transactions were objectively fair to Sinven. In this case, as in most, it mattered quite a lot which standard applied. As is often the case, the party bearing the burden of proof on a given dispute lost.

Under *Sinclair Oil*, a court will apply the intrinsic fairness standard, as opposed to the business judgment rule, when the parent has received a benefit "to the exclusion and at the expense of the subsidiary." In other words, the fiduciary obligations owed by a parent corporation are limited to self-dealing. The more exacting intrinsic fairness standard comes into play only when the parent is on both sides of the transaction and, moreover, used its position to extract nonpro rata benefits from a transaction to the minority shareholders' detriment.

The *Sinclair Oil* opinion began with a summary of the court's prior decision in *Getty Oil Co. v. Skelly Oil Co.*[72] In that case, a regulatory agency overseeing oil imports concluded that Skelly was controlled by Getty. As a result, the agency further determined that Skelly was no longer entitled to a separate allocation of imported crude oil. Skelly sued Getty, contending that it was entitled to a share of Getty's allocation. The court upheld Getty's refusal to share its allocation with Skelly, applying the business judgment rule. Intrinsic fairness was inapplicable, because Getty had not received a benefit at the expense of Skelly. Getty gained nothing to which it was not already entitled. Accordingly, no self-dealing, no intrinsic fairness review, and no liability.

The *Sinclair Oil* opinion then turned to whether Sinven's dividend payment policy violated Sinclair's fiduciary duties. Sinven had paid out large amounts of dividends during the applicable period—dividends that in fact exceeded its earnings. Plaintiff contended that the dividends resulted from an improper motive; namely, Sinclair's need for cash. The court applied the business judgment rule to this dispute. Because the minority shareholders had received a pro rata share of the dividends, Sinclair did not receive a nonpro rata benefit at their expense. The dividends were within the limits proscribed by the relevant legal capital statute and were not so large as to amount to a waste of corporate assets. Accordingly, plaintiff was unable to rebut the business judgment

---

[72] 267 A.2d 883 (Del.1970).

rule's presumption of good faith. In dicta, the court suggested that the intrinsic fairness test would be applied to dividend decisions in which there are two classes of stock and dividends are paid on the class owned by the parent but not on the class owned by the minority. This example implicates the conflict of classes discussed in the next section.

The court next took up plaintiff's claim that Sinclair Oil had prevented Sinven from expanding. The Chancellor had applied the intrinsic fairness standard to this issue, concluding that Sinclair had improperly and unfairly denied Sinven opportunities to expand its operations outside of Venezuela. On appeal, the Delaware supreme court reversed, identifying the business judgment rule as the proper standard of review. Plaintiff could point to no opportunities that Sinclair had usurped from Sinven. Absent the taking of a corporate opportunity properly belonging to Sinven, the decision of which subsidiary would be allowed to act outside of Venezuela was a business judgment for Sinclair Oil to make.[73] Again, the key consideration was that Sinclair Oil did not take anything away from Sinven that belonged to Sinven.

Finally, the court turned to a contract between another Sinclair Oil subsidiary and Sinven. Sinclair Oil had used its power to cause Sinven to enter into a contract to exclusively sell oil to a wholly-owned Sinclair Oil subsidiary. When that subsidiary breached the contract, Sinclair Oil prevented Sinven from suing to enforce its contract rights. According to the court, this issue properly was reviewed under the intrinsic fairness standard. Forcing Sinven to contract with a Sinclair Oil entity was itself self-dealing. Because the contract was breached and not enforced, moreover, Sinclair Oil had gotten a nonpro rata benefit from the contract at the expense of the minority. Accordingly, Sinclair Oil had to show that its failure to enforce the contract was intrinsically fair to Sinven, which it could not do.

> 2.   Zahn v. Transamerica *and Conflicts Between Classes of Stock*

It is instructive to compare *Sinclair Oil* with the Third Circuit's decision in *Zahn v. Transamerica Corp.*[74] At first blush, *Zahn* seems to present the same sort of issues discussed in *Sinclair Oil*—a majority shareholder who benefited itself at the minority's expense. On closer examination, however, there are some interesting complications. In particular, *Zahn* posed the question:

---

[73] See David J. Greene & Co. v. Dunhill Int'l, Inc., 249 A.2d 427 (Del.Ch.1968) (invoking corporate opportunity doctrine to hold parent liable for usurping an opportunity from a majority-owned subsidiary).

[74] 162 F.2d 36 (3d Cir.1947).

What obligations does the board of directors have when there is more than a single class of stock?

Plaintiff was a minority shareholder of Axton-Fisher Tobacco Co., a Kentucky corporation. Plaintiff challenged a decision by Axton-Fisher's board to redeem a class of Axton-Fisher shares prior to liquidation of the firm. It is important to understand the capital and ownership structure of Axton-Fisher in order to understand the case and the holding. Axton-Fisher had 3 class of shares: (1) Preferred shares with a par value of $100, a cumulative dividend preference of $6 per year, and a liquidation preference of $105 plus accrued dividends; (2) Class A common stock; and (3) Class B common stock.

In the case at bar, only the latter two classes were in play. The rights of those two classes differed in five significant areas: (1) The Class A stock had an annual cumulative dividend of $3.20, while the Class B stock had a $1.60 annual dividend. If dividends above the specified minimums were paid, such dividends were shared equally by the two classes. (2) The Class A could be called (a mandatory redemption) by the firm on 60 days' notice at $60 per share plus accrued dividends. The Class B could not be called. (3) If the firm was liquidated, the Class A was entitled to receive twice as much per share as the Class B (e.g., if Class B was to get $50 per share on liquidation, Class A would be entitled to $100). (4) Class A shares were convertible into Class B shares at the option of the holder at any time on a share for share basis. (5) The Class A stock had no voting rights, unless there were four successive failures to pay quarterly dividends, in which case it would receive equal voting rights with the Class B. As of the time of this dispute, Class A had such voting rights. The Class B had full voting rights.

Transamerica owned almost all of the Class B shares and about two-thirds of the Class A stock. Most members of the board were officers or agents of Transamerica.

Axton-Fisher's main asset was leaf tobacco. Because of rationing and shortages caused by the Second World War, the value of its tobacco inventory had risen from about $6 million to about $20 million. Plaintiff alleged that Transamerica devised a scheme to appropriate to itself most of that increase in value. The scheme called for Axton-Fisher's board to call the Class A shares at a price of about $80. Following the redemption, the firm was to be liquidated with the remaining assets being distributed to the Class B shareholders—thus, mainly to Transamerica. If the Class A shares had not been redeemed, they would have received around $240 upon liquidation of the firm.

Once a decision was made to liquidate the firm, the directors had three options: (1) Redeem the Class A shares without disclosing the extent of the appreciation of the inventory and without disclosing their intent to liquidate the firm. (2) Disclose the firm's true value and the liquidation plan, give notice of intent to redeem the Class A stock, then liquidate. (3) Decline to redeem the Class A shares and simply liquidate the company, thereby giving the Class A shareholders twice as much as the Class B shareholders. The issue in this case, put simply, was whether the directors breached their fiduciary duty to the minority shareholders by selecting the first option.

The court held that there was a breach of fiduciary duty. The Class A redemption was effected at the direction of the principal Class B shareholder in order to benefit the Class B stock in preference to the Class A. The *Sinclair Oil* court doubtless would have reached the same result. The directors took an action intended to extract a nonpro rata benefit for the parent at the expense of the minority.

Does this result mean that a similarly placed board is obliged to choose the third option? Put another way, would the result have changed if the directors had selected option 2, disclosed all material facts, and then called the Class A shares for redemption? There is some broad language in the opinion implying that the directors had a fiduciary duty to select option 3—i.e., to liquidate without redemption. But that dictum makes no sense.

Suppose the board had selected option 2. After the board announced its plans, rational Class A shareholders would exercise their conversion rights and become Class B shareholders, sharing equally in the redemption. Option 2 thus gives the minority shareholders a chance to participate equally through exercise of their conversion rights. In such a case, the parent would not be getting anything at the expense of the minority.

There is an even more fundamental reason why the directors should be permitted to follow option 2. The firm's organic documents governing the Class A shares' rights included a provision giving the firm the option of redeeming those shares at a fixed price if the board saw fit to do so. This term allocated risk between the two classes. The Class A stock had certain dividend and liquidation preferences over the Class B, and thus was a safer stock to be holding if things went badly for the firm. In contrast, the Class B was designed to take second place in many respects, but was to garner the lion's share of the profits if the company was successful. As a result, the Class A stock is more akin to preferred stock than to true common stock.

One purpose of the redemption provisions of the Class A stock was to enable the Class B stock to buy out the former if things went well. If you give someone an option to buy shares at a fixed price, you can hardly complain if that person exercises the option if the shares go up in value. Management's primary duty is to the residual claimants—here, the Class B shareholders. Management had a duty to fulfill its contractual obligations to the Class A holders, including giving them an option to convert their shares, but its primary duty was to maximize the value of the Class B shares. It could balance its obligations to all parties by selecting option 2. The fact that a majority shareholder is in the mix does not change that analysis. In a subsequent decision on damages, the Third Circuit in fact affirmed that what we have called option 2 would be consistent with the board's fiduciary duties.[75]

D. Sales of Control

Suppose a parent corporation or other controlling shareholder wishes to sell its stock in the subsidiary to an outsider. In all probability, this "control block" will sell at a price substantially higher than the market price for the stock. Or, in the case of a close corporation without an active market for its stock, at a price higher than that which minority shares would command. Can the selling shareholder be held liable for failing to share the control premium with the minority?

1. *The General Rule*

As a general rule, controlling shareholders are free to dispose of their stock as they see fit and on such terms as a willing buyer offers.[76] One of the risks incident to owning a minority interest in a corporation is that the majority may decide to sell without consulting the minority. The cases setting out the general rule, however, typically go on to identify a number of exceptions, such as a sale under circumstances indicating that the purchasers intend to loot or mismanage the corporation, the sale involves fraud or misuse of confidential information, the sale amounts to a wrongful appropriation of corporate assets that properly belong to the corporation, or the sale includes a premium for the sale of office.

---

[75] Speed v. Transamerica Corp., 235 F.2d 369, 373 (3d Cir.1956).

[76] For statements of the general rule, see Treadway Companies, Inc. v. Care Corp., 638 F.2d 357, 375 (2d Cir.1980); Clagett v. Hutchison, 583 F.2d 1259, 1262 (4th Cir.1978); Zetlin v. Hanson Holdings, Inc., 397 N.E.2d 387, 388 (N.Y.1979); Tryon v. Smith, 229 P.2d 251, 254 (Or.1951); Glass v. Glass, 321 S.E.2d 69, 74 (Va.1984).

2.   Sale to a Looter

Suppose that Susan Stockholder, the controlling shareholder of Acme Inc., sells her control block to Lorraine Looter. Looter then proceeds to loot Acme—she liquidates all the assets, steals the cash from the bank account, and absconds to some Pacific island where she sets up a satellite dish and spends her ill-gotten gains in general debauchery. Looter then dies from one of those nasty diseases to which debauchery so often leads. After casting about for a deep pocket to sue, the minority shareholders sue Susan Stockholder. Liability?

There are few true sale to looter cases. In the leading *DeBaun v. First Western Bank and Trust Co.* decision, the controlling shareholder was aware of considerable information that should have alerted it to potential problems. A credit report on the prospective buyer indicated a large number of business failures. The purchase price was so high that the buyer would have to tap corporate assets in order to make the required payments. The selling shareholder had obtained but not collected a fraud judgment against the buyer. "Armed with knowledge of these facts," the seller knew or should have known that a sale would be detrimental to the minority shareholders' interests.[77] So, as a general rule, there is no duty to investigate. Where the controlling shareholder is presented with a suspicious character and/or a suspiciously high price, however, the controlling shareholder has a duty to reasonably investigate the buyer's plans.[78]

3.   Sale of Office

Suppose Lorraine Looter agrees to purchase a control block of stock from Susan Stockholder. As part of their agreement, Stockholder promises to transfer control of the board to new directors of Looter's choosing. They effect the transfer through sequential resignations. Assume there are three directors: Stockholder, Frank Flunky, and Corrine Crony. Flunky resigns, which he may do at any time under DGCL § 141(b). Per DGCL § 223(a)(1), vacancies may be filled by a majority vote of the

---

[77] DeBaun v. First Western Bank and Trust Co., 120 Cal.Rptr. 354, 360 (Cal.App.1975).

[78] See, e.g., Harris v. Carter, 582 A.2d 222, 235 (Del.Ch.1990) (although the seller is "not a surety for his buyer, when the circumstances would alert a reasonably prudent person to a risk that his buyer is dishonest or in some material respect not truthful, a duty devolves upon the seller to make such inquiry as a reasonably prudent person would make"); see also Gerdes v. Reynolds, 28 N.Y.S.2d 622 (Sup.Ct.1941) (gross inadequacy of price could put seller on inquiry notice); but see Clagett v. Hutchison, 583 F.2d 1259, 1262 (4th Cir.1978) ($34.75 per share price for stock trading at $7.50 to $10 "cannot be said to be so unreasonable as to place [the seller] on notice of the likelihood of fraud on the corporation or the remaining shareholders").

remaining directors. Acting pursuant to that statutory grant of authority, Stockholder and Crony then appoint Looter to the board. Crony then resigns, creating a vacancy to be filled by Stockholder and Looter. And so on, until Looter and her nominees hold all board spots. The new board then appoints Looter and her cronies as officers and day-to-day control has changed hands without a formal shareholder vote. Liability?

As a general rule, sales of corporate office are voidable as contrary to public policy. Any portion of the control premium attributable to the sale of office must be forfeited to the minority shareholders.[79] Hence, liability seemingly should arise when sequential resignations are used to effect a change in the board and officers. But consider the practicalities of the issue. Suppose the buyer acquired a majority of the voting stock. The buyer could wait until the next annual meeting of the shareholders. Absent cumulative voting, the buyer's holdings will suffice to elect the entire board. If the buyer did so, the minority shareholders would have no cause for complaint. Alternatively, even before the next annual meeting, the new controlling shareholder could call a special meeting to remove the existing board and elect replacements. Assuming the board may be removed without cause, or is willing to resign en masse, the minority again would have no cause for complaint. Imposing liability on a majority block seller and/or buyer who accomplish the same result by sequential resignations simply elevates form over substance and thus makes little policy sense. But what if the control block is less than a majority of the shares? At least in theory, if the issue were put before them at a meeting, the other shareholders could vote for other directors. In that case, perhaps liability should be imposed where sequential resignations are used to transfer control without a shareholder vote.

In the leading decision, *Essex Universal Corp. v. Yates*,[80] a high-powered three judge panel of the Second Circuit splintered three different ways on this question. Chief Judge Lumbard said there should be no liability if the buyer purchased more than 50 percent of the voting stock, because the buyer would eventually get control of the board anyway. If the buyer purchased less than 50 percent, however, liability for sale of office should be imposed unless the buyer "would as a practical certainty have been guaranteed of the stock voting power to choose a majority of the directors." Because the 28.3 percent block acquired by the purchaser is "usually tantamount to majority control" Chief Judge Lumbard would put the burden of proof on the challenger. In

[79] See, e.g., Brecher v. Gregg, 392 N.Y.S.2d 776 (Sup.Ct.1975); Gerdes v. Reynolds, 28 N.Y.S.2d 622 (Sup.Ct.1941).

[80] 305 F.2d 572 (2d Cir.1962).

contrast, Judge Friendly would hold a sequential resignation plan voidable as contrary to public policy except "when it was entirely plain that a new election would be a mere formality—i.e., when the seller owned more than 50% of the stock." Where the buyer purchases less than 50 percent of the shares, after all, it is not certain that its slate would in fact be elected. Finally, Judge Clark thought such arrangements are not per se unlawful. Instead, their legality was a question of fact to be determined at trial. Query: How?

4. *Usurping a Corporate Opportunity*

We come at last to one of corporate law's hoariest chestnuts: *Perlman v. Feldmann.*[81] Newport Steel Corporation, as its name suggests, was a steel manufacturer. During the Korean War demand for steel was very high relative to the available supply of steel. Basic economics tells us that the price of steel should have risen substantially. It did not, however, because the Truman administration had imposed price controls on steel. Newport Steel's dominant shareholder, one C. Russell Feldmann, devised the so-called Feldmann plan, pursuant to which steel purchasers were obliged to extend interest free loans to Newport Steel. The effective price Newport Steel received thus included both the nominal purchase price and the present value of the interest charges it avoided. This was a legal—but somewhat shady—way of getting around the price controls on steel.

A consortium of manufacturers decided to ensure their access to steel by purchasing a steel company. One way to do so, of course, would be to acquire a steel company by means of a merger or tender offer in which all shareholders of the target steel manufacturer would share equally in any premium the consortium was willing to pay. Instead, the consortium formed the Wilport Company, a Delaware corporation, which then purchased Feldman's controlling block of Newport Steel shares at a substantial premium over market. The minority shareholders got nothing and sued. On those facts, the court held for the minority, opining that "siphoning off for personal gain corporate advantages to be derived from a favorable market situation" violated Feldmann's fiduciary duties to the minority.

A simplified example may be helpful. Assume there are 10 Newport Steel shares outstanding, of which Feldmann owns 3. Each year for the next ten years Newport Steel is expecting to sell $120 worth of steel. Ignoring expenses, assume projected annual earnings of $120 or $12 per share, $10 per share of which

---

[81] 219 F.2d 173 (2d Cir.1955).

represents the sale of steel at the controlled price, and $2 per share of which represents cash flows generated by the Feldmann Plan. How much is one share of stock worth? In the real world, we would have to take into account the time value of money and risk by projecting the cash flow into the future and discounting the anticipated cash flows back to present value. To keep the problem simple, we will ignore that complication and assume each share of stock is worth $120 ($12 earnings per year per shore times ten years). If Wilport obtains control by purchasing Feldman's stock, it will get to decide who may purchase Newport Steel's output. Presumably, Wilport will force Newport Steel to sell all of its output to Wilport, a fact of which the court made much. But so what? As long as Newport is operating at full capacity and Wilport pays the maximum controlled price, the minority are no worse off under Wilport than they were under Feldmann. The kicker therefore is that Wilport also gets to decide whether or not to keep the Feldmann plan in place. If Wilport buys Newport and keeps the plan in place, it will pay $120 per year for steel. If Wilport buys Newport and cancels the plan, it will only pay $100 per year for Steel. Suppose Wilport pays Feldmann $150 per share ($450) for his stock and then cancels the Feldmann plan. Feldmann received $30 more than the stock is worth on a per share basis—a control premium. Everybody else now has stock that is worth only $100 ($10 earnings per year per share, reflecting loss of Feldmann plan revenues, times ten years). Wilport thus paid $450 for stock that is only worth $300, but Wilport will save $20 per year on the price it pays for Steel, which translates into $200 over the ten year period for which we are projecting earnings. So Wilport is better off by a net of $50. The decline of $150 in the value of its Newport shares is off-set by the $200 it saves in costs.

Perlman v. Feldmann thus presented a very unique set of facts: (1) A unique profit making opportunity was available to the corporation only because of the government price controls. (2) The value of that profit making opportunity could be capitalized and divided between the purchaser and seller of the control block. (3) The minority shareholders thus lost significant sums that otherwise would have come to them in the ordinary course. So understood, *Perlman* is a very simple case. *Perlman* does not stand for the proposition that a controlling shareholder must give all other shareholders an equal opportunity to sell their stock on a pro rata basis. Instead, it simply stands for the proposition that a controlling shareholder may not usurp an opportunity that should be available to all shareholders. One could have reached the very same result under a *Sinclair Oil*-style analysis. The controlling shareholder received a benefit "to the exclusion and at the expense" of the minority. Not only were the minority excluded from the opportunity to sell at a premium, they were left worse off as a result.

Beyond *Perlman*'s unique facts, where are corporate opportunity issues most likely to arise? Probably in connection with structuring of acquisitions. Suppose Lorraine Looter approaches Susan Stockholder with an offer to buy Stockholder's control block at a premium. Should there be liability? Not if we adopt the *Sinclair Oil* analogy. The majority shareholder can do whatever she wants as long as she does not deprive the minority shareholders of something to which they are entitled. On these facts, there is no corporate opportunity to be usurped. But suppose Looter approached Stockholder with a slightly different proposal, under which Acme would be merged into a corporation owned by Looter. Stockholder rejects the merger proposal, but offers to sell Looter her control block at a premium. On these facts, the *Perlman* court likely would impose liability. The *Perlman* court found that Feldmann breached his fiduciary duty to the minority shareholders by arranging the transaction so that only Feldmann and his cronies shared in the premium. Susan Stockholder has done essentially the same thing. The original offer was a merger in which all shareholders would have a chance to participate. But the controlling shareholder refused to go along, effectively saying: "if you don't buy me out at a premium over what everybody else gets— no deal." Looter had no choice but to go along, thereby denying the minority shareholders an opportunity to share in the control premium. Stockholder abused her position to usurp an opportunity available to all shareholders.

5.   Refusals to Sell

Courts make cases like *Sinclair Oil* or *Perlman* unnecessarily difficult by blurring the distinction between director and shareholder fiduciary duties. Consider the sale of office cases: The real problem in these cases is not the sale of a control block, but rather the directors' abdication of their duty to make an informed business judgment. Instead of exercising their best individual business judgment, they mindlessly followed a contractual obligation.

Only rarely do you get cases that starkly present the question of shareholder duties without any intervening issue of director duties. Delaware Chancellor Allen's decision in *Mendel v. Carroll* is about as clear an example of such a case as one can ever expect to get. The Carroll Family collectively controlled Katy Industries, Inc., owning at various times 48 to 52% of the stock. Even when they did not have an outright majority, their status as the largest shareholder ensured that they had effective control.

The Carroll family proposed a freeze-out merger that would have cashed out the minority shareholders at about $26 per share. The board set up a special committee comprised of independent directors to consider the offer. A competing offer was made by a group organized by a fellow named Sanford Pensler at about $28 per share. The Carroll Family withdrew their merger proposal, but also announced they had no interest in selling their shares. Their opposition to the Pensler proposal effectively precluded it from going forward. Minority shareholders sued, alleging both that the Carroll Family violated its fiduciary duties and that the board of directors violated its fiduciary duties.

If Carroll Family directors had voted on the proposal, the Carroll Family would have been on both sides of the deal. Because the board used a special committee of independent directors to make the decision, however, thereby keeping the Carroll Family out of the board's decisionmaking process, there are no complicating issues of whether any member of the Carroll Family had director duties. Instead, we have two distinct issues: (1) did the directors violate their fiduciary duties by failing to act against the majority shareholders' interests; (2) did the majority shareholder violate its fiduciary duty to the minority?

As to the board's duties, plaintiff argued that the originally proposed freeze-out merger amounted to a shift in control. Under Delaware law governing corporate takeovers, where such a shift in control occurs the board of directors has a fiduciary duty to maximize immediate shareholder value.[82] The Carroll Family proposal was only $26, Pensler offered $28. The Pensler deal therefore was the better deal and the board had a duty to take it. The board responded by arguing that the Carroll Family would not sell their shares. If the family will not go along, a deal cannot be done. Consequently, the board's duty to the shareholders is limited to getting the best deal possible given the Carroll Family's intransigence. Plaintiff replied that the board was obligated under these circumstances to act against the majority shareholders' interest. Plaintiff suggested the board sell additional shares to the Pensler group, thereby diluting the Carroll Family holdings to the point at which they no longer had control.

Chancellor Allen left open the possibility that a board might sometimes be required to act against the majority's interest. Because the board also owes fiduciary duties to the majority, however, he limited this possibility to cases in which the majority shareholder is overreaching and trying to injure the minority. On

---

[82] See Revlon, Inc. v. MacAndrews & Forbes Holdings, Inc., 506 A.2d 173 (Del.1985).

the facts, this was not such a case. Allen pointed out that the plaintiff's argument broke down at several points. First, because the Carroll Family already had effective control at all relevant times, nothing they did amounted to a shift of control, and the takeover precedents were irrelevant. Second, Allen also took issue with the proposition that $28 was a better deal for the shareholders than $26. The Carroll Family already had control. Their offer thus would not include a control premium. The Pensler group was trying to buy control. The fact that they were only willing to pay a $2 control premium suggests that they might be low-balling the shareholders. Of course, Allen did not need to decide whether $28 from Pensler was in fact better or worse for the shareholders than $26 from the Carroll Family. In the absence of a showing that the board acted from conflicted interests, he properly left that issue to the board.

Turning to the fiduciary duties of controlling shareholders, the majority opinion in *Perlman v. Feldmann* had analogized shareholders to partners, drawing special attention to the broad dicta Judge Cardozo's famous *Meinhard v. Salmon* opinion. If we take Cardozo literally, partners may not behave selfishly towards one another. If we take *Perlman* literally, neither may "corporate fiduciaries." If we apply *Meinhard* and *Perlman* to the facts of *Mendel*, surely we conclude that the Carroll Family was acting selfishly, probably motivated by their desire to retain control over the firm's free cash flow.

Allen touched on the sale of control cases in passing. On the one hand, he recognized the legitimacy of sales of control at a premium. At the same time, however, he noted that liability for sale of control at a premium over market could be imposed in the usual cases of sale to looters, sale of office, or usurpation of corporate opportunity. In any event, *Mendel* involved the reverse situation: where the controlling shareholder refused to sell and, by that refusal, prevented a takeover. In that context, Allen held that self-sacrifice is not required. The family had no obligation to sell.

E. Freeze-Outs

In a freeze-out transaction, the controlling shareholder buys out the minority shareholders, even if the minority object. The transaction typically is effected using a so-called triangular merger in which the corporation is merged with a wholly owned subsidiary of the controlling shareholder. A merger combines two corporations to form a single firm. After a merger, only one of the two companies will survive, but that survivor succeeds by operation of law to all of the assets, liabilities, rights, and obligations of the two constituent corporations. In addition, a merger also converts the shares of each constituent corporation into whatever consideration was specified in the merger agreement. Suppose the merger agreement provided that minority shareholders were to receive $50 per share in cash. After the merger takes place, their shares are transformed by operation of law into a mere IOU for the promised cash payment.

Corporate law originally required unanimous shareholder approval of mergers. The unanimity requirement created serious holdout problems, allowing dissenting minorities to block desirable transactions. In the 1800s, the necessary vote was reduced in most states to a majority of the outstanding shares. A few states have slightly higher vote requirements, such as two-thirds, but none retains the old unanimity requirement.

Taken together, these rules provide the controlling shareholder with a form of private eminent domain. Its shares standing alone may suffice to approve the merger, even if every other shareholder votes against it. Assuming the merger is approved, the minority shareholders will be forced to accept the consideration specified in the merger agreement.

Although minority shareholders have no power to block a freeze-out merger, they are not wholly lacking in remedies. When states began moving away from the unanimity requirement, they also created the statutory appraisal proceeding. In brief, appraisal rights give dissenting shareholders the right to have the fair value of their shares determined and paid to them in cash, provided that the dissenting shareholder complies with specified procedures. In practice, however, appraisal is not a very attractive remedy. Getting a shareholder to the point where the statutes permit exercise of the appraisal rights tends to be like working one's way through a labyrinth. There are many traps for the unwary—the most significant of which is the requirement that a shareholder perfect his appraisal rights by giving the corporation written notice of his intent to do so before the shareholder vote on the merger. Facts tending to show that the price was unfair often will not be discovered until after the shareholder vote. In addition, many jurisdictions do not permit the use of class actions in appraisal proceedings. Accordingly, it can be very expensive to exercise appraisal rights because each dissenting shareholder must hire his own lawyer. In contrast, if he can bring a fraud or fiduciary duty claim outside the appraisal statute he can do so via a class or derivative action. Finally, it also is possible that he will get greater relief in a cause of action for damages than under appraisal.

Because of the advantages class and derivative actions possess over appraisal proceedings, the exclusivity of such proceedings is the critical issue. Should appraisal be regarded as the exclusive remedy or should unhappy shareholders be allowed to challenge the merger even if they were not eligible to make use of the appraisal remedy? This issue tends to come up most often in going private or freeze-out transactions where the buyer is either management and/or a controlling shareholder. Plaintiffs claim that there has been a breach of fiduciary duty or fraud or what have you. The question then becomes whether they are entitled to a remedy outside the appraisal process.

Current Delaware law on these issues originated with the supreme court's decision in *Weinberger v. UOP.*[83] A conglomerate named The Signal Companies purchased 50.5% of UOP's stock. Sometime thereafter Signal decided to acquire the remaining 49.5% of UOP's shares at $21 per share through a freeze-out merger between a wholly owned Signal subsidiary and UOP. Plaintiff challenged the fairness of the merger on a variety of grounds. In a far-reaching opinion, the court laid out a number of important principles. Although some of its pronouncements have undergone substantial subsequent modification, *Weinberger* remains the starting point for any discussion of freeze-out mergers.

1.   The Business Purpose Test

In *Singer v. Magnavox*, shareholders of Magnavox challenged the corporation's agreement to be acquired by North American Philips in a reverse triangular merger.[84] Because North American indirectly owned 84.1% of Mangnavox's outstanding shares by virtue of a prior tender offer, the outcome of the shareholder vote on the merger proposal was a foregone conclusion. After the merger became effective, plaintiff shareholders sought an order nullifying the merger and awarding compensatory damages on the grounds that the merger was fraudulent and constituted a breach of duty by the defendant directors and by North American as the controlling shareholder.

In *Singer*, the challenged freeze-out merger fully complied with the relevant Delaware merger statutes. The supreme court, however, held that compliance with the form of the statute did not end the inquiry: "inequitable action does not become permissible simply because it is legally possible." Accordingly, the court imposed certain limitations on the acquiring company's ability to freeze-out minority shareholders. Among these was the so-called business purpose test, which held that a merger could not be effected for the "sole purpose of freezing out minority shareholders."

---

[83]   457 A.2d 701 (Del.1983).

[84]   380 A.2d 969 (Del.1977).

If the business purpose test is based solely on the target corporation's interests, effecting a freeze-out merger becomes quite difficult. In many cases, the advantages of a going private transaction accrue mainly to the controlling shareholder. In subsequent decisions, however, the Delaware supreme court effectively eviscerated the business purpose test by requiring only that the merger serve some bona fide purpose of the parent corporation.[85] Because competent transaction planners easily could create a paper trail showing the merger promoted some business interest of the parent, the test was left as mere formalism. Recognizing that the business purpose test afforded minority shareholders no meaningful protections, the Delaware supreme court abandoned it in *Weinberger*.[86]

2. Freeze-Outs and Fairness

According to *Weinberger*, a freeze-out merger must satisfy an "entire fairness" standard.[87] In turn, entire fairness has two components: fair price and fair dealing. The controlling shareholder's obligation to pay a fair price raises valuation issues discussed in Chapter 12. Here we focus on the controlling shareholder's duty to deal fairly with the minority.

Even after acquiring a majority position in UOP, Signal still was sitting on a pile of excess cash for which it had been unable to find profitable uses. Illustrating the agency costs inherent in free cash flow, Signal's board failed to pay out the cash to the shareholders via a dividend or stock repurchase. Instead, after considering and rejecting many options, Signal turned its attention

---

[85] See, e.g., Tanzer v. International General Industries, Inc., 379 A.2d 1121 (Del.1977).

[86] Weinberger v. UOP, Inc., 457 A.2d 701, 715 (Del.1983). In Coggins v. New England Patriots Football Club, Inc., 492 N.E.2d 1112 (Mass.1986), the Massachusetts court declined to follow *Weinberger* in this regard. The Massachusetts court both retained the business purpose test and interpreted that test to require the merger serve some legitimate business interest of the target subsidiary. As is often the case, the challenged merger's benefits flowed to the controlling shareholder, which the court deemed improper. Even in *Coggins*-like jurisdictions, however, careful transaction planning often can create the requisite paper trail showing a purported interest of the target subsidiary served by the freeze-out merger.

[87] The entire fairness standard applies only where the majority shareholder seeks to freeze-out the minority via a merger. According to the Delaware supreme court, "Delaware law does not impose a duty of entire fairness on controlling stockholders making a non-coercive tender or exchange offer to acquire shares directly from the minority holders." Solomon v. Pathe Communications Corp., 672 A.2d 35, 39 (Del.1996) (citations and quotations omitted). In place of an entire fairness standard, the Delaware courts examine both the structure of the transaction to insure that it is voluntary in nature and information disclosed to insure its adequacy and completeness. Where an offer is found to be both structurally non-coercive and fully disclosed, the court will leave the decision whether to tender or not up to the stockholders. See, e.g., In re Pure Resources, Inc., Shareholders Litig., 808 A.2d 421, 433–46 (Del.Ch.2002); In re Aquila Inc. Shareholders Litig., 805 A.2d 184 (Del.Ch.2002); In re Siliconix Inc. Shareholders Litig., 2001 WL 716787 (Del.Ch. 2001).

back to UOP. Signal's board ordered that a feasibility study be prepared relating to the possible acquisition by Signal of the remaining minority UOP shares. Messrs. Arledge and Chitiea prepared the study. They were both officers of Signal and also directors of both UOP and Signal. Using confidential UOP information, Arledge and Chitiea concluded that buying the remaining 49.5% of UOP's stock at any price up to $24 per share would be a good investment for Signal. After the feasibility study was completed, Signal's executive committee decided to effect a freeze-out merger at $21 per share, which the committee purportedly believed would be a fair price.

Negotiations between Signal and UOP were conducted on the latter's behalf by one Crawford, who was UOP's president but also had been a long-time Signal employee. Indeed, the court described Crawford as "Signal's man at UOP." When the matter was laid before UOP's board, the UOP board members who had been nominated by Signal were present at the meeting in person or by telephone conference call. They left the meeting to permit free discussion by the non-Signal directors, but returned before the final vote. Although they did not vote, the record showed that they would have voted affirmatively.

The court concluded that this course of conduct violated the duty of fair dealing in at least three respects. First, the Arledge-Chitiea report was prepared using confidential UOP information. It is perfectly permissible for someone to be a director of two corporations simultaneously, even if those corporations are related as parent and subsidiary. "But such common directors owe the same fidelity to both corporations."[88] Consequently, Arledge and Chitiea could not use their positions as UOP directors to benefit Signal.

Second, there was a lack of candor. As a controlling shareholder seeking to effect a freeze-out transaction, Signal's fiduciary duties to the minority included an obligation to fully disclose all material facts. The Arledge-Chitiea report was clearly material—the reasonable investor would consider both the information therein and the manner in which it was prepared to be important in deciding how to vote—but the report was not disclosed either to the independent UOP directors or to the minority shareholders.

Finally, there was a lack of arms-length bargaining. As a prudential matter, Crawford and the Signal-affiliated board members should have recused themselves from the negotiations. A

---

[88] San Diego, Old Town, and Pacific Beach R.R. Co. v. Pacific Beach Co., 44 P. 333, 334 (Cal.1896).

special committee of UOP's independent directors then should have been appointed to study the offer and conduct any negotiations. As the court explained: "Although perfection is not possible, or expected, the result here could have been entirely different if UOP had appointed an independent negotiating committee of its outside directors to deal with Signal at arm's length."[89] Instructively, the court went on to equate "fairness in this context" to the conduct that might be expected from "a theoretical, wholly independent, board of directors acting upon the matter before them." Notice how this expectation squares with the authority/accountability dichotomy we have developed in connection with judicial oversight of board decisionmaking. Only where there is evidence of possible self-dealing do accountability concerns trump the null hypothesis of preserving the board's discretionary authority from judicial review. If independent and disinterested directors have conducted the transaction, accountability concerns are minimized, and the court appropriately will give more deference to the board's decisions.

Unlike some duty of loyalty settings, however, approval of a freeze-out merger by the disinterested directors (or shareholders for that matter) does not change the applicable standard of review to, say, the business judgment rule. As the Delaware court explained in *Kahn v. Lynch Communication Systems*,[90] "approval of the transaction by an independent committee of directors or an informed majority of minority shareholders shifts the burden of proof on the issue of fairness from the controlling or dominating shareholder to the challenging shareholder-plaintiff. Nevertheless, even when an interested cash-out merger transaction receives the informed approval of a majority of minority stockholders or an independent committee of disinterested directors, an entire fairness analysis is the only proper standard of judicial review." The court went on to emphasize that the burden shifts to plaintiff only if the majority shareholder does not dictate the terms of the merger and the independent committee has "real bargaining power that it can exercise with the majority shareholder on an arm length basis."

3.   *Freeze-Outs, Fiduciary Duties, and Appraisal*

Weinberger's basic requirement of entire fairness was not a novel development, although the emphasis on fair dealing constituted an important refinement of the standard.[91] What good is a fairness requirement, however, if there is no effective remedy? Under *Singer* and its pre-*Weinberger* progeny, the statutory

---

[89] Weinberger v. UOP, Inc., 457 A.2d 701, 709 n. 7 (Del.1983).

[90] 638 A.2d 1110, 1117 (Del.1994).

[91] See, e.g., Singer v. Magnavox Co., 380 A.2d 969, 980 (Del.1977) (requiring that freeze-out mergers satisfy an "entire fairness" standard).

appraisal proceeding was not the sole remedy available for mergers failing to satisfy the entire fairness test. Instead, aggrieved shareholders could bring a class action for money damages, even if they were not eligible for appraisal. This had the significant advantage of permitting shareholders who voted for the merger to change their minds and seek damages if they subsequently decided the merger was unfair.

In contrast, the *Weinberger* court ruled that any future challenges to a merger's fairness generally must be made by means of an appraisal proceeding. (Cases then pending were allowed to proceed as class actions.) As the court explained, "a plaintiff's monetary remedy ordinarily should be confined to the more liberalized appraisal proceeding herein established." The court acknowledged that appraisal might not be "adequate in certain cases, particularly where fraud, misrepresentation, self-dealing, deliberate waste of corporate assets, or gross and palpable overreaching are involved." But while the chancery court was authorized to provide alternative measures of damages in those cases, such as by granting rescissory damages,[92] the court was to do so within the confines of the appraisal process.

Weinberger appeared to unequivocally leave appraisal as the exclusive remedy in freeze-out mergers. If a minority shareholder thought a merger was unfair, his remedy was to bring an appraisal proceeding, which meant there would be no class action and the shareholder would have to perfect his appraisal rights. In its subsequent *Rabkin* opinion, however, the Delaware supreme court took it all back—or, at least, most of it.

On March 1, 1983, the Olin Corporation bought 63 percent of the outstanding stock of the Philip A. Hunt Chemical Corporation from a company called Turner & Newall. Olin paid Turner & Newall $25 per share. The parties agreed that, if Olin bought the remainder of Hunt stock within one year, Olin would pay the minority shareholders $25 as well. At the time, Olin stated it had "no present intention" to buy the remaining shares. The court observed, however, that "it is clear that Olin always anticipated owing 100 percent of Hunt." In any case, just over one year later, on

---

[92] Rescissory damages give shareholders the value of their stock measured at the time of judgment, thereby giving the shareholders a share of the gains from the merger. This, at least in theory, was supposed to deter the practice of "low-balling," in which the bidder offered a price less than that which likely would be available in an appraisal proceeding on the theory that few if any shareholders would exercise their appraisal rights. In practice, however, it gives shareholders a put option. In other words, the dissenter can elect to be treated as though he had been a shareholder in the firm all along. This allows the dissenter to free ride on the majority shareholder's efforts to enhance share value. If the firm does worse than the market, however, he'll probably get at least the appraisal price plus interest. As a result, the availability of rescissory damages makes appraisal a no-risk proposition.

March 23, 1984, Olin met with its investment banking firm to plan its purchase of the remaining stock at $20 per share. Within a short time, it had engineered a freeze-out merger at $20.

Disgruntled shareholders plaintiffs rejected an appraisal and brought a class action challenging the merger as unfair. The defendants moved to dismiss on grounds that appraisal is the exclusive remedy. The chancery court agreed with the defendants and dismissed. The Delaware supreme court reversed, however, holding that the chancery court's view "render[ed] meaningless our extensive discussion of fair dealing" in *Weinberger*.[93] To be sure, *Weinberger* contemplated that the chancery court could take into account breaches of fiduciary duty when valuing stock in an appraisal proceeding. Ultimately, however, appraisal is concerned mainly with the adequacy of the price. If there is to be a successful collateral attack on the manner in which the controlling shareholder dealt with the minority, a class action for damages provides a far more effective tool. *Rabkin* implicitly recognized this truth, leaving appraisal a very limited scope of action. After *Rabkin*, appraisal apparently is exclusive only when plaintiff's claims go solely to the fairness of the price.[94] Although the court did not say so expressly, this conclusion follows inexorably from three aspects of the decision: (1) the supreme court's rejection of the chancery court's "narrow" interpretation of *Weinberger*; (2) the supreme court's emphasis that the case involved charges of "unfair dealing"; (3) the fact that plaintiff's allegation of unfair dealing was enough to defeat dismissal of the class action. In other words, Delaware has come full circle. In order to ensure that minority shareholders have an effective remedy in freeze-out mergers, the court has reopened the courthouse door to class and derivative actions.[95]

In contrast, the Model Act has moved in just the opposite direction. Subject to two exceptions, MBCA § 13.02(d) states that a shareholder entitled to appraisal rights "may not challenge" a completed merger. One exception authorizes suit to remedy serious procedural errors in the decisionmaking process, such as a failure to obtain the required votes. The other permits a class action outside of appraisal where shareholder approval of the merger was procured by fraud. Note also the implicit exception for equitable relief sought prior to the merger's completion. Finally, the exclusivity principle does not preclude a class action for damages

---

[93] Rabkin v. Philip A. Hunt Chemical Corp., 498 A.2d 1099, 1104 (Del.1985).

[94] See Cede & Co. v. Technicolor, Inc., 542 A.2d 1182 (Del.1988).

[95] The Delaware courts' evisceration of the appraisal remedy became very nearly complete when Vice Chancellor Strine held that shareholders who vote in favor of a merger are not barred either from being members of the class or even from serving as lead plaintiffs in the class action. In re JCC Holding Co., Inc., 843 A.2d 713 (Del.Ch. 2003).

brought against directors for violating their duties of care and loyalty.

4.   *Effect of Shareholder Ratification*

As with other duty of loyalty claims, shareholder approval and/or ratification is not claim preclusive. Instead, valid shareholder action shifts the burden of proof from defendants to plaintiffs. Given the outcome determinative potential of assigning the burden of proof, of course, this is a nontrivial benefit for the defendants.

In a freeze-out merger, the controlling shareholder's conflict of interest is imputed to the target subsidiary's board. Accordingly, such a merger is treated as a type of self-dealing transaction and the burden of proof is on the defendant controlling shareholder and/or the controlled directors to prove that the transaction was fair to the minority. If a freeze-out merger is approved by a majority of the disinterested shareholders—the so-called "majority of the minority," however, the burden of proof shifts to the plaintiff to show that the merger was unfair. The standard of review remains entire fairness, with its integral fair price and fair dealing components, but the burden is now on plaintiff to show lack of fairness on one or both grounds.[96]

---

[96] See In re Wheelabrator Technologies, Inc. Shareholders Litigation, 663 A.2d 1194, 1203 (Del.Ch.1995); see also Kahn v. Lynch Communication Sys., 638 A.2d 1110 (Del.1994); Rosenblatt v. Getty Oil Co., 493 A.2d 929 (Del.1985). In Kahn v. M&F Worldwide Corp., 88 A.3d 635 (Del. 2014), however, the Delaware Supreme Court held that a freeze-out merger would be reviewed under the business judgment rule rather than the fairness standard if six conditions are met: (1) the controlling stockholder conditions the transaction on the approval of both a special committee and the majority of the minority stockholders, (2) the special committee is independent, (3) the special committee is empowered to select its own advisors and to say no definitively, (4) the special committee meets its duty of care in negotiating a fair price, (5) the vote of the minority stockholders is informed, and (6) there is no coercion of the minority stockholders.

Chapter 8

SHAREHOLDER LITIGATION

§ 8.1 Introduction

In the preceding chapters, we reviewed the fiduciary duties corporate law imposes on corporate management and the board of directors that supervises those managers. In this chapter, we take up the mechanism by which those duties are enforced.

In general, fiduciary duties of officers and directors are owed to the corporation as an entity, rather than to individual shareholders. Accordingly, this chapter focuses on the mechanism by which those duties typically are enforced—the derivative suit.[1]

The law governing derivative litigation has many complexities, most of which result from the collision of two basic principles. On the one hand, the derivative cause of action belongs to the corporation. The board of directors is charged with running the corporation and therefore ought to control corporate litigation. On the other hand, when it is the directors or their associates who are on trial, we may not trust them to make unbiased decisions. Consequently, like the substantive content of fiduciary duties, the law governing derivative litigation must balance the competing policies of deference to the board's decisionmaking authority and the need to hold erring directors accountable.

§ 8.2 Direct v. Derivative Litigation

"Direct" shareholder suits arise out of causes of action belonging to the shareholders in their individual capacity. It is typically premised on an injury directly affecting the shareholders and must be brought by the shareholders in their own name. In contrast, a "derivative" suit is one brought by the shareholder on behalf of the corporation. The cause of action belongs to the corporation as an entity and arises out of an injury done to the corporation as an entity. The shareholder is merely acting as the firm's representative.

Distinguishing direct and derivative suits is easier said than done. The ALI PRINCIPLES posit two basic tests: (1) Who suffered the most immediate and direct injury? Note that it is not enough for a shareholder to allege that the challenged conduct resulted in a

---

[1] In theory, of course, a derivative suit may be brought by any shareholder who meets the specified procedural requirements to redress any injury done the corporation by any party. As noted, however, its most important function is providing a mechanism by which breaches of fiduciary duty are remedied.

drop in the corporation's stock market price. (2) To whom did the defendant's duty run?[2] In *Grimes v. Donald*, the Delaware supreme court favorably cited the ALI standards, but also added yet another test based on the nature of the relief being sought. In *Grimes*, plaintiff alleged that the board of directors had improperly abdicated its authority to the chief executive officer. Plaintiff's only requested relief was "a declaration of the invalidity" of the employment agreements by which the board delegated power to the officer. Accordingly, the court held, those claims could proceed directly because no monetary recovery would accrue to the corporation as a result of the suit.[3] The commentary to the ALI PRINCIPLES confirms that "courts have been more prepared to permit the plaintiff to characterize the action as direct when the plaintiff is seeking only injunctive or prospective relief."[4]

The Delaware supreme court addressed this issue in *Tooley v. Donaldson, Lufkin & Jenrette, Inc.*[5] The court recognized that many prior decisions used the so-called "special injury" test to determine whether a suit was direct or derivative. A special injury was defined as a wrong that "is separate and distinct from that suffered by other shareholders, ... or a wrong involving a contractual right of a shareholder, such as the right to vote, or to assert majority control, which exists independently of any right of the corporation."[6] In *Tooley,* the Delaware supreme court rejected the special injury test, in favor of the following two-pronged standard: (1) who suffered the alleged harm, the corporation or the suing stockholders, individually; and (2) who would receive the benefit of any recovery or other remedy, the corporation or the stockholders, individually. This is a potentially easier standard to apply than the ALI version, since it eliminates the need to determine the party to whom the defendant owed duties.

Specific suits that have been characterized as derivative in nature include claims involving corporate rights arising out of tort

---

[2] ALI PRINCIPLES § 7.01. When the defendants are corporate directors or officers, it is particularly important identify the party to whom the defendants owed the relevant duty, because they owe duties to both the corporation as an entity and the shareholders as individuals. Because of this dual loyalty, a particular course of conduct sometimes will violate two or more duties owed by the same defendant—one to the corporation and a different one owed to the shareholders as individuals. Insider trading, for example, can violate both a duty owed to the corporation as an entity and a separate duty owed to the shareholder who is selling the securities. In such a case, the shareholders may bring a direct action to redress their own injuries, while also bringing a derivative action to redress the injury to the corporation. ALI PRINCIPLES § 7.01(c).

[3] Grimes v. Donald, 673 A.2d 1207, 1213 (Del.1996).

[4] ALI PRINCIPLES § 7.01 cmt. d.

[5] 845 A.2d 1031 (Del.Sup.2004).

[6] Moran v. Household Int'l, Inc., 490 A.2d 1059, 1070 (Del.Ch.1985), aff'd 500 A.2d 1346 (Del.1985).

or contract, monetary damages based on corporate mismanagement, executive compensation, waste of corporate assets, and the adequacy of consideration for issuance of corporate stock. Suits that may be brought directly include claims involving oppression of minority shareholders, a proposed reorganization favoring one class of shares over another, compelling declaration of a dividend, inspection of corporate books and records, shareholder voting rights, preemptive rights, and injunctive relief where the board of directors improperly abdicated its authority to corporate officers. Examples of conduct simultaneously giving rise both to derivative and direct causes of action include sale of corporate offices and violations of the federal proxy rules. In close cases, as already suggested, courts are often willing to accept a plaintiff's characterization of the suit as direct, at least where plaintiff is seeking only injunctive or prospective relief.[7] Note that in diversity actions brought in federal court, state law controls whether a suit is direct or derivative.[8]

§ 8.3   Attorney's Fees: Herein of Strike Suits and Their Converse

In 1949, the U.S. Supreme Court observed:

> This [derivative suit] remedy, born of stockholder helplessness, was long the chief regulator of corporate management and has afforded no small incentive to avoid at least grosser forms of betrayal of stockholders' interests. . . . Unfortunately, the remedy itself provided opportunity for abuse, which was not neglected. Suits sometimes were brought not to redress real wrongs, but to realize upon their nuisance value. . . . These litigations were aptly characterized in professional slang as "strike suits."[9]

As the Supreme Court elsewhere explained, strike suits are nonmeritorious actions brought "by people who might be interested in getting quick dollars by making charges without regard to their truth so as to coerce corporate managers to settle worthless claims in order to get rid of them."[10]

The basic problem is that the real party in interest is the plaintiffs' attorney rather than the plaintiff-shareholders themselves. Because the derivative cause of action belongs to the corporation, any monetary recovery belongs to the corporation and

---

[7] ALI PRINCIPLES § 7.01 cmt. d.

[8] Sax v. World Wide Press, Inc., 809 F.2d 610, 613 (9th Cir.1987).

[9] Cohen v. Beneficial Indus. Loan Corp., 337 U.S. 541, 548 (1949).

[10] Surowitz v. Hilton Hotels Corp., 383 U.S. 363, 371 (1966).

normally will be paid into the corporate treasury. The sole benefit the representative shareholder-plaintiff receives is the increase in share price, if any, resulting from that recovery and/or from any improved management that results from the suit.

Why would a shareholder expend sizeable legal fees and other costs in an effort to achieve such an uncertain reward? It was early recognized that shareholders would not bring derivative suits if they were obliged to bear the legal costs of suit in all cases. As a result, both federal and state law provide for payment of the plaintiff's legal fees in derivative litigation.

The usual American Rule, of course, is that each party pays its own legal fees and other expenses. In the derivative suit context, however, the corporation may be ordered to pay the plaintiff-shareholder's fees and expenses if the litigation results in a monetary recovery or confers a substantial nonmonetary benefit on the corporation. Courts are quite generous in finding a substantial benefit, even in cases where the outcome clearly had little effect on the corporation's finances or stock price.

It is for this reason that the real party in interest—i.e., the party on the plaintiffs' side with the greatest personal interest in the outcome of the litigation—is the plaintiff's attorney rather than the nominal shareholder-plaintiff. Consequently, those attorneys have little incentive to refrain from bringing strike suits. The fee regime encourages them to bring nuisance suits in the hope that management will settle just so that the case will go away, while the shareholders ultimately bear any expenses incurred in the settlement.

Conversely, however, the shareholder-plaintiffs' attorney may be too eager to settle a meritorious suit. Recall that all corporate statutes allow the corporation to indemnify management for expenses incurred in defending or settling suits brought against them in their official capacity. The corporation, moreover, must indemnify managers who succeed "on the merits or otherwise."[11] A manager who is dismissed from the litigation, for whatever reason, without having to make a monetary payment is deemed to have "succeeded" for this purpose.[12] As a result, it may be in the interests of both the plaintiff-shareholders' attorney and the managerial defendants to settle meritorious litigation before trial. The settlement can be crafted in such a way as to exonerate the individual defendants, while still permitting payment of plaintiffs' legal fees. The individual defendants face no risk of personal liability or expense, because the firm will reimburse them, and

---

[11] See, e.g., DGCL § 145(c).

[12] See, e.g., Waltuch v. Conticommodity Servs., Inc., 88 F.3d 87 (2d Cir.1996).

plaintiffs' counsel is assured of some payment. In contrast, taking the case to trial significantly increases the uncertainty and, hence, the risks facing both sides. Plaintiff's counsel will get no fee if the trial does not result in some "substantial benefit," but defendants who lose at trial may have to pay a judgment without benefit of indemnification.

The corporation and its shareholders lose under either settlement scenario. A rational shareholder would not bring strike suits, absent some sort of side payment or other nonpro rata benefit, because any expenses incurred by the corporation reduce the value of the residual claim and, accordingly, come out of the shareholder's pocket. Because the real party in interest is the plaintiffs' attorney, who will not own stock in the affected corporation and thus will lack any economic incentive to maintain the value of the residual claim, however, there is no disincentive to bringing nonmeritorious suits and plenty of incentive to do so. Conversely, rational shareholders would not want to settle meritorious suits for less than their (discounted) full value, but again the real parties in interest have incentives to do so. Many of the rules governing derivative litigation are best understood as a response to these concerns.

§ 8.4 Procedural Aspects

A. FRCP 23.1

Derivative suits have some unique procedural aspects, most of which are nicely captured by Federal Rule of Civil Procedure 23.1:

> In a derivative action brought by one or more shareholders or members to enforce a right of a corporation or of an unincorporated association, the corporation or association having failed to enforce a right which may properly be asserted by it, the complaint shall be verified and shall allege (1) that the plaintiff was a shareholder or member at the time of the transaction of which the plaintiff complains or that the plaintiff's share or membership thereafter devolved on the plaintiff by operation of law, and (2) that the action is not a collusive one to confer jurisdiction on a court of the United States which it would not otherwise have. The complaint shall also allege with particularity the efforts, if any, made by the plaintiff to obtain the action the plaintiff desires from the directors or comparable authority and, if necessary, from the shareholders or members, and the reasons for the plaintiff's failure to obtain the action or for not making the effort. The derivative action may not be maintained if it

appears that the plaintiff does not fairly and adequately represent the interests of the shareholders or members similarly situated in enforcing the right of the corporation or association. The action shall not be dismissed or compromised without the approval of the court, and notice of the proposed dismissal or compromise shall be given to shareholders or members in such manner as the court directs.

Many states, including Delaware, have comparable rules. The following sections break out the various elements of Rule 23.1, as well as describing some additional procedural rules imposed by various states. Because the seemingly trivial provision for demand on the board of directors has assumed great doctrinal significance, that requirement is deferred for separate consideration.

B. Choice of Law and Forum

As a preliminary matter, we must address the conflict of law and federalism issues posed by the intersection of Federal Rule 23.1 and substantive state corporate law. Consider, for example, the problems presented by *Cohen v. Beneficial Industrial Loan Corp.*[13] Cohen filed, in federal district court in New Jersey, a derivative action claiming that Beneficial's directors had committed various breaches of fiduciary duty. Because a breach of fiduciary duty implicates state rather than federal law, subject matter jurisdiction rested solely on diversity of citizenship. Under a New Jersey security for expenses statute, shareholder-plaintiffs who lost a derivative action were liable for the corporation's reasonable expenses and attorney's fees. In addition, the statute authorized defendants to require plaintiffs who owned less than $50,000 worth of stock to post a bond ensuring payment of such expenses. Federal Rule 23.1 lacks any such requirement, as does Delaware law—the state in which Beneficial was incorporated. Under standard choice of law rules, Delaware law provided the governing substantive law. But what about that pesky New Jersey security for expenses statute? Did it apply to Cohen's suit?

The Supreme Court held that under *Erie Railroad Co. v. Tompkins*,[14] in diversity actions, "mere rules of procedure" are governed by federal law but "rules of substantive law" are provided by state law. Consequently, for example, "questions of whether or not a stockholder may bring a derivative action are governed by state law."[15] As for the securities for expense statute, the Supreme

---

[13] 337 U.S. 541 (1949).

[14] 304 U.S. 64 (1938).

[15] Galef v. Alexander, 615 F.2d 51, 58 (2d Cir.1980).

Court deemed it to be substantive in nature for *Erie* purposes, because the statute created both a potential liability and a mechanism for recovering any such liability. In contrast, the various requirements set forth in Federal Rule 23.1 are procedural in nature. A federal court sitting in diversity therefore will apply Rule 23.1 rather than any inconsistent state rules.[16]

A different question is presented when federal subject matter jurisdiction over a derivative action is based on a federal cause of action. Suits involving federal questions, of course, are not subject to the *Erie* regime. Courts have thus held, for example, that state security for expenses statutes do not apply to such suits.[17]

A choice of law problem nevertheless persists in derivative actions involving federal questions. In *Burks v. Lasker*,[18] a shareholder of a federally regulated investment company brought suit under the federal securities laws against the company's board of directors. The Supreme Court held that state law controls the board of directors' ability to use a special litigation committee to terminate the litigation. In *Kamen v. Kemper Financial Services, Inc.*,[19] the Court extended *Burks*, describing the federal law governing derivative suits brought under the Investment Company Act as a species of federal common law, and incorporating state law governing excusal of the demand requirement in such suits. Unless there is a clear inconsistency between the federal and state law, or the state law would frustrate relevant federal policies, state law thus controls most aspects of derivative litigation in federal question cases except for basic substantive issues of liability.

Although the law of the state of incorporation thus controls most questions, there generally has been no requirement that a derivative suit be brought in the state courts of the state of incorporation. Instead, the plaintiff could file in any federal or state court having the requisite personal and subject matter jurisdiction. In *Boilermakers Local 154 Ret. Fund v. Chevron Corp.*,[20] however, the Delaware Chancery Court upheld a so-called "exclusive forum" bylaw, which required that both direct and derivative shareholder suits be filed solely in Delaware Chancery Court. The bylaw in

---

[16] Sax v. World Wide Press, Inc., 809 F.2d 610, 613 (9th Cir.1987).

[17] See, e.g., McClure v. Borne Chem. Co., 292 F.2d 824 (3d Cir.), cert. denied, 368 U.S. 939 (1961). Such statutes will apply to any pendent state claims, however. See, e.g., Weisfeld v. Spartans Indus., Inc., 58 F.R.D. 570, 578 (S.D.N.Y.1972) (holding that "[t]he law is clear that state security requirements for shareholders' derivative actions should be enforced by the federal courts in both pendent and diversity jurisdiction cases but as to *State* causes of action only.").

[18] 441 U.S. 471 (1979).

[19] 500 U.S. 90 (1991).

[20] 73 A. 3d 934 (Del. Ch. 2013).

question had been unilaterally adopted by the board of directors without shareholder approval and provided that:

> Unless the Corporation consents in writing to the selection of an alternative forum, the Court of Chancery of the State of Delaware shall be the sole and exclusive forum for (i) any derivative action or proceeding brought on behalf of the Corporation, (ii) any action asserting a claim of breach of a fiduciary duty owed by any director, officer or other employee of the Corporation to the Corporation or the Corporation's stockholders, (iii) any action asserting a claim arising pursuant to any provision of the Delaware General Corporation Law, or (iv) any action asserting a claim governed by the internal affairs doctrine. Any person or entity purchasing or otherwise acquiring any interest in shares of capital stock of the Corporation shall be deemed to have notice of and consented to the provisions of this [bylaw].

DGCL § 109(a) gives the board power to unilaterally adopt bylaws provided the articles of incorporation grant that power to the board, which was the case in Chevron. Section 109(b) provides that the bylaws of a corporation "may contain any provision, not inconsistent with law or with the certificate of incorporation, relating to the business of the corporation, the conduct of its affairs, and its rights or powers or the rights or powers of its stockholders, directors, officers or employees." Because the court deemed forum selection bylaws to relate to the corporation's affairs, the bylaw was valid.

Since the *Boilermakers'* decision, courts in at least 3 other states (California, Louisiana, and New York) have held such bylaws to be valid and enforced them by requiring plaintiffs to file their lawsuit in Delaware.[21]

C. Verification

Federal Rule 23.1 and the corporation statutes of about 20 states require verification of the complaint. To verify the complaint, the plaintiff swears that the allegations in the complaint are true. The verification requirement's supposed purpose has been stated as follows: "The verification of the complaint in a shareholder derivative action may appear at first blush to be a purely technical requirement, but it serves the important purpose of ensuring 'that the plaintiff or some other person has investigated the charges and found them to have substance,' and thereby prevent the filing of

---

[21] Groen v. Safeway Inc., 763 F.Supp.2d 1170 (N.D. Cal. 2011); Genoud v. Edgen Group, Inc., 2014 WL 2782221 (La.Dist.Ct. Jan. 17, 2014)); Hemg Inc. v. Aspen University, 2013 WL 5958388 (N.Y. Sup. Ct., Nov. 4, 2013).

strike suits."[22] On the other hand, courts have emphasized that the verification requirement is "not to be a general impediment to shareholder derivative actions."[23]

Courts routinely grant plaintiffs leave to replead and properly verify a deficient complaint. Courts have likewise waived the verification requirement when it was apparent from a plaintiff's deposition that he was sufficiently cognizant of the complaint's allegations.[24] Courts have also waived the requirement if plaintiff filed an affidavit verifying the complaint and further swearing the failure to properly verify the complaint was a mere oversight.[25] Finally, courts have held that plaintiffs' failure to comply with the verification requirement at the time the complaint was filed is not a jurisdictional defect, such that defendant waives the objection if it is not made on a timely basis.[26]

The U.S. Supreme Court dealt a body blow to the verification requirement when it deemed that requirement to be satisfied where plaintiff "verified the complaint, not on the basis of her own knowledge and understanding, but in the faith that her son-in-law had correctly advised her either that the statements in the complaint were true or to the best of his knowledge he believed them to be true."[27] As a result, the verifying plaintiff no longer need have detailed personal knowledge of the events that gave rise to the suit. Instead, it suffices that "some person, party, attorney, advisor, or otherwise has responsibly investigated the allegations at the behest of the named plaintiff, who then stands behind the merits of the complaint."[28]

Given the verification requirement's substantial erosion, it now seems wholly pointless. The MBCA has eliminated its former verification requirement. The ALI PRINCIPLES substituted a requirement of attorney certification for that of verification by the plaintiff. ALI PRINCIPLES § 7.04(b) thus provides that counsel must certify that every pleading and motion is well grounded in fact and is warranted by existing law or by a good faith argument for the extension, modification, or reversal of existing law, and further that the filing is not made for any improper purpose, such as to cause unnecessary delay. As the commentary to § 7.04(b) indicates, this standard essentially tracks the sanction provisions of Federal Rule

---

[22] Smachlo v. Birkelo, 576 F.Supp. 1439, 1442 (D.Del.1983).

[23] See, e.g., Lewis v. Curtis, 671 F.2d 779, 787 (3d Cir.1982).

[24] See, e.g., Deaktor v. Fox Grocery Co., 332 F.Supp. 536, 541 (W.D.Pa.1971).

[25] See, e.g., Markowitz v. Brody, 90 F.R.D. 542, 549 n. 2 (S.D.N.Y.1981); Weisfeld v. Spartans Indus., Inc., 58 F.R.D. 570, 577–58 (S.D.N.Y.1972).

[26] See, e.g., Alford v. Shaw, 398 S.E.2d 445, 447 (N.C.1990).

[27] Surowitz v. Hilton Hotels Corp., 383 U.S. 363, 370–71 (1966).

[28] Rogosin v. Steadman, 65 F.R.D. 365, 367 (S.D.N.Y.1974).

of Civil Procedure 11. If preventing strike suits is the goal, the ALI's approach seems a more effective solution than Federal Rule 23.1's verification requirement.

D. Contemporaneous Ownership

1. *The Basic Requirement*

Federal Rule 23.1's contemporaneous ownership provision requires the verified complaint to allege that the plaintiff was a shareholder at the time of the challenged or event. MBCA § 7.41 elevates the contemporaneous ownership requirement into a rule of standing. Under it, shareholders may not "commence or maintain" a derivative suit unless they were shareholders "at the time of the act or omission complained of." The phrase "commence or maintain" codifies the long-standing common law rule that standing to sue derivatively is limited to those who are shareholders both at the time the cause of action was arose and when the suit was filed.[29] In some states, moreover, one must also be a shareholder when judgment is entered,[30] or even through the appeals process.[31]

Both Federal Rule 23.1 and MBCA § 7.41 provide limited exceptions to the contemporaneous ownership requirement. Both grant standing to shareholders who received their shares by operation of law—e.g., via bequest—from a contemporaneous shareholder. In addition, both provide that plaintiff need not be a record owner of shares—beneficial ownership suffices.

Various common law exceptions to the contemporaneous ownership requirement also have been created. Some courts, for example, recognize a quasi-exemption to the requirement by allowing so-called double derivative suits in which a shareholder of a parent corporation sues on behalf of a wholly-owned subsidiary.

---

[29] See, e.g., Hawes v. Oakland, 104 U.S. 450, 461 (1881); Werfel v. Kramarsky, 61 F.R.D. 674 (S.D.N.Y.1974); Green v. Bradley Const., Inc., 431 So.2d 1226 (Ala.1983); but cf. Bateson v. Magna Oil Corp., 414 F.2d 128 (5th Cir.1969), which held that a shareholder who inadvertently sold his stock but shortly thereafter reacquired stock for very purpose of filing a previously planned derivative suit had standing. Id. at 131.

[30] See, e.g., Sorin v. Shahmoon Indus., Inc., 220 N.Y.S.2d 760, 781 (Sup.Ct.1961); but see Alford v. Shaw, 398 S.E.2d 445, 449 (N.C.1990) (holding "there is no requirement of continuing share ownership in order for an individual who is a shareholder at the time of the transaction about which he is complaining and at the time the action is filed, to proceed with a derivative action").

[31] See Schilling v. Belcher, 582 F.2d 995 (5th Cir.1978), interpreting Florida law as providing that shareholder who sells his stock while an appeal from a favorable judgment is pending loses standing to further prosecute the case except to extent that the judgment runs personally to his favor. Id. at 996. This holding was rejected by ALI PRINCIPLES § 7.02(a)(2) and, in any event, would be inapplicable as to jurisdictions in which shareholders are not obliged to hold their stock through judgment.

Both corporations must be made party to such a suit and demand must be made on both boards of directors.[32]

Some courts have also recognized a so-called continuing wrong exception to the contemporaneous ownership requirement.[33] The cases are all over the map, however, and many courts apply this exception quite conservatively. "The effects of an act can ripple through decades. But that fact does not mean that the act itself continues . . . so as to entitle later purchasers of the stock to sue on earlier wrongs."[34]

What if the would-be plaintiffs involuntarily lost their status as shareholders as a result of corporate action, perhaps even the action of which plaintiffs complain, as where the shareholders were forced out by a freeze-out merger? In *Lewis v. Anderson*,[35] the Delaware supreme court held that such a shareholder lacks standing. It is hard to see any justification for the *Lewis* rule, other than the highly formalistic notion that the cause of action belongs to the corporation. The rule is "tantamount to paving the way for deliberate corporate pilfering by management and then for the immunization of the guilty officers from liability therefor by their arranging for a merger or consolidation of the corporation into or with another corporation."[36]

The continuous ownership requirement is sometimes justified as being necessary to ensure that the plaintiff will adequately represent interests of all shareholders. Because any recovery in derivative litigation normally is paid to the corporation, someone who is not now a shareholder will not benefit from a successful suit. A former shareholder thus supposedly has an incentive to negotiate an inadequate settlement that confers some personal benefit on the shareholder. Because it is the shareholder-plaintiff's lawyer who is the real party in interest, however, this justification for the rule has little merit.

The contemporaneous ownership requirement also is often justified as necessary to prevent courts from being used as a forum for purchased grievances or speculative suits.[37] Hence, for example,

---

[32] Cochran v. Stifel Fin. Corp., 2000 WL 286722 (Del.Ch.); Flocco v. State Farm Mut. Auto. Ins. Co., 752 A.2d 147, 154 (D.C.2000) (interpreting Illinois law).

[33] See, e.g., Valle v. North Jersey Auto. Club, 376 A.2d 1192 (N.J.1977).

[34] Thorpe v. CERBCO, Inc., 1993 WL 35967 at *4 (Del.Ch.).

[35] 477 A.2d 1040 (Del.1984). Two exceptions recognized by Delaware to the *Lewis* rule are: "(1) where the merger itself is the subject of a claim of fraud; and (2) where the merger is in reality a reorganization which does not affect plaintiff's ownership." Lewis v. Anderson, 477 A.2d 1040, 1046 n. 10 (Del.1984).

[36] Platt Corp. v. Platt, 249 N.Y.S.2d 75, 83 (App.Div.1964), aff'd mem., 256 N.Y.S.2d 335 (1965).

[37] Cohen v. Beneficial Industrial Loan Corp., 337 U.S. 541, 556 (1949). See also Bank of Santa Fe v. Petty, 867 P.2d 431 (N.M.App.1993) (noting that requirement is intended to prevent champerty).

the rule prevents "an outsider from buying or acquiring shares for the purpose of seeking to upset an action that had been taken by the corporation at some previous time."[38] According to some courts, those who bring such suits would be unjustly enriched by a recovery under the circumstances.[39] As long as any recovery is paid into the corporate treasury, however, concerns over potential unjust enrichment seem misplaced. All current shareholders are benefited by such a recovery, without regard to when they acquired their shares. If the company is publicly held, moreover, the correct question is not when the challenged event occurred but when it became public knowledge. A public company's stock price will adjust immediately after wrongdoing becomes public. Barring shareholders who acquired their stock in the interim from suing derivatively thus bars suit by persons who were doubtless injured. ALI PRINCIPLES § 7.02(a)(1) correctly grants standing to persons who acquired their shares before the material facts were disclosed to the public or otherwise known by the purchaser.

2.   *Bondholder Standing to Sue Derivatively*

Federal Rule 23.1's contemporaneous ownership provision requires an allegation "that the plaintiff was a *shareholder*" at the requisite times. MBCA § 7.40 likewise refers solely to shareholders when discussing the right to sue derivatively. Do these seemingly procedural provisions imply a further standing limitation? Specifically, does the contemporaneous ownership requirement deny standing to bondholders?

Although the MBCA's statutory text does not speak directly to this issue, the statute's drafters assert that MBCA § 7.41 implicitly limits derivative standing to shareholders. Consequently, "creditors or holders of options, warrants, or conversion rights" lack standing to sue derivatively.[40] In *Harff v. Kerkorian*,[41] the Delaware chancery court likewise limited standing under its derivative litigation statute to shareholders.

In *Harff*, holders of MGM convertible bonds claimed that MGM's directors had breached their fiduciary duty to the corporation by paying an excessive dividend. Although suits to enforce a dividend right are treated as direct, this lawsuit was derivative because it involved claims that a dividend was paid improperly. Convertible bonds generally have a lower coupon rate

---

[38] Kaplus v. First Continental Corp., 711 So.2d 108, 112 (Fla.App.1998).

[39] See Bangor Punta Operations, Inc. v. Bangor & Aroostook R.R., 417 U.S. 703, 711 (1974) (rule prevents a windfall).

[40] MBCA § 7.41 cmt.

[41] 324 A.2d 215 (Del.Ch.1974), rev'd in part on other grounds, 347 A.2d 133 (Del.1975).

than regular bonds. To the extent that the conversion feature has value to the debtholders, that value is part of the economic return on their investment. Accordingly, the debtholders will not demand as high a rate of interest as will the holder of a nonconvertible bond. The allegedly excessive dividend reduced the value of the common stock and, indirectly, injured the bondholders by reducing the value of their conversion feature.

Neither the corporation nor its directors owe any fiduciary duties to bondholders, at least so long as the corporation is solvent. In this case, however, the issue was whether bondholders have the right to sue derivatively on behalf of the corporate enterprise. *Harff* held that bondholders have no standing to sue derivatively, even if their bonds have a conversion feature. Even if the word "shareholder" in the relevant statutes is broadly interpreted to include holders of all equity securities, a convertible bond remains purely a debt security until such time as it is converted into stock.[42]

The leading case holding to the contrary is *Hoff v. Sprayregan*,[43] which involved a claim that the directors had wasted corporate assets by issuing stock for inadequate consideration to a person who thereby became a controlling shareholder. As with *Harff*, the transactions at issue made exercising the conversion feature less attractive and thus reduced the value of that feature, reducing the return to investors. First, the transactions entailed creation of a new class of preferred stock with rights superior to the common into which the debentures were convertible. Second, the issuance of stock below market value had a dilutive effect, which lowered the value of the common. Finally, the transaction resulted in Sprayregan becoming the dominant shareholder of the firm.

Hoff held that holders of convertible bonds have standing to sue derivatively on behalf of the corporation. The *Hoff* court finessed the apparent standing limitation imposed by FRCP 23.1's reference to shareholders by defining that term to include holders of convertible bonds. The underlying cause of action was based on the federal Securities Exchange Act, which includes convertible bonds within its definition of equity securities.[44] It is not self-evident that the definitions of equity securities and shareholder are co-extensive, but without any real explanation or justification the court nevertheless equated them. Accordingly, the court held that the convertible bondholders had standing to sue derivatively.

---

[42] In Simons v. Cogan, 549 A.2d 300 (Del.1988), the Delaware supreme court endorsed *Harff*.

[43] 52 F.R.D. 243 (S.D.N.Y.1971).

[44] Securities Exchange Act § 3(a)(11).

Note that, even if it was correctly decided, *Hoff* thus does not grant standing to holders of nonconvertible bonds. One also could argue that *Hoff*'s analysis is mere dicta. As an alternative holding, the court noted that the convertible bondholders had exercised their conversion rights in July 1969. Certain aspects of the challenged transactions were not completed until August of that year. Invoking the continuing wrong principle, the court held that the former bondholders—who were now shareholders—were entitled to sue. In any event, the subsequent *Brooks v. Weiser* decision limited *Hoff* to its specific legal setting—i.e., a federal claim arising under a statute including convertible securities within the definition of equity securities. Where state corporate law provides the underlying substantive legal regime, standing before a federal court sitting in diversity is determined by reference to state law definitions of the term shareholder.[45]

3.   Director qua Director Standing

Assume an injury to the corporation giving rise to a claim belonging to the corporation. Obviously, the board of directors, acting collectively, could authorize the corporation's agents to bring the lawsuit in question. Suppose, however, the board has not acted. An individual director who is also a shareholder obviously could bring a derivative cause of action in the latter capacity. But does a director qua director have standing? The logical answer is no, although that answer is based on the implications of several distinct principles rather than a single statement of doctrine. First, both MBCA § 7.41 and Federal Rule 23.1 speak only of shareholders. As we have seen, other corporate constituents (such as creditors) lack standing. Second, under AGENCY RESTATEMENT § 14 C, an individual director is not an agent of the corporation. Indeed, comment b to that section states that the individual director "has no power of his own to act on the corporation's behalf, but only as one of the body of directors acting as a board." Taken together, these principles logically suggest that a director acting alone has no standing to sue qua director.

A few states, most notably New York, confer standing by statute on individual directors to bring derivative proceedings.[46] A director may not initiate a derivative action after leaving office, but neither removal nor expiration of the director's term of office extinguishes the director's standing to continue a previously filed suit. ALI PRINCIPLES § 7.02(c) adopted the same rule.[47]

---

[45] 57 F.R.D. 491, 494 (S.D.N.Y.1972).

[46] N.Y. Bus. Corp. Law § 720.

[47] In Schoon v. Smith, 953 A.2d 196 (Del.2008), the court held that the judiciary has the power to create standing for a director suing in his capacity as

E. Collusive Jurisdiction and Realignment of Parties

Federal Rule 23.1 requires that the plaintiff verify that the suit is "not a collusive one to confer jurisdiction on a court of the United States. . . ." For our purposes, the significant questions posed by this requirement are (1) whether the corporation is a necessary party to the litigation and (2) whether the corporation should be aligned as a plaintiff or defendant.

The corporation is deemed an indispensable party who must be joined to the litigation.[48] Accordingly, plaintiffs normally start out by naming the corporation as a defendant, so as to ensure it is joined to the litigation. In theory, courts then should realign the corporation as a plaintiff, because any recovery normally will be paid to the corporation. If the corporation's board of directors is actively opposing the shareholder-plaintiff, however, such that the corporation is "antagonistic" to the lawsuit, courts will align the corporation as a defendant.[49]

> The question of whether to realign the corporation as a plaintiff or allow it to remain as a defendant is "a practical not a mechanical determination and is resolved by the pleadings and the nature of the dispute." Thus, if the complaint in a derivative action alleges that the controlling shareholders or dominant officials of the corporation are guilty of fraud or malfeasance, then antagonism is clearly evident and the corporation remains a defendant. On the other hand, if the individual plaintiff is the majority stockholder or a controlling officer, then the corporation cannot be deemed antagonistic to the suit and it should be realigned as a plaintiff.[50]

F. Fair and Adequate Representation

Under both Federal Rule 23.1 and MBCA § 7.41(2), the named shareholder-plaintiff must be a fair and adequate representative. But of what? Under the Rule, the plaintiff must fairly and adequately represent the interests of similarly situated shareholders. Under MBCA § 7.41(2), the plaintiff must fairly and adequately represent the corporation's interests. Given that the

---

such, but that at present "no new exigencies" required an "extension of equitable standing to . . . a director."

[48] See, e.g., Liddy v. Urbanek, 707 F.2d 1222, 1224 (11th Cir.1983); Dean v. Kellogg, 292 N.W. 704, 707 (Mich.1940); but cf. Weinert v. Kinkel, 71 N.E.2d 445 (N.Y.1947) (dissolved corporation was not an indispensable party).

[49] Smith v. Sperling, 354 U.S. 91, 95 (1957).

[50] Liddy v. Urbanek, 707 F.2d 1222, 1224–25 (11th Cir.1983) (citations omitted).

derivative suit conceptually "belongs" to the corporation and not the shareholders, the latter approach seems preferable.

In practice, would-be plaintiffs are most commonly disqualified under the fairness and adequacy standard where they brought the derivative suit for strategic purposes relating to other disputes with the corporation or its management. In *Recchion v. Kirby*,[51] for example, the would-be plaintiff-shareholder owned only one share of stock, brought the suit six years after he learned of the allegedly wrongful conduct, was supported by no other shareholders, and had a pending personal lawsuit against the corporation. Concluding that the derivative action was brought for use as leverage in plaintiff's personal lawsuit, the court disqualified the plaintiff.

In several cases brought by shareholder-plaintiffs who were pursuing an attempted acquisition of the corporation, the would-be plaintiffs have been disqualified.[52] In contrast, courts have divided on whether shareholders who have tried to compel the corporation or its other shareholders to buy their shares at an above-market price should be disqualified.[53]

Plaintiffs also will be disqualified where they participated in, knowingly acquiesced in, or voted to ratify the challenged conduct. In *Recchion*, for example, the court held that plaintiff had unclean hands because he had participated in some of the alleged misconduct knowing that his actions were improper and inconsistent with generally accepted accounting practices. Plaintiff was therefore estopped to bring a derivative suit.[54]

Given that the real party in interest usually is the plaintiff's lawyer rather than the nominal shareholder-plaintiff, it is noteworthy that at least one court has disqualified a plaintiff on grounds that she possessed "little, if any, comprehension of the litigation" and "that total control as well as financing of the action rests with the lawyers."[55] Conversely, however, a named plaintiff who is not an attorney may not proceed pro se.[56] The resulting

---

[51] 637 F.Supp. 1309 (W.D.Pa.1986).

[52] See, e.g., Nolen v. Shaw-Walker Co., 449 F.2d 506 (6th Cir.1971); Adiel v. Electronic Fin. Systems, Inc., 513 So.2d 1347 (Fla.App.1987).

[53] Compare Vanderbilt v. Geo-Energy Ltd., 725 F.2d 204 (3d Cir.1983) (not disqualified) with Steinberg v. Steinberg, 434 N.Y.S.2d 877 (Sup.Ct.1980) (disqualified).

[54] Recchion v. Kirby, 637 F.Supp. 1309, 1316 (W.D.Pa.1986).

[55] Mills v. Esmark, Inc., 573 F.Supp. 169, 176 (N.D.Ill.1983). Other courts have indicated that plaintiff's knowledge and the degree of control exercised by counsel are factors to be considered. See, e.g., Rothenberg v. Security Mgmt. Co., Inc., 667 F.2d 958, 961 (11th Cir.1982); Davis v. Comed, Inc., 619 F.2d 588, 593–94 (6th Cir.1980).

[56] Pridgen v. Andresen, 113 F.3d 391, 393 (2d Cir.1997); In re Texaco Inc. Shareholder Derivative Litig., 123 F.Supp.2d 169, 172 (S.D.N.Y.2000).

problem is solved by combining a knowledgeable named plaintiff with competent legal counsel.

In general, the adequacy of the named plaintiff is determined under the totality of the circumstances. In doing so, courts consider a number of factors: (1) economic or other conflicts between the named plaintiff and other shareholders; (2) evidence that the named plaintiff was not the driving force behind the litigation, especially with respect to the degree of control exercised by counsel; (3) plaintiff's lack of familiarity with the litigation; (4) pendency of other litigation between the named plaintiff and the individual defendants and/or the corporation; (5) evidence of personal vindictiveness toward the defendants; and (6) the support plaintiff receives from other shareholders, if any.[57]

G. Judicial Approval of Settlements

Federal Rule 23.1 and MBCA § 7.45 require judicial approval before a derivative suit may be settled and notice of a proposed settlement must be given to the shareholders. To be approved, the settlement is supposed to be fair, reasonable and adequate.[58] The settlement must not be collusive, but rather the product of arm's length negotiations following adequate discovery. Courts purportedly consider a wide range of factors in deciding whether to approve a settlement, including: (1) the maximum and likely recovery; (2) the complexity, expense, and duration of continued litigation; (3) the probability of success; (4) the stage of the proceedings; (5) the ability of the defendants to pay a larger judgment; (6) the adequacy of the settlement terms; (7) whether the settlement vindicates important public policies; (8) whether the settlement was approved by disinterested directors; and (9) whether other shareholders have objected.[59] Cases in which objecting shareholders intervene to challenge a settlement likely get far more exacting scrutiny than those in which the other shareholders remain quiescent. If objecting shareholders are able to force a better deal, they are entitled to their own legal fees.[60]

---

[57] See, e.g., Rothenberg v. Security Mgmt. Co., Inc., 667 F.2d 958, 961 (11th Cir.1982); Davis v. Comed, Inc., 619 F.2d 588, 593–94 (6th Cir.1980).

[58] See 2 ALI PRINCIPLES at 188; cf. Desimone v. Indus. Bio-Test Labs., Inc., 83 F.R.D. 615, 618 (S.D.N.Y.1979) (discussing comparable rules governing settlement of class actions).

[59] See, e.g., Shlensky v. Dorsey, 574 F.2d 131 (3d Cir.1978); Krasner v. Dreyfus Corp., 500 F.Supp. 36 (S.D.N.Y.1980); see also Polk v. Good, 507 A.2d 531, 536 (Del.1986) (holding that the chancellor "exercises a form of business judgment to determine the overall reasonableness of the settlement").

[60] White v. Auerbach, 500 F.2d 822 (2d Cir.1974) (remanding for evidentiary hearing on issue).

The judicial approval requirement is especially significant in light of the claim preclusive effect of settlements.[61] In theory, judicial approval acts as a check on both the incentive to bring strike suits and the incentive to settle meritorious claims too cheaply. In practice, however, trial courts possess broad discretion to approve derivative suit settlements.[62] Settlements imposing minimal sanctions on individual defendants and conferring nominal benefits on the corporation, if any, but large legal fees for the plaintiffs' lawyers are routinely approved. The judicial approval requirement commonly seems all bark and no bite.

H. Recovery

In general, any monetary recovery from a derivative lawsuit will be paid over to the corporation rather than either the named shareholder-plaintiff or the shareholders as a class. In many cases, of course, the individual defendant directors or officers will also be shareholders and therefore will benefit along with all other shareholders from the resulting increase in value of the residual claim. Although it is often said that individual shareholder recovery is appropriate in derivative proceedings when necessary to prevent a wrongdoer from benefiting by a corporate recovery, in practice that fact alone rarely results in individual recovery.[63] Among other things, because corporate creditors have a prior claim on the firm's assets, individual recovery by shareholders would be inconsistent with the creditors' rights.

Courts have done a lousy job of specifying when individual recovery is appropriate. In trying to summarize the few and often conflicting cases, the ALI PRINCIPLES' drafters seemingly just threw up their hands, as they merely suggested that individual recovery should be ordered when it is "equitable in the circumstances and adequate provision has been made for the creditors of the corporation."[64]

Where individual recovery is ordered, it should be on a pro rata basis. In *Perlman v. Feldmann*, for example, the plaintiff-shareholders owned approximately 63% of the corporation's stock. Having determined defendant's potential liability to be just under $2,126,280.91, the trial court awarded the plaintiffs 63% thereof— $1,339,769.62—plus interest and costs.[65] Notice that corporate

---

[61] Cf. Matsushita Elec. Indus. Co. v. Epstein, 516 U.S. 367 (1996) (giving full faith and credit to a state court settlement purporting to release both state and federal claims).

[62] In re General Tire & Rubber Co. Sec. Litig., 726 F.2d 1075 (6th Cir.1984).

[63] See, e.g., Glenn v. Hoteltron Systems, Inc., 547 N.Y.S.2d 816 (1989).

[64] ALI PRINCIPLES § 7.18(e).

[65] Perlman v. Feldmann, 154 F.Supp. 436 (D.Conn.1957). Similarly, in Lynch v. Patterson, 701 P.2d 1126 (Wyo.1985), plaintiff owned 30% of the corporation's

recovery thus would have subjected the defendants to greater total liability. Indeed, that fact formed part of the appellate court's sparse justification for the imposition of individual recovery.

I.   Jury Trial

In *Ross v. Bernhard*,[66] the U.S. Supreme Court held that the Seventh Amendment right to jury trial potentially applied to derivative proceedings in federal court. The test is whether there would have been a right to trial by jury if the corporation had brought the suit. If so, the equitable nature of the derivative suit does not eliminate the constitutional requirement of trial by jury. State court decisions vary widely. New York recognizes a right to jury trial in derivative suits, for example, while California does not.[67]

§ 8.5   Demand and Board Control of Derivative Litigation

A.   The Demand Requirement

Because the derivative suit is premised on a cause of action belonging to the corporation, one might assume that the corporation would simply bring the lawsuit itself. Derivative suits in fact are relatively rare; most corporate lawsuits are brought by the entity, rather than its shareholders. The derivative suit, of course, was devised so as to permit shareholders to seek relief on behalf of the firm in those cases where the corporation's management for some reason elected not to pursue the claim. Logically, however, it would seem that the corporation should be given an opportunity to decide whether to bring suit before a shareholder is allowed to file a derivative suit.

Accordingly, Federal Rule 23.1 provides that shareholders may not bring suit unless they first make demand on the board of directors or demand is excused.[68] The requisite demand can take any form, although most jurisdictions require that it be in writing. The demand need not be in the form of a pleading nor a detailed as a complaint, but rather simply must request that the board bring

---

stock, with the remaining 70% owned by the defendants. Having successfully established that the defendants had paid themselves excess compensation in the amount of $266,000, plaintiff was awarded 30% of that amount.

[66] 396 U.S. 531 (1970).

[67] Compare Fedoryszyn v. Weiss, 310 N.Y.S.2d 55 (Sup.Ct.1970) with Metcalf v. Shamel, 333 P.2d 857 (Cal.App.1959).

[68] Federal Rule 23.1 contemplates that demand may be made on shareholders in appropriate cases. A few jurisdictions require demand on shareholders, at least in some cases. See, e.g., Heilbrunn v. Hanover Equities Corp., 259 F.Supp. 936 (S.D.N.Y.1966) (demand on shareholders excused where wrongdoers hold a majority of corporation's stock); Mayer v. Adams, 141 A.2d 458 (Del.Supr.1958) (demand on shareholders excused where alleged wrong could not be ratified by shareholders).

suit on the alleged cause of action. To be sure, the demand must be sufficiently specific as to apprise the board of the nature of the alleged cause of action and to evaluate its merits. "At a minimum, a demand must identify the alleged wrongdoers, describe the factual basis of the wrongful acts and the harm caused to the corporation, and request remedial relief."[69] The demand must be directed to the board of directors as a whole, and not merely to the chairman of the board, senior officers, or a majority shareholder.[70] Hence, for example, a fax sent to the office of the corporation's chairman of the board did not satisfy the demand requirement.[71]

Although the demand requirement looks like a mere procedural formality, it has evolved into the central substantive rule of derivative litigation.[72] The foundational question in derivative litigation is the extent to which the corporation, acting through the board of directors or a committee thereof, is permitted to prevent or terminate a derivative action. Put another way, who gets to control the litigation—the shareholder or the corporation's board of directors? Curiously, the answer to that question depends mainly on the procedural posture of the particular case with respect to the demand requirement.

We take up the substantive implications of the demand requirement below. In this section, we focus on the procedural issue of when a shareholder is required to make demand. In particular, we contrast the two leading approaches to the problem—those of New York and Delaware.

1.   New York's Demand Futility Standard

Demand is required in all cases, except those in which it is excused. In turn, demand is excused when it is futile. New York restated its demand futility standard in *Marx v. Akers*.[73] Plaintiff filed a derivative suit against IBM and its directors alleging that the directors had authorized excessive compensation both for

---

[69] Allison v. General Motors Corp., 604 F.Supp. 1106, 1117 (D.Del.), aff'd mem., 782 F.2d 1026 (3d Cir.1985). Accord Lewis v. Sporck, 646 F.Supp. 574, 577–78 (N.D.Cal.1986).

[70] See, e.g., Kaster v. Modification Systems, Inc., 731 F.2d 1014, 1017–19 (2d Cir.1984) (holding that demand on an individual who was president, chairman of the board, and 71% stockholder did not satisfy demand requirement under FRCP 23.1); Shlensky v. Dorsey, 574 F.2d 131, 141 (3d Cir.1978) (four letters sent to the company's president did not satisfy FRCP 23.1).

[71] Equitec-Cole Roesler LLC v. McClanahan, 251 F.Supp.2d 1347 (S.D.Tex.2003).

[72] See Levine v. Smith, 591 A.2d 194, 207 (Del.1991) ("The demand requirement is not a 'mere formalit[y] of litigation,' but rather an important 'stricture[ ] of substantive law.' "); see also Barr v. Wackman, 368 N.Y.S.2d 497, 505 (1975) ("demand is generally designed to weed out unnecessary or illegitimate shareholder derivative suits").

[73] 644 N.Y.S.2d 121 (1996).

themselves and IBM executives. The defendants moved to dismiss on the ground that plaintiff had failed to make demand. As to plaintiff's claim that the board had approved excessive executive salaries, the court agreed that demand was required. As to the claim that the directors had approved excessive compensation for themselves, however, demand was excused.

The court identified three bases on which demand is excused under New York law: First, the complaint alleges with particularity that a majority of the board of directors is interested in the challenged transaction. Director interest obviously is present where the directors have a personal self-interest in the challenged transaction. Directors who cause the corporation to enter into a transaction from which they financially benefit, for example, are clearly interested for this purpose.[74] Alternatively, however, director interest may be present where the director has no personal interest in a transaction but is dominated or controlled by a self-interested director.[75]

Second, demand is excused if the complaint alleges with particularity that the board of directors did not fully inform themselves about the challenged transaction to the extent reasonably appropriate under the circumstances. Directors who "passively rubber-stamp" management decisions have not made an informed judgment. (Notice the implicit parallel to Delaware's decision in *Smith v. Van Gorkom*[76] that the business judgment rule does not protect directors who have made an uninformed judgment.)

Finally, demand is excused where the complaint alleges with particularity that the challenged transaction was so egregious on its face that it could not have been the product of sound business judgment of the directors. Note the parallel to cases like *Litwin v. Allen*,[77] which supposedly withdraw the business judgment rule's protections from directors who have acted irrationally.

It is not enough that one director is interested in the transaction or even if several directors are interested (or failed to inform themselves). Instead, demand is excused only when one of the three *Marx* prongs is satisfied with respect to a majority of the board.[78] The mere fact that a majority of the board is named as defendants does not make them interested for purposes of demand futility. Although being named as defendants may give them a stake in the lawsuit, the requisite interest must be one in the

---

[74] Barr v. Wackman, 368 N.Y.S.2d 497 (1975).

[75] Marx v. Akers, 644 N.Y.S.2d. 121, 128 (1996).

[76] 488 A.2d 858 (Del.1985).

[77] 25 N.Y.S.2d 667 (Sup.Ct.1940).

[78] Marx v. Akers, 644 N.Y.S.2d 121, 127–28 (1996).

underlying transaction or event. Finally, and perhaps most significantly in light of prior more lenient precedents to the contrary, the mere fact that a majority of the board acquiesced in or approved the transaction is insufficient.

As applied to the case at bar, demand was required with respect to the claim of excessive executive compensation. Only three of the 18 directors were executives and only they had a direct personal interest in such compensation. There was no showing that the 15 outsiders were dominated by interested parties and plaintiff's "conclusory allegations" that the board had used faulty procedures to calculate executive salaries did not suffice with respect to either of the latter two Marx prongs. With respect to the allegedly excessive director compensation, however, demand was excused. The court adopted a virtual per se rule that directors are interested in their own compensation. Defendants, however, had also moved to dismiss for failure to state a claim. Taking back with one hand what it had given with the other, the court agreed that plaintiff's "conclusory allegations" did not state a claim.

2.   Delaware's Demand Futility Standard

As with New York, Delaware requires demand in all cases except those in which it is excused on grounds of futility. In the seminal *Aronson v. Lewis* decision, the Delaware supreme court set forth the following test for demand futility:

> [T]he Court of Chancery in the proper exercise of its discretion must decide whether, under the particularized facts alleged, a reasonable doubt is created that: (1) the directors are disinterested and independent and (2) the challenged transaction was otherwise the product of a valid exercise of business judgment.[79]

Several important questions immediately arise. First, did the court really mean to phrase the standard in the conjunctive? Must plaintiff create a reasonable doubt as to both prongs? In its subsequent *Levine v. Smith* opinion, the court made clear that the test is in the disjunctive, such that satisfying either prong suffices.[80]

Second, and more significant, how does "reasonable doubt" come into it? This odd phrasing has been sharply criticized:

> The reference to "reasonable doubt" summons up the standard applied in criminal law. It is a demanding standard, meaning at least a 90% likelihood that the defendant is guilty. If "reasonable doubt" in the *Aronson*

---

[79] Aronson v. Lewis, 473 A.2d 805, 814 (Del.1984).
[80] 591 A.2d 194, 205 (Del.1991).

formula means the same thing as "reasonable doubt" in criminal law, then demand is excused whenever there is a 10% chance that the original transaction is not protected by the business judgment rule. Why should demand be excused on such a slight showing? Surely not because courts want shareholders to file suit whenever there is an 11% likelihood that the business judgment rule will not protect a transaction. *Aronson* did not say, and later cases have not supplied the deficit. If "reasonable doubt" in corporate law means something different from "reasonable doubt" in criminal law, however, what is the difference?, and why use the same term for two different things?[81]

In its most recent defense of the reasonable doubt standard, the Delaware supreme court rather weakly countered that "the term is apt and achieves the proper balance."[82] Somewhat more helpfully, the court rephrased the test by reversing it: "the concept of reasonable doubt is akin to the concept that the stockholder has a 'reasonable belief' that the board lacks independence or that the transaction was not protected by the business judgment rule."

Let's now turn to the pleading stage. Because the relevant facts must be plead with particularity, prolix pastiches of conclusory allegations will not cut it.[83] If plaintiffs file without first making pre-suit demand, and defendant(s) move to dismiss for failure to do so, however, the issue of demand futility is decided on the pleadings—plaintiffs are not entitled to discovery.[84] What then is the plaintiff to do? For the most part, plaintiffs must rely on what the Delaware supreme court calls "the tools at hand";[85] i.e., external sources of information, such as media reports and corporate regulatory filings. In appropriate cases, shareholder-plaintiffs also may invoke their inspection rights to demand pre-suit access to corporate books and records.

As for the substantive standard for demand futility, the *Aronson* test was helpfully restated in *Grimes v. Donald*:

> One ground for alleging with particularity that demand would be futile is that a "reasonable doubt" exists that the board is capable of making an independent decision to assert the claim if demand were made. The basis for claiming excusal would normally be that: (1) a majority of

---

[81] Starrels v. First Nat'l Bank of Chicago, 870 F.2d 1168, 1175 (7th Cir.1989) (Easterbrook, J., concurring) (citations omitted).

[82] Grimes v. Donald, 673 A.2d 1207, 1217 (Del.1996).

[83] Brehm v. Eisner, 746 A.2d 244, 249 (Del.2000).

[84] Rales v. Blasband, 634 A.2d 927, 934 n. 10 (Del.1993); Levine v. Smith, 591 A.2d 194, 208–10 (Del.1991).

[85] Brehm v. Eisner, 746 A.2d 244, 249 (Del.2000).

the board has a material financial or familial interest; (2) a majority of the board is incapable of acting independently for some other reason such as domination or control; or (3) the underlying transaction is not the product of a valid exercise of business judgment. If the stockholder cannot plead such assertions consistent with Chancery Rule 11, after using the "tools at hand" to obtain the necessary information before filing a derivative action, then the stockholder must make a pre-suit demand on the board.[86]

As to the first prong, directors are interested if they have a personal financial stake in the challenged transaction or otherwise would be materially affected by the board's actions. Consequently, for example, the chancery court excused demand on director interest grounds where five of nine directors approved a stock appreciation rights plan likely to benefit them.[87]

Under the second *Grimes* prong, the key doctrinal question is whether the directors can base their judgment on the merits rather than on extraneous considerations. Again, demand is not excused simply because the plaintiff has named a majority of the board as defendants.[88] Indeed, it is not enough even to allege that a majority of the board approved of, acquiesced in, or participated in the challenged transaction. In other words, merely being named as defendants or participants does not render the board incapable, as a matter of law, of objectively evaluating a pre-suit demand and, accordingly, does not excuse such a demand. Instead, demand typically will be excused under this prong only if a majority of the board was dominated or controlled by someone with a personal financial stake in the transaction.[89] Directors whose independence is compromised by undue influences exerted by interested parties are presumed, as a matter of law, of being incapable of exercising valid business judgment.

Turning to the third *Grimes* prong, should one rephrase it to ask whether the business judgment rule applies to the underlying challenged transaction? Some cases have done so. In *Zupnick v. Goizueta*,[90] plaintiff conceded that the board was disinterested and

---

[86] Grimes v. Donald, 673 A.2d 1207, 1216 (Del.1996). The term "majority" should be taken literally. In Kohls v. Duthie, 791 A.2d 772 (Del.Ch.2000), for example, demand was excused even though half of the board was deemed capable of impartially assessing the litigation. Id. at *7.

[87] Bergstein v. Texas Int'l Co., 453 A.2d 467, 471 (Del.Ch.1982).

[88] Grimes v. Donald, 673 A.2d 1207, 1216 n. 8 (Del.1996).

[89] See Aronson v. Lewis, 473 A.2d 805, 814 (Del.1984) ("where officers and directors are under an influence which sterilizes their discretion, they cannot be considered proper persons to conduct litigation on behalf of the corporation").

[90] 698 A.2d 384 (Del.Ch.1997).

independent. Under those circumstances, the court phrased the test as whether the "particularized factual allegations of the complaint create a reason to doubt" that the board's decision "was entitled to the protection of the business judgment rule." In *Brehm v. Eisner*, the Delaware supreme court adopted a similar approach, emphasizing that the inquiry under this prong focuses on "the directors' decisionmaking process, *measured by concepts of gross negligence.*"[91]

In both *Zupnick* and *Brehm*, however, plaintiff's complaint challenged a specific board action; namely, allegedly excessive executive compensation. What about the important class of cases in which plaintiff alleges that the board failed to exercise proper oversight? Recall that the business judgment rule is inapplicable where the board did not exercise business judgment. Is demand therefore automatically excused in oversight cases?

The Delaware supreme court first addressed this question in *Rales v. Blasband*. Plaintiff brought a double derivative suit on behalf of a parent corporation with respect to the sale of subordinated debentures by its wholly owned subsidiary. Because the derivative suit did not challenge a decision by the parent corporation's board, the court held that the *Aronson* standard did not apply:

> Instead, it is appropriate in these situations to examine whether the board that would be addressing the demand can impartially consider its merits without being influenced by improper considerations. Thus, a court must determine whether or not the particularized factual allegations of a derivative stockholder complaint create a reasonable doubt that, as of the time the complaint is filed, the board of directors could have properly exercised its independent and disinterested business judgment in responding to a demand. If the derivative plaintiff satisfies this burden, then demand will be excused as futile.[92]

The court noted three scenarios in which this test is to be used in lieu of the *Aronson* standard: (1) where a majority of the board that made the challenged transaction has been replaced by disinterested and independent members; (2) where the litigation arises out of some transaction or event not involving a business decision by the board; and (3) where the challenged decision was made by the board of a different corporation.

---

[91] 746 A.2d 244, 259 (Del.2000) (emphasis in original).
[92] Rales v. Blasband, 634 A.2d 927, 934 (Del.1993).

The *Rales* standard makes sense as applied to derivative suits brought to enforce corporate rights as against wrongdoers outside the corporation. If the shareholder-plaintiff sued a third party for breach of contract vis-à-vis the corporation, for example, the board obviously ought to have a chance to evaluate the suit before it goes forward. It is less obvious that *Rales* should apply where the shareholder-plaintiff alleges, for example, that the board failed to adequately supervise corporate employees. Yet, post-*Rales* decisions have applied its standard to such board oversight cases.[93]

Finally, we turn to appellate review of a chancery court decision on demand futility. Until quite recently, it was assumed that the chancery court's decision on demand futility was subject to review by the Delaware supreme court solely for abuse of discretion. In *Brehm v. Eisner*,[94] however, the Delaware supreme court held that, because demand futility is decided on the pleadings, the chancery court's decision is subject to de novo review on appeal.

B.   Board Control of Derivative Litigation

It is curious that the seemingly technical requirement of demand on the board has become the critical issue in derivative litigation. If demand is required, the shareholder-plaintiff has very little prospect of success. If demand is excused, the shareholder-plaintiff's prospects improve—albeit not by much. Derivative litigation thus bifurcates at the demand stage. If demand is required, two questions arise: What happens if the board accepts the demand? Conversely, what happens if the demand is rejected? If demand is excused, the key issue is whether the board can wrest control of the litigation back from the shareholder-plaintiff.

1.   *Demand Required Cases*

At least in Delaware, a plaintiff who makes demand is deemed to concede that demand was required.[95] Accordingly, due to the demand required/demand excused bifurcation of substantive standards, which make it very difficult for plaintiffs to prevail in the former, well-counseled plaintiffs almost never make demand. The initial issue in almost all derivative suits therefore is whether

---

[93] See, e.g., Kohls v. Duthie, 791 A.2d 772 (Del.Ch.2000); Seminaris v. Landa, 662 A.2d 1350, 1354 (Del.Ch.1995).

[94] 746 A.2d 244, 254–54 (Del.2000).

[95] Rales v. Blasband, 634 A.2d 927, 935 n. 12 (Del.1993); Spiegel v. Buntrock, 571 A.2d 767, 775 (Del.1990). Note that making demand only concedes the board's ex ante good faith and independence. If the board refuses the demand, the plaintiff is entitled to argue that the board's refusal was wrongful, as where the board lacked independence or acted in bad faith. Scattered Corporation v. Chicago Stock Exchange, 701 A.2d 70 (Del.1997).

Conversely, however, appointment by the board of a special committee to investigate the challenged transaction is not deemed a concession that demand would be futile. Seminaris v. Landa, 662 A.2d 1350, 1353 (Del.Ch.1995).

demand is required under the standards described in the preceding section.

If the court concludes that demand was required, what happens next? In theory, failure to make demand is grounds for dismissal with prejudice. In practice, however, the court likely will either stay further proceedings or, at worst, dismiss without prejudice while plaintiff made the required demand.[96] The case would then go forward as described below.

Where the shareholder makes demand, either pre-suit or after a judicial determination that demand was required, the board is expected to undertake a two-step process. The board must first inform itself of the relevant facts relating to the challenged transaction or other alleged wrongdoing, as well as the legal and business considerations attendant to resolving the matter. Any factual investigation must be reasonable and conducted in good faith, but within those parameters the board has great discretion.

When that process is complete, the board must elect amongst the three principal alternatives available to it: (1) accepting the demand and prosecuting the action; (2) resolving the matter internally without resort to litigation; or (3) refusing the demand.

If the board accepts the demand and then attempts to resolve the matter through a settlement of the derivative claim with the shareholder-plaintiff, the parties must comply with the judicial approval requirement of Federal Rule 23.1 or its relevant state counterpart. Suppose, however, that the corporation resolves the matter through a settlement with the alleged wrongdoers. In that case, the judicial approval requirement under Federal Rule 23.1 and its state counterparts does not apply. If the corporation gives the defendants a sweetheart deal, of course, the shareholder-plaintiff could initiate a new derivative suit for "fraud or waste in releasing corporate claims for inadequate payment."[97] Presumably the same would be true if the corporation accepted demand but then lost the case due to a failure to vigorously prosecute it.

Anecdotal evidence strongly suggests that the board's typical response, however, is to refuse the demand. If the board does so, the shareholder may seek judicial review of that refusal, but the plaintiff bears the burden of proving that the refusal was wrongful. Worse yet, at least from plaintiff's perspective, the relevant

---

[96] See, e.g., Elfenbein v. Gulf & Western Indus., Inc., 590 F.2d 445, 450 (2d Cir.1978) (opining that dismissal with "leave to replead within a specified time period" is the preferable disposition).

[97] Wolf v. Barkes, 348 F.2d 994, 996 (2d Cir.), cert. denied, 382 U.S. 941 (1965).

standard of review is the business judgment rule.[98] Worst of all, at least from the plaintiff's perspective, plaintiff is not entitled to discovery.[99]

Some suggest that the wrongful refusal inquiry should be directed at the business judgment rule's applicability to the underlying challenged transaction where that transaction "was approved by the same directors who are reviewing the plaintiff's demand."[100] In *Grimes*, however, the Delaware supreme court made clear that the inquiry is directed to whether "the board in fact acted independently, disinterestedly, or with due care *in response to the demand.*"[101] Note the potential for a clear case of self-dealing, such as an interested director transaction, to be immune from challenge through a derivative suit. A disinterested and independent majority of the board is deemed capable of deciding whether to refuse demand, at least where the decision does not involve fraud, illegality or self-dealing on the part of a majority of the board. A demand refusal by such a board will be protected by the business judgment rule.

2. *Demand Excused Cases*

Anecdotal evidence suggests that boards generally settle demand excused cases. The incentives for both sides to settle before a decision on the merits are just too strong. Yet, a recalcitrant board intent upon resisting a derivative suit has a weapon by which it can regain control of the litigation even when demand is excused; namely, the so-called special litigation committee (SLC).

The SLC emerged in response to a sharp rise in derivative litigation during the 1970s. In demand excused cases, the board would appoint a committee to investigate the challenged transaction or event and make a recommendation to the court as to whether or not the litigation was in the firm's best interests. The committee members were specially chosen for their independence and disinterest (or so corporations said). Indeed, the committee typically was comprised of newly appointed board members chosen specifically to serve on the committee. The committee was vested with all of the board's powers for the limited purpose of deciding

---

[98] Spiegel v. Buntrock, 571 A.2d 767, 776 (Del.1990); Aronson v. Lewis, 473 A.2d 805, 813 (Del.1984); Zapata Corp. v. Maldonado, 430 A.2d 779, 784 n. 10 (Del.1981) (dicta).

[99] Scattered Corporation v. Chicago Stock Exchange, 701 A.2d 70, 77 (Del.1997) ("The law in Delaware is settled that plaintiffs in a derivative suit are not entitled to discovery to assist their compliance with the particularized pleading requirement of Rule 23.1 in a case of demand refusal. A plaintiff's standing to sue in a derivative suit, whether based on demand-refused or demand-excused, must be determined on the basis of the well-pleaded allegations of the complaint.").

[100] Michael P. Dooley, Fundamentals of Corporation Law 334 (1995).

[101] Grimes v. Donald, 673 A.2d 1207, 1219 (Del.1996) (emphasis supplied).

what position the corporation should take in connection with the litigation. The theory explained to the courts was that the committee could take over and prosecute meritorious suits, while seeking dismissal of frivolous actions. The principal legal issue thus was whether the court should defer to a committee recommendation that the suit be dismissed.

New York law. New York's answer to that question was handed down in *Auerbach v. Bennett.*[102] Agents of GTE had paid out some $11 million in illegal bribes and kickbacks. Four of GTE's directors were personally involved in the misconduct. A GTE shareholder brought a derivative action against GTE, all of its directors, and its outside auditor for breach of fiduciary duty to the corporation. The board responded to the litigation by appointing a SLC, which concluded that none of the defendants had violated their statutory duty of care, none had profited personally from the incidents and that the claims were without merit. The committee therefore recommended that the court dismiss the suit. Noting that the business judgment doctrine generally bars judicial inquiry into actions of corporate directors taken in good faith and in the exercise of honest judgment in the lawful furtherance of corporate purposes, the court opined that analysis of the case at bar turned on whether the business judgment rule applied to such a recommendation by a SLC.

Judicial review of a SLC recommendation to terminate derivative litigation implicates a two-tiered set of questions. The first tier is the challenged transaction; here the illegal payments. The second tier is the committee's recommendation that the action be dismissed. The *Auerbach* defendants argued that the second tier action insulated the first tier from judicial review because the business judgment rule mandates judicial deference to the committee's recommendation. We might call this the Tootsie Pop defense—you cannot see the chewy center (the first tier wrongdoing) because the hard candy shell (the second tier committee recommendation) blocks your view.

The Court of Appeals agreed that the committee's ultimate substantive decision to dismiss the litigation is protected from review. Judicial inquiry is permissible with respect to two aspects of the committee's work, however: (1) the committee's disinterested independence; and (2) the adequacy and appropriateness of the procedures by which the decision was made. It seems that plaintiff has the ultimate burden of proof with respect to the committee's independence and the adequacy of their procedures, although there

---

[102] 419 N.Y.S.2d 920 (1979).

is language in the opinion suggesting that the committee may have the initial burden of showing that its procedures were reasonable.

If the court is not satisfied as to either the SLC's disinterested independence or the adequacy of its procedures, the suit will not be dismissed and review of the first tier decision will not be foreclosed. If the court is satisfied on both scores, however, the case must be dismissed without reaching the merits. In *Auerbach*, accordingly, in which there apparently was no question that the payments were illegal, the challenged misconduct thus was not to be reviewed so long as the committee was independent and used proper procedures in reaching its decision. (Of course, if one thinks that directors and officers can violate the law without necessarily violating their fiduciary duties, this outcome will not seem problematic.)

On the facts before it, the court determined that the committee was independent. None of the committee members were members of the board when the illegal payments took place and none had any prior affiliation with the firm. The latter point—lack of prior affiliation—seems to be the key. As long as the committee members have no demonstrable contact with the corporation or the board, they likely will be deemed independent.

In examining the committee's procedures, *Auerbach* teaches that a reviewing court may explore whether the areas and subjects the committee investigated were reasonably complete. The court may also determine whether the inquiry was conducted in good faith. The court will be looking for proof that the investigation was restricted in scope, shallow in execution, pro forma or half-hearted. Relevant factors thus include such matters as the number of hours spent on the matter, whether the committee had independent legal counsel and other advisers, who was interviewed, and the like. On the other hand, the court may not consider the evidence the committee uncovered, the factors the committee considered, the relative weight accorded to those factors in the committee's decisionmaking process, or even whether the evidence supports the conclusion. The following analogy may be useful—the court may ensure all the proper papers are in the file, but is forbidden from reading the papers to see what they say.

Delaware law. The Delaware supreme court took a less deferential approach to this issue in *Zapata Corp. v. Maldonado*.[103] In *Zapata*, the Delaware supreme court specifically rejected *Auerbach*'s conclusion that the business judgment rule applies to a SLC's recommendations. Instead, the court laid out a new set of

---

[103] 430 A.2d 779 (Del.1981). In Alford v. Shaw, 358 S.E.2d 323 (N.C.1987), North Carolina adopted a *Zapata*-based standard for all derivative suits, without regard to whether demand is excused or required.

procedures to be followed in such cases. After an "objective and thorough investigation," the committee may cause the corporation to file a motion to dismiss the derivative action.[104] The motion should include a written record of the committee's investigation and its findings and recommendations. Each side is given a limited opportunity for discovery with respect to the court's mandated areas of inquiry.

In deciding whether to dismiss the action, the court is to apply a two-step test: (1) The court should inquire into the independence and good faith of the committee. The court also should inquire into the bases supporting the committee's recommendations. The corporation will have the burden of proving independence, good faith, and a reasonable investigation. (2) If the first step is satisfied, the court may but need not go on to apply its own business judgment to the issue of whether or not the case is to be dismissed.

The first step differs from *Auerbach* in that the Delaware court looks not only at the procedures used, but also at the reasonableness of the basis for the committee's decision—something *Auerbach* expressly forbids.[105] In other words, Delaware judges not only make sure all the papers are in the file, they also read the papers to see if the investigative results support the committee's conclusions.

The second step is intended to catch cases complying with the letter, but not the spirit, of the first step.[106] In other words, the court is saying that judges should not dismiss meritorious derivative suits merely because the board and its committee jumped through the correct procedural hoops. Unfortunately, *Zapata* gave no real standards by which judges should apply their own business judgment in the second-step. The supreme court simply opined that the trial court should consider such things as the corporation's interest in having the suit dismissed and "matters of law and public policy,"[107] which could mean everything under the sun. In its subsequent *Kaplan v. Wyatt* decision, moreover, the court made clear that the chancellors are not obliged to conduct the second step

---

[104] "The general rule that a stay should issue [while a SLC reviews the matter and prepares its recommendation] is subject to exception in an atypical case when, based on the undisputed facts in the stay motion record, the committee's later decision to terminate the litigation could not command respect under *Zapata*." Biondi v. Scrushy, 820 A.2d 1148, 1165 (Del.Ch.2003).

[105] Several other states also require their courts to determine whether the committee's recommendation has a reasonable basis. See, e.g., Houle v. Low, 556 N.E.2d 51 (Mass.1990); Lewis v. Boyd, 838 S.W.2d 215 (Tenn.App.1992).

[106] Cf. Johnson v. Hui, 811 F.Supp. 479, 490 (N.D.Cal.1991) (describing second step of *Zapata* as a "smell test").

[107] Zapata Corp. v. Maldonado, 430 A.2d 779, 789 (Del.1981).

inquiry and that a refusal to do so was subject to review under the abuse of discretion standard.[108]

In *Joy v. North*,[109] a diversity case arising under Connecticut law, federal Circuit Judge Ralph Winter held that Connecticut courts would follow *Zapata*, rather than *Auerbach*, but thought it necessary to lay out more determinate guidelines for judicial review of SLC recommendations. The central question under *Joy* is whether the litigation is in the best interests of the corporation. The burden is on the corporation to demonstrate that the litigation is more likely than not to be against its interests. The court will examine the underlying data developed by the committee, the adequacy of the committee's procedures, and whether there is a reasonable basis for the committee's recommendation. Again, note the difference from *Auerbach*. As in *Zapata*, Judge Winter looks behind the procedures to see what the committee actually found.

The break with *Zapata* came when Judge Winter articulated a methodology not unlike the Hand Formula familiar from tort law. If the cost of litigation to the corporation exceeds the product of the likely recoverable damages times the probability of liability, suit must be dismissed. The costs that may be considered include attorney's fees, out of pocket expenses, time spent by corporate personnel preparing for and participating in trial, and potential mandatory indemnification (discounted by the probability of liability). On the cost side, the court may not consider discretionary indemnification or insurance.[110] Where the likely recovery to the corporation is small in comparison to total shareholders' equity, the court may also consider two other factors: (1) the degree to which key personnel may be distracted from corporate business by the litigation and (2) the potential for lost business.

3.   Judicial Concern with Structural Bias

The significantly less deferential approach taken by *Zapata* and *Joy*, relative to *Auerbach*, resulted from the former courts' heightened sensitivity to the potential for bias on the part of SLC members. Because the members of the committee typically are appointed by the defendants to the derivative litigation, there is a natural concern that the persons selected will be biased in favor of

[108] 499 A.2d 1184, 1192 (Del.1985).

[109] 692 F.2d 880 (2d Cir.1982), cert. denied, 460 U.S. 1051 (1983). As a diversity case applying the law of another state, of course, *Joy* is not binding on the Delaware courts.

[110] Suppose plaintiff's claim is for $1 million. Defendant director has personal assets of $100,000, but is covered by a D & O liability policy that will pay up to $20 million per incident. Can the existence of that policy be considered by the court and, if so, for what purposes? Insurance is relevant to the likely recovery side of the equation, but not to the costs side of the formula. Thus, the court cannot consider either past premiums or future premium increases in its calculation of costs.

the defendants. The requirements of independence and disinterest purportedly eliminate the risk of actual bias. Because the persons selected frequently are directors or senior officers of other corporations, however, there is a concern that the SLC's members will have excessive sympathy for colleagues facing personal liability. As the Delaware supreme court put it: "The question naturally arises whether a 'there but for the grace of God go I' empathy might not play a role."[111] The legitimacy of this concern is supported by the fact that in only one of the first 20 reported SLC decisions did the committee determine that the suit should proceed.[112]

Despite the potential for actual or structural bias, neither *Auerbach*, *Zapata*, nor *Joy* accepted their respective plaintiffs' arguments that the defendant board of directors was per se disabled from appointing a SLC and delegating to that committee power to act on the corporation's behalf. In *Miller v. Register and Tribune Syndicate, Inc.*,[113] by way of contrast, the Iowa supreme court concluded that the structural bias purportedly inherent in the SLC process incapacitated directors charged with misconduct from appointing a SLC. Instead, the board may petition the court to appoint a special panel, to whose recommendations the court will defer.

C. The ALI and MBCA Universal Demand Alternatives

As noted above, the demand requirement is, at least in part, a corollary of the basic proposition that a derivative action is representative in nature. The demand requirement thus allows the corporation to take over the cause of action or to resist it, according to the judgment of the directors. Under both Delaware and New York law, however, the demand requirement has been charged with an additional task; namely, functioning as the principal sieve by which meritorious shareholder litigation is separated from the chaff. If the board of directors is so clearly disabled by conflicted interests that its judgment cannot be trusted, the shareholder should be permitted to go forward, absent intervention by a special litigation committee. If not, the board should be allowed to decide whether the litigation should proceed.

---

[111] Zapata Corp. v. Maldonado, 430 A.2d 779, 787 (Del.1981). Or, as Judge Winter put it in *Joy*: "It is not cynical to expect that such committees will tend to view derivative actions against the other directors with skepticism. Indeed, if the involved directors expected any result other than a recommendation of termination at least as to them, they would probably never establish the committee." 692 F.2d 880, 888 (2d Cir.1982), cert. denied, 460 U.S. 1051 (1983).

[112] See James D. Cox, Searching for the Corporation's Voice in Derivative Suit Litigation: A Critique of *Zapata* and the ALI Project, 1982 Duke L.J. 959.

[113] 336 N.W.2d 709 (Iowa 1983).

Although an inquiry into the board's ability to exercise disinterested judgment seems warranted, it is not at all clear that the demand requirement is a necessary—or even appropriate—vehicle for undertaking said inquiry. Both the ALI PRINCIPLES and the Model Business Corporation Act have done away with the demand futility inquiry. In its place, both have imposed a universal demand requirement, while preserving, albeit in different forms, a sieve to identify cases in which the board's conflicted interests preclude deference to board decisions.

1.   MBCA § 7.44

MBCA § 7.42 requires a written demand upon the board in all cases and, further, precludes a shareholder from bringing suit for 90 days after the demand is made unless irreparable injury would result or the board rejects demand. MBCA § 7.44 then takes over, providing two alternatives for internal corporate review of the demand: If the independent and disinterested directors constitute a quorum, the demand may be reviewed by the board. Whether or not the independent directors constitute a quorum, the independent directors may appoint by majority vote a committee of two or more independent directors.[114]

As under both New York and Delaware law, directors can be deemed independent even if they were nominated by the defendants, are named as a defendants, or they approved the challenged transaction. If either the board or committee "determined in good faith after conducting a reasonable inquiry upon which its conclusions are based that the maintenance of the derivative proceeding is not in the best interests of the corporation" the court "shall" dismiss the complaint.[115] If a majority of the board was independent at the time that determination was made, the burden of proof with respect to the board's independent disinterest and the adequacy of its investigation is on plaintiff; if a majority of the board was not independent, the burden of proof is on the defendant. The comments to § 7.44 make clear that the MBCA's drafters rejected *Zapata*: "Section 7.44 does not authorize the court to review the reasonableness of the determination" made by the board or committee. So long as the determination has "some support" in the findings of the inquiry, the standard is satisfied.

---

[114] Interestingly, the MBCA partially followed the Iowa Supreme Court's *Miller* decision by providing a third alternative. Under MBCA § 7.44(f), upon motion by the corporation, the court may appoint a panel of one or more independent persons to determine whether the suit should go forward. If that panel recommends dismissal, the court shall dismiss the action unless plaintiff can prove the independent panel failed to act in good faith or failed to conduct a reasonable inquiry upon which its conclusions were based. Unlike *Miller*, however, this option is not exclusive of the SLC process.

[115] MBCA § 7.44(a).

2. ALI PRINCIPLES Part VII

As for the ALI PRINCIPLES, years of controversy and repeated drafting efforts, including last-minute amendments from the floor, produced an astonishingly long and complex set of rules and commentary that basically tracks Delaware law, albeit adding (among other wrinkles) a universal demand requirement.[116] PRINCIPLES § 7.03(b) requires demand in all cases, excepting only those in which plaintiff demonstrates that irreparable injury to the corporation would result. In the following sections, covering well over 100 pages (counting commentary and reporters' notes), the PRINCIPLES distinguish and provide for judicial review of two basic categories of cases.

The first set of cases is comprised of proceedings against persons other than directors, senior executives, or controlling persons of the corporation. A board recommendation to dismiss a derivative suit against such non-insiders is reviewed under the business judgment rule.[117] The second set comprises suits against directors, senior executives, or controlling persons of the corporation. Judicial review of a derivative proceeding against such insiders is further bifurcated, with the scope of review effectively depending on whether the cause of action is premised on a breach of the duty of care or the duty of loyalty. In the former case, the court should apply the business judgment rule to a recommendation to dismiss made by the disinterested directors (acting either as the board or a committee thereof).[118] In the latter case, subject to a convoluted exception for certain cases in which defendants would retain an improper personal benefit, the court should dismiss the proceeding upon such a recommendation "if the court finds . . . that the board or committee was adequately informed under the circumstances and reasonably determined that dismissal was in the best interests of the corporation, based on grounds that the court deems to warrant reliance."[119]

3. Evaluating Universal Demand

The demand futility inquiry mandated by both New York and Delaware law has been subjected to considerable criticism. Judge Frank Easterbrook contends, for example, that the demand futility inquiry produces "gobs of litigation" collateral to the merits. In a

---

[116] See generally Carol B. Swanson, Juggling Shareholder Rights and Strike Suits in Derivative Litigation: The ALI Drops the Ball, 77 Minn. L. Rev. 1339 (1993). Pennsylvania has adopted the ALI approach *in toto*. Cuker v. Mikalauskas, 692 A.2d 1042 (Pa.1997).

[117] ALI PRINCIPLES § 7.07(a)(1).

[118] ALI PRINCIPLES §§ 7.07(a)(2) and 7.10(a)(1).

[119] Id. at § 7.10(a)(2).

derivative proceeding under the federal Investment Company Act against fund directors, Easterbrook therefore fashioned a federal common law of derivative proceedings that included a universal demand requirement.[120] "The usually highly perceptive Judge Easterbrook [was led into this] reversible error" by a misunderstanding of the demand futility inquiry's function.[121]

Determining the scope of judicial review of any board of director decision requires one to make trade-offs between preserving the board's decisionmaking authority and ensuring that the board has not misused its authority for the personal benefit of board members. In the derivative litigation context, New York and Delaware have used the demand futility inquiry as the vehicle by which those trade-offs are made. Replacing the demand futility inquiry with a universal demand requirement does not eliminate the need to separate out those cases in which conflicted interests have so tainted the board's decisionmaking processes as to preclude giving the resulting decisions the deference usually accorded them by corporate law. Instead, as the drafters of both the ALI PRINCIPLES and the MBCA appear to have recognized, it simply shifts the task of effecting such a separation to a different stage of the process.

The only justification for a universal demand therefore seems to be the claim that it conserves judicial resources. In reversing Judge Easterbrook, the Supreme Court explained that a universal demand requirement was unlikely to produce much in the way of judicial economy. In support of Easterbrook's universal demand rule, the defendants contended such a rule "would force would-be derivative suit plaintiffs to exhaust their intracorporate remedies before filing suit and would spare both the courts and the parties the expense associated with the often protracted threshold litigation that attends the collateral issue of demand futility." In rejecting defendants' argument, the Court first noted the federalism implications of creating universal demand requirement as a matter of federal common law. "Under KFS' proposal, federal courts would be obliged to develop a body of principles that would replicate the substantive effect of the State's demand futility doctrine but that would be applied *after* demand has been made and refused." Doing so would impinge on the states' power to regulate corporations, as well as subjecting corporations to conflicting standards in state and federal litigation. The court then turned to the purported judicial economies of a federal universal demand rule:

---

[120] Kamen v. Kemper Fin. Servs., Inc., 908 F.2d 1338 (7th Cir.1990), rev'd, 500 U.S. 90 (1991).

[121] Michael P. Dooley, Two Models of Corporate Governance, 47 Bus. Law. 461, 502 (1992).

Requiring demand in all cases, it is true, might marginally enhance the prospect that corporate disputes would be resolved without resort to litigation; however, nothing disables the directors from seeking an accommodation with a representative shareholder even after the shareholder files his complaint in an action in which demand is excused as futile. At the same time, the rule proposed by KFS is unlikely to avoid the high collateral litigation costs associated with the demand futility doctrine. So long as a federal court endeavors to reproduce through independent review standards the allocation of managerial power embodied in the demand futility doctrine, KFS' universal-demand rule will merely shift the focus of threshold litigation from the question whether demand is excused to the question whether the directors' decision to terminate the suit is entitled to deference under federal standards. Under these circumstances, we do not view the advantages associated with KFS' proposal to be sufficiently apparent to justify replacing "the entire corpus of state corporation law" relating to demand futility.[122]

---

[122] Kamen v. Kemper Fin. Servs., Inc., 500 U.S. 90, 106 (1991).

Chapter 9

THE LIMITS OF
FIDUCIARY OBLIGATION

§ 9.1   Introduction

What is the social role of the corporation? What goals should corporate directors and managers pursue? Managerialist schools of thought claim that managers are autonomous actors free to pursue whatever interests they choose (or society directs). Shareholder primacy theorists believe that corporations should be run so as to maximize shareholder wealth. Proponents of corporate social responsibility argue that directors and managers should consider the interests of all corporate constituencies in making corporate decisions. Hence, stakeholderists define the "socially responsible firm" as "one that becomes deeply involved in the solution of society's major problems."[1] In particular, they emphasize the corporation's obligation to consider the impact of its actions on nonshareholder corporate constituents, such as employees, customers, suppliers, and local communities.

§ 9.2   Corporate Social Responsibility and the Law

In general, corporate law does not mandate corporate social responsibility. Instead, the question is whether the law even permits corporate social responsibility. Put another way, to what extent do the fiduciary duties of corporate directors permit them to consider nonshareholder interests when making corporate decisions?

A.   Case Law

Despite the obvious centrality of this problem to the operation of business corporations, there are surprisingly few authoritative precedents on point. The law's basic position on corporate social responsibility famously was articulated in *Dodge v. Ford Motor Co.*[2] In 1916, Henry Ford owned 58% of the stock of Ford Motor Co. The Dodge brothers owned 10%. The remainder was owned by five other individuals. Beginning in 1908, Ford Motor paid a regular annual dividend of $1.2 million. Between 1911 and 1915 Ford Motor also regularly paid huge "special dividends," totaling over $40 million. In

---

[1] Robert Hay and Ed Gray, Social Responsibilities of Business Managers, in Managing Corporate Social Responsibility 8, 11 (Archie B. Carroll ed. 1977).

[2] 170 N.W. 668 (Mich.1919).

1916, Henry Ford announced that the company would stop paying special dividends. Instead, the firm's financial resources would be devoted to expanding its business. Ford also continued the company's policy of lowering prices, while improving quality. The Dodge brothers sued, asking the court to order Ford Motor to resume paying the special dividends and to enjoin the proposed expansion of the firm's operations. At trial, Ford testified to his belief that the company made too much money and had an obligation to benefit the public and the firm's workers and customers.

The plaintiff Dodge brothers contended an improper altruism towards his workers and customers motivated Ford. The court agreed, strongly rebuking Ford:

> A business corporation is organized and carried on primarily for the profit of the stockholders. The powers of the directors are to be employed for that end. The discretion of directors is to be exercised in the choice of means to attain that end, and does not extend to a change in the end itself, to the reduction of profits, or to the nondistribution of profits among stockholders in order to devote them to other purposes.

Consequently, "it is not within the lawful powers of a board of directors to shape and conduct the affairs of a corporation for the merely incidental benefit of shareholders and for the primary purpose of benefiting others."

Despite its strong rhetoric, *Dodge* does not stand for the proposition that directors will be held liable for considering the social consequences of corporate actions. To be sure, having found that Ford had failed to pursue shareholder wealth maximization, the court ordered Ford Motor to resume paying its substantial special dividends. Invoking the business judgment rule, however, the *Dodge* court declined to interfere with Ford's plans for expansion and dismissed the bulk of plaintiff's complaint. The shareholder wealth maximization norm set forth in *Dodge* thus can be understood as a standard of conduct, while the business judgment rule remains the standard of review. Consequently, *Dodge* does not stand for the proposition that courts will closely supervise the conduct of corporate directors to ensure that every decision maximizes shareholder wealth. As the court's refusal to enjoin Ford Motor's proposed expansion illustrates, courts generally will not substitute their judgment for that of the board of directors. If a proposed course of action plausibly relates to long-term shareholder wealth maximization, courts will not intervene. Ford's proposed expansion plans did so, and thus were allowed to go forward. Ford's refusal to pay a special dividend, while simultaneously lowering prices, compounded by his anti-profitmaking trial testimony, did not. Accordingly, the court ordered him to pay the requested dividend. As always, authority and accountability are in tension. We have consistently argued that, absent self-dealing or other unusual circumstances, authority should prevail. Ford's conduct lay at the outer boundary of defensible exercises of authority and the court appropriately slapped his wrist.

As the law evolved, corporate altruism began to be seen as proper so long as it was likely to provide direct benefits to the corporation and its shareholders. Applying the business judgment rule, moreover, many courts essentially presumed that an altruistic decision was in the corporation's best interests. *Shlensky v. Wrigley*[3] exemplifies this approach. Recall that Shlensky, a minority shareholder in the Chicago Cubs, challenged the decision by Wrigley, the majority shareholder, not to install lights at Wrigley Field. Shlensky claimed the Cubs were persistent money losers, which he attributed to poor home attendance, which in turn he attributed to the board's refusal to install lights and play night baseball. According to Shlensky, Wrigley was indifferent to the effect of his continued intransigence on the team's finances. Instead, Shlensky argued, Wrigley was motivated by his beliefs that baseball was a day-time sport and that night baseball might have a deteriorating effect on the neighborhood surrounding Wrigley Field.

Despite Shlensky's apparently uncontested evidence that Wrigley was more concerned with interests other than those of the shareholders, the court did not even allow him to get up to bat. Instead, the court presumed that Wrigley's decision was in the firm's best interests. Indeed, the court basically invented reasons why a director might have made an honest decision against night baseball. The court opined, for example, "the effect on the surrounding neighborhood might well be considered by a director." Again, the court said: "the long run interest" of the firm "might demand" protection of the neighborhood. Accordingly, Shlensky's case was dismissed for failure to state a claim upon which relief could be granted.

The rhetorical emphasis shifted significantly between *Dodge* and *Shlensky*. Where *Dodge* emphasized the directors' duty to maximize profits, *Shlensky* emphasized the directors' authority and discretion. Ultimately, however, they are consistent. The Illinois Appellate Court did not reject the profit-maximizing norm laid down by *Dodge*, but rather followed *Dodge* in holding that the

---

[3] 237 N.E.2d 776 (Ill.App.1968), see § 6.2. Accord Ella M. Kelly & Wyndham, Inc. v. Bell, 266 A.2d 878, 879 (Del.1970); Union Pac. R.R. Co. v. Trustees, Inc., 329 P.2d 398, 401–02 (Utah 1958).

business judgment rule immunized the directors' decision from judicial review.

To be sure, a few cases posit that directors need not treat shareholder wealth maximization as their sole guiding star. *A. P. Smith Manufacturing Co. v. Barlow*, the most frequently cited example, upheld a corporate charitable donation on the ground, inter alia, that "modern conditions require that corporations acknowledge and discharge social as well as private responsibilities as members of the communities within which they operate."[4] Ultimately, however, the differences between *Barlow* and *Dodge* have little more than symbolic import. As the *Barlow* court recognized, shareholders' long-run interests are often served by decisions (such as charitable giving) that appear harmful in the short-run. Because the court acknowledged that the challenged contribution thus could be justified on profit-maximizing grounds, its broader language on corporate social responsibility is arguably mere dictum.

In any event, *Dodge*'s theory of shareholder wealth maximization has been widely accepted by courts over an extended period of time. Almost three quarters of a century after *Dodge*, the Delaware chancery court similarly opined: "It is the obligation of directors to attempt, within the law, to maximize the long-run interests of the corporation's stockholders."[5]

In sum, the law governing operational decisions has a somewhat schizophrenic feel. In most jurisdictions, courts will exhort directors to use their best efforts to maximize shareholder wealth. In a few, courts may exhort directors to consider the corporation's social responsibility. In either case, however, the announced principle is no more than an exhortation. The court may hold forth on the primacy of shareholder interests, or may hold forth on the importance of socially responsible conduct, but ultimately it does not matter. Under either approach, directors who consider nonshareholder interests in making corporate decisions, like directors who do not, will be insulated from liability by the business judgment rule.[6]

---

[4] 98 A.2d 581, 586 (N.J.1953). See also Theodora Holding Corp. v. Henderson, 257 A.2d 398, 404 (Del.Ch.1969) (opining that corporate social responsibility is a desirable goal).

[5] Katz v. Oak Indus., Inc., 508 A.2d 873, 879 (Del.Ch.1986).

[6] The principal exception to this rule is where directors rely on nonshareholder interests to justify takeover defenses, which do not necessarily get business judgment rule protection. See, e.g., Revlon, Inc. v. MacAndrews & Forbes Holdings, Inc., 506 A.2d 173 (Del.1985).

B. Nonshareholder Constituency Statutes

Over thirty states have purported to address the corporate social responsibility debate by adopting so-called nonshareholder constituency statutes. Typically, these statutes amend the existing statutory statement of the director's duty of care. They commonly authorize the board of directors, in discharging its duty of care, to consider the impact a decision will have on not only shareholders, but also on a list of other constituency groups, such as employees, suppliers, customers, creditors, and the local communities in which the firm does business. In addition to the laundry list of constituency factors, some statutes more generally authorize directors to consider both the long-and short-term effects of the decision.

Most nonshareholder constituency statutes are permissive. Directors "may," but need not, take nonshareholder interests into account. There are no express constraints on the directors' discretion in deciding whether to consider nonshareholder interests and, if they decide to do so, which constituency groups' interests to consider. As a result, the statutes should not be interpreted as creating new director fiduciary duties running to nonshareholder constituencies and the latter should not have standing under these statutes to seek judicial review of a director's decision.[7]

Beyond this, however, the nonshareholder constituency statutes uniformly are silent on many key issues. Among the issues left open by almost all statutes are such critical questions as: How should directors decide whether particular claimants fall into one of the protected constituent categories, some of which, such as customers and communities, are very amorphous? What weight should directors assign to shareholder and nonshareholder interests? What should directors do when those interests cannot be reconciled? What should directors do when the interests of various nonshareholder constituencies conflict amongst themselves? What standards should courts use in reviewing a director's decision not to consider nonshareholder interests? What standards of review apply to director action claimed to be motivated by concern for nonshareholder constituents? Nor is there, as yet, any significant guidance from the courts. The statutes have rarely been cited outside the takeover setting, and even there they have not received authoritative interpretation. To the contrary, the decisions

---

[7] Although most statutes are silent on this point, the New York and Pennsylvania statutes explicitly state that they create no duties towards any party. N.Y. Bus. Corp. Law § 717(b); 15 Pa. Cons. Stat. § 1717. Where statutes are silent, it is important to note that at common law the board of directors has no duty to consider nonshareholder interests. See, e.g., Local 1330, United Steel Workers v. U.S. Steel Corp., 631 F.2d 1264, 1280–82 (6th Cir.1980). Accordingly, judicial creation of such a duty should require a clearer legislative statement.

generally are limited to the not very startling observation that the statutes permit director consideration of stakeholder interests.[8] The waters thus remain quite murky.

Plausible interpretations of nonshareholder constituency statutes fall on a spectrum between two extremes. At one end of the spectrum is a reading that allows directors to ignore shareholder interests in making corporate decisions. At the other end is a reading under which the statutes simply codify the pre-existing common law, including an unmodified shareholder wealth maximization norm. Neither extreme seems likely to emerge as the prevailing interpretation. Instead, we will end up somewhere in the middle. But where?

At a minimum, if the statutes do anything beyond merely codifying present law, they presumably permit directors to select a plan that is second-best from the shareholders' perspective, but which alleviates the decision's impact on the firm's nonshareholder constituencies. In other words, the directors may balance a decision's effect on shareholders against its effect on stakeholders. If the decision would harm stakeholders, the directors may trade-off a reduction in shareholder gains for enhanced stakeholder welfare.

This interpretation is virtually compelled by the statutory language. What purpose is there in giving the directors the right to consider nonshareholder interests if the directors cannot protect those interests? Without the right to act on their deliberations, the right to include stakeholder interests in those deliberations is rendered nugatory. If the statutes are to have any meaning, they must permit directors to make some trade-offs between their various constituencies.

How then might these statutes change the outcome of specific cases, if at all? Assume the XYZ Company operates a manufacturing plant nearing obsolescence in an economically depressed area. XYZ's board of directors is considering three plans for the plant's future. Plan A will keep the plant open, which will preserve the jobs of two hundred fifty workers, but will reduce earnings per share by ten percent as long as the plant remains open. Plan B will close the plant immediately, which will put the two hundred fifty plant employees out of work in an area where manufacturing jobs are scarce, but will cause earnings per share to rise by ten percent. Plan C contemplates closing the plant, but implementing a job training and relocation program for its workers

---

[8] See, e.g., Keyser v. Commonwealth Nat'l Fin. Corp., 675 F.Supp. 238, 265–66 (M.D.Pa.1987); Baron v. Strawbridge & Clothier, 646 F.Supp. 690, 697 (E.D.Pa.1986).

as a supplement to state-provided programs. Plan C will cause a ten percent reduction in earnings per share for one year.

A shareholder threatens to bring a derivative action against the directors charging breach of their duty of care if they pick any plan other than Plan B. Under traditional corporate law principles, as espoused by *Dodge*, XYZ's board is required to choose the plan that maximizes shareholder wealth: Plan B. However, because the statutes permit directors to balance shareholder and stakeholder interests, the board should be free to adopt either Plan A or Plan C without fear of liability if a shareholder challenges the board's decision.

As a practical matter, however, the result would be no different under traditional common law rules. The business judgment rule undoubtedly would preclude judicial review of the board's decision. In *Shlensky v. Wrigley*,[9] Wrigley's stubborn opposition to lights probably cost the shareholders money over the short term, but the business judgment rule prevented Shlensky's lawsuit from going forward. In *Dodge v. Ford Motor Co.*,[10] Ford's concern for his workers and customers likewise may have harmed the other shareholders, but again the business judgment rule shielded him from liability in connection with the plant expansion decision. Just so, the business judgment rule would shield our hypothetical XYZ board's decision from judicial review. In theory, of course, absent a nonshareholder constituency statute, a shareholder might be able to rebut the business judgment rule's presumption of good faith and hold directors liable for considering nonshareholder interests. In practice, however, cases in which the business judgment rule does not shield operational decisions from judicial review are so rare as to amount to little more than aberrations. In sum, the probability of holding directors liable for operational decisions was so low before the nonshareholder constituency statutes came along that the statutes could not further lower it.

C. Benefit Corporations

In 2013 Delaware enacted new provisions to its General Corporation Law allowing the formation of a new hybrid type of entity called a "public benefit corporation" (PBC). A PBC is defined in § 362 as a "for-profit corporation . . . that is intended to produce a public benefit or benefits and to operate in a responsible and sustainable manner." The "public benefit" must be specified in the firm's certificate of incorporation and consist of "a positive effect . . . on one or more categories of persons, entities, communities or

---

[9] 237 N.E.2d 776 (Ill.App.1968).

[10] 170 N.W. 668 (Mich.1919).

interests (other than stockholders in their capacities as stockholders) including, but not limited to, effects of an artistic, charitable, cultural, economic, educational, environmental, literary, medical, religious, scientific or technological nature." Existing for-profit corporations may convert to PBCs only with the approval of 90 percent of outstanding shares, with the dissenting shareholders entitled to appraisal (that is, the right to be cashed out at fair market value). The PBC must, at least biennially, provide its shareholders with a statement that includes "objective factual information . . . regarding [its] success in meeting [its] objectives for promoting [its specified] public benefits and interests." Other states have adopted similar provisions, with variations, particularly as to public disclosure, and third-party assessment, of the public benefit. These benefit corporations are becoming increasingly common vehicles for social entrepreneurship.

§ 9.3   Extra-Contractual Duties to Bondholders

As with any long-term relational contract, bond indentures inevitably prove incomplete. In a world characterized by uncertainty, complexity, and bounded rationality, it cannot be otherwise. Where the bond indenture is silent, should the law invoke fiduciary duties or other extra-contractual rights as gap fillers?

The majority view is that neither the corporation itself nor its officers and directors owe fiduciary duties to bondholders, as the leading cases hold.[11] Instead, "the relationship between a corporation and the holders of its debt securities, even convertible debt securities, is contractual in nature."[12] The indenture thus both defines and confines the scope of the corporation's obligations to its bondholders.

To be sure, a few cases purportedly hold to the contrary. The leading precedents, however, relate to insolvent corporations.[13] Outside the insolvency context, there is little support for fiduciary

---

[11] See, e.g., Metropolitan Life Ins. Co. v. RJR Nabisco, Inc., 716 F.Supp. 1504, 1524–25 (S.D.N.Y.1989); Simons v. Cogan, 549 A.2d 300, 304 (Del.1988); Revlon, Inc. v. MacAndrews & Forbes Holdings, Inc., 506 A.2d 173, 182 (Del.1985).

[12] Katz v. Oak Indus., Inc., 508 A.2d 873, 879 (Del.Ch.1986).

[13] See FDIC v. Sea Pines Co., 692 F.2d 973, 976–77 (4th Cir.1982) (stating that "when the corporation becomes insolvent, the fiduciary duty of the directors shifts from the stockholders to the creditors"); Production Resources Group, LLC v. NCT Group, Inc., 863 A.2d 772, 790–91 (Del.Ch.2004) ("When a firm has reached the point of insolvency, it is settled that under Delaware law, the firm's directors are said to owe fiduciary duties to the company's creditors. This is an uncontroversial proposition. . . ."); Geyer v. Ingersoll Publications Co., 621 A.2d 784, 787 (Del.Ch.1992) (observing that "when the insolvency exception does arise, it creates fiduciary duties for directors for the benefit of creditors").

duties to bondholders.[14] Most of the cases opining to the contrary involved fraudulent schemes or conveyances actionable outside the bounds of corporate fiduciary obligation.[15] Other cases in this genre involve recharacterization of nominal debt securities as equity.[16] Still others are mere dicta.[17]

The limited extra-contractual rights of bondholders are provided by the implied covenant of good faith found in all contracts. *Katz v. Oak Industries*, for example, held that the implied covenant is breached when it is clear from the express terms of the indenture that the parties would have prohibited the challenged act if they had thought to negotiate about it:

> [T]he appropriate legal test is not difficult to deduce. It is this: is it clear from what was expressly agreed upon that the parties who negotiated the express terms of the contract would have agreed to proscribe the act later complained of as a breach of the implied covenant of good faith—had they thought to negotiate with respect to that matter. If the answer to this question is yes, then, in my opinion, a court is justified in concluding that such act constitutes a breach of the implied covenant of good faith.[18]

The oft-cited *Met Life* decision likewise invoked an implied covenant of good faith, although its treatment of that covenant differed

---

[14] In North American Catholic Educational Programming Foundation, Inc. v. Gheewalla, 930 A.2d 92 (Del.2007), the Delaware supreme court resolved a longstanding debate by holding that directors of a corporation in the "zone of insolvency" do not owe direct fiduciary duties to creditors.

[15] See Metropolitan Life Ins. Co. v. RJR Nabisco, Inc., 716 F.Supp. 1504, 1524 (S.D.N.Y.1989) (analyzing cases).

[16] Cf. Eliasen v. Green Bay & W.R.R. Co., 569 F.Supp. 84 (E.D.Wis.1982) (discussing theory and cases). In *Eliasen*, the Class B debentures in question had economic rights more closely resembling those of common stock than normal debt. The Class B debentures had no right to regular payment of interest, but were paid interest only when the board chose and only after the nominal stockholders had been paid, and the debentures came last in a liquidation. The court nevertheless declined to treat the debentures as the equivalent of stock because the Class B debentures had no voting rights and, moreover, were originally issued in a reorganization of an insolvent debtor to creditors who would have been entitled to nothing in a liquidation. Id.

[17] The classic example is Green v. Hamilton Int'l Corp., 437 F.Supp. 723 (S.D.N.Y.1977), in which the court held that "[a]s holders of convertible debentures, plaintiffs were part of 'the entire community of interests in the corporation— creditors as well as stockholders' to whom the fiduciary duties of directors and controlling shareholders run." Id. at 729 n.4 (quoting Justice Douglas' famous dictum in Pepper v. Litton, 308 U.S. 295, 307 (1939)). The passage from *Green* is mere dicta because the court simply determined that plaintiff's claim of fraud under Securities Exchange Act Rule 10b–5 could survive a FRCP 12(b)(6) motion to dismiss. In addition, while *Green* purported to interpret Delaware law, the Delaware supreme court specifically disavowed *Green* in Simons v. Cogan, 549 A.2d 300, 303–04 (Del.1988).

[18] Katz v. Oak Indus., Inc., 508 A.2d 873, 880 (Del.Ch.1986).

somewhat from *Katz.*[19] In the latter, the chancery court suggested that an implied covenant of good faith is part of every contract. In *Met Life*, however, the court suggested that a covenant of good faith is implied only when necessary to ensure that neither side deprives the other side of the "fruits of the agreement." The court then seemingly limited the fruits of the bond indenture to regular payment of interest and ultimate repayment of principal. In any case, the court made clear that "the implied covenant will only aid and further the explicit terms of the agreement and will never impose an obligation which would be inconsistent with other terms of the contractual relationship." Consequently, the implied covenant will not give bondholders any extra-contractual rights inconsistent with those set out in the indenture.

Assuming the two tests are different, does the difference matter? *Katz* seems a bit broader, perhaps applying the covenant to conduct that does not directly threaten either the repayment of principal or regular payment of interest. In particular, *Katz* seemingly allows the covenant of good faith to address matters that affect the market price of the bonds. In order to do so, of course, the court would require express terms in the indenture addressing such matters, because only then could one draw the inferences necessitated by the decision's hypothetical bargain-like standard.

Despite this potential difference, however, the two cases are quite similar in a number of respects. In particular, both *Katz* and *Met Life* constrain the implied covenant of good faith by reference to the express terms of the contract. Taken together, the two decisions reflect a basic principle, which can be expressed colloquially as "you made your bed, now you have to lie in it."

§ 9.4   Extra-Contractual Duties to Preferred Shareholders

Unlike bondholders, who are creditors of the corporation, holders of preferred stock are nominally shareholders. In addition, while bond indentures tend to be lengthy and highly detailed, the organic documents governing preferred stock tend to be bare-bones affairs. To what extent are preferred stockholders therefore entitled to the benefits of fiduciary duties or other extra-contractual protections?

Jedwab v. MGM Grand Hotels, Inc.,[20] split the baby in an interesting way. A prospective buyer of MGM, Bally Manufacturing, made a total offer for the company, leaving to MGM's board the task

---

[19] Metropolitan Life Ins. Co. v. RJR Nabisco, Inc., 716 F.Supp. 1504 (S.D.N.Y.1989).

[20] 509 A.2d 584 (Del.Ch.1986).

of dividing the proceeds between the common and the preferred. The preferred shareholders objected to the division set by the board. Did the board owe the preferred shareholders fiduciary duties of care and loyalty with respect to division of the deal?

The chancery court's opinion acknowledged a number of prior Delaware decisions holding that "preferential rights are contractual in nature."[21] The chancellor rejected, however, the defendants' asserted corollary that all rights of preferred stock are contractual in nature. Instead, the chancellor drew a distinction between the preferential rights and special limitations associated with preferred stock, which are created by the articles of incorporation or other organic corporate documents, and rights that both the preferred and common shares possess by virtue of being stock. The former are contractual in nature and, as such, the board's sole obligation is to give the preferred their contract rights. The latter, however, may give rise to fiduciary obligations. The disputed merger implicated none of the relevant preferential rights or special limitations of MGM's preferred. Accordingly, the court identified three aspects of the preferred holders' complaint as implicating fiduciary duties: "(a) to a 'fair' allocation of the proceeds of the merger; (b) to have the defendants exercise appropriate care in negotiating the proposed merger; and (c) to be free of overreaching by Mr. Kerkorian [a controlling shareholder]. . . ."

Jedwab has a certain superficial plausibility, but proves unpersuasive on closer examination. First, a number of Delaware supreme court precedents in fact suggest that all of the rights of preferred stockholders are contractual in nature, not just those relating to their preferential rights and special limitations.[22] The supreme court's holding in *Wood v. Coastal States Gas Corp.*[23] seems particularly problematic for *Jedwab*'s viability. In *Coastal*, plaintiff-preferred shareholders challenged a spin-off transaction as violating the provision of Coastal's articles of incorporation governing conversion of their stock to common. Holding that its duty was to interpret the contract created by the conversion provision, the court concluded that the preferred stockholders' rights were not violated. To be sure, *Coastal* involved a preferential right and thus fell into the category of rights that even *Jedwab* acknowledges to be contractual in nature. The *Coastal* court,

[21] See, e.g., Rothschild Int'l Corp. v. Liggett Group, Inc., 474 A.2d 133, 136 (Del.1984).

[22] See, e.g., Judah v. Delaware Trust Co., 378 A.2d 624, 628 (Del.1977) ("Generally, the provisions of the certificate of incorporation govern the rights of preferred shareholders, the certificate . . . being interpreted in accordance with the law of contracts, with only those rights which are embodied in the certificate granted to preferred shareholders.").

[23] 401 A.2d 932 (Del.1979).

however, used very broad language in defining the rights of preferred stockholders: "For most purposes, the rights of the preferred shareholders as against the common shareholders are fixed by the contractual terms agreed upon when the class of preferred stock is created." The qualifier, "for most purposes," does not leave a lot of wiggle room for *Jedwab* to sneak through. Even more significantly, however, the *Coastal* court expressly rejected the plaintiff-preferred shareholders' claim that the spin-off unjustly enriched the common stockholders. In so holding, the court opined that whatever participation rights the preferred stockholders possessed must be created by the articles of incorporation. By thus rejecting an extra-contractual remedy, the *Coastal* court further confirmed the essentially contractual nature of preferred stockholders' rights.

Second, *Jedwab* depends on the proposition that preferred stock is granted certain rights by statute and common law even where the corporation's organic documents are silent. The chancellor cited two such examples: Where the contract is silent, preferred stock get the same voting rights as common stock. Where the contract is silent, preferred stock participates pro rata with the common in a liquidation.[24] Neither of these examples, however, rise to the same level as conferring the benefits of fiduciary obligation on preferred stockholders. Neither entails the sort of open-ended inquiry required by fiduciary obligation, nor does either entail the same risk of conflicting interests.

Finally, from a policy perspective, several objections to *Jedwab* can be noted. First, *Jedwab* does not eliminate potential conflicts of interest between the holders of preferred and common. Whose interests must the board maximize when those interests clash? On a related note, the *Jedwab* opinion makes clear that the preferred are not entitled to an equal share in the merger consideration—only to a fair share. Yet, how does the board decide what is fair ex ante? Even if the board makes a good faith effort to set a fair price, the indeterminacy of valuation means that reasonable people could differ. Conversely, if the prospective buyer proposed the division to be made between the common and the preferred, the board likely would escape liability. Among other things, the board could defend itself on causation grounds—i.e., whether or not the board breached its fiduciary duties, that breach was not the cause of plaintiff's injuries.[25] Finally, *Jedwab* implies that the preferred may have

---

[24] Jedwab v. MGM Grand Hotels, Inc., 509 A.2d 584, 593–94 (Del.Ch.1986).

[25] See, e.g., Dalton v. American Inv. Co., 490 A.2d 574 (Del.Ch.), aff'd, 501 A.2d 1238 (Del.1985) (declining to reach issue of fiduciary obligation to preferred stockholders as there was no causal link between alleged breach and alleged injury).

greater rights with respect to nonpreference issues than with respect to preferences, which seems odd at best.[26]

In fairness, *Jedwab* wrestled with a persistent problem in the preferred stock area. As noted, bond indentures are hundreds of pages long and deal with virtually every conceivable contingency. In contrast, preferred stock certificates of designation tend to be relatively short and to deal with only a few issues. Which leaves unresolved a nagging question; namely, how do you deal with issues that come up that the contract does not cover? The answer, by analogy to the bond setting, is to use an implied covenant of good faith rather than fiduciary duties. In this context, such a covenant would preclude the board from taking action that deprives the preferred of the benefit of their bargain. To the extent that covenant fails to provide adequate protections, portfolio theory teaches that the preferred stockholders should engage in self-help by diversifying their portfolio.

§ 9.5   The "Special" Problem of Corporate Philanthropy

As we have seen, *A. P. Smith Manufacturing Co. v. Barlow*,[27] is often cited as a leading corporate social responsibility decision. Ironically, however, the specific question presented therein—the validity of corporate philanthropy—has been resolved in a more narrow way. Corporate charitable donations are subject to attack under two doctrines: ultra vires and breach of fiduciary duty. Neither is likely to succeed, so long as the amount in question is reasonable and some plausible corporate purpose may be asserted.

Virtually all states have adopted statutes specifically granting corporations the power to make charitable donations,[28] which eliminates the ultra vires issue. Although these statutes typically contain no express limit on the size of permissible gifts, courts interpreting the statutes require corporate charitable donations to be reasonable both as to the amount and the purpose for which they are given.[29] The federal corporate income tax code's limits on the

---

[26] The Delaware chancery court continues to follow *Jedwab*. See, e.g., Jackson Nat'l Life Ins. Co. v. Kennedy, 741 A.2d 377, 386–87 (Del.Ch.1999) ("fiduciary duties as well may be owed to preferred stockholders in limited circumstances. . . . Whether a given claim asserted by preferred stockholders is governed by contract or fiduciary duty principles, then, depends on whether the dispute arises from rights and obligations created by contract or from a right or obligation that is not by virtue of a preference but is shared equally with the common") (footnotes and internal quotation marks omitted).

[27] 98 A.2d 581, 586 (N.J.1953).

[28] See, e.g., DGCL § 122(9); MBCA § 3.02(13).

[29] See, e.g., Memorial Hospital Ass'n v. Pacific Grape Products Co., 290 P.2d 481 (Cal.1955); Kahn v. Sullivan, 594 A.2d 48 (Del.1991); Theodora Holding Corp. v. Henderson, 257 A.2d 398 (Del.Ch.1969); Union Pac. R. Co. v. Trustees, Inc., 329 P.2d 398 (Utah 1958).

deductibility of corporate charitable giving are often used by analogy by courts seeking guidance on whether a gift was reasonable in amount.

As for breach of fiduciary duty claims, the principles announced in *Dodge v. Ford Motor Co.*[30] arguably require that corporate philanthropy redound to the corporation's benefit. As *Shlensky v. Wrigley*[31] suggests, however, reasonable corporate donations should be protected by the business judgment rule.[32] Consequently, *Barlow*'s discourse on corporate social responsibility properly is regarded as mere dicta.

---

[30] 170 N.W. 668 (Mich.1919).

[31] 237 N.E.2d 776 (Ill.App.1968).

[32] See, e.g., Ella M. Kelly & Wyndham, Inc. v. Bell, 266 A.2d 878, 879 (Del.1970); Union Pac. R. Co. v. Trustees, Inc., 329 P.2d 398, 401–02 (Utah 1958).

Chapter 10

SHAREHOLDER VOTING

§ 10.1 Introduction

Shareholder voting can serve three different purposes, depending upon the nature of the firm in question. Consider, as the first category, firms with a small number of shareholders all of whom have ready access to firm information and homogeneous preferences. In such a case, voting is effectively an exercise of managerial power. Both strategic and tactical business decisions can be made efficiently through voting, because in such a firm there is no need to incur the costs of retaining specialized managers. Accordingly, such a firm usually will lack the separation of ownership and control characteristic of public corporations.

A second category of firms include those that are more complex, but in which there are controlling shareholders. Such a firm displays partial separation of ownership and control. Controlling shareholders of such firms have substantial access to firm information and retain incentives to cast informed votes. Although the firm probably will have a professional managing body, the managers face a real possibility of being voted out of office by the controlling shareholder if their performance is sub-par. Hence, voting again has both managerial and oversight functions.

In the final category of cases, the firm is highly complex, the shareholders are numerous and have diverse preferences, and the shareholders lack both the knowledge and incentives necessary to exercise an informed vote. Such a firm displays complete separation of ownership and control.

In all corporations, statutory shareholder voting rights are quite limited. Recall that, under DGCL § 141, the corporation's business and affairs are "managed by or under the direction of a board of directors." The vast majority of corporate decisions accordingly are made by the board of directors acting alone, or by persons to whom the board has properly delegated authority. Shareholders have virtually no right to initiate corporate action and, moreover, are entitled to approve or disapprove only a very few board actions. The statutory decisionmaking model thus is one in which the board acts and shareholders, at most, react. In the first two classes of corporations, however, it is possible for shareholders to depart from the statutory rules by agreement. We take up such agreements in Chapter 14.

§ 10.2 State Law

A. Overview

Shareholders normally vote only at properly noticed and called shareholder meetings.[1] All statutes require that there be at least one shareholder meeting a year (called, logically enough, the annual meeting of shareholders). In addition, all statutes have some provision for so-called special meetings—i.e., meetings held between annual meetings to consider some extraordinary matter that cannot wait. Who is entitled to call a special meeting varies from state to state. Almost all state corporation laws allow the board to call a special meeting. Most allow a specified percentage of the shareholders acting together to call a special meeting. A few allow a specified corporate officer, such as the president or chairman of the board, to call a special meeting. MBCA § 7.02(a)(1) empowers the board of directors and any other person authorized by the articles or bylaws to call a special meeting. MBCA § 7.02(a)(2) empowers the holders of at least 10% of the voting shares to call a special meeting. The articles may specify a lower or higher percentage, but not to exceed, 25% of the voting power. In contrast, per DGCL § 211(d) special meetings may be called only by the board of directors and any other person authorized by the articles or bylaws.

Whether it is an annual or special meeting, most shareholders will not show up. Large corporations with thousands of shareholders frequently hold their shareholder meetings in small halls or even just a very large conference room. Most shareholders vote by proxy. (In a sense, proxy voting is the corporate law equivalent of absentee voting.) Since the 1930s, proxy voting has been extensively regulated by the federal securities laws. Hence, many of the mechanics of shareholder voting are governed by federal rather than state law. Generally speaking, state law governs substantive aspects of shareholder voting, such as how many votes a shareholder gets, when they get to vote, and the types of questions on which they get to vote. Federal law governs the procedures by which shareholders vote and the disclosures to which shareholders are entitled.

B. Notice, Quorum, and Votes Required

Virtually all state corporate codes adopt one vote per common share as the default rule, but allow corporations to depart from the norm by adopting appropriate provisions in their organic

---

[1] A majority of states allow shareholders to act without a meeting by unanimous written consent. See, e.g., MBCA § 7.04. A substantial minority, including Delaware, permit shareholders to act by written consent even if the shareholders are not unanimous. See, e.g., DGCL § 228.

documents. Firms have devised at least three variants on the traditional model, each of which in some way repackages the bundle of rights associated with common stock: non-voting stock, dual class stock in which each class has different voting rights, and common stock having only voting rights. All of the major stock exchanges, however, have adopted listing standards severely restricting the use of such variants and they are therefore rare.

Whether shareholders will vote in person or by proxy, statutory notice and quorum requirements must be satisfied if their action is to be valid. MBCA § 7.05(a), for example, requires no less than 10 but no more than 60 days' notice for both annual and special meetings. Under MBCA § 7.05(b), notice of an annual meeting need not state the purposes for which the meeting is called, although the federal proxy rules mandate such notice. Under MBCA § 7.05(c), by contrast, only those matters specified in the notice may be taken up at a special meeting.

The Model Act's default quorum is a majority of the shares entitled to vote, although the articles of incorporation can specify either a higher or lower figure.[2] Although there is some case law to the contrary, the Model Act effectively precludes a shareholder from "breaking the quorum" by leaving the meeting. If a shareholder's stock is represented at the meeting in person or by proxy for any reason, that shareholder's stock is deemed to be present for quorum purposes for the remainder of the meeting.[3]

Subject to the special rules governing election of directors and group voting, which are discussed in subsequent sections, MBCA § 7.25(c) provides that "action on a matter . . . is approved if the votes cast . . . favoring the action exceed the votes cast opposing the action." In contrast, DGCL § 216 states that "the affirmative vote of the majority of shares present in person or represented by proxy at the meeting and entitled to vote on the subject matter shall be the act of the stockholders." The distinction between the two formulations is subtle but significant. Suppose there are 1000 shares entitled to vote, 800 of which are represented at the meeting either in person or by proxy, and which are voted as follows:

In Favor	399
Opposed	398
Abstain	3

---

[2] MBCA § 7.25(a). Delaware law is similar, except it forbids the articles from setting a quorum of less than one-third the shares entitled to vote. DGCL § 216.

[3] See MBCA § 7.25(b); but see, e.g., Levisa Oil Corp. v. Quigley, 234 S.E.2d 257 (Va.1977) (shareholder may break quorum by departing meeting); see also Textron, Inc. v. American Woolen Co., 122 F.Supp. 305 (D.Mass.1954) (shareholder present before a quorum is established may depart and, if so, may not be counted towards a quorum).

Under the MBCA, the motion carries, as more shares were voted in favor of the motion than against it. Under the Delaware statute, however, a majority of the shares present at the meeting—401— must be voted in favor of the motion for it to carry, and this motion therefore fails. In effect, Delaware treats abstentions as no votes, while the MBCA ignores them.

The articles of incorporation may require a higher vote than the default statutory minimum, either across the board or on specified issues. State corporation laws also typically provide that certain extraordinary actions require approval by a higher vote. MBCA § 10.03 requires, for example, that amendments to the articles of incorporation be approved by a majority of the shares entitled to vote. Again, suppose there are 1000 shares entitled to vote, 800 of which are represented at the meeting either in person or by proxy. In order for the amendment to be adopted, 501 shares must be voted in favor. The same vote is required for approval of a merger (per § 11.04) or sale of all or substantially all the corporation's assets (per § 12.02). Delaware law is similar.

C.   Election of Directors

1.   Plurality Versus Majority Vote

One of the curiosities of the corporate electoral system is that it traditionally did not provide for a straight up or down—for or against—vote for directors. Instead, shareholders typically are given three options: vote for all of the nominees for director, withhold support for all of them, and withhold support from specified directors.

Withholding support from a director candidate is not the same as a vote against that candidate. Delaware General Corporation Law § 216(3) provides: "Directors shall be elected by a plurality of the votes of the shares present in person or represented by proxy at the meeting and entitled to vote on the election of directors." The Comments to Model Business Corporation Act § 7.28(a), which also uses a "plurality" standard, explain that: "A 'plurality' means that the individuals with the largest number of votes are elected as directors up to the maximum number of directors to be chosen at the election." Say the firm had 10 vacancies to be filled and there were exactly ten candidates. Hence, an unpopular director would be reelected even if holders of a majority of the shares withheld their votes from him.[4]

---

[4] A potential complication is caused because the DGCL and MBCA formulations with respect to election of directors have the same "cast" versus "present" dichotomy as their respective formulations with respect to matters other than the election of directors. Does the phrasing of § 216(3) therefore suggest that Delaware would treat a proxy withholding authority to vote for a director the same

In 2006, however, Delaware amended the statutory provisions on director election to accommodate majority voting. Section 141(b) of the Delaware General Corporation Law was amended by adding the following sentences: "A resignation [of a director] is effective when the resignation is delivered unless the resignation specifies a later effective date or an effective date determined upon the happening of an event or events. A resignation which is conditioned upon the director failing to receive a specified vote for reelection as a director may provide that it is irrevocable." This amendment was designed to validate bylaws that had been voluntarily adopted by a number of companies, most notably Pfizer, pursuant to which directors who received a majority of withhold "votes" are required to submit their resignation to the board.[5]

Section 216 was amended at the same time by adding the following sentence: "A bylaw amendment adopted by stockholders which specifies the votes that shall be necessary for the election of directors shall not be further amended or repealed by the board of directors." This amendment validates bylaw provisions requiring that a director receive a majority vote in order to be elected. Under such provisions, it is now possible to vote "against" a director. The MBCA has adopted a similar provision authorizing use of a majority vote rule on an opt-in basis. As of late 2006, more than 250 companies—including 31% of Fortune 500 firms—had adopted some form of majority voting bylaw.[6]

Critics of majority voting schemes contend that failed elections can have a destabilizing effect on the corporation. Selecting and vetting a director candidate is a long and expensive process, which

---

way it treats abstentions as to other matters, in which case a director would not be reelected if the holders of a majority of the shares withheld support? The logical answer is no, but there does not seem to be definitive authority.

[5] One question presented by these so-called Pfizer or plurality-plus policies is whether the board retains authority to turn down the resignation of a director who fails to get the requisite majority vote. In City of Westland Police & Fire Retirement System v. Axcelis Technologies, Inc., 1 A.3d 281 (Del. 2010), the Delaware Supreme Court confirmed that the board has substantial discretion to do just that. Axcelis Technologies had a seven-member board staggered into three classes. In 2008, all three of the incumbent directors up for reelection failed to receive a majority of the votes cast. Pursuant to the company's plurality-plus policy, all three submitted their resignations. The board rejected all three resignations. A shareholder initiated a § 220 request to inspect the relevant books and records of the company preparatory to filing a derivative suit challenging the board's decision. In order to prevent shareholders from conducting fishing expeditions, Delaware courts will grant such inspection requests only where there is a credible basis from which to infer that some wrongdoing may have occurred. In acknowledging that § 220 requests sometimes can be meritorious in this context, the Court observed that "the question arises whether the directors, as fiduciaries, made a disinterested, informed business judgment that the best interests of the corporation require the continued service of these directors, or whether the Board had some different, ulterior motivation." It thus seems fair to infer that the business judgment rule will be the standard by which courts evaluate board decisions under such policies.

[6] William J. Sjostrom, Jr. & Young Sang Kim, Majority Voting for the Election of Directors, 40 Conn. L. Rev. 459 (2007).

has become even more complicated by the new stock exchange listing standards defining director independence. Suppose, however, that the shareholders voted out the only qualified financial expert sitting on the audit committee. The corporation immediately would be in violation of its obligations under those standards.

Critics also complain that qualified individuals would be deterred from service. The enhanced liability and increased workload imposed by Sarbanes-Oxley and related regulatory and legal developments has made it much harder for firms to recruit qualified outside directors. The risk of being singled out by shareholders for a no vote presumably will make board service even less attractive, especially in light of the concern board members demonstrate for their reputations.

2.   Cumulative Voting

Under the standard voting rules, a majority shareholder can elect the entire board of directors. This is why prospective buyers place a higher value on control blocks vis-à-vis shares owned by noncontrolling shareholders. Cumulative voting provides an alternative mechanism for electing the board of directors that can assure board representation for the minority. An example will be helpful.

Assume ABC Corporation has 3 shareholders: A, who owns 250 shares; B, who owns 300 shares; C, who owns 650.[7] The bylaws specify a four-member board of directors. Under standard voting procedures, directors are elected by a plurality of the votes cast at the meeting on a one share-one vote basis.[8] Suppose, for example, that each of A, B and C are supporting four different candidates for director. The following will result:

A–1: 250 for	B–1: 300 for	C–1: 650 for; elected
A–2: 250 for	B–2: 300 for	C–2: 650 for; elected
A–3: 250 for	B–3: 300 for	C–3: 650 for; elected
A–4: 250 for	B–4: 300 for	C–4: 650 for; elected

Consequently, C elects the entire board of directors. This is of vital importance, because directors make most corporate decisions. In this example, the board will be composed entirely of people nominated by C.

---

[7] The example is taken from Michael P. Dooley, Fundamentals of Corporation Law 376 (1995).

[8] See, e.g., MBCA § 7.28(a). It might help if you think of director balloting as voting for a slate: Each share entitles its owner to cast one vote towards determining which slate will be elected. Alternatively, you can think of each director position as a seat that can be filled by only one person. Each share entitles its owner to cast one vote towards determining the occupant of that seat.

In cumulative voting, by contrast, the number of votes each shareholder may cast is determined by multiplying the number of shares owned by the number of director positions up for election. Each shareholder then may concentrate his votes by casting all of his votes for one candidate (or distributing his votes among two or more candidates).[9] The directors receiving the highest number of votes will be elected. In this example, A has 1000 votes available to be cast; B has 1200 votes; and C has 2600 votes. A and B each nominate themselves and cast all of their votes for themselves on their respective ballots. A receives 1000 votes. B receives 1200 votes. C nominates herself and her friends C–1, C–2, and C–3. But C cannot cast her votes so as to elect all four of her nominees. C might, for example, cast 1100 votes for herself and 1000 votes for C–1. Both C and C–1 will be elected. Unfortunately for C, however, she has only 500 votes left to divide between C–2 and C–3. Accordingly, they cannot be elected.

The following formula is used to determine the number of directors a given shareholder may elect under cumulative voting:

$$X = \frac{[(DN \times TN)]}{N+1} + 1$$

Where N is the total number of directors to be elected; DN is the number of directors a shareholder wishes to elect; TN is the total number of voting shares outstanding; and X is the number of shares needed to elect the desired number of directors. If you solve this equation for directors DN = 4; you will find that C needs 961 shares in order to elect all 4 directors. Notice that even if B and C cumulated their votes together, they could not prevent A from electing at least one director. If you work out all the permutations, you will find that in this hypothetical A can elect one director, B can elect one, and C can elect two. Unless all three agree, no combination of shareholders can elect all four directors.

Cumulative voting was very much in vogue in the late 1800s. A number of states adopted mandatory cumulative voting as part of their state constitutions. Others did the same by statute. During the last few decades, however, cumulative voting in public corporations has increasingly fallen out of favor. Opponents of cumulative voting argue it produces an adversarial board and results in critical decisions being made in private meetings held by the majority faction before the formal board meeting. Today, most states—including Delaware and MBCA jurisdictions—allow cumulative voting on an opt-in basis. In other words, standard voting is the default rule in these states but the corporation may

---

[9] See, e.g., MBCA § 7.28(c).

provide for cumulative voting in its articles of incorporation. In all states, of course, cumulative voting is limited to the election of directors—shareholders are not allowed to cumulate votes as to other types of shareholder decisions.[10]

3. Classified Boards

Typically, the entire board of directors is elected annually, whether by standard or cumulative voting, to a one-year term.[11] Alternatively, however, the articles of incorporation or bylaws may provide for a classified or staggered board of directors.[12] In this model, the board is divided into two or three classes. In a board with two classes of directors, the members serve two-year terms so that only half the board is up for election in any given year. In a board with three classes, directors serve three year terms and only a third of the board is up for election annually.

Classified boards have significant change of control implications and are often used as a defense against proxy contests and corporate takeovers. Under a staggered board with three classes, for example, the shareholders must wait two annual meeting cycles before they can replace a majority of the board. In order for the classified board to actually delay a change of control, of course, the classification scheme must be protected from the possibility that the shareholders will remove the directors without cause or pack the board with new appointments. Classified board provisions in articles of incorporation therefore typically are coupled with additional terms reserving to the board the sole right to determine the number of directors and to fill any vacancies. If permitted by state law, drafters of a classified board scheme also limit or abolish the right of shareholders to call a special shareholders meeting or to remove directors without cause.

Notice that by decreasing the number of directors up for election in any given year classification of a board of directors can

---

[10] The California Corporations Code provides for application of various code provisions to a foreign corporation if the firm does a majority of its business in California and if a majority of the record holders of their shares are California residents. In Wilson v. Louisiana-Pacific Res., Inc., 187 Cal.Rptr. 852 (Cal.App.1982), application of California's cumulative voting provisions to a Utah corporation meeting the foregoing test was upheld against a dormant commerce clause challenge. The court opined: "A corporation can do a majority of its business in only one state at a time; and it can have a majority of its shareholders resident in only one state at a time. If a corporation meets those requirements in this state, no other state is in a position to regulate the method of voting by shareholders on the basis of the same or similar criteria. It might also be said that no state could claim as great an interest in doing so." Id. at 860.

[11] Under MBCA § 8.05(b), the directors' term in office technically expires at the next annual shareholders' meeting following their election. Under DGCL § 141(b), a director's term continues until his successor is elected.

[12] See, e.g., DGCL § 141(d). Curiously, MBCA § 8.06 permits staggered boards only if there are nine or more directors.

substantially increase the number of shares that must be cumulated to elect a director. This effect is nicely illustrated by *Coalition to Advocate Public Utility Responsibility, Inc. v. Engels*.[13] Northern States Power Company (NSP) had 14 directors, each elected annually for a one-year term by means of cumulative voting. In 1973, CAPUR (a coalition of consumer and environmental groups) sought to elect to the board a "public interest" candidate named Alpha Smaby (really).[14] Smaby promised that, if elected to the board, she would promote the "public interest" with special concern for environmental and consumer issues. NSP's board opposed Smaby's election and sought to prevent it by (1) reducing the number of directors to 12 and (2) classifying the board into three groups of four directors with staggered three-year terms. As a result, only four directors would be up for election in any given year. Under the old rules, Smaby needed the cumulated votes of just over 7% of the shares to be elected. The changes made by the board raised the number of shares needed to assure her election to about 20%.

Both changes were permitted by statute. Most corporate law codes give the board power to make unilateral changes in its size. Most likewise permit the corporation to have a staggered board. The trial court nonetheless granted a preliminary injunction against the board. Why? Basically because it is inequitable to change the rules in the middle of the game—or so the court opined. Consistent with well-established principles of Delaware law,[15] the court held that otherwise lawful actions can be enjoined as if they unfairly injure rights of minority shareholders. By implementing these changes in the middle of an election campaign, without disclosure, and for the purpose of defeating a minority candidate, the board breached its fiduciary duties. Although the election thus went forward under the old rules, Smaby ultimately did not receive a sufficient number of votes to be elected.[16] The case nevertheless reaffirms the principle that otherwise lawful board action becomes impermissible if undertaken in the midst of an election campaign for the purpose of obstructing a legitimate effort by dissident shareholders to obtain board representation. From the perspective of corporate counsel working with the incumbent directors, of course, the transactional

---

[13] 364 F.Supp. 1202 (D.Minn.1973).

[14] Smaby's obituary does not relate whether Alpha was her original birth name, but does tell us that she was "a former Minnesota state lawmaker active in opposing the Vietnam War and in promoting liberal causes. . . . Smaby served two terms in the state House of Representatives. During the 1968 presidential campaign, she was a delegate to the Democratic National Convention and supported anti-war candidate Eugene McCarthy." Orlando Sentinel Trib., July 20, 1991, at A16.

[15] See, e.g., Schnell v. Chris-Craft Indus., Inc., 285 A.2d 437 (Del.1971); Condec Corp. v. Lunkenheimer, 230 A.2d 769 (Del.Ch.1967).

[16] Michael P. Dooley, Fundamentals of Corporation Law 382–85 (1995).

implication is that such changes should be undertaken in mid-year long before any insurgent shareholders begin making noise.

D. Group Voting

Ordinarily all shares with voting rights vote as a single group. In some circumstances, however, the shareholders may be divided into two or more voting groups with each group consisting of one or more classes or series of stock. For example, where an amendment to the articles of incorporation or a proposed reorganization affects a particular class or series of stock, that class or series likely will have the right to vote on the proposed amendment as a separate group. Indeed, the group may be entitled to vote even if the class or series otherwise has no voting rights.

MBCA § 10.04(a) details eight distinct changes to the articles that trigger group voting: (1) an exchange or reclassification of all or part of the shares of the class into shares of another class; (2) an exchange or reclassification of all or part of the shares of another class into shares of the class; (3) a change in the rights, preferences, or limitations of all or part of the shares of the class; (4) changing the shares of all or part of the class into a different number of shares of the same class; (5) creating a new class of shares having rights or preferences with respect to distributions or to dissolution that are prior or superior to the shares of the class; (6) increasing the rights, preferences, or number of authorized shares of any class that, after giving effect to the amendment, will have rights or preferences with respect to distributions or to dissolution that are prior or superior to the shares of the class; (7) limiting or denying an existing preemptive right of all or part of the shares of the class; or (8) canceling or otherwise affecting rights to distributions that have accumulated but not yet been authorized on all or part of the shares of the class. Per § 10.04(b), if the amendment would affect a series of stock in one of the specified ways, the series is entitled to vote as a separate group. Conversely, per subsection (c), if an amendment that effects two or more classes or series in substantially similar ways, the affected classes or series must vote as a single group. Finally, subsection (d) grants voting rights to affected classes even though the articles of incorporation provide that the shares are nonvoting. MBCA § 10.04 similarly requires group voting on a merger if the plan of merger would affect one or more classes or series of stock in any of the foregoing ways.

In contrast, DGCL § 242(b)(2) only triggers group voting if the class is affected adversely. Specifically, the statute provides for group voting on an amendment to the articles "if the amendment would increase or decrease the aggregate number of authorized shares of such class, increase or decrease the par value of the shares of such class, or alter or change the powers, preferences, or special rights of the shares of such class so as to affect them adversely." The analysis does not change if the class lacks voting rights, as is often the case with preferred stock, because § 242(b) confers group voting rights even if the group is otherwise denied voting rights by the articles.

Delaware's "adversely affect" language is less determinate than the more specific MBCA formulations and, hence, more likely to produce litigation. In *Dalton v. American Investment Co.*,[17] for example, AIC was acquired by Leucadia, Inc. in a triangular merger between AIC and a wholly owned Leucadia subsidiary. AIC was the surviving entity. AIC's common shareholders were cashed out, but AIC's preferred shareholders were left in place. Certain of AIC preferred's holders sued. Because the plan of merger would amend AIC's articles of incorporation, the preferred claimed a right to vote on the plan of merger as a separate group. The pre-merger articles contained two relevant provisions: (1) The board was authorized to redeem—but not to call—the preferred. (2) If the board offered to buy back some (but not all) of the preferred shares, and the offer was over-subscribed, the shares to be redeemed were to be determined by lot. The plan of merger replaced these provisions with a sinking fund coupled with a call provision. Under the sinking fund provision, the board would retire 5% of the preferred annually for 20 years. To the extent that board repurchased preferred shares on the open market during a given year, those shares would count as a credit against the redemption obligation. The Chancellor determined that the amendment did not adversely affect the preferred and, accordingly, they were not entitled to vote as a separate group. To be sure, if the market price of the preferred was below the redemption price specified in the articles, the board could satisfy its obligation under the sinking fund by buying stock on the market. As a result, the apparent opportunity to get cashed out at a premium proved illusory. Yet, as the Chancellor pointed out, the amendment did not deprive the preferred of any rights they had previously possessed.

How then would the "adversely affect" phraseology impact other cases? Suppose the corporation's board of directors proposed an amendment that would cut the preferred stock's dividend from 8% to 5%. The amendment doubtless adversely affects the preferred and that class' holders would be entitled to vote as a separate group. Assume the requisite majority of the class of common stock votes yes, but that the proposed amendment is not approved by the requisite majority of the class of preferred. What happens? The

---

[17] 490 A.2d 574 (Del.Ch.), aff'd, 501 A.2d 1238 (Del.1985).

amendment is not approved. Approval of this amendment requires approval by both classes.

Now suppose the corporation's board of directors proposed an amendment to create a new class of preferred stock with rights superior to those of the existing class of preferred. This amendment adversely affects the interests of the existing class of preferred, whose claims have been subordinated to a prior claimant, but the amendment does not "alter or change the powers, preferences, or special rights of the preferred." Although creation of a class with superior rights may redound to the economic detriment of both the existing common and the existing preferred, it does not "alter or change" the rights of either class. As an old Delaware case explained, "the relative position of one class of shares in the scheme of capitalization is not to be confused with rights incident to that class as compared with other classes of shares."[18] The amendment in question affects the former, rather than the latter, but only the latter is covered by the statute.

E. Shareholder Inspection Rights

An insurgent shareholder conducting a proxy contest typically wants to communicate directly with his fellow shareholders. In addition, the shareholder may want access to other corporate books and records, so as to gain information that might bolster his arguments. The federal proxy rules provide limited mailing rights for an insurgent, but no other inspection rights. Consequently, the insurgent must look to state law inspection rights.

State shareholder inspection rights statutes must balance two competing concerns. On the one hand, shareholders have a legitimate interest in using the proxy system to hold the board accountable. On the other hand, nobody wants a junk mail distributor to get access to the shareholder list or a competitor to get access to the corporation's trade secrets and other proprietary information.[19] DGCL § 220(b) balances these concerns by requiring a shareholder asserting inspection rights to make a written demand setting forth a "proper purpose" for the request. The statute further defines a "proper purpose" as one "reasonably related to such person's interest as a stockholder." If the corporation denies the shareholder access to its records, the shareholder may sue in the Chancery Court. Under subsection (c), where the shareholder only

---

[18] Hartford Accident & Indemnity Co. v. W. S. Dickey Clay Mfg. Co., 24 A.2d 315, 318 (Del.1942).

[19] Cf. Cooke v. Outland, 144 S.E.2d 835, 842 (N.C.1965) ("Considering the huge size of many modern corporations and the necessarily complicated nature of their bookkeeping, it is plain that to permit their thousands of stockholders to roam at will through their records would render impossible not only any attempt to keep their records efficiently, but the proper carrying on of their businesses.").

seeks access to the shareholder list or stock ledger, the burden of proof is on the corporation to show that the shareholder is doing so for an improper reason. Where the shareholder seeks access to other corporate records, however, the shareholder must prove that he is doing so for the requisite proper purpose.[20]

The statutory framework poses several questions. First, what reasons for seeking access to a shareholder list constitute proper purposes? Attempts to investigate alleged corporate mismanagement are usually deemed proper, although the shareholder must have some factual basis for making the request and is not allowed to conduct a fishing expedition.[21] Collecting information relevant to valuing shares is a proper purpose.[22] A tender offeror stated a proper purpose in desiring to inform other shareholders of the pending offer and soliciting tenders from them.[23] Most pertinently for purposes of this Chapter, communicating with fellow shareholders in connection with a planned proxy contest is a proper purpose.[24] Improper purposes include attempting to discover proprietary business information for the benefit of a competitor, to secure prospects for personal business, to institute strike suits, and to pursue one's own social or political goals.[25]

---

[20] DGCL § 220(b) makes clear that shareholder inspection rights are not limited to the stockholder list, but rather extend to "other books and records." The extent to which a shareholder is entitled to rummage through corporate files under this provision, however, is poorly defined. At a bare minimum, it would seem likely that a shareholder is entitled to inspect the articles of incorporation, bylaws, minutes of board and shareholder meetings, board or shareholder actions by written consent, SEC filings and other public records. See, e.g., MBCA § 16.01(e) (requiring such records to be maintained for inspection). Where a shareholder seeks to prove director or officer mismanagement in connection with a particular transaction or event, the shareholder likely is entitled to inspect relevant contracts, correspondence, and the like. The Delaware supreme court has held, however, that a request to access such records must be very narrowly tailored: "A Section 220 proceeding should result in an order circumscribed with rifled precision." Security First Corp. v. U.S. Die Casting and Development Co, 687 A.2d 563 (Del.1997).

[21] See, e.g., Nodana Petroleum Corp. v. State, 123 A.2d 243, 246 (Del.1956); Helmsman Mgmt. Servs., Inc. v. A & S Consultants, Inc., 525 A.2d 160, 165 (Del.Ch.1987); Skouras v. Admiralty Enters., Inc., 386 A.2d 674, 678 (Del.Ch.1978). Recall that the Delaware supreme court has emphasized that shareholders should make use of the § 200 inspection right to investigate alleged misconduct before filing a derivative suit. See, e.g., Rales v. Blasband, 634 A.2d 927 (Del.1993).

[22] See, e.g., State ex rel. Nat'l Bank of Del. v. Jessup & Moore Paper Co., 88 A. 449 (Del.Super.1913).

[23] Crane Co. v. Anaconda Co., 382 N.Y.S.2d 707 (N.Y.1976).

[24] See, e.g., Hatleigh Corp. v. Lane Bryant, Inc., 428 A.2d 350 (Del.Ch.1981).

[25] Tatko v. Tatko Bros. Slate Co., 569 N.Y.S.2d 783 (App.Div.1991). Once the shareholder has demonstrated a proper purpose, the shareholder is entitled to "all of the documents in the corporation's possession, custody, or control, that are necessary to satisfy that proper purpose." Saito v. McKesson HBOC, Inc., 806 A.2d 113, 115 (Del.2002). Consequently, a shareholder may not be denied access to "necessary documents solely because the documents were prepared by third parties or because the documents predate the stockholder's first investment in the corporation." Id.

The latter improper purpose—pursuit of noneconomic social or political goals—has proven an especially problematic subject for Delaware courts. In the well-known *State ex rel. Pillsbury v. Honeywell, Inc.* decision,[26] plaintiff belonged to an antiwar group trying to stop Honeywell from producing anti-personnel fragmentation bombs for the military. After buying some Honeywell stock, plaintiff requested access to Honeywell's shareholder list and to corporate records relating to production of such bombs. In denying plaintiff access to those records, the court emphasized that plaintiff's stated reasons were based on his pre-existing social and political views rather than any economic interest. Accordingly, the court carefully limited its holdings to the facts at bar: "We do not mean to imply that a shareholder with a bona fide investment interest could not bring this suit if motivated by concern with the long-or short-term economic effects on Honeywell resulting from the production of war munitions." The court further noted that the "suit might be appropriate when a shareholder has a bona fide concern about the adverse effects of abstention from profitable war contracts on his investment in Honeywell." As such, *Honeywell* puts more emphasis on proper phrasing of one's statement of purpose than on the validity of the purpose itself. So long as one's social agenda can be dressed up in the language of economic consequences, one gets access to the list.[27] Does this formalistic approach make sense? The Delaware chancery court seems to think not, as at least one chancery decision opines that Delaware law has de facto rejected *Honeywell*'s requirement that the shareholder's purpose must relate to the "enhancement of the economic value of the corporation."[28]

Second, to what extent will the court scrutinize the shareholder's stated reasons? On the one hand, Delaware courts expressly retain the right to scrutinize the shareholder's stated purpose to determine whether it is the real reason for which he seeks access. On the other hand, Delaware courts have made clear that the existence of an improper secondary purpose is not enough to deny the shareholder access. Because "a shareholder will often have more than one purpose, [§ 220(b)] has been construed to mean that the shareholder's *primary* purpose must be proper; any *secondary* purpose, whether proper or not, is irrelevant."[29]

[26] 191 N.W.2d 406 (Minn.1971) (interpreting Delaware law).

[27] See, e.g., Conservative Caucus Research, Analysis & Education Foundation, Inc. v. Chevron Corp., 525 A.2d 569 (Del.Ch.1987) (a political group successfully sought access to Chevron's shareholder list for the stated purpose of warning its fellow "stockholders about the allegedly dire economic consequences which will fall upon Chevron if it continues to do business in Angola").

[28] Food & Allied Serv. Trades Dep't, AFL-CIO v. Wal-Mart Stores, Inc., 1992 WL 111285 at *4 (Del.Ch.1992).

[29] BBC Acquisition v. Durr-Fillauer Medical, 623 A.2d 85, 88 (Del.Ch.1992). On yet another hand, however, where the corporation is able to show an improper

Third, where the plaintiff-shareholder seeks to use an inspection of corporate books and records as one of the "tools at hand" for developing allegations that will satisfy the pleading obligation in fiduciary duty litigation, how colorable must plaintiff's claims of wrongdoing be? In *Seinfeld v. Verizon Communications, Inc.*,[30] the Delaware supreme court held that reaffirmed that this was a proper purpose for seeking inspection, "because where the allegations of mismanagement prove meritorious, investigation furthers the interest of all stockholders and should increase stockholder return." The trouble is that while seeking evidence of mismanagement or wrongdoing can benefit the corporation, "indiscriminate fishing expeditions" do not. "At some point, the costs of generating more information fall short of the benefits of having more information. At that point, compelling production of information would be wealth-reducing, and so shareholders would not want it produced." To strike the appropriate balance between these concerns, the court adopted a standard pursuant to which the plaintiff must show, by a preponderance of the evidence, that there is some evidence providing a credible basis from which the chancery court can infer that the claims warrant further investigation. The requisite showing must be more than a mere suspicion, but may "fall well short of demonstrating that anything wrong [in fact] occurred." This standard may be "satisfied by a credible showing, through documents, logic, testimony or otherwise, that there are legitimate issues of wrongdoing."

Finally, to which shareholder list is the plaintiff entitled? All corporations maintain a list of shareholders of record. When investors buy stock of public corporations through a broker, however, their shares typically are registered in so-called "street name." The broker places shares in the custody of depository firms, such as Depository Trust Co., which then uses a so-called "nominee" to register the shares with the issuer. The broker, of course, retains records identifying the beneficial owner of the shares. As a result, a public corporation's list of record shareholders will consists mostly of street names—i.e., the names of the nominees used by the various depository firms—not the names of the actual beneficial owners. A so-called CEDE list identifies the brokerage firms on whose behalf the depository institution's nominee holds shares.[31] A nonobjecting beneficial owner (NOBO) list pierces the street name by providing a list of the names and addresses of beneficial owners

---

secondary purpose, the court may circumscribe the shareholder's access so as to protect legitimate corporate interests. Safecard Servs., Inc. v. Credit Card Serv. Corp., 1984 WL 8265 (Del.Ch.1984).

　[30]　909 A.2d 117 (Del.2006).

　[31]　The list's name comes from the fact that the largest depository firm, Depository Trust Co., uses Cede & Co. as its nominee name.

who have not objected to being identified as such.[32] The U.S. Second Circuit Court of Appeals interpreted prior New York state law as entitling a shareholder to both the CEDE and NOBO lists and, moreover, if the corporation had not already compiled such lists, interpreted New York law as entitling a shareholder to demand that the corporation do so. This holding, however, was subsequently reversed by statute.[33] Delaware law grants the shareholder access to pre-existing lists of both types, it does not require the issuer to compile a NOBO list on shareholder request.[34]

§ 10.3 Federal Regulation of Proxies

A. Origins

Most shareholders attend neither the corporation's annual meeting nor any special meetings. Instead, they are represented—and vote—by proxy. Shareholders send in a card (called a proxy card) on which they have marked their vote. The card authorizes a proxy agent to vote the shareholder's stock as directed on the card. The proxy card may specify how the shares are to be voted or may simply give the proxy agent discretion to decide how the shares are

---

[32] SEC Exchange Act Rule 14b–1 requires brokers to assemble a NOBO list at the issuer's request. The question of whether a shareholder is entitled to demand that the issuer request the creation of such a list or to access to a pre-existing NOBO list, however, is left to state corporate law.

[33] Sadler v. NCR Corp., 928 F.2d 48 (2d Cir.1991). Subsequently to *Sadler*, New York law was amended to provide that, in response to shareholder requests for information:

Any person who shall have been a shareholder of record of a corporation upon at least five days' written demand shall have the right to examine in person or by agent or attorney, during usual business hours, its minutes of the proceedings of its shareholders and record of shareholders and to make extracts therefrom for any purpose reasonably related to such person's interest as a shareholder. Holders of voting trust certificates representing shares of the corporation shall be regarded as shareholders for the purpose of this section. Any such agent or attorney shall be authorized in a writing that satisfies the requirements of a writing under paragraph (b) of section 609 (Proxies). A corporation requested to provide information pursuant to this paragraph shall make available such information in written form and in any other format in which such information is maintained by the corporation and shall not be required to provide such information in any other format. If a request made pursuant to this paragraph includes a request to furnish information regarding beneficial owners, the corporation shall make available such information in its possession regarding beneficial owners as is provided to the corporation by a registered broker or dealer or a bank, association or other entity that exercises fiduciary powers in connection with the forwarding of information to such owners. *The corporation shall not be required to obtain information about beneficial owners not in its possession.*

McKinney's Business Corporation Law § 1315(a) (emphasis supplied).

[34] RB Assocs. of N.J., L.P. v. Gillette Co., 1988 WL 27731 (Del.Ch.1988). See also Luxottica Group S.p.A. v. U.S. Shoe Corp., 919 F.Supp. 1091, 1093 (S.D.Ohio 1995) (because Ohio statute only authorized inspection of records, "if any, on file with the corporation," the court declined to order issuer to compile a NOBO list for shareholder to inspect); Cenergy Corp. v. Bryson Oil & Gas P.L.C., 662 F.Supp. 1144 (D.Nev.1987) (corporation is not obliged to produce information it did not possess). The Delaware supreme court has made clear that shareholders are entitled to inspect books and records prepared before the shareholder's first investment in the firm. Saito v. McKesson HBOC, Inc., 806 A.2d 113 (Del.2002).

to be voted. (Confusingly, older materials sometimes refer to both the proxy card and the proxy agent as a proxy without explanatory qualification.)

In 1934, when the federal Securities Exchange Act was first adopted, state corporate law was largely silent on the issue of corporate communications with shareholders. Typical state statutes required only that the corporation send shareholders notice of a shareholders meeting, stating where and when the meeting would be held. Under most state laws, the notice merely was required to briefly identify the issues to be voted on—and some states did not even require that minimal disclosure in connection with annual meetings. (In most states, the corporation statute still does not require much more than this minimal notice.)

By 1934, however, we had already seen the development of large public corporations having thousands of shareholders and using the proxy system of voting. Congressional hearings on the Exchange Act presented numerous allegations that incumbent managers used the corporate shareholder list and corporate funds to solicit proxies in connection with a shareholder meeting. Obviously, because the incumbents were the ones asking for proxies, the proxy cards and soliciting materials were designed to encourage shareholders to vote as the incumbents desired. The proxy system thus allegedly helped incumbent directors and managers to perpetuate themselves in office.

Congress ultimately settled on disclosure as the principal vehicle by which the proxy system was to be regulated at the federal level. Incumbent corporate managers and directors were not to solicit proxies from shareholders without giving the shareholders enough information on which to make an informed voting decision. Comparable disclosures were to be required from insurgents soliciting proxies in opposition to the incumbents, as well.

After several legislative false starts, however, the Congress ultimately dumped the job of creating a disclosure-based proxy regime in the SEC's lap. As adopted, Exchange Act § 14(a) provides:

> It shall be unlawful for any person, by use of the mails or by any means or instrumentality of interstate commerce or of any facility of a national securities exchange or otherwise, in contravention of such rules and regulations as the Commission may prescribe as necessary or appropriate in the public interest or for the protection of investors, to solicit or to permit the use of his name to solicit any proxy or consent or authorization in respect of any security (other than an exempted security) registered pursuant to Section 12 of this title.

Notice that § 14(a) is not self-executing. It proscribed nothing until the SEC adopted implementing rules and regulations. Pursuant to this broad grant of authority, the SEC has created a complex regulatory scheme governing the manner in which proxies are solicited and, therefore, the manner in which shareholder decisions are made.

B. The Regulatory Framework

Per Exchange Act § 14(a), federal proxy regulation extends only to corporations registered with the SEC under § 12 of that Act, which means that virtually all public corporations are picked up by this requirement, while most close corporations are exempt. Because § 14(a) simply states that it shall be unlawful to solicit proxies in contravention of such rules as the SEC may proscribe, however, the rest of the regulatory framework is provided not by statute but entirely by SEC rules.

1. What Is a Solicitation of Proxies?

Given the wording of Exchange Act § 14(a), the definition of "solicit" is the linchpin of the entire regulatory structure. The standard judicial definition of "solicit" includes not only "direct requests to furnish, revoke or withhold proxies, but also ... communications which may indirectly accomplish such a result or constitute a step in a chain of communications designed ultimately to accomplish such a result."[35] The basic question is whether a communication is reasonably calculated to influence a shareholder's vote. If so, subject to the exceptions discussed below, it is a proxy solicitation.

The proxy rules include a number of exceptions to the definition of solicitation, which are designed to encourage communication between shareholders. Among the more important exemptions of general application are:

- Rule 14a–1(l)(2)(iv) exempts public statements of how the shareholder intends to vote and its reasons for doing so.

- Rule 14a–2(b)(1), subject to numerous exceptions, exempts persons who do not seek "the power to act as

---

[35] Long Island Lighting Co. v. Barbash, 779 F.2d 793, 796 (2d Cir.1985). In *LILCO*, an environmentalist group ran newspaper and radio ads critical of the defendant electrical utility's management. The utility managers alleged that the group was acting in conjunction with an insurgent shareholder conducting a proxy contest. The incumbent managers sued the environmentalists, alleging that their ads constituted a proxy solicitation. Over a strong dissent by Judge Ralph Winter (a former professor of corporate law at Yale), the court declined to reach the obvious First Amendment issues posed by the case. Instead, having adopted the definition of a solicitation quoted in the text, the court remanded for a determination of whether the defendants had solicited proxies under that definition.

proxy for a security holder" and do not furnish or solicit "a form of revocation, abstention, consent or authorization." Consequently, for example, a newspaper editorial advising a vote against incumbent managers is now definitively exempted.[36] Note that the Rule thus addresses—although hardly eliminates—the obvious First Amendment concerns implicated by regulating speech in connection with shareholder voting.

- Rule 14a–2(b)(2) preserves the long-standing exemption for solicitations of 10 or fewer persons.

- Rule 14a–2(b)(3) exempts the furnishing of proxy voting advice by someone with whom the shareholder has a business relationship. (A number of firms now provide such voting advice to institutional investors.)

2.   The Proxy Rules

Under SEC Rule 14a–3, the incumbent board of directors' first step in soliciting proxies must be the distribution to shareholders of the firm's annual report.[37] The annual report contains detailed financial statements and a discussion by management of the firm's business. It is intended to give shareholders up-to-date information about what the firm is doing and to give shareholders a basis on which to assess how well management is performing.

Once the annual report is in the shareholders' hands, the proxy solicitation process can begin. The solicitor's goal is to get the shareholder to sign and date a proxy card, voting his shares in the manner the solicitor desires. Because the end goal of this process is the proxy card, it may be helpful to focus initially on a simplified example of a proxy card that complies with the applicable rules. (See Figures 1 and 2. Obviously, the figures are not to scale.)

---

[36] Note that all of the exemptions under Rule 14a–2(b) are limited in that they do not exempt the communication from Rule 14a–9's prohibition of fraudulent and misleading proxy solicitations.

[37] The annual report may be sent to the shareholders before proxies are solicited or may be sent in the same package as the proxy solicitation materials. The main point is that the annual report must be in the shareholder's hands when they make voting decisions.

Figure 1. Simplified sample proxy card conforming to Rule 14a–4 (front)

———

THIS PROXY IS SOLICITED ON BEHALF OF THE BOARD OF DIRECTORS.

Alice Able, Bill Black, and Candice Charles and each of them, each with the power of substitution, are hereby authorized to represent and to vote the stock of the undersigned in ACME CORPORATION at the Annual Meeting of its stockholders to be held on April 29, 200X and any adjournments thereof.

MANAGEMENT RECOMMENDS AND WILL VOTE FOR THE ELECTION OF THE FOLLOWING AS DIRECTORS (UNLESS OTHERWISE DIRECTED):

1.   Alice Able, Bill Black, Candice Charles, Delta Dawn, Eddie Eagle, and Fred MacFred.

To vote for all nominees, check this box. [ ]

To withhold authority to vote for all nominees, check this box. [ ]

To withhold authority to vote for any individual nominee while voting for the

remainder, write this nominee's name in the space following:

MANAGEMENT RECOMMENDS AND WILL VOTE FOR THE FOLLOWING (UNLESS OTHERWISE DIRECTED):

2.   Appointment of Dewey Cheatem & Howe LLP as Independent Public Accountants.

FOR [ ] AGAINST [ ] ABSTAIN [ ]

MANAGEMENT DOES NOT RECOMMEND AND WILL VOTE AGAINST THE FOLLOWING STOCKHOLDER PROPOSAL (UNLESS OTHERWISE DIRECTED):

3.   Provide information about toxic chemicals.

FOR [ ] AGAINST [ ] ABSTAIN [ ]

(OVER)

———

Figure 2. Simplified sample proxy card conforming to Rule 14a 4 (back)

----

4.   In their discretion, the Proxies are authorized to vote upon such other business as may properly come before the meeting.

You are encouraged to specify your choices by marking the appropriate boxes on the reverse side, but you need not mark any boxes. If you wish to vote in accordance with the board of directors' recommendations, simply sign and date this form in the space below. The proxies cannot vote your shares unless you sign and return this card.

Signature: _____

Date: _____

The sample card has been designed to comply with the requirements of SEC Rule 14a–4, which governs the form of the proxy card. The first item of interest can be found at the top of Figure 1 (the card's front), where the card identifies the party soliciting the shareholder's proxy. In this case, it is the incumbent board of directors. This statement is mandated by SEC Rule 14a–4(a)(1), which requires that the proxy card clearly state whether or not is being solicited by the current board of directors.[38]

The second point to be noticed can be found in the paragraph just below that line. By signing the card, the shareholder appoints three people—Able, Black, and Charles—as proxies (i.e., proxy agents) and authorizes them to vote the shareholder's stock in accordance with the instructions on the card. Note that this proxy card is not a permanent delegation of authority—the proxy agents only have authority to vote the shares at the specified shareholder meeting.

Now look at the portion of the card relating to the election of directors (i.e., the first numbered paragraph in Figure 1). Under SEC Rule 14a–4(b), the solicitor must give shareholders three options: vote for all of the nominees for director, withhold support for all of them, and withhold support from specified directors by

---

[38] In addition, SEC Rule 14a–9 provides that failure to clearly distinguish one party's proxy card from that of another party constitutes fraud. When a proxy contest occurs, for example, the two sides typically use different colored cards.

striking out their names. Note that provision need not be made for write-in candidates.[39]

Now look at the next two numbered paragraphs. With respect to any other matters to be voted on at the meeting, the solicitor again must give shareholders three options. But this time the options are: vote for, vote against, or abstain.

Now look at Figure 2 (the back of the card). The first paragraph (numbered 4) gives the proxy agents authority to use their discretion to vote on any other business to come before the meeting. Under SEC Rule 14a–4(c), unless the proxy card contains an express statement like the one in this card, the shareholder's stock may not be voted on any matters other than the specific matters enumerated on the card. Discretionary authority can be very important. Suppose an insurgent shows up at the meeting and makes a motion to which the incumbent board objects. If the board has been granted the discretionary authority conveyed in numbered paragraph 4 of this card, all of the shares represented by those cards can be voted against the motion. If not, the board may have to scrounge up votes from those shareholders who attended in person. (If the party soliciting the proxies knew in advance that a particular issue would come before the meeting, however, the grant of discretionary authority will not be valid.)

The statement in the next paragraph tells shareholders how their stock will be voted if they return a signed card containing no instructions. This is to deal with the common problem of apathetic shareholders who simply sign the card and mail it back in, without ever indicating how their shares are to be voted. In such cases, a statement of this sort gives the proxy agents authority under SEC Rule 14a–4(e) to vote the shares in the indicated manner.

The signature block may seem purely ministerial, but even it has a substantive component. Proxies of the sort at issue here are revocable. Shareholders are free to change their minds and revoke previously granted proxies at any time up to the moment of the election. In practice, there are two ways shareholders revoke prior proxies: (1) by showing up at the shareholders' meeting and voting the shares in person; or (2) by giving a later dated proxy. Where the shareholder signs more than one proxy card, only the most recent

---

[39] Under SEC rules adopted in 2003, the corporation's proxy statement must provide the following disclosures with respect to the process by which directors are nominated: (1) whether the corporation's board of directors has a separate nominating committee; (2) whether the nominating committee has a written charter and, if so, what the charter provides; (3) the processes followed by the nominating committee in identifying and evaluating candidates; and (4) the minimum qualifications required by the nominating committee for proposed board members to possess.

card counts—all earlier cards are thereupon revoked. Hence, the significance of the date.

Along with the proxy card, the SEC requires that the solicitor provide solicited shareholders with a proxy statement containing mandated disclosures relating to the matters to be acted upon. The cover page of the proxy statement typically includes the state law-required notice of where and when the meeting is to be held, and will also state what issues are to be decided at the meeting. A proxy statement relating to an annual meeting, at which directors are being elected, will typically open with biographical information about the candidates. The proxy statement will also include disclosures about board of director committees, board and executive compensation, relationships between the firm and its directors and senior officers, and a description of any other matters to come before the shareholders.

Per Rule 14a–6, a preliminary proxy card and statement must be filed with the SEC at least 10 calendar days before proxies are first solicited. Filing of preliminary materials is not required, however, with respect to an uncontested annual meeting at which only basic matters such as election of directors and appointment of an independent auditor are to be decided. In either case, definitive copies of the proxy card, proxy statement, and any other soliciting materials (such as letters to shareholders) must be filed with the SEC no later than the day they are first used.

In a proxy contest, a key factor will be the insurgent's ability to communicate directly with the shareholders. Towards that end, the insurgent will want access to the corporation's list of shareholders. SEC Rule 14a–7, however, does not require the incumbent board to provide a copy of the shareholder list to the insurgent. The incumbents are given an alternative: they can provide the shareholder list to the insurgent or they can require that the insurgent provide its proxy materials to the corporation, which is obligated to promptly mail those materials to the shareholders (at the insurgent's expense). The incumbents usually prefer the latter route, as it gives them greater control over the process by which proxies are solicited. Commonly, however, insurgents are able to circumvent this restriction by seeking access to the shareholder list under state law.

C.   Proxy Contests

In the usual case, only the incumbent board of directors solicits proxies and the board's recommendations usually get overwhelming support from the shareholders. Occasionally, however, an independent shareholder (often called an insurgent) may solicit proxies in opposition to management. Usually the insurgent is putting forward a slate of directors as an alternative to the slate proposed by management. Rarely, the insurgent may solicit proxies in opposition to some proposal made by management. In either case, the process is doubled. Both sides independently prepare proxy cards and proxy statements that are separately sent to the shareholders.[40]

Historically, proxy contests were "the most expensive, the most uncertain, and the least used of the various techniques" for acquiring corporate control.[41] Insurgents contemplating a proxy battle face a host of legal and economic disincentives. In recent years, however, proxy contests have become somewhat more common as a new set of countervailing incentives favoring proxy contests have emerged.

1.   *Disincentives to Proxy Campaigns*

A would-be insurgent's obstacles are legion. Various state statutes permit corporations to adopt measures—so-called shark repellents—making it more difficult for an insurgent to gain control of the board of directors via a proxy contest. Among the more important of these are classified boards, the elimination of cumulative voting, and dual class stock plans. Other impediments include management's informational advantages and investor perceptions that proxy insurgents are not serious contenders for control. The two most important obstacles for a would-be insurgent, however, are probably the rules governing reimbursement of expenses and shareholder apathy.

2.   *Reimbursement of Expenses*

Proxy contests are enormously expensive. Any serious contest requires the services of lawyers, accountants, financial advisers, printers, and proxy solicitors.[42] None of these folks come cheap. Even incidental costs, such as mailing expenses, mount up very quickly when one must communicate (usually several times) with the thousands of shareholders in the typical public corporation. As it is always more pleasant to spend someone else's money than it is to spend one's own, both incumbents and insurgents will want the corporation to pay their expenses.

---

[40] See generally Randall S. Thomas & Catherine T. Dixon, Aranow & Einhorn on Proxy Contests for Corporate Control § 2.01 (1998) (describing types of proxy contests).

[41] Henry G. Manne, Mergers and the Market for Corporate Control, 73 J. Pol. Econ. 110, 114 (1965).

[42] See generally Randall S. Thomas & Catherine T. Dixon, Aranow & Einhorn on Proxy Contests for Corporate Control § 2.03[C][1] (1998) (listing potential expenses).

In theory, incumbent directors do not have unbridled access to the corporate treasury. In practice, however, incumbents rarely pay their own expenses. Under state law, the board of directors may use corporate funds to pay for expenses incurred in opposing the insurgent, provided the amounts are reasonable and the contest involves policy questions rather than just a "purely personal power struggle."[43] Only the most poorly advised of incumbents find it difficult to meet this standard. The board merely needs have its lawyers parse the insurgent's proxy materials for policy questions on which they differ. Such a search is bound to be successful: if the insurgent agrees with all of management's policies, why is it trying to oust them?

In contrast, insurgents initially must bear their own costs. Insurgents have no right to reimbursement out of corporate funds. Rather, an insurgent will be reimbursed only if an appropriate resolution is approved by a majority of both the board of directors and the shareholders.[44] If the incumbents prevail, of course, they are unlikely to look kindly on an insurgent's request for reimbursement of expenses. In effect, the insurgent must win to have any hope of getting reimbursed.

The rules on reimbursement of expenses take on considerable importance when coupled with the rules on standing in proxy litigation. In *J. I. Case Co. v. Borak*,[45] the Supreme Court held that proxy claims under § 14(a) are both direct and derivative in nature. Consequently, *Borak* gives management standing to sue the insurgent in the corporation's name.[46] As a practical matter, the incumbent board thus has another weapon with which to fend off insurgent shareholders. If the Supreme Court had treated proxy litigation as direct in nature, only shareholders would have standing to sue for violations of the proxy rules. Although the board still could bring suit against the insurgent, it would have to do so in the directors' individual capacity as shareholders. As such, they could not use firm resources to finance the litigation. Because the firm is permitted to sue in its own name for violations of the proxy rules, however, the board can use the firm's deep pocket to pay for legal expenses incurred in such suits. In contrast, because of the rules on reimbursement of expenses, the insurgent's litigation costs come out of its own pocket.

---

[43] E.g., Rosenfeld v. Fairchild Engine & Airplane Corp., 128 N.E.2d 291 (N.Y.1955), reh'g denied, 130 N.E.2d 610 (N.Y.1955).

[44] E.g., Steinberg v. Adams, 90 F.Supp. 604 (S.D.N.Y.1950); Grodetsky v. McCrory Corp., 267 N.Y.S.2d 356 (Sup.Ct.1966).

[45] 377 U.S. 426 (1964).

[46] E.g., Studebaker Corp. v. Gittlin, 360 F.2d 692 (2d Cir.1966).

An important development in this area took place in 2008, when the Delaware Supreme Court ruled on a shareholder proposed bylaw governing reimbursement of proxy expenses. AFSCME's pension fund invoked Rule 14a–8 to propose an amendment to CA's bylaws pursuant to which a shareholder who successfully conducted a short slate proxy contest would be entitled to reimbursement of its reasonable expenses. CA objected to inclusion in the proxy statement of the proposal and asked the SEC for a no-action letter supporting exclusion.[47]

Before answering CA's request, the SEC invoked Delaware's new constitutional provision allowing the SEC to certify questions of law to the Delaware Supreme Court. The SEC certified two questions: (1) Was AFSCME's proposal a proper subject for shareholder action under Delaware law and (2) would the proposal, if adopted, cause CA to violate any Delaware law?

The Delaware Supreme Court held that the proposal is a proper subject of shareholder action. The Court recognized that there is a recursive loop between DGCL § 109, which empowers both directors (so long as the articles of incorporation so provide, as CA's did) and shareholders of a Delaware corporation to adopt, amend, or repeal bylaws, and § 141(a), which vests the board of directors with exclusive authority to manage the business and affairs of the corporation. The problem arises because § 109(b) imposes an important limitation on the otherwise sweeping scope of permissible bylaws: "The bylaws may contain any provision, not inconsistent with law or with the certificate of incorporation, relating to the business of the corporation, the conduct of its affairs, and its rights or powers or the rights or powers of its stockholders, directors, officers or employees." Clear conflicts between the statute or articles and the bylaws present little difficulty. But what if the bylaw nominally complies with the letter of the law, but conflicts with its spirit?

The circularity arises here because, on the one hand, § 141(a) provides that "[t]he business and affairs of every corporation organized under this chapter shall be managed by or under the direction of a board of directors." A bylaw that restricts the board's managerial authority thus seems to run afoul of § 109(b)'s prohibition of bylaws that are "inconsistent with law." On the other hand, § 141(a) also provides that the board's management powers are plenary "except as may be otherwise provided in this chapter."

---

[47] CA, Inc. v. AFSCME Employees Pension Plan, 953 A.2d 227 (Del. 2008). Under SEC Rule 14a–8, shareholders meeting specified eligibility requirements may a proposal and accompanying supporting statement not exceeding 500 words in length for inclusion in the company's proxy statement and on the company's proxy card. An included proposal must then be brought up at the shareholder meeting for a vote.

Does an otherwise valid bylaw adopted pursuant to § 109 squeeze through that loophole?

The Supreme Court declined to "articulate with doctrinal exactitude a bright line" that would divide those bylaws that shareholders may permissibly adopt from those that go too far in infringing upon the directors' right to manage the corporation. Bylaws that relate to the process for electing directors, however, go to "a subject in which shareholders of Delaware corporations have a legitimate and protected interest." Accordingly, the AFSCME proposal was a proper subject for stockholder action.

On the other hand, the court also noted that, if adopted, the proposal would cause CA to violate Delaware law in some cases. The proposal could require the board to reimburse a successful short slate proxy contestant even if a proper application of fiduciary principles would preclude the board from doing so. As examples of such cases, the Court pointed to a proxy contest undertaken for "personal or petty concerns, or to promote interests that do not further, or are adverse to, those of the corporation." In order not to violate the board's fiduciary duties under Delaware law, the proposal therefore would have to include a fiduciary out.

In response to *CA*, the Delaware legislature adopted new DGCL § 113. The new statute expressly authorizes proxy expense reimbursement bylaws. The bylaw must be adopted prior to the record date of the meeting at which the insurgent solicited proxies, thereby preventing an insurgent from seeking to simultaneously elect directors and amend the bylaws. Section 113 also permits the bylaw to impose a number of conditions on reimbursement. The bylaw may condition reimbursement on the insurgent seeking to elect a short slate rather than to replace the entire board. The amount to be reimbursed can be determined based on the proportion of votes received by the insurgent's candidate(s). The list of conditions is non-exclusive.

Although § 113 mostly codifies the *CA* decision, the statute does not expressly require a fiduciary out. Whether courts will follow the *CA* decision and continue to require that a bylaw include a fiduciary out in order to be valid remains uncertain.

3.   *Shareholder Apathy and Related Problems*

The insurgent's problems are said to be compounded by the other shareholders' rational apathy. As the theory goes, a rational shareholder will expend the effort to make an informed decision only if the expected benefits of doing so outweigh its costs. Given the length and complexity of proxy statements, especially in a proxy contest where the shareholder is receiving multiple communications from the contending parties, the opportunity cost entailed in reading the proxy statements before voting is quite high and very apparent. Shareholders also probably do not expect to discover grounds for opposing management from the proxy statements. Finally, most shareholders' holdings are too small to have any significant effect on the vote's outcome. Accordingly, shareholders can be expected to assign a relatively low value to the expected benefits of careful consideration. Shareholders are thus rationally apathetic. For the average shareholder, the necessary investment of time and effort in making informed voting decisions simply is not worthwhile.[48]

Instead of carefully considering the contending parties' arguments, shareholders typically adopt the so-called Wall Street Rule: it's easier to switch than fight. To the extent the shareholders are satisfied, they will vote for management. Disgruntled shareholders, in contrast, will have long since sold out. As a result, shareholders are likely to vote for management even where that is not the decision an informed shareholder would reach. The insurgent thus risks laying out considerable funds for no return on that investment.

4.   Proxy Contests and Takeover Bids

In the last few years, various factors combined to make hostile tender offers a much less attractive, and proxy contests a much more attractive, acquisition technique than they were during most of the 1980s. Perhaps the most important factors in the proxy contest's resurgence were two supreme court decisions. *Paramount Communications, Inc. v. Time Inc.*,[49] by the Delaware Supreme Court, significantly weakened the standards by which target takeover defenses are measured. Under Delaware law, incumbent directors must show that the hostile offer poses a threat to corporate policy and that their response was reasonable in relation to the threat.[50] *Time* both recognized a much broader class of cognizable threats and weakened the proportionality requirement. As a result, effective management takeover defenses should pass muster more easily. Not only does this trend make hostile tender offers more difficult, it also encourages bidders to conduct a proxy contest before making a tender offer. If elected, the bidder's

---

[48] Frank H. Easterbrook and Daniel R. Fischel, Voting in Corporate Law, 26 J. L. & Econ. 395, 402 (1983); Martin Lipton, Corporate Governance in the Age of Finance Corporatism, 136 U. Penn. L. Rev. 1, 66–67 (1987). The problem is compounded by the likelihood that a substantial number of shareholders will attempt to freeride on the efforts of the few informed shareholders.

[49] 571 A.2d 1140 (Del.1989).

[50] See Unocal Corp. v. Mesa Petroleum Co., 493 A.2d 946 (Del.1985).

nominees often can lower the target's defenses and thereby permit the tender offer to go forward.

In *CTS Corp. v. Dynamics Corp.*,[51] the U.S. Supreme Court for the first time upheld a state takeover law against constitutional challenge. Since *CTS*, state takeover laws have routinely withstood constitutional scrutiny. By erecting new barriers to hostile tender offerors, they make tender offers less attractive. Because most permit the target's board of directors to waive their application to a particular bid, they also encourage pre-offer proxy contests.

Proxy contests probably will never become commonplace. They remain expensive and risky. Yet, they also are an essential part of the market for corporate control. So long as outsiders want to buy companies whose incumbent directors and officers want to remain independent, proxy contests will be part of the buyer's toolkit.

D. Proxy Litigation

There are many ways to violate the proxy rules, because there are so many technical rules that must be complied with, but the likeliest source of liability is an illegal proxy solicitation. It is illegal to solicit proxies until the solicitor has delivered a proxy statement to the shareholders. It also is illegal to solicit proxies using materials that have not been filed with the SEC. Finally, it is illegal to solicit proxies using false or misleading soliciting materials. In examining these issues, we focus on several questions: (1) Does a cause of action exist for violations of the proxy rules and, if so, who has standing to bring such an action? (2) What must the plaintiff show in order to prevail in such a cause of action? (3) What remedies are available to injured parties?

1.   *The Implied Private Right of Action*

No matter how closely one scrutinizes Securities Exchange Act § 14(a), one will not find anything relating to a private party cause of action under the statute or rules. In *J. I. Case Co. v. Borak*,[52] however, the Supreme Court implied a private right of action from the statute. Case proposed to merge with American Tractor Co. Borak owned around 2000 shares of Case stock and sought to enjoin the merger on the grounds, inter alia, that the company's proxy materials were false and misleading. Borak claimed that the merger was approved by a small margin and would not have been approved but for the false and misleading statements. Case argued that Borak had no standing to sue, as the federal proxy rules provided no private party cause of action.

---

[51] 481 U.S. 69 (1987).

[52] 377 U.S. 426 (1964).

Despite the lack of any statutory authorization for a private party cause of action, Justice Clark's opinion for the Court found that such an action in fact existed. To be sure, Justice Clark purported to find a statutory basis for the cause of action in Exchange Act § 27. Noting that § 27 gives district courts jurisdiction over "all suits in equity and actions at law brought to enforce any liability or duty" under the Act, Justice Clark contended that "[t] he power to enforce implies the power to make effective the right of recovery afforded by the Act. And the power to make the right of recovery effective implies the power to utilize any of the procedures or actions normally available to the litigant. . . ." The trouble with that argument is that Section 27 speaks of liabilities imposed by the Act, but nothing in § 14(a) or the rules thereunder creates such liabilities vis-à-vis shareholders.

Borak is better understood as an exercise of judicial fiat. A private right of action exists not because Congress intended it, but because a majority of the Supreme Court said so. The general legitimacy of implied private rights of action is beyond our purview, however.[53] Instead, we are concerned solely with Justice Clark's policy justification for this particular cause of action.

Justice Clark was quite above-board as to his motivation—he wanted to deter fraud and other proxy violations. According to Justice Clark, private enforcement provides "a necessary supplement" to SEC efforts. He implied that shareholders are in a better position than the SEC to detect proxy violations—they have fewer proxy statements to review and presumably are better informed about the company. Again, however, the argument is spurious. Most shareholders do not carefully review proxy materials. Instead, they are rationally apathetic. They lack both the desire and the incentive to closely monitor the firm. Justice Clark doubtless knew that individual shareholders were unlikely to emerge as champions of corporate truth and justice. Instead, it seems probable that he was trying to provide incentives for the plaintiffs' bar to become more active in proxy litigation.

This inference is supported by Clark's characterization of the implied private right of action as being both direct and derivative in nature. Strikingly, he did so over Borak's strong argument that the suit was only direct in nature. At the time *Borak* was decided, the modern federal class action procedure had not yet been adopted. If proxy actions were allowed to proceed only directly, and plaintiffs' lawyers were limited to representing individual shareholders, the

---

[53] See Reschini v. First Fed. Sav. & Loan Ass'n of Ind., 46 F.3d 246, 255 (3d Cir.1995) (*Borak* "is still good law as a construction of the 1934 Act and Rule 14a–9. However, it is not clear that *Borak*, if it arose for the first time today, would be decided the same way.").

contingent fees generated by proxy litigation would be insufficient to attract quality lawyers. (The situation would be even worse in cases like *Borak*, where plaintiff sought only equitable relief.) Because the implied cause of action had a derivative element, however, a plaintiffs' lawyer could effectively sue on behalf of all shareholders, by nominally suing in the corporation's name, generating larger damage claims and bigger contingent fees.[54]

The Supreme Court's emphasis on promoting private attorneys general became even more pronounced in its next major proxy decision, *Mills v. Electric Auto-Lite Co.*[55] Mergenthaler Linotype Company owned over 50% of Auto-Lite's stock. About one-third of Mergenthaler's voting stock, in turn, was owned by American Manufacturing Co. American had voting control of Mergenthaler and through it Auto-Lite. Auto-Lite and Mergenthaler agreed to merge. The merger agreement required approval by two-thirds of Auto-Lite's outstanding shares, which therefore required affirmative votes from at least some of the minority shareholders. Plaintiffs alleged that the proxy materials used to solicit those votes were false and misleading and sued to enjoin the shareholder vote.

In the portion of its opinion dealing with remedies, the Supreme Court created a strong incentive for members of the plaintiffs' bar to act as private attorneys general. The Court opined that shareholder-plaintiffs "who have established a violation of the securities laws by their corporation and its officials, should be reimbursed by the corporation or its survivor for the costs of establishing the violation." Note carefully that plaintiffs' counsel was entitled to attorney's fees simply for finding a violation—there was no requirement that the plaintiff ultimately prevail in the sense of recovering damages. Indeed, in *Mills*, the shareholders ultimately recovered nothing, but the plaintiffs' attorneys' fees were still paid by the corporation.[56] *Mills* thus created a powerful economic incentive for lawyers to sue even in cases where it was clear that no injury had been caused by the violation.

The sweeping mandate in *Mills* to plaintiff's attorneys to go forth and uncover proxy rule violations was somewhat pared back

---

[54] *Borak* held that proxy suits can be brought either directly or derivatively. With the development of the modern class action, the characterization of proxy litigation as derivative became less important. For example, even though state law will govern some aspects of a proxy suit brought derivatively (such as whether demand is required), this is not the showstopper that requirement can be for fiduciary litigation because the proxy suit can also be brought directly. On the other hand, the characterization of proxy litigation does allow management standing to sue insurgents at corporate expense.

[55] 396 U.S. 375 (1970).

[56] Mills v. Eltra Corp., 663 F.2d 760 (7th Cir.1981); Mills v. Electric Auto-Lite Co., 552 F.2d 1239 (7th Cir.1977).

by later Supreme Court decisions.[57] Today, the case law requires that the plaintiff's cause of action must create either a common fund from recovered damages or some substantial nonmonetary benefit in order for fees to be awarded.[58] Because injunctive relief likely satisfies the "substantial benefit" standard, however, there is still an incentive to sue even where it seems unlikely that monetary damages ultimately will be forthcoming.

2. Key Elements of the Proxy Cause of Action

When proxy litigation is grounded on an allegation of fraud, four key elements must be considered: (1) the materiality of the alleged misrepresentation or omission; (2) causation; (3) reliance; and (4) the defendant's state of mind. We consider these elements seriatim in the sections that follow.

3. Materiality

Recall that in *Mills v. Electric Auto-Lite Co.*,[59] the plaintiffs were shareholders of Auto-Lite, which was controlled by Mergenthaler Linotype Company, which in turn was controlled by American Manufacturing Co. Plaintiffs alleged that the proxy materials used in connection with the shareholder vote on a proposed merger between Auto-Lite and Mergenthaler were false and misleading because they failed to disclose that all of Auto-Lite's directors were Mergenthaler nominees.

Under *Mills*, a statement or omission is material when "it might have been considered important by a reasonable shareholder who was in the process of deciding how to vote." In other words, the statement or omission must have "a significant propensity to affect the voting process." Today, it is still the case that materiality is an essential element of the cause of action, but the definition of materiality has changed. In the *TSC Industries* case, the Supreme Court adopted a uniform standard of materiality under the securities laws: whether "there is a substantial likelihood that a reasonable shareholder would consider it important in deciding how to vote."[60]

---

[57] See, e.g., Alyeska Pipeline Service Co. v. Wilderness Society, 421 U.S. 240 (1975) (holding that absent statutory authorization, courts should not award attorney's fees to a plaintiff simply because plaintiff he served as a private attorney general).

[58] See, e.g., Goldberger v. Integrated Resources, Inc., 209 F.3d 43 (2d Cir.2000); Amalgamated Clothing and Textile Workers Union v. Wal-Mart Stores, Inc., 54 F.3d 69 (2d Cir.1995); Smillie v. Park Chemical Co., 710 F.2d 271 (6th Cir.1983).

[59] 396 U.S. 375 (1970).

[60] TSC Indus., Inc. v. Northway, Inc., 426 U.S. 438, 449 (1976).

Would the *Mills* omission be material under today's standard? On the one hand, the proxy statement did inform shareholders that Mergenthaler owned over 50% of Auto-Lite and that the boards of both companies had approved the merger. Arguably, reasonable shareholders should have been able to figure out for themselves that all of Auto-Lite's directors were elected by Mergenthaler. On the other hand, facts tending to show that the merger was approved by a board subject to a conflict of interest likely would be considered important by a reasonable shareholder. If the proxy statement had highlighted the fact that all of Auto-Lite's directors were Mergenthaler nominees, the conflict of interest would have been flagged, and the shareholders might have assessed the merger more carefully. (Note that in assessing materiality of disclosures, courts ignore the fact that most shareholders are rationally apathetic.)

In *Virginia Bankshares, Inc. v. Sandberg*,[61] the Supreme Court further refined the materiality standard by addressing its application to statements of belief or opinion. First American Bancshares (FABI) owned 100 percent of Virginia Bankshares (VBI). In turn, VBI owned 85 percent of First American Bank of Virginia (Bank). VBI merged Bank into itself, and paid Bank shareholders $42 per share. Under Virginia law (the applicable standard), the merger required a two-thirds vote. Because VBI owned 85 percent of the voting stock, a proxy solicitation was unnecessary to effect the transaction. Nevertheless, VBI solicited proxies from the other shareholders. In pertinent part, the proxy statement opined: "The Plan of Merger has been approved by the Board of Directors because it provides an opportunity for the Bank's public shareholders to achieve a high value for their shares." Plaintiff Sandberg (a minority shareholder) claimed that the shares were worth $60, that the directors knew $42 was a low price, and that the directors nevertheless went along with a low-priced merger because they hoped not to lose their seats on the board. Justice Souter's majority opinion concluded that the statement was material, but only after an astonishingly tortuous analysis. Justice Scalia's concurring opinion summed up the resulting rule of law far more succinctly:

> As I understand the Court's opinion, the statement "In the opinion of the Directors, this is a high value for the shares" would produce liability if in fact it was not a high value and the directors knew that. It would not produce liability if in fact it was not a high value but the directors honestly believed otherwise. The statement "The Directors voted to accept the proposal because they believe it offers a high

---

[61] 501 U.S. 1083 (1991).

value" would not produce liability if in fact the directors' genuine motive was quite different—except that it would produce liability if the proposal in fact did not offer a high value and the Directors knew that.

Justice Scalia went on to caution, however:

[N]ot every sentence that has the word "opinion" in it, or that refers to motivation for directors' actions, leads us into this psychic thicket. Sometimes such a sentence actually represents facts as facts rather than opinions— and in that event no more need be done than apply the normal rules for § 14(a) liability. I think that is the situation here. In my view, the statement at issue in this case is most fairly read as affirming *separately* both the fact of the Directors' opinion *and* the accuracy of the facts upon which the opinion was assertedly based.

4. Reliance and Causation

According to the prevailing view, reliance is not an essential element of the plaintiff's cause of action under the proxy rules.[62] In contrast, the law is well-settled that a proxy litigation plaintiff seeking monetary damages must show that the violation caused an injury to the shareholders—but it is a funny kind of causation. In *Mills*, the Supreme Court held that a plaintiff proves causation by showing that the proxy solicitation itself (as opposed to the defect) was an "essential link" in the accomplishment of the transaction.[63] Note that under this standard almost any violation "causes" an injury. In most transactions requiring shareholder approval, the proxy solicitation will be an essential link in accomplishing the transaction, because the solicitation was necessary to obtain the requisite shareholder vote.

In *Mills*, the Supreme Court left open the question of "whether causation could be shown where the management controls a sufficient number of shares to approve the transaction without any votes from the minority." In *Virginia Bankshares*, whose facts were recounted in the preceding section, the Supreme Court concluded that the requisite causation could not be shown in that situation.[64] Plaintiff advanced two explanations for VBI's decision to solicit proxies, both of which plaintiff argued supported a finding of causation. First, plaintiff argued that FABI wanted minority shareholder approval for reasons of goodwill, an explanation the court deemed too speculative to provide the requisite causation.

[62] See, e.g., Cowin v. Bresler, 741 F.2d 410 (D.C.Cir.1984).
[63] Mills v. Electric Auto-Lite Co., 396 U.S. 375, 385 (1970).
[64] Virginia Bankshares, Inc. v. Sandberg, 501 U.S. 1083 (1991).

Second, and far more significantly, plaintiff argued that VBI sought shareholder ratification to insulate the transaction from challenge under state law fiduciary duty rules. On the facts at bar, the Court also rejected this argument. Under Virginia law, VBI would be immunized from breach of fiduciary duty claims only if the transaction was approved by a majority of the minority shareholders after full disclosure. If VBI lied in the proxy material, there could be no valid approval. Absent valid approval, VBI gets no protection from the shareholder vote, and the proxy solicitation could not have been an essential step in the merger. Absent that showing, plaintiff cannot prove causation.[65]

5. State of Mind

In both *Virginia Bankshares* and *TSC Industries*, the Supreme Court declined to decide whether the defendant must have acted with scienter or merely negligently in order to be held liable for fraud in a § 14(a) action.[66] As to issuer liability, and that of officers and directors, courts generally hold that negligence suffices.[67] As to collateral participants, such as accountants who certify financial statements contained in a proxy statement (as is done when a merger is to be voted on), at least one court has held that plaintiff must prove scienter.[68]

6. Remedies

Probably the most common remedy in proxy litigation is some form of prospective relief, such as an ex ante injunction against the shareholder vote. The court typically forbids the company from going forward with the shareholder meeting until the party soliciting proxies provides a new proxy statement, correcting whatever violation has been identified, and resolicits the proxies. Retrospective monetary relief, however, is available in appropriate cases. Damages must be shown, which means that plaintiff must establish a monetary injury. Because the violation itself is not an

---

[65] If VBI had been honest, there might have been ratification and the proxy might have been an essential step, but because there would not have been a misleading statement, the plaintiff would still lose. Cf. Howing Co. v. Nationwide Corp., 972 F.2d 700 (6th Cir.1992) (upon remand by the Supreme Court for reconsideration in light of *Virginia Bankshares*, holding that loss of a state law appraisal remedy in a freeze-out merger satisfies the causation requirement).

[66] Note that the *Virginia Bankshares* approach to opinions and statements of belief makes the state of mind issue—why the board voted in favor of the merger— irrelevant with respect to such opinions. The question in such cases becomes simply: did the board knowingly misstate the underlying facts? If VBI's stock is worth $60 and the board members announce that it is worth $42 when they know it is worth $60, the plaintiff can sue.

[67] See, e.g., Wilson v. Great American Indus., Inc., 855 F.2d 987 (2d Cir.1988); Gerstle v. Gamble-Skogmo, 478 F.2d 1281 (2d Cir.1973); see also Shidler v. All American Life & Fin. Corp., 775 F.2d 917 (8th Cir.1985) (rejecting an argument that strict liability was the standard).

[68] Adams v. Standard Knitting Mills, 623 F.2d 422 (6th Cir.1980).

injury, plaintiff must show some sort of actual loss or harm resulting from the violation.

The most drastic option, at least from the firm's perspective, is a setting aside of the transaction. In *Mills*, for example, the merger could be undone and the two firms restored to their prior position as separate entities. This option is chosen very rarely. Courts tend to look at mergers and similar transactions the way a cook looks at an omelet: once the eggs have been scrambled, you can't put them back in the shells. When a merger takes place, all sorts of commingling takes place. Employees are fired or transferred, assets (such as bank accounts) are mixed up and reallocated, operating procedures are changed, and the like. The courts are very aware of this commingling process and therefore will set aside a merger only where it is possible to do so without harming the overall value of the firms and no other remedy can make the injured parties whole.

§ 10.4 Shareholder Proposals Under Rule 14a–8

The phenomenon of rational shareholder apathy suggests that most shareholders will have little interest in exercising a greater voice in corporate decisionmaking via the proxy process. In the name of shareholder democracy, however, the SEC nevertheless periodically tries to encourage shareholder participation in corporate policymaking. One of the SEC's chief vehicles in this endeavor is the shareholder proposal rule—Rule 14a–8.

Absent Rule 14–8, there would be no vehicle for shareholders to put proposals on the firm's proxy statement. Shareholders' only practicable alternative would be to conduct a proxy contest in favor of whatever proposal they wished to put forward. The chief advantage of the shareholder proposal rule, from the perspective of the proponent, thus is that it is cheap. The proponent need not pay any of the printing and mailing costs, all of which must be paid by the corporation, or otherwise comply with the expensive panoply of regulatory requirements.

Shareholder proposals traditionally were used mainly by social activists. Prior to the end of apartheid in South Africa, for example, many proposals favored divestment from South Africa. The rule is still widely used by social activists, but the rule also is increasingly being used by institutional investors to press matters more closely related to corporate governance. For example, proposals in recent years have included such topics as repealing takeover defenses, confidential proxy voting, regulating executive compensation, and the like.

Not all shareholder proposals must be included in the proxy statement. Rule 14a–8 lays out various eligibility requirements, which a shareholder must satisfy in order to be eligible to use the rule. The rule also lays out various procedural hurdles the shareholder must clear. Finally, the Rule identifies a number of substantive bases for excluding a proposal.

A. SEC Review

The SEC referees the shareholder proposal process, albeit sometimes reluctantly. If the subject corporation's management believes the proposal can be excluded from the proxy statement, management must notify the SEC that the firm intends to exclude the proposal. A copy of the notice must also be sent to the proponent.[69] Management's notice must be accompanied by an opinion of counsel if any of the stated grounds entail legal issues, such as when management claims the proposal is improper under state corporate law. Although the rule does not require the proponent to reply, the SEC staff will consider any arguments the proponent may wish to make in support of the resolution's eligibility for inclusion in management's proxy statement.

If the SEC staff agrees that the proposal can be excluded, it issues a so-called no action letter, which states that the staff will not recommend that the Commission bring an enforcement proceeding against the issuer if the proposal is excluded.[70] On the other hand, if the staff determines that the proposal should be included in management's proxy statement, the staff notifies the issuer that the SEC may bring an enforcement action if the proposal is excluded. The SEC staff can also take an intermediate position; in effect, it says to the proponent: "As your proposal or your supporting statement are presently drafted, they can be excluded under Rule 14a–8. However, if you revise them as follows, we believe that management must include the proposal." Whichever side loses at the staff level can ask the Commissioners to review the staff's decision. After review by the Commissioners, the losing party can seek judicial review by the United States Circuit Court of Appeals for the District of Columbia. These reviews are very rare. If management is the losing party, it typically acquiesces in the staff's decision. If the shareholder proponent loses, he typically seeks injunctive relief in federal district court.[71]

---

[69] Rule 14a–8(j). Under Rule 14a–8(f)(1), if the alleged defect is potentially remediable, the company must reply within 14 calendar days after receiving the proposal. If the proponent can remedy the alleged deficiency, it must do so within 14 calendar days. This process is separate from the procedure under which management notifies the SEC of its intent to exclude the proposal.

[70] On no action letters, see generally Donna M. Nagy, Judicial Reliance on Regulatory Interpretations in SEC No-action Letters: Current Problems and a Proposed Framework, 83 Cornell L. Rev. 921 (1998).

[71] Although the proxy solicitation process itself is quite expensive, the marginal cost of any one proposal is small. Why then do corporate officials waste

B. Eligibility

Under Rule 14a–8(b)(1), a shareholder-proponent must have owned at least 1% or $2,000 (whichever is less) of the issuer's voting securities for at least one year prior to the date on which the proposal is submitted. What happens if the individual shareholder cannot satisfy these requirements? (1) Suppose three shareholders want to jointly support a proposal: A, who has owned $800 in stock for 2 years; B, who has owned $900 in stock for 18 months; and C, who has owned $500 in stock for 13 months. (2) D and E want to sponsor a separate proposal. D has owned $1200 in stock for two years; E has owned $1200 in stock for two months.

The SEC permits aggregation of shareholdings for purposes of meeting the dollar limit but not the time limit. In case 1 above, A, B, and C satisfy the eligibility standard because they jointly own more than $2000 in stock and have all held stock for more than one year. In case 2, however, D and E would not meet the eligibility test. Although they collectively satisfy the $2,000 requirement, they cannot satisfy the time period requirement because E has held stock for less than a year. In order for their proposal to be included, they would have to find a third shareholder who has held at least $800 in stock for at least one year.

C. Procedural Issues

1. Number of Submissions

Per Rule 14a–8(c), the proponent may only submit one proposal per corporation per year. There is no limit to the number of companies to which a proponent can submit proposals in a given year, however. As long as the proponent meets the eligibility requirements for each firm, an activist thus may press the same proposal at multiple firms.

2. Prior Submissions

The proponent may continue to submit the same proposal to the same firm year after year in the hopes that it will eventually be adopted by the shareholders, provided the proposal annually

---

time and money fighting these proposals? One suspects part of the reason is managerial dislike for people they regard as pests, paranoids, bubble-heads, self-righteous protectors of the public morality, and self-appointed shareholder spokesmen. Another reason may be managerial suspicion that proponents are using proposals for purposes unrelated to the merits of the proposal, as where union pension funds make corporate governance proposals. Finally, some proposals can negatively impact the corporation, even if only indirectly. As the result of an anti-affirmative action shareholder proposal put forward by a white supremacist group, for example, AT & T received considerable negative attention and ultimately felt obliged to issue a statement deploring "hate-filled proposals." Social Activists Fighting Gag Rule SEC Seeks Limits On Proxy Issues, The Record, May 17, 1992, at B1.

receives a specified level of support. A resubmitted proposal (or a substantially similar one) must be included if it was submitted: (i) once during the preceding five years and received 3% or more of the vote; (ii) twice in the preceding five years and received 6% or more of the vote the last time it was submitted; or (iii) 3 or more times in the preceding five years and received 10% or more of the vote the last time it was submitted.[72]

3. *Attendance*

Although the proxy system generally is designed to facilitate participation by shareholders who choose not to attend the shareholders' meeting, the shareholder proposal rule requires the proponent to present the proposal in person at the meeting. If the proponent fails to show up, Rule 14a 8(h) bars the proponent from using the rule at that company for the following two years.

4. *Timing*

The proposal must be submitted to the corporation at least 120 days before the date on which proxy materials were mailed for the previous year's annual shareholder's meeting.[73] For example, if the firm mailed its proxy materials on May 1, 2010, one counts back 120 days from May 1 to determine when a proposal must be submitted to be included in the 2011 proxy statement, which works out to January 2, 2011. The SEC is surprisingly strict in enforcing this requirement.

5. *Length*

Under Rule 14a–8(d), a proposal and any accompanying supporting statement may not exceed 500 words in length. (There is no length restriction on rebuttal statements by management.) In the past, a shareholder who wished to make a more expansive case for his proposal thus was required to conduct a full-fledged proxy solicitation, with all the expense and regulatory burden associated therewith.

D. **Substantive Grounds for Excluding a Proposal**

1. *Proper Subjects for Shareholder Action*

Most shareholder proposals are phrased as recommendations. The use of precatory language follows from Rule 14a–8(i)(1), which provides that a shareholder proposal must be a proper subject of action for security holders under the law of the state of incorporation. Recall that under state law, all corporate powers

---

[72] Rule 14a–8(i)(12).
[73] Rule 14–8(e).

shall be exercised by or under the authority of the board.[74] Consequently, state corporate law commits most powers of initiation to the board of directors—the shareholders may not initiate corporate actions, they may only approve or disapprove of corporate actions placed before them for a vote. The SEC's explanatory note to Rule 14a–8(i)(1) recognizes this aspect of state law by explaining that mandatory proposals may be improper. The note goes on, however, to explain the SEC's belief that a shareholder proposal is proper if phrased as a request or recommendation to the board.

If a precatory proposal passes, the board is not obligated to implement it. Indeed, a board decision not to do so should be protected by the business judgment rule. On the other hand, the risk of adverse publicity and poor shareholder relations may encourage a board to implement an approved precatory proposal even where the board opposes the proposal on the merits.

Shareholder amendments to the bylaws may constitute an exception to the general rule that proposals cannot mandate board action. A bylaw that relates only to a specific business decision probably is invalid, as an improper intrusion on the board's exclusive power to make ordinary business decisions. Broader, more fundamental bylaws, especially ones that impose constraints rather than order the board to take action, however, pose a more difficult set of problems. The legality of such bylaws under state corporate law is sharply contested.[75] Where lawful, however, a mandatory shareholder proposal to adopt such a bylaw presumably could not be excluded under Rule 14a–8(i)(1).

2.   *False or Misleading Proposals*

Rule 14a–8(i)(3) provides that a proposal may be omitted if it violates any of the proxy rules, including Rule 14a–9 which prohibits false or misleading statements. Consequently, the issuer may exclude proposals containing misrepresentations or groundless assertions. For example, SEC explanatory note (b) to Rule 14a–9 provides that material impugning character or personal reputation violates Rule 14a–9 if made without factual foundation. Where the proposal impugns management's character, the SEC staff usually will require that the proposal can be included in the proxy statement if the proponent agrees to drop the offensive language or is able to factually demonstrate that it is true. If the proponent fails

---

[74] See, e.g., DGCL § 141(a).

[75] Conversely, it seems clear that a corporate bylaw cannot trump the federal securities laws. Hence, bylaws that impede shareholders from making use of Rule 14a–8 appear to be invalid. See SEC v. Transamerica Corp., 163 F.2d 511, 518 (3d Cir.1947) (holding that the SEC's regulatory powers "cannot be frustrated by a corporate bylaw").

to provide the requisite factual basis for his assertion, and also refuses to revise the supporting statement, the whole proposal can be excluded.

3. Not Otherwise Significant

Rule 14a–8(i)(5) provides that a proposal relating to operations accounting for less than 5 percent of the firm's assets, earnings or sales, and that is not otherwise significantly related to the firm's business, may be omitted from the proxy statement. The principal problem here is deciding whether a proposal falling short of the various 5% thresholds is "otherwise significantly related to the firm's business." The classic case is *Lovenheim v. Iroquois Brands, Ltd.*[76] The defendant imported various food stuffs into the United States, including pâté de foie gras from France. Lovenheim suspected that Iroquois Brands' French suppliers forced fed their geese, which produces larger livers, and which Lovenheim believed was a form of animal cruelty. Lovenheim proposed that Iroquois Brands form a committee to investigate the methods used by the firm's suppliers in producing pâté and report its findings to the shareholders.

Iroquois Brands pâté operations clearly did not satisfy Rule 14a–8(i)(5)'s five percent threshold tests. Pâté sales constituted a mere $79,000 per year, on which Iroquois Brands lost money, relative to annual revenues of $141 million and profits of $6 million. The result therefore turned on whether the pâté operations were "otherwise significantly related" to its business.[77] Iroquois Brands contended that the phrase related to economic significance.

---

[76] 618 F.Supp. 554 (D.D.C.1985).

[77] Courts have not always applied the 5% standards as precisely as they should. In New York City Employees' Retirement System v. Dole Food Co., Inc., 795 F.Supp. 95 (S.D.N.Y.1992), for example, the New York City employees' pension fund petitioned Dole to include a proposal recommending that Dole form a committee to study the impact of various national health care reform proposals would have on Dole.

The district court ordered Dole to include the proposal in the proxy statement. In rejecting Dole's arguments under Rule 14a–8(i)(5), the court held that health care reform had economic significance because health insurance and care imposed large financial costs on Dole. Specifically, the court opined: "It is substantially likely that Dole's health insurance outlays constitute more than five percent of its income." The opinion does not set out any evidence as to Dole's health insurance expenses. Query whether courts ought to simply assume away a critical element of the standard. In any event, the court also misconstrued Rule 14a–8(i)(5). The rule does not speak of expenses that represent more than 5 percent of income. The Rule talks about operations—lines of business—that represent 5 percent of the company's total business, measured in various ways, none of which include expenditures. Despite the court's flawed reasoning, however, the result is probably right. Employee health benefits (or the decision not to provide such benefits) are a matter of considerable economic significance. Federal changes to the health insurance system doubtless would have had a major economic impact on employers. Accordingly, the proposal arguably had economic significance even though it did not satisfy any of the 5% thresholds.

Lovenheim contended that noneconomic tests of a proposal's significance were appropriate.

The court agreed with Lovenheim, holding that while the proposal related "to a matter of little economic significance,"[78] the term "otherwise significantly related" is not limited to economic significance. Rather, matters of ethical and social significance also can be considered. The court articulated four rationales for its interpretation: (1) the rule itself was ambiguous; (2) the SEC previously had required inclusion of important social policy questions even where less than 1% of the firm's assets or earnings were implicated by the question; (3) in adopting the present 5% threshold tests, the SEC said proposals falling short of the thresholds still must be included if their significance appeared on the face of the proposal; (4) the earlier Medical Committee decision implied that proposals involving general political and social concerns were acceptable.[79]

As evidence that Lovenheim's proposal had "ethical or social" significance, the court observed that humane treatment of animals was one of the foundations of western civilization, citing various old and new statutes, ranging from the Seven Laws of Noah to the Massachusetts Bay Colony's animal protection statute of 1641 to modern federal and state humane laws. Additional support came from the fact that "leading organizations in the field of animal care" supported measures aimed at eliminating force feeding.

4. Ordinary Business

Rule 14a–8(i)(7) allows the issuer to exclude so-called ordinary business matters. The question here is whether a proposal is an ordinary matter for the board or an extraordinary matter on which shareholder input is appropriate. The answer hinges on whether the proposal involves significant policy questions. As for deciding whether a policy question is significant, most courts assume that *Lovenheim*-style ethical or social significance suffices.

The SEC's policy on enforcing Rule 14a–8(i)(7) with respect to shareholder proposals concerned mainly with social—rather than economic—issues has fluctuated over the years. The SEC long handled such proposals on a case-by-case basis. In 1992, however, it departed from that practice and adopted a bright-line position that for the first time effectively excluded an entire category of social issue proposals. Cracker Barrel Old Country Stores attempted to exclude a shareholder proposal calling on the board of directors to

---

[78] Lovenheim v. Iroquois Brands, Ltd., 618 F.Supp. 554, 559 (D.D.C.1985).

[79] See Medical Comm. for Human Rights v. SEC, 432 F.2d 659, 680 (D.C.Cir.1970), vacated as moot, 404 U.S. 403 (1972).

include sexual orientation in its anti-discrimination policy. In a no action letter issued by the SEC's Division of Corporation Finance, the Commission took the position that all employment-related shareholder proposals raising social policy issues could be excluded under the "ordinary business" exclusion.

Subsequent litigation developed two issues. First, if a shareholder proponent sued a company whose management relied on *Cracker Barrel* to justify excluding an employment-related proposal from the proxy statement, should the reviewing court defer to the SEC's position? In *Amalgamated Clothing and Textile Workers Union v. Wal-Mart Stores, Inc.*,[80] a federal district court held that deference was not required and, moreover, that proposals relating to a company's affirmative action policies were not per se excludible as ordinary business under Rule 14a–8(i)(7).

Second, was the SEC's *Cracker Barrel* position valid? In other words, could the SEC properly apply the *Cracker Barrel* interpretation in internal agency processes, such as when issuing a no action letter? In *New York City Employees' Retirement System v. SEC*, the district court ruled that the SEC's *Cracker Barrel* position was itself invalid because the SEC had failed to comply with federal administrative procedures in promulgating the position. The Second Circuit reversed, thereby allowing the SEC to apply *Cracker Barrel* internally, but in doing so concurred with the trial court's view that *Cracker Barrel* was not binding on courts.[81]

In 1998, the SEC adopted amendments to Rule 14a–8 that, among other things, reversed its *Cracker Barrel* position.[82] In promulgating this change, the SEC emphasized that employment discrimination was a consistent topic of public debate, thereby highlighting the on-going importance of *Lovenheim*-style social and ethical considerations. Indeed, the SEC explicitly noted its belief that the Rule 14a–8(i)(7) exception did not justify excluding proposals that raise significant social policy issues.

Reversal of the *Cracker Barrel* position returned the SEC to its prior case-by-case approach. Specific management decisions relating to employment, such as hiring, promotion, and termination of employees, as well as other business decisions, such as product lines and quality, remain excludable. The SEC does not want shareholders to "micro-manage" the company. Proposals broadly relating to such matters but focusing on significant social policy

---

[80]   21 F.Supp. 877 (S.D.N.Y.1993).

[81]   New York City Employees' Retirement Sys. v. SEC, 45 F.3d 7 (2d Cir.1995).

[82]   Amendments To Rules On Shareholder Proposals, Exchange Act Release No. 40018 (May 21, 1998).

issues, such as affirmative action and other employment discrimination matters, generally are not excludable.[83]

We are thus returned to the task of deciding whether a particular proposal is "significant." On this issue, the federal district court decision in *Austin v. Consolidated Edison Company of New York, Inc.*[84] is both instructive and troubling. The plaintiffs put forward a proposal that the issuer provide more generous pension benefits to its employees. The court authorized the issuer to exclude the proposal as impinging on an ordinary business matter. Acknowledging that shareholder proposals relating to senior executive compensation were not excludable, the court observed that the issue of "enhanced pension rights" for workers "has not yet captured public attention and concern as has the issue of senior executive compensation." Does this mean that the significance of a proposal turns on whether its subject matter has become a routine story for CNBC or CNN?

---

[83] See, e.g., New York City Employees' Retirement Sys. v. Dole Food Co., 795 F.Supp. 95 (S.D.N.Y.1992), in which the proponent offered a proposal requesting Dole to study the potential impact on the company of various pending national health care reform proposals. Dole relied on Rule 14an8(i)(7) to exclude the proposal, among other provisions. The court rejected Dole's argument. Although employee benefits generally are an ordinary business matter, "a significant strategic decision" as to employee benefits fell outside the scope of ordinary business matters.

[84] 788 F.Supp. 192 (S.D.N.Y.1992).

Chapter 11

INSIDER TRADING AND SECURITIES FRAUD

§ 11.1 Introduction

The term insider trading is something of a misnomer. It conjures up images of corporate directors or officers using secret information to buy stock from (or sell it to) unsuspecting investors. To be sure, the modern federal insider trading prohibition proscribes a corporation's officers and directors from trading on the basis of material nonpublic information about their firm, but it also casts a far broader net. Consider the following people who have been convicted of illegal insider trading over the years:

- A partner in a law firm representing the acquiring company in a hostile takeover bid who traded in target company stock.

- A Wall Street Journal columnist who traded prior to publication of his column in the stock of companies he wrote about.

- A psychiatrist who traded on the basis of information learned from a patient.

- A financial printer who traded in the stock of companies about which he was preparing disclosure documents.

As you can see, the insider trading laws thus capture a wide range of individuals who trade in a corporation's stock on the basis of material information unknown by the investing public at large.

Insider trading is covered by a number of legal regimes, of which no less than 5 are important for our purposes:

- The disclose or abstain rule under § 10(b) of the Securities Exchange Act of 1934 and Securities and Exchange Commission Rule 10b–5 thereunder, which is principally concerned with classic insiders such as corporate officers and directors;

- The misappropriation theory under § 10(b) and Rule 10b–5, which deals mainly with persons outside the company in whose stock they traded;

- SEC Rule 14e–3 under Exchange Act § 14(e), which is limited to insider trading in connection with a tender offer;

- Section 16(b) of the Exchange Act, which prohibits corporate directors, officers, and shareholders owning more than 10% of the firm's stock from earning "short swing profits" by buying and selling stock in a six month period;

- State corporate law, which principally targets corporate officers and directors who buy stock from shareholders of their company in face-to-face transactions.

All five regulatory schemes are discussed below, but our attention will focus mainly on the federal prohibition under SEC Rule 10b–5.

At the beginning of the 1900s, state corporate law was the only legal regime regulating insider trading. At that time, as is still true in some states, corporate law allowed insider trading. Federal securities law, especially Rule 10b–5, however, has largely superseded the state common law of insider trading. To be sure, the state rules are still on the books and are still used in a few cases that fall through the cracks of the federal regulatory scheme, but federal law offers regulators and plaintiffs so many procedural and substantive advantages that it has become the dominant legal regime in this area. The most important feature of federal law, however, may be that it put a cop on the beat. State law relied on firms and shareholders to detect and prosecute insider trading. Under federal law, the SEC and the Justice Department can prosecute inside traders, which has substantially increased the likelihood it will be detected and successfully prosecuted.

A truly significant distinguishing feature of the federal insider trading prohibition has been change. Although the prohibition is only about four decades old, it has seen more shifts in doctrine than most corporate law rules have seen in the last century. Exploring this rich history is a useful exercise—in many respects you cannot understand today's issues without the historical background—but is also is fraught with danger: you must draw clear distinctions between what *was* the law and what *is* the law.

One point requiring particular attention is the evolution of new theories on which insider trading liability can be based. We shall see two very important cases in which the Supreme Court restricted the scope of the traditional disclose or abstain rule. In response to those cases, the SEC and the lower courts developed two new theories on which liability could be imposed. As we move through this material, pay close attention to which theory is being discussed at any given moment and consider how that theory differs from the others.

§ 11.2   Origins of the Insider Trading Prohibition

Although we now take it for granted that regulating insider trading is a job for the SEC under federal law, it was not always so. Until the 1960s, insider trading was as a matter of state corporate law. Since then, of course, the federal prohibition has largely eclipsed state law in this area, but the older state rules are still worth studying.

A.   State Common Law

Our overview of the state common law of insider trading is both historical and functional. We'll look first at the three different insider trading rules states adopted in the early 1900s. It turns out that these rules were largely limited to face-to-face transactions, however, so we will then look at how states regulated insider trading in the context of stock market transactions. Completing those two tasks will carry us through the 1930s, when Congress adopted the federal securities laws, but we will defer development of federal law in order to look at how state corporate law treats insider trading today.

1.   Face-to-Face Transactions

Prior to 1900 it was treatise law that "[t]he doctrine that officers and directors [of corporations] are trustees of the stockholders . . . does not extend to their private dealings with stockholders or others, though in such dealings they take advantage of knowledge gained through their official position."[1] Under this so-called "majority" or "no duty" rule, liability was imposed solely for actual fraud, such as misrepresentation or fraudulent concealment of a material fact. As one court explained, liability arose only where the defendant said or did something "to divert or prevent, and which did divert or prevent, the plaintiff from looking into, or making inquiry, or further inquiries, as to the affairs or condition of the company and its prospects for dividends. . . ."[2]

The first tentative step towards the modern prohibition came in *Oliver v. Oliver*,[3] in which the Georgia Supreme Court announced the so-called "minority" or "duty to disclose" rule. Under *Oliver*, directors who obtained inside information by virtue of their position

---

[1] H. L. Wilgus, Purchase of Shares of a Corporation by a Director from a Shareholder, 8 Mich. L. Rev. 267 (1910).

[2] Carpenter v. Danforth, 52 Barb. 581, 589 (N.Y.Sup.Ct.1868).

[3] 45 S.E. 232 (Ga.1903).

held the information in trust for the shareholders. Accordingly, directors had a duty to disclose all material information to shareholders before trading with them.

In *Strong v. Repide*,[4] the U.S. Supreme Court offered a third approach to the insider-trading problem. The court acknowledged the majority rule, but declined to follow it. Instead, the court held that, under the particular factual circumstances of the case at bar, "the law would indeed be impotent if the sale could not be set aside or the defendant cast in damages for his fraud." Thus was born the so-called "special facts" or "special circumstances" rule, which holds that although directors generally owe no duty to disclose material facts when trading with shareholders, such a duty can arise in—as the name suggests—"special circumstances." What facts were sufficiently "special" for a court to invoke the rule? *Strong v. Repide* identified the two most important fact patterns: Concealment of identity by the defendant and failure to disclose significant facts having a dramatic impact on the stock price.

As state law evolved in the early 1900s, both the special circumstances and minority rules rapidly gained adherents. Every court faced with the issue during this period felt obliged to discuss all three rules. While many courts adhered to the majority rule, they typically went out of their way to demonstrate that the case at bar in fact did not involve any special facts. Even more strikingly, during this period no court deciding the issue as a matter of first impression adopted the old majority rule. As a result, by the late 1930s, a headcount of cases indicated that the special circumstances rule prevailed in a plurality of states, the older no duty rule no longer commanded a majority, and the duty to disclose rule had been adopted in a substantial number—albeit, still a minority—of states.[5]

2. Do Selling Directors Owe a Fiduciary Duty to Their Nonshareholder Purchasers?

Given that both the special circumstances and minority rules were based on the director or officer's fiduciary duties, a problem arose: What happened when a director sold shares, rather than buying them? A director who buys shares is trading with someone who is already a shareholder of the corporation and, as such, someone to whom the director has fiduciary obligations. A director who sells shares, however, likely is dealing with a stranger, someone not yet a shareholder and, as such, not yet someone to whom the director owes any duties. Assuming *arguendo* that the

---

[4] 213 U.S. 419 (1909).

[5] I. Beverly Lake, The Use for Personal Profit of Knowledge Gained While a Director, 9 Miss. L.J. 427, 448–9 (1937).

director's fiduciary duties to shareholders proscribe buying shares from them on the basis of undisclosed material information, the logic of that rule does not necessarily extend to cases in which the director sells to an outsider. As with most questions of state law in this area, the issue is not solely of historical or academic interest. As we shall see, the modern federal insider trading prohibition is also premised on a violation of fiduciary duty. Unfortunately, while the federal prohibition indisputably applies both to insiders who buy and those who sell,[6] state law remains uncertain.

3.   Stock Market Transactions

Both the special circumstances and minority rules were more limited in scope than may appear at first blush. Most of the cases in which plaintiffs succeeded involved some form of active fraud, not just a failure to disclose. More important, all of these cases involved face-to-face transactions. The vast majority of stock transactions, both then and now, take place on impersonal stock exchanges. In order to be economically significant, an insider trading prohibition must apply to such transactions as well as face-to-face ones.

The leading state case in this area, still found in most corporations casebooks, is *Goodwin v. Agassiz.*[7] Ignoring some factual complexities unnecessary to understanding the opinion, what happened here is a classic insider-trading story: Defendants were directors and senior officers of a mining corporation. A geologist working for the company advanced a theory suggesting there might be substantial copper deposits in northern Michigan. The company thought the theory had merit and began securing mineral rights on the relevant tracts of land. Meanwhile, the defendants began buying shares on the market. Plaintiff was a former stockholder who had sold his shares on the stock market. The defendants apparently had bought the shares, although neither side knew the identity of the other party to the transaction until much later. When the true facts became known, plaintiff sued the directors, arguing that he would not have sold if the geologist's theory had been disclosed. The court rejected plaintiff's claim, concluding that defendants had no duty to disclose the theory before trading.

Goodwin is commonly read as standing for the proposition that directors and officers trading on an impersonal stock exchange owe no duty of disclosure to the persons with whom they trade.

---

[6] See, e.g., SEC v. Texas Gulf Sulphur Co., 401 F.2d 833 (2d Cir.1968), cert. denied, 394 U.S. 976 (1969) (where insiders purchased stock on inside information); SEC v. Adler, 137 F.3d 1325 (11th Cir.1998) (where defendant sold shares of stock based on his possession of material nonpublic information).

[7] 186 N.E. 659 (Mass.1933).

Although that reading is correct as a bottom line matter, it ignores some potentially important doctrinal complications. The Massachusetts Supreme Judicial court's analysis begins with a nod to the old majority rule, opining that directors generally do not "occupy the position of trustee toward individual stockholders in the corporation." The court went on, however, to note that "circumstances may exist . . . [such] that an equitable responsibility arises to communicate facts," which sounds like the special circumstances rule. Indeed, the court made clear that Massachusetts would apply the special circumstances rule to face-to-face transactions: "where a director personally seeks out a stockholder for the purpose of buying his shares without making disclosure of material facts within his peculiar knowledge and not within reach of the stockholder, the transaction will be closely scrutinized and relief may be granted in appropriate instances." Was the court likewise applying the special circumstances rule to stock market transactions? Perhaps. The court took pains to carefully analyze the nature of the information in question, concluding that it was "at most a hope," and was careful to say that there was no affirmative duty to disclose under the circumstances at bar. At the same time, however, the dispositive special circumstance clearly was the stock market context. As to transactions effected on an impersonal exchange, no duty to disclose would be imposed.

Given that federal law later imposed just such a duty, it is instructive to examine carefully the court's explanation for its holding:

> Purchases and sales of stock dealt in on the stock exchange are commonly impersonal affairs. An honest director would be in a difficult situation if he could neither buy nor sell on the stock exchange shares of stock in his corporation without first seeking out the other actual ultimate party to the transaction and disclosing to him everything which a court or jury might later find that he then knew affecting the real or speculative value of such shares. Business of that nature is a matter to be governed by practical rules. Fiduciary obligations of directors ought not to be made so onerous that men of experience and ability will be deterred from accepting such office. Law in its sanctions is not coextensive with morality. It cannot undertake to put all parties to every contract on an equality as to knowledge, experience, skill and shrewdness. It cannot undertake to relieve against hard bargains made between competent parties without fraud.

The insider trading prohibition's defenders find much that is contestable in the court's rationale. Two observations suffice for present purposes: First, notice the strongly normative (and strongly laissez faire) tone of the quoted passage. Why can't the law undertake to ensure that all parties to stock market transaction have at least roughly equal access to information? This question turns out to be one of insider trading jurisprudence's recurring issues. Second, consider the "difficult situation" the court claims an insider trading prohibition would create for "honest directors." Even at its most expansive, the federal insider trading prohibition never required directors to seek out individually those with whom they trade and personally make disclosure of "everything" they know about the company. A workable insider trading prohibition simply requires directors to disclose publicly all material facts in their possession before trading or, if they are not able to do so, to refrain from trading. Corporate policies could be developed to limit director and officer trading to windows of time in which there is unlikely to be significant undisclosed information, such as those following dissemination of periodic corporate disclosures. An inconvenience for all concerned, to be sure, but hardly enough to keep able people from serving as directors of publicly traded corporations. Not surprisingly, this aspect of the court's rationale has gotten short shrift from later courts.

4.   State Common Law Today

About the same time as *Goodwin* was decided, the New Deal Congresses began adopting the federal securities laws. Although those laws did not preempt state corporate law, federal regulation has essentially superseded them insofar as insider trading is concerned. State law is not just a historical footnote, however. Some cases still fall though the federal cracks, being left for state law to decide. Plaintiffs still sometimes include a state law-based count in their complaints. Most important, we will see that state law ought to provide the basic analytical framework within which the federal regime operates. Having said that, however, it must be admitted that the ever-increasing focus of regulators and litigators on federal law aborted the evolution of state common law in this area. With one important exception, discussed below, we are still more or less where we were in the late 1930s.

Although both the special circumstances and minority rules continued to pick up adherents during the decades after *Goodwin* was decided,[8] a number of states continue to adhere to the no duty

---

[8] See, e.g., *Broffe v. Horton*, 172 F.2d 489 (2d Cir.1949) (diversity case); *Childs v. RIC Group, Inc.*, 331 F.Supp. 1078, 1081 (N.D.Ga.1970), aff'd, 447 F.2d 1407 (5th Cir.1971) (diversity case); *Hobart v. Hobart Estate Co.*, 159 P.2d 958 (Cal.1945). An early line of federal cases arising under Rule 10b–5 applied the special circumstances

rule.[9] Insofar as stock market transactions are concerned, moreover, *Goodwin* apparently remains the prevailing view.[10] The leading cases are of considerable antiquity, however, so one can easily imagine lawyers arguing that the old no duty precedents should not be followed today. As they might point out, the American Law Institute's Principles of Corporate Governance opine that a duty to disclose exists in both face-to-face and stock market transactions,[11] albeit as yet without much case law support.

5. *Derivative Liability for Insider Trading Under State Corporate Law*

Although the Massachusetts court in *Goodwin* rejected the argument that directors "occupy the position of trustee towards individual stockholders,"[12] it also recognized that directors are fiduciaries of the corporate enterprise. Its holdings barring shareholders from seeking direct relief thus did not prohibit corporate actions against insider traders. Although a leading case did not emerge until the 1960s, litigators eventually stumbled on the possibility of derivative litigation against inside traders.

All of the cases we have been discussing thus far were brought as direct actions; i.e., cases in which the plaintiff shareholder sued in his own name seeking compensation for the injury done to him by the insider with whom he traded. In derivative litigation, by contrast, the cause of action belongs to the corporation and any recovery typically goes into the corporate treasury rather than directly to the shareholders. One would normally expect the corporation's board or officers to prosecute such suits. Corporate law recognizes, however, that a corporation's managers sometimes may be reluctant to enforce the corporation's rights. This seems especially likely when the prospective defendant is a fellow director or officer. The derivative suit evolved to deal with such situations, providing a procedural device for shareholders to enforce rights belonging to the corporation.

In *Diamond v. Oreamuno*,[13] the leading insider trading derivative case, defendants Oreamuno and Gonzalez were respectively the Chairman of the Board and President of

---

and, more often, the fiduciary duty rules to face-to-face insider trading transactions. See, e.g., *Speed v. Transamerica Corp.*, 99 F.Supp. 808 (D.Del.1951).

[9] See, e.g., *Goodman v. Poland*, 395 F.Supp. 660, 678–80 (D.Md.1975); *Fleetwood Corp. v. Mirich*, 404 N.E.2d 38, 46 (Ind.App.1980); Yerke v. Batman, 376 N.E.2d 1211, 1214 (Ind.App.1978).

[10] 3A FLETCHER CYC CORP. ¶ 1168.1 (Perm. Ed. 1986).

[11] AMERICAN LAW INSTITUTE, PRINCIPLES OF CORPORATE GOVERNANCE: ANALYSIS AND RECOMMENDATIONS § 5.04 (1992).

[12] *Goodwin*, 186 N.E. at 660.

[13] 248 N.E.2d 910 (N.Y.1969).

Management Assistance, Inc. ("MAI"). MAI was in the computer leasing business. It sub-contracted maintenance of leased systems to IBM. As a result of an increase in IBM's charges, MAI's earnings fell precipitously. Before these facts were made public, Oreamuno and Gonzalez sold off 56,500 shares of MAI stock at the then-prevailing price of $28 per share. Once the information was made public, MAI's stock price fell to $11 per share. A shareholder sued derivatively, seeking an order that defendants disgorge their allegedly ill-gotten gains to the corporation.[14] The court held that a derivative suit was proper in this context and, moreover, that insider trading by corporate officers and directors violated their fiduciary duties to the corporation.

Diamond has been a law professor favorite ever since it was decided. A plethora of law review articles have been written on it, mostly in a favorable vein. *Diamond* also still shows up in most corporations case books. In the real world, however, *Diamond* has proven quite controversial. A number of leading opinions in other jurisdictions have squarely rejected its holdings.[15]

In *Freeman v. Decio*,[16] for example, the court held that corporate officers and directors could not be held liable for insider trading to the corporation under state corporate law via derivative litigation without a showing that the corporation was injured by their conduct. *Freeman* conceded that if all confidential information relating to the firm were a corporate asset, plaintiffs would not need to show an injury to the corporation in order for the insider's trades to constitute a breach of duty. The court said, however, such a view puts the cart before the horse. One should first ask whether there was any potential loss to the corporation before deciding whether to treat the information in question as a firm asset. The court further concluded that most instances of insider trading did not pose any cognizable risk of injury to the firm. According to the court, any harm caused by insider trading was borne mainly by the investors with whom the insider trades, rather than the firm.

B.   Origins of the Federal Prohibition

The modern federal insider trading prohibition has its statutory basis in the federal securities laws—principally the Securities Exchange Act of 1934. As with the other New Deal-era

---

[14] In everyday speech, the word "profit" connotes having more money than you started out with. Not so in the world of insider trading, where it is possible to profit by avoiding a loss. Courts have treated the use of inside information to avoid a loss as legally indistinguishable from the use of inside information to make a profit in the more conventional sense.

[15] See, e.g., *Freeman v. Decio*, 584 F.2d 186 (7th Cir.1978) (Indiana law); *Schein v. Chasen*, 313 So.2d 739, 746 (Fla.1975).

[16] 584 F.2d 186 (7th Cir.1978).

securities laws, the Exchange Act was a response to the 1929 stock market crash and the subsequent depression. Congress hoped these laws would ameliorate the economic crisis caused by the crash. Towards that end, all of the various statutes shared two basic purposes: protecting investors engaged in securities transactions and assuring public confidence in the integrity of the securities markets.

From the beginning, disclosure was Congress' favorite tool for regulating securities. As the Supreme Court later stated, the federal securities statutes' fundamental aim was "to substitute a philosophy of full disclosure for the philosophy of *caveat emptor* and thus achieve a high standard of business ethics in the securities industry."[17] Accordingly, prohibitions of fraud and manipulation in connection with the purchase or sale of securities buttressed the Exchange Act's disclosure requirements.

Is insider trading a breach of the disclosure obligations created by the Exchange Act? If not, is it otherwise captured by the Act's prohibition of fraud and manipulation? The United States Supreme Court, among others, thinks so: "A significant purpose of the Exchange Act was to eliminate the idea that use of inside information for personal advantage was a normal emolument of corporate office."[18]

The core of the modern federal insider trading prohibition derives its statutory authority from § 10(b) of the Exchange Act, which provides in pertinent part that:

> It shall be unlawful for any person, directly or indirectly, by the use of any means or instrumentality of interstate commerce or of the mails, or of any facility of any national securities exchange . . .

> (b) To use or employ, in connection with the purchase or sale of any security registered on a national securities exchange or any security not so registered, any manipulative or deceptive device or contrivance in contravention of such rules and regulations as the Commission may prescribe as necessary or appropriate in the public interest or for the protection of investors.

Notice that this text is not self-executing. Section 10(b) gives the SEC authority to prohibit "any manipulative or deceptive device or contrivance" and then makes the use of such proscribed devices illegal. Until the SEC exercises its rulemaking authority, however, the statute is unavailing.

---

[17] *SEC v. Capital Gains Research Bureau, Inc.*, 375 U.S. 180, 186 (1963).

[18] *Dirks v. SEC*, 463 U.S. 646, 653 n. 10 (1983).

In 1942, the SEC adopted Rule 10b–5, which became the foundation on which the modern insider trading prohibition rests. The Rule provides:

> It shall be unlawful for any person, directly or indirectly, by the use of any means or instrumentality of interstate commerce, or of the mails or of any facility of any national securities exchange,
>
> > (a) To employ any device, scheme, or artifice to defraud,
> >
> > (b) To make any untrue statement of a material fact or to omit to state a material fact necessary in order to make the statements made, in the light of the circumstances under which they were made, not misleading, or
> >
> > (c) To engage in any act, practice, or course of business which operates or would operate as a fraud or deceit upon any person,
>
> in connection with the purchase or sale of any security.

Note that, as with § 10(b) itself, the rule on its face does not prohibit (or even speak to) insider trading. Nor was Rule 10b–5 initially used against insider trading on public secondary trading markets. Instead, like state common law, the initial Rule 10b–5 cases were limited to face-to-face and/or control transactions.[19] Not until 1961 did the SEC finally conclude that insider trading on an impersonal stock exchange violated Rule 10b–5.[20] Only then did the modern federal insider trading prohibition at last begin to take shape.

In sum, the modern prohibition is a creature of SEC administrative actions and judicial opinions, only loosely tied to the statutory language and its legislative history. U.S. Supreme Court Chief Justice William Rehnquist famously observed that Rule 10b–5 is a judicial oak which has grown from little more than a legislative acorn.[21] Nowhere in Rule 10b–5 jurisprudence is this truer than where the insider trading prohibition is concerned, given the tiny (even nonexistent) legislative acorn on which it rests.

---

[19] See, e.g., Speed v. Transamerica Corp., 99 F.Supp. 808 (D.Del.1951) (omissions in connection with what amounted to tender offer); Kardon v. National Gypsum Co., 73 F.Supp. 798 (E.D.Pa.1947) (sale of control negotiated face to face); In re Ward La France Truck Corp., 13 S.E.C. 373 (1943) (same).

[20] In re Cady, Roberts & Co., 40 S.E.C. 907 (1961).

[21] Blue Chip Stamps v. Manor Drug Stores, 421 U.S. 723, 737 (1975).

C.   A Rule 10b–5 Primer

Before tracing the evolution of the insider trading prohibition under Rule 10b–5, however, a brief overview of the rule itself is in order. The rule's three subsections outlaw three types of conduct in connection with the purchase or sale of a security: the use of any device, scheme or artifice to defraud; material misstatements and omissions; and any act, practice or course of business that operates as a fraud. In general, however, the differences (if any) between the various rule's subsections do not matter very much—Rule 10b–5 is generally treated as broad prohibition of fraud in securities transactions and no one cares very much about whether the conduct in question is an artifice to defraud or a practice that operates as a fraud.

On its face, the rule does not tell us very much other than that fraud in connection with securities transactions is a bad thing. What elements does one have to prove in order to show a violation of the rule? Who has standing to sue violators? What remedies can they seek? The plain text of the rule answers few of these questions.[22] Instead, these issues were resolved in a long series of decisions, including a number of important Supreme Court decisions.

1.   Standing

Both the United States Justice Department (typically acting through local U.S. Attorney's offices) and the SEC clearly have standing to sue those who violate Rule 10b–5. The more interesting question is whether private parties have standing to sue under the rule. Nothing in either the rule or the statute explicitly authorizes such a private party cause of action. Lower federal courts recognized an implied right of action under Rule 10b–5 as early as 1946,[23] however, and the Supreme Court followed suit in 1971.[24] Today, of course, judicial implication of private rights of action is highly controversial and the current Supreme Court seems less inclined to create or preserve such rights of action than any of its recent predecessors. The private right of action under Rule 10b–5 nevertheless remains quite firmly established. As former Justice

---

[22] Both the statute and the rule plainly require a jurisdictional nexus; i.e., there must be a use of a means or instrumentality of interstate commerce, the mails, or any facility of a national securities exchange in order for the statute to be applicable. In most cases, this requirement is easily satisfied: basically, if the defendant made a phone call or sent a letter in connection with the fraud, § 10(b) can apply. Section 10(b) will also apply if the defendant takes either of those steps indirectly; for example, if the defendant orders his broker to sell shares, and the broker uses the phone or the mails, the statute is triggered.

[23] Kardon v. National Gypsum Co., 69 F.Supp. 512 (E.D.Pa.1946).

[24] Superintendent of Insurance v. Bankers Life & Cas. Co., 404 U.S. 6, 13 n. 9 (1971).

Thurgood Marshall once observed, the "existence of this implied remedy is simply beyond peradventure."[25]

Although the Supreme Court has confirmed the implied right of action under Rule 10b–5, it has limited private party standing to persons who actually buy or sell a security.[26] This may seem trivial or obvious, but it is not. Suppose the executives of a company wanted to drive down the price of the firm's stock so that they could buy it for themselves. They put out false bad news about the company. You were considering buying stock in the company but were dissuaded by the bad news put out by the executives. If you later try to sue, arguing that but for the executives' misconduct you would have bought some of the company's stock, the Supreme Court's standing rules will bar you from bringing suit.

Although one must have either purchased or sold a security in order to have standing to sue under Rule 10b–5, one need not have purchased or sold in order to be a proper party defendant. In the seminal insider trading case, *SEC v. Texas Gulf Sulphur Co.*,[27] the defendant corporation issued a misleading press release. Because the corporation had neither bought nor sold any securities during the relevant period, it argued it could not be held liable under Rule 10b–5. The court rejected this argument, observing that Rule 10b–5 on its face prohibits fraud "in connection with the purchase or sale of any security." The court interpreted this language as requiring "only that the device employed, whatever it might be, be of a sort that would cause reasonable investors to rely thereon, and, in connection therewith, so relying, cause them to purchase or sell a corporation's securities."

Although the Rule 10b–5 implied right of action long has been a major weapon in the arsenal of defrauded investors, it is less important in insider trading than in other contexts. First, private party litigation against inside traders is rare—at least compared to other types of securities fraud—and is usually parasitic on SEC enforcement actions. Second, Congress has created a special express cause of action for those who trade contemporaneously with inside traders. Our discussion of Rule 10b–5's elements thus can focus on those applicable to actions brought by the government.

2.   *Application to Omission Cases*

Rule 10b–5 applies to both affirmative misrepresentations and passive omissions. For our purposes, however, issues relating to omissions are far more important than are those relating to

---

[25] Herman & MacLean v. Huddleston, 459 U.S. 375, 380 (1983).

[26] Blue Chip Stamps v. Manor Drug Stores, 421 U.S. 723 (1975).

[27] 401 F.2d 833 (2d Cir.1968), cert. denied, 394 U.S. 976 (1969).

misrepresentations. Most insider trading cases today involve trading on impersonal stock exchanges in which the alleged inside trader allegedly bought or sold stock without first disclosing nonpublic information she knew when she traded.

Two aspects of Rule 10b–5, as applied to omission cases, are especially important. First, not all omissions give rise to liability. Instead, liability arises only if the defendant had a duty to speak. As we shall see, this requirement has been the central feature of the Supreme Court's insider trading jurisprudence. Second, reliance and transaction causation are presumed in omission cases. In private party litigation under Rule 10b–5, plaintiff generally must prove that he or she reasonably relied upon the defendant's fraudulent words or conduct.[28] Plaintiff also must prove both transaction causation and loss causation. The former is analogous to but for causation in tort law—it is a showing that defendant's words or conduct caused plaintiff to engage in the transaction in question. Loss causation is somewhat analogous to the tort law concept of proximate causation—it involves showing that the defendant's words or conduct caused plaintiff's economic loss. In omission cases, both transaction causation and reliance generally are presumed so long as plaintiff can show defendant had a duty to disclose and failed to do so.[29]

3. *Materiality*

Under Rule 10b–5, only material misrepresentations or omissions are actionable. Materiality is determined by asking whether there is a substantial likelihood that a reasonable investor would consider the information important in deciding how to act. When one is dealing with speculative or contingent facts, of course, this test can be hard to apply. Recall that in *Goodwin v. Agassiz*, for example, the defendants were buying stock based on a theory that land in the area the company worked might have commercially significant copper deposits. At the time the defendants traded, the theory was just that—a theory, which had not been verified. Was it material, as defined by the federal securities law?

In *Basic Inc. v. Levinson*,[30] the Supreme Court adopted what it called a "highly fact-dependent probability/magnitude balancing approach" to materiality in the context of contingent facts. Although

---

[28] In some misrepresentation cases, reliance and transaction causation may be presumed under the so-called "fraud on the market" theory. A rebuttable presumption arises under this theory if plaintiff can prove defendant made material public misrepresentations, the security was traded on an efficient market, and plaintiff traded in the security between the time the misrepresentations were made and the truth was revealed. Basic Inc. v. Levinson, 485 U.S. 224 (1988).

[29] Affiliated Ute Citizens v. United States, 406 U.S. 128 (1972).

[30] 485 U.S. 224 (1988).

Basic in fact was secretly negotiating a possible merger with another company, it issued three public denials that any such negotiations were underway. When the merger was finally announced, a class action was brought on behalf of those investors who had sold Basic stock during the period between the false denials and the merger announcement. The plaintiff class allegedly received a lower price for their shares than would have been the case if Basic had told the truth.

The core issue was whether the denials were material. When the denials were made, it had not been certain that the merger would go through. The probability/magnitude balancing test was thus appropriate. As to the probability part of the equation, the court looked to "indicia of interest in the transaction at the highest corporate levels." Evidence such as "board resolutions, instructions to investment bankers, and actual negotiations between principals or their intermediaries may serve as indicia of interest." As to magnitude, the court deemed it quite high, opining that a merger is "the most important event that can occur in a small corporation's life, to wit, its death. . . ." Notice, however, that magnitude appears to have both a relative and an absolute component. A merger of a small company into a large company, for example, is a big deal for the target, but may be insignificant from the acquirer's perspective.

Although the probability/magnitude language sounds technically sophisticated and precise, in fact it is inherently subjective and indeterminate. You may recall the famous Hand Formula from torts—multiply the probability of injury times the magnitude of the likely resulting injury; if the product is less than the benefits of adequate precautions, liability for allegedly negligent conduct may be imposed.[31] At first glance, the *Basic* test sounds like the Hand formula, but on closer examination, there is no magic product to serve as a threshold above which information becomes material. The court never tells us how high a probability nor how large a magnitude is necessary for information to be deemed material. One thus inside trades on the basis of speculative information knowing that a jury, acting with the benefit of hindsight, may reach a different conclusion about how probability and magnitude should be balanced than you did.

A major issue in insider trading cases is whether the allegedly illegal insider trading behavior can serve as proof that the facts on which the insider traded were material. The problem, of course, is the potential for bootstrapping: if the allegedly illegal trade proves that the information is material, the materiality requirement becomes meaningless—all information in the defendant's possession

[31] See United States v. Carroll Towing Co., 159 F.2d 169 (2d Cir.1947).

when he or she traded would be material. Nonetheless, a footnote in the Supreme Court's *Basic* opinion flatly stated that "trading and profit making by insiders can serve as an indication of materiality."

4. Scienter

One can easily mislead investors without intending to do so. Even an honest mistake might cause some to be misled. As such, it is not apparent that liability for securities fraud should be premised on intent. Tort law encourages drivers to drive more safely, because they can be held liable for negligent accidents. Tort law also encourages manufacturers to put out safer products by imposing strict liability for defective products. Should securities law be any less rigorous in encouraging accurate disclosure?

Liability in fact can be imposed for unintentional misrepresentations under some securities law provisions. Sections 11 and 12(a)(2) of the 1933 Securities Act, for example, require no evidence from plaintiff with respect to the defendant's state of mind. Instead, state of mind is at most an affirmative defense under these provisions. In order to make out the state of mind defense, moreover, defendants must show that they were non-negligent.

Under Rule 10b–5, however, the Supreme Court has held that plaintiff's prima facie case must include proof defendant acted with scienter, which the court defined as a mental state embracing intent to deceive, manipulate or defraud.[32] Although this formulation clearly precludes Rule 10b–5 liability for those who are merely negligent, the Supreme Court left open the issue of whether recklessness alone met the scienter requirement. Subsequent lower court decisions have generally held that recklessness suffices.

5. The Limits of Rule 10b–5: The Need for Deception

In *Santa Fe Industries, Inc. v. Green*,[33] Santa Fe effected a short-form merger with a subsidiary corporation. Minority shareholders of the subsidiary were dissatisfied with the consideration they were paid for their stock. Although plaintiffs had state law remedies, such as the statutory appraisal proceeding, they opted to sue under Rule 10b–5. Plaintiffs claimed that the merger violated Rule 10b–5 because it was effected without prior notice to the minority shareholders and was done without any legitimate business purpose. They also claimed that their shares had been undervalued. Both claims raised, quite directly, the question of what conduct is covered by the rule. The Supreme Court held that plaintiffs had not stated a cause of action under Rule 10b–5.

---

[32] Aaron v. SEC, 446 U.S. 680 (1980); Ernst & Ernst v. Hochfelder, 425 U.S. 185 (1976).

[33] 430 U.S. 462 (1977).

Drawing on the plain text and legislative history of the rule, the court concluded that a Rule 10b–5 cause of action arises only out of deception or manipulation. Deception requires a misrepresentation or omission. Because the *Santa Fe* plaintiffs received full disclosure, there was no misrepresentation or omission. In addition, neither of plaintiffs' claims went to disclosure violations; rather, both went to the substance of the transaction. Plaintiffs were not claiming that Santa Fe lied to them, but that the transaction was unfair. In other words, they were claiming that a breach of fiduciary duty gives rise to a cause of action under Rule 10b–5. The Supreme Court held that a mere breach of duty will not give rise to liability under 10b–5.

Manipulation is conduct intended to mislead investors by artificially affecting market activity. In other words, defendant must engage in conduct that creates artificial changes in the price of a security or artificially changes the volume of trading in a security. Again, Santa Fe was mainly being charged with a breach of the state law fiduciary duties a majority shareholder owes to minority shareholders. Nothing Santa Fe did constituted unlawful manipulation.

In addition to its textual arguments, the Supreme Court also relied on policy considerations grounded in federalism. The court clearly was concerned that allowing plaintiffs to go forward in this case would federalize much of state corporate law, in many cases overriding well-established state policies of corporate regulation. In the court's view, if the *Santa Fe* plaintiffs were allowed to sue, every breach of fiduciary duty case would give rise to a federal claim under Rule 10b–5. The court refused to give the Rule 10b–5 such an expansive reach, instead holding that it did not reach "transactions which constitute no more than internal corporate mismanagement."

Santa Fe was a critical holding in Rule 10b–5's evolution, putting the substantive fairness of a transaction outside the rule's scope. The rule henceforth was limited to disclosure violations. *Santa Fe* also implied a second—and potentially even more significant—constraint on the rule in suggesting that misconduct covered by state corporate law should be left to state law. As we have seen, insider trading long has fallen within the regulatory purview of state corporate law. As such, *Santa Fe* could have (and perhaps should have) constrained much of the federal insider trading prohibition's growth. As we shall see, however, later courts have largely ducked this issue.

6.   Secondary Liability and the Plain Meaning Issue

In *Central Bank of Denver v. First Interstate Bank*,[34] the Supreme Court held that there was no implied private right of action against those who aid and abet violations of Rule 10b–5. *Central Bank* thus substantially limited the scope of secondary liability under the rule, at least insofar as private party causes of action are concerned. For our purposes, however, the case is more significant for its methodology than its holding.

Until quite recently, courts and commentators viewed Rule 10b–5 as an example of interstitial lawmaking in which courts used common-law adjudicatory methods to flesh out the text's bare bones. In *Central Bank*, however, the Supreme Court held the scope of conduct prohibited by § 10(b) (and thus the rule) is controlled by the text of the statute. Where the plain text does not resolve some aspect of the Rule 10b–5 cause of action, courts must "infer 'how the 1934 Congress would have addressed the issue had the 10b–5 action been included as an express provision in the 1934 Act.' " The court elsewhere acknowledged this is an "awkward task," but Justice Scalia put it more colorfully: "We are imagining here."[35] *Central Bank* constrained this imaginative process by requiring courts to "use the express causes of action in the securities acts as the primary model for the § 10(b) action."[36] As we shall see, *Central Bank* poses a significant threat to the further evolution of the federal insider trading prohibition, although thus far its potential remains unrealized.

D.   *Cady, Roberts*

The modern federal insider trading prohibition fairly can be said to have begun with *In re Cady, Roberts & Co.*,[37] an SEC enforcement action. Curtiss-Wright Corporation's board of directors decided to reduce the company's quarterly dividend. One of the directors, J. Cheever Cowdin, was also a partner in Cady, Roberts & Co., a stock brokerage firm. Before the news was announced, Cowdin informed one of his partners, Robert M. Gintel, of the impending dividend cut. Gintel then sold several thousand shares of Curtiss-Wright stock held in customer accounts over which he had discretionary trading authority. When the dividend cut was announced, Curtiss-Wright's stock price fell several dollars per share. Gintel's customers thus avoided substantial losses.

---

[34] 511 U.S. 164 (1994).

[35] Lampf, Pleva, Lipkind, Prupis & Petigrow v. Gilbertson, 501 U.S. 350 (1991).

[36] Central Bank, 511 U.S. at 178.

[37] 40 S.E.C. 907 (1961).

Cady, Roberts involved what is now known as tipping: an insider (the tipper) who knows confidential information does not himself trade, but rather informs (tips) someone else (the tippee) who does trade. It also involved trading on an impersonal stock exchange, instead of a face-to-face transaction. As the SEC acknowledged, this made *Cady, Roberts* a case of first impression. Prior 10b–5 cases in which inside information was used for personal gain had involved issues of tortious fraudulent concealment little different from the sorts of cases with which the state common law had dealt. Notwithstanding that limitation, the SEC held that Gintel had violated Rule 10b–5. In so doing, it articulated what became known as the disclose or abstain rule: An insider in possession of material nonpublic information must disclose such information before trading or, if disclosure is impossible or improper, abstain from trading.

E.   *Texas Gulf Sulphur*

It was not immediately clear what precedential value *Cady, Roberts* would have. It was an administrative ruling by the SEC, not a judicial opinion. It involved a regulated industry closely supervised by the SEC. There was the long line of precedent, represented by *Goodwin v. Agassiz*, to the contrary. In short order, however, the basic *Cady, Roberts* principles became the law of the land.

In March of 1959, agents of Texas Gulf Sulphur Co. (TGS) found evidence of an ore deposit near Timmins, Ontario.[38] In October 1963, Texas Gulf Sulphur began ground surveys of the area. In early November, a drilling rig took core samples from depths of several hundred feet. Visual examination of the samples suggested commercially significant deposits of copper and zinc. TGS's president ordered the exploration group to maintain strict confidentiality, even to the point of withholding the news from other TGS directors and employees. In early December, a chemical assay confirmed the presence of copper, zinc, and silver. At the subsequent trial, several expert witnesses testified that they had never heard of any other initial exploratory drill hole showing comparable results. Over the next several months, TGS acquired the rights to the land under which this remarkable ore deposit lay. In March and early April 1964, further drilling confirmed that TGS had made a significant ore discovery. After denying several rumors about the find, TGS finally announced its discovery in a press conference on April 16, 1964.

---

[38] SEC v. Texas Gulf Sulphur Co., 401 F.2d 833 (2d Cir.1968), cert. denied, 394 U.S. 976 (1969).

Throughout the fall of 1963 and spring of 1964, a number of TGS insiders bought stock and/or options on company stock. Others tipped off outsiders. Still others accepted stock options authorized by the company's board of directors without informing the directors of the discovery. Between November 1963 and March 1964, the insiders were able to buy at prices that were slowly rising, albeit with fluctuations, from just under $18 per share to $25 per share. As rumors began circulating in late March and early April, the price jumped to about $30 per share. On April 16th, the stock opened at $31, but quickly jumped to $37 per share. By May 15, 1964, TGS's stock was trading at over $58 per share—a 222% rise over the previous November's price. Any joy the insiders may have taken from their profits was short-lived, however, as the SEC sued them for violating Rule 10b–5.

Texas Gulf Sulphur is the first of the truly seminal insider trading cases. It is still widely taught, in large part because it presents such a stark and classic fact pattern. In examining *Texas Gulf Sulphur*, however, it is critical to distinguish between what the law *was* and what the law *is*—although much of what was said in that opinion is still valid, the core insider trading holding is no longer good law.

The Second Circuit Court of Appeals held that when an insider has material nonpublic information the insider must either disclose such information before trading or abstain from trading until the information has been disclosed. Thus was born what is now known as the "disclose or abstain" rule. The name is something of a misnomer, of course. The court presumably phrased the rule in terms of disclosure because this was an omissions case under Rule 10b–5. In such cases, the defendant must owe a duty of disclosure to some investor in order for liability to be imposed.[39] As a practical matter, however, disclosure will rarely be an option.

During the relevant time period, TGS had no affirmative duty to disclose the ore strike. As the Second Circuit correctly noted, the timing of disclosure is a matter for the business judgment of corporate managers, subject to any affirmative disclosure requirements imposed by the stock exchanges or the SEC. In this case, moreover, a valuable corporate purpose was served by delaying disclosure: confidentiality prevented competitors from

---

[39] See e.g., Chiarella v. United States, 445 U.S. 222, 230 (1980) (stating that liability for nondisclosure "is premised upon a duty to disclose arising from a relationship of trust and confidence between parties to a transaction"); see also Dirks v. SEC, 463 U.S. 646, 654 (1983) (stating that there is no general duty to disclose and the duty to disclose must arise from a fiduciary relationship); SEC v. Switzer, 590 F.Supp. 756, 766 (W.D.Okla.1984) (holding that overhearing inadvertently revealed inside information does not create a duty to disclose before trading because for a fiduciary duty to run to a tippee, the inside information must be disclosed for an improper purpose).

buying up the mineral rights and kept down the price landowners would charge for them. The company therefore had no duty to disclose the discovery, at least up until the time that the land acquisition program was completed.

Given that the corporation had no duty to disclose, and had decided not to disclose the information, the insiders' fiduciary duties to the corporation would preclude them disclosing it for personal gain. In this case, the company's president had specifically instructed insiders in the know to keep the information confidential, but such an instruction was not technically necessary. Agency law precludes a firm's agents from disclosing confidential information that belongs to their corporate principal, as all information relating to the ore strike clearly did.[40]

Disclosure by an insider who wishes to trade thus is only feasible if there is no legitimate corporate purpose for maintaining secrecy. These situations, however, presumably will be relatively rare—it is hard to imagine many business developments that can be disclosed immediately without working some harm to the corporation. In most cases, the disclose or abstain rule really does not provide the insider with a disclosure option: generally the duty will be one of complete abstention.

The policy foundation on which the Second Circuit erected the disclose or abstain rule was equality of access to information. The court contended that the federal insider trading prohibition was intended to assure that "all investors trading on impersonal exchanges have relatively equal access to material information." Put another way, the majority thought Congress intended "that all members of the investing public should be subject to identical market risks."

The equality of access principle admittedly has some intuitive appeal. The implications of the equal access principle, however, become troubling when we start dealing with attenuated circumstances, especially with respect to market information. Suppose a representative of TGS had approached a landowner in the Timmins area to negotiate purchasing the mineral rights to the land. TGS' agent does not disclose the ore strike, but the landowner turns out to be pretty smart. She knows TGS has been drilling in the area and has heard rumors that it has been buying up a lot of mineral rights. She puts two and two together, reaches the obvious conclusion, and buys some TGS stock. Under a literal reading of *Texas Gulf Sulphur*, has our landowner committed illegal insider trading?

---

[40] Restatement (Second) of Agency § 395 (1958).

The surprising answer is "probably." The *Texas Gulf Sulphur* court stated that the insider trading prohibition applies to "anyone in possession of material inside information," because § 10(b) was intended to assure that "all investors trading on impersonal exchanges have relatively equal access to material information." The court further stated that the prohibition applies to any persons who have "access, directly or *indirectly*" to confidential information (here is the sticking point) if they know that the information is unavailable to the investing public. The only issue thus perhaps would be a factual one turning on the landowner's state of mind: Did she know she was dealing with confidential information? If so, the equal access policy would seem to justify imposing a duty on her. Query whether the insider trading prohibition should stretch quite that far? Ultimately, the Supreme Court concluded that it should not.

§ 11.3   The Disclose or Abstain Rule

Texas Gulf Sulphur sent the insider trading prohibition down a path on which insider trading was deemed a form of securities fraud and, accordingly, within the SEC's regulatory jurisdiction. There was nothing inevitable about that choice, however. State corporate law had been regulating insider trading for decades before *Texas Gulf Sulphur* was decided. Well-established state precedents treated the problem as one implicating not concepts of deceit or manipulation, but rather the fiduciary duties of corporate officers and directors. To be sure, many states held that insider trading did not violate those duties, especially with respect to stock market transactions, but so what? In light of those precedents, the Second Circuit could have held that insider trading was not within Rule 10b–5's regulatory purview. If it had done so, the prohibition would have evolved along a far different path than the one it actually followed.

A.   *Chiarella*

1.   *The Facts*

Vincent Chiarella was an employee of Pandick Press, a financial printer that prepared tender offer disclosure materials, among other documents.[41] In preparing those materials Pandick used codes to conceal the names of the companies involved, but Chiarella broke the codes. He purchased target company shares before the bid was announced, then sold the shares for considerable profits after announcement of the bid. He was caught and indicted for illegal insider trading. He was thereafter convicted of violating

---

[41] Chiarella v. United States, 445 U.S. 222 (1980).

Rule 10b–5 by trading on the basis of material nonpublic information. The Second Circuit affirmed his conviction, applying the same equality of access to information-based disclose or abstain rule it had created in Texas Gulf Sulphur.

Chiarella was one of the first of a series of high profile takeover-related insider trading cases during the 1980s. Obviously, one can significantly increase takeover profits if one knows in advance that a takeover will be forthcoming. If you know of an impending bid prior to its announcement, you can buy up stock at the low pre-announcement price and sell or tender at the higher post-announcement price. The earlier one knows of the bid, of course, the greater the spread between your purchase and sale prices and the greater the resulting profit. By using options, rather than actually buying target stock, you can further increase your profits, because options permit one to control larger blocks of stock for the same investment.

2.   Inside Versus Market Information

Nonpublic information, for purposes of Rule 10b–5, takes two principal forms: inside information and market information. Inside information typically comes from internal corporate sources and involves events or developments affecting the issuer's assets or earnings. Market information typically originates from sources other than the issuer and involves events or circumstances concerning or affecting the price or market for the issuer's securities and does not concern the issuer's assets or earning power. The information at issue in *Chiarella* thus was a type of market information. This distinction is unimportant for our purposes because insider trading liability can be imposed on those who trade while in possession of either type.

3.   The Holding

Relative to some of those who followed him into federal court, Vincent Chiarella was small fry. But his case produced the first landmark Supreme Court insider trading ruling since *Strong v. Repide*.[42] As noted, in affirming Chiarella's conviction the Second Circuit had invoked *Texas Gulf Sulphur*'s equality of access to information-based disclose or abstain rule. Under the equal access-based standard, Chiarella clearly loses: he had greater access to information than those with whom he traded. But notice: Chiarella was not an employee, officer, or director of any of the companies in whose stock he traded. He worked solely for Pandick Press, which in turn was not an agent of any of those companies. Pandick worked

---

[42] 213 U.S. 419 (1909).

for acquiring companies—not the takeover targets in whose stock Chiarella traded.

Chiarella's conviction demonstrated how far the federal insider trading prohibition had departed from its state common law predecessors. Recall that state common law had required, where it imposed liability at all, a fiduciary relationship between buyer and seller. The mere fact that one party had more information than the other was not grounds for setting aside the transaction or imposing damages. Yet, it was for that reason alone that the Second Circuit upheld Chiarella's conviction.

The Supreme Court reversed.[43] In doing so, the court squarely rejected the notion that § 10(b) was intended to assure all investors equal access to information. The Court said it could not affirm Chiarella's conviction without recognizing a general duty between all participants in market transactions to forego trades based on material, nonpublic information, and it refused to impose such a duty.

Chiarella thus made clear that the disclose or abstain rule is not triggered merely because the trader possesses material nonpublic information. When a 10b–5 action is based upon nondisclosure, there can be no fraud absent a duty to speak, and no such duty arises from the mere possession of nonpublic information. Instead, the disclose or abstain theory of liability for insider trading was now premised on the inside trader being subject to a duty to disclose to the party on the other side of the transaction that arose from a relationship of trust and confidence between the parties thereto.

Chiarella radically limited the scope of the insider trading prohibition as it had been defined in *Texas Gulf Sulphur*. Consider the landowner hypothetical discussed above: Under an equal access to information-based standard, she is liable for insider trading because she had material information unavailable to those with whom she traded. Under *Chiarella*, however, she cannot be held liable. She is (by hypothesis) not the agent or fiduciary of TGS shareholders and, presumably, has no other special relationship of trust and confidence with them. Accordingly, she is free to trade on the basis of what she knows without fear of liability. The policy conundrum is now flipped, of course: after *Texas Gulf Sulphur*, the question was how large a net should the prohibition cast; after *Chiarella*, the question was how broad should be the scope of immunity created by the new fiduciary relationship requirement.

---

[43] Chiarella v. United States, 445 U.S. 222 (1980).

B. *Dirks*

The Supreme Court tackled that question three years later in *Dirks v. SEC*.[44] Raymond Dirks was a securities analyst who uncovered the massive Equity Funding of America fraud. Dirks first began investigating Equity Funding after receiving allegations from Ronald Secrist, a former officer of Equity Funding, that the corporation was engaged in widespread fraudulent corporate practices. Dirks passed the results of his investigation to the SEC and the Wall Street Journal, but also discussed his findings with various clients. A number of those clients sold their holdings of Equity Funding securities before any public disclosure of the fraud, thereby avoiding substantial losses. After the fraud was made public and Equity Funding went into receivership, the SEC began an investigation of Dirk's role in exposing the fraud. One might think Dirks deserved a medal (certainly Mr. Dirks seems to have felt that way), but one would be wrong. The SEC censured Dirks for violating the federal insider trading prohibition by repeating the allegations of fraud to his clients.

Under the *Texas Gulf Sulphur* equal access to information standard, tipping of the sort at issue in *Dirks* presented no conceptual problems. The tippee had access to information unavailable to those with whom he traded and, as such, was liable. After *Chiarella*, however, the tipping problem was more complex. Neither Dirks nor any of his customers were agents, officers, or directors of Equity Funding. Nor did they have any other form of special relationship of trust and confidence with those with whom they traded.

In reversing Dirk's censure, the Supreme Court expressly reaffirmed its rejection of the equal access standard:

> We were explicit in *Chiarella* in saying that there can be no duty to disclose where the person who has traded on inside information "was not [the corporation's] agent, . . . was not a fiduciary, [or] was not a person in whom the sellers [of the securities] had placed their trust and confidence." Not to require such a fiduciary relationship, we recognized, would "[depart] radically from the established doctrine that duty arises from a specific relationship between two parties" and would amount to "recognizing a general duty between all participants in market transactions to forgo actions based on material, nonpublic information."

---

[44] 463 U.S. 646 (1983).

Recognizing that this formulation posed problems for tipping cases, the court held that a tippee's liability is derivative of that of the tipper, "arising from [the tippee's] role as a participant after the fact in the insider's breach of a fiduciary duty." A tippee therefore can be held liable only when the tipper breached a fiduciary duty by disclosing information to the tippee, and the tippee knows or has reason to know of the breach of duty.

On the *Dirks* facts, this formulation precluded imposition of liability. To be sure, Secrist was an employee and, hence, a fiduciary of Equity Funding. But the mere fact that an insider tips nonpublic information is not enough under *Dirks*. What *Dirks* proscribes is not merely a breach of confidentiality by the insider, but rather the breach of a fiduciary duty of loyalty to refrain from profiting on information entrusted to the tipper.[45] Looking at objective criteria, courts must determine whether the insider-tipper personally benefited, directly or indirectly, from his disclosure. Secrist tipped off Dirks in order to bring Equity Funding's misconduct to light, not for any personal gain. Absent the requisite personal benefit, liability could not be imposed.[46]

In *Dirks*, the Supreme Court identified several situations in which the requisite personal benefit could be found. The most obvious is the quid pro quo setting, in which the tipper receives some form of pecuniary gain. Nonpecuniary gain can also qualify, however. Suppose a corporate CEO discloses information to a wealthy investor not for any legitimate corporate purpose, but solely to enhance her own reputation. *Dirks* would find a personal benefit on those facts. Finally, *Dirks* indicated that liability could be imposed where the tip is a gift. A gift satisfies the breach element

---

[45] To be clear, Rule 10b–5 liability is grounded not on a breach of fiduciary duty but on violation of a disclosure obligation. Under *Dirks*, the tippee has a duty of disclosure to those with whom he trades where the tipper breach a fiduciary duty by making the tip. Hence, the tippee does not succeed to any fiduciary duty. Instead, it is the tippee's duty of disclosure that is said to be derivative of the tipper's breach of duty.

In the misappropriation context, however, the trend is to say that breach of a mere duty of confidentiality suffices. See SEC Rule 10b5–2(b)(1) (stating that the requisite "duty of trust or confidence" exists whenever "a person agrees to maintain information in confidence."); see also SEC v. Yun, 327 F.3d 1263, 1272–73 (11th Cir.2003) (holding that "a spouse who trades in breach of a reasonable and legitimate expectation of confidentiality held by the other spouse sufficiently subjects the former to insider trading liability . . .. Of course, a breach of an agreement to maintain business confidences would also suffice."); SEC v. Kirch, 263 F.Supp.2d 1144 (N.D.Ill.2003) (holding "that the 'duty of loyalty and confidentiality' owed by the outsider . . . to the person . . . who shared confidential information with him or her . . . is not limited to fiduciary relationships in the limited sense that requires such factors as control and dominance on the part of the fiduciary. Instead that 'duty of loyalty and confidentiality' can be (and is) created by precisely the type of [confidentiality] policy and expectations that are present . . . here . . . .").

[46] The SEC has argued that the personal benefit requirement does not apply to tipping cases brought under the misappropriation theory of liability. The Eleventh Circuit has rejected that argument. SEC v. Yun, 327 F.3d 1263 (11th Cir.2003).

because it is analogous to the situation in which the tipper trades on the basis of the information and then gives the tippee the profits.[47]

1.   Selective Disclosure and Regulation FD

The SEC long has been concerned that selective disclosure to analysts undermines public confidence in the integrity of the stock markets:

> [M]any issuers are disclosing important nonpublic information, such as advance warnings of earnings results, to securities analysts or selected institutional investors or both, before making full disclosure of the same information to the general public. Where this has happened, those who were privy to the information beforehand were able to make a profit or avoid a loss at the expense of those kept in the dark.

> We believe that the practice of selective disclosure leads to a loss of investor confidence in the integrity of our capital markets. Investors who see a security's price change dramatically and only later are given access to the information responsible for that move rightly question whether they are on a level playing field with market insiders.[48]

Unfortunately for the SEC, the *Dirks'* tipping regime was an inadequate constraint on the selective disclosure practice because, inter alia, it can be difficult to prove that the tipper received a personal benefit in connection with a disclosure. In 2000, the SEC adopted Regulation FD to create a noninsider trading-based mechanism for restricting selective disclosure. If someone acting on behalf of a public corporation discloses material nonpublic information to securities market professionals or "holders of the issuer's securities who may well trade on the basis of the information," the issuer must also disclose that information to the public. Where the issuer intentionally provides such disclosure, it must simultaneously disclose the information in a manner designed to convey it to the general public. Hence, for example, if the issuer holds a briefing for selected analysts, it must simultaneously

---

[47] In a tipping case brought under the classic disclose or abstain theory, it seems that the tipper must know that the tippee intends to use the information to inside trade. In the misappropriation context, the Second Circuit has held that no such explicit *quid pro quo* is required. Instead, it suffices if the tipper knows that the tippee will put the tipped information "to some kind of a misuse." U.S. v. Libera, 989 F.2d 596, 600 (2d Cir.1993). See also U.S. v. Falcone, 257 F.3d 226 (2d Cir.2001) (reaffirming *Libera* against defendant's claim *Libera* had been implicitly overruled by *O'Hagan*).

[48] Exchange Act Rel. No. 43,154 (Aug. 15, 2000).

announce the same information through, say, a press release to "a widely disseminated news or wire service." The SEC encouraged issuers to make use of the Internet and other new information technologies, such as by webcasting conference calls with analysts. Where the disclosure was not intentional, as where a corporate officer "let something slip," the issuer must make public disclosure "promptly" after a senior officer learns of the disclosure.

2. Tipping Chains

At least in theory, it is possible for a tipper to be liable even if the tippee is not liable. The breach of duty is enough to render the tipper liable, but the tippee must know of the breach in order to be held liable. Notice also that it is possible to have chains of tipping liability: Tipper tells Tippee #1 who tells Tippee #2 who trades. Tippee #2 can be held liable, so long as she knew or had reason to know that the ultimate source of the information had breached his fiduciary duties by disclosing it.

§ 11.4   The Misappropriation Theory and Rule 14e–3: Post-*Chiarella* Gap-Fillers

Chiarella created a variety of significant gaps in the insider trading prohibition's coverage. Consider this standard law school hypothetical: A law firm is hired by Raider Corporation to represent it in connection with a planned takeover bid for Target Company. Ann Associate is one of the lawyers assigned to the project. Before Raider publicly discloses its intentions, Associate purchases a substantial block of Target stock. Under the disclose or abstain rule, she has not violated the insider trading prohibition. Whatever the scope of the duties she owed Raider, she owed no duty to the shareholders of Target. Accordingly, she owes no duty of disclosure to those shareholders. Rule 14e–3 and the misappropriation theory were created to fill this gap.

A.   Rule 14e–3

Rule 14e–3 was the SEC's immediate response to *Chiarella*.[49] The Rule was specifically intended to reach the wave of insider trading activity associated with the increase in merger and acquisition activity during the 1980s. The rule prohibits insiders of the bidder and target from divulging confidential information about a tender offer to persons that are likely to violate the rule by trading on the basis of that information. This provision (Rule 14e–3(d)(1)) does not prohibit the bidder from buying target shares or

---

[49] 17 C.F.R. § 240.14e–3. In fact, Rule 14e–3 was pending at the time *Chiarella* was decided, see Chiarella v. United States, 445 U.S. 222, 234 n. 18 (1980), almost as though the Commission knew that its attempts to reach warehousing of takeover securities under Rule 10b–5 were of questionable validity.

from telling its legal and financial advisers about its plans. What the rule prohibits is tipping of information to persons who are likely to buy target shares for their own account. In particular, the rule was intended to strike at the practice known as warehousing. Anecdotal evidence suggests that before Rule 14e–3 was on the books bidders frequently tipped their intentions to friendly parties. Warehousing increased the odds a hostile takeover bid would succeed by increasing the number of shares likely to support the bidder's proposal.

Rule 14e–3 also, with certain narrow and well-defined exceptions, prohibits any person that possesses material information relating to a tender offer by another person from trading in target company securities if the bidder has commenced or has taken substantial steps towards commencement of the bid. The requisite "substantial step" can be found even if formal announcement of a tender offer has not yet occurred and, perhaps, even if a tender offer never takes place. Substantial steps include such things as voting on a resolution by the offering person's board of directors relating to the tender offer; the formulation of a plan or proposal to make a tender offer by the offering person; activities which substantially facilitate the tender offer, such as arranging financing for a tender offer, or preparing or directing or authorizing the preparation of tender offer materials.[50] The trader must know or have reason to know that the information is nonpublic. The trader also must know or have reason to know the information was acquired from the bidder or the target company or agents of either.

Unlike both the disclose or abstain rule and the misappropriation theory under Rule 10b–5, Rule 14e–3 liability is not premised on a fiduciary relationship. There is no need for a showing that the trading party or tipper was subject to any duty of confidentiality, and no need to show that a tipper personally benefited from the tip. In light of the well-established fiduciary duty requirement under Rule 10b–5, however, the rule arguably ran afoul of *Schreiber v. Burlington Northern, Inc.*,[51] in which the Supreme Court held that § 14(e) was modeled on § 10(b) and, like that section, requires a showing of misrepresentation or nondisclosure. If the two sections are to be interpreted in pari

---

[50] SEC Release No. 34–17,120 (1980). See, e.g., SEC v. Maio, 51 F.3d 623 (7th Cir.1995) (signing a confidentiality agreement constituted a substantial step where one of the corporate parties had earlier solicited a tender offer); SEC v. Musella, 578 F.Supp. 425 (S.D.N.Y.1984) (retaining law firm to advise on an impending offer constituted a substantial step); Camelot Indus. Corp. v. Vista Resources, Inc., 535 F.Supp. 1174 (S.D.N.Y.1982) (meeting between target managers, prospective acquiror, and an investment banker deemed a substantial step); O'Connor & Assoc. v. Dean Witter Reynolds, Inc., 529 F.Supp. 1179 (S.D.N.Y.1981) (Rule 14e–3 can be violated even if offer never becomes effective).

[51] 472 U.S. 1 (1985).

materia, as *Shreiber* indicated, and § 10(b) requires a fiduciary relationship in order for liability to arise, the SEC appeared to have exceeded its statutory authority by adopting a rule that makes illegal a variety of trading practices that do not involve any breach of duty. In *United States v. O'Hagan*,[52] however, the Supreme Court upheld Rule 14e–3 as a valid exercise of the SEC's rulemaking authority despite the absence of a fiduciary relationship element.

While Rule 14e–3 thus escapes the fiduciary duty-based restrictions of the *Chiarella/Dirks* regime, the Rule nevertheless is quite limited in scope. One prong of the rule (the prohibition on trading while in possession of material nonpublic information) does not apply until the offeror has taken substantial steps towards making the offer. More important, both prongs of the rule are limited to information relating to a tender offer. As a result, most types of inside information remain subject to the duty-based analysis of *Chiarella* and its progeny.

Although most lawsuits under 14e–3 have been brought by the SEC, it seems likely that a private right of action exists under the rule and is available to investors trading in the target's securities at the same time as the persons who violated the rule.[53]

B.   Misappropriation

In response to the set-backs it suffered in *Chiarella* and *Dirks*, the SEC began advocating a new theory of insider trading liability: the misappropriation theory. Unlike Rule 14e–3, the SEC did not intend for the misappropriation theory to be limited to tender offer cases (although many misappropriation decisions have in fact involved takeovers). Accordingly, the Commission posited misappropriation as a new theory of liability under Rule 10b–5. Which meant, in turn, that the SEC had to find a way of finessing the fiduciary duty requirement imposed by *Chiarella* and *Dirks*.

1.   Origins

The misappropriation theory is commonly (but incorrectly) traced to Chief Justice Burger's *Chiarella* dissent. Burger contended that the way in which the inside trader acquires the nonpublic information on which he trades could itself be a material circumstance that must be disclosed to the market before trading. Accordingly, Burger argued, "a person who has misappropriated nonpublic information has an absolute duty [to the persons with whom he trades] to disclose that information or to refrain from

---

[52]   521 U.S. 642, 666–76 (1997).

[53]   See, e.g., O'Connor & Assoc. v. Dean Witter Reynolds, Inc., 529 F.Supp. 1179 (S.D.N.Y.1981).

trading."[54] The majority did not address the merits of this theory; instead rejecting it solely on the ground that the theory had not been presented to the jury and thus could not sustain a criminal conviction.

Consequently, the way was left open for the SEC to urge, and the lower courts to adopt, the misappropriation theory as an alternative basis of insider trading liability. The Second Circuit swiftly moved to take advantage of that opportunity. In *United States v. Newman*,[55] employees of an investment bank misappropriated confidential information concerning proposed mergers involving clients of the firm. As was true of Vincent Chiarella, the Newman defendants' employer worked for prospective acquiring companies, while the trading took place in target company securities. As such, the Newman defendants owed no fiduciary duties to the investors with whom they traded. Moreover, neither the investment bank nor its clients traded in the target companies' shares contemporaneously with the defendants.

Unlike Chief Justice Burger's *Chiarella* dissent, the Second Circuit did not assert that the Newman defendants owed any duty of disclosure to the investors with whom they traded or had defrauded. Instead, the court held that by misappropriating confidential information for personal gain, the defendants had defrauded their employer and its clients, and this fraud sufficed to impose insider trading liability on the defendants with whom they traded.[56] As eventually refined, the (pre-*O'Hagan*) misappropriation theory thus imposed liability on anyone who: (1) misappropriated material nonpublic information; (2) thereby breaching a fiduciary duty or a duty arising out of a similar relationship of trust and confidence; and (3) used that information in a securities transaction, regardless of whether he owed any duties to the shareholders of the company in whose stock he traded.[57]

Like the traditional disclose or abstain rule, the misappropriation theory thus contemplated a disclosure obligation arising out of a fiduciary relationship.[58] The fiduciary relationship in question, however, was a quite different one. Under the misappropriation theory, the defendant did not need to owe a fiduciary duty to the investor with whom he traded, nor did he need

---

[54] Chiarella v. United States, 445 U.S. 222, 240 (1980) (Burger, C.J., dissenting).

[55] 664 F.2d 12 (2d Cir.1981).

[56] See U.S. v. Newman, 664 F.2d 12, 17 (2d Cir.1981); see also United States v. Carpenter, 791 F.2d 1024 (2d Cir.1986), aff'd on other grounds, 484 U.S. 19 (1987); SEC v. Materia, 745 F.2d 197 (2d Cir.1984), cert. denied, 471 U.S. 1053 (1985).

[57] See United States v. Bryan, 58 F.3d 933, 945 (4th Cir.1995).

[58] See SEC v. Switzer, 590 F.Supp. 756, 766 (W.D.Okla.1984) (stating that it is not unlawful to trade on the basis of inadvertently overheard information).

to owe a fiduciary duty to the issuer of the securities that were traded. Instead, the misappropriation theory applied when the inside trader violated a fiduciary duty owed to the source of the information.[59] Had the misappropriation theory been available against Chiarella, for example, his conviction could have been upheld even though he owed no duties to those with whom he had traded. Instead, the breach of the duty he owed to Pandick Press would have sufficed.

The misappropriation theory should be seen as the vehicle by which the SEC sought to recapture as much as possible the ground it had lost in *Chiarella* and *Dirks*. In the years following those decisions, the SEC (and the lower courts) seemed to view the fiduciary duty element as a mere inconvenience that should not stand in the way of expansive insider trading liability. They consistently sought to evade the spirit of the fiduciary duty requirement, while complying with its letter. Even a former SEC Commissioner admitted as much, acknowledging that the misappropriation theory was "merely a pretext for enforcing equal opportunity in information."[60] Put another way, the SEC used the misappropriation theory as a means of redirecting the prohibition back towards the direction in which *Texas Gulf Sulphur* had initially set it.

2.   Called into Question

The Supreme Court first took up the misappropriation theory in *Carpenter v. United States*,[61] in which a Wall Street Journal reporter and his confederates misappropriated information belonging to the Journal. The Supreme Court upheld the resulting convictions under the mail and wire fraud statutes, holding that confidential business information is property protected by those statutes from being taken by trick, deceit, or chicanery.[62] As to the defendants' securities fraud convictions, however, the court split 4–

---

[59] See, e.g., United States v. Carpenter, 791 F.2d 1024, 1028–29 (2d Cir.1986) (applying misappropriation theory to a journalist who breaches his duty of confidentiality to his employer).

[60] Charles C. Cox & Kevin S. Fogarty, Bases of Insider Trading Law, 49 Ohio St. L.J. 353, 366 (1988).

[61] 484 U.S. 19 (1987).

[62] The federal mail and wire fraud statutes, 18 U.S.C. §§ 1341 and 1343, respectively prohibit the use of the mails and "wire, radio, or television communication" for the purpose of executing any "scheme or artifice to defraud." The mail and wire fraud statutes protect only property rights, McNally v. United States, 483 U.S. 350 (1987), but confidential business information is deemed to be property for purposes of those statutes. Carpenter v. United States, 484 U.S. 19, 25 (1987). Hence, the Supreme Court held, the Wall Street Journal owned the information used by Winans and his co-conspirators and, moreover, that their use of the mails and wire communications to trade on the basis of that information constituted the requisite scheme to defraud. Arguably, after *Carpenter* and *O'Hagan*, if there is a Rule 10b–5 violation there will also be a mail and wire fraud violation and vice-versa.

4. Following the long-standing tradition governing evenly divided Supreme Court decisions, the lower court ruling was affirmed without opinion, but that ruling had no precedential or stare decisis value.

The way was thus left open for lower courts to reject the misappropriation theory, which the Fourth and Eighth Circuits subsequently did in, respectively, *United States v. Bryan*[63] and *United States v. O'Hagan*.[64] These courts held that Rule 10b–5 imposed liability only where there has been deception upon the purchaser or seller of securities, or upon some other person intimately linked with or affected by a securities transaction. Because the misappropriation theory—at last as read most broadly—involved no such deception, but rather simply a breach of fiduciary duty owed to the source of the information, the theory could not stand. The Supreme Court took cert in *United States v. O'Hagan* to resolve the resulting split between these circuits and the prior Second Circuit holdings validating the misappropriation theory.

3. O'Hagan: *Facts*

James O'Hagan was a partner in the Minneapolis law firm of Dorsey & Whitney. In July 1988, Grand Metropolitan PLC (Grand Met), retained Dorsey & Whitney in connection with its planned takeover of Pillsbury Company. Although O'Hagan was not one of the lawyers on the Grand Met project, he learned of their intentions and began buying Pillsbury stock and call options on Pillsbury stock. When Grand Met announced its tender offer in October, the price of Pillsbury stock nearly doubled, allowing O'Hagan to reap a profit of more than $4.3 million.

O'Hagan was charged with violating 1934 Act § 10(b) and Rule 10b–5 by trading on misappropriated nonpublic information. As with Chiarella and the *Newman* defendants, O'Hagan could not be held liable under the disclose or abstain rule because he worked for the bidder but traded in target company stock. He was neither a classic insider nor a constructive insider of the issuer of the securities in which he traded.

4. O'Hagan: *Issues*

Both § 10(b) and Rule 10b–5 sweep broadly, capturing "any" fraudulent or manipulative conduct "in connection with" the purchase or sale of "any" security. Despite the almost breath-taking expanse of regulatory authority Congress thereby delegated to the

---

[63] 58 F.3d 933 (4th Cir.1995).

[64] 92 F.3d 612 (8th Cir.1996), rev'd, 521 U.S. 642 (1997).

Commission, the Supreme Court has warned against expanding the concept of securities fraud beyond that which the words of the statute will reasonably bear.[65] The validity of the misappropriation theory thus depends upon whether (1) the deceit, if any, worked by the misappropriator on the source of the information constitutes deception as the term is used in § 10(b) and Rule 10b–5 and (2) any such deceit is deemed to have occurred "in connection with" the purchase or sale of a security.

Deceit on the source of the information; herein of Santa Fe. In *Bryan*, the Fourth Circuit defined fraud—as the term is used in § 10(b) and Rule 10b–5—"as the making of a material misrepresentation or the nondisclosure of material information in violation of a duty to disclose."[66] So defined, fraud is present in a misappropriation case only in a technical and highly formalistic sense. Although a misappropriator arguably deceives the source of the information, any such deception is quite inconsequential. The source of the information presumably is injured, if at all, not by the deception, but by the conversion of the information by the misappropriator for his own profit. Hence, it is theft—and any concomitant breach of fiduciary duty—by the misappropriator that is truly objectionable. Any deception on the source of the information is purely incidental to the theft. Accordingly, the Fourth Circuit held, the misappropriation theory runs afoul of the Supreme Court's holding in *Santa Fe* that a mere breach of duty cannot give rise to Rule 10b–5 liability.

Recall that Santa Fe had attempted to freeze out minority shareholders of one of its subsidiaries by means of a statutory short-form merger. While plaintiff-shareholders had a state law remedy available in the statutory appraisal rights provision, they sought redress under Rule 10b–5 instead. They claimed that the merger violated Rule 10b–5 because the deal was effected without prior notice to the minority shareholders and was done without any legitimate business purpose. They also claimed that their shares had been fraudulently under-valued. In holding that plaintiffs had failed to state a cause of action under Rule 10b–5, the Supreme Court opined that § 10(b) and Rule 10b–5 were only intended to reach deception and manipulation—neither of which was present in the case at bar.

Santa Fe's requirement that conduct involve deception in order to fall within Rule 10b–5's scope featured prominently in the reasoning of those circuit courts that rejected the misappropriation theory. In *Bryan*, for example, the Fourth Circuit opined that "the

---

[65] Central Bank of Denver v. First Interstate Bank, 511 U.S. 164, 174 (1994).

[66] U.S. v. Bryan, 58 F.3d 933, 946 (4th Cir.1995).

misappropriation theory does not even require deception, but rather allows the imposition of liability upon the mere breach of fiduciary relationship or similar relationship of trust and confidence."[67] And, as such, ran afoul of *Santa Fe*.

Of even greater potential relevance to the problem at hand, however, is the *Santa Fe* Court's concern that a decision in favor of the plaintiffs would result in federalizing much of state corporate law.[68] *Santa Fe* is part of a long line of securities law cases in which the Supreme Court came down on the states' side of federalism disputes. For example, the Court has emphasized that "state regulation of corporate governance is regulation of entities whose very existence and attributes are a product of state law,"[69] from which the Court extrapolated the proposition that "it ... is an accepted part of the business landscape in this country for States to create corporations, to prescribe their powers, and to define the rights that are acquired by purchasing their shares." In keeping with that principle, the Court emphasized that state law governs the rights and duties of corporate directors: "As we have said in the past, the first place one must look to determine the powers of corporate directors is in the relevant State's corporation law. . . . 'Corporations are creatures of state law' ... and it is state law which is the font of corporate directors' powers."[70]

The insider trading prohibition co-exists uneasily with these principles, at best. In *Santa Fe*, for example, the Court held that Rule 10b–5 did not reach claims "in which the essence of the complaint is that shareholders were treated unfairly by a fiduciary."[71] Yet, this is the very essence of the complaint made in insider trading cases. The Court also held that extension of Rule 10b–5 to breaches of fiduciary duty was unjustified in light of the state law remedies available to plaintiffs. Likewise, insider trading plaintiffs have available state law remedies. Granted, these remedies vary from state to state and are likely to prove unavailing in many cases. The same was true, however, of the state law remedy at issue in *Santa Fe*. Finally, the Court expressed reluctance "to federalize the substantial portion of the law of

---

[67] U.S. v. Bryan, 58 F.3d 933, 949 (4th Cir.1995). This interpretation of the misappropriation theory is clearly incorrect post-*O'Hagan*, in light of the Supreme Court's requirement that the source of the information be deceived, and arguably misreads the pre-*O'Hagan* circuit court decisions endorsing the theory. Although courts adopting the misappropriation theory recognized that Rule 10b–5 only encompasses fraud and manipulation, they held that the deception the misappropriator works on the source of the information suffices to impose liability on him. See, e.g., United States v. Chestman, 947 F.2d 551, 566 (2d Cir.1991).

[68] See Santa Fe Industries, Inc. v. Green, 430 U.S. 462, 478–79 (1977).

[69] CTS Corp. v. Dynamics Corp., 481 U.S. 69, 89 (1987).

[70] Burks v. Lasker, 441 U.S. 471, 478 (1979) (citations omitted).

[71] Santa Fe Industries, Inc. v. Green, 430 U.S. 462, 477 (1977).

corporations that deals with transactions in securities, particularly where established state policies of corporate regulation would be overridden." But this is precisely what the federal insider trading prohibition did.

Santa Fe thus loomed as a substantial obstacle for proponents of an insider trading prohibition grounded in securities fraud. As the Fourth Circuit put it: "the misappropriation theory transforms Section 10(b) from a rule intended to govern and protect relations among market participants who are owed duties under the securities laws into a federal common law governing and protecting any and all trust relationships."[72] It thus amounts to "the effective federalization of [fiduciary] relationships historically regulated by the states," which is precisely what *Santa Fe* was intended to prevent.

The "in connection with" requirement; herein of Central Bank. According to the Eighth Circuit's *O'Hagan* opinion, "the misappropriation theory does not require 'deception,' and, even assuming that it does, it renders nugatory the requirement that the 'deception' be 'in connection with the purchase or sale of any security,' " as required by the text of § 10(b).[73] As such, the Eighth Circuit held that the theory ran afoul of the Supreme Court's *Central Bank*[74] decision.

Recall that *Central Bank* held the text of § 10(b) to be dispositive with respect to the scope of conduct regulated by that section. The Eighth Circuit interpreted the statutory prohibition of fraud created by § 10(b) narrowly to exclude conduct constituting a "mere breach of a fiduciary duty," but rather to capture only conduct constituting a material misrepresentation or the nondisclosure of material information in violation of the duty to disclose. Insofar as the misappropriation theory permits the imposition of § 10(b) liability based upon a breach of fiduciary duty without any such deception, the Eighth Circuit held that the theory was inconsistent with the plain statutory text of § 10(b) and, accordingly, invalid as per *Central Bank*.

The Eighth Circuit's principal rationale for rejecting the misappropriation theory, however, was based on the statutory limitation that the fraud be committed "in connection with" a securities transaction. Again relying upon the Supreme Court's *Central Bank* decision, the *O'Hagan* court gave this provision a narrow interpretation. Specifically, the court held that § 10(b) reaches "only a breach of a duty to parties to the securities

---

[72] See U.S. v. Bryan, 58 F.3d 933, 950 (4th Cir.1995).

[73] U.S. v. O'Hagan, 92 F.3d 612, 617 (8th Cir.1996), rev'd, 521 U.S. 642 (1997).

[74] Central Bank of Denver v. First Interstate Bank, 511 U.S. 164 (1994).

transaction or, at the most, to other market participants such as investors."[75] Absent such a limitation, the court opined, § 10(b) would be transformed "into an expansive 'general fraud-on-the-source theory' which seemingly would apply infinite number of trust relationships." Such an expansive theory of liability, the court further opined, could not be justified by the text of statute.

In the typical misappropriation case, of course, the source of the information is not the affected purchaser or seller. Often the source is not even a contemporaneous purchaser or seller and frequently has no stake in any affected securities transaction. In *Carpenter*, for example, the Wall Street Journal was neither a purchaser nor seller of the affected securities, nor did it have any financial stake in any of the affected transactions. Similarly, in *Bryan*, the state of West Virginia was not a purchaser or seller, and had no direct stake in Bryan's securities transactions. In neither case did the defendant fail to disclose material information to a market participant to whom he owed a duty of disclosure. One thus must stretch the phrase "in connection with" pretty far in order to bring a misappropriator's alleged fraud within the statute's ambit, even assuming the misappropriator has deceived the source of the information. As the Fourth Circuit put it: "The misappropriation of information from an individual who is in no way connected to, or even interested in, securities is simply not the kind of conduct with which the securities laws, as presently written, are concerned."[76]

The Eighth and Fourth Circuits' interpretation of § 10(b) has much to commend it. The courts carefully considered the Supreme Court's relevant precedents, especially *Santa Fe* and *Central Bank*. Insofar as the misappropriation theory imposes liability solely on the basis of a breach of fiduciary duty to the source of the information, without any requirement that the alleged perpetrator have deceived the persons with whom he traded or other market participants, it arguably ran afoul of those precedents. As the Eighth Circuit opined, the lower court decisions endorsing the misappropriation theory had generally failed to conduct a rigorous analysis of § 10(b)'s text or the pertinent Supreme Court decisions. Indeed, in a telling passage of his partial dissent to a leading Second Circuit opinion endorsing and fleshing out the misappropriation theory, Judge Winter (a former corporate law professor at Yale) stated the misappropriation theory lacked "any obvious relationship" to the statutory text of § 10(b) because "theft

---

[75] U.S. v. O'Hagan, 92 F.3d 612, 618 (8th Cir.1996), rev'd, 521 U.S. 642 (1997). In *Bryan*, the Fourth Circuit similarly opined § 10(b) is primarily concerned with deception of purchasers and sellers of securities, and at most extends to fraud committed against other persons closely linked to, and with a stake in, a securities transaction. U.S. v. Bryan, 58 F.3d 933, 946 (4th Cir.1995).

[76] U.S. v. Bryan, 58 F.3d 933, 950 (4th Cir.1995).

rather than fraud or deceit" had become "the gravamen of the prohibition."[77] In light of these considerations, reconciling the insider trading prohibition with *Central Bank* loomed as one of the major doctrinal problems facing the Supreme Court in *O'Hagan*.

5.   O'Hagan: *Holding*

In *O'Hagan*, a majority of the Supreme Court upheld the misappropriation theory as a valid basis on which to impose insider trading liability. A fiduciary's undisclosed use of information belonging to his principal, without disclosure of such use to the principal, for personal gain constitutes fraud in connection with the purchase or sale of a security, the majority (per Justice Ginsburg) opined, and thus violates Rule 10b–5.[78]

The court acknowledged that misappropriators such as O'Hagan have no disclosure obligation running to the persons with whom they trade. Instead, it grounded liability under the misappropriation theory on deception of the source of the information. As the majority interpreted the theory, it addresses the use of "confidential information for securities trading purposes, in breach of a duty owed to the source of the information." Under this theory, the majority explained, "a fiduciary's undisclosed, self serving use of a principal's information to purchase or sell securities, in breach of a duty of loyalty and confidentiality, defrauds the principal of the exclusive use of that information." So defined, the majority held, the misappropriation theory satisfies § 10(b)'s requirement that there be a "deceptive device or contrivance" used "in connection with" a securities transaction.[79]

Status of Central Bank: As we have just seen, the tension between *Central Bank* and the insider trading prohibition was a major doctrinal issue facing the court in *O'Hagan*. Surprisingly, however, the majority essentially punted on this issue. The majority ignored the statutory text, except for some rather glib assertions about the meaning of the phrases "deception" and "in connection with." The Supreme Court also ignored the cogent arguments advanced by both the Eighth and Fourth Circuits with respect to the implications of *Central Bank* for the misappropriation theory. To the extent the majority discussed *Central Bank*'s implications for

---

[77] United States v. Chestman, 947 F.2d 551, 578 (2d Cir.1991) (Winter, J., concurring in part and dissenting in part).

[78] United States v. O'Hagan, 521 U.S. 642 (1997).

[79] The Supreme Court thus rejected Chief Justice Burger's argument in *Chiarella* that the misappropriation theory created disclosure obligation running to those with whom the misappropriator trades. United States v. O'Hagan, 521 U.S. 642, 655 n. 6 (1997). Instead, it is the failure to disclose one's intentions to the source of the information that constitutes the requisite disclosure violation under the *O'Hagan* version of the misappropriation theory. Id. at 653–55.

the problem at hand, it focused solely on the Eighth Circuit's argument that *Central Bank* limited Rule 10b–5's regulatory purview to purchasers and sellers. The interpretive methodology expounded in *Central Bank* was essentially ignored. One is therefore left to wonder whether the strict textualist approach taken by *Central Bank* was a one time aberration.

The majority's failure to more carefully evaluate *Central Bank*'s implications for the phrase "in connection with," as used in § 10(b), is especially troubling. By virtue of the majority's holding that deception on the source of the information satisfies the "in connection with" requirement, fraudulent conduct having only tenuous connections to a securities transaction is brought within Rule 10b–5's scope. There has long been a risk that Rule 10b–5 will become a universal solvent, encompassing not only virtually the entire universe of securities fraud, but also much of state corporate law. The minimal contacts *O'Hagan* requires between the fraudulent act and a securities transaction substantially exacerbate that risk.[80] In addition to the risk that much of state corporate law may be preempted by federal developments under Rule 10b–5, the uncertainty created as to Rule 10b–5's parameters fairly raises vagueness and related due process issues, despite the majority's rather glib dismissal of such concerns.

Status of Santa Fe: The majority opinion treated *Santa Fe* as a mere disclosure case, asserting: "in *Santa Fe Industries*, all pertinent facts were disclosed by the persons charged with violating § 10(b) and Rule 10b–5; therefore, there was no deception through nondisclosure to which liability under those provisions could attach." Having done so, the majority then evaded the *Santa Fe* problem by redefining the misappropriation theory. The majority makes clear that the misappropriation theory is grounded not a breach of fiduciary duty, as some lower court precedents implied, but on nondisclosure. Under *O'Hagan,* liability potentially arises only where the misappropriator has a duty of disclosure to the source of the information. In turn, that duty arises out of a fiduciary relationship between the misappropriator and the source. Liability ultimately depends not on a breach of duty arising out of that relationship, however, but rather on the misappropriator's failure to disclose to the source his trading intentions.

The majority's analysis is problematic on at least two scores. First, the court's reconceptualization of *Santa Fe* as a disclosure case wholly ignored the important federalism concerns upon which *Santa Fe* rested and which are implicated by the misappropriation

---

[80] See also SEC v. Zandford, 535 U.S. 813 (2002) (holding that the "in connection with" requirement must be given a broad interpretation so as to achieve the remedial purposes of the Exchange Act).

theory (indeed, by the insider trading prohibition as a whole). Second, as we have noted at several points, different fiduciary relationships impose different obligations. In assuming that a duty of disclosure arises out of all fiduciary relationships, the majority comes perilously close to creating the very federal fiduciary principle *Santa Fe* was intended to preclude.

6.   Open Questions

In many respects, *O'Hagan* posed more new questions than it answered old ones. Here are some of the more interesting and important issues it left open:

Liability for brazen misappropriators? The *O'Hagan* majority made clear that disclosure to the source of the information is all that is required under Rule 10b–5. If a brazen misappropriator discloses his trading plans to the source, and then trades on that information, Rule 10b–5 is not violated, even if the source of the information refused permission to trade and objected vigorously.[81] This holding was necessitated by the court's need to finesse *Santa Fe*, as discussed above. If the brazen misappropriator were to be held liable, it could only be on the basis of a breach of fiduciary duty, since disclosure had been made. Hence, the brazen misappropriator must walk. If this rule seems odd, so did the majority's justification for it.

According to the majority, "investors likely would hesitate to venture their capital in a market where trading based on misappropriated nonpublic information is unchecked by law," because they suffer from "a disadvantage that cannot be overcome with research or skill." As such, the majority claimed, the misappropriation theory advances "an animating purpose of the Exchange Act: to ensure honest securities markets and thereby promote investor confidence."

The difficulties with this argument should be readily apparent. Investors who trade with a brazen misappropriator presumably will not feel any greater confidence in the integrity of the securities market if they later find out that the misappropriator had disclosed his intentions to the source of the information. Worse yet, both the phraseology and the substance of the majority's argument plausibly could be interpreted as resurrecting the long-discredited equal access test.[82] If the goal of insider trading law in fact is to insulate

---

[81] United States v. O'Hagan, 521 U.S. 642, 655 (1997) ("full disclosure forecloses liability under the misappropriation theory . . . if the fiduciary discloses to the source that he plans to trade on the nonpublic information, there is no 'deceptive device' and thus no § 10(b) violation").

[82] For an argument that *O'Hagan* is premised on equal access-related concerns, see Elliott J. Weiss, United States v. O'Hagan: Pragmatism returns to the Law of Insider Trading, 23 J. Corp. L. 395 (1998).

investors from information asymmetries that cannot be overcome by research or skill, the equal access test is far better suited to doing so than the current test.

Merely requiring the prospective misappropriator to disclose his intentions before trading also provides only weak protection of the source of the information's property rights in the information. To be sure, because of the disclosure requirement concerns about detecting improper trading are alleviated. As the majority pointed out, moreover, the source may have state law claims against the misappropriator. In particular, the agency law prohibition on the use of confidential information for personal gain will often provide a remedy to the source. In some jurisdictions, however, it is far from clear whether inside trading by a fiduciary violates state law. Even where state law proscribes such trading, the Supreme Court's approach means that in brazen misappropriator cases we lose the comparative advantage the SEC has in litigating insider trading cases and, moreover, also lose the comparative advantage provided by the well-developed and relatively liberal remedy under Rule 10b–5.

These issues received some treatment in *SEC v. Rocklage*,[83] in which the SEC brought a misappropriation theory-based insider trading charge against the spouse of a CEO who had passed material nonpublic information about her husband's company to her brother and his friend who then traded. As the court summarized the issue:

> The defendants' view is that a pre-tip disclosure to the source of an intention to trade or tip completely eliminates any deception involved in the transaction. They rely on O'Hagan's language that "if the fiduciary discloses to the source that he plans to trade on the nonpublic information, there is no 'deceptive device' and thus no § 10(b) violation." The defendants argue that O'Hagan put no qualifiers on what is meant by "disclos[ure] to the source" of a plan to trade on nonpublic information, and so the SEC is not free to qualify the concept.

> The SEC disagrees, arguing that the disclosure referenced in *O'Hagan* must mean disclosure that is "useful" to the fiduciary's principal. The SEC draws support from a footnote in *O'Hagan* which may be read as implying that disclosure enables a source to take remedial action. As the SEC sees it, disclosure to the source serves a useful purpose when "the source of material non-public information reasonably could be expected to, and

---

[83] 470 F.3d 1 (1st Cir.2006).

reasonably could, prevent the unauthorized use of the information for securities trading."

The First Circuit rejected both positions. Instead, the court opined that:

Unlike this case, *O'Hagan* was not a case which involved the deceptive acquisition of information. Arguably, the language in O'Hagan can be read to create a "safe harbor" if there is disclosure to the fiduciary principal of an intention to trade on or tip legitimately acquired information. This is because under O'Hagan's logic such a "safe harbor" applies, if at all, when the alleged deception is in the undisclosed trading or tipping of information. In those cases, disclosure of the intent to trade arguably will eliminate the sole source of deception. But a case of deceptive acquisition of information followed by deceptive tipping and trading is different. It makes little sense to assume that disclosure of an intention to tip using deceptively acquired information would necessarily negate the original deception.

This reading of *O'Hagan* likely guts the brazen misappropriator loophole. If the "safe harbor" is limited to cases in which the alleged misappropriator "legitimately" acquires the information, the vast majority of misappropriation cases likely will be ineligible for the safe harbor.

Suppose for example the following: CEO discloses to CLO material nonpublic information. At the time the CLO receives the information, she plans to trade on the basis of it, but she does not disclose that intent to the CEO at that time. Sometime later, just as the CLO is about to trade, she discloses her plans to the CEO. Presumably, the First Circuit would tell us that the failure to disclose her intentions at the time she first received the information meant that she committed deception in acquiring the information and that her subsequent disclosure therefore does not preclude liability.

Liability for authorized trading? Suppose a takeover bidder authorized an arbitrageur to trade in a target company's stock on the basis of material nonpublic information about the prospective bidder's intentions. Warehousing of this sort is proscribed by Rule 14e–3, but only insofar as the information relates to a prospective tender offer. Whether such trading in a nontender offer context violated Rule 10b–5 was unclear before *O'Hagan*.

The *O'Hagan* majority at least implicitly validated authorized trading. It approvingly quoted, for example, the statement of the government's counsel that to satisfy the common law rule that a trustee may not use the property that [has] been entrusted [to] him, there would have to be consent.[84] On the facts of *O'Hagan*, as the majority indicated, insiders would need approval from both Dorsey & Whitney and Grand Met in order to escape Rule 10b–5 liability. Is it plausible that Grand Met would have given such approval? Maybe. Warehousing of takeover stocks and tipping acquisition plans to friendly parties were once common—hence the need for Rule 14e–3—and probably still occurs.

Notice the interesting question presented by the requirement that O'Hagan disclose his intentions to Dorsey & Whitney. Given that O'Hagan was a partner in Dorsey & Whitney, query whether his knowledge of his intentions would be imputed to the firm. As a practical matter, of course, O'Hagan should have informed the lawyer with the principal responsibility for the Grand Met transaction and/or the firm's managing partner.

The authorized trading dictum has significant, but as yet little-noticed, implications. Query, for example, whether it applies to all insider trading cases or just to misappropriation cases. Suppose that in a classic disclose or abstain case, such as *Texas Gulf Sulphur*, the issuer's board of directors adopted a policy of allowing insider trading by managers. If they did so, the corporation has consented to any such inside trading, which under Justice Ginsburg's analysis appears to vitiate any deception. The corporate policy itself presumably would have to be disclosed, just as broad disclosure respecting executive compensation is already required, but the implication is that authorized trading should not result in 10b–5 liability under either misappropriation or disclose or abstain theory of liability.

On the other hand, the two theories can be distinguished in ways that undermine application of the authorized trading dictum to disclose or abstain cases. In a misappropriation case, such as *Carpenter*, liability is premised on fraud on the source of the information. In *Carpenter*, acting through appropriate decision making processes, the Journal could authorize inside trading by its agents. By contrast, however, *Chiarella* focused the classic disclose or abstain rule on fraud perpetrated on the specific investors with whom the insiders trade. Authorization of inside trading by the issuer's board of directors, or even a majority of the shareholders, does not constitute consent by the specific investors with whom the insider trades. Nothing in *O'Hagan* explicitly suggests an intent to undermine the *Chiarella* interpretation of the traditional disclose or abstain rule. To the contrary, Justice Ginsburg expressly states that

---

[84] United States v. O'Hagan, 521 U.S. 642, 654 (1997).

the two theories are "complementary." Because the disclose or abstain rule thus remains conceptually distinct from the misappropriation theory, the authorized trading dictum can be plausibly limited to the latter context.

The fiduciary relationship requirement. Does a duty to disclose to the source of the information arise before trading in all fiduciary relationships? Consider ABA Model Rule of Professional Conduct 1.8(b), which states: "A lawyer shall not use information relating to representation of a client to the disadvantage of the client unless the client consents after consultation. . . ." Does a lawyer's use of confidential client information for insider trading purposes always operate to the client's disadvantage? If not, and assuming the Model Rule accurately states the lawyer's fiduciary obligation, O'Hagan did not violate § 10(b).

The *O'Hagan* majority, however, failed to inquire into the nature of O'Hagan's duties, if any, to Grand Met. Instead, the majority assumed that lawyers are fiduciaries, all fiduciaries are subject to a duty to refrain from self-dealing in confidential information, and, accordingly, that the misappropriation theory applies to lawyers and all other fiduciaries. The majority's approach, of course, begs the question—how do we know O'Hagan is a fiduciary?

Criminal or civil? In rejecting the Eighth Circuit's argument that Rule 10b–5 is primarily concerned with deception of market participants, the majority noted that the discussion in *Central Bank* upon which the Eighth Circuit relied dealt only with private civil litigation under § 10(b). The court then went on to discuss its holding in *Blue Chip Stamps*[85] that only actual purchasers or sellers of securities have standing to bring private causes of action under Rule 10b–5. The court concluded: "Criminal prosecutions do not present the dangers the Court addressed in *Blue Chip Stamps*, so that decision is 'inapplicable' to indictments for violations of § 10(b) and Rule 10b–5."[86]

This passage opens the door for misappropriators to argue that *O'Hagan* should be limited to criminal prosecutions, because the majority acknowledged the limitations imposed by *Central Bank* and *Blue Chip Stamps* on private party litigation. Such a limitation on private party litigation, however, seems unlikely. Although the majority declined to address the significance of the 1988 statute and its legislative history for the validity of the misappropriation theory, interpreting *O'Hagan* as validating the misappropriation theory

---

[85] Blue Chip Stamps v. Manor Drug Stores, 421 U.S. 723 (1975).

[86] United States v. O'Hagan, 521 U.S. 642, 665 (1997).

only as to criminal actions would render the private party cause of action created by Exchange Act § 20A nugatory.

§ 11.5   Elements of the Modern Prohibition

A. Material Nonpublic Information

In cases arising under § 10(b) and Rule 10b–5, liability arises only with respect to the misuse of material information. Materiality is defined for this purpose as whether there is a substantial likelihood that a reasonable investor would consider the omitted fact important in deciding whether to buy or sell securities.[87] Where a fact is contingent or speculative, such as was the case in *Texas Gulf Sulphur*, materiality is determined by balancing the indicated probability that the event will occur and the anticipated magnitude of the event in light of the totality of the company's activity.

In a case like *Texas Gulf Sulphur*, it is just as important to determine when the information in question became material as it is to determine whether the information was material. Consider how the materiality standard would apply at two critical dates: November 12, when the visual assay indicated a potentially significant ore strike, and April 7, when the results of additional test holes confirmed that mining would be commercially viable.

Under these standards, the ore discovery was certainly material as of April 7. The additional test holes had confirmed that the initial core sample was not an aberration—TGS really had a major find on its hands. After April 7, the critical issue is not whether the strike will pay off, but when. The balancing test thus is not at issue, because we are no longer dealing with a contingent fact. Given the size of the discovery, this was certainly information any reasonable investor would consider significant.

It is less clear that the information known on November 12th would be regarded as material as of that date. Before April there was only one core sample. While that sample was remarkable, only a highly trained geologist would be able to draw conclusions from it. Since it would take a highly sophisticated investor with considerable expertise in mining operations to understand the relevance of the find, perhaps the hypothetical reasonable investor would not consider it important. On the other hand, however, there was testimony from a stock broker that one good test hole was a signal to buy mining stock.[88]

---

[87] Basic Inc. v. Levinson, 485 U.S. 224, 231–32 (1988).

[88] SEC v. Texas Gulf Sulphur Co., 401 F.2d 833, 850–51 (2d Cir.1968), cert. denied, 394 U.S. 976 (1969).

One might also consider the response of the company and the insiders. The firm's decision to acquire options on the surrounding land tends to point towards a finding of materiality. According to the court, so did the insiders' own trading conduct, although this is a somewhat dubious proposition in view of the resulting bootstrapping effect.

B. The Requisite Fiduciary Relationship

After *Chiarella*, liability for insider trading could be imposed only on persons who owe fiduciary duties to those with whom they trade: agents, fiduciaries, persons in whom the investors had placed their trust and confidence.[89] Unfortunately, the Supreme Court has failed to do a very good job of fleshing out this requirement. Is it enough that a fiduciary relationship exist, without any breach of the duties arising out of it? If a breach is required, which duty must be breached? What law determines whether the requisite fiduciary relationship and/or breach of duty is present in a particular fact pattern? Under state law, for example, corporate officers and directors generally owe no fiduciary duty to bondholders. Can insiders therefore inside trade in debt securities with impunity? Although corporate officers and directors owe fiduciary duties to their shareholders, we've seen that in many states insider trading does not breach those duties. Can insiders of firms incorporated in those states inside trade with impunity?

In both *Chiarella* and *Dirks*, the Supreme Court frequently spoke of the need to show the existence of a "fiduciary relationship" as a predicate to liability.[90] Yet, surely that is not enough. As Justice Frankfurter put it, albeit in a different context, "to say that a man is a fiduciary only begins analysis; it gives direction to further inquiry. To whom is he a fiduciary? What obligations does he owe as a fiduciary? In what respect has he failed to discharge those obligations?"[91] In other words, it should not be enough to establish the existence of a fiduciary relationship. Before liability can be imposed one must also establish that the defendant violated

---

[89] "When an allegation of fraud is based upon nondisclosure, there can be no fraud absent a duty to speak," and no such duty arises "from the mere possession of nonpublic market information." Chiarella v. United States, 445 U.S. 222, 235 (1980). Thus, there can be no duty to disclose where the person who has traded on or tipped inside information "was not [the corporation's] agent, ... was not a fiduciary, [or] was not a person in whom the sellers [of the securities] had placed their trust and confidence." Id. at 232; accord Dirks v. SEC, 463 U.S. 646, 653–55 (1983).

[90] E.g., Dirks v. SEC, 463 U.S. 646, 654 (1983); Chiarella v. United States, 445 U.S. 222, 232 (1980).

[91] SEC v. Chenery Corp., 318 U.S. 80, 85–86 (1943).

a fiduciary duty arising out of the fiduciary relationship in question.[92]

In any fiduciary relationship, however, a variety of duties may arise. Which is the duty whose violation triggers insider trading liability? Again, the Court has not been very precise on this score. It has spoken mainly of a duty to disclose before trading arising out of a relationship of trust and confidence. While so describing the duty perhaps sufficed for purposes of applying the disclose or abstain rule to trading insiders, it created analytical problems when the insider tipped information rather than trading on it. The duty to disclose phraseology created even greater problems when the misappropriation theory was created. Given that Chiarella owed no fiduciary duties to the investors with whom he traded, for example, he plainly owed those investors no duty to disclose nonpublic information before trading.

Faced with these problems, some lower courts switched the inquiry to whether the defendant was subject to a duty of confidentiality.[93] Using a duty of confidentiality as the requisite fiduciary duty, however, makes little sense in the insider trading context. Unlike most types of tangible property, the same piece of information can be used by more than one person at the same time; an insider's use of the information, moreover, does not necessarily lower its value to its owner. When an executive that has just negotiated a major contract for his employer thereafter inside trades in the employer's stock, for example, the value of the contract to the employer has not been lowered nor, absent some act of disclosure, has the executive violated his duty of confidentiality. Using nonpublic information for personal gain thus is not inconsistent with a duty of confidentiality, unless one's trades somehow reveal the information.[94]

---

[92] This conclusion is supported by the Supreme Court's treatment of tippee liability. It is not enough to show that the tipper was party to a fiduciary relationship with the source of the information. As we have seen, there must also be a breach of the tipper's fiduciary duty before tippee liability can result. That this requirement extends to insider trading liability generally seems reasonably clear from *Dirks'* discussion of *Chiarella*. See Dirks v. SEC, 463 U.S. 646, 653–54 (1983).

[93] See, e.g., United States v. Libera, 989 F.2d 596 (2d Cir.1993), cert. denied, 510 U.S. 976 (1993); United States v. Carpenter, 791 F.2d 1024, 1034 (2d Cir.1986), aff'd on other grounds, 484 U.S. 19 (1987). Note that these cases arose in the employment context, in which it is thought that an implicit duty to refrain from self-dealing is created by agency law. Those courts thus did not have to face, let alone resolve, the potential disparity between a duty of confidentiality and a duty to refrain from self-dealing.

[94] See, e.g., U.S. v. Kim, 184 F.Supp.2d 1006, 1010 (N.D.Cal.2002) (holding that "exchange of confidential information, alone, does not give rise to a fiduciary-like relationship"). Having said that, however, one is constrained to note that in the misappropriation context there seems to be a growing judicial acceptance, reinforced by recent SEC regulatory action, that a duty of confidentiality suffices. In the misappropriation context, however, the trend is to say that breach of a mere duty of confidentiality suffices. See, e.g., SEC v. Yun, 327 F.3d 1263, 1272–73 (11th

The fiduciary duty requirement therefore should be satisfied only by a duty to refrain from self-dealing in nonpublic information. This conclusion finds considerably greater support in *Dirks* than does the duty of confidentiality approach. Justice Powell, for example, described the elements of an insider trading violation as: "(i) the existence of a relationship affording access to inside information intended to be available only for a corporate purpose, and (ii) the unfairness of allowing a corporate insider to take advantage of that information by trading without disclosure." Another passage likewise described insider trading liability as arising from "the 'inherent unfairness involved where one takes advantage' of 'information intended to be available only for a corporate purpose and not for the personal benefit of anyone.'" Yet another noted that insiders are "forbidden by their fiduciary relationship from personally using undisclosed corporate information to their advantage." The focus in each instance is on the duty to refrain from self-dealing.

The emphasis on self-dealing, rather than confidentiality, is further confirmed by the result in *Dirks*. Secrist violated his duty of confidentiality by disclosing the information to Dirks. Yet, the fact of the tip alone did not suffice for liability to be imposed. Rather, as we have seen, the court held that liability could be imposed only if Secrist had made the tip for personal gain, in other words, only if the tip involved self-dealing. Hence, mere violation of the duty of confidentiality is not enough. Rather, a duty to disclose before trading arises only if trading would violate a duty to refrain from self-dealing in confidential information owed by the trader to the owner of that information.

To be clear, I am not arguing that liability under the classic disclose or abstain theory is based on a breach of fiduciary duty. Any such implication in *Dirks* or *Chiarella* was clearly laid to rest by *O'Hagan*'s emphasis on nondisclosure as the basis of liability under Rule 10b–5. Instead, I am suggesting that the duty to disclose arises under the classical disclose or abstain theory where (1) the insider has a fiduciary relationship to those with whom he trades and/or the issuer of the securities in which he trades and (2) the obligations inherent in that relationship include a duty to

Cir.2003) (holding that "a spouse who trades in breach of a reasonable and legitimate expectation of confidentiality held by the other spouse sufficiently subjects the former to insider trading liability .... Of course, a breach of an agreement to maintain business confidences would also suffice."); SEC v. Kirch, 263 F.Supp.2d 1144 (N.D.Ill.2003) (holding "that the 'duty of loyalty and confidentiality' owed by the outsider ... to the person ... who shared confidential information with him or her ... is not limited to fiduciary relationships in the limited sense that requires such factors as control and dominance on the part of the fiduciary. Instead that 'duty of loyalty and confidentiality' can be (and is) created by precisely the type of [confidentiality] policy and expectations that are present ... here ...."). The SEC has now codified this position in Rule 10b5–2(b).

refrain from self-dealing in confidential information. In turn, liability under Rule 10b–5 is based not on a breach of that duty but rather on the failure to make the requisite disclosure.

C. Who Is an Insider?

The term insider trading is something of a misnomer. It conjures up images of corporate directors or officers using secret information to buy stock from (or sell it to) unsuspecting investors. To be sure, the modern federal insider trading prohibition proscribes a corporation's officers and directors from trading on the basis of material nonpublic information about their firm, but it also casts a far broader net. Consider the following people who have been convicted of insider trading:

- A partner in a law firm representing the acquiring company in a hostile takeover bid who traded in target company stock.[95]

- A Wall Street Journal columnist who traded prior to publication of his column in the stock of companies he wrote about.[96]

- A psychiatrist who traded on the basis of information learned from a patient.[97]

- A financial printer who traded in the stock of companies about which he was preparing disclosure documents.[98]

Consequently, the phrase insider trading thus includes a wide range of individuals who trade in a corporation's stock on the basis of material information unknown by the investing public at large.

It seems reasonably clear that the principal task in this area is to determine whether a fiduciary relationship exists between the inside trader and the person with whom he trades. Whether that determination is made as a matter of state or federal law, unfortunately, remains unclear. *O'Hagan* confirms that the attorney-client relationship is a fiduciary one. Dictum in all three Supreme Court precedents tells us that corporate officers and directors are fiduciaries of their shareholders. Beyond these two categories we must make educated guesses. Until a majority of the Supreme Court has held that a particular relationship is fiduciary in nature, however, we cannot know for sure.

---

[95] U.S. v. O'Hagan, 521 U.S. 642 (1997).

[96] United States v. Carpenter, 791 F.2d 1024 (2d Cir.1986), aff'd on other grounds, 484 U.S. 19 (1987).

[97] United States v. Willis, 737 F.Supp. 269 (S.D.N.Y.1990).

[98] Chiarella v. United States, 445 U.S. 222 (1980).

1.   Classic Insiders

At common law, the insider trading prohibition focused on corporate officers and directors. The short-swing profit insider trading restrictions provided by § 16(b) similarly are limited to officers, directors, and shareholders owning more than 10 percent of the company's stock. One of the many issues first addressed in the seminal *Texas Gulf Sulphur* case was whether § 10(b) was restricted to that class of persons. Some of the *Texas Gulf Sulphur* defendants were middle managers and field workers. The *Texas Gulf Sulphur* court had little difficulty finding that such mid-level corporate employees were insiders for purposes of § 10(b). But that holding followed directly from the court's equal access test: "Insiders, as directors or management officers are, of course, by this Rule, precluded from [insider] dealing, but the Rule is also applicable to one possessing [nonpublic] information who may not be strictly termed an 'insider' within the meaning of [section] 16(b) of the Act."[99] *Chiarella's* rejection of the equal access test thus reopened the question of how far down the corporate ladder Rule 10b–5 extended.

Recall that the Supreme Court had said Chiarella could not be held liable under Rule 10b–5 because, as to the target companies' shareholders, "he was not their agent, he was not a fiduciary, [and] he was not a person in whom the sellers had placed their trust and confidence."[100] Were the TGS geologists who discovered the ore deposit persons in whom TGS' shareholders placed their trust and confidence? Presumably not, because TGS' shareholders likely did not even know of their existence. On the other hand, the geologists were agents of TGS and, as such, likely would be deemed fiduciaries of TGS' shareholders for purposes of Rule 10b–5. Although the question of whether all corporate employees will be deemed insiders remains open, there seems little doubt that the insider trading prohibition includes not only directors and officers, but also at least those key employees who have been given access to confidential information for corporate purposes. In *Chiarella*, the majority opinion implied that the duty to disclose or abstain applies to anyone in "a relationship [with the issuer] affording access to inside information intended to be available only for a corporate purpose." The Second Circuit likewise has stated that: "it is well settled that traditional corporate 'insiders'—directors, officers and persons who have access to confidential corporate information—must preserve

---

[99] SEC v. Texas Gulf Sulphur Co., 401 F.2d 833, 848 (2d Cir.1968), cert. denied, 394 U.S. 976 (1969).

[100] Chiarella v. United States, 445 U.S. 222, 232 (1980).

the confidentiality of nonpublic information that belongs to and emanates from the corporation."[101]

Suppose, however, that the TGS geologists had written a memo to their supervisor describing the ore discovery. A TGS janitor discovered a draft of the memo in the trash and bought a few shares. Although the janitor may be an agent of TGS, the janitor is not a key employee given access to confidential information for a corporate purpose. It is therefore doubtful whether the janitor should be regarded as an insider for Rule 10b–5 purposes.

2. Constructive Insiders

In *Dirks*, the Supreme Court made clear that the disclose or abstain rule picks up a variety of nominal outsiders whose relationship to the issuer is sufficiently close to justify treating them as "constructive insiders":

> Under certain circumstances, such as where corporate information is revealed legitimately to an underwriter, accountant, lawyer, or consultant working for the corporation, these outsiders may become fiduciaries of the shareholders. The basis for recognizing this fiduciary duty is not simply that such persons acquired nonpublic corporate information, but rather that they have entered into a special confidential relationship in the conduct of the business of the enterprise and are given access to information solely for corporate purposes. . . . For such a duty to be imposed, however, the corporation must expect the outsider to keep the disclosed nonpublic information confidential, and the relationship at least must imply such a duty.[102]

A firm's outside legal counsel are widely assumed to be paradigmatic constructive insiders.[103] Yet, there still must be a relationship with the issuer. In *O'Hagan*, for example, the defendant could not be held liable under the disclose or abstain rule as a constructive insider because he worked for the bidder but traded in target company stock.

Although *Dirks* clearly requires that the recipient of the information in some way agree to keep it confidential, courts have sometimes overlooked that requirement. In *SEC v. Lund*,[104] for example, Lund and another businessman discussed a proposed joint

---

[101] Moss v. Morgan Stanley Inc., 719 F.2d 5, 10 (2d Cir.1983), cert. denied, 465 U.S. 1025 (1984).

[102] Dirks v. SEC, 463 U.S. 646, 655 n. 14 (1983).

[103] See, e.g., United States v. Elliott, 711 F.Supp. 425, 432 (N.D.Ill.1989).

[104] 570 F.Supp. 1397 (C.D.Cal.1983).

venture between their respective companies. In those discussions, Lund received confidential information about the other's firm. Lund thereafter bought stock in the other's company. The court determined that by virtue of their close personal and professional relationship, and because of the business context of the discussion, Lund was a constructive insider of the issuer. In doing so, however, the court focused almost solely on the issuer's expectation of confidentiality. It failed to inquire into whether Lund had agreed to keep the information confidential.

Lund is usefully contrasted with *Walton v. Morgan Stanley & Co.*[105] Morgan Stanley represented a company considering acquiring Olinkraft Corporation in a friendly merger. During exploratory negotiations Olinkraft gave Morgan confidential information. Morgan's client ultimately decided not to pursue the merger, but Morgan allegedly later passed the acquired information to another client planning a tender offer for Olinkraft. In addition, Morgan's arbitrage department made purchases of Olinkraft stock for its own account. The Second Circuit held that Morgan was not a fiduciary of Olinkraft: "Put bluntly, although, according to the complaint, Olinkraft's management placed its confidence in Morgan Stanley not to disclose the information, Morgan owed no duty to observe that confidence." Although *Walton* was decided under state law, it has been cited approvingly in a number of federal insider trading opinions and is generally regarded as a more accurate statement of the law than *Lund*.[106] Indeed, a subsequent case from the same district court as *Lund* essentially acknowledged that it had been wrongly decided:

> What the Court seems to be saying in *Lund* is that anytime a person is given information by an issuer with an expectation of confidentiality or limited use, he becomes an insider of the issuer. But under *Dirks*, that is not enough; the individual must have expressly or impliedly entered into a fiduciary relationship with the issuer.[107]

Even this statement does not go far enough, however, because it does not acknowledge the additional requirement of an affirmative assumption of the duty of confidentiality.[108]

---

[105] 623 F.2d 796 (2d Cir.1980).

[106] See, e.g., Dirks v. SEC, 463 U.S. 646, 662 n. 22 (1983); United States v. Chestman, 947 F.2d 551, 567–68 (2d Cir.1991), cert. denied, 503 U.S. 1004 (1992); Moss v. Morgan Stanley Inc., 719 F.2d 5 (2d Cir.1983), cert. denied, 465 U.S. 1025 (1984).

[107] SEC v. Ingram, 694 F.Supp. 1437, 1440 n. 3 (C.D.Cal.1988).

[108] SEC Rule 10b5–2(b)(1) states that the requisite "duty of trust or confidence" exists whenever "a person agrees to maintain information in confidence." While the Rule thus suggests that a mere contractual confidentiality obligation suffices, the Rule preserves the requirement of an affirmative assumption of that obligation. In

3.   Tippers and Tippees

Recall that under *Dirks* tippees are only liable if two conditions are met: (1) the tipper breached a fiduciary duty to the corporation by making the tip and (2) the tippee knew or had reason to know of the breach. The requirement that the tip constitute a breach of duty on the tipper's part eliminates many cases in which an insider discloses information to an outsider. Hence, the SEC's decision to adopt Regulation FD as a mechanism for proscribing selective disclosure without reliance on the *Dirks* formulation.

Indeed, not every disclosure made in violation of a fiduciary duty constitutes an illegal tip. What *Dirks* proscribes is not just a breach of duty, however, but a breach of the duty of loyalty forbidding fiduciaries to personally benefit from the disclosure. An instructive case is *SEC v. Switzer*,[109] which involved Barry Switzer, the well-known former coach of the Oklahoma Sooners and Dallas Cowboys football teams. Phoenix Resources Company was an oil and gas company. One fine day in 1981, Phoenix's CEO, one George Platt, and his wife attended a track meet to watch their son compete. Coach Switzer was also at the meet, watching his son. Platt and Switzer had known each other for some time. Platt had Oklahoma season tickets and his company had sponsored Switzer's television show. Sometime in the afternoon Switzer laid down on a row of bleachers behind the Platts to sunbathe. Platt, purportedly unaware of Switzer's presence, began telling his wife about a recent business trip to New York. In that conversation, Platt mentioned his desire to dispose of or liquidate Phoenix. Platt further talked about several companies bidding on Phoenix. Platt also mentioned that an announcement of a "possible" liquidation of Phoenix might occur the following Thursday. Switzer overheard this conversation and shortly thereafter bought a substantial number of Phoenix shares and tipped off a number of his friends. Because Switzer was neither an insider or constructive insider of Phoenix, the main issue was whether Platt had illegally tipped Switzer.

Per *Dirks*, the initial issue was whether Platt had violated his fiduciary duty by obtaining an improper personal benefit: "Absent some personal gain, there has been no breach of duty to stockholders. And absent a breach by the insider [to his stockholders], there is no derivative breach [by the tippee]." The court found that Platt did not obtain any improper benefit. The court further found that the information was inadvertently (and unbeknownst to Platt) overheard by Switzer. Chatting about

---

any event, the Rule is limited on its face to cases arising under the misappropriation theory.

[109] 590 F.Supp. 756 (W.D.Okla.1984).

business with one's spouse in a public place may be careless, but it is not a breach of one's duty of loyalty.

The next issue is whether Switzer knew or should have known of the breach. Given that there was no breach by Platt, of course, this prong of the *Dirks* test by definition could not be met. But it is instructive that the court went on to explicitly hold that "Rule 10b–5 does not bar trading on the basis of information inadvertently revealed by an insider."

4.   *Nontraditional Relationships*

Once we get outside the traditional categories of Rule 10b–5 defendants—insiders, constructive insiders, and their tippees— things get much more complicated. Suppose a doctor learned confidential information from a patient, upon which she then traded? Is she an insider? As the Second Circuit observed in *United States v. Chestman*:

> [F]iduciary duties are circumscribed with some clarity in the context of shareholder relations but lack definition in other contexts. Tethered to the field of shareholder relations, fiduciary obligations arise within a narrow, principled sphere. The existence of fiduciary duties in other common law settings, however, is anything but clear. Our Rule 10b–5 precedents . . ., moreover, provide little guidance with respect to the question of fiduciary breach, because they involved egregious fiduciary breaches arising solely in the context of employer/employee associations.[110]

At issue in that case was inside trading by a member of the Waldbaum family in stock of a corporation controlled by that family. Ira Waldbaum was the president and controlling shareholder of Waldbaum, Inc., a publicly-traded supermarket chain. Ira decided to sell Waldbaum to A & P at $50 per share, a 100% premium over the prevailing market price. Ira informed his sister Shirley of the forthcoming transaction. Shirley told her daughter Susan Loeb, who in turn told her husband Keith Loeb. Each person in the chain told the next to keep the information confidential. Keith passed an edited version of the information to his stockbroker, one Robert Chestman, who then bought Waldbaum stock for his own account and the accounts of other clients. Chestman was accused of violating Rule 10b–5. According to the Government's theory of the case, Keith Loeb owed fiduciary duties to his wife Susan, which he violated by trading and tipping Chestman.

---

[110] 947 F.2d 551, 567 (2d Cir.1991) (citations omitted), cert. denied, 503 U.S. 1004 (1992).

The Second Circuit held that in the absence of any evidence that Keith regularly participated in confidential business discussions, the familial relationship standing alone did not create a fiduciary relationship between Keith and Susan or any members of her family. Accordingly, Loeb's actions did not give rise to the requisite breach of fiduciary duty.

In reaching that conclusion, the court laid out a general framework for dealing with nontraditional relationships. The court began by identifying two factors that did not, standing alone, justify finding a fiduciary relationship between Keith and Susan. First, unilaterally entrusting someone with confidential information does not by itself create a fiduciary relationship.[111] This is true even if the disclosure is accompanied by an admonition such as "don't tell," which Susan's statements to Keith included. Second, familial relationships are not fiduciary in nature without some additional element.

Turning to factors that could justify finding a fiduciary relationship on these facts, the court first identified a list of "inherently fiduciary" associations:

> Counted among these hornbook fiduciary relations are those existing between attorney and client, executor and heir, guardian and ward, principal and agent, trustee and trust beneficiary, and senior corporate official and shareholder. While this list is by no means exhaustive, it is clear that the relationships involved in this case—those between Keith and Susan Loeb and between Keith Loeb and the Waldbaum family—were not traditional fiduciary relationships.

A rather serious problem with the *Chestman* court's glib assertion that the specified relationships are "inherently fiduciary" is the resulting failure to seriously evaluate whether any duty arising out of such relationships was violated by the defendant's conduct. In *United States v. Willis*,[112] for example, the court determined that a psychiatrist violated the prohibition by trading on information learned from a patient. In determining that the requisite breach of fiduciary duty had occurred, the court relied in large measure on the Hippocratic Oath. In relevant part, the Oath reads: "Whatsoever things I see or hear concerning the life of men, in my attendance on the sick or even apart therefrom, which ought not to

---

[111] Repeated disclosures of business secrets, however, could substitute for a factual finding of dependence and influence and, accordingly, sustain a finding that a fiduciary relationship existed in the case at bar. U.S. v. Chestman, 947 F.2d 551, 569 (2d Cir.1991), cert. denied, 503 U.S. 1004 (1992). Hence, the court's emphasis on the absence of such repeated disclosures as between Keith and Susan or her family.

[112] 737 F.Supp. 269 (S.D.N.Y.1990).

be noised abroad, I will keep silence thereon, counting such things to be as sacred secrets." While the Oath thus imposes a duty of confidentiality on those who take it, it does not forbid them from self-dealing in information learned from patients so long as the information is not thereby disclosed. As such, it is not at all clear that the requisite breach of duty was present in *Willis*. Unfortunately, as *Willis* illustrates, these issues routinely are swept under the rug.

In any event, once one moves beyond the class of "hornbook" fiduciary relationships, *Chestman* held that the requisite relationship will be found where one party acts on the other's behalf and "great trust and confidence" exists between the parties:

> A fiduciary relationship involves discretionary authority and dependency: One person depends on another—the fiduciary—to serve his interests. In relying on a fiduciary to act for his benefit, the beneficiary of the relation may entrust the fiduciary with custody over property of one sort or another. Because the fiduciary obtains access to this property to serve the ends of the fiduciary relationship, he becomes duty-bound not to appropriate the property for his own use.[113]

In the insider trading context, of course, the relevant property is confidential information belonging to the principal. Because the relationship between Keith and Susan did not involve either discretionary authority or dependency of this sort, their relationship was not fiduciary in character.

In 2000, the SEC addressed the *Chestman* problem by adopting Rule 10b5–2, which provides "a nonexclusive list of three situations in which a person has a duty of trust or confidence for purposes of the 'misappropriation' theory...."[114] First, such a duty exists whenever someone agrees to maintain information in confidence.[115] Second, such a duty exists between two people who have a pattern or practice of sharing confidences such that the recipient of the information knows or reasonably should know that the speaker

---

[113] U.S. v. Chestman, 947 F.2d 551, 569 (2d Cir.1991), cert. denied, 503 U.S. 1004 (1992). But see SEC v. Kirch, 263 F.Supp.2d 1144 (N.D.Ill.2003) (holding "that the 'duty of loyalty and confidentiality' . . . is not limited to fiduciary relationships in the limited sense that requires such factors as control and dominance on the part of the fiduciary").

[114] Exchange Act Rel. No. 43,154 (Aug. 15, 2000).

[115] Rule 10b5–2's imposition of liability whenever someone agrees to maintain information in confidence is inconsistent with the emphasis in *Chiarella* and its progeny on the need for a duty of disclosure that arises out of a relationship of trust and confidence. Whether the SEC has authority to create a rule imposing misappropriation liability on the basis of an arms-length contractual duty of confidentiality—as opposed to a fiduciary duty-based duty of confidentiality—has not been tested.

expects the recipient to maintain the information's confidentiality. Third, such a duty exists when someone receives or obtains material nonpublic information from a spouse, parent, child, or sibling. On the facts of *Chestman*, accordingly, Rule 10b5–2 would result in the imposition of liability because Keith received the information from his spouse who, in turn, had received it from her parent.

    5.   *What Does "Other Relationship of Trust and Confidence" Mean?*

    In *Chiarella*, the Supreme Court referred to a disclosure obligation arising out of a relationship of trust and confidence.[116] In *Chestman*, the Second Circuit juxtaposed that phrase with the related concept of fiduciary relationships. Consequently, the court observed, the requisite relationship could be satisfied either by a fiduciary relationship or by a "similar relationship of trust and confidence."[117]

    So expanding the class of relationships that can give rise to liability may lead to a results-oriented approach. If a court wishes to impose liability, it need simply conclude that the relationship in question involves trust and confidence, even though the relationship bears no resemblance to those in which fiduciary-like duties are normally imposed. Accordingly, courts should be loath to use this phraseology as a mechanism for expanding the scope of liability. The *Chestman* court was sensitive to this possibility, holding that a relationship of trust and confidence must be "the functional equivalent of a fiduciary relationship" before liability can be imposed. *Chestman* also indicates that regardless of which type of relationship is present the defendant must be shown to have been subject to a duty (incorrectly described by the court as one of confidentiality) and to have breached that duty. Finally, the court indicated that at least as to criminal cases, it would not expand the class of relationships from which liability might arise to encompass those outside the traditional core of fiduciary obligation. Accordingly, for most purposes it should be safe to disregard any possible distinction between fiduciary relationships and other relationships of "trust and confidence."

D. Possession or Use?

    The SEC long has argued that trading while in knowing possession of material nonpublic information satisfies Rule 10b–5's scienter requirement. In *United States v. Teicher*,[118] the Second

---

[116] Chiarella v. United States, 445 U.S. 222, 230 (1980).

[117] U.S. v. Chestman, 947 F.2d 551, 568 (2d Cir.1991), cert. denied, 503 U.S. 1004 (1992).

[118] 987 F.2d 112 (2d Cir.1993).

Circuit agreed, albeit in a passage that appears to be dictum. An attorney tipped stock market speculators about transactions involving clients of his firm. On appeal, defendants objected to a jury instruction pursuant to which they could be found guilty of securities fraud based upon the mere possession of fraudulently obtained material nonpublic information without regard to whether that information was the actual cause of their transactions. The Second Circuit held that any error in the instruction was harmless, but went on to opine in favor of a knowing possession test. The court interpreted *Chiarella* as comporting with "the oft-quoted maxim that one with a fiduciary or similar duty to hold material nonpublic information in confidence must either 'disclose or abstain' with regard to trading." The court also favored the possession standard because it "recognizes that one who trades while knowingly possessing material inside information has an informational advantage over other traders." The difficulties with the court's reasoning should be apparent. In the first place, a mere possession test is inconsistent with Rule 10b–5's scienter requirement, which requires fraudulent intent (or, at least, recklessness). In the second, contrary to the court's view, *Chiarella* simply did not address the distinction between a knowing possession and a use standard. Finally, the court's reliance on the trader's informational advantage is inconsistent with *Chiarella's* rejection of the equal access test.

In *SEC v. Adler*,[119] the Eleventh Circuit rejected *Teicher* in favor of a use standard. Under *Adler*, "when an insider trades while in possession of material nonpublic information, a strong inference arises that such information was used by the insider in trading. The insider can attempt to rebut the inference by adducing evidence that there was no causal connection between the information and the trade—i.e., that the information was not used." Although defendant Pegram apparently possessed material nonpublic information at the time he traded, he introduced strong evidence that he had a plan to sell company stock and that that plan predated his acquisition of the information in question. If proven at trial, evidence of such a pre-existing plan would rebut the inference of use and justify an acquittal on grounds that he lacked the requisite scienter.

In 2000, the SEC tried to resolve this issue by adopting Rule 10b5–1, which states that Rule 10b–5's prohibition of insider trading is violated whenever someone trades "on the basis of"

---

[119] 137 F.3d 1325 (11th Cir.1998). The Ninth Circuit subsequently agreed with *Adler* that proof of use, not mere possession, is required. The Ninth Circuit further held that in criminal cases no presumption of use should be drawn from the fact of possession—the government must affirmatively prove use of nonpublic information. United States v. Smith, 155 F.3d 1051 (9th Cir.1998).

material nonpublic information.[120] Because one is deemed, subject to certain narrow exceptions, to have traded "on the basis of" material nonpublic information if one was aware of such information at the time of the trade, Rule 10b5–1 formally rejects the *Adler* position. In practice, however, the difference between *Adler* and Rule 10b5–1 may prove insignificant. On the one hand, *Adler* created a presumption of use when the insider was aware of material nonpublic information. Conversely, Rule 10b5–1 provides affirmative defenses for insiders who trade pursuant to a pre-existing plan, contract, or instructions. As a result, the two approaches should lead to comparable outcomes in many cases.

E. Is There Liability for Trading in Debt Securities?

One of the areas in which the Supreme Court's failure to specify the source and nature of the fiduciary obligation underlying the disclose or abstain rule has proven especially problematic is insider trading in debt securities. Yet, the prohibition's application to debt securities has received surprisingly little judicial attention. One court has held that insider trading in convertible debentures violates Rule 10b–5,[121] but this case is clearly distinguishable from nonconvertible debt securities. Because they are convertible into common stock at the option of the holder, both the market price and interest rate paid on such instruments are affected by the market price of the underlying common stock. Federal securities law recognizes the close relationship of convertibles to common stock by defining the former as equity securities. As such, the status of nonconvertible debt remains unresolved. A strong argument can be made, however, that the prohibition should not extend to trading in nonconvertible debt.

In most states, neither the corporation nor its officers and directors have fiduciary duties to debtholders. Instead, debtholders' rights are limited to the express terms of the contract and an implied covenant of good faith.[122] Cases in a few jurisdictions purport to recognize fiduciary duties running to holders of debt securities, but the duties imposed in these cases are more accurately characterized as the same implied covenant of good faith found in most other jurisdictions.[123]

---

[120] Exchange Act Rel. No. 43,154 (Aug. 15, 2000).

[121] In re Worlds of Wonder Securities Litigation, [1990–1991 Trans. Binder] Fed. Sec. L. Rep. (CCH) ¶ 95,689, 1990 WL 260675 (N.D.Cal.1990).

[122] See, e.g., Metropolitan Life Ins. Co. v. RJR Nabisco, Inc., 716 F.Supp. 1504 (S.D.N.Y.1989); Katz v. Oak Indus., 508 A.2d 873 (Del.Ch.1986).

[123] See, e.g., Broad v. Rockwell Int'l Corp., 642 F.2d 929 (5th Cir.), cert. denied, 454 U.S. 965 (1981); Gardner & Florence Call Cowles Found. v. Empire, Inc., 589 F.Supp. 669 (S.D.N.Y.1984), vacated, 754 F.2d 478 (2d Cir.1985); Fox v. MGM Grand Hotels, Inc., 187 Cal.Rptr. 141 (Cal.Ct.App.1982).

The distinction between this implied covenant and a fiduciary duty is an important one for our purposes. An implied covenant of good faith arises from the express terms of a contract and is used to fulfill the parties' mutual intent. In contrast, a fiduciary duty has little to do with the parties' intent. Instead, courts use fiduciary duties to protect the interests of the duty's beneficiary. Accordingly, a fiduciary duty requires the party subject to the duty to put the interests of the beneficiary of the duty ahead of his own, while an implied duty of good faith merely requires both parties to respect their bargain.

A two-step move thus will be required if courts are to impose liability under the disclose or abstain rule on those who inside trade in debt securities. First, the clear holdings of *Chiarella* and *Dirks* must be set aside so that the requisite relationship can be expanded to include purely contractual arrangements and the requisite duty expanded to include mere contractual covenants. Second, the implied covenant of good faith must be interpreted as barring self-dealing in nonpublic information by corporate agents. In that regard, consider the leading *Met Life* decision, which indicates that a covenant of good faith will be implied only when necessary to ensure that neither side deprives the other of the fruits of the agreement.[124] The fruits of the agreement are limited to regular payment of interest and ultimate repayment of principal. Because insider trading rarely affects either of these fruits, it does not violate the covenant of good faith.[125]

To be sure, the courts could simply ignore state law. Yet, the Supreme Court has consistently held that insider trading liability requires an agency or fiduciary relationship. As to common stock, *Dirks* created what appears to be a federal fiduciary obligation, but recall that that obligation was extrapolated from state common law. It seems unlikely that the courts will treat the state law status of debtholders as irrelevant.

F. Remedies and Penalties

Woe unto those who violate the insider trading prohibition, for the penalties are many, cumulative, and severe. The Justice Department may pursue criminal charges. The SEC may pursue a

---

[124] Metropolitan Life Ins. Co. v. RJR Nabisco, Inc., 716 F.Supp. 1504, 1517 (S.D.N.Y.1989).

[125] Various alternative theories of liability may come into play in this context. In particular, the misappropriation theory might apply. Suppose a corporate officer traded in the firm's debt securities using material nonpublic information belonging to the corporation. As the argument would go, even though the officer owes no fiduciary duties to the bondholders, he owes fiduciary duties to the corporation. The violation of those duties might suffice for liability under the misappropriation theory. The misappropriation theory clearly would not reach trading by an issuer in its own debt securities, which would come under the disclose or abstain rule.

variety of civil penalties. Private party litigants may bring damage actions under both federal and state law.

The SEC has no authority to prosecute criminal actions against inside traders, but it is authorized by Exchange Act § 21(d)(1) to ask the Justice Department to initiate a criminal prosecution. In addition, the Justice Department may bring such a prosecution on its own initiative. Under § 32(a), a willful violation of Rule 10b–5 or 14–3 is a felony that can be punished by a $5 million fine ($25 in the case of corporations) and up to 20 years in jail. Since the mid-1980s insider trading scandals, criminal prosecutions have become fairly common in this area.

The SEC long has had the authority to pursue various civil penalties in insider trading cases. Under Exchange Act § 21(d), the SEC may seek a permanent or temporary injunction whenever "it shall appear to the Commission that any person is engaged or is about to engage in any acts or practices constituting a violation" of the Act or any rules promulgated thereunder. Courts have made it quite easy for the SEC to obtain injunctions under § 21(d). The SEC must make a "proper showing," but that merely requires the SEC to demonstrate a violation of the securities laws occurred and there is a reasonable likelihood of future violations.[126] The SEC is not required to meet traditional requirements for equitable relief, such as irreparable harm.[127] The SEC is not required to identify particular individuals who were wronged by the conduct, moreover, but only that the violation occurred.

"Once the equity jurisdiction of the district court has been properly invoked by a showing of a securities law violation, the court possesses the necessary power to fashion an appropriate remedy."[128] Thus, in addition to or in place of injunctive relief, the SEC may seek disgorgement of profits, correction of misleading statements, disclosure of material information, or other special remedies. Of these, disgorgement of profits to the government is the most commonly used enforcement tool.

The SEC may also punish insider trading by regulated market professionals through administrative proceedings. Under § 15(b)(4) of the 1934 Act, the SEC may censure, limit the activities of, suspend, or revoke the registration of a broker or dealer who willfully violates the insider trading prohibition. Similar sanctions

---

[126] See SEC v. Commonwealth Chem. Sec., Inc., 574 F.2d 90, 99–100 (2d Cir.1978). But cf. SEC v. Lund, 570 F.Supp. 1397, 1404 (C.D.Cal.1983) (court denied an injunction on the grounds that the defendant's action was "an isolated occurrence" and that his "profession [was] not likely to lead him into future violations").

[127] See SEC v. Management Dynamics, Inc., 515 F.2d 801 (2d Cir.1975); SEC v. Manor Nursing Centers, Inc., 458 F.2d 1082 (2d Cir.1972).

[128] SEC v. Manor Nursing Centers, 458 F.2d 1082, 1103 (2d Cir.1972).

may be imposed on those associated with the broker or dealer in such activities. The SEC may issue a report of its investigation of the incident even if it decides not to pursue judicial or administrative proceedings, which may lead to private litigation.

During the 1980s, Congress significantly expanded the civil sanctions available to the SEC for use against inside traders. The Insider Trading Sanctions Act of 1984 created a civil monetary penalty of up to three times the profit gained or loss avoided by a person who violates Rules 10b–5 or 14e–3 "by purchasing or selling a security while in the possession of material nonpublic information." An action to impose such a penalty may be brought in addition to or in lieu of any other actions that the SEC or Justice Department is entitled to bring. Because the SEC thus may seek both disgorgement and treble damages, an inside trader faces potential civil liability of up to four times the profit gained.

In the Insider Trading and Securities Fraud Act of 1988 (ITSFEA), Congress made a number of further changes designed to augment the enforcement resources and penalties available to the SEC. Among other things, it authorized the SEC to pay a bounty to informers of up to 10 percent of any penalty collected by the SEC. The treble money fine was extended to controlling persons, so as to provide brokerage houses, for example, with greater incentives to monitor the activities of their employees.

Although it has long been clear that persons who traded contemporaneously with an inside trader have a private cause of action under Rule 10b–5 (and perhaps Rule 14e–3), and may also have state law claims, private party litigation against inside traders has been rare and usually parasitic on SEC enforcement actions. Private party actions were further discouraged by the Second Circuit's decision in *Moss v. Morgan Stanley Inc.*,[129] which held that contemporaneous traders could not bring private causes of actions under the misappropriation theory. ITSFEA attempted to encourage private actions by overruling *Moss*. Under Exchange Act § 20A, contemporaneous traders can sue to recover up to the amount of profit gained or loss avoided. Tippers and tippees are jointly and severally liable. The amount recoverable is reduced by any amounts disgorged to the Commission. As yet, however, it does not appear that plaintiffs have made very frequent use of § 20A.

§ 11.6 Section 16(b)

In addition to the complicated insider trading rules under 10(b), Congress has also provided a much simpler prophylactic rule under Securities Exchange Act § 16(b). In brief, § 16(b) holds that

---

[129] 719 F.2d 5 (2d Cir.1983).

any profits an insider earns on purchases and sales that occur within six months of each other must be forfeited to the corporation.[130] As with all prophylactic rules, § 16(b) is both over- and under-inclusive. It captures all sorts of trades unaffected by the use of inside information, while missing many trades flagrantly based on nonpublic information.

Section 16(a) requires insiders to report their holdings in the issuer's equity securities within 10 days after they first become subject to Section 16. Thereafter, an insider must report any transactions in the issuer's equity securities within two business days of their occurrence. The report must be filed electronically with the SEC. In addition, the report must be posted to the issuer's corporate website.[131]

Under § 16(b), any profits earned on purchases and sales within a six month period must be disgorged to the issuer. Shareholders of the issuer may sue insiders derivatively and a shareholder's lawyer can get a contingent fee out of any recovery or settlement.

A. Matching Transactions

Although there must be both a sale and a purchase within six months of each other in order to trigger § 16(b), it applies whether the sale follows the purchase or vice versa. Accordingly, shares are fungible for § 16(b) purposes. The trader thus need not earn his or her gains from buying and selling specific shares of stock. Instead, if the trader unloads 10 shares of stock and buys back 10 different

---

[130] Section 16(b) provides:

For the purpose of preventing the unfair use of information which may have been obtained by such beneficial owner, director, or officer by reason of his relationship to the issuer, any profit realized by him from any purchase and sale, or any sale and purchase, of any equity security of such issuer (other than an exempted security) or a security-based swap agreement (as defined in section 206B of the Gramm-Leach-Bliley Act) involving any such equity security within any period of less than six months, unless such security or security-based swap agreement was acquired in good faith in connection with a debt previously contracted, shall inure to and be recoverable by the issuer, irrespective of any intention on the part of such beneficial owner, director, or officer in entering into such transaction of holding the security or security-based swap agreement purchased or of not repurchasing the security or security-based swap agreement sold for a period exceeding six months. Suit to recover such profit may be instituted at law or in equity in any court of competent jurisdiction by the issuer, or by the owner of any security of the issuer in the name and in behalf of the issuer if the issuer shall fail or refuse to bring such suit within sixty days after request or shall fail diligently to prosecute the same thereafter; but no such suit shall be brought more than two years after the date such profit was realized. This subsection shall not be construed to cover any transaction where such beneficial owner was not such both at the time of the purchase and sale, or the sale and purchase, of the security or security based swap agreement (as defined in section 206B of the Gramm-Leach-Bliley Act) involved, or any transaction or transactions which the Commission by rules and regulations may exempt as not comprehended within the purpose of this subsection.

[131] Note that only transactions in stock of the executive company have to be disclosed. Hence, an executive of Acme who owns stock in Ajax may buy or sell Ajax stock without having to file a Form 4.

shares of stock in the same company at a cheaper price, he or she is liable.

Examples: (1) Susan is chief financial officer of Acme, Inc. She buys 1,000 Acme shares at $8 on February 1. She sells 1,000 shares at $10 on May 1. Because the sale and purchase took place within six months, § 16(b) is triggered. She has earned a $2 profit per share and therefore must disgorge $2,000 to Acme.

(2) Sam is senior vice president of Ajax, Inc. He has owned 10,000 shares for many years. On June 1 he sells 1,000 shares at $10. On September 15 he buys 1,000 shares at $8. He also must disgorge $2,000 to Ajax ($2 per share times 1000 shares).

Courts interpret the statute to maximize the amount the company recovers. They do not use any of the standard accounting tools (e.g., FIFO: first in, first out). Much less do they let shareholders identify specific shares of stock (e.g., "In November I sold the share I bought in January, not the share I bought in October.") Instead, they match the lowest priced purchases and the highest priced sales.[132] Again, an example will be helpful:

Example: Shania is president of Acme, Inc. Her transactions were as follows:

- March 1: bought 100 shares at $10
- April 1: sold 70 shares at $12
- May 1: bought 50 shares on May 1 at $9
- May 15: sold 25 shares at $13
- December 31: sold 35 shares at $20

The December 31 sale cannot be matched with either the March 1 or May 1 purchase, because they are more than six months apart. The other transactions are all matchable. A court will match them in the way that maximizes Acme's recovery:

- Match the 25 shares sold on May 15 with 25 of the shares bought on May 1, because they have the largest price differential. With a $4 profit per share ($13 minus $9) times 25 shares, Shania owes Acme $100.
- Next match 25 of the shares sold on April 1 with the remaining 25 shares purchased on May 1 for a profit of $75 ($3 per share ($12 minus $9) times 25 shares).

---

[132] See, e.g., Smolowe v. Delendo Corp., 136 F.2d 231 (2d Cir.), cert. denied, 320 U.S. 751 (1943).

- Now match the remaining 45 shares sold on April 1 with 45 of the shares bought on March 1 for a profit of $90 ($2 per share ($12 minus $10) times 45 shares).

- Shania therefore owes Acme a total of $265.

B. Officers, Directors, and 10% Shareholders

Unlike Rule 10b–5, § 16(b) applies only to officers, directors, or shareholders who own more than 10% of the company's stock. Determining whether or not one is a shareholder or director is straightforward, of course. In contrast, determining whether one is an officer can be tricky. Securities Exchange Act Rule 3b–2 defines an officer as a "president, vice president, secretary, treasury or principal financial officer, comptroller or principal accounting officer, and any person routinely performing corresponding functions. . . ." The latter catchall phrase is the potential trouble spot. Should the statutory term "officer" be construed narrowly so that objective factors, especially one's title, determine whether one was subject to § 16(b)? Or should the term be interpreted more broadly, so as to take into account subjective considerations such as the nature of one's functions and/or whether one's role gave one access to inside information?

An early decision, *Colby v. Klune*,[133] expressed doubt as to whether the SEC had authority to adopt Rule 3b–2. Instead, the court adopted a formulation that looked to subjective considerations, which defined an officer as "a corporate employee performing important executive duties of such character that he would be likely, in discharging those duties, to obtain confidential information that would aid him if he engaged in personal market transactions." The Ninth Circuit later concurred with the view that title alone is not dispositive, but focused on access to information as the relevant consideration: "Liability under § 16(b) is not based simply upon a person's title within his corporation; rather, liability follows from the existence of a relationship with the corporation that makes it more probable than not that the individual has access to inside information."[134]

The SEC ultimately intervened by adopting Rule 16a–1(f), under which either one's title or one's function could result in officer status:

> The term "officer" shall mean an issuer's president, principal financial officer, principal accounting officer (or, if there is no such accounting officer, the controller), any

---

[133] 178 F.2d 872 (2d Cir.1949).

[134] Merrill Lynch, Pierce, Fenner & Smith, Inc. v. Livingston, 566 F.2d 1119 (9th Cir.1978).

vice president of the issuer in charge of a principal business unit, division or function (such as sales, administration or finance), any other officer who performs a policy making function, or any other person who performs similar policy making functions for the issuer. Officers of the issuer's parent(s) or subsidiaries shall be deemed officers of the issuer if they perform such policy making functions for the issuer. In addition, when the issuer is a limited partnership, officers or employees of the general partner(s) who perform policy making functions for the limited partnership are deemed officers of the limited partnership.

Someone who holds one of the listed titles is likely to be deemed an officer, whether or not he has access to inside information, subject to a "very limited exception applicable only where the title is essentially honorary or ceremonial."[135] (Conversely, the mere fact that one's position is described in, say, the corporate bylaws as that of an officer does not suffice to make one an officer for this purpose.[136]) An executive with policymaking functions that give the executive access to inside information, however, will be deemed an officer even if the executive lacks one of the formal titles usually associated with that position.

Section 16(b) treats officers and directors on the one hand and shareholders on the other differently. Under Rule 16a–2, you cannot match a transaction by an officer or director made prior to his or her appointment as an officer or director to one made after he or she is appointed. You can, however, match transactions that occur after he or she ceases to be an officer or director with those made while he or she still held office.

In contrast, a shareholder has § 16(b) liability only if she owned more than 10 percent of the company's shares both at the time of the purchase and of the sale. In *Reliance Electric Co. v. Emerson Electric Co.*,[137] Emerson bought 13.2 percent of Dodge Manufacturing Co. stock in a hostile tender offer. To avoid being taken over by Emerson, Dodge agreed to merge with Reliance. Emerson gave up the fight and decided to sell its Dodge shares. In an attempt to minimize any potential § 16(b) liability, Emerson first sold Dodge shares representing 3.24 percent of the outstanding common stock. It then sold the remainder, which represented 9.96 percent of the outstanding. When Reliance sued under § 16(b), the

---

[135] National Medical Enterprises, Inc. v. Small, 680 F.2d 83 (9th Cir.1982).

[136] Lockheed Aircraft Corp. v. Campbell, 110 F.Supp. 282 (S.D.Cal.1953) (assistant treasurer and assistant secretary not officers for § 16(b) purposes even though their positions were described in the bylaws as those of officers).

[137] 404 U.S. 418 (1972).

Supreme Court held that shareholders are subject to the statute only if they own more than 10 percent of the stock immediately before the sale. Emerson therefore had no liability with respect to its sale of the final 9.96 percent. *Reliance* is a good example of how form prevails over substance in § 16(b)—even though Emerson's two sales were part of a related series of transactions effected pursuant to a single plan, which plausibly could have been deemed a step transaction, the court treated the second sale as having independent legal significance.

Notice that Emerson did not raise, and the Supreme Court thus did not address, the significance of the fact that Emerson had not been a 10 percent shareholder at the time it made its initial tender offer. Instead, that issue came up in *Foremost-McKesson, Inc. v. Provident Securities Co.*,[138] in which the Supreme Court held that a purchase by which a shareholder crosses the 10% threshold cannot be matched with subsequent sales for § 16(b) purposes. Again, an example may be helpful.

Example: Selena is not an officer or director of Ajax, Inc. At all relevant times, Ajax has 1,000 shares outstanding. Selena's transactions are as follows:

- January 1: buys 50 shares at $10
- February 1: buys 55 shares at $10
- April 1: buys 50 shares at $10.
- May 1: sells 60 shares at $15
- May 2: sells 55 shares at $20

Liability equals $250 (50 shares times ($15–$10)). The January 1 purchase cannot be matched with either sale, because on January 1 Selena was not yet a 10 percent shareholder. The February 1 purchase cannot be matched with either sale because it is the transaction by which Selena became a (more than) 10 percent shareholder. Only the April 1 purchase is potentially matchable, because only at the time of that purchase did Selena own more than 10 percent of Ajax's stock. As to the sales, only the May 1 sale can be matched with the April 1 purchase. On May 2, Selena owned less than 10 percent of Ajax's stock.

C. Limited Scope

Besides the smaller class of prospective defendants, there are several other important limitations on § 16(b)'s scope relative to Rule 10b–5. Section 16(b), for example, applies only to insider transactions in their own company's stock. There is no tipping

---

[138] 423 U.S. 232 (1976).

liability, no misappropriation liability, and no constructive insider doctrine. Second, § 16(b) applies only to firms that must register under the Securities Exchange Act.[139] Finally, it applies only to equity securities, such as stocks and convertible debt.[140]

D.   Form Versus Substance

Form usually triumphs over substance in § 16(b) cases. There are some exceptions, however, the most notable of which is the unconventional transaction doctrine. The Exchange Act defines "sale" very broadly: it includes every disposition of a security for value. For purposes of § 16(b), however, certain transactions are not deemed sales; namely, so-called unconventional transactions.

The leading case in this area is *Kern County Land Co. v. Occidental Petroleum Corp.*[141] In 1967, Occidental launched a tender offer for 500,000 shares of Kern County Land Co. (Old Kern). The offer later was extended and the number of shares being sought was increased. When the offer closed in June, Occidental owned more than 10% of Old Kern's stock. To avoid being taken over by Occidental, Old Kern negotiated a defensive merger with Tenneco. Under the merger agreement, Old Kern stock would be exchanged for Tenneco stock. In order to avoid becoming a minority shareholder in Tenneco, Occidental sold to a Tenneco subsidiary an option to purchase the Tenneco shares Occidental would acquire in the merger, which could not be exercised until the § 16(b) six month period had elapsed. Tenneco and Old Kern merged during the six-month period following Occidental's tender offer. Somewhat later, more than 6 months after the tender offer, Occidental sold Tenneco stock pursuant to the option.

The successor corporation to Old Kern (New Kern) sued under § 16(b). It offered two theories. First, the merger and resulting exchange of Old Kern for Tenneco stock constituted a sale, which had occurred less than six months after the purchase effected by the tender offer. Second, the tender offer constituted a purchase and that the grant of the option (rather than the exercise of the option)

---

[139] These include companies with stock traded on a national exchange, and companies with assets of at least $10 million and 500 or more shareholders. See Securities Exchange Act § 12(g); Rule 12g–1.

[140] Exchange Act § 3(a)(11) defines "equity security" as "any stock or similar security; or any security convertible, with or without consideration, into such a security, or carrying any warrant or right to subscribe to or purchase such a security; or any such warrant or right." In addition, Rule 3a11–1 includes limited partnership interests, interests in a joint venture, voting trust certificates, and options as equity securities.

SEC Rule 16a–1(d) defines equity security of an issuer to mean "any equity security or derivative security relating to an issuer, whether or not issued by that issuer." Accordingly, an option on an issuer's shares even though issued by a third party, would be treated as an equity security for purposes of Section 16.

[141] 411 U.S. 582 (1973).

constituted a sale. Because the option was granted less than six months after the tender offer, New Kern argued that Occidental was liable for any profit earned on the shares covered by the option. The Supreme Court rejected both of New Kern's arguments, holding that Occidental had no § 16(b) liability. Both the merger and the grant of the option were unconventional transactions and, as such, were not deemed a sale for § 16(b) purposes.

Courts consider three factors in deciding whether a transaction is conventional or unconventional: (1) whether the transaction is volitional; (2) whether the transaction is one over which the beneficial owner has any influence; and (3) whether the beneficial owner had access to confidential information about the transaction or the issuer. In the case at bar, Occidental was a hostile bidder with no access to confidential information about Old Kern or Tenneco. In addition, as to the merger, the exchange was involuntary—because the other shareholders had approved the merger, Occidental had no option but to exchange its shares.

Although *Kern* still stands for the proposition that substance sometimes triumphs over form even in § 16(b), it no longer states the rule for options. Instead, the SEC treats the acquisition of an option as the purchase (or sale) of the underlying stock. Thus, the purchase of an option to buy stock (a call) could be matched either with a sale of the underlying stock or with the purchase of an option to sell the stock (a put). For example, suppose an investor bought call options on 10 shares for $1 each, exercisable at $50 per share. If he exercised the options and sold the stock for $60 a share, he would have § 16(b) liability of $60 x 10 — (10 x $1 + 10 x $50) = $90. A purchase of stock could similarly be matched with the purchase of a put.

E.   Impact of Sarbanes-Oxley

As we have seen, federal law prohibits insider trading by employees, officers, and directors, among others, of the corporation that issued the stock being traded. Not all insider transactions are illegal, of course. Instead, insider trading is banned only when the insider trades while in possession, and on the basis, of material nonpublic information. Information is material for this purpose if there is a substantial likelihood that a reasonable investor would consider the information important in deciding how to act. Information remains nonpublic until it is disclosed in a manner that ensures its availability to the investing public. Merely waiting until a press release is read to reporters at a news conference, for example, is not enough. The information must have been widely disseminated and public investors must have an opportunity to act on it.

As a matter of good corporate practice, all publicly held corporations should adopt policies designed to prevent illegal trading by insiders. Such policies protect the insiders by providing guidance as to when trading is least likely to result in liability. Given the severe penalties for inside trading, and the inevitable temptation to profit from access to inside information, such policies are necessary to, in a sense, protect insiders from themselves. Equally important, moreover, such policies also protect the issuer itself from potential liability.

An effective blackout policy obviously must preclude insiders from trading stock they hold directly. In order to ensure compliance, however, it should also apply to stock held indirectly, such as stock held in a 401(k) plan or other employee benefit program.

Abuse of just such a blackout policy was one of the most unsavory features of the infamous Enron scandal. As Enron was going down the tubes, rank-and-file Enron employees were prevented from selling Enron stock held in their 401(k) plans during a lengthy blackout period imposed while the plan changed administrators. At the same time, however, top Enron executives were selling large amounts of stock they owned directly.

Section 306 of the Sarbanes-Oxley Act was adopted in direct response to this part of the Enron saga. Under it, directors and executive officers of a corporation are forbidden from trading any of their company's equity securities during any blackout period in which 50% or more of the issuer's employees are banned from trading stocks held in pension and benefit accounts. In addition, subject to some minor exceptions, employees must be given 30 days' notice before a blackout period commences.

If an executive officer or director violates the trading ban, the company can sue to recover any profit the executive earns from the trade. If the company fails to do so, § 306 expressly authorizes shareholders of the company to sue derivatively on the company's behalf to force the executive to disgorge profits.

Sarbanes-Oxley also accelerated the deadlines for reporting insider transactions. Pre-SOX, executives filed a Form 4 within 10 days after the end of any month in which the executive purchased or sold some of his company's stock. Under SOX, reporting must take place much more quickly. As noted above, a covered insider now must file a Form 4 disclosing his or her trades within two business days following the transaction. In addition, SOX required that the Form must be filed electronically. Finally, under SOX, a copy of the Form 4 must be posted to the company's website within one day after it is filed with the SEC.

Chapter 12

MERGERS AND ACQUISITIONS

§ 12.1 Introduction

The corporation's legal personhood is a fiction, of course, but it is a very useful one. Among the powers thereby granted corporations are the rights to hold, acquire, and dispose of stock of other corporations. As a result, one corporation can acquire control of another through a merger or other acquisition device. To be sure, natural persons and many other entities also can acquire corporations, but the vast majority of corporate takeovers are effected by another corporation.

Corporate acquisitions provide transactional lawyers many opportunities to create value for their clients. One of the most basic is regulatory arbitrage in the choice of acquisition form. If a given substantive deal structure necessarily led to a single legal structure, there would be no issue. But the law provides a number of acquisition forms, providing multiple ways of structuring any given deal. Each form has its own advantages or disadvantages—or, put in economic terms, each form has its own transaction cost schedule. The transaction planner's task is to identify, in the context of a particular transaction, the legal form imposing the lowest costs for the deal at hand.

A. Classifying Acquisition Techniques

Acquisition techniques can be classified in various ways. One might, for example, distinguish between negotiated and hostile acquisitions. Negotiated acquisitions are those in which the target is willing to be bought—indeed, the target may have initiated the transaction by searching out a buyer. Here the focus is on the mechanics by which the acquisition takes place, the duties of management in selecting and negotiating with a bidder, and the risk that competing bidders will try to buy the target out from under the initial bidder. Hostile acquisitions are those in which the target company's board of directors is unwilling to be acquired. Here the focus will be on how the target can defend itself against the bidder and what the bidder can do to defeat those defenses.

A more useful classification system, however, distinguishes between statutory and nonstatutory acquisition techniques.[1] The

---

[1] The statute in question is the corporation code of the relevant state. Although the so-called nonstatutory techniques are largely unregulated by state corporation codes, they are governed by various other statutes, such as the federal securities laws.

former category includes the merger, its variants, and the sale of all or substantially all corporate assets. The latter includes the proxy contest, the tender offer, and stock purchases. The role of the target board of directors is the chief distinction between the two categories. Statutory forms, such as a merger or asset sale, require approval by the target's board of directors. In contrast, the nonstatutory techniques do not. A proxy contest obviously does not require board approval, although a shareholder vote is still required. A tender offer or stock purchase require neither board approval nor a shareholder vote—if the buyer ends up with a majority of the shares, it will achieve control.

The need for board approval creates insurmountable barriers to use of a statutory form if the bidder is unable to secure board cooperation. The nonstatutory forms eliminate this difficulty by permitting the bidder to bypass the target's board and obtain control directly from the stockholders. But why would a board be unwilling to cooperate? Several reasons suggest themselves: (1) The board may refuse to sell at any price, perhaps out of concern for their positions and perquisites. (2) The board may hold out for a price higher than the bidder is willing to pay. (3) The board may hold out for side-payments.

B. A Preliminary Overview of Acquisition Mechanics

There are five principal ways of acquiring control of a corporation: merger; purchase of all or substantially all of the target's assets; proxy contest; tender offer; negotiated or open market stock purchases. Subsequent sections will describe their mechanics in more detail, but a quick overview may be helpful.

1. *The Merger*

Although much planning and preparatory work must take place beforehand, a merger actually occurs when a document called the articles of merger is filed with the appropriate officials of the states of incorporation of the corporate parties to the transaction. At that instant, two companies magically become one. This happens because a number of events take place by operation of law and without the need for further action after the merger becomes effective, including most notably: (1) the separate existence of all corporate parties, with the exception of the surviving corporation, comes to an end; (2) title to all property owned by each corporate party is automatically vested in the surviving corporation; (3) the surviving company succeeds to all liabilities of each corporate party; and (4) the consideration passes to non-dissenting shareholders.

Before it may take effect, a merger must be approved by the board of directors and shareholders of each of the constituent corporations (i.e., the corporations that are party to the transaction). In most states the requisite vote is a majority of the outstanding shares. The requirement of shareholder approval can be a significant disadvantage to the merger in comparison to some other acquisition devices. Where public corporations are involved the process of obtaining shareholder approval is cumbersome and expensive. One must hire accountants to prepare the financial statements and to give an accounting opinion. Lawyers must be paid to prepare opinion letters on corporate, securities and tax law questions. The lawyers will also draft, or at least review, the proxy statement that must be disseminated to shareholders in order to solicit their votes. A proxy solicitation firm usually will be retained to run the shareholder meeting and to solicit proxies. Finally, senior corporate officers must expend considerable time and effort. As a result, the cost of the shareholder approval process can easily run into seven figures. After all of that, moreover, shareholders occasionally do something silly like not approving the acquisition.

A consolidation is a merger-like transaction that differs mainly in the identity of the surviving company. In a merger, two (or more) corporations combine with one of the constituent corporations surviving. In a consolidation, two (or more) corporations combine with none of the constituent corporations surviving. Instead, an entirely new corporation is created. The approval requirements and other procedural aspects are otherwise the same as for a merger.[2]

In most mergers, the shareholders of the target corporation receive a premium for their shares over the market price that prevailed before the deal was announced. In the famous merger case of *Smith v. Van Gorkom*,[3] for example, the pre-announcement price was around $38 but the buyer paid $55 in the merger. Where two or more corporations combine in a so-called merger of equals, however, none of the constituent corporations' shareholders receive

---

[2] Another transaction closely related to the merger is the so-called compulsory share exchange. In a share exchange, the acquiring corporation buys all of the outstanding shares of one or more classes of target corporation stock. Unlike a tender offer or other stock purchase transaction, in which each individual shareholder decides whether or not to sell, a share exchange is binding on all shareholders of the affected class of stock. See, e.g., MBCA § 11.03. As with a merger or consolidation, the share exchange must be approved by the board of directors and, subject to a limited but important exception, the shareholders of all constituent corporations. See, e.g., MBCA § 11.04. The exception just mentioned provides that shareholders of the acquiring corporation are not entitled to vote if the acquirer's articles of incorporation will not change, there is no change in the shareholders stock or rights, and the number of shares to be issued does not exceed 20% of the outstanding shares. See, e.g., MBCA § 11.04(g). Although the Model Act provision for compulsory share exchanges has been adopted by over 40 states, Delaware has no comparable provision. Even in states where the procedure is available, moreover, it is rarely used.

[3] 488 A.2d 858 (Del.1985).

a premium for their shares. Instead, they all end up as shareholders of the combined entity.

2.   The Sale of All or Substantially All Assets

An acquisition by asset sale differs from a merger mainly in that the two companies do not combine. The target company remains in existence at least for a little while after the asset sale has been completed. Only title to the assets change hands, both corporations remain alive. As a result, the mechanics of transferring control and consideration are more complex. Documents of transfer must be prepared with respect to every asset being sold and those documents must be filed with every applicable agency. For example, a deed of transfer will have to be properly filed with every county in which the target owns real estate. There must be a written assumption of liabilities. Finally, the process of distributing the consideration to the target's shareholders is more complicated. Since the target is still in existence one option is to distribute the consideration as a dividend. More often the target is formally dissolved and its remaining assets (including the consideration paid in the acquisition) are distributed to its shareholders in a final liquidating dividend.

3.   The Tender Offer

An offer to purchase shares made by a bidder directly to the stockholders of a target company, sometimes subject to a minimum or a maximum number of shares that the bidder will accept, communicated to the shareholders by means of newspaper advertisements and (in most cases) by a general mailing to the entire list of shareholders, with a view to acquiring control of the target company.

An exchange offer is simply a tender offer in which all or part of the consideration is paid in the form of acquiring company stock or debt securities, rather than all in cash. As such, an exchange offer also can be structured as a partial or two-tier bid. This option is most often used by acquirers who are established public corporations; target shareholders are unlikely to want stock or debt issued by some brand new company neither they nor their advisers have ever heard of. The other disadvantage associated with exchange offers is that the securities almost certainly will have to be registered with the SEC under the 1933 Act, adding to the delay period before the offer can be made. Delay is deadly to the hostile offer, because it allows time for management to erect takeover defenses and creates greater opportunities for competing bids.

4. Negotiated or Open Market Purchases

Securities Exchange Act § 13(d), adopted as part of the Williams Act, requires that any person who acquires more than 5% of a class of equity securities of a public corporation must file a disclosure statement on Schedule 13D disclosing his holdings and intentions. Once the Schedule 13D is filed, the market price of the target's stock tends to increase substantially as speculators anticipate a future merger or tender offer at a premium above the market price. For this reason, acquisition of control by open market purchases of stock is rare. The bidder will buy up as many shares as possible before being obliged to file its Schedule 13D and then shift gears to effect a merger, tender offer, or proxy contest. (Because the bidder is not obliged to file its Schedule 13D for 10 days after crossing the 5% threshold, bidders frequently acquire substantially more than 5% before disclosing their holdings.)

The short-swing profit provision of Securities Exchange Act § 16(b) provides another disincentive to acquiring control through stock purchases. Once the bidder crosses the 10% threshold, its profits on subsequent sales within the next six months may have to be disgorged to the target corporation. "Because a bidder typically realizes that it may be outbid if a bidding contest develops, it realizes that it may wish to sell out to the high bidder in the reasonably near future."[4] Consequently, most bidders are only willing to cross the 10% threshold in a transaction that will give it control of the target in a single step, such as a merger or tender offer.

Where a single shareholder (or, perhaps, a small and cohesive shareholder group) owns a controlling block of shares, however, a negotiated purchase of that block may be desirable. Acquisition of that block will give the purchaser immediate control of the corporation without the risks associated with a lengthy merger or tender offer process. As we shall see, however, such transactions entail significant fiduciary obligations on the part of both the selling and acquiring shareholders.

5. The Proxy Contest

In a proxy contest, the prospective acquirer nominates a slate of directors to be elected at the annual meeting of the shareholders. The contest arises because the insurgent slate is offered as an alternative to the incumbent members of the board. Alternatively, the insurgent shareholder may seek to hold a special shareholders meeting to remove the incumbent board and replace it with his nominees. Proxy contests, like tender offers, permit a bidder to end-

---

[4] William J. Carney, Mergers and Acquisitions: Cases and Materials 15 (2000).

run management. Proxy contests, however, suffer from a number of other drawbacks that render them the most expensive and the most uncertain, and therefore the least used, of the various techniques for acquiring corporate control. Among other things, the incumbent board's ability to use the corporate treasury to finance its reelection campaign gives the incumbents a significant advantage. In addition, the phenomenon of rational shareholder apathy, pursuant to which many shareholders pay little attention to the campaign, makes it difficult for the insurgent to make a persuasive case.

§ 12.2 Statutory Acquisition Techniques

A. The Merger

In a merger, two corporations combine to form a single entity. Suppose, for example, Acme Company and Ajax Corporation are about to combine via merger. Their merger is effected by filing the requisite documentation—typically so-called "articles of merger"—with the appropriate state official, not unlike the incorporation process by which the two companies were formed. After the merger, only one of the two companies will survive. But the survivor will have succeeded by operation of law to all of the assets, liabilities, rights, and obligations of the two constituent corporations.[5]

As MBCA § 11.07 more specifically explains, a merger has no fewer than 8 distinct effects on the merging corporations:

- The corporation designated in the merger agreement as the surviving entity continues its existence.

- The separate existence of the corporation or corporations that are merged into the survivor ceases.

- All property owned by, and every contract right possessed by, each constituent corporation is vested in the survivor.

- All liabilities of each constituent corporation are vested in the survivor.

- The surviving corporation's name may be substituted in any pending legal proceeding for the name of any constituent corporation that was a party to the proceeding.

---

[5] As a technical matter, a merger is defined as a combination of two or more corporations in which one of the constituent parties survives. In a consolidation, two or more corporations combine to form a new corporation. Because the articles of consolidation serve as the new entity's articles of incorporation, the distinction is mostly semantic from a corporate law perspective.

- The articles of incorporation and bylaws of the survivor are amended to the extent provided in the merger agreement.

- The articles of incorporation or organizational documents of any entity that is created by the merger become effective.

- The shares of each constituent corporation are converted into whatever consideration was specified in the merger agreement and the former shareholders of the constituent corporations are entitled only to the rights provided them in the merger agreement or by statute.

Under the Model Act, effecting a merger requires four basic steps. First, a plan of merger must be drafted, specifying the deal's terms and conditions.[6] The board of directors must approve the plan of merger.[7] The shareholders then must approve the plan.[8] Unlike most corporate actions, which only require approval by a majority of those shares present and voting, a merger requires approval by a majority of the outstanding shares.[9] Finally, articles of merger must be filed with the requisite state agency—usually the Secretary of State.

The process is essentially the same in non-Model Act states, with the principal variation being the vote required for the merger to receive shareholder approval. At early common law, a merger required unanimous shareholder approval. The unanimity requirement created the potential for hold up problems, as a dissenting minority could block a transaction in hopes of being assuaged by side-payments. Unanimity gradually gave way to supermajority voting requirements, which in Delaware and Model Act states have further eroded into a mere majority of the outstanding shares. About one-third of the states retain some form of supermajority voting requirement, however, typically two-thirds of the shares entitled to vote.[10]

---

[6] MBCA § 11.02(c).

[7] MBCA § 11.04(a).

[8] MBCA § 11.04(b)–(d).

[9] MBCA § 11.04(e). The voting requirements become more complex, of course, if group voting is required or if the terms of the deal trigger voting rights for classes of stock that otherwise lack such rights.

[10] The most prominent supermajority holdout, New York, amended its statute in 1998 to require approval by a majority of the shares entitled to vote with respect to subsequently formed corporations. N.Y. Bus. Corp. L. § 903. In addition, the New York statute allows pre-existing corporations to opt for a majority vote rule by amending their articles. Id. Given New York's long prominence as a holdout jurisdiction, this action may presage a gradual further erosion of supermajority vote requirements in the remaining holdouts.

In most states, a shareholder vote is not required if the transaction qualifies as a so-called short-form merger. The short-form merger statute is a special provision for a merger between a parent corporation and one of its subsidiaries. The statute may be invoked only if the parent corporation owns a high percentage—typically 90%—of the subsidiary's outstanding stock.[11] Early short-form merger statutes typically required the transaction to be approved by the board of directors of each corporation. Neither corporation's shareholders were allowed to vote. MBCA § 11.05(a) and DGCL § 253(a), however, reflect a modern trend towards even more liberal short-form mergers. Both statutes authorize a short-form merger when the parent owns at least 90% of the subsidiary's stock. If that threshold is met, only the parent corporation's board need approve the merger.[12] Neither the subsidiary's board nor its minority shareholders have any say. The assumption seems to be that both votes would be foregone conclusions.

Under Delaware law, shareholder voting rights also may be eliminated for certain transactions that do not qualify for treatment as short-form mergers if three conditions are met: (1) the agreement of merger does not amend the surviving corporation's articles of incorporation; (2) the outstanding shares of the surviving corporation are unaffected by the transaction;[13] and (3) the transaction does not increase the number of outstanding shares by more than 20%. If all three conditions are satisfied, approval by the surviving corporation's shareholders is not required. Approval by any other constituent corporation's shareholders is still required, however.[14]

B. The Sale of All or Substantially All Corporate Assets

The board of directors has essentially unconstrained authority to sell, lease, mortgage, or otherwise dispose of corporate assets

---

[11] The statutory elimination of shareholder voting rights makes sense in this context because the outcome of any vote by the subsidiary's shareholders would be a foregone conclusion and because how a parent corporation votes shares of a subsidiary is a business decision for the parent's board rather than the parent's shareholders.

[12] If the parent will not survive or the articles of merger will effect a change in the parent's articles of incorporation, however, the parent's shareholders must approve the transaction. DGCL § 253(c); MBCA § 11.05(c).

[13] Specifically, DGCL § 251(f) provides that "each share of stock of such constituent corporation outstanding immediately prior to the effective date of the merger is to be an identical outstanding or treasury share of the surviving corporation after the effective date of the merger." This curious language was intended to preclude the use of § 251(f) in so-called reverse triangular mergers. In such a transaction, the target corporation is merged with a subsidiary of the acquiring corporation, with the target surviving. Absent the quoted language, § 251(f) could be invoked to prevent the target corporation's shareholders from voting, provided the other two conditions were satisfied.

[14] DGCL § 251(f). Under DGCL § 262, shareholders of the surviving company are denied appraisal rights in such transactions.

except where the board attempts to dispose of all or substantially all corporate assets. In the latter case, shareholder approval is required.[15] Under DGCL § 271(a), the required vote is a majority of the outstanding voting shares. Under MBCA § 12.02(e), by contrast, the requisite vote is only a majority of those present and voting. In both cases, only the selling corporation's shareholders are entitled to vote.[16]

1.   What Does "All or Substantially All" Mean?

"All or substantially all" is not exactly a bright-line standard. Given the expense and other burdens associated with shareholder approval, and the potentially severe consequences of guessing wrong, determining whether the sale qualifies as "all or substantially all" becomes a critical issue for transaction planners. Two classic Delaware opinions usefully illustrate the problem.

In *Gimbel v. Signal Companies*, the defendant conglomerate had multiple lines of business, including aircraft and aerospace technology, truck manufacturing, and oil.[17] The latter once was Signal's core business, but over time had become something of a side line. The board of directors decided to sell the oil division at a price exceeding $480 million. The plaintiff shareholder challenged the sale on various grounds, including a claim that the transaction constituted a sale of substantially all Signal's assets. The Chancellor used a number of metrics to determine the percentage of assets being sold: revenues, earnings, assets, net worth, return on assets, and return on net worth. In each case, the contribution of the oil business was compared to the other lines of business. The precise percentage attributable to the oil business varied substantially depending on which metric was chosen. For example, the oil business represented 41% of Signal's total net worth, but represented only 26% of total assets, and generated only 15% of revenues and earnings. As a purely quantitative matter, the court therefore held, the sale did not entail a disposition of all or substantially all of Signal's assets. In dicta, however, the court went

---

[15] DGCL § 271. In 1999, the Model Act adopted amendments incorporating a new terminology. Under revised MBCA § 12.02(a), shareholder approval is required if the transaction "would leave the corporation without a significant continuing business activity."

[16] Note that we are discussing only dispositions of assets in this section. The decision to purchase assets is vested solely in the board, although shareholder action may be required indirectly by ancillary legal regimes. This is especially likely to be true if the acquiring corporation will issue a substantial amount of stock in connection with the transaction. Under MBCA § 6.21(f)(1)(ii), for example, shareholders must approve an issuance of stock for consideration other than cash if the shares to be issued "will comprise more than 20 percent of the voting power of the shares of the corporation that were outstanding immediately before the transaction." The major stock exchanges impose similar requirements in their listing standards.

[17] 316 A.2d 599 (Del.Ch.1974).

on to apply a second standard based on qualitative considerations. Signal had become a conglomerate whose main occupation was buying, operating, and selling businesses of various types. Oil may have been where the company started, but it was now just one line of business among many. Selling off the oil subsidiary did not mean that the company was going out of business or even changing the nature of its business. Consequently, the court indicated, the sale did not rise to the level of a sale of all or substantially all Signal's assets.

In *Katz v. Bregman*, the corporation sold off a series of unprofitable divisions.[18] When it proposed to sell one of its principal remaining subsidiaries, however, a shareholder sued claiming the transaction would entail a sale of all or substantially all the remaining assets. Through its various subsidiaries, the company had been in the business of manufacturing steel storage and shipping drums. Using the proceeds of its various sales, the company planned to go into the business of manufacturing plastic shipping and storage drums. In assessing whether shareholder approval was required, the Chancellor began with quantitative metrics. The subsidiary to be sold represented 51% of the firm's remaining assets, which generated 44.9% of total revenues and 52.4% of pre-tax earnings. Turning to qualitative measures, the court opined that the planned switch from steel to plastic drums would be "a radical departure," by which the corporation would sell off the core part of the business in order to go into an entirely new line of business. Taken together, the nature of the transaction, plus the fairly high percentage of assets being sold, satisfied the "all or substantially all" standard and shareholder approval therefore was required.

The *Katz* opinion seems problematic from a number of perspectives. On the one hand, switching from steel to plastic drums hardly seems like a "radical departure." Imagine a company that for many years profitably manufactured wooden baseball bats. Because almost nobody except professional players uses wooden bats anymore, the business has suffered. The company therefore decides to sell its wood lathes and other manufacturing equipment and to invest the proceeds in equipment for manufacturing aluminum baseball bats. Making this sort of product line decision is a quintessential business judgment for the board of directors. In relying on qualitative considerations, the *Katz* opinion thus

---

[18] 431 A.2d 1274 (Del.Ch.1981).

improperly inserted shareholders into a decision reserved by statute for the board.[19]

As a transactional planning matter, the absence of a bright-line rule creates unfortunate complications. Consider the plight of a transactional lawyer asked by the seller's board of directors to opine as to the necessity of a shareholder vote. A well-known rule of thumb suggests assuming that a sale of more than 75% of balance sheet assets by market value is a sale of substantially all corporate assets and that a sale of less than 25% is not.[20] Between those yard lines, one must make an educated guess based on qualitative considerations of the sort identified by *Gimbel* and *Katz*.

2.   *Choosing Between a Merger and an Asset Sale*

A given transaction often can be accomplished in more than one way. For example, suppose Ajax, Inc., is a unitary corporation with 5 unincorporated divisions: Defense; Consumer Electronics; Computers; Automotive; Trucking. Ajax proposes to sell the Defense division to the Acme Company. Because the divisions are part of a single corporation, it may seem that a sale of assets is the only choice. But the transaction readily could be structured as a merger. The transaction planner will cause Ajax to set up a shell corporation called NewCo. Ajax will then transfer the assets of the Defense division to NewCo in return for NewCo's stock. NewCo and Acme will then merge. Having said that, however, mergers and asset sales do differ in some rather fundamental ways, of which the following seem most significant:

Ease of transferring control: When a merger becomes effective, the separate existence of constituent corporations, except the

---

[19] See DGCL § 141(a) ("The business and affairs of every corporation organized under this chapter shall be managed by or under the direction of a board of directors").

[20] Leo Herzel et al., Sales and Acquisitions of Divisions, 5 Corp. L. Rev. 3, 25 (1982). The 1999 amendments to the Model Act create a formal safe harbor for transactions below the 25% threshold: "If a corporation retains a business activity that represented at least 25% of total assets at the end of the most recently completed fiscal year, and 25% of either income from continuing operations before taxes or revenues from continuing operations for that fiscal year, in each case of the corporation and its subsidiaries on a consolidated basis, the corporation will conclusively be deemed to have retained a significant continuing business activity." MBCA § 12.02(a).

In general, corporate assets are carried on the books at their historical cost, but current market value obviously is more important and, usually, more accurate. The sale price offers a good proxy for the market value of the assets being sold, of course. As for the value of the assets being retained, one typically obtains an appraisal by an investment banking firm. If litigation results, of course, a battle of expert witnesses as to proper valuation follows. If the assets being sold constitute an identifiable line of business, such as a specific subsidiary or division, some other metrics become available. In these cases, you can often figure out what percentage of your earnings, revenues or sales the assets produce. For example, in *Gimbel*, the firm was selling off its oil subsidiary. So it was fairly easy to compute the percentage of revenues and earnings the subsidiary produced.

surviving corporation, comes to an end. As we have seen, a number of key events thereupon take place by operation of law and without the need for further action. In an asset sale, the target company remains in existence with its incumbent directors and shareholders. Virtually nothing happens by operation of law, which significantly raises transaction costs.

Ease of transferring assets: In a merger, title to all property owned by each constituent corporation is automatically vested in the surviving corporation. In an asset sale, documents of transfer must be prepared with respect to each and every asset being sold and those documents must be filed with every applicable agency. For example, a deed of transfer will have to be properly filed with every county in which the target owns real estate.

Ease of passing consideration: In a merger, the consideration passes directly to nondissenting shareholders. In an asset sale, the process of distributing the consideration to the target's shareholders is more complicated. (Assuming this is desired. In some cases, the proceeds will be invested in a new line of business.) Because the selling corporation still exists, one option is to distribute the consideration as a dividend. More often, the target is formally dissolved and liquidated. After creditors have been paid off, any remaining assets (including the consideration paid in the acquisition) are distributed to its shareholders in a final liquidating dividend.

Successor liability: In a merger, the surviving company succeeds to all liabilities of each constituent corporation. In an asset sale, subject to some emerging exceptions in tort law, the purchaser does not take the liabilities of the selling company unless there has been a written assumption of liabilities.

Shareholder voting: Avoiding shareholder voting is the goal of most transaction planners most of the time. In the case of public corporations, the process of obtaining shareholder approval is cumbersome and expensive. Proxies must be solicited, which requires preparation of a proxy statement. Accountants must prepare financial statements and give an accounting opinion. Lawyers must prepare opinion letters on corporate, securities and tax law questions. The lawyers will also draft, or at least review, the proxy statement. The firm typically will hire a proxy solicitation firm to run the shareholder meeting and to solicit proxies. Senior corporate officers must expend time going over documents and gathering materials. And so on. As a result, the cost of the shareholder approval process easily can run well into seven figures. After all of that, moreover, shareholders occasionally do something silly—like not approving the acquisition. In a straight two-party merger, approval by both company's boards and by both company's shareholders is required. In an asset sale, by contrast, the purchasing corporation's shareholders generally are not entitled to vote on the transaction.

Appraisal rights: Appraisal rights give dissenting shareholders the right to demand that the corporation buy their shares at a judicially determined fair market value. The prospect that a significant number of shareholders might force the firm to buy them out for cash can threaten the acquisition, especially if the buyer is strapped for cash. So the transaction planner tries to minimize the availability of appraisal rights. In a straight two-party merger, shareholders of both corporations are eligible for appraisal rights. In most states, shareholders of the selling company are entitled to appraisal rights in a sale of all or substantially all corporate assets, but not the purchasing corporation's shareholders. In Delaware, appraisal is limited solely to mergers. In an asset sale, neither corporation's shareholders are entitled to appraisal.

Summary: On the last three criteria, a sale of all or substantially all corporate assets seems preferable to a merger. An asset sale minimizes successor liability problems and restricts both shareholder voting and appraisal rights relative to a straight two-party merger. Is there a way to get these transaction cost-minimizing advantages of an asset sale, while also getting the advantages of a merger? Indeed, there is a simple solution: the triangular merger.[21]

C. Triangular Transactions

In a triangular merger, the acquiring corporation sets up a shell subsidiary. The shell is capitalized with the consideration to be paid to target shareholders in the acquisition—such as cash or securities of the acquiring corporation.[22] The shell is then merged with the target corporation. In a forward triangular merger, the shell is the surviving entity. In a reverse triangular merger, the target survives. The point is the same in either case. The target company ends up as a wholly owned subsidiary of the acquirer. The former target shareholders either become shareholders of the acquirer or are bought out for cash.

In a triangular merger, nothing changes from the target's perspective. Exactly the same approval process must be followed. From the acquiring corporation's perspective, however, much has changed. Only shareholders of a constituent corporation are entitled

---

[21] Note that an asset sale also can be structured as a triangular transaction.

[22] Formally, the acquiring corporation transfers the consideration to the shell, which in turn issues all of its shares to the parent acquiring company.

to vote or to exercise appraisal rights. In a triangular transaction, the constituent parties are the target and the shell. As a result, the parent acquiring corporation is not a formal party to the transaction, and its shareholders are entitled neither to voting nor appraisal rights.

A triangular merger also addresses the problem of successor liability. After a triangular merger, the target remains in existence as a wholly owned subsidiary of the true acquirer. As such, the target remains solely responsible for its obligations. Unless a plaintiff is able to pierce the corporate veil, and thus reach the parent, the parent acquiring corporation's exposure to successor liability is limited to its investment in the acquired subsidiary.

Finally, leaving the target in place as a separate entity may have other advantages in terms of employee and customer relations.

Again, the take home lesson is that there are many forms a given deal can take. To the extent the law elevates form over substance, as it generally does in this area, the transaction planner has substantial opportunity to engage in regulatory arbitrage. This potentially permits the planner to add substantial value to a transaction. Contrary to conventional wisdom, good lawyering actually can create wealth.

D.   Ensuring Exclusivity

Announcement of a pending acquisition often leads other bidders to make competing unsolicited offers. Although it is difficult to gauge accurately the likelihood of a competing takeover proposal, conventional takeover wisdom treats competing bids as a serious risk for the initial bidder. The prospective acquirer incurs substantial up-front costs in making the offer, among which are: Search costs entailed in identifying an appropriate target, which can be significant in some circumstances. Once an appropriate target is identified, preparation of the offer typically requires the services of outside legal, accounting, and financial advisers. If all or part of the purchase price is to be paid from sources other than cash reserves, a likely scenario, the bidder incurs commitment and other financing fees. Finally, the bidder may pass up other acquisition opportunities while negotiating with the target. Unfortunately for the bidder, however, the emergence of a competing bid may reduce or eliminate the expected return on its sunk costs. Second bidders prevail in a substantial majority of competitive bidding contests. Even if the initial bidder prevails, the ultimate acquisition price is likely to be substantially higher than the initial bid.

Exclusivity provisions in corporate merger agreements are intended to prevent (or, at least, discourage) competing bids from interfering with the planned transaction. Such provisions may be conveniently divided into two basic categories: performance promises, wherein the target's board agrees to engage (or agrees not to engage) in certain types of conduct prior to the shareholder vote; and cancellation fees, typically a specified amount the target agrees to pay the favored bidder if the transaction does not go forward.

Performance promises can be further broken down into best efforts clauses and the various forms of no shop covenants. A best efforts clause requires both parties to use their "best efforts" to consummate the transaction.[23] It is intended to assure that the target's board of directors will not attempt to back out of the agreement. The best efforts clause also typically imposes corresponding obligations on the favored bidder's board with respect to its shareholders. Even in cases where approval by the bidder's shareholders is not required, such as in a triangular merger, the favored bidder may still agree to use its best efforts to assure that the transaction is consummated.

No shop clauses prohibit the target corporation from soliciting a competing offer from any other prospective bidders, although they allow the target to consider an unsolicited bid and even negotiate with the competing bidder. In contrast, the no negotiation covenant prohibits such negotiations. An intermediary version, the no merger provision, permits the target to negotiate with a prospective competing offeror, but prohibits it from entering into a merger agreement with the competitor until the initial bid has been brought before the shareholders.

Provisions for monetary compensation of the favored bidder in the event the transaction fails to go forward are common in negotiated acquisitions.[24] Cancellation fees, the most widely used member of this category, essentially are liquidated damages payable if the acquirer fails to receive the expected benefits of its agreement. A variation of the cancellation fee arrangement, closely akin to stock lockups, involves giving an option to the acquirer pursuant to which the acquirer has the right to purchase a specified number of target shares and also a right to resell those shares to the target at a price higher than the exercise price in the event that an alternative bid is accepted. As such, the target is required to pay some specified dollar amount to the acquirer in the event that the

---

[23] In this context, "best efforts" imposes "at a minimum a duty to act in good faith toward the party to whom it owes a 'best efforts' obligation." Jewel Cos., Inc. v. Pay Less Drug Stores Northwest, Inc., 741 F.2d 1555, 1564 n. 11 (9th Cir.1984). But see Great Western Producers Co-op. v. Great Western United Corp., 613 P.2d 873, 878 (Colo.1980) (holding, under Delaware law, that a best efforts clause merely imposed an obligation to "make a reasonable, diligent, and good faith effort").

[24] See, e.g., Cottle v. Storer Communication, Inc., 849 F.2d 570, 578 (11th Cir.1988); Beebe v. Pacific Realty Trust, 578 F.Supp. 1128, 1150 n. 7 (D.Or.1984).

transaction is not consummated, reimbursing the acquirer for out of pocket costs associated with making the offer and perhaps also including an increment reflecting the acquirer's lost time and opportunities. The fee ordinarily falls in a range of 1 to 5% of the proposed acquisition price. Payment of the fee is commonly triggered by the acquisition of a specified amount of target stock by a third party.[25] Variants include termination of the merger agreement by the target or shareholder rejection of the acquisition proposal.[26]

Although exclusive merger agreements are common they increasingly include a self-defeating provision known as a "fiduciary out." A fiduciary out may be simply a proviso stating that nothing contained in the merger agreement shall relieve the board of directors of its fiduciary duty to the shareholders.[27] Alternatively, the fiduciary out may expressly retain a right for the target's board to solicit other offers or to negotiate with other bidders if its fiduciary duties so require. The most potent version relieves the target board of its obligation to recommend the initial offer to the shareholders if a better offer is made or permits the target to terminate the merger agreement if a higher offer is received. Delaware decisions have indicated that a target board may be obliged to include a fiduciary out in an exclusive merger agreement, at least where the exclusivity provisions have sufficient teeth to present the shareholders with a *"fait accompli."*[28]

§ 12.3 The Appraisal Remedy

Mergers and sales of all or substantially all corporate assets can be likened to a form of private eminent domain. If the transaction is approved by the requisite statutory number of shares, dissenting shareholders have no statutory basis for preventing the merger. Granted, some of the minority shareholders may believe that the merger which is being forced upon them is unfair. They may want to retain their investment in the target or they may believe that the price is unfair. Corporate statutes give hold-out shareholders no remedy where they simply want to keep their target shares—the statutes permit majority shareholders to effect a

[25] See, e.g., Revlon, Inc. v. MacAndrews & Forbes Holdings, Inc., 506 A.2d 173, 178 (Del.1985); Hanson Trust PLC v. ML SCM Acquisition Inc., 781 F.2d 264, 269 (2d Cir.1986).

[26] See, e.g., Cottle v. Storer Communication, Inc., 849 F.2d 570, 572 (11th Cir.1988); Beebe v. Pacific Realty Trust, 578 F.Supp. 1128, 1150 (D.Or.1984).

[27] See, e.g., ConAgra, Inc. v. Cargill, Inc., 382 N.W.2d 576, 582 (Neb. 1986); Smith v. Van Gorkom, 488 A.2d 858, 879 (Del. 1985).

[28] Omnicare, Inc. v. NCS Healthcare, Inc., 818 A.2d 914, 938 (Del. 2003) (holding that: "Instead of agreeing to the absolute defense of the Genesis merger from a superior offer, however, the NCS board was required to negotiate a fiduciary out clause to protect the NCS stockholders if the Genesis transaction became an inferior offer.").

freeze-out merger to eliminate the minority. All the statute gives disgruntled shareholders is a right to complain about the fairness of the price being paid for their shares; namely, the appraisal remedy.

In theory, appraisal rights are quite straightforward. Briefly, they give shareholders who dissent from a merger the right to have the fair value of their shares determined and paid to them in cash, provided the shareholders comply with the convoluted statutory procedures. Unfortunately, putting this simple theory into practice has proven surprisingly difficult. Indeed, the current status of the appraisal doctrine is best described as "tattered."[29]

All appraisal statutes authorize appraisal rights in statutory mergers of close corporations. Beyond that, however, it is impossible to generalize. Whether appraisal rights are available for any other type of transaction depends on which state's law governs. In many states, appraisal is available in connection with a wide range of fundamental transactions, including mergers, sales of all or substantially all corporate assets, and even certain amendments to the articles of incorporation. For example, MBCA § 13.02(a)(4) provides appraisal rights in connection with article amendments effecting a reverse stock split.

In contrast, under DGCL § 262, Delaware law provides appraisal rights only in connection with statutory mergers.[30] But not even all mergers are covered. Section 262(b)(1) provides that appraisal rights shall not be available for companies whose stock is listed on a national securities exchange or which has more than 2,000 record shareholders. However, § 262(b)(2) then restores appraisal rights for such firms' shareholders if the consideration paid in the merger is anything other than stock of the surviving corporation, stock of another corporation that is listed on a national securities exchange or held by more than 2,000 record shareholders,[31] and/or cash in lieu of fractional shares.[32]

In order to be eligible to make use of the appraisal remedy, Delaware 262(a) requires that a stockholder: (1) hold shares continuously through the effective date of the merger; (2) perfect his

[29] The fiduciary duties of controlling shareholders have laid a significant gloss on the appraisal remedy. The result has been most unfortunate, at least insofar as doctrinal clarity is concerned. See Chapter 7.

[30] Appraisal rights, however, are not available in connection with a short form merger. See DGCL § 262; see also Glassman v. Unocal Exploration Corp., 777 A.2d 242 (Del. 2001) (holding that "absent fraud or illegality, appraisal is the exclusive remedy available to a minority shareholder who objects to a short-form merger").

[31] This provision would come into play in a triangular merger, in which the surviving corporation ends up as a wholly owned subsidiary of the acquirer. This provision allows the use of acquiring company stock as consideration.

[32] The Model Act provides a similar market out, although its version is far more complex by virtue of various exceptions for conflicted interest transactions. MBCA § 13.02(b).

appraisal rights by complying with the provisions of Delaware
§ 262(d) by sending written notice to the corporation, prior to the
shareholder vote, that he intends to exercise his appraisal rights (it
is not sufficient to merely vote against the merger at the meeting);
and (3) neither vote in favor of nor consent in writing to the merger.
MBCA § 13.21 is substantially similar.

A key question is whether appraisal is the exclusive remedy by
which a shareholder may challenge a merger. The Delaware
supreme court's *Weinberger* decision indicated appraisal would be
exclusive except in cases of fraud, misrepresentation, self-dealing,
deliberate waste of corporate assets or gross and palpable overreaching.[33] The subsequent *Rabkin* decision, however, allows
plaintiffs to bring a class action for damages whenever the plaintiffs
can prove a breach of the duty of fair dealing.[34] Consequently,
appraisal is exclusive only in cases in which plaintiff's claims go
solely to the adequacy of the price.

§ 12.4   De Facto Mergers

Transaction planning does not take place in a vacuum, of
course. Shareholders denied voting and/or appraisal rights by virtue
of the deal's structure may seek to reclaim those rights by invoking
the de facto merger doctrine. This doctrine is based on the principle
of equivalence—like things ought to be treated alike. Put another
way, the de facto merger doctrine sounds the clarion call of
elevating substance over form.

Assume that Buyer Corporation and Target Inc. agree that
Buyer will acquire Target via a reverse triangular merger. As a
result, Buyer's shareholders will not be entitled to vote on the
merger nor will they be eligible for appraisal rights. Disgruntled
Buyer shareholders sue, arguing that the reverse triangular merger
is a de facto merger. If the court agrees, the court will ignore the
form of the transaction, treat the deal as a standard two-party
merger, and grant both Buyer and Target shareholders the right to
vote and the right to dissent.

In *Hariton v. Arco Electronics*, the Delaware supreme court
emphatically rejected the de facto merger doctrine.[35] Arco agreed to
sell all of its assets to Loral Electronics in return for 283,000 Loral
shares. Arco then planned to dissolve, distributing the Loral shares

---

[33] Weinberger v. UOP, Inc., 457 A.2d 701 (Del.1983).

[34] Rabkin v. Philip A. Hunt Chemical Corp., 498 A.2d 1099 (Del.1985). One of
the key advantages of a class action vis-à-vis appraisal is that shareholders who vote
in favor of the merger are not barred either from being members of the class or even
from serving as lead plaintiffs in the class action. In re JCC Holding Co., Inc., 843
A.2d 713 (Del.Ch.2003).

[35] 188 A.2d 123 (Del.1963).

to its shareholders as a final liquidating dividend. An Arco shareholder sued, claiming that the nominal asset sale was, in substance, a merger. The court agreed "that this sale has achieved the same result as a merger," but held that form was to be elevated over substance. The de facto merger doctrine offended the equal dignity of the merger and asset sale provisions of the corporation code. Put another way, the legislature has provided multiple vehicles by which to achieve the same substantive outcome. Each statutory acquisition method had "independent legal significance," and the court could not gainsay the legislative decisions to provide different acquisition forms carrying different levels of shareholder protection.

In contrast, the Pennsylvania courts latched onto the doctrine at an early date. Indeed, many of the classic cases are Pennsylvania cases. In 1957, the Pennsylvania legislature amended the state's corporation code with the self-evident intent of eliminating the de facto merger doctrine. Despite clear legislative history indicating such an intent, the Pennsylvania supreme court in *Farris v. Glen Alden Corp.* held that the de facto merger doctrine survived the amendment.[36] In 1959, the legislature again amended the statute, this time explicitly entitling the act as "abolishing the doctrine of de facto mergers or consolidation." The Pennsylvania courts subsequently ignored the de facto merger doctrine, leaving it for the Third Circuit sitting in a diversity proceeding to pronounce the doctrine's demise.[37]

Although the de facto merger doctrine apparently is no longer good law in Pennsylvania, the *Glen Alden* decision remains worthy of study. It involved an interestingly structured transaction, which resulted from the planner's imaginative exercise in statutory construction. A company called List owned 38.5% of Glen Alden and wanted to combine the two companies. In order to do so, List sold its assets to Glen Alden in return for Glen Alden stock. List then liquidated and distributed the Glen Alden stock to its shareholders. Because List was much larger than Glen Alden, the List shareholders wound up owning 76.5% of the Glen Alden stock. The plaintiff, a Glen Alden shareholder, claimed that he was entitled to appraisal rights.

The transaction was structured to fall between the cracks of Delaware and Pennsylvania law. Under Delaware law, shareholders in a merging corporation had appraisal rights, but shareholders in a corporation selling all of its assets did not. Under Pennsylvania law, appraisal rights were available to both constituent parties to a

---

[36] 143 A.2d 25 (Pa.1958).

[37] Terry v. Penn Central Corp., 668 F.2d 188, 192 (3d Cir.1981).

merger, the selling company's shareholders in an asset sale, but not to the purchasing corporation's shareholders in an asset sale. Glen Alden was a Pennsylvania corporation. List was a Delaware corporation. Consequently, if the two companies had merged, both companies' shareholders would get appraisal rights. If Glen Alden sold its assets to List, the Glen Alden shareholders would have appraisal rights under Pennsylvania law. If List sold its assets to Glen Alden, however, neither firm's shareholders would be entitled to appraisal.[38]

In states where the de facto merger doctrine remains good law, courts support the doctrine mainly by platitudes: form should not be elevated over substance, like transactions should be treated alike, and so on. The problem is deciding when two transactions are alike, such that they should be treated alike. The general rule is to ask whether a transaction so fundamentally changes the nature of the business as to cause the shareholder to give up his shares in one company and against his will accept shares in a different enterprise. A relatively standard laundry list of factors to be considered has evolved, including: distribution of consideration to the shareholders; change in board composition; change in shareholder composition; significant changes in share value; and significant changes in the company's lines of business.[39]

Turning to policy concerns, does the de facto merger doctrine make sense? Put another way, why did the Delaware courts and the Pennsylvania legislature reject the de facto merger doctrine? Is it simply that they prefer corporate interests to shareholder interests? No. The statute provides various ways of accomplishing an acquisition. It does so because no one acquisition technique is always appropriate. If we let courts recharacterize the statutory alternatives, we increase uncertainty and we eliminate the wealth-creating advantages of having multiple acquisition formats.

§ 12.5 The Target Board's Proper Role in Statutory Acquisitions

The target board of directors' gate-keeping role in statutory acquisitions creates a potential conflict of interest. Because approval by the target's board of directors is a necessary prerequisite to these acquisition methods, the bidder may seek to purchase the board's cooperation by offering directors and/or senior

---

[38] Ordinarily, the Glen Alden board alone would have approved the purchase. In this case, however, Glen Alden apparently had insufficient authorized but unissued shares of stock to distribute to List. Accordingly, the shareholders of Glen Alden were allowed to indirectly vote on the transaction, as their approval of an amendment to the articles of incorporation was necessary to authorize more shares.

[39] See, e.g., Hariton v. Arco Elec., Inc., 188 A.2d 123 (Del.1963); Good v. Lackawanna Leather Co., 233 A.2d 201, 207–08 (N.J.Ch.1967).

managers side payments, such as an equity stake in the surviving entity, employment or noncompetition contracts, substantial severance payments, continuation of existing fringe benefits or other compensation arrangements.[40] Although it is undoubtedly rare for side payments to be so large as to materially affect the price the bidder would otherwise be able to pay target shareholders, side payments may affect target board decisionmaking by inducing it to agree to an acquisition price lower than that which could be obtained from hard bargaining or open bidding.[41] Even where the board is not consciously seeking side-payments from the bidder, a conflict of interest can still arise: "There may be at work a force more subtle than a desire to maintain a title or office in order to assure continued salary or perquisites. Many people commit a huge portion of their lives to a single large-scale business organization. They derive their identity in part from that organization and feel that they contribute to the identity of the firm. The mission of the firm is not seen by those involved with it as wholly economic, nor the continued existence of its distinctive identity as a matter of indifference."[42] Although such motivations are understandable, they conflict with the shareholders' economic interests.

Modern corporation statutes nevertheless give primary responsibility for negotiating a merger agreement to the target's board of directors. The board possesses broad authority to determine whether to merge the firm and to select a merger partner. The initial decision to enter into a negotiated merger transaction is thus reserved to the board's collective business judgment, shareholders having no statutory power to initiate merger negotiations.[43] The board also has sole power to negotiate the terms on which the merger will take place and to arrive at a definitive merger agreement embodying its decisions as to these matters.[44]

To be sure, most mergers require shareholder approval. Yet, if the target's board rejects the initial bidder, the merger process

---

[40] E.g., Samjens Partners I v. Burlington Indus., Inc., 663 F.Supp. 614 (S.D.N.Y.1987) (white knight offered target management equity stake); Singer v. Magnavox Co., 380 A.2d 969 (Del.1977) (target directors offered employment contracts); Gilbert v. El Paso Co., 490 A.2d 1050 (Del.Ch.1984) (plaintiff alleged tender offeror modified bid to benefit target managers).

[41] E.g., Pupecki v. James Madison Corp., 382 N.E.2d 1030 (Mass.1978) (plaintiff claimed that consideration for sale of assets was reduced due to side-payments to controlling shareholder); Barr v. Wackman, 368 N.Y.S.2d 497 (N.Y.1975) (plaintiff claimed target directors agreed to low acquisition price in exchange for employment contracts).

[42] Paramount Communications, Inc. v. Time Inc., [1989] Fed. Sec. L. Rep. (CCH) ¶ 94,514, at 93,268–69, 1989 WL 79880 (Del.Ch.1989), aff'd, 571 A.2d 1140 (Del.1989).

[43] Smith v. Van Gorkom, 488 A.2d 858, 873 (Del.1985).

[44] DGCL § 251(b).

comes to a halt without shareholder involvement. If the board approves a merger agreement, the shareholders become somewhat more involved, but only slightly. Shareholders have no statutory right to amend or veto specific provisions, their role being limited to approving or disapproving the merger agreement as a whole, with the statute requiring only approval by a majority of the outstanding shares.

Allocating the principal decisionmaking role to the board of directors makes sense. The board knows much more than its shareholders about the company's business goals and opportunities. The board also knows more about the extent to which a proposed merger would promote accomplishment of those goals. The board also is a more manageable body. The familiar array of collective action problems that plague shareholder participation in corporate decisionmaking obviously preclude any meaningful role for shareholders in negotiating a merger agreement. Rational shareholders will expend the effort to make an informed decision only if the expected benefits of doing so outweigh its costs. Because merger proxy statements are especially long and complicated, there are unusually high opportunity costs entailed in attempting to make an informed decision. In contrast, shareholders probably do not expect to discover grounds for opposing the proposed transaction in the proxy statement. Frequently there are none, and even where grounds exist they will often be very difficult to discern from the proxy statement. Accordingly, shareholders can be expected to assign a relatively low value to the expected benefits of careful consideration. As a result, negotiated acquisitions are likely to be approved even where approval is not the decision an informed shareholder would reach. This is why corporate law gives the board sole power to negotiate mergers. It is also why corporate law requires shareholders to vote on the merger agreement as a whole, rather than allowing them to approve or disapprove specific provisions.

As with any conferral of plenary authority, the board's power to make decisions about negotiated acquisitions gives rise to the potential for abuse. Because mergers must be approved by the target's board of directors before being submitted for shareholder approval, the bidder at the very least may have to compensate the incumbents for the loss of the rents associated with their offices, thereby reducing the amount that can be paid to the target shareholders for the sale of the firm. At the extreme, incumbents may be unwilling to surrender their positions on any terms that are acceptable to the bidder. Despite these concerns, the Delaware cases consistently apply the business judgment rule to board decisions to approve a merger. In the setting at hand, however, the prerequisite of an informed decision takes on particular import. As illustrated by the Delaware supreme court's canonical decision in *Smith v. Van Gorkom*,[45] if the board is grossly negligent in failing to adequately inform itself prior to approving a merger proposal, liability can result. Absent such facts, however, even clear mistakes of judgment thus will not result in liability.

In most cases, the business judgment rule thus ensures that the considerable latitude conferred upon the board by statute may be exercised without significant risk of judicial intervention. Why? In an arms-length merger, the board's potential conflict of interest is policed by a variety of nonlegal constraints. Independent directors and shareholders must be persuaded to approve the transaction. The reputational consequences of self-dealing may cause both the directors and managers problems in the internal and external job markets. Ill-advised acquisitions are likely to cause the acquiring firm problems in the capital markets, which may constrain its willingness to divert gains from target shareholders to the target's board and managers. In addition to those monitoring mechanisms, negotiated acquisitions are subject to the constraining influences of the market for corporate control. Where side payments persuade the target's board to accept a low initial offer, a second bidder may—and often does—succeed by offering shareholders a higher-priced alternative. Indeed, to the extent side payments affect the initial bidder's ability to raise its offer in response to a competing bid, the threat of competing bids becomes particularly important. In such cases, the second bidder is almost certain to prevail. True, the competing bidder's transaction cannot be structured as a merger or asset sale if it is unable to persuade target management to change sides. But the intervenor has a formidable alternative: the tender offer, which eliminates the need for target board cooperation by permitting the bidder to buy a controlling share block directly from the stockholders.

§ 12.6 Nonstatutory Acquisition Techniques

As we have seen, the target corporation's board of directors serves as a gatekeeper in all of the statutory acquisition forms. Target board approval is a condition precedent to putting the transaction to a shareholder vote and, of course, to ultimately closing the transaction to occur. If the board disapproves of a prospective acquisition, an outsider must resort to one of the three nonstatutory acquisitions devices: proxy contests, share purchases, or tender offers.

---

[45] 488 A.2d 858 (Del.1985).

A. Share Purchases v. Tender Offers

Absent cumulative voting, ownership of 50.1% of the outstanding voting stock guarantees one the right to elect the entire board of directors. Once the acquirer replaces the incumbent board with new members, the old board's opposition is moot. The acquirer could obtain the necessary shares through purchases on the open market or privately negotiated block transactions. These techniques have significant disadvantages. They are time consuming. The acquisition program eventually must be disclosed, as SEC regulations require disclosure by holders of more than 5% of a company's stock, and may leak even earlier. In either case, news of an acquisition program typically drives up the stock price. Search and other transaction costs may be significant. Privately negotiated block transactions at a premium over market raise fiduciary duty concerns. And so on.

The tender offer was devised as a shortcut to bypass such concerns. A tender offer is a public offer to shareholders of the target corporation in which the prospective acquirer offers to purchase target company shares at a specified price and upon specified terms. The offer is made during a fixed period of time. The offer may be for all or only a portion of a class or classes of securities of the target corporation. Shareholders wishing to accept the offer are said to "tender" their shares to the bidder. Tendered shares are held in escrow until the offer ends. At that time, the bidder may—but need not—"take down" the tendered shares. If the bidder does so, the escrow agent releases the promised consideration to the shareholders. Otherwise, the escrow agent returns the tendered shares to the owners.

B. Tender Offers v. Proxy Contests

Proxy contests long have been "the most expensive, the most uncertain, and the least used of the various techniques" for acquiring corporate control.[46] Insurgents contemplating a proxy battle face a host of legal and economic disincentives: The incumbents' informational advantages. Long-standing investor perception that proxy insurgents are not serious contenders for control. Classified boards of directors, which mean that even a successful proxy contest can only unseat a minority of the board. Restrictions on reimbursement of the insurgent's expenses, while the incumbent board is allowed essentially unfettered access to the corporate treasury. Rational shareholder apathy. And so on.

---

[46] Henry G. Manne, Mergers and the Market for Corporate Control, 73 J. Pol. Econ. 110, 114 (1965).

During the 1960s, the cash tender offer emerged as a potent alternative that suffered from relatively few of these disadvantages. At the time, a principal advantage was the almost total absence of regulation. Since the 1930s, proxy contests have been subject to numerous federal rules imposing substantial disclosure obligations on prospective acquirers. The expensive process of preparing and vetting the requisite disclosure documents directly increases the transaction costs associated with such acquisitions. More subtly, mandatory disclosure rules decrease an insurgent's profit margin by forcing it to reveal the anticipated sources of gain to be had from a change of control.[47] Prior to the 1968 adoption of the Williams Act, in contrast, cash tender offers were essentially unregulated. Accordingly, offers slightly over market could succeed and bidders thus reaped a non-pro rata share of the gains.

After passage of the Williams Act, tender offerors faced disclosure obligations (and thus transaction costs) comparable to those under the proxy rules. Tender offers nevertheless still remained more profitable than proxy contests. Although the Williams Act undoubtedly reduced offerors' profit margins, the tender offeror is still able to reap a non-pro rata share of the gains from a change in control. The changes made by the Williams Act thus reduced, but did not eliminate, the cash tender offer's advantages.

Assume, for example, that the target company has 110 outstanding shares, currently trading at $10 per share, of which the bidder owns ten. The bidder correctly believes that under its management the firm's shares would be worth $20. If the bidder successfully gains control through a proxy contest, its ten shares will produce a $100 profit when the stock price rises to reflect the company's value under its management. All the other shareholders, however, will also automatically receive a pro rata share of those gains. There is nothing the bidder lawfully can do to capture a non-pro rata share of the gains. As a result, the bidder confers a $1,000

---

[47] Two factors are at work here. First, not only target shareholders but also incumbent target managers receive the information. More extensive disclosure of the bidder's plans, coupled with the delay imposed by the Williams Act's minimum tender offer period, means that the incumbent managers will be in a better position to resist an unfriendly offer. In addition, the disclosures are also accessible by potential competing bidders. The more information the initial bidder must disclose, the greater the extent to which competing bidders are able to free-ride on the first bidder's investment in search costs. Second, assuming the target's stock is traded in an efficient secondary market, not all shareholders need to analyze the information in order for it to be factored into the corporation's stock price. Hence, the "ordinary joe" shareholders are irrelevant to the price-setting process. In any event, one effect of a tender offer is to concentrate the target's stock in the hands of professional investors, as risk averse individual investors capture profits by selling as the price rises in response to the bid. As a result, the remaining investors are better able to analyze tender offer disclosures than would be the run of the mill investor.

benefit on the other shareholders (many of whom undoubtedly voted for management).

In contrast, if the tender offeror is able to purchase all the outstanding shares it does not already own at a price below $19 per share, its profit will exceed the $100 figure available from a successful proxy contest. To do so, of course, it need not persuade all of the other shareholders to sell. As long as the holders of at least 46 shares are willing to tender at a price below $19 per share, our hypothetical bidder will obtain voting control. It may then freeze out the remaining minority shareholders in a subsequent merger at approximately the same price.

How likely is this scenario? Quite likely. Unlike the proxy contest, the tender offer does not automatically confer a pro rata share of the gains from a change of control on the target's shareholders. Instead, their share of the gains is now determined by the size of the premium paid by the bidder. No rule requires that the premium constitute a pro rata share of the gains. Instead, the premium will be no larger than necessary to obtain a controlling block of target stock. Granted, the disclosures mandated by the Williams Act may enable shareholders to estimate the gains anticipated by the bidder. It is unlikely, however, that shareholders will obtain all of those gains. For one thing, collective action problems preclude the hard bargaining needed to extract a full share of the gains. Absent competing bids or successful management resistance, there is no mechanism for the shareholders to demand a bigger piece of the pie. Rational shareholders thus can be expected to accept a premium reflecting a less than pro rata sharing of the gains, reasoning that some profit is better than none.

In addition to enabling the bidder to obtain a greater share of the gains from a change of control, the tender offer (if followed by a freeze-out merger) enables the bidder to eliminate the complications caused by controlling a company with minority shareholders. With minority shareholders remaining in place after a proxy contest, the firm's directors may not benefit the controlling shareholder to the exclusion or at the expense of the minority. With the minority eliminated by a tender offer and freeze-out merger, the bidder may do with the target as it will.

In sum, these factors predict that tender offers should succeed far more often than proxy contests. The data confirm this prediction. Proxy contests tend to succeed less than half the time. In contrast, tender offers succeed in the majority of cases. When the tender offer's greater probability of success is coupled with its higher profitability, one would expect bidders to prefer it to proxy contests. Again the data confirm this expectation, both on an absolute scale and when compared to the frequency of tender offers. Although there was an up-tick in proxy contest activity during the 1990s, much of that activity was attributable to the general rise in takeover activity. Indeed, many proxy contests during that period were made in conjunction with tender offers.

§ 12.7   Federal Regulation of Tender Offers

Prior to the 1968 passage of the Williams Act, neither federal securities nor state corporate law regulated tender offers. As already noted, this absence of regulation was one of the intrinsic advantages the tender offer possessed over other acquisition forms and thus led to the enormous growth in the volume of tender offers during the early and middle part of that decade. In 1965, Senator Harrison Williams of New Jersey proposed federal legislation to protect target companies from what he called "industrial sabotage" of hostile corporate raids on "proud old companies."[48] Although the 1965 legislation was not adopted, a second bill was introduced in 1967. The 1967 bill was considerably more balanced and focused primarily on disclosure and antifraud. As Senator Williams and others emphasized, the bill attempted to favor neither the target nor the offeror. As subsequently amended, the Williams Act has four components of principal interest for our purposes:

1. Securities Exchange Act § 13(d) regulates beachhead acquisitions of target stock. (The term beachhead acquisition refers to purchases of an initial block of target stock, either on the open market or privately, before the bidder announces its intent to conduct a tender offer.)

2. Securities Exchange Act § 13(e) regulates self-tender offers by issuers. Among the powers of a corporation is the right to buy its own stock. Stock redemptions and repurchases are subject to the legal capital statute of the state of incorporation. Where effected by means of a tender offer, however, they must also comply with § 13(e).

3. Securities Exchange Act § 14(d) regulates tender offers generally. The statute and the SEC regulations thereunder impose both disclosure and procedural requirements on the offer.

---

[48] Corporate raider is a pejorative dating from the 1960s to describe bidders, especially those who do not actually acquire target companies but rather use the tender offer process to make quick profits through greenmail or by selling blocks of target stocks to other bidders.

4.   Securities Exchange Act § 14(e) prohibits fraud in connection with a tender offer.

There is no doubt that the Williams Act dramatically changed the takeover game. It eliminated such favorite raider tactics as the "Saturday night special"—the surprise offer made over a weekend. It significantly increased the amount of information available to target shareholders, predictably driving up the average control premium paid in takeovers. Finally, it significantly expanded the federal government's role in corporate governance.

A.   Beachhead Acquisitions

For the would-be acquirer, keeping its interest in the target and takeover plans secret for as long as possible is crucial. As soon as a possible bid is disclosed, the target's stock price jumps. Target management may begin erecting defenses against the bid or seeking alternative transactions. Other potential acquirers may begin looking at the target with the idea of making a competing bid, such that the initial bidder's disclosures may simply serve to identify the target and publicize its vulnerability. In pre-Williams Act days, it was common for a prospective acquirer to quietly buy up substantial amounts of target stock before initiating its public offer. In some cases, bidders managed to acquire de facto control before going public. Today, however, Securities Exchange Act § 13(d) and the SEC rules thereunder form an early warning system effectively mandating early disclosure of impending control contests.

1.   The Obligation to Disclose

Securities Exchange Act § 13(d) requires that any person who acquires beneficial ownership of more than 5% of the outstanding shares of any class of voting equity securities registered under Securities Exchange Act § 12 must file a Schedule 13D disclosure statement within 10 days of such acquisition with the SEC, the issuer, and the exchanges on which the stock is traded.[49] Amendments must be filed within 10 days of any material change in the information in the prior filing. Let's break this requirement down into its component pieces:

---

[49] The § 13(d) reporting requirement also applies to acquisitions of more than 5% of the outstanding shares of any class of voting equity securities of a closed-end investment company registered under the Investment Company Act of 1940 or of an insurance company exempted from registration by Securities Exchange § 12(a)(2)(G).

Certain institutional investors who hold shares with no intent of affecting the control of the issuer may file a short form Schedule 13G, which essentially requires disclosure only of the amount of shares held and the nature of the holder. Rule 13d–1(b). All other 5% holders must file the longer Schedule 13D. Schedule 13D requires substantially greater disclosure (including the purpose of the holding) and must be amended more frequently. (Schedule 13G typically is filed on an annual basis.)

Any person: Suppose two corporations or individuals are working together to acquire the target corporation. Each plans to buy just under 5% of the target's stock, thinking that they will thereby get almost 10% without having to file a Schedule 13D disclosure statement. This plan will not work. Section 13(d)(3) provides that when two or more persons act as a group for the purpose of acquiring, holding or disposing of shares of the issuer they will collectively be deemed a "person" under the statute. Accordingly, such a group must file a Schedule 13D report if the members' aggregate holdings exceed the 5% threshold.

Generally speaking, some kind of agreement is necessary before it can be said that a group exists. Not only must there be an agreement, but the agreement must go to certain types of conduct. The relevant statutory provision, Securities Exchange Act § 13(d)(3) identifies "acquiring, holding, or disposing" of stock as the requisite purposes. Shortly after the Williams Act was adopted, the question arose whether two or more persons acting together for the purpose of voting shares, as when they cooperate in conducting a proxy contest, form a group for purposes of this provision. The courts split on that question.[50] The SEC subsequently adopted Rule 13d–5(b)(1), which expanded the statutory list of purposes to include voting. Consequently, a group is formed when two or more shareholders agree to act together for the purposes of voting their shares, even if they do not intend to buy any additional shares. The rule's adoption seems to have resolved the controversy, even if the SEC's authority to effectively amend the statute remains somewhat obscure.

Proving the existence of the requisite agreement is a complex and potentially difficult question of fact. On the one hand, "Section 13(d) allows individuals broad freedom to discuss the possibilities of future agreements without filing under securities laws."[51] On the other hand, an agreement to act in concert need not be formal or written. The existence of such an agreement may be proven by circumstantial evidence. Taken together, these factors create substantial uncertainty for putative group members. Given the minimal penalties for violating § 13(d), one suspects many groups err on the side of not filing.

Who acquires: In cases where a group is at issue, the meaning of the statutory term "acquires" takes on particular import. Suppose the group members' aggregate holdings exceed five percent when they enter into the agreement by which the group is formed for § 13(d) purposes. None of the group members, however, buy any

---

[50] Compare GAF Corp. v. Milstein, 453 F.2d 709 (2d Cir.1971) (group exists) with Bath Indus., Inc. v. Blot, 427 F.2d 97 (7th Cir.1970) (no group).

[51] Pantry Pride, Inc. v. Rooney, 598 F.Supp. 891, 900 (S.D.N.Y.1984).

additional shares. Do they have an immediate filing obligation or is their filing obligation only triggered by further acquisitions of additional shares? The Seventh Circuit early held that the group must acquire additional shares, over and above the shares they own at the time the agreement is made, before the filing obligation is triggered.[52] In contrast, the Second Circuit held that the group acquires stock, and thus triggers the filing obligation, at the moment they enter into an agreement to act in concert, even if the members do not intend to acquire additional shares.[53] In promulgating Rule 13d–5(b), the SEC adopted the Second Circuit position by providing that a group is formed "when two or more persons agree to act together for the purpose of acquiring, holding, voting or disposing of" stock.

Beneficial ownership of more than 5% of any equity security registered under Exchange Act § 12: Rule 13d–3(a) deems a person to be the beneficial owner of stock if he has the power (by contract, understanding, arrangement, relationship or otherwise) to vote or dispose of (or to direct the voting or disposition of) the securities in question. Rule 13d–3(d) further provides that a person shall be deemed the beneficial owner of a security if he has the right to acquire ownership of the security within 60 days (e.g., by exercise of an option, conversion of a convertible security, or revocation or termination of a trust) or acquires such a right (whether or not exercisable within 60 days) with a purpose of affecting control of the issuer. Brokers, pledgees and underwriters are not deemed the beneficial owners of securities when they hold them in the ordinary course of their business. Finally, the SEC long has taken the position that a holding company is the indirect beneficial owner of the securities held by its subsidiaries, so that if the holding company and its subsidiaries hold an aggregate of more than 5% of the outstanding shares of the class in question, they must report. All of the statutory jargon boils down to a very simple point: Beneficial ownership is a broader concept than having title to the securities. Someone can be the beneficial owner of securities even if somebody else actually has title to them. If someone has or shares the power to vote or dispose of the shares, he is their beneficial owner.

Within 10 days after such person crosses the five percent threshold: Under § 13(d), the acquirer has 10 days before it must file a Schedule 13D disclosure statement. The 10-day window begins to run on the day the acquiring person makes an acquisition which puts his holdings over the five percent threshold. Where a

---

[52] Bath Indus., Inc. v. Blot, 427 F.2d 97, 109 (7th Cir.1970).

[53] GAF Corp. v. Milstein, 453 F.2d 709, 715 (2d Cir.1971).

group is formed, the 10-day window begins to run on the day they enter into the requisite agreement to act in concert, provided their aggregate holdings exceed 5% on that date.

The statutory framework had a predictable timing effect. A bidder who intends or expects to make a hostile takeover will buy up to 4.9% as quietly as possible. It will not cross the 5% threshold until all its preparations are completed. Once it crosses that threshold, it will begin actively buying stock, attempting to acquire as many shares as possible without alerting the target during the 10-day window. Pre-filing acquisitions of 10% of the issuer's stock are common and there are anecdotal accounts of pre-filing acquisitions of as much as 25% or more of the stock.

Amending the disclosure statement: Rule 13d–2(a) requires reporting parties to file an amendment to their Schedule 13D promptly in the event of any material change in the facts set forth in the statement. "Material" is defined to include (but is not limited to) any acquisition or disposition of at least 1% or more of the class of securities in question. "Promptly" is not the most precise term the drafters might have chosen, of course, as it creates a question of fact to be determined on a case-by-case basis.[54] As a rule of thumb, most practitioners assume that "promptly" means no more than a couple of days.[55]

2.   The Content of a Schedule 13D Disclosure Statement

As with other SEC forms, Schedule 13D does not follow the "fill in the box" format familiar from tax returns. Three of the required disclosure items are significant for our purposes: Item 2 on disclosure of identity; Item 4 on disclosure of intent; and Item 6 on disclosure of agreements or understandings.

Item 2—Identity: For individuals, Item 2 disclosure presents no real problem. The individual must disclose such basic items as name, business address, occupation, and whether the individual has ever been found in violation of specified laws. As to the latter point, Item 2 specifically requires disclosure of whether the filer, during the preceding five years, has been convicted in any criminal proceeding, excluding traffic violations or similar misdemeanors. If so, the filer must provide disclosure of the nature and date of the conviction, the name and location of the court, and any penalty imposed. Item 2 also requires disclosure of whether the filer, during

---

[54] Scott v. Multi-Amp Corp., 386 F.Supp. 44, 61 (D.N.J.1974); SEC v. GSC Enterprises, 469 F.Supp. 907, 914 (N.D.Ill.1979).

[55] See, e.g., Kamerman v. Steinberg, 123 F.R.D. 66, 72–73 (S.D.N.Y.1988) (denying motion for summary judgment on ground that a jury reasonably could find that weekend events should have been disclosed at the start of business on the following Monday).

the preceding five years, was the subject of a judgment or consent decree enjoining the filer from violating the securities laws in the future or finding a past of such laws.

For corporate parties things get more complicated. In addition to such basic items as identifying the state of incorporation and the like, Instruction C requires Item 2 disclosures with respect to each executive officer and director, and each controlling person. If the controlling person is itself a corporation, Item 2 disclosures are required with respect to each intermediary corporation and each officer and director of the ultimate parent controlling corporation. Surprisingly, it is not clear whether Item 2 disclosures are required with respect to executive officer and director of intermediary corporations.

Item 4—Intent: Item 4 is the heart of any Schedule 13D and, along with deciding who is a member of the group, the source of most § 13(d) litigation. The instructions require disclosure of "any plans or proposals which the reporting persons may have which relate to or would result in" any of 9 specified actions or, in a tenth catch-all provision, any "action similar to any of those enumerated above." Among the enumerated actions are: (1) acquisition or disposition of the target's securities; (2) a merger or other extraordinary transaction involving the target or any of its subsidiaries; (3) a sale or transfer of a material amount of the target's assets; (4) changes in the composition of the target's board of directors or management; and so on. In addition to the numerous specifics required by the instructions to Item 4, courts have held that the reporting person must explicitly state whether it intends to seek or is considering seeking control of the issuer.[56]

In practice, Item 4 disclosures tend to be boilerplate and to throw in every possible purpose except the proverbial kitchen sink. The reporting person discloses what options it is considering, but buries its true intent in a lengthy statement of everything it might conceivably do someday. Although courts have occasionally criticized the kitchen sink approach, it remains the safest and most common form of Item 4 disclosure.

Item 6—Contracts and understandings: Item 6 requires disclosure of any contracts, arrangements, understandings, or relationships with respect to the securities of the issuer. At a minimum, Item 6 requires disclosure of the terms of an agreement or understanding among the members of a reporting group. If such an agreement has been reduced to writing, a copy of the agreement

---

[56] See, e.g., Dan River, Inc. v. Unitex Ltd., 624 F.2d 1216, 1226 n. 9 (4th Cir.1980); Chromalloy American Corp. v. Sun Chem. Corp., 611 F.2d 240, 247 (8th Cir.1979); SEC v. Amster & Co., 762 F.Supp. 604, 613–14 (S.D.N.Y.1991).

must be attached to the disclosure statement as an exhibit pursuant to Item 7.

3.   Section 13(d) Litigation

Nobody likes to be fired, so it is hardly surprising that target directors and managers frequently resist unsolicited takeover bids. Among the most common takeover defenses is litigation under § 13(d), typically alleging some form of nondisclosure. Suppose Bidder filed a Schedule 13D disclosure document containing the following Item 4 disclosure: "Bidder has determined to make a large equity investment in Target. From time to time, as market conditions warrant in its view, Bidder may purchase or sell shares of Target's common stock on the open market." Shortly before filing the initial schedule 13D, Bidder entered into a brokerage contract with a well known brokerage firm specializing in takeover stocks. The contract provides: (1) the broker will purchase up to 4.9% of Target's outstanding common stock; (2) Bidder will reimburse the broker for any losses suffered in connection with those acquisitions; and (3) the broker will pay over to Bidder any profits realized in connection with those acquisitions, less its usual brokerage fee plus an additional 5%, including any profits realized by tendering or otherwise selling the shares to Bidder. This so-called "parking" agreement was not disclosed in any of Bidder's filings. The target sues, alleging that Bidder violated 13(d) by not disclosing the parking arrangement and by not adequately disclosing whether it intended to seek control of Target.

Obviously, the SEC has standing to prosecute violations of the tender offers rules. In a civil proceeding, the SEC may seek a variety of sanctions ranging from disgorgement of profits to corrective disclosures. To be sure, the SEC cannot conduct a criminal prosecution, but the SEC can refer cases to the Justice Department for criminal prosecution, as it frequently did in connection with the insider trading scandals of the 1980s.

Targets of an unsolicited offer frequently inform the SEC of alleged violations and ask that the SEC bring charges against the bidder. This is largely a pro forma act, as the SEC only rarely takes an aggressive posture in prosecuting § 13(d) violations. Instead, most § 13(d) litigation is brought by the target.

Standing presents the initial hurdle for private party litigation under § 13(d). More precisely, there are two distinct issues here, which all too often get bollixed up: (1) Is there an implied private right of action under § 13(d), at all? (2) Assuming that there is an implied private right of action under § 13(d), does this plaintiff have standing to assert that right of action in this case? As to the former question, most courts have found that there is an implied private right of action under § 13(d). As to the latter, we must bifurcate the inquiry. Do shareholders of the target corporation have standing under § 13(d)? Does the target corporation have standing under § 13(d)?

As for shareholder standing, most courts hold that shareholders have standing to seek injunctive but not monetary relief under § 13(d). As a result, shareholders generally cannot receive damages for § 13(d) violations.[57] Shareholders who wish to sue for false or misleading § 13(d) reports thus are relegated to the damage remedies provided by Securities Exchange Act § 18(a) and/or Rule 10b–5. Section 18(a) usually is of limited utility to investors. To recover under Section 18(a), an investor must show actual "eyeball" reliance on the false or misleading report, namely that the investor actually saw the report and relied on it.[58] This requirement has precluded the enforcement of claims under § 18(a) by class action, the only efficient means of litigating such claims. In addition, it can be difficult to show damages under § 18(a), because that section requires the misstatement to have affected the price of the securities (i.e., a causal nexus must be proven between the misrepresentation and the loss or diminishment of the plaintiff's investment).[59] Rule 10b–5 is also potentially available, but is of limited utility in this context because the investor must prove scienter and must be a purchaser or seller of the security.[60]

As for target corporations, they too lack standing to seek damages for § 13(d) violations.[61] Initially, federal courts almost uniformly granted issuers standing to seek injunctive relief under § 13(d).[62] In the oft-cited *Liberty National* case, however, the standing issue got bollixed up with the issue of allowable remedies. A bit of background on the latter issue is necessary. In *Rondeau v. Mosinee Paper Corp.*, the issuer brought suit for the defendant's failure to file a Schedule 13D. The Seventh Circuit granted an

---

[57] See, e.g., Sanders v. Thrall Car Mfg. Co., 582 F.Supp. 945, 960n61 (S.D.N.Y.1983), aff'd, 730 F.2d 910 (2d Cir.1984); Rosenbaum v. Klein, 547 F.Supp. 586, 591 (E.D.Pa.1982); Issen v. GSC Enterprises, Inc., 508 F.Supp. 1278, 1295 (N.D.Ill.1981); Myers v. American Leisure Time Enterprises, Inc., 402 F.Supp. 213, 214 (S.D.N.Y.1975), aff'd mem., 538 F.2d 312 (2d Cir.1976).

[58] See, e.g., Gross v. Diversified Mortgage Investors, 438 F.Supp. 190, 195 (S.D.N.Y.1977).

[59] Cramer v. General Telephone & Elec., 443 F.Supp. 516, 525 (E.D.Pa.1977), aff'd, 582 F.2d 259 (3d Cir.1978).

[60] See Ernst & Ernst v. Hochfelder, 425 U.S. 185, 193 (1976).

[61] See, e.g., Hallwood Realty Partners, L.P. v. Gotham Partners, L.P., 286 F.3d 613 (2d Cir.2002) (holding that a target has no private cause of action for damages under § 13(d)).

[62] See, e.g., Florida Commercial Banks v. Culverhouse, 772 F.2d 1513, 1519 n. 2 (11th Cir.1985) (citing cases in 1st, 2d, 4th, 7th, 8th and 9th Circuits); Portsmouth Square Inc. v. Shareholders Protective Comm., 770 F.2d 866, 871 n. 8 (9th Cir.1985); Gearhart Indus., Inc. v. Smith Int'l, Inc., 741 F.2d 707, 714 (5th Cir.1984).

injunction that for a period of 5 years would have prevented the defendant from voting any shares purchased between the date when a Schedule 13D should have been filed and the date on which it was in fact filed. The Supreme Court reversed, on the grounds that the plaintiff had not shown such irreparable harm that a sterilizing injunction was appropriate. The Court suggested that less severe remedies might be available under appropriate fact settings, such as enjoining the defendant from voting, acquiring additional shares or commencing a takeover bid pending compliance.[63] Since *Rondeau*, however, courts finding a § 13(d) violation generally have been quite conservative in fashioning a remedy. Typically, they merely issue an order directing that the violation be cured, either by amending the filing or by filing a Schedule 13D not previously filed. Courts have been unwilling, in the belief that they are unauthorized, to grant more effective relief.[64]

In *Liberty National*, the target corporation sought an aggressive equitable remedy ordering the bidder to divest all of its target stock holdings. In broad language, which lay extensive emphasis on the conflict of interest between target corporation managers and shareholders in the hostile takeover setting, the Eleventh Circuit held that "no cause of action under section 13(d) exists *for the relief Liberty requests.*"[65] Notice how the court blurred three distinct inquiries: the existence of a cause of action; standing of the party at bar; and the remedy being sought. Instructively, a subsequent Eleventh Circuit decision limited *Liberty National* to the relief being sought. Where the target corporation sought only corrective disclosure, the target corporation had standing.[66]

B. Tender Offer Disclosure and Procedural Rules

The Williams Act's announced goal is protection of target shareholders.[67] Disclosure provided the principal vehicle by which this goal was to be achieved; consequently, the Act imposes substantial disclosure requirements on both target management and the bidder. To be sure, the Williams Act also provides a number of procedural protections for shareholders. In general, however, the Act's procedural requirements mainly serve to make the disclosure

---

[63] 422 U.S. 49 (1975).

[64] See, e.g., Treadway Companies, Inc. v. Care Corp., 638 F.2d 357, 380 (2d Cir.1980) (refusing an injunction where defective filing was cured and "shareholders had ample time to digest th[e] information").

[65] Liberty Nat'l Ins. Holding Co. v. Charter Co., 734 F.2d 545, 567 (11th Cir.1984) (emphasis supplied).

[66] Florida Commercial Banks v. Culverhouse, 772 F.2d 1513, 1519 (11th Cir.1985).

[67] S. Rep. No. 550, 90th Cong., 1st Sess. 3 (1967); H.R. Rep. No. 1711, 90th Cong., 2d Sess. 3 (1968). See also Rondeau v. Mosinee Paper Corp., 422 U.S. 49, 58 (1975).

requirements more effective, as they principally "require or prohibit certain acts so that investors will possess additional time within which to take advantage of the disclosed information."[68]

Accordingly, the bidder must disseminate a Schedule TO disclosure statement containing, among other things, information relating to the bidder's identity, the source of its funds and any plans to merge with or otherwise make material changes in the target if the bid is successful. If all or part of the tender offer price is to be paid in the form of securities, rather than purely in cash, the bidder likely also will be required to incorporate a Securities Act registration statement in its offering materials and to generally comply with the Securities Act and state blue sky laws on offering securities. Similarly, if the company makes a tender offer for its own shares, it is subject to a series of SEC rules under Exchange Act § 13(e) that basically track the disclosure and procedural rules applicable to third-party tender offers under §§ 14(d) and 14(e).

1. *Definition of Tender Offer*

Although the Williams Act establishes an extensive regulatory scheme governing tender offers, the Act never actually defines what constitutes a tender offer subject to the statute and the rules thereunder. The obvious rationale for this failure has been a desire on the part of Congress and the SEC to retain regulatory flexibility to deal with novel transactions that might fall outside the scope of a statutory definition, while still raising the same regulatory concerns as covered transactions. Nobody doubts that the Williams Act applies to "conventional" tender offers, which might be defined as: A public offer to purchase at a specified price and terms during a specified period of time all or part of a class or classes of securities of a publicly held corporation. But what about privately negotiated block purchases or secondary market purchases, as well as other "unconventional" acquisition techniques?

The issue arose during the 1970s and 1980s in connection with two stock purchase techniques: the creeping tender offer and the street sweep. The term "creeping tender offer" is actually a misnomer. The bidder never makes a conventional tender offer. Rather, the bidder directly purchases a sufficient number shares on the open market to give it effective control over the target. Once the bidder has working control over the target, it then effects a merger with the target in order to solidify its control and to eliminate remaining minority shareholders.

In contrast, a street sweep begins with a conventional tender offer that is subsequently withdrawn. The tactic was devised to take

---

[68] Schreiber v. Burlington Northern, Inc., 472 U.S. 1, 9 (1985).

advantage of the takeover arbitrageur phenomenon. Arbitrageurs seek profit by buying target company stock on the open market and subsequently tendering the stock to the bidder at the higher tender offer price. Risk averse target shareholders commonly are prompted to sell by the price increase that generally follows announcement of a tender offer. Arbitrageurs, who are willing to take the risk that the deal will not go forward, therefore can acquire substantial blocks of the target's stock. In a street sweep, the nominal bidder withdraws the tender offer and purchases a controlling block of target shares directly from arbitrageurs through open market or privately negotiated transactions. In *Hanson Trust PLC v. SCM Corp.*,[69] for example, Hanson (and affiliated companies) launched a tender offer for all outstanding shares of SCM. After Hanson terminated the tender offer in response to defensive moves by SCM, Hanson made five privately negotiated and one open market purchase from arbitrageurs, totaling 25% of SCM's outstanding common stock.

To determine whether these types of transactions should be deemed tender offers—and thereby subject to § 14(d) and the underlying rules—courts have frequently looked to the eight factors of the so-called *Wellman* test:

> (1) active and widespread solicitation of public shareholders; (2) for a substantial percentage of the issuer's stock; (3) at a premium over the prevailing market price; (4) offer terms fixed, rather than negotiable; (5) offer contingent on the tender of a fixed minimum or limited to a maximum number of shares to be purchased; (6) offer open for only a limited time period; (7) offeree subjected to pressure to sell; and (8) public announcement of a purchasing program preceding or accompanying a rapid accumulation of a large amount of the target's securities.[70]

Not all factors need be present for a transaction to be deemed a tender offer. Indeed, one may not even need a majority to be present, as the court emphasized that identifying the determinative factors is to be done on a case-by-case basis. Having said that, however, the factors that usually seem most important are publicity and pressure to sell. These are the factors that make a purchase program most look like a tender offer.

The ambiguity inherent in the *Wellman* test has not precluded its widespread use. Although the SEC has not formally adopted the *Wellman* test, the test was developed by the SEC enforcement staff

---

[69] 774 F.2d 47 (2d Cir.1985).

[70] Wellman v. Dickinson, 475 F.Supp. 783, 823 (S.D.N.Y.1979), aff'd on other grounds, 682 F.2d 355 (2d Cir.1982).

for use in litigation and the SEC staff has often urged its adoption by the courts on a case-by-case basis. The Ninth Circuit, for example, relied on the *Wellman* test in determining that a creeping tender offer by Carter Hawley Hale was not a tender offer within the meaning of the Act.[71]

In *Hanson Trust*, however, the Second Circuit called the validity of the *Wellman* test into question, arguing that a "mandatory 'litmus test' appears to be both unwise and unnecessary."[72] The issue at bar was whether a street sweep constituted a tender offer subject to the disclosure and procedural mandates of the Williams Act. After Hanson's rapid block purchases following the termination of its tender offer, SCM sought injunctive relief, including enjoining Hanson from acquiring additional shares or voting the shares it held, alleging that Hanson's block purchases were a tender offer in violation of 14. In lieu of the *Wellman* factors, the Second Circuit invoked the guidelines used to determine whether an offering of securities is eligible for the private placement exemption under Securities Act § 4(1). As such, the main issue is whether the offerees are sophisticated investors who do not need the Williams Act's protections. Applying that standard, the court determined that Hanson Trust's street sweep was neither a new tender offer nor a "de facto" continuation of the withdrawn tender offer. The offerees from whom Hanson Trust bought were all professional investors fully capable of looking out for themselves.

2. Commencement of a Tender Offer

Determining when a tender offer commences is critical for several reasons. For one thing, it tells the bidder when its disclosure obligation triggers. For another, many tender offer rules contain time periods that run from the commencement date. Rule 14d–2 governs the commencement of a tender offer:

> A bidder will have commenced its tender offer for purposes of section 14(d) of the Act ... and the rules under that section at 12:01 a.m. on the date when the bidder has first published, sent or given the means to tender to security holders. For purposes of this section, the means to tender includes the transmittal form or a statement regarding how the transmittal form may be obtained.

---

[71] The offer in question actually was a defensive stock purchase program effected on the secondary market by the target company for its own stock—a creeping self-tender offer, if you will. SEC v. Carter Hawley Hale Stores, Inc., 760 F.2d 945 (9th Cir.1985).

[72] Hanson Trust PLC v. SCM Corp., 774 F.2d 47, 57 (2d Cir.1985).

Pre-offer communications are exempted if they (1) do not include the means by which target shareholders may tender their stock and (2) all written communications are filed with the SEC and issuer.

3.   Content of Required Disclosure

On the day the offer commences, the bidder must file a disclosure document on Schedule TO with the SEC. Most of the information contained in the Schedule TO also must be disseminated to the target's shareholders, but the Williams Act gives the offeror two options as to how to effect that distribution. The first, and least used option, is so-called long-form publication of the offer in a newspaper. Typically one prepares an advertisement containing all the necessary disclosures and then runs the ad in the Wall Street Journal, New York Times and perhaps one or two other papers of national distribution. This option is unpopular because it is extremely expensive to buy the necessary ad space and, more important, because there is no guarantee that a substantial number of target shareholders will notice the ad or pay much attention to it.

Alternatively, and more commonly, the offeror publishes a summary of the proposal in a newspaper advertisement and then mails a more detailed disclosure statement directly to the shareholders. Although this option is probably at least as expensive as the first, if not more so, there is a fair degree of certainty that all target shareholders will receive notice of the proposal by this means. As with a proxy statement, the issuer must either provide the bidder with a copy of the shareholder list or agree to mail the tender offer materials on behalf of the offeror and at his or her expense.

Most of the disclosures in a tender offer are similar to those required in a Schedule 13D, albeit more detailed, and are fairly mechanical. Counsel just follows the instructions, inserting the usual boilerplate. The most technically difficult issue is the question of soft information disclosure. Consider two companies: Target Corp. and Acquirer Co. Suppose that Target's stock currently is trading at $15 per share. Acquirer does an extensive evaluation of Target. Acquirer prepares business plans for incorporating Target into the existing company, it commissions appraisals of Target's assets, it prepares projections of future income and operating results, and the like. At the end of this process, Acquirer determines on a reservation price of $25 per share. In other words, Acquirer concludes that an acquisition of Target would be profitable at any price up to $25 per share. Clearly, Acquirer is not obliged to disclose its actual reservation price. But what about the appraisals and forecasts from which that price was determined? Must they be disclosed?

Historically, disclosure of soft information was disfavored. In recent years, the SEC has adopted safe harbor rules permitting disclosure of certain soft information, such as appraisals and projections.[73] Because that rule does not mandate disclosure, however, it does not resolve the question at hand. Note that the issue here is different from the run of the mill omissions case under the securities laws, where the initial issue is whether the defendant had a duty to speak. In this context, the bidder has an affirmative obligation to file a Schedule TO containing significant disclosures. The question here therefore is whether the soft information in question is material, such that it also must be disclosed. Before the Third Circuit's decision in *Flynn v. Bass Brothers*,[74] most courts held that there is no affirmative duty to disclose soft information. In other words, the failure to disclose soft information was not regarded as a material omission. In *Flynn*, however, the Third Circuit held that courts must make a case-by-case determination of whether soft information, such as asset appraisals and projections of future earnings are material. The standard to be applied is whether the benefits to the shareholders will outweigh the harm to the shareholders. The factors the court will consider include: the qualifications of those who prepared the information; the purpose for which it was intended; its relevance to the decision; the degree of subjectivity in its preparation; the degree to which the information is unique; and the availability of other more reliable sources of information.

4. Procedural Rules

In addition to the basic disclosure provisions, the Williams Act provides a number of procedural protections for target shareholders. For example, shareholders are permitted to withdraw shares tendered to the bidder at any time prior to the closing of the offer. In Section 14(d)(5), the statute actually provides that tendered shares may only be withdrawn during the 7 days after the offer commences and at any time 60 days after commencement of the bid (assuming that the offer has not been closed and the shares taken up during that 60 day period). SEC Rule 14d–7, however, permits withdrawal for up to 15 days after commencement of the offer. The rule triggers withdrawal rights if a competing bid is made during the tender offer period. Shareholders thus have substantial opportunity to change their minds, especially if a better offer comes along.

Rule 14e–1 obligates the bidder to keep the tender offer open for at least 20 business days. In addition, the bidder must further

---

[73] The relevant Securities Exchange Act rule is Rule 3b–6.

[74] 744 F.2d 978, 988 (3d Cir.1984).

extend the tender offer period by at least 10 business days after material changes in the offer's terms. In particular, the bidder must extend the offer by 10 days if it raises the offering price.

In partial tender offers, if more than the specified number of shares are tendered Rule 14d–8 requires the offeror to take up the tendered shares on a pro rata basis. This ensures that all shareholders who tender get a chance to receive a premium for at least part of their shares. The rule eliminates a favorite pre-Williams Act tactic, in which bidders made a partial offer on a first come-first served basis. This tactic pressures shareholders to tender, so as to avoid being left as minority shareholders in a company under new control. To eliminate a similar tactic, Rule TOO provides that if the bidder, during the pendency of the offer, increases the consideration to be paid, shareholders who have already tendered their shares are entitled to receive that additional consideration.

5. Target Obligations

As long as they are acting in good faith, the target's directors have no legal duty to negotiate with a prospective acquirer. The target's board likewise has no duty to make a detailed response to hypothetical questions or hypothetical offers. Once a firm, bona fide offer is on the table, however, the target's board has a state corporate law-based fiduciary obligation to consider carefully the proposed acquisition.[75] To be sure, the "business judgment" rule "leaves relatively wide discretion in management to act in what it considers to be the best interests of the corporation."[76] Recall, however, that an informed decision is an essential prerequisite for the rule's application.

In evaluating a bona fide proposal, the following factors are legitimate and relevant considerations:

1.   The adequacy of the offering price in terms of variables such as (i) current and past market prices of the target's stock, (ii) book value and replacement cost of assets, (iii) earnings projections, (iv) "hidden" or off balance sheet assets, (v) future prospects for improvements in earnings or market value, (vi) market conditions, (vii) liquidation value of assets, (viii) if all shares are sought, the potential

---

[75] See, e.g., Norlin Corp. v. Rooney, Pace Inc., 744 F.2d 255, 267 (2d Cir.1984) ("we have required corporate managers to examine carefully the merits of a proposed change in control . . . [and] have also urged consultation with investment specialists in undertaking such analysis. . . . [t]he purpose of this exercise . . . is to insure a reasoned examination of the situation before action is taken, not afterwards").

[76] Berman v. Gerber Products Co., 454 F.Supp. 1310, 1319 (W.D.Mich.1978).

sales price of the business (a full financial picture of the target should be prepared), (ix) recent sales prices of other similarly situated companies, (x) premiums over book value paid in recent "friendly" acquisitions and hostile takeovers of other similar companies, and (xi) the probability that a higher price could be obtained from another offeror.

2.   The nature of the consideration offered, e.g., cash or securities (and, if securities, the prospects of the company to which they relate).

3.   Whether the acquirer is seeking all or a portion of the target stock; if a partial offer, the effect upon remaining shareholders, i.e., what generally would be the prospects for the minority in the case of a successful partial offer, and in particular, whether there would be a subsequent merger and if so, on what terms.[77]

4.   If applicable, the regulatory implications of the offer and the likelihood that the suitor could obtain regulatory approvals.

5.   The offeror's background, business practices and intention towards the company.

The latter two considerations are especially pertinent with respect to the target board's potential duty to affirmatively oppose an offer. Where the directors know or have reason to know that a potential acquirer would loot or mismanage the target company, for example, they have a duty to oppose the offer.[78] Likewise, where the target's directors believe that an offer is illegal for regulatory reasons, they also have a duty to oppose it.[79]

Where the initial offer by the suitor includes an invitation to negotiate, the directors of the target may enter into negotiations if they so choose, of course. Negotiation may disclose useful information, as well as providing the target company more time to evaluate and respond to the situation. The target company may condition its willingness to enter into negotiations on the suitor's agreement not to make an unfriendly offer. On the other hand, there are several potential disadvantages to entering into

---

[77] For example, the directors should consider the likely market liquidity of the shares held by the remaining shareholders, and whether this is the first step in a "freeze-out" of the minority in light of Weinberger v. UOP, Inc., 457 A.2d 701 (Del.1983).

[78] Harman v. Willbern, 374 F.Supp. 1149, 1158–59 (D.Kan.1974), aff'd, 520 F.2d 1333 (10th Cir.1975).

[79] Panter v. Marshall Field & Co., 646 F.2d 271, 297 (7th Cir.1981); Berman v. Gerber Products Co., 454 F.Supp. 1310, 1323 (W.D.Mich.1978).

negotiations with an unwanted suitor. Negotiating could also give the suitor the impression that an offer might be accepted if the terms were different. This could encourage the suitor to disbelieve management objections and to pursue its proposal persistently when it might otherwise withdraw. Any counter-offer made by the target could undermine subsequent arguments to shareholders attacking the suitor. If discussions included a consideration of management's or the directors' future with the target company, claims could be raised that management or directors received improper benefits.

If a tender offer is made, the Williams Act mandates a target board disclosure statement on Schedule 14D–9.[80] Before filing the Schedule 14D–9, the target may only send communications to its shareholders if those communications are limited to three matters: (i) identifying the offeror; (ii) stating that the target is studying the tender offer and will, before a specified date, advise as to its position; and (iii) requesting shareholders to defer making a determination on whether to accept or reject the tender offer until they have been advised of the target's position. Under SEC Rule 14e–2, the target must disclose to shareholders within 10 business days of the commencement of a tender offer whether the target's board: (i) recommends acceptance or rejection of the tender offer; (ii) expresses no opinion and is remaining neutral with respect to the tender offer; or (iii) is unable to take a position with respect to the tender offer. The statement also must include the board's reason or reasons for its position. Pursuant to Rule 14d–9(f), this communication is deemed to be a recommendation or solicitation and therefore requires the filing of Schedule 14D–9 with the SEC. The Schedule 14D–9 must disclose: (i) the reasons supporting the board's recommendations, (ii) any arrangements or understandings between members of management or the board and the offeror, (iii) the identity and employment capacity of the persons making the recommendations, and (iv) information as to all transactions by officers or directors effected during the 60 days prior to the filing of the Schedule 14D–9 in the securities that are the subject of the offer.

§ 12.8 Takeover Defenses: The Arsenal

As we have seen, the target's board of directors functions as a sort of gatekeeper in statutory acquisitions. A key feature of the nonstatutory acquisition forms, from the acquirer's perspective,

---

[80] Before the offer has actually commenced, the issue is whether a proposal is material information the target is required to disclose. In general, no announcement need be made of invitations to negotiate or of casual inquiries. Panter v. Marshall Field & Co., 646 F.2d 271, 296 (7th Cir.1981) ("Directors are under no duty to reveal every approach made by a would-be acquiror or merger partner.").

thus is the ability to bypass the target board and make an offer directly to the target's shareholders. When the hostile tender offer emerged in the 1970s as an important acquirer tool, lawyers and investment bankers working for target boards began to develop defensive tactics designed to impede such offers. Takeover defenses reasserted the board's primacy, by extending their gatekeeping function to the nonstatutory acquisition setting. The takeover arms race remains unrelenting. As fast as new acquisition techniques are developed, new defenses spring up.

A. Shark Repellents

A shark repellent is an amendment to the firm's articles of incorporation designed to persuade potential bidders to look elsewhere. Broadly speaking, shark repellents fall into two principal categories: provisions relating to the board of directors and supermajority voting requirements for certain transactions.

1. Classified Boards

Classified board provisions, which are also known as staggered boards, divide the board of directors into three classes of which only one is elected annually. The offeror thus must go through two annual meeting cycles before it has elected a majority of the board. This defense will be most effective as to an acquirer who needs quick access to target assets to pay off acquisition debt. If the acquirer can wait out the current board, the provisions will be of little benefit. Many factors will tend to lead the current board to play along with a successful acquirer—even if the board has the right to hold-out. Why should any director, except maybe an insider, risk being sued by the acquirer every time they do something he or she opposes?

The classification scheme must be protected from the possibility that the acquirer will (1) remove the directors without cause or (2) pack the board with his or her own appointments. This can be done by reserving to the board the sole right to determine the number of directors and the sole right to fill any vacancies. If permitted by state law, a classified board shark repellent can be further strengthened by limiting or abolishing the right of shareholders to call a special shareholders meeting or to remove directors without cause (defining cause as narrowly as possible).

Delaware permits a classified board to be created either in the articles of incorporation or in the bylaws.[81] In contrast, the MBCA requires that a classified board be created through the articles.[82] In

---

[81] DGCL § 141(d).

[82] MBCA § 8.06.

general, a classified board scheme established in the articles will be more difficult for to a hostile bidder to undo. Because shareholders may initiate changes to the bylaws, but initial board approval is required to amend the articles, a classified board scheme contained solely in the bylaws is more vulnerable to repeal than a classified board scheme contained in solely in the articles.

2.   *Supermajority Vote Requirements*

Supermajority provisions focus on preventing back-end freeze-out mergers. It is rare for even a highly successful hostile tender offeror to purchase 100% of the shares. The bidder therefore will usually follow a successful offer with a freeze-out merger to eliminate any remaining minority shareholders.

In some cases, a bidder may intentionally use a back-end merger to ensure success. In a so-called "two-tier offer," the bidder makes a partial tender offer and simultaneously announces its intention to subsequently acquire the remaining shares of the company in a subsequent merger. Often, the price paid in the second step merger will be lower than the tender offer price and/or be paid in a less desirable form of consideration. Such offers are said to be structurally coercive.[83] Such an offer works because collective action problems preclude shareholders from communicating with each other and from credibly binding themselves to reject offers not in their collective best interests. Suppose the bidder makes a tender offer for 51% of the target's stock at $50 per share in cash, while announcing an intent to follow up a successful offer with a freeze-out merger at $40 per share to be paid in the form of subordinated debt securities. An individual shareholder might believe that the offer is unacceptable, but worry that a majority of the other stockholders will accept the offer. A shareholder who does not tender thus risks having all of his shares acquired in the less desirable back-end transaction, which creates an incentive to tender into the front-end transaction. If the shareholder tenders, however, some pro rata portion of his shares will be taken up in the higher paying front-end.

A freeze-out merger generally only requires approval by a majority of the outstanding shares. As a result, the outcome of the shareholder vote often will be a foregone conclusion in light of the acquirer's holdings. Supermajority voting shark repellents erect barriers to second-step transactions by imposing a supermajority voting requirement for mergers, asset sales, and like transactions. A typical formulation requires that any merger be approved by 80% of all outstanding shares and a majority of the outstanding shares

---

[83] See, e.g., Chesapeake Corp. v. Shore, 771 A.2d 293, 331 (Del.Ch.2000); City Capital Assoc. Ltd. Partnership v. Interco Inc., 551 A.2d 787, 797 (Del.Ch.1988).

not owned by the bidder. Such provisions are authorized by DGCL § 102(b)(4), which authorizes the articles of incorporation to include: "Provisions requiring for any corporate action, the vote of a larger portion of the stock or of any class or series thereof. . . ."[84]

Supermajority vote shark repellents usually provide that the supermajority provision can be deleted or amended only by a vote equal to the supermajority vote. Hence, for example, amending an 80% vote requirement would have to be approved by 80% of all outstanding shares. This requirement is obviously intended to prevent the offeror from avoiding the supermajority vote by the simple expedient of amending the charter. In order to permit friendly transactions, most of these provisions provide that transactions approved by a majority or supermajority of the continuing directors—those in office when the raider first acquired a substantial interest in the target (say 10%)—shall not be subject to the supermajority shareholder vote requirement.

3.   *The Fair Price Variant*

Fair price shark repellents are a variant on the supermajority vote provision. This version exempts transactions from the supermajority vote where the price to be paid exceeds a specified amount. The specified "fair price" usually is not less than the price paid in the first-step transaction. In addition, fair price provisions also typically require that the second-step payment be made in the same form of consideration. Hence, they prevent the offeror from paying cash in the first-step and junk bonds in the second. A related alternative is a compulsory redemption provision that allows minority shareholders to demand to be bought out at a price at least equal to the price paid in the first-step transaction.

B.   Poison Pills

Poison pills take a wide variety of forms, but today most are based on the class of security known as a right. Hence, the pill's official name, the "shareholder rights plan." A traditional right, such as a warrant, grants the holder the option to purchase new shares of stock of the issuing corporation. The modern poison pill adds three additional elements not found in traditional rights: a "flip-in" element; a "flip-over" element; and a redemption provision.[85]

---

[84] See Seibert v. Milton Bradley Co., 405 N.E.2d 131 (Mass.1980) (upholding bylaw requiring 75% approval of a merger unless the merger was approved by a two-thirds vote of the board of directors); Seibert v. Gulton Indus., Inc., 1979 WL 2710 (Del.Ch.1979) (upholding a supermajority vote shark repellent requiring an 80% vote to approve mergers with another person or entity owning 5% or more of the outstanding stock).

[85] Warrants are traded as separate securities, having value because they typically confer on the holder the right to buy issuer common stock at a discount

1.   Flip-Over Pills

As noted, rights are corporate securities that give the holder of the right the option of purchasing shares. Because issuance of rights does not require shareholder approval, a rights-based pill may be adopted by the board of directors without any shareholder action.[86] When adopted as part of a poison pill plan, the rights initially attach to the corporation's outstanding common stock, cannot be traded separately from the common stock, and are priced so that exercise of the option would be economically irrational. The rights become exercisable, and separate from the common stock, upon a so-called distribution event, which is typically defined as the acquisition of, or announcement of an intent to acquire, some specified percentage of the issuer's stock by a prospective acquirer. (Twenty percent is a commonly used trigger level.) Although the rights are now exercisable, and will remain so for the remainder of their specified life (typically ten years), they remain out of the money.

The pill's flip-over feature typically is triggered if, following the acquisition of a specified percentage of the target's common stock, the target is subsequently merged into the acquirer or one of its affiliates. In such an event, the holder of each right becomes entitled to purchase common stock of the acquiring company, typically at half-price, thereby impairing the acquirer's capital structure and drastically diluting the interest of the acquirer's other stockholders. In other words, once triggered, the flip-over pill gives target shareholders the option to purchase acquiring company shares at a steep discount to market. As with the older style preferred stock pills, this causes dilution for the bidder's pre-existing shareholders and may have undesirable balance sheet effects.

In *Moran v. Household International*, the Delaware supreme court upheld a flip-over pill against challenges based on both the board's authority and the board's fiduciary duties.[87] Household's poison pill was a flip-over pill, albeit with a few bells and whistles. There were two triggering events: (1) the making of a tender offer for 30 percent or more of Household's shares; and (2) the acquisition of 20% or more of Household's outstanding shares by any person or group. If issued, the rights were immediately exercisable and would entitle the holders to purchase 1/100th of a share of Household

---

from the prevailing market price. In contrast, the poison pill right usually is "stapled" to the common stock and does not trade separately until some triggering event occurs.

[86] See Account v. Hilton Hotels Corp., 780 A.2d 245 (Del.2001) (noting the power of "directors of a Delaware corporation" to "adopt a rights plan unilaterally").

[87] 500 A.2d 1346 (Del.1985).

preferred stock at a price of $100. Because that price was way out of the money, there was no expectation that the rights would be exercised.

Why were the underlying rights initially stapled to the common stock? This common provision is intended to ensure that the rights trade with the common. If the rights traded separately, the potential target corporation would have to issue a separate security. More important, if the rights did not trade with the common, holders might sell common without selling the rights—or vice-versa if a separate secondary trading market developed for the rights.

Why did the rights detach from the stock in a way that initially made them unattractive to exercise? By detaching the rights once a bidder is on the scene, the target ensures that the bidder has to buy up the rights separately. Some stockholders will tender their common or sell their common shares on the market, but retain the rights. Consequently, the bidder has to deal with two distinct groups. As for the provision under which the rights are initially convertible into preferred (out of the money) and only convertible into common (in the money) in the event of a second-step transaction, it is intended to preclude an argument that the right was a sham security. DGCL § 157 allows the corporation to issue rights, but does not facially authorize the issuance of rights for takeover defenses purposes. Presumably, the transaction planner who devised the pill intended that this provision would make it appear as though the rights had economic value.

Note that the Household pill, if triggered by the making of a tender offer for 30% or more of the stock, was redeemable. The board could redeem the rights at a price of 50 cents per right at any time prior to their being exercised. If the pill was triggered by the acquisition of 20% or more of the stock, however, the rights were not redeemable. The transaction planner presumably intended this distinction to deter hostile beachhead acquisitions exceeding 20% of the shares, while still allowing a friendly deal to be accomplished by means of a tender offer.

In *Moran*, plaintiff argued that the board lacked authority to adopt a poison pill. Plaintiff contended, for example, that Delaware law, if it allowed poison pills, would be preempted by the Williams Act. The Delaware court brushed this argument off by positing that there was no state action where private parties act pursuant to a state statute authorizing their conduct.

Plaintiff also contended that DGCL § 157 did not authorize the issuance of the rights. As we've already seen, Household's poison pill was structured so as to avoid the anticipated § 157-based claim that the rights were a sham security. A second issue, however, was presented by § 157's authorization of rights "entitling the holders thereof to purchase from the corporation any shares of *its* capital stock."[88] How could Household issue rights that purport to give its shareholders the right to buy shares of another corporation? In *Moran*, the court analogized the Household pill to the anti-destruction provisions commonly found in convertible securities. Anti-destruction clauses are a common feature of convertible securities. They give holders of target company convertible securities the right to convert their securities into whatever securities the acquiring company is offering in exchange for target company common stock. Because anti-destruction provisions are valid, and the right was not a sham security, the court upheld the pill.

Plaintiffs' final broad category of authority arguments asserted that the board has no power to block shareholders from receiving tender offers. Although the *Moran* decision recognized that the board can erect defenses that deter certain types of bids, it implied that the board must leave some mechanism by which the bidder can present an offer to the shareholders. The court thus upheld the Household pill because there were several methods by which one could structure the offer so as to avoid the pill's poisonous effects, including conditioning the offer on redemption of the pill by board, soliciting written consents to remove the board at same time that the offer is made, and conducting a proxy contest to oust the incumbent board.[89]

2. Flip-In Pills

A pill with only a flip-over provision is vulnerable. The classic example of a bidder turning such a pill to its own advantage was Sir James Goldsmith's takeover of Crown Zellerbach. Like most first generation pills, the Crown Zellerbach pill only kicked in if the bidder sought to effect a freeze-out merger. Goldsmith acquired a controlling interest in Crown Zellerbach, but decided not to squeeze out the remaining Crown Zellerbach shareholders. This had a rather nifty effect. Since Goldsmith wasn't going to do a merger, he

---

[88] DGCL § 157 (emphasis supplied).

[89] Plaintiff argued that Household's pill precluded shareholders from exercising their right to conduct a proxy contest. Delaware law provides that a board may not erect takeover defenses that disenfranchise its shareholders without a "compelling justification." See, e.g., Unitrin, Inc. v. American Gen. Corp., 651 A.2d 1361, 1379 (Del.1995); Stroud v. Grace, 606 A.2d 75, 92 n. 3 (Del.1992); Blasius Indus., Inc. v. Atlas Corp., 564 A.2d 651 (Del.Ch.1988). While the board thus cannot preclude proxy contests, the *Moran* court concluded that Household's pill did not do so. Soliciting proxies did not trigger the pill, even if the challenger held proxies for more than 20% of the shares. Moreover, the court concluded that even though the pill would effectively prohibit one from buying more than 20% of the shares before conducting a proxy contest that restriction was unlikely to have a significant impact on the success rate of such contests. Moran v. Household Int'l, Inc., 500 A.2d 1346, 1355 (Del.1985).

didn't suffer any poisonous effects. On the other hand, since the rights were now exercisable in the event of a merger, what had happened? The pill had become a double-edged sword, which Goldsmith had redirected at the target's throat. By triggering the pill, Goldsmith precluded anyone from merging with Crown Zellerbach—any merger partner would suffer the poisonous effects. As a result, he had effectively precluded the board from attracting a white knight.

In response, transaction planners developed the flip-in pill. The flip-in element is typically triggered by the actual acquisition of some specified percentage of the issuer's common stock. (Again, 20 percent is a commonly used trigger.) If triggered, the flip-in pill entitles the holder of each right—except, and this is key, the acquirer and its affiliates or associates—to buy shares of the target issuer's common stock or other securities at half price. In other words, the value of the stock received when the right is exercised is equal to two times the exercise price of the right. The flip-in plan's deterrent effect thus comes from the dilution caused in the target shares held by the acquirer. For example, in Grand Metropolitan's bid for Pillsbury, Pillsbury's flip-in plan would have reduced Grand Met's interest in Pillsbury from 85% to 56 percent. The value of Grand Met's holdings would have declined by more than $700 million dollars.

3.   Redemption Provisions

Proponents of poison pills argue that such plans give the target bargaining leverage that it can use to extract a higher price in return for redeeming the pill. Because the rights trade separately from the issuer's common stock, an acquirer remains subject to the pill's poisonous effects even if an overwhelming majority of the target's shareholders accept the bidder's tender offer. In the face of a pill, a prospective acquirer thus has a strong incentive to negotiate with the target's board.

Flexible redemption provisions are imperative for this purpose; the transaction planner must give the board the option of redeeming the rights at a nominal cost in order to allow desirable acquisitions to go forward. Typical redemption provisions include: the window redemption provision, in which the board retains the ability to redeem the rights for a specified time period following the issuance of the rights, and the white knight redemption provision, in which the target may redeem the rights in connection with a transaction approved by a majority of the continuing directors.

Note that combining a poison pill with a classified board shark repellent gives the board an especially powerful negotiating device. The pill will deter the bidder from buying a control block of stock prior to the pill being redeemed. Instead, in the face of board resistance, the acquirer must go through two successive proxy contests in order to obtain a majority of the board. Prevailing in two such successive contests, without owning a controlling block of stock, would be a significant obstacle.

4.   Modern Pills

Today, poison pills typically include all three elements: a flip in right, a flip-over right, and a redemption provision. In combination, they make a highly effective anti-takeover device.

C.   Other Defenses

The most common response to a hostile takeover bid is litigation, usually raising some violation or another of the tender offer rules we studied earlier. In this section, we consider some other commonly used defenses.

1.   Defensive Acquisitions

In the old days, a potential target would try to create barriers for potential purchasers by acquiring companies that cause antitrust problems for the most likely bidders. In the 1970s, for example, the Marshall Field & Co. department store chain acquired numerous other retail chains for the purpose of creating such antitrust barriers. Although the acquisitions were uniformly unprofitable, the acquired chains operated in the same geographic areas as the most probable potential bidders for Marshall Field.[90] An obvious problem with this tactic is that unprofitable defensive acquisitions will cause the target's stock price to fall, which may make the target more vulnerable to potential buyers who will not face antitrust concerns.[91]

2.   Dual Class Stock Plans

In the early decades of the last century, the capital structure of many corporations included multiple classes of common stock having disparate voting rights. Classes of nonvoting common were especially common. Such dual class stock capital structures fell into disfavor around the time of the Great Depression but returned to prominence in the 1980s due to their considerable potential as an anti-takeover device. An incumbent who cannot be outvoted, after all, cannot be ousted. In the early 1980s, a growing number of companies therefore adopted dual class capital structures to concentrate voting control in management's hands. This effect is

---

[90] Panter v. Marshall Field & Co., 646 F.2d 271 (7th Cir.1981) (holding that the defensive acquisition strategy did not violate the target board's fiduciary duties).

[91] See Mark L. Mitchell & Kenneth Lehn, Do Bad Bidders Become Good Targets?, 98 J. Pol. Econ. 372 (1990).

most easily demonstrated by considering the simplest type of disparate voting rights plan—a charter amendment creating two classes of common stock. The Class A shares are simply the preexisting common stock, having one vote per share. The newly created Class B shares, distributed to the shareholders as a stock dividend, have most of the attributes of regular common stock, but possess an abnormally large number of votes (usually 10) per share. Class B shares typically are not transferable, but may be converted into Class A shares for sale. Normal shareholder turnover thus concentrates the superior voting shares in the hands of long-term investors, especially incumbent managers, giving them voting control without the investment of any additional funds.

As a result of regulatory developments in the late 1980s, dual class stock has lost much of its utility as a takeover defense. Under current stock exchange listing standards, dual class stock plans generally must be implemented before the corporation goes public. Post-IPO charter amendments effecting a disparate voting rights plan thus are precluded. The difficulty of marketing dual class stock in an IPO has largely limited this technique to companies whose existing dual class structures was grandfathered by the stock exchanges.

3. Stock Repurchases

Stock repurchase programs involve setting up a regular program to buy target shares on the open market from time to time. Such programs should have the desirable effect of supporting the company's stock price by (1) lessening the number of outstanding shares and (2) acting as a signal that management is supportive of shareholder interests. As a high stock price is an excellent takeover defenses, such repurchase programs have become a common feature of corporate governance.

As a takeover defense, stock repurchases will be most effective when the corporation has a large amount of free cash (cash for which there are no positive net present value investments available), but no substantial free cash flows. If the corporation has on-going free cash flows, a one-time stock repurchase is unlikely to have a permanent stock price effect. In order to make such a target a less attractive takeover candidate, an on-going program of regular stock repurchases will be necessary.

There are some potential problems associated with stock repurchase programs. Securities fraud liability is a major risk. Issuers can be held liable for securities fraud under Rule 10b–5 when they purchase shares while in possession of material nonpublic information, just as officers and directors can be held liable for inside trading. In any repurchase plan, the corporation therefore must be careful to analyze whether there would be any basis for an insider trading claim. In large companies with diverse information flows, this can obviously be very difficult. The best times to engage in repurchases are therefore immediately after annual and quarterly disclosure reports are filed with the SEC, as there is somewhat less likelihood of undisclosed material information at those times.

A stock repurchase plan reduces the number of shares the bidder has to buy in order to achieve control. If the price effect of the repurchase plan is not substantial, the plan may backfire. This risk can be alleviated by having a friendly or controlled entity purchase the stock. Some firms therefore effect repurchases through a pension plan or employee stock ownership plan. In that way, the shares remain outstanding, with full voting rights, instead of becoming nonvoting treasury shares.

4. Lockups

Both negotiated acquisitions and unsolicited tender offers may trigger competitive bidding for control of the target. Like exclusivity provisions in a merger agreement, the lockup developed as a response to these risks. A lockup is any arrangement or transaction by which the target corporation gives the favored bidder a competitive advantage over other bidders.[92] So defined the term includes such tactics as an unusually large cancellation fee or an agreement by the target to use takeover defenses to protect the favored bid from competition. Lockup options refer more narrowly to agreements (usually separate from the merger agreement) granting the acquirer an option to buy shares or assets of the target. The option commonly becomes exercisable upon the acquisition by some third party of a specified percentage of the target's outstanding shares.[93]

Stock lockup options give the favored bidder an option to purchase treasury or authorized but unissued target shares. If the option is exercised prior to the shareholder vote on the merger agreement, the favored bidder can vote the additional shares in favor of the merger, helping to assure that the requisite approval will be obtained. If a competing bidder prevails, the favored bidder can exercise the option and sell the additional shares on the open market or tender them to the successful bidder, thereby recouping some or all of its sunk costs. Finally, the risk that the option will be

---

[92] See generally Stephen M. Bainbridge, Exclusive Merger Agreements and Lock-Ups in Negotiated Corporate Acquisitions, 75 Minn. L. Rev. 239 (1990).

[93] E.g., Hanson Trust PLC v. ML SCM Acquisition, Inc., 781 F.2d 264, 267 (2d Cir.1986); Mobil Corp. v. Marathon Oil Co., 669 F.2d 366 (6th Cir.1981), cert. denied, 455 U.S. 982 (1982); DMG, Inc. v. Aegis Corp., 1984 WL 8228 (1984).

exercised, thereby driving up the number of shares that must be acquired in order to obtain control and thus increasing the overall acquisition cost, may deter competing bids in the first instance.

Asset lockup options grant the favored bidder an option to purchase a significant target asset. While asset lockups often are used to entice a prospective bidder, they are principally intended to end or prevent competitive bidding for the target. Accordingly, the subject of the option is usually either the assets most desired by a competing bidder or those essential to the target's operations.[94] Asset lockups are sometimes referred to as "crown jewel options," the name coming from the notion that the asset subject to the option is the target's crown jewel, i.e., its most valuable or desirable asset.

§ 12.9 The Propriety of Target Board Resistance to Unsolicited Offers

The takeover defenses just reviewed create a very serious conflict between the interests of shareholders and corporate management. Successful takeover bids produce substantial gains for target shareholders. In contrast, in today's hostile takeover environment, target directors and officers know that a successful bidder is likely to fire many of them. Any defensive actions by the incumbent board and management are thus tainted by the specter of self-interest. As Judge Richard Posner explained:

> When managers are busy erecting obstacles to the taking over of the corporation by an investor who is likely to fire them if the takeover attempt succeeds, they have a clear conflict of interest, and it is not cured by vesting the power of decision in a board of directors in which insiders are a minority. . . . No one likes to be fired, whether he is just a director or also an officer. The so-called outsiders moreover are often friends of the insiders. And since they spend only part of their time on the affairs of the corporation, their knowledge of those affairs is much less than that of the insiders, to whom they are likely therefore to defer.[95]

In light of this conflict, courts have had to evolve a workable standard for reviewing takeover defenses.

---

[94] See, e.g., Hanson Trust PLC v. ML SCM Acquisition, Inc., 781 F.2d 264, 267 (2d Cir.1986); Mobil Corp. v. Marathon Oil Co., 669 F.2d 366 (6th Cir.1981), cert. denied, 455 U.S. 982 (1982).

[95] Dynamics Corp. of Am. v. CTS Corp., 794 F.2d 250, 256 (7th Cir.1986), rev'd on other grounds, 481 U.S. 69 (1987).

A. Cheff v. Mathes

Holland Furnace marketed its products using a set of remarkably fraudulent tactics. Holland salesmen went door to door posing as government or utility inspectors. Once they had received access to the homeowner's furnace, the salesmen would dismantle the furnace and refuse to reassemble it. The salesmen would inform the homeowner that the furnace was unsafe and that parts necessary to make it safe were unavailable. The homeowner would then be sold a replacement Holland furnace.[96] Because of government investigations into these unsavory practices, the firm was under-performing.

Arnold Maremont proposed a merger between Holland and Maremont's Motor Products Corporation. Holland's president, one Cheff, rejected Maremont's overtures. Maremont then began buying Holland stock. When he announced his purchase publicly and demanded a place on the board, Cheff again refused. Holland claimed Maremont often bought corporations to liquidate them for a profit. Because of this reputation, Cheff claimed, Holland employees who were aware of Maremont's interest were beginning to show signs of discontent.

Having met resistance, Maremont offered to sell his stock to the firm at a premium over his purchase price and over the current market price.[97] Holland's board agreed, causing the corporation to repurchase Maremont's shares using corporate funds. Other shareholders then challenged that repurchase transaction in a derivative suit.

---

[96] Holland Furnace Co. v. FTC, 295 F.2d 302 (7th Cir.1961).

[97] During the 1980's, the purchase by a corporation of a potential acquirer's stock, at a premium over the market price, came to be called "greenmail." Buying off one person, however, provides no protection against later pursuers, except possibly to the extent that the premium paid to the first pursuer depletes the corporate resources and makes it a less attractive target. Such reduction in corporate resources could, of course, be achieved by managers simply by paying a dividend to all shareholders or by buying the corporation's shares from all shareholders wanting to sell. Section 5881 of the Internal Revenue Code, enacted in 1987, imposes a penalty tax of 50 percent on the gain from greenmail, which is defined as gain from the sale of stock that was held for less than two years and sold to the corporation pursuant to an offer that "was not made on the same terms to all shareholders." Despite its many critics, greenmail actually may be beneficial in that it may allow the board to seek higher bids or to enhance value (above the greenmail bidder's price) by making changes in management or strategy. The question whether greenmail deserves its bad reputation therefore is essentially an empirical one. The evidence supports the proposition that greenmail actually benefits nonparticipating shareholders overall, and does not appear to be a device for entrenching incumbent management. Consequently, a greenmailer may be a catalyst for change from within or for a bidding war and may therefore deserve to make a profit. Jonathan R. Macey & Fred S. McChesney, A Theoretical Analysis of Corporate Greenmail, 95 Yale L.J. 13 (1985); Fred S. McChesney, Transaction Costs and Corporate Greenmail: Theory, Empirics, and a Mickey Mouse Case Study, 14 Managerial & Decision Econ. 131 (1993).

In *Cheff v. Mathes*, the Delaware supreme court announced the so-called "primary purpose test" for review of takeover defenses. Under that standard, the court did not give the directors the immediate benefit of the business judgment rule's presumption of good faith. Rather, the directors had the initial burden of showing that they had reasonable grounds to believe that a danger to corporate policy and effectiveness existed and did not act for the primary purpose of preserving their own incumbency. Only if the board could make such a showing would they be entitled to the business judgement rule's protection. However, the directors merely had to show good faith and reasonable investigation; they could not be held liable for an honest mistake of judgment.

The *Cheff* court was well aware of the conflict of interest inherent in target resistance to unsolicited bids. Hence, its imposition of the primary purpose test. To be sure, the Court downplayed the conflict slightly by comparing the conflict posed by takeovers to that "present, for example, when a director sells property to the corporation." As we shall see below, however, this comparison is a perfectly plausible one, although it also is one that has essentially escaped most academic commentators.

In practice, however, the burden placed on target directors by the primary purpose test proved illusory. Liability could be imposed only if entrenching the incumbent officers and directors in office was the primary motive for the defensive actions.[98] Management therefore simply directed its counsel to carefully scrutinize the bidder's tender offer documents to find some issue of policy as to which they differed. And, of course, it was always possible to find some policy disagreement between incumbent management and the outside bidder. Why else would the bidder be trying to oust the incumbents? Once found, such a policy difference was all that was necessary to justify the use of defensive tactics, because the board could not be held liable for its actions, even if hindsight showed them to be unwise, so long as they were motivated by a sincere belief that they were necessary to maintain proper business policy and practices. The primary purpose analysis thus added little to the highly deferential treatment of board decisions mandated by the traditional business judgment rule and therefore proved an ineffective response to the conflict of interest present when target boards and management respond to a takeover bid.

---

[98] Royal Industries, Inc. v. Monogram Industries, Inc., [1976–1977 Transfer Binder] Fed. Sec. L. Rep. (CCH) ¶ 95,863 at 91,136–38, 1976 WL 860 (C.D.Cal.1976) (applying Delaware law); Condec Corp. v. Lunkenheimer Co., 230 A.2d 769 (Del.Ch.1967).

B. *Unocal*

The Delaware supreme court eventually recognized that the traditional doctrinal options were inadequate to the task at hand. Characterizing the action of a corporation's board of directors as a question of care or of loyalty has vital—indeed, potentially outcome determinative—consequences. If the court treated takeover defenses as a loyalty question, with its accompanying intrinsic fairness standard, takeover defenses would rarely pass muster. The defendant directors would be required, subject to close and exacting judicial scrutiny, to establish that the transaction was objectively fair to the corporation. Because this burden is an exceedingly difficult one to bear, and thus would likely result in routine judicial invalidation of takeover defenses, a duty of loyalty analysis makes sense only if we think all takeovers are socially desirable and that all takeover defenses are therefore bad social policy.

On the other hand, if the court treated takeover defenses as a care question, virtually all takeover defenses would survive judicial review. Before the target's directors could be called to account for their actions, plaintiff would have to rebut the business judgment rule's presumptions by showing that the decision was tainted by fraud, illegality, self-dealing, or some other exception to the rule. Absent the proverbial smoking gun, plaintiff is unlikely to prevail under this standard. A duty of care analysis thus makes sense only if we think management resistance to takeovers is always appropriate.

Cheff had attempted to split the difference by creating an intermediate standard of review. As we have seen, however, that effort proved illusory. In *Unocal v. Mesa Petroleum*,[99] the Delaware supreme court tried again.

Unocal attempted to steer a middle course by promulgating what has been called an "intermediate" or "enhanced business judgment" standard of judicial review, but is perhaps best described as a "conditional business judgment rule."[100] Famed corporate raider T. Boone Pickens, whom the court referred to as having "a national reputation as a 'greenmailer,'" controlled Mesa, which in turn owned 13% of Unocal's voting stock. Mesa launched a hostile two-tiered tender offer, pursuant to which it initially offered to buy slightly over 37% of the remaining shares for $54 per share.

---

[99] 493 A.2d 946 (Del.1985).

[100] Michael P. Dooley, Fundamentals of Corporation Law 547 (1995). Like the traditional business judgment rule, the conditional *Unocal* rule can be applied only to actions that are within the power or authority of the board. As a preliminary inquiry one thus must ask whether the board had the authority under the governing statutes and the corporation's organic documents to take this specific action. 500 A.2d 1346, 1350 (Del.1985).

According to Mesa, if the initial bid succeeded, Mesa would then eliminate the remaining shares by means of a freeze-out merger, in which the consideration would be junk bonds ostensibly worth $54 per Unocal share.

Two-tier offers like Mesa's are generally regarded as being structurally coercive. Suppose Target's pre-bid stock price was $50. Bidder 1 makes a two-tier offer with differing prices: $80 cash in the first step tender offer and $60 cash in the second step freeze-out merger. Assuming the first step tender offer seeks 50% of the shares plus one, the blended offer price is $70 with a blended premium of $20 per share (calculated by taking the weighted average of the two steps). Bidder 2 offers $75 in cash for any and all shares tendered, a premium of $25 per share. As a group shareholders are better off with Bidder 2. Yet, Bidder 1's offer creates a prisoners' dilemma. Those shareholders who "cheat," by taking Bidder 1's front end offer, end up with $80 rather than $75. With a large noncohesive group in which defectors bear no cost—such as shame or reprisals—rational investors should defect. Because everyone's individual incentive is to defect, the shareholders end up with the offer that is worst for the group. Mesa's offer differed from this example by offering the same price in both steps, but the far less attractive form of consideration to be paid in the second step would have similarly coercive effects.

In hopes of fending off Mesa's bid, Unocal's board of directors authorized a discriminatory self-tender offer for Unocal's own stock. Under Unocal's counter offer, if Mesa's front-end tender offer succeeded in giving Mesa a majority of Unocal's stock, Unocal would then offer to repurchase the remaining minority shares with debt securities purportedly worth $72 per share. Unocal's self-tender offer was intentionally discriminatory in that any shares tendered by Pickens would not be accepted. If effected, the self-tender offer would drain Unocal of most of its significant assets and leave it burdened by substantial debt. Even more cleverly, however, Unocal might never need actually complete the self-tender offer. Its offer only applied if Mesa acquired more than 50% of Unocal's voting stock. Because Unocal offered a higher price than did Mesa, however, Unocal's shareholders were likely to tender to it rather than to Mesa. If no shareholders tendered to Mesa, Mesa would not acquire 50%, and Unocal would be able close its offer without taking down any of the tendered shares. When Unocal's shareholders complained about this aspect of the defense, Unocal agreed to buy 50 million of the shares tendered to it the stock tendered to it even if Mesa did not acquire 50%.

Mesa sued to enjoin the self-tender offer, alleging that Unocal's board of directors had violated its fiduciary duties to both Mesa and

Unocal's other shareholders. In particular, Mesa objected to the discriminatory nature of the proposed self-tender offer. The Delaware supreme court rejected Mesa's arguments. Given the coercive nature of Mesa's bid, the bid's probable price inadequacy, and Pickens' reputation as a greenmailer, Unocal was entitled to take strong measures to defeat the Mesa offer. Because excluding Mesa from the self-tender offer was essential to making the defense work, the directors could discriminate against Mesa without violating their fiduciary duties.[101]

Although the Delaware supreme court thus reaffirmed the target's board general decisionmaking primacy, in light of the board's potential conflict of interest vis-à-vis the shareholders, judicial review was to be somewhat more intrusive than under the traditional business judgment rule: "Because of the omnipresent specter that a board may be acting primarily in its own interests, rather than those of the corporation and its shareholders, there is an enhanced duty which calls for judicial examination at the threshold before the protections of the business judgment rule may be conferred."

The initial burden of proof is on the directors, who must first show that they had reasonable grounds for believing that a danger to corporate policy or effectiveness existed. The directors satisfy this burden by showing good faith and reasonable investigation. The good faith element requires a showing that the directors acted in response to a perceived threat to the corporation and not for the purpose of entrenching themselves in office. The reasonable investigation element requires a demonstration that the board was adequately informed, with the relevant standard being one of gross negligence. Assuming the directors carry their initial burden, they next must prove that the defense was reasonable in relationship to the threat posed by the hostile bid. Note that both the decision to adopt and any subsequent decision to implement a set of takeover defenses are subject to challenge and judicial review.[102]

Not surprisingly, the board's "initial" burden of proof quickly became the whole ball game. If the directors carried their two-step

---

[101] After the *Unocal* decision, the SEC demonstrated its disapproval of discriminatory tender offers by amending its Williams Act rules to prohibit tender offers other than those made to all shareholders. See Exchange Act Rule 13e–4(f)(8) (issuer self-tender offers); Exchange Act Rule 14d–10 (third party offers).

[102] In Moran v. Household Int'l, Inc., 500 A.2d 1346 (Del.1985), plaintiffs sued when the poison pill was first adopted, before any takeover bid had been made. The court upheld the pill as valid, but explained that: "When the Household Board of Directors is faced with a tender offer and a request to redeem the [pill], they will not be able to arbitrarily reject the offer. They will be held to the same fiduciary standards any other board of directors would be held to in deciding to adopt a defensive mechanism, the same standard as they were held to in originally approving the [pill]." Id. at 1355.

burden, the business judgment rule applied, but if the directors failed to carry their initial burden, the duty of loyalty's intrinsic fairness test applied.[103] It is for this reason that the *Unocal* test is more properly seen as a conditional version of the business judgment rule, rather than an intermediate standard. The *Unocal* rule solved the problem of outcome determination not so much by creating a different standard of review, as by creating a mechanism for determining on an individual basis which of the traditional doctrinal standards was appropriate for the particular case at bar.

C. *Revlon*

In *Revlon v. MacAndrews & Forbes Holdings*, the Delaware supreme court developed a modified version of the *Unocal* to deal with a particular problem; namely, the use of takeover defenses to ensure that a white knight would prevail in a control auction with the hostile bidder.[104] In response to an unsolicited tender offer by Pantry Pride, Revlon's board undertook a variety of defensive measures, culminating in the board's authorization of negotiations with other prospective bidders. Thereafter the board entered into a merger agreement with a white knight, which included a lockup arrangement, as well as other measures designed to prevent Pantry Pride's bid from prevailing. Revlon's initial defensive tactics were reviewed (and upheld) under standard *Unocal* analysis. In turning to the lockup arrangement, however, the Court struck out in a new direction:

> The Revlon board's authorization permitting management to negotiate a merger or buyout with a third party was a recognition that the company was for sale. The duty of the board had thus changed from the preservation of Revlon as a corporate entity to the maximization of the company's value at a sale for the stockholders' benefit. This significantly altered the board's responsibilities under the *Unocal* standards. It no longer faced threats to corporate policy and effectiveness, or to the stockholders' interests, from a grossly inadequate bid. The whole question of defensive measures became moot. The directors' role changed from defenders of the corporate bastion to auctioneers charged with getting the best price for the stockholders at a sale of the company.

Because the lockup ended the auction in return for minimal improvement in the final offer, it was invalidated.

---

[103] Shamrock Holdings, Inc. v. Polaroid Corp., 559 A.2d 257, 271 (Del.Ch.1989).
[104] 506 A.2d 173 (Del.1985).

Revlon proved surprisingly troublesome. For example, did it establish special duties to govern control auctions or were the so-called "*Revlon* duties" really just the general *Unocal* rules applied to a special fact situation? The courts have waffled on this issue, although the latter interpretation seems to have ultimately prevailed. In 1987, for example, the Delaware supreme court drew a rather sharp distinction between the *Unocal* standard and what it then called "the *Revlon* obligation to conduct a sale of the corporation."[105] Two years later, however, the court indicated that *Revlon* is "merely one of an unbroken line of cases that seek to prevent the conflicts of interest that arise in the field of mergers and acquisitions by demanding that directors act with scrupulous concern for fairness to shareholders."[106] Even so, the doctrinal differences between *Unocal* and *Revlon* still loom quite large at times.

Whether the *Revlon* duties were distinct or just a sub-set of *Unocal*, what exactly were directors supposed to do once their role changes from "defenders of the corporate bastion to auctioneers"? Prior to the pivotal *Paramount* decisions discussed below, we thought a few things could be said with confidence. We knew, for example, that target directors need not be passive observers of market competition.[107] The board's objective, however, "must remain the enhancement of the bidding process for the benefit of the stockholders."[108] Favored treatment of one bidder at any stage of the process was therefore subjected to close scrutiny. Ultimately, the board's basic task was to get the best possible deal, which usually but not always meant the best possible price, for their shareholders. Directors did not need to blindly focus on price to the exclusion of other relevant factors. The board could evaluate offers on such grounds as the proposed form of consideration, tax consequences, firmness of financing, antitrust or other regulatory obstacles, and timing.[109] Easy standards to state perhaps, but often quite difficult ones to apply.

Finally, and even more fundamentally, when did directors stop being "defenders of the corporate bastion" and become "auctioneers"? Again, prior to the *Paramount* decisions, it seemed well-settled that the auctioneering duty is triggered when (but apparently only when) a proposed transaction would result in a

---

[105] Ivanhoe Partners v. Newmont Mining Corp., 535 A.2d 1334, 1338 (Del.1987).

[106] Barkan v. Amsted Indus., Inc., 567 A.2d 1279, 1286 (Del.1989).

[107] CRTF Corp. v. Federated Dep't Stores, Inc., 683 F.Supp. 422, 441 (S.D.N.Y.1988) (applying Delaware law).

[108] Mills Acquisition Co. v. Macmillan, Inc., 559 A.2d 1261, 1287 (Del.1989).

[109] Cottle v. Storer Communication, Inc., 849 F.2d 570, 577 (11th Cir.1988).

change of control of the target corporation. For example, if a defensive recapitalization, which most of these cases involved, transferred effective voting control to target management, or some other identifiable control block, the courts treated the transaction as a "change in control" of the corporation requiring adherence to *Revlon*'s auction rule.[110] If no identifiable control block formed (or changed hands), however, defensive measures were subject solely to standard *Unocal* review.[111]

D. The Paramount Cases

As the *Unocal* regime evolved, two recurring questions arose. First, what threats to the corporation and its shareholders were legally cognizable under the first prong? Second, what defenses were proportional to a given threat?

At least for a time, the Delaware chancery court defined the category of cognizable threats quite narrowly. Only threats to shareholder interests had any real analytical significance. Nor were all threats to shareholder interests cognizable. Rather, at least in the context of an offer for all of the target's outstanding shares, the trend was towards limiting cognizable threats to inadequate value and structural coercion.[112] Inadequate value refers, obviously enough, to a claim that the price offered by the bidder is too low. Structural coercion refers to bidder tactics creating a "risk that disparate treatment of non-tendering shareholders might distort shareholders' tender decisions."[113]

The Delaware courts gave target directors a more-or-less free hand to deal with structurally coercive bidder tactics. Defenses designed to preclude such offers, to minimize their coercive effect, or

---

[110] Mills Acquisition Co. v. Macmillan, Inc., 559 A.2d 1261, 1285 (Del.1989) (holding that the requisite "sale" could take "the form of an active auction, a management buyout or a 'restructuring'"); see also Robert M. Bass Group, Inc. v. Evans, 552 A.2d 1227, 1243 (Del.Ch.1988); cf. Ivanhoe Partners v. Newmont Mining Corp., 535 A.2d 1334, 1345 (Del.1987) (*Revlon* not triggered where management ally had less than 50% voting control after defensive recapitalization); accord Black & Decker Corp. v. American Standard, Inc., 682 F.Supp. 772, 781 (D.Del.1988) (reading Delaware law to require directors of a company to maximize the amount received by shareholders once it is clear to them that the "corporation is to be subject to a change of control").

[111] Paramount Communications, Inc. v. Time Inc., [1989 Transfer Binder] Fed. Sec. L. Rep. (CCH) ¶ 94,514 at 93,279–80, 1989 WL 79880 (Del.Ch.), aff'd on other grounds, 571 A.2d 1140 (Del.1989).

[112] See, e.g., City Capital Assoc. Ltd. Partnership v. Interco Inc., 551 A.2d 787, 797 (Del.Ch.1988).

[113] Ronald J. Gilson & Reinier Kraakman, Delaware's Intermediate Standard for Defensive Tactics: Is there Substance to Proportionality Review, 44 Bus. Law. 247, 267 (1989). Two-tier tender offers are perhaps the most commonly recognized form of structural coercion. If shareholders believe that the offeror is likely to obtain a controlling interest in the front-end transaction, they face the risk that they will be squeezed out in the back-end for less desirable consideration. Thus they are coerced into tendering into the front-end to avoid that risk, even if they believe the front-end transaction itself is undesirable.

to provide a more viable alternative to the shareholders all were deemed proportional. Indeed, when structural coercion was the identified threat, proportionality review usually was perfunctory at best.

When inadequate value was the sole threat, however, proportionality review became more exacting. As most observers interpreted the so-called poison pill cases,[114] *Unocal* permitted target management to use takeover defenses as negotiating leverage to obtain a better deal for the shareholders or, more realistically, to delay the hostile offer while an alternative transaction was arranged. In either case, however, target management supposedly had to let the shareholders make the ultimate decision.[115] According to the conventional wisdom, once it became clear the best possible alternatives were on the table, the board was required to redeem the pill and permit the shareholders to choose between the available alternatives. The target board could neither "just say no," nor could it structure the transaction in such a way as to force shareholders to accept a management-sponsored alternative.

This straightforward approach took a beating from the Delaware supreme court in a pair of cases involving Paramount Communications. In the first of these cases, *Paramount Communications v. Time Inc.*,[116] the Delaware courts addressed a takeover struggle between Time, Warner Communications, and Paramount. After first developing a long-term strategic plan and searching for acquisitions that would advance that plan, Time's board of directors agreed to a merger with Warner Communications in which former Warner shareholders would receive newly issued Time shares representing approximately 62 percent of the shares of the combined entity. As is typical in negotiated acquisitions, the parties also sought "to discourage any effort to upset the transaction" by agreeing to a lockup option giving each party the option to trigger an exchange of shares. In addition, the merger agreement included a no shop clause in the merger agreement,

---

[114] The name refers to a group of cases in which targets used poison pills to protect a restructuring plan from interference by a hostile bidder. See, e.g., Grand Metropolitan PLC v. Pillsbury Co., 558 A.2d 1049 (Del.Ch.1988); City Capital Assoc. Ltd. Partnership v. Interco Inc., 551 A.2d 787 (Del.Ch.1988); see also BNS Inc. v. Koppers Co., Inc., 683 F.Supp. 458 (D.Del.1988) (applying Delaware law); CRTF Corp. v. Federated Dep't Stores, Inc., 683 F.Supp. 422 (S.D.N.Y.1988) (same).

[115] Cases purporting to stand for the proposition that the board must ultimately permit the shareholders to choose include: Shamrock Holdings, Inc. v. Polaroid Corp., 559 A.2d 257 (Del.Ch.1989); Grand Metropolitan PLC v. Pillsbury Co., 558 A.2d 1049, 1058 (Del.Ch.1988); City Capital Assoc. Ltd. Partnership v. Interco Inc., 551 A.2d 787, 799–800 (Del.Ch.1988); AC Acquisitions Corp. v. Anderson, Clayton & Co., 519 A.2d 103, 113–14 (Del.Ch.1986). But see Moran v. Household Int'l, Inc., 490 A.2d 1059, 1070 (Del.Ch.), aff'd, 500 A.2d 1346 (Del.1985).

[116] [1989 Transfer Binder] Fed. Sec. L. Rep. (CCH) ¶ 94,514, 1989 WL 79880 (Del.Ch. 1989), aff'd, 571 A.2d 1140 (Del.1989).

which they supplemented by obtaining commitments from various banks that they would not finance a takeover bid for Time.

Shortly before Time' shareholders were to vote on the merger agreement,[117] Paramount made a cash tender offer for Time. Time's board rejected the offer as inadequate, without entering into negotiations with Paramount. To forestall Paramount, the Time and Warner boards then agreed to a new structure for the transaction, under which Time would make a cash tender offer for a majority block of Warner shares to be followed by a merger in which remaining Warner shares would be acquired, thus obviating the need for shareholder approval. The new plan required Time to incur between 7 and 10 billion dollars in additional debt. Finally, and perhaps most damningly from the perspective of a Time shareholder, it foreclosed the possibility of a sale to Paramount. If the new plan succeeded, Time's shareholders therefore would end up as minority shareholders in a company saddled with substantial debt and whose stock price almost certainly would be lower in the short run than the Paramount offer.

The substantial differences in shareholder wealth likely to result from a decision to merge with Warner rather than to sell to Paramount forcefully presented the question of who should make that decision. As Chancellor Allen put it, the "overarching question is where legally (an easy question) and equitably (more subtle problem) the locus of decisionmaking power does or should reside in circumstances of this kind." Paramount naturally insisted that Time's board had an obligation to give the "shareholders the power and opportunity to decide whether the company should now be sold." Chancellor Allen, however, squarely rejected that proposition. Allen acknowledged that reasonable people could believe that the Paramount offer was the better deal for the shareholders, that many of Time's shareholders undoubtedly so believed, and that the Time directors' preference for the Warner deal might turn out to be a terrible mistake. Having said all that, however, the board nonetheless had the authority to go forward with the Warner acquisition:

> [T]he financial vitality of the corporation and the value of the company's shares is in the hands of the directors and management of the firm. The corporation law does not operate on the theory that directors, in exercising their powers to manage the firm, are obligated to follow the

---

[117] The plan of merger called for Warner to be merged into a Time subsidiary in exchange for Time common stock. Although Time was not formally a party to the merger and approval by its shareholders therefore was not required under Delaware law, New York Stock Exchange rules required a vote of Time shareholders because of the number of shares to be issued.

wishes of a majority of shares. In fact, directors, not shareholders, are charged with the duty to manage the firm.[118]

Although Time board was comprised principally of outsiders with no readily apparent conflicts of interest, their response to the Paramount bid was a major change in the form of the transaction whose sole purpose was preventing their shareholders from accepting Paramount's offer. This attempt to foreclose shareholder choice without first conducting a fair competition for control reasonably might lead one to infer they were acting from selfish interests.

Both decisions in *Time* responded at least implicitly to this concern. Both the chancery and supreme courts concluded that the Time board's initial decision to merge with Warner was protected by the business judgment rule. Both courts also concluded that the lockup, the decision to recast the transaction as a tender offer for Warner, and the various other measures undertaken to stave off Paramount's competing bid involved a conflict of interest sufficiently severe to require application of a more exacting standard of review. The preliminary question then was whether the *Unocal* or *Revlon* standard governed.

For somewhat different reasons both Chancellor Allen and the supreme court concluded that *Revlon* had not triggered. Chancellor Allen followed the poison pill cases by holding that *Revlon* applies to any transaction constituting a change in control, but he determined that the merger agreement would not result in a transfer of control because control of the combined entity remained "in a large, fluid, changeable and changing market."

Although the Delaware supreme court indicated Allen's analysis was correct "as a matter of law," it rejected plaintiff's *Revlon* claims on "different grounds":

> Under Delaware law there are, generally speaking and without excluding other possibilities, two circumstances which may implicate *Revlon* duties. The first, and clearer one, is when a corporation initiates an active bidding process seeking to sell itself or to effect a business reorganization involving a clear break-up of the company.

---

[118] Paramount Communications, Inc. v. Time Inc., [1989 Transfer Binder] Fed. Sec. L. Rep. (CCH) ¶ 94,514 at 93,284, 1989 WL 79880 (Del.Ch.1989). The supreme court agreed: "Delaware law confers the management of the corporate enterprise to the stockholders' duly elected board representatives. . . . That duty may not be delegated to the stockholders." Paramount Communications, Inc. v. Time Inc., 571 A.2d 1140, 1154 (Del.1989). The supreme court further observed that courts should not substitute their "judgment as to what is a 'better' deal for that of a corporation's board of directors." Id. at 1153.

> However, *Revlon* duties may also be triggered where, in
> response to a bidder's offer, a target abandons its long-
> term strategy and seeks an alternative transaction also
> involving the breakup of the company.[119]

This passage is not exactly crystal clear. What are the other
possibilities the court did not exclude? What is the difference
between the first and second identified possibilities? If they were
deciding the case on broader grounds than Allen, can change of
control transactions not involving a break-up of the company still
trigger *Revlon*? In particular, does *Revlon* apply when the target
"initiates an active bidding process seeking to sell itself," but the
auction participants do not contemplate breaking-up the company?
What does the Court mean by a break-up of the company? As we'll
see, later cases mooted these questions, but at the time they loomed
large.

Despite having decided that *Revlon* was inapplicable, the *Time*
courts did not leave the lockup and other bid-preclusive measures
immune from challenge. Instead, both courts concluded that the
lockup and Time's subsequent recasting of the acquisition as a
tender offer were defensive measures to be analyzed under
Unocal.[120] Relying on *Interco* and its progeny, Paramount argued
that bid-preclusive defensive tactics were excessive in light of the
minimal threat of inadequate value posed by a non-coercive tender
offer at a substantial premium. Chancellor Allen distinguished
those cases on the grounds that the original decision to merge with
Warner was motivated by Time's long-term business plan. Unlike
the poison pill cases, in which the management-sponsored
transaction was principally intended to defeat an unsolicited tender
offer, Chancellor Allen saw the revised structure of the Time-
Warner transaction as being principally intended to facilitate
accomplishment of the board's long-term strategy. Given that the
tender offer thus arose out of preexisting legitimate, non-defensive
business considerations, Time had a "legally cognizable interest" in
going forward with the acquisition of Warner, which satisfied the
first prong of *Unocal*.

Allen believed the second prong of the *Unocal* analysis required
him to evaluate, among other things, the importance of the
corporate policy at stake and the impact of the board's actions. With
respect to the first point, Chancellor Allen reiterated his view that

---

[119] Paramount Communications, Inc. v. Time Inc., 571 A.2d 1140, 1150
(Del.1989).

[120] The Delaware supreme court has since confirmed that lockups and other so-
called "deal protection devices" are to be reviewed under the *Unocal* standard, even
in the context of a negotiated acquisition. Omnicare, Inc. v. NCS Healthcare, Inc.,
818 A.2d 914, 932–34 (Del. 2003).

pursuing the board's long-term strategy was a legitimate and important corporate goal. As to the latter, he observed that the offer for Warner "was effective, but not overly broad." Time's board thus "did only what was necessary to carry forward a preexisting transaction in an altered form."

As with Allen's *Revlon* analysis, the supreme court affirmed his *Unocal* analysis, but once again did so with important differences. The supreme court expressly rejected Paramount's argument that structural coercion and inadequate value were the only threats cognizable under *Unocal*. Instead, *Unocal* was to be applied on a case-by-case basis and in a flexible, open-ended manner. Among the flexible, open-ended threats the court identified in this case were the possibility that shareholders might incorrectly value the benefits of sticking with management's long-term business plan, the difficulty of comparing Paramount's bid to the benefits of the Warner acquisition, and the possibility that Paramount's bid might "upset, if not confuse," the shareholder vote. Applying the second, proportionality prong of the *Unocal* analysis, the court found that Time's recasting of the transaction was a reasonable response to the identified threats.

Just as had been the case with its analysis of *Revlon*, the supreme court's approach marked a major turning point in the evolution of *Unocal*. It expanded the list of cognizable threats and arguably weakened the proportionality standard. In doing so, it appeared to undermine the ability of the *Unocal* framework to capture cases in which conflicted interests drove the board's decisionmaking process.

Consider, for example, that many commentators concluded that *Time* validated the so-called "just say no" defense, pursuant to which the target's board simply refuses to allow the firm to be acquired, backing up that refusal by a poison pill or other takeover defenses. We find this reading unpersuasive. At the Chancery Court level, Allen's analysis hinged on his observation that Time's acquisition of Warner did not legally preclude "the successful prosecution of a hostile tender offer" for the resulting entity. More important, he also indicated that defensive tactics used against a hostile offer by Paramount or some other bidder for the combined entity after Time's acquisition of Warner would present a different issue.

The supreme court's opinion is similarly limited. While it is true that the court rejected any inference that directors are obliged to abandon a pre-existing business plan in order to permit short-term shareholder gains, Time's plan was deemed reasonable and proportionate to the Paramount threat precisely because it was "not aimed at 'cramming down' on its shareholders a management-sponsored alternative," but was only intended to carry forward "a preexisting transaction in an altered form." The supreme court also expressly affirmed Chancellor Allen's finding that Time's actions "did not preclude Paramount from making an offer for the combined Time-Warner company."

These limitations on the court's holding are important, because they eliminate the just say no defense, as well as some of the other more apocalyptic interpretations of *Time*. The just say no defense does cram down a particular result—independence—on the shareholders, and also attempts to preclude anyone from making an offer for the combined company, both of which the court said management could not do. *Time* thus does not necessarily compel one to conclude that the just say no defense will be deemed to be proportional to an adequate, non-coercive offer.

The trouble is that this limitation on *Time*'s scope is not sufficient, because it in fact creates its own problems. The courts' concern with the legal effect of Time's actions appeared to signal a retreat from the use of *Unocal* to constrain target defensive measures. Consider, for example, the poison pill cases. Suppose management responds to an unsolicited tender offer by proposing a restructuring that effectively transfers voting control to the incumbent management team. The target's board endorses this proposal and, to insure its success, refuses to redeem the target's outstanding poison pill. Because of the substantial financial injury a pill would work on the bidding company and its shareholders, a bidder rarely seeks to complete its tender offer while an effective pill remains in place. Unless there has been a fair competition between the competing proposals, this course of conduct necessarily permits an inference of management self-interest. Yet, just as Time's actions did not legally preclude Paramount from pursuing a bid for the combined Time-Warner entity, a poison pill does not legally preclude a bidder from going forward. Accordingly, one could have plausibly argued that it was proper under *Time*'s interpretation of *Unocal*.

Although *Time*'s doctrinal implications are troubling, the actual result in that case is far less troubling. In most of the poison pill cases, for example, the pill was deployed in order to delay a hostile bid while the target undertook a defensive restructuring intended to give management effective voting control or to otherwise make the target unpalatable to potential bidders.[121] Such

---

[121] In a typical defensive restructuring, the target company pays a dividend consisting of cash (often borrowed) and debt securities, reducing the post-dividend value of the target's stock to the extent of the distribution. While the process is usually rather complex, target managers and/or the target's employee stock ownership plan effectively receive the dividend in the form of stock, rather than cash

a restructuring's deterrent effect is not dependent upon the target's size; it works even for very small companies. In contrast, the success of Time's defensive actions depended almost wholly on the combined entity's great size. While the extent of the combined entity perhaps made it unlikely that a subsequent buyer would emerge to unwind the transaction, the possibility existed. The market for corporate control thus could exert some constraining influence on Time's board, which reduced the likelihood that the board was acting for improper motives, especially in comparison to the defensive restructurings just described.

A variety of other factors could be cited to distinguish *Time* from *Macmillan*, *Interco*, and their ilk. Time's business strategy was motivated by a desire to advance legitimate corporate interests; in particular, it had not been cobbled together simply to justify takeover defenses. As a result, Paramount was essentially asking the court to enjoin Time's board from continuing to operate the corporation's business and affairs during the pendency of the takeover bid. The Delaware courts were properly reluctant to do so, as a hostile bidder has no right to expect the incumbent board of directors to stop an ongoing business strategy in mid-stream.[122]

In sum, *Time* presented a highly unusual set of facts, which rebutted the inference that the board acted from improper motives and rendered the result—if not the reasoning—in that particular case relatively unobjectionable. Many fruitful avenues for limiting *Time*'s reasoning thus presented themselves. The question was whether the Delaware supreme court would avail themselves of those options or would continue down the road of retreat *Time*'s reasoning appeared to mark out.

---

or debt, at an exchange rate based on the stock's post-dividend value. E.g., Black & Decker Corp. v. American Standard, Inc., 682 F.Supp. 772 (D.Del.1988); Ivanhoe Partners v. Newmont Mining Corp., 535 A.2d 1334, 1345 (Del.1987); Robert M. Bass Group, Inc. v. Evans, 552 A.2d 1227, 1243 (Del.Ch.1988). Alternatively, the target may conduct a tender offer in which public shareholders exchange their stock for cash and debt. E.g., AC Acquisitions Corp. v. Anderson, Clayton & Co., 519 A.2d 103 (Del.Ch.1986). In either case, management's equity interest increases substantially vis-a-vis public shareholders. In *AC Acquisitions*, for example, the restructuring would have transferred 25% of the firm's voting stock to a newly formed employee stock ownership plan. Coupled with management's stock holdings, this would have created a formidable barrier for any post-transaction bidder.

[122] *Time* also was distinguishable from negotiated acquisitions in which the target board used a lockup to preclude competing bids. Time was the putative acquirer in what was really a merger of equals, unlike the typical fact pattern, in which the competing bid is directed to the shareholders of the merger target. As such, there is a lower than normal risk that the merger was motivated by side payments to Time's managers. Moreover, Time's board could have structured the Warner acquisition as a tender offer from the outset, borrowing several billion dollars in the junk bond market to pay cash for Warner's shares, and thereby complete the acquisition without ever having to getting shareholder approval. Had they done so, Paramount would have been powerless to prevent the acquisition except by getting control of Time's board before the Warner acquisition could be completed.

Ironically, the vehicle by which the Delaware supreme court revisited its *Time* decision was provided by Paramount, which now found itself playing Time's role and advocating the very same arguments that had been its downfall in the prior case.[123] Paramount, run by Martin Davis, entered into merger negotiations with Viacom, run and largely owned by Sumner Redstone. The parties sought to preclude competing bids with an array of defensive measures, including: (1) A no shop clause in their merger agreement, pursuant to which Paramount's board could not discuss any business combination with a third party unless (i) the third party could show that its proposal was not subject to financial contingencies, and (ii) the Paramount board decided that its fiduciary duties required it to talk to the third party. (2) A termination fee, under which Paramount was obliged to pay Viacom $100 million if the Paramount-Viacom deal fell through. The termination fee was payable regardless of whether the deal cratered because Paramount terminated the Viacom deal to accept a competing offer or the Paramount stockholders voted down the Viacom deal. (3) A stock lockup option, under which, if the Viacom deal fell through for any reason that triggered the termination fee, Viacom would have the option of buying 24 million shares of outstanding Paramount stock at $69 per share (roughly 20% of the outstanding shares). Viacom could buy these shares with a senior subordinated note or could demand instead that Paramount pay it the difference between $69 and the market price of the stock for 24 million shares.

Despite this seemingly formidable array of defenses, QVC made a competing offer. Hollywood egos seem to have played some role, as QVC's CEO and major shareholder, Barry Diller, had once been fired by Davis and the two apparently hated each other. Following several rounds of bidding, Paramount's board announced that it would recommend acceptance of the Viacom proposal and would continue to resist QVC's offer.

In the inevitable litigation, Paramount relied on *Time* to argue that the *Revlon* duties had not triggered. Given *Time*'s description of the requisite triggering events, this was not an implausible argument. Paramount had neither initiated an active bidding process nor approved a breakup of the company.

QVC thus sharply illustrated the potential mischief done by *Time*. Assuming that *Revlon* had not triggered, the issue would be whether Paramount's defensive actions could be sustained under a *Unocal*-style analysis, which would have raised the distinction

---

[123] Paramount Communications, Inc. v. QVC Network Inc., 637 A.2d 34 (Del.1994).

between legally and factually precluding competing bids. A successful Paramount-Viacom merger would not have legally precluded QVC from attempting to purchase the combined Viacom-Paramount entity. Accordingly, there was a strong argument that Paramount's actions should pass muster under *Time*'s reading of *Unocal*.

The Delaware supreme court rejected Paramount's reading of *Time*. Recall the relevant passage from *Time*: "Under Delaware law there are, generally speaking and *without excluding other possibilities*, two circumstances which may implicate *Revlon* duties," which are initiation of an active bidding process and approval of a break-up of the company.[124] In *QVC*, the court emphasized the phrase "without excluding other possibilities." In this case, the court opined, one of the other possibilities was present; namely, a change of control. Accordingly, *Revlon* was triggered.[125]

The court's analysis of *Time*, of course, was disingenuous at best. In *Time*, the court had passed over the change of control test in favor of the break-up and self-initiated auction triggers. The "other possibilities" language was little more than judicial boilerplate. Yet, from a precedential perspective, that boilerplate became the mechanism by which the court was able to avoid the need to overrule its own *Time* decision while still repairing the damage that decision had done to *Unocal* and *Revlon*.

The end, however, perhaps justifies the means. By rehabilitating Chancellor Allen's *Time* opinion, which the *QVC* court went out of its way to describe as "well-reasoned," and by resurrecting the change of control test, *QVC* specifically addressed the potential for conflicted interests on the part of directors in transactions like the one at hand. Indeed, the court laid great stress on the fact that a transaction in which control changes hands to an identifiable owner leaves the target's shareholders vulnerable to both ex ante and ex post misconduct by the incumbent directors and the new owner.

In addition to consigning *Time*'s interpretation of *Revlon* to the dust bin of history, the court made a subtle but very important doctrinal shift. Where *Time* had treated *Unocal* and *Revlon* as involving separate modes of inquiry directed at distinct issues, *QVC* restored the pre-*Time* view that they are part of a single line of cases in which the significant conflict of interest found in certain control transactions justified enhanced judicial scrutiny. The court,

---

[124] Paramount Communications, Inc. v. Time Inc., 571 A.2d 1140, 1150 (Del.1989) (emphasis supplied).

[125] Paramount Communications Inc. v. QVC Network Inc., 637 A.2d 34, 46–48 (Del.1994).

for example, opined that "the general principles announced in *Revlon*, in *Unocal v. Mesa Petroleum Co.*, and in *Moran v. Household International, Inc.* govern this and every case in which a fundamental change of corporate control occurs or is contemplated."

Likewise, while *Time* had emphasized the formal tests announced in *Unocal* and *Revlon*, the *QVC* court struck out in a less rigid direction. As described by *QVC*, the enhanced scrutiny test is basically a reasonableness inquiry to be applied on a case-by-case basis: "The key features of an enhanced scrutiny test are: (a) a judicial determination regarding the adequacy of the decisionmaking process employed by the directors, including the information on which the directors based their decision; and (b) a judicial examination of the reasonableness of the directors' action in light of the circumstances then existing." The burden of proof is on the directors with respect to both issues. They need not prove that they made the right decision, but merely that their decision fell within the range of reasonableness.

The implicit assumption seems to be that a reasonable decision is unlikely to be motivated by conflicted interest or, at least, that improper motives are irrelevant so long as the resulting decision falls within a range of reasonable outcomes. The operating norm seems to be "no harm, no foul," which seems sensible enough.

QVC, moreover, strongly indicated that a court should not second-guess a board decision that falls within the range of reasonableness, "even though it might have decided otherwise or subsequent events may have cast doubt on the board's determination." In *Interco*, Chancellor Allen had warned that "Delaware courts have employed the Unocal precedent cautiously. . . . The danger that it poses is, of course, that courts—in exercising some element of substantive judgment—will too readily seek to assert the primacy of their own view on a question upon which reasonable, completely disinterested minds might differ."[126] *QVC* made clear that, so long as the board's conduct falls within the bounds of reasonableness, Delaware courts will not second-guess the board's decisions.

E.   *Unitrin*

If that point was insufficiently clear after *QVC*, it was driven home in unmistakable terms by the Delaware supreme court's subsequent decision in *Unitrin v. American General Corp.*, in which the court approved an everything but the kitchen sink array of defensive tactics.[127] Unitrin's board adopted a poison pill, amended

---

[126] City Capital Assoc. Ltd. Partnership v. Interco, Inc., 551 A.2d 787, 796 (Del.Ch.1988).

[127] 651 A.2d 1361 (Del.1995).

the bylaws to add some shark repellent features, and initiated a defensive stock repurchase. The chancery court found the latter "unnecessary" in light of the poison pill. The supreme court reversed. The court deemed "draconian" defenses—those which are "coercive or preclusive"—to be invalid. (Note the parallel to our discussion of the post-*Time* status of the just say no defense.) Defenses that are not preclusive or coercive are to be reviewed under *QVC*'s "range of reasonableness" standard. On the facts before it, the court concluded that the shareholders were not foreclosed from receiving a control premium in the future and that a change of control was still possible. Accordingly, the defensive tactics were neither coercive nor preclusive. More important, the supreme court held that the chancery court had "erred by substituting its judgment" for that of the board. The court explained:

> The *ratio decidendi* for the "range of reasonableness" standard is a need of the board of directors for latitude in discharging its fiduciary duties to the corporation and its shareholders when defending against perceived threats. The concomitant requirement is for judicial restraint. Consequently, if the board of directors' defensive response is not draconian (preclusive or coercive) and is within a "range of reasonableness," a court must not substitute its judgment for the board's.

Note, once again, how the balance tips towards deference to the board even in a context charged with conflicts of interest. Given the significant conflicts of interest posed by takeovers, courts recognize the need for some review. But the Delaware courts also seemingly recognize that their power of review easily could become the power to decide. To avoid that result, they are exercising appropriate caution in applying the *Unocal* standard.

§ 12.10 Consideration of Nonshareholder Constituency Interests

The takeover wars of the 1980s produced a host of target corporation defensive tactics. Early on, so-called nonmonetary factor provisions were a fairly common variant on the shark repellent theme. They permit, and in some cases require, directors to consider a variety of nonprice factors in evaluating a proposed acquisition. In particular, most allow directors to consider "the social, legal and economic effects of an offer upon employees, suppliers, customers and others having similar relationships with the corporation, and the communities in which the corporation conducts its business."[128]

From management's perspective, nonmonetary factor provisions have two principal drawbacks. First, except in the case of a newly incorporated firm, they must be adopted as amendments to the corporation's charter, which requires shareholder approval. Shareholder resistance to shark repellents steadily grew throughout the 1980s, especially among institutional investors. By 1989, for example, over half of the institutional investors responding to an industry survey reported that they had opposed some nonmonetary factors provisions, while another one-quarter reported that they did so routinely.[129] This growing opposition made nonmonetary factors provisions far less attractive and helped contribute to their apparent decline in popularity.

Second, and more seriously, state law arguably does not permit corporate organic documents to redefine the directors' fiduciary duties. In general, a charter amendment may not derogate from common law rules if doing so conflicts with some settled public policy.[130] In light of the well-settled shareholder wealth maximization policy, nonmonetary factors charter amendments therefore appeared vulnerable. As the 1980s wound down, this problem seemed especially significant for Delaware firms, as Delaware law became increasingly hostile to directorial consideration of nonshareholder interests in the takeover decisionmaking process.

A. Delaware Case Law

The business judgment rule typically precludes courts from reviewing board of director decisions that take into account the interests of nonshareholder constituencies. Once Delaware adopted *Unocal*'s conditional business judgment rule as the standard of review for management resistance to takeovers, however, such decisions were no longer automatically protected. To be sure, under its first prong, *Unocal* apparently allowed directors to consider interests other than short-term shareholder wealth maximization. Under *Unocal*, target directors may balance the takeover premium a bidder offers shareholders against the bid's potential effects on the corporate entity. Among other factors, the board was explicitly

---

[128] Proxy Statement and Text of Amendment for Nortek, Inc. (May 26, 1982), reprinted in Robert L. Winter et al., 1 Shark Repellents and Golden Parachutes: A Handbook for the Practitioner 197 (1983 and supp.)

[129] Lauren Krasnow, Voting by Institutional Investors on Corporate Governance Issues in the 1989 Proxy Season 37 (1989).

[130] Sterling v. Mayflower Hotel Corp., 93 A.2d 107, 118 (Del.1952); Ernest L. Folk, III, The Delaware General Corporation Law: A Commentary and Analysis 10 (1972).

permitted to consider "the impact of the bid on 'constituencies' other than shareholders (i.e., creditors, customers, employees, and perhaps even the community)."[131]

Unfortunately, *Unocal* was not entirely clear as to what the language just quoted meant. Unocal's board was faced with a structurally coercive bid by "a corporate raider with a national reputation as a 'greenmailer.' "[132]Accordingly, the directors reasonably believed that the bid was not in the best interests of any corporate constituency and, on the facts before the court, there arguably was no conflict between shareholder and stakeholder interests. Other situations are less clear-cut. Suppose, for example, the bidder makes a fairly priced, noncoercive offer, but also announces plans to close plants and lay off numerous workers. The target's board of directors reasonably concludes that the negative impact on its employees exceeds the gains shareholders will garner. Did *Unocal* permit the board to turn down such an offer?

In *Revlon, Inc. v. MacAndrews and Forbes Holdings, Inc.*, the Delaware supreme court concluded that *Unocal* did not.[133] *Revlon* added two crucial provisos to *Unocal*'s treatment of nonshareholder constituencies. The first is of general applicability, dealing with all structural decisions except those in which the so-called *Revlon* duties have triggered. If *Unocal* arguably allowed target boards to trade off a decrease in shareholder wealth for an increase in stakeholder wealth, *Revlon* forecloses that interpretation. *Revlon* expressly forbids management from protecting stakeholder interests at the expense of shareholder interests. Rather, any management action benefiting stakeholders must produce ancillary shareholder benefits.[134] In other words, directors may only consider stakeholder interests if doing so would benefit shareholders.[135]

---

[131] Unocal Corp. v. Mesa Petroleum Co., 493 A.2d 946, 955 (Del.1985). Several judicial opinions outside Delaware suggest that nonshareholder interests may be considered in making structural decisions. See, e.g., Norlin Corp. v. Rooney, Pace Inc., 744 F.2d 255 (2d Cir.1984); Herald Co. v. Seawell, 472 F.2d 1081 (10th Cir.1972); GAF Corp. v. Union Carbide Corp., 624 F.Supp. 1016 (S.D.N.Y.1985); Enterra Corp. v. SGS Assoc., 600 F.Supp. 678 (E.D.Pa.1985); Abramson v. Nytronics, Inc., 312 F.Supp. 519 (S.D.N.Y.1970).

[132] Unocal Corp. v. Mesa Petroleum Co., 493 A.2d 946, 956 (Del.1985).

[133] 506 A.2d 173 (Del.1985).

[134] "A board may have regard for various constituencies in discharging its responsibilities, provided there are rationally related benefits accruing to the stockholders." Revlon, Inc. v. MacAndrews & Forbes Holdings, Inc., 506 A.2d 173, 182 (Del.1985). A somewhat weaker formulation was used in Mills Acquisition Co. v. Macmillan, Inc., 559 A.2d 1261 (Del.1989), which allows consideration of nonshareholder interests provided they bear "some reasonable relationship to general shareholder interests." Id. at 1282 n. 29.

[135] Compare Buckhorn, Inc. v. Ropak Corp., 656 F.Supp. 209, 231–32 (S.D.Ohio), aff'd, 815 F.2d 76 (6th Cir.1987) (employee stock ownership plan invalidated because there was "no evidence in the record as to how the ESOP would benefit the stockholders nor as to how Ropak's tender offer posed a threat to Buckhorn's employees") with Shamrock Holdings, Inc. v. Polaroid Corp., 559 A.2d

Second, where the *Revlon* duties have triggered, stakeholders become entirely irrelevant. Once a *Revlon* auction begins, it no longer matters whether benefiting nonshareholder interests may also benefit shareholders. Instead, shareholder wealth maximization is the board's only appropriate concern.[136] Indeed, in *Revlon* land,[137] considering any factors other than shareholder wealth violates the board's fiduciary duties.[138]

In sum, *Revlon* sharply limits directors' ability to consider nonshareholder interests in structural decisions. Moreover, by withholding the business judgment rule's protections from directors, *Revlon* puts considerable teeth into the shareholder wealth maximization norm. Unlike the operational context, directors who make structural decisions based on stakeholder interests rather than shareholder interests face the very real threat of personal liability.

B. Nonshareholder Constituency Statutes

Over 30 states have adopted nonshareholder constituency statutes that authorize directors to consider nonshareholder interests when making corporate decisions, typically by amending the existing statutory statement of the director's duty of due care. These statutes provide that, in discharging their duty of care, directors may consider the effects of a decision on not only shareholders, but also on a laundry list of other constituency groups, commonly including employees, suppliers, customers, creditors, and the local communities in which the firm does business. As such, these statutes seemingly reject *Revlon*'s command that short-term shareholder wealth maximization be the director's sole concern once a corporate control auction begins. Unfortunately, there is essentially no case law authoritatively interpreting any of these statutes, so their precise impact remains uncertain.

§ 12.11 State Anti-Takeover Legislation

A. The First Generation and MITE

Simultaneously with Congress' adoption of the Williams Act, the states began adopting what are now known as first generation

---

257, 276 (Del.Ch.1989) (employee stock ownership plan upheld because it was "likely to add value to the company and all of its stockholders").

[136] Revlon, Inc. v. MacAndrews & Forbes Holdings, Inc., 506 A.2d 173, 182 (Del.1985).

[137] *"Revlon* land" is a term of art for corporate control contests in which the so-called *Revlon* duties have triggered.

[138] Black & Decker Corp. v. American Standard, Inc., 682 F.Supp. 772, 786–87 (D.Del.1988); C-T of Virginia, Inc. v. Barrett, 124 Bankr. 689 (W.D.Va.1990); Revlon, Inc. v. MacAndrews & Forbes Holdings, Inc., 506 A.2d 173, 185 (Del.1985).

state takeover laws. Like the Williams Act, the first generation state laws were mainly disclosure statutes. Unlike the Williams Act, the first generation statutes also imposed certain procedural and substantive requirements creating substantial obstacles for takeover bidders.

The Illinois Business Takeover Act (IBTA), which the Supreme Court invalidated in *Edgar v. MITE Corp.*,[139] was typical of the first generation statutes. It differed from the Williams Act in three critical ways. First, the IBTA required bidders to notify the target and the Illinois Secretary of State twenty days before the offer's effective date. Second, the IBTA permitted the Secretary of State to delay a tender offer by holding a hearing on the offer's fairness. Moreover, the Secretary was required to hold such a hearing if one was requested by shareholders owning ten percent of the class of securities subject to the offer. Finally, the Secretary of State could enjoin a tender offer on a variety of bases, including substantive unfairness.

1. Preemption Standards

Three basic preemption tests are currently in use. First, the federal regulatory scheme may so thoroughly pervade the field as to suggest Congress left no room for concurrent state regulation.[140] Nobody seriously contends that state takeover regulation is preempted by the Williams Act under this standard. Congress has never attempted broadly to supplant state regulation of corporate governance.[141] A cursory comparison of the federal tender offer rules and any state's corporation code demonstrates that the former occupies only a relatively small portion of the field. Among the many issues left to state law are the fiduciary duties of managers, the validity of post-offer freeze-out mergers, and so on. Federal regulation is thus by no means sufficiently pervasive as to justify preemption under this prong.

Second, where it is physically impossible for an actor to comply with both federal and state regulations, the supremacy of federal law requires that the actor comply with the federal rule.[142] This is a fairly constrained standard, however. The question here is not whether the state statute deters rational actors from going forward. Rather, the question is whether an actor could comply with both the federal and state laws if it chose to make the attempt.

---

[139] 457 U.S. 624 (1982).

[140] Rice v. Santa Fe Elevator Corp., 331 U.S. 218, 230 (1947) (whether federal regulation is "so pervasive as to make reasonable the inference that Congress left no room for the States to supplement" federal law).

[141] CTS Corp. v. Dynamics Corp. of Am., 481 U.S. 69, 85–86 (1987); Business Roundtable v. SEC, 905 F.2d 406, 411–13 (D.C.Cir.1990).

[142] Florida Lime & Avocado Growers, Inc. v. Paul, 373 U.S. 132, 142–43 (1963).

Finally, state statutes are preempted by federal law if they are inconsistent with the purposes of the relevant federal law. Here the relevant standard is whether the state law "stands as an obstacle to the accomplishment and execution of the full purposes and objectives of Congress."[143] This preemption standard requires a court to resolve two questions: (1) What are the intended Congressional purposes of federal tender offer regulation? (2) Does the state statute under review interfere with the accomplishment of those purposes?

2. *Did the Williams Act Preempt the IBTA?*

Lower courts were divided on the constitutionality of state takeover legislation pre-*MITE*, but the trend was decidedly hostile towards state regulation.[144] Courts found such statutes problematic under both the physical incompatibility and frustration of Congressional intent standards. The potential for delay inherent in the advance filing and the administrative review requirements of many state statutes were found to excessively tilt the balance sought by the Williams Act to the side of target management.[145] The administrative review process, which could result in the state barring the tender offer on "fairness" or other grounds, was also found to conflict with a purported Congressional intent that shareholders make the decision as to whether to tender or not.

On January 19, 1979, MITE Corporation filed a Schedule TO with the SEC, indicating its intent to make a $28 per share cash tender offer for Chicago Rivet & Machine Company. On February 1, 1980, Illinois officials notified MITE that the proposed offer violated the IBTA and issued a cease and desist order and a notice of an administrative hearing. Chicago Rivet then notified MITE that it would file suit under the IBTA to restrain the tender offer. MITE thereupon sued in federal court, seeking to have the IBTA declared unconstitutional on both preemption and commerce clause grounds.

---

[143] Hines v. Davidowitz, 312 U.S. 52, 67 (1941).

[144] Pre-*MITE* decisions invalidating state takeover statutes included: Kennecott Corp. v. Smith, 637 F.2d 181 (3d Cir.1980); Natomas Co. v. Bryan, 512 F.Supp. 191 (D.Nev.1981); Canadian Pac. Enter. (U.S.) Inc. v. Krouse, 506 F.Supp. 1192 (S.D.Ohio 1981); Kelly v. Beta-X Corp., 302 N.W.2d 596 (Mich.Ct.App.1981). But see AMCA Int'l Corp. v. Krouse, 482 F.Supp. 929 (S.D.Ohio 1979); City Investing Co. v. Simcox, 476 F.Supp. 112 (S.D.Ind.1979), aff'd, 633 F.2d 56 (7th Cir.1980).

[145] In 1979, the SEC had promulgated Rule 14d–2(b), which requires that a bidder meet the SEC's dissemination and Schedule TO disclosure requirements within five days of the announcement of the offer. The rule created a direct conflict between the federal tender offer rules and the first generation of state takeover laws. Because most first generation statutes required a substantial delay between the announcement and dissemination of the offer, it was no longer possible to time an offer to comply with both federal and state law. After Rule 14d–2(b) was promulgated, the clear trend was towards finding state takeover statutes unconstitutional. See Mark A. Sargent, On the Validity of State Takeover Regulation: State Responses to *MITE* and *Kidwell*, 42 Ohio St. L.J. 689, 696–97 (1981).

The district court struck down the statute on both grounds and the Seventh Circuit affirmed.

Although the circuit court recognized that the federal scheme of regulating tender offers is not so pervasive that an implicit congressional intent to preempt parallel state legislation could be inferred from the Williams Act, it found that the IBTA empowered the Illinois Secretary of State to pass upon the substantive fairness of a tender offer and to prohibit it from going forward, if the Secretary judged the offer inequitable. Thus, the circuit court stated, "Illinois' substitution of the judgment of its Secretary of State for an investor's own assessment of the equitability of a tender offer is patently inconsistent with the Williams Act, . . . which contemplates unfettered choice by well-informed investors." Consequently, the IBTA was preempted by the Williams Act. The circuit court also found that the IBTA unconstitutionally burdened interstate commerce. The circuit court relied on the balancing standard set forth by the Supreme Court in *Pike v. Bruce Church*: "Where the statute regulates evenhandedly to effectuate a legitimate local public interest, and its effects on interstate commerce are only incidental, it will be upheld unless the burden imposed on such commerce is clearly excessive in relation to the putative local benefits."[146] Illinois asserted two interests: protection of resident shareholders and regulation of the internal affairs of Illinois corporations. The circuit court rejected both arguments. It found that the IBTA provided shareholders "marginal" benefits and that Illinois' "tenuous interest" was counterbalanced by the statute's "global impact" and its "significant potential to cause commercial disruption" by blocking an offer "even if it received the enthusiastic endorsement of all other States." Consequently, because the IBTA substantially obstructed interstate commerce, without significant countervailing local benefits, it violated the dormant commerce clause.

The Supreme Court affirmed in a badly divided opinion.[147] Rejecting an argument that the preliminary injunction rendered the case moot, the plurality reached the constitutional issues. Among the substantive portions of Justice White's opinion, only the *Pike* commerce clause analysis commanded a majority. On that issue, the Court found that Illinois had "no legitimate interest in protecting non-resident shareholders," and offered only "speculative"

---

[146] 397 U.S. 137, 142 (1970) (citation omitted).

[147] Edgar v. MITE Corp., 457 U.S. 624 (1982). In his lead opinion, Justice White determined that the IBTA was preempted by the Williams Act and also invalid under the commerce clause because (1) the IBTA directly regulated interstate commerce and (2) the IBTA's legitimate local benefits did not outweigh its indirect burden on interstate commerce. Only the latter holding, however, commanded a majority of the Court.

protection for resident shareholders. The Court agreed with the circuit court "that the possible benefits of the potential delays as required by the Act may be outweighed by the increased risk that the tender offer will fail due to defensive tactics employed by incumbent management." The Court also rejected Illinois' "internal affairs" argument, noting that: "[t]ender offers contemplate transfers of stock by stockholders to a third party and do not themselves implicate the internal affairs of the target company. Furthermore, . . . Illinois has no interest in regulating the internal affairs of foreign corporations." The Court therefore concluded that the IBTA was unconstitutional under the dormant commerce clause because it imposed a substantial burden on interstate commerce that outweighed the putative local benefits.

Writing for a plurality of the court, Justice White also argued that the Williams Act preempted IBTA. According to White, the Williams Act adopted a policy of neutrality as between bidders and targets. In an oft-used metaphor, Congress supposedly intended to create a level playing field for takeover contests. The IBTA's prenotification and hearing requirements imposed significant delays before a bid could commence, during which management could erect defenses and take other measures designed to prevent the offer from going forward, and thus frustrated Congressional purpose by tipping the playing field in target management's favor. Drawing on the Williams Act's legislative history, White noted that Congress had rejected an advance filing requirement precisely because "Congress itself 'recognized that delay can seriously impede a tender offer' and sought to avoid it." In addition, White concluded that the administrative veto granted the Secretary of State conflicted with a Congressional intent that shareholders be allowed make the final decision as to whether to accept a tender offer.

The *MITE* decision's immediate impact was unclear. Only those statutes with similarly "global" ability to block tender offers were directly rendered unconstitutional by the opinion of the Court. Because Justice White's preemption analysis commanded the votes of only two other Justices, it seemed possible that state statutes with a more narrow jurisdictional basis but still having a pro-target bias could pass constitutional muster. Indeed, in refusing to join the preemption analysis, Justice Stevens expressly stated that he was "not persuaded . . . that Congress' decision to follow a policy of neutrality in its own legislation is tantamount to a federal prohibition against state legislation designed to provide special protection for incumbent management." Similarly, Justice Powell declined to join the preemption analysis, observing that the Court's "Commerce Clause reasoning leaves some room for state regulation" and that "the Williams Act's neutrality policy does not necessarily imply a congressional intent to prohibit state legislation [protecting] interests that include but are often broader than those of incumbent management." Surprisingly, however, subsequent lower court decisions almost uniformly adopted the plurality's preemption analysis.

B.   The Second Generation and CTS

Justice White's *MITE* opinion left open a narrow window of opportunity for states to regulate takeovers: the internal affairs doctrine, pursuant to which the state of incorporation's law governs questions of corporate governance. The second generation of state takeover statutes was carefully crafted to fit within that loophole.

1.   *The Second Generation Statutes*

The so-called "second generation" statutes were, for the most part, cautiously tailored to avoid direct regulation of tender offers. Instead, they addressed issues purporting to fall within the sphere of corporate governance concerns traditionally subject to state law. In the years between 1983 and 1987, many of these statutes were challenged and almost uniformly were struck down by the lower courts as unconstitutional. That trend was reversed following the Supreme Court's decision in *CTS Corp. v. Dynamics Corp.*,[148] however.

There are four principal variants of "second generation" statutes: Control share acquisition statutes rely on the states' traditional power to define corporate voting rights as a justification for regulating the bidder's right to vote shares acquired in a control transaction. A "control share acquisition" is typically defined as the acquisition of a sufficient number of target company shares to give the acquirer control over more than a specified percentage of the voting power of the target. The triggering level of share ownership is usually defined as an acquisition which would bring the bidder within one of three ranges of voting power: 20 to 33 1/3%, 33 1/3 to 50% and more than 50%. Most control share acquisition laws provide that shares acquired in a control share acquisition shall not have voting rights unless the shareholders approve a resolution granting voting rights to the acquirer's shares.[149] The shares owned by the acquirer, officers of the target and directors who are also employees of the target may not be counted in the vote on the resolution.

---

[148]   481 U.S. 69 (1987).

[149]   E.g., Ind. Code Ann. § 23–1–42. A few states took a slightly different approach, under which the shareholders determine whether or not the proposed acquisition may be made. E.g., Ohio Rev. Code Ann. § 1701.831. This is a slightly more aggressive position than the more usual approach, which simply requires shareholder approval for voting rights to be accorded to the acquirer's shares.

The stated purpose of control share statutes is providing shareholders with an opportunity to vote on a proposed acquisition of large share blocks which may result in or lead to a change in control of the target. These statutes are premised on the assumption that individual shareholders are often at a disadvantage when faced with a proposed change in control. If the target's shareholders believe that a successful tender offer will be followed by a purchase by the offeror of non-tendered shares at a price lower than that offered in the initial bid, for example, individual shareholders may tender their shares to protect themselves from such an eventuality, even if they do not believe the offer to be in their best interests.

By requiring certain disclosures from the prospective purchaser and by allowing the target's shareholders to vote on the acquisition as a group, control share acquisition statutes supposedly provide the shareholders a collective opportunity to reject an inadequate or otherwise undesirable offer. For example, since control share acquisition statutes generally require the offeror to disclose plans for transactions involving the target that would be initiated after the control shares are acquired, shareholders presumably would be unlikely to approve a creeping tender offer or street sweep which would be followed by a squeezeout back-end merger at a price less than or in a consideration different than that paid by the acquirer in purchasing the initial share block.

Fair price statutes are modeled on the approach taken in company charters that include fair price provisions. These statutes provide that certain specified transactions, sometimes called "Business Combinations," involving an "interested shareholder" must be approved by a specified supermajority shareholder vote unless certain minimum price and other conditions are met. The term "interested shareholder" is typically defined by statute as a shareholder owning more than some specified percentage, often 10%, of the outstanding shares of the target.

Business combination statutes are an extension of the fair price statute concept, providing substantially greater teeth. The typical statute prohibits a target from engaging in any business combination with an interested shareholder of the target corporation for a set period of time, often five years, following the date on which the interested shareholder achieved such status. Following the initial freeze period, a business combination with an interested shareholder is still prohibited unless the business combination is approved by a specified vote of the outstanding shares not beneficially owned by the interested shareholder or the business combination meets specified fair price and other criteria.[150] The definition of interested shareholder typically is comparable to that used in fair price statutes. As with fair price statutes, the term "business combination" typically is defined to include a broader variety of transactions than just a statutory merger.

Cash-out statutes require an acquirer of more than a threshold percentage of a target's stock to offer to purchase the remaining shares of all of the other shareholders at a price which reflects the highest premium paid by the acquirer in accumulating target stock. Cash-out statutes typically apply to so-called "control transactions," which are defined as acquisitions by a person or group who, after the acquisition, will have the status of a "controlling person or group." A "controlling person or group" is a person who has, or a group of persons acting in concert that has, voting power over voting shares that would entitle the holders thereof to cast at least a specified percentage of votes that all shareholders would be entitled to cast in the election of directors.

2.   Powell's CTS Opinion

In *CTS Corp. v. Dynamics Corp.*,[151] the Supreme Court upheld an Indiana control share acquisition statute. Justice Powell's majority opinion began by noting that the *MITE* plurality's preemption analysis was not binding on the Court, but he declined to explicitly overrule it. Instead, Powell claimed that the Indiana Act passed muster even under White's interpretation of the Williams Act's purposes. It is perhaps instructive, however, that Justice White was the lone dissenter from Powell's preemption holding.

In fact, *CTS'* preemption analysis differed from *MITE*'s in at least two key respects. Where Justice White emphasized Congress' neutrality policy, Justice Powell emphasized Congress' desire to protect shareholders.[152] Where Justice White would preempt any state statute favoring management, Justice Powell upheld the

---

[150] See, e.g., N.Y. Bus. Corp. Law § 912(c). Delaware § 203 is similar to the original business combination statutes in a number of respects, but there is no requirement of shareholder approval after the freeze period expires. Shareholder voting may still occur, however, because the freeze period will be waived if at any time during it a proposed transaction is approved by the board of directors and by the two-thirds of the outstanding shares not owned by the bidder. DGCL § 203.

[151] 481 U.S. 69 (1987).

[152] In dissent, Justice White argued that the Williams Act was primarily intended to protect individual investors. CTS Corp. v. Dynamics Corp. of Am., 481 U.S. 69, 98–99 (1987) (White, J., dissenting). In contrast, Justice Powell believed that the Williams Act was intended to protect shareholders. Id. at 82. The difference between investors and shareholders is more than just semantic. Under Justice White's view, a statute will be preempted if it interferes with an individual investor's ability to freely make his own decision. In contrast, Justice Powell would uphold state takeover statutes that make shareholders as a group better off, even if the wishes of some individual investors are thereby frustrated.

Indiana Act even though he recognized that it would deter some takeover bids. Justice Powell did so because he believed that, despite the Indiana statute's deterrent effect. Justice Powell believed that it protected shareholders by permitting them collectively to evaluate an offer's fairness. He laid particular emphasis on a bidder's ability to coerce shareholders into tendering, such as by making a two-tier tender offer. By allowing shareholders collectively to reject such offers, the Indiana statute defuses their coercive effect. That the statute also deters takeovers and thereby protects incumbent managers is merely incidental to its primary function of protecting shareholders. The Indiana act therefore did not conflict with the Williams Act; to the contrary, Justice Powell concluded that it furthered Congress' goal of protecting shareholders.

Although Justice Powell acknowledged the Indiana act imposed a substantial delay on bidders, he reinterpreted *MITE* to only bar states from injecting unreasonable delay into the tender offer process. He then concluded that a potential 50 day waiting period was not unreasonable. Justice Powell noted that a variety of state corporate laws, such as classified board and cumulative voting statutes, limit or delay the transfer of control following a successful tender offer: "[T]he Williams Act would pre-empt a variety of state corporate laws of hitherto unquestioned validity if it were construed to pre-empt any state statute that may limit or delay the free exercise of power after a successful tender offer. . . . The longstanding prevalence of state regulation in this area suggests that, if Congress had intended to pre-empt all state laws that delay the acquisition of voting control following a tender offer, it would have said so explicitly."

Justice White's analysis implied that the Williams Act's neutrality policy meant that any state laws which derogated from the level playing field established by the Williams Act were to be preempted. However, there was another, perhaps equally plausible, interpretation of the Act; namely, that Congress wanted to assure that the Act itself not affect the balance of power between bidders and targets but did not intend to prohibit all state laws that affected that balance. Powell's opinion implicitly embraced the latter view.

Turning to the commerce clause issues, Powell held that the Indiana statute also passed muster under the dormant commerce clause. The statute did not discriminate against out of state entities. It did not bar tender offers, leaving a meaningful opportunity for the offeror to succeed. Because the statute was limited to Indiana corporations, the statute did not have significant extraterritorial effects. As to the local benefits aspect of the balancing test, Justice Powell held that the state had a legitimate interest in defining the attributes of its corporations and protecting shareholders of its corporations. He opined, for example, that "[n]o principle of corporation law and practice is more firmly established than a State's authority to regulate domestic corporations, including the authority to define the voting rights of shareholders."[153] Accordingly, it "is an accepted part of the business landscape in this country for States to create corporations, to prescribe their powers, and to define the rights that are acquired by purchasing their shares."

C. Interpreting CTS

Clearly *CTS* contemplated a greater degree of state regulation than did *MITE*, but how much greater remained uncertain. Because Justice Powell so narrowly focused on the specific provisions of the Indiana Act, he failed to provide a generally applicable analysis. Indeed, both proponents and opponents of state takeover legislation can mine *CTS* for support for their arguments. Faced with this uncertainty, two distinct lower court readings of *CTS's* preemption analysis developed.

1. *A Meaningful Opportunity for Success*

The more restrictive interpretation of *CTS* requires states to preserve a meaningful opportunity for successful hostile bids. This standard is most fully developed in a trilogy of cases involving the Delaware takeover statute's constitutionality.[154] DGCL § 203 is a variant on the older business combination statutes. Section 203 prohibits a Delaware corporation from entering into a business combination for a period of three years after an offeror becomes an interested stockholder. Business combination is defined to include freeze-out mergers and other common post-acquisition transactions.[155] Interested shareholder is defined, subject to various exceptions, as the owner of 15% or more of the target's outstanding shares.

Unlike the older business combination statutes, the Delaware statute does not impose either a supermajority approval or a fair price requirement in connection with business combinations after the freeze period expires. Thus, once the three-year period expires,

---

[153] CTS Corp. v. Dynamics Corp. of Am., 481 U.S. 69, 89 (1987).

[154] City Capital Assoc. Ltd. v. Interco, Inc., 696 F.Supp. 1551 (D.Del.1988), aff'd on other grounds, 860 F.2d 60 (3d Cir.1988); RP Acquisition Corp. v. Staley Cont'l, Inc., 686 F.Supp. 476 (D.Del.1988); BNS Inc. v. Koppers Co., Inc., 683 F.Supp. 458 (D.Del.1988).

[155] Section 203 puts fewer restrictions on the raider's use of target assets to finance an acquisition than do the older business combination statutes. For example, it permits the raider to sell off target assets to third parties (subject to the usual fiduciary duty and voting rules).

the interested stockholder may complete a second-step business combination on whatever terms and conditions would be lawful under applicable corporate and securities law provisions. In addition, the three-year freeze period is waived if any of four conditions are satisfied: (1) prior to the date on which the bidder crosses the 15% threshold, the business combination or the triggering acquisition is approved by the target's board of directors; (2) the bidder, in a single transaction, goes from a stock ownership level of less than 15% to more than 85% of the target's voting stock (not counting shares owned by inside directors or by employee stock plans in which the employees do not have the right to determine confidentially whether shares held by the plan will be tendered); (3) during the three year freeze period, the transaction is approved by the board of directors and by two-thirds of the outstanding shares not owned by the bidder; or (4) the target's board of directors approves a white knight transaction. Section 203(b) also sets forth various other conditions under which the statute will not apply, most prominently an opt-out provision pursuant to which a corporation may exempt itself from the statute through appropriate charter or bylaw provisions.

In the leading case of the trilogy, *BNS Inc. v. Koppers Co.*,[156] Chief District Judge Schwartz began by interpreting *CTS* as meaning that neutrality between bidders and targets was no longer regarded as a purpose of the Williams Act in itself, but rather merely as a means towards the true congressional end of shareholder protection. State statutes having a substantial deterrent effect are now permissible, as are statutes favoring management, so long as these effects are merely incidental to protecting shareholders.[157] This proviso, however, is critical. As Chief Judge Schwartz saw it, *CTS* does not permit states to eliminate hostile takeovers. Rather, states must preserve a "meaningful opportunity" for hostile offers that are beneficial to target shareholders to succeed. Chief Judge Schwartz offered a four part test to decide whether a state law did so: (1) does the state law protect independent shareholders from coercion; (2) does it give either side an advantage in consummating or defeating an offer; (3) does it impose an unreasonable delay; and (4) does it permit a state official to substitute his views for those of the shareholders. Concluding that Section 203 probably satisfied these standards, Chief Judge Schwartz declined to enjoin its enforcement.

---

[156] 683 F.Supp. 458 (D.Del.1988).

[157] Accord Hyde Park Partners, L.P. v. Connolly, 839 F.2d 837, 850 (1st Cir.1988) ("protection of management that is incidental to protection of investors does not per se conflict with the purpose or purposes of the Williams Act.").

2.   Amanda *Acquisition*

In contrast, Judge Frank Easterbrook's decision in *Amanda Acquisition Corp. v. Universal Foods Corp.*[158] provided a much more state statute-friendly approach to the preemption issue. Like most post-*MITE* state takeover statutes, the Wisconsin law in question deters tender offers by regulating freeze-out mergers and other post-acquisition transactions. Like most business combination statutes, it imposes a statutory freeze period, here three years, following the acquisition during which business combinations are prohibited. The sole viable exception to the freeze period is prior approval by the incumbent directors: "In Wisconsin it is management's approval in advance, or wait three years."

Judge Easterbrook began with the Williams Act's neutrality policy. Congress unquestionably expected the federal tender offers rules to be neutral as between bidders and targets. In *MITE*, Justice White read that expectation as forbidding state statutes from tipping the balance between them. Both Justices Powell and Stevens rejected that reading in their concurrences. And, of course, *CTS* implicitly backpedals from the spirit of Justice White's analysis. Judge Easterbrook recognized that all of this might open the door for nonneutral state laws, but he claimed to "stop short of th[at] precipice." At a minimum, however, *Amanda Acquisition* implicitly treats neutrality as a means rather than an end in itself. Easterbrook's decision to uphold the Wisconsin statute in the face of its admitted deterrent effects only makes sense if he has rejected Justice White's analysis in *MITE* of the neutrality policy's preemptive power.

In any case, Judge Easterbrook thereafter essentially ignored the Williams Act's neutrality policy. Instead, he asserted that Congress intended the Williams Act to regulate the process by which tender offers take place and the disclosures to which shareholders are entitled. He then used this reading of congressional purpose to distinguish *MITE* from *CTS*. The IBTA threatened to preclude a bidder from purchasing target shares even if the bidder complied with federal law. In contrast, the Indiana control share acquisition statute did not interfere with the federally mandated tender offer process; indeed, it did not even come into play until that process was completed and the shares acquired.

The Wisconsin business combination statute, like the Indiana Act, left the tender offer process alone. According to Judge Easterbrook, the Wisconsin statute therefore could be preempted only if the Williams Act gives investors a federal right to receive

---

[158] 877 F.2d 496 (7th Cir.1989).

tender offers. He determined, however, that no such federal right exists: "Investors have no right to receive tender offers. More to the point—since Amanda sues as bidder rather than as investor seeking to sell—the Williams Act does not create a right to profit from the business of making tender offers. It is not attractive to put bids on the table for Wisconsin corporations, but because Wisconsin leaves the process alone once a bidder appears, its law may coexist with the Williams Act." The state statute need not even leave the bidder an opportunity—meaningful or otherwise—for success. Accordingly, the issue is not whether the statute deters tender offers. The issue is whether the state law directly interferes with an undeterred bidder's ability to go forward on schedule and in compliance with federal law.

3.   Commerce Clause Issues

As illustrated by both *CTS* and *MITE*, challenges to state takeover laws typically entail not only preemption but also dormant commerce clause claims. Recall that there are three core commerce clause questions: (1) does the state statute discriminate against interstate commerce; (2) does the state statute subject interstate commerce to inconsistent regulation; and (3) do the local benefits of the statute outweigh the burdens it places on interstate commerce (the legitimacy of this third test is a matter of considerable debate among constitutional scholars, but let's leave it in their capable hands).[159] Post-*CTS*, commerce clause challenges have not had much traction. As long as the state statute treats in-state bidders and out-of-state bidders the same, the statute will pass muster under the first test. Provided the state law applies only to firms incorporated within the regulating state, there is no possibility of inconsistent regulation and it will pass muster under the second test. Some state takeover law decisions have declined to apply the third test, concluding that even statutes whose costs exceed their benefits are constitutional.[160] Even those that retain the third test, however, generally uphold state takeover laws in light of the substantial state interest in regulating corporate governance.[161]

---

[159] See CTS Corp. v. Dynamics Corp. of Am., 481 U.S. 69, 87–93 (1987).

[160] E.g., Amanda Acquisition Corp. v. Universal Foods Corp., 877 F.2d 496, 505–09 (7th Cir.1989).

[161] See, e.g., City Capital Assoc. L.P. v. Interco, Inc., 696 F.Supp. 1551, 1555 (D.Del.1988), aff'd on other grounds, 860 F.2d 60 (3d Cir.1988); RP Acquisition Corp. v. Staley Cont'l, Inc., 686 F.Supp. 476, 487–88 (D.Del.1988).

Chapter 13

DIVIDENDS AND OTHER LEGAL CAPITAL ARCANA

§ 13.1 Introduction

A corporation's balance sheet balances when assets (the left side) equal the sum of liabilities and shareholder equity (the right side). Shareholder equity thus consists of the corporation's net assets—the (hopefully positive) difference between assets and liabilities. Consequently, we speak of an "equity cushion." Because creditors have a prior claim on the corporation's assets, a fall in the value of those assets comes out of shareholder equity before it impairs the corporation's ability to repay its liabilities.

At common law, the corporation's shareholder equity thus was viewed as a "trust fund" held by the corporation for the benefit of its creditors. This doctrine received its classic expression in the early 19th century decision of *Wood v. Dummer*.[1] The Hallowell and Augusta Bank paid out the bulk of its assets in dividends to its shareholders. As a result, when the Bank later became insolvent, insufficient assets remained to pay its creditors. Trying the case in his capacity as a circuit judge, U.S. Supreme Court Justice Story held that "the capital stock of banks is to be deemed a pledge or trust fund for the payment of the debts contracted by the bank." Suppose, for example, that the Bank issued 2,000 shares of common stock having a par value of $100. On those facts, its capital equaled $200,000. Accordingly, the Bank was obliged to maintain net assets of at least $200,000.

The trust fund doctrine likely was intended to deter opportunistic conduct by shareholders vis-à-vis creditors. The corporation's decisionmaking and financial apparatus is controlled by the board of directors, elected by and responsible to the shareholders. In close corporations, the problem is especially pronounced because the shareholders and the board members likely will be one and the same. One obvious risk is that shareholders will divert cash flows to their own pockets in the form of salaries, bonuses, dividends, and the like. A more subtle problem is that limited liability creates incentives for shareholders to cause the company to invest in higher risk projects than the firm's creditors would like. As the firm's residual claimants, shareholders will not be paid until all creditor claims are satisfied. Shareholders thus will

---

[1] 30 F.Cas. 435 (C.C.D.Me.1824).

prefer that the corporation select high risk projects that promise high returns. Because limited liability means that shareholders only put at risk what funds they have invested in the firm, moreover, they are able to effectively externalize some of the risk associated with such projects to creditors. If the high risk project fails, the creditors may not be paid, but cannot collect any unpaid debt from the shareholders.

In the nineteenth century, many states gave teeth to the trust fund doctrine through minimum capital requirements, which specified the minimum amount shareholders had to initially invest in the company. Over time, however, it became obvious that one size does not fit all and minimum capital requirements have faded from view. Few states have them today and those that do set the minimum at nominal amounts.

Instead, legal capital rules tried to implement the trust fund concept by deterring shareholders from impairing the corporation's equity cushion. One prong of this approach regulated the flow of money into the corporation, while the other regulated the flow of money out. Requiring that stock be fully paid and nonassessable was an effort to ensure that the assets of which the corporation's shareholder equity purportedly consisted actually existed and, in fact, had been paid in. Restricting the payment of dividends was an effort to ensure that the corporation maintained some equity cushion. Neither effort turned out very well, however, and today the once proud trust fund doctrine is but a tattered shadow of its former self. Instead, modern creditors must rely on self-help. They protect themselves through private contracting (such as negative pledge covenants in bond indentures or loan agreements), credit investigations, and charging higher interest rates.

§ 13.2 Money In: Herein of Watered Stock

If the corporation wishes to raise capital by selling equity securities, it is the board of directors that makes that determination and also decides the amount and form of consideration to be received in exchange for the shares to be issued.[2] Accordingly, so long as the charter authorizes the class of shares in question and there are sufficient authorized but unissued shares, the board is free to sell shares for any lawful purpose, provided that the corporation receives adequate consideration for the shares. That latter proviso leads us to the questions of par value and watered stock.

At one time, all stock had a "par value," stated in the articles of incorporation, which was the price at which the corporation initially

---

[2] DGCL § 153(a).

sold shares to the public. A firm could not sell shares for less than par value and, at least in its initial offering, usually did not sell shares for more than par value. A vast and arcane body of law grew up to implement these so-called legal capital requirements. Today, however, most of that law has fallen into decrepitude. Virtually all states allow one to sell stock with low or even no par value. The MBCA has gone even further and simply abolished the entire concept of par value. Yet, because it is difficult to understand today's legal capital regime without understanding that regime's historical antecedents, we begin with a brief lesson on the history of par value and "watered stock."

Recall that the corporation's capital—i.e., the aggregate par value of its outstanding stock—was viewed as a trust fund for the protection of creditors. If a corporation claimed that it had sold 2,000 shares of stock with a par value of $100 per share, for a total capital of $200,000, the trust fund concept necessitated some mechanism for ensuring that the full value of the purported capital in fact had been paid into the corporation. Suppose Shareholder bought 100 shares of the corporation's stock. Shareholder should have paid at least $10,000 for her shares. If Shareholder paid less than that amount, her stock was said to be "watered." If Shareholder actually paid only $4,000, for example, she could be held liable to the firm's creditors for the $6,000 "water."[3]

Failure to pay in full for shares probably was rare. Because corporation statutes allowed corporations to issue stock in return for noncash forms of consideration, such as property or services rendered, however, disputes over the valuation of such consideration were not uncommon.[4] Suppose the board accepted an offer from a prospective shareholder to exchange an acre of land for 500 shares of stock having a par value of $100 per share. The corporation later became insolvent and creditors claimed that the acre of land in question was really worth only $20,000. If true, the shareholder's stock was watered to the tune of $30,000.

Several factors combined to effectively eliminate the watered stock problem. One was the decline of par value as a meaningful concept. Par value always was an arbitrary figure. With the development of secondary trading markets for corporate stock, the market price (and thus the value) of outstanding corporate stock rarely coincided with its par value. As a result, par value simply had no relation whatsoever to the price shares would command on a

---

[3] They still arise today. See, e.g., Hanewald v. Bryan's Inc., 429 N.W.2d 414 (N.D.1988).

[4] Valuation disputes were (and are) especially likely when a promoter receives stock from the corporation in return for noncash consideration. These situations are governed by the fiduciary duties of promoters.

secondary trading market or the price at which shares subsequently might be issued by the corporation. States began to permit corporations to issue low par value stock (such as shares with par value of a penny) and most states eventually permitted corporations to issue shares having no par value whatsoever.

Another factor related to the manner in which noncash consideration is valued. When a corporation issues shares for unlawful or inadequate consideration, the other shareholders are injured because the value of their stock is diluted. This is of particular concern when shares are issued for noncash consideration, because of the potential for valuation disputes. Traditional legal capital statutes require the board of directors to place a value on noncash consideration. In the absence of actual fraud, however, the value set by the board is conclusive on all parties—the corporation, its shareholders and its creditors.[5] Obviously, water cannot exist if the board has conclusively determined that the price paid equals the price required. Allegations that the board acted improperly in assigning a value to the consideration are therefore relegated to tort fraud rules and corporate fiduciary duties.

Consequently, today, watered stock is largely a dead issue. Corporations issue no par or low par stock and sell it at the highest price the shares will bring in the primary market. As long as the investor pays something for his shares, the par value requirement will be satisfied.

A. Watered Stock in Delaware Law Today

All statutes permit the corporation to issue shares in return for not only cash, but also property and past uncompensated services. Traditional legal capital statutes prohibit a corporation, however, from accepting certain forms of consideration for shares. Until recently, Delaware's statute was typical of this group: only cash, services rendered, and personal or real property constituted lawful consideration for stock.[6] Other forms of consideration were not permitted. In particular, Delaware did not permit its corporations to issue stock in return for a promise of future services, which had significant planning consequences.[7]

In 2004, however, Delaware amended § 152 to eliminate the prohibition on issuing stock "except for money paid, labor done or personal property, or real estate or leases thereof actually acquired

---

[5] DGCL § 152. In most states, constructive fraud can be found where the board grossly overvalued the property. See, e.g., McManus v. American Exp. Tax and Business Services, Inc., 67 F.Supp.2d 1083, 1089 (D.Ariz.1999).

[6] DGCL § 152.

[7] See, e.g., Maclary v. Pleasant Hills, Inc., 109 A.2d 830 (Del.Ch.1954).

by such corporation." With the elimination of that provision, the Delaware General Corporation Law now simply provides that stock will be considered fully paid and non-assessable upon receipt by the corporation of the consideration determined by the board of directors.

B. Watered Stock Under the MBCA Today

The trend away from par value was taken to its logical conclusion in the MBCA, under which par value has no legal significance. MBCA § 6.21(b), moreover, expressly allows the corporation to accept just about any form of consideration: tangible or intangible property, cash, promissory notes, services performed, contracts for future services or other securities of the corporation. Section 6.21(c) then provides that the board must determine whether the consideration is adequate. If the board so determines, their conclusion is conclusive. Once the corporation receives the agreed consideration, the shares are regarded as fully paid and nonassessable.

§ 13.3   Money Out: Dividend Statutes

From the trust fund perspective, it is not enough to ensure that the corporation's allegedly paid-in capital actually exists, one must also prevent the shareholders from draining assets out of the corporation. Preventing shareholders from doing so in the form of dividends is the function of the second set of legal capital rules—the dividend statutes.

A. Modern Dividend Statutes

Our analysis focuses on two representative examples of modern dividend statutes—the MBCA and Delaware. In working through the statutes, we will concentrate on two issues: (1) when may the corporation properly pay dividends; and (2) who can be held liable if dividends are paid improperly.

The following sample problem will facilitate our discussion of the statutes: Assume Acme Corporation issued 1,000 shares of stock (par value $1.00). Five years later the balance sheet reads as follows:

Assets		Liabilities and Shareholder Equity	
Cash	$ 2,000	Current liabilities	$ 2,000
Accounts receivable	$ 2,000	Long-term liabilities	$13,000
Inventory	$ 6,000	Total liabilities	$15,000
Total current assets	$10,000	Capital	$ 1,000
		Surplus	$ 4,000
Building	$10,000	Total shareholder equity	$ 5,000
Total fixed assets	$10,000		
Total assets	$20,000		

Can Acme pay a dividend under these circumstances? If Acme pays an illegal dividend, who can be held liable by whom?

1.   Delaware

DGCL § 170(a)(1) provides, in pertinent part:

> The directors of every corporation, subject to any restrictions contained in its certificate of incorporation, may declare and pay dividends upon the shares of its capital stock ... either (1) out of its surplus ... or (2) in case there shall be no such surplus, out of its net profits for the fiscal year in which the dividend is declared and/or the preceding fiscal year.

Some of the statutory terminology should be familiar from our treatment of corporate finance, but understanding how the statute works requires us to use the more precise definitions set out in DGCL § 154.

Capital: the amount allocated to the capital account depends on whether the stock has a par value. In the case of par value shares, the minimum amount of capital is determined by multiplying the number of shares issued by their par value. In addition, the board may (but need not) designate an additional portion of the consideration received by the corporation when shares are issued as capital. In the case of no-par shares, capital is simply that part of the consideration received designated by the board as capital. If the board fails to designate part of the consideration as capital, than capital is determined by the amount of the consideration received. Notice the potential trap for the unwary. It is important for the board to always designate some portion of the consideration as capital or all of the consideration goes into capital.

Net assets: the difference between total assets and total liabilities.

Surplus: The difference between the corporation's net assets at any time and the amount of capital. The following examples may shed some light on how these statutes work in practice:

1.   At t=0, ABC Corporation has no assets, no liabilities, and no shareholder equity. At t=1, ABC sells 1,000 shares of common stock at the stock's par value of $1 per share. After giving effect to this transaction, ABC's balance sheet will read as follows:

   Assets   *Liabilities + Shareholder Equity*

   Cash $1,000   Liabilities 0

                              Capital $1,000

   Legal capital statutes, such as Delaware's, divide shareholder equity into two basic categories: capital and surplus. Per DGCL § 154, capital, in the case of par value shares, is the aggregate par value of the outstanding shares. Accordingly, ABC has capital of $1,000 (1000 shares issued x $1 per share par value).

2.   At t=0, XYZ Corporation has no assets, no liabilities, and no shareholder equity. At t=1, XYZ sells 1,000 shares of common stock. Each share of stock has a par value of $1. XYZ is able to sell the stock for more than par value: $10 per share. (No law says a corporation cannot sell stock for more than its par value.) After giving effect to that transaction, XYZ's balance sheet will read as follows:

   Assets   *Liabilities + Shareholder Equity*

   Cash $10,000   Liabilities 0

                              Capital $1,000

                              Surplus $9,000

   Again, because we are dealing with par value shares, capital is the aggregate par value of the outstanding shares, which here is $1,000 (1000 shares issued x $1 per share par value). In addition, because XYZ sold the shares for more than their par value, the board had the option to designate as capital an additional portion of the consideration received. Assume XYZ's board did not do so. Accordingly, the remainder of the consideration XYZ received for its shares ($9,000) will be allocated to the surplus account.

3. At t=0, 123 Corporation has no assets, no liabilities, and no shareholder equity. At t=1, 123 sells 1,000 shares of "no par" common stock. 123 is able to sell the stock at $10 per share. In the case of no-par shares, capital is simply that portion of the consideration received designated by the board as capital. The board could put as little as $1 into the capital account. If the board fails to designate part of the consideration as capital, however, the entire consideration received is deemed to be capital.

Pursuant to DGCL § 170, the board of directors may cause the corporation to pay a dividend out of the corporation's surplus up to the full amount of any such surplus. If the corporation has no surplus, or has negative surplus, the board can cause the corporation to pay a so-called nimble dividend out of its net profits for the fiscal year in which the dividend is paid or for the preceding fiscal year.[8]

In our principal example, Acme has net assets of $5,000. How did we determine that amount? The accounting distinction between current and fixed assets has no legal significance under Delaware law, so we have total assets of $20,000. Likewise, the accounting distinction between current and long-term liabilities has no legal significance, so we have total liabilities of $15,000. Subtracting total liabilities from total assets gives us net assets of $5,000. Subtracting the $1,000 capital (1,000 shares times a par value of $1 per share) from our net assets of $5,000, leaves us with a total of $4,000 in surplus. Hence, Acme can pay a dividend of up to $4,000 out of surplus.

DGCL § 174 provides that if there is a willful or negligent illegal dividend payment the directors under whose administration the payment occurs are jointly and severally liable to the corporation or directly to its creditors in the event of dissolution or

---

[8] Note the nimble dividend provision raises the prospect of double-dipping for dividends. Assume the corporation has both surplus and net profits in the current fiscal year. A fair reading of DGCL suggests that such a corporation could maximize its dividend by breaking the dividend declaration process into two stages. The corporation's board of directors would first declare a dividend under DGCL § 170(a)(1) equal to the full amount of the corporation's surplus. At that point, the corporation no longer has any surplus. Accordingly, DGCL § 170(a)(2) permits the corporation to pay a nimble dividend out of its profits for the current fiscal year. Nothing on the face of § 170(a) prohibits such a tactic, although there are no reported decisions on point.

insolvency. A director can avoid liability by timely causing his dissent to be noted on the corporation's books. Section 172 also protects a director who in good faith relies on reports of corporate officers, legal counsel or accountants. The amount for which directors can be held liable is the amount of the dividend that was improperly paid plus prejudgment interest. There is no express provision for holding liable those shareholders who receive the improper dividend, although directors are entitled to contribution from shareholders who knowingly received the illegal dividend. Worse yet, from the creditor's perspective, standing under 174 is limited to the corporation (and, presumably, shareholders suing derivatively). Creditors are given standing only where the corporation is insolvent. In effect, creditors are limited to their fraudulent conveyance remedies.

2.   MBCA: Old and New

The 1969 version of the MBCA was a legal capital statute, not unlike (but somewhat more complicated than) the Delaware statute. The MBCA (1969), like Delaware, used surplus as the basic test for the legality of dividends. The MBCA (1969), however, recognized two distinct types of surplus: earned surplus and capital surplus. The definition of capital surplus was straightforward: it was any surplus that was not earned surplus. Earned surplus was a somewhat complex concept, but basically one added up all of the corporation's profits and other gains (if any) from the date of incorporation. One then subtracted from that figure any losses from the date of incorporation. Finally, one further deducted any distributions to shareholders or amounts transferred to stated capital or capital surplus. What was left was earned surplus.

Under the MBCA (1969), there were two distinct tests for the legality of dividends. First, an equity insolvency test that prohibited the corporation from paying dividends if the firm was insolvent or if the payment would render the corporation insolvent. Second, a balance sheet test that allowed dividends to be paid only out of surplus. Earned surplus could be freely used for dividends, up to the full amount thereof. In contrast, MBCA (1969) § 46 permitted a "distribution" to be paid out of capital surplus only if a number of conditions were satisfied, most importantly: (1) no dividend could be paid if the corporation was insolvent or the payment would render the corporation insolvent; (2) the articles of incorporation authorized the board to pay dividends out of capital surplus or, in the alternative, the shareholders approved such payment by a majority of the outstanding shares; and (3) the rights of preferred shareholders were protected.

All such complications went out the window with the 1984 promulgation of the MBCA's current version. Indeed, MBCA § 6.40 is the simplest of all the modern statutory limitations on the payment of dividends. Section 6.40 governs a class of transactions referred to as "distributions," a term defined in § 1.40(6) to include not only the traditional cash dividend but also any direct or indirect transfer of money or other property (except the firm's own shares) or incurrence of debt to or on behalf of shareholders. The term thus includes cash dividends, distribution of noncash assets, repurchase or redemption of shares, and distribution of debt securities.

Like the MBCA (1969), the current version imposes a two-part test to determine the legality of a distribution. First, an equity insolvency test under which the corporation, after giving effect to the distribution,[9] must be able to pay its debts as they become due in the usual course of business.[10] Second, a balance sheet test under which, after giving effect to the distribution, the corporation's total assets must exceed the sum of total liabilities plus the amount required to satisfy any liquidation preference of preferred stock.[11] Both tests must be satisfied, as MBCA § 6.40(c) is phrased in the disjunctive, or the distribution may not be made. In our principal example, assuming Acme can satisfy the equity insolvency test and has no preferred stock to worry about, Acme could make a distribution of up to $5,000, which is the amount by which total assets exceed total liabilities.

MBCA § 8.33(a) provides that a director who votes for, or assents to, an improper distribution is personally liable to the corporation for the amount of the distribution that exceeds that which could have properly been paid out. Plaintiff must also show that the director did not comply with the standards of conduct set forth in § 8.30. In turn, MBCA § 8.30(a) requires that the director act in good faith, with the care that an ordinarily prudent person in a like position would exercise under similar circumstances and in a manner he reasonably believes to be in the best interests of the corporation. MBCA § 8.30(e) further provides that a director is entitled to rely on reports from corporate officers, legal counsel and accountants. A director who relies in good faith on an accounting opinion stating that neither of the § 6.40(b) tests are met and a legal opinion that the dividend is proper therefore may not be held liable.

---

[9] Under MBCA § 6.40(e)(3), when the effect of a cash dividend is measured depends on the time span between the date the distribution is authorized and the date it is actually paid. If that time span is less than 120 days, the effect is measured as of the date of authorization; if the span is more than 120 days, however, the effect is measured on the date of payment.

[10] MBCA § 6.40(c)(1).

[11] MBCA § 6.40(c)(2).

As an example, assume that prior to making a distribution, Acme Corporation had total assets of $10,000 and total liabilities of $8,000. Assume that payment of the distribution will not prevent the corporation from paying its debts as they come due. If the corporation makes a $4,000 distribution, the directors' potential § 8.33(a) liability is $2,000. The MBCA's liability provision thus takes into account that some portion of the distribution may have been proper. The corporation could properly make a $2,000 distribution, because that is the amount by which total assets exceeded total liabilities, and only the excess over that amount is the extent of the liability.

MBCA § 8.33(b) provides that a director who is held liable for an unlawful distribution is entitled to contribution from (1) any other director who voted for or assented to the distribution and also failed to live up to the standards of § 8.30, and (2) from each shareholder who accepted the distribution knowing that it was improper. Although the MBCA imposes a contribution obligation on shareholders who knowingly receive an improper distribution, it does not otherwise impose any liability on shareholders. If a creditor wishes to recover the amount of the unlawful distribution from the shareholders, its remedy lies in the fraudulent conveyance laws, not the MBCA. This is a significant change from the common law rule that all shareholders had corporate law liability for improper distribution.

It is noteworthy that under MBCA § 8.33, the cause of action for an unlawful distribution belongs to the corporation. A shareholder therefore could bring a derivative action against the responsible directors. Because creditors generally have no standing to sue derivatively, however, only rarely will they be able to bring suit under MBCA § 8.33. The MBCA's distribution rules thus provide creditors with few protections.

B. Dividends and Asset Revaluation

Consider a relatively simple balance sheet:

Assets		*Liabilities and Shareholder equity*	
Land	$ 9,000	Total liabilities:	$38,000
Other	$24,000	Capital:	$15,000
Total	$33,000	Surplus	($20,000)
		Total shareholder equity	($ 5,000)

This corporation could not pay a dividend under either the MBCA or Delaware approach. Under the MBCA, total liabilities already exceed total assets, so a distribution could not be made. Under Delaware law, the corporation has no surplus and, assuming it could not pay a nimble dividend, thus could not pay a dividend.

Notice, however, that the corporation owns real property being carried on the balance sheet at $9,000. Because assets generally are carried on the books at their historical cost, and land tends to appreciate in value, it is a fair supposition that the land may be worth much more than $9,000. Suppose the fair market value of the land in fact is $30,000. If we "write up" the value of the land to $30,000, the corporation will have total assets of $54,000, and now may pay a dividend. Under the MBCA, total assets exceed total liabilities by $16,000, which is available for distribution. Under Delaware law, net assets are now $16,000, which results in a surplus of $1,000, which is available for payment of a dividend.

Generally accepted accounting principles (GAAP) require that most assets be carried on the books at historical cost less depreciation. Accordingly, you may not write up assets to reflect an increase in their fair market value, but must write them down to reflect depreciation. In contrast, state corporate law generally does not require adherence to GAAP in determining whether a dividend lawfully may be paid. Indeed, MBCA § 6.40(d) expressly authorizes a corporation to use "a fair valuation or other method that is reasonable under the circumstances" in determining the amount of total assets and total liabilities. Accordingly, while the corporation may rely on financial statements prepared in accordance with GAAP, there is no requirement that it do so. The drafters' comments on § 6.40, moreover, go on to state that the statute authorizes departures from historical cost accounting in determining the funds available for distribution. The comments further indicate that a corporation generally may not selectively revalue assets, however. If it is going to revalue some assets, all must be reappraised and adjusted to their fair market value. Delaware and New York reach the same result through case law.[12]

§ 13.4   Redemptions and Repurchases

Redemptions and repurchases by a corporation of its own stock are an alternative way of getting funds out of the corporation and

---

[12] See, e.g., Morris v. Standard Gas & Electric, 63 A.2d 577, 582 (Del.Ch.1949) (the board of directors has a "duty to evaluate the assets on the basis of acceptable data and by standards which they are entitled to believe reasonably reflect present values"); Randall v. Bailey, 23 N.Y.S.2d 173, 183 (N.Y.Sup.1940) (rejecting contention that "cost and not value must be used in determining whether or not there exists a surplus out of which dividends can be paid"); see also Klang v. Smith's Food & Drug Centers, Inc., 702 A.2d 150 (Del.1997) (authorizing revaluation of assets for purposes of determining whether a repurchase of shares complied with DGCL § 160).

into the hands of shareholders. Again, we will focus on the Delaware and MBCA statutes as examples.

A. Delaware Law

DGCL § 160 provides that a corporation may repurchase its own stock, provided that it may not do so if its capital is impaired or if the redemption would cause its capital to be impaired.[13] This means, in effect, that repurchases are made out of surplus rather than capital. Note that there is no equivalent of the nimble dividend concept, so a corporation with no surplus may not repurchase shares. Presumably this requirement reflects some residual notion of capital as a trust fund for the benefit of creditors.

Suppose the corporation has 4,000 shares of stock outstanding, each share of stock having a par value of $5. Prior to the repurchase the corporation's balance sheet read as follows:

Assets	*Liabilities/Shareholder Equity*	
Cash $100,000	Liabilities	$50,000
	Capital	$20,000
	Surplus	$30,000

The corporation then redeems 1,000 shares, paying $10 per share.[14] After giving effect to that transaction, the balance sheet will read as follows:

Assets	*Liabilities/Shareholder Equity*	
Cash $90,000	Liabilities	$50,000
	Capital	$20,000
	Surplus	$20,000

Unless the firm reduces its capital pursuant to DGCL §§ 243 and 244, the stated capital for the repurchased shares thus remains on the books.

Suppose the corporation in our example subsequently wanted to issue the repurchased shares for less than par value and/or for an impermissible form of consideration (such as a promise of future services). Ordinarily such a sale would present watered stock

---

[13] Section 160 does permit the corporation to repurchase its own stock out of capital provided the corporation reduces its capital pursuant to DGCL §§ 243 and 244.

[14] Note that there is no legal obstacle to paying more than par value in a repurchase transaction. Par value solely relates to the price that the corporation must receive when it sells shares.

problems, but the use of repurchased shares can obviate those concerns. Recall that authorized but unissued shares are shares authorized by the charter that have not been sold by the firm. Suppose the charter authorizes the firm to issue up to 20,000 common shares. The firm sells 4,000 shares to investors. At that point it has 4,000 outstanding shares and 16,000 authorized but unissued shares. Treasury shares are shares which were once issued and outstanding, but have been repurchased by the corporation. If, in the preceding example, the corporation bought back 1,000 of its outstanding shares, it would now have 3,000 outstanding shares, 16,000 authorized but unissued shares, and 1,000 treasury shares. Treasury shares may not be voted, do not count towards a quorum, and do not receive dividends.[15] The stated capital for those shares is still on the books, however, so treasury shares are still deemed fully paid and nonassessable even after they are repurchased. Accordingly, "[t]reasury shares may be disposed of by the corporation for such consideration as may be determined from time to time by the board of directors. . . ."[16] The statute thus allows the board to issue treasury shares for less than their par value and/or in return for forms of consideration not lawful with respect to newly-issued shares.

B. MBCA

MBCA § 1.40(6) defines the term distribution to include a redemption of shares. Consequently, redemptions are subject to the same statute § 6.40—as dividends. Returning to the example used in the preceding section, the firm could lawfully repurchase the shares in question. After giving effect to the transaction, which you will recall requires payment of $10,000 to the shareholders, total assets would still exceed total liabilities. Consistent with its abolition of the par value concept, the MBCA has also eliminated the concept of treasury shares. Reacquired shares under the RMBCA are simply classified as authorized but unissued shares.

C. Note on Related Legal Issues

Courts sometimes order an involuntary redemption of stock as a remedy in close corporation cases. Redemption is commonly ordered as an alternative to dissolution of the corporation in cases in which a minority shareholder has been oppressed by the majority.[17] Redemption is also sometimes used as a remedy for breach of the fiduciary duties owed by controlling shareholders.

---

[15] DGCL § 160(c).

[16] DGCL § 153(c).

[17] See, e.g., Alaska Plastics, Inc. v. Coppock, 621 P.2d 270 (Alaska 1980); see also MBCA § 14.34 (authorizing such a remedy).

Where the corporation voluntarily goes into the market to repurchase stock a couple of issues may arise. One is the validity of selective repurchases from specific shareholders, which is mostly a problem in close corporations. In *Donahue v. Rodd Electrotype*,[18] for example, Electrotype's controlling shareholder, Harry Rodd, wished to retire from the business. Harry gave some his stock to his sons and daughter. One of his sons, Charles Rodd, was then elected president of the corporation. Harry and Charles (the latter acting on behalf of the firm) reached an agreement whereby the corporation purchased the remainder of Harry's stock. Donahue, a minority shareholder, asked that his shares be redeemed by the corporation on the same terms as those given Harry, but was refused. Donahue claimed this selective repurchase violated the fiduciary duties owed by the controlling shareholders of a closely held corporation to the minority shareholders thereof. The Massachusetts court agreed, holding that shareholders of a close corporation must deal with one another with "utmost good faith and loyalty."[19] The purchase of Harry's shares, coupled with the refusal to buy Donahue's shares, constituted a breach of this duty because it gave Harry (but only Harry) a market for his shares and also constituted a diversion of corporate assets to the personal use of a controlling shareholder. While *Donahue* thus suggests that majority shareholders cannot use their control of the firm to, in effect, create a market for their shares without extending the same opportunity to the minority,[20] one should not treat *Donahue* as precluding selective repurchases. *Donahue* arose in the close corporation context and the court's decision is expressly limited to that context. Subsequent Massachusetts decisions, moreover, have backed away from the strong fiduciary duty announced in *Donahue*.[21]

Selective repurchases by a public corporation are generally insulated from judicial review by the business judgment rule. Challenges to such repurchases, moreover, bump up against the various obstacles to derivative litigation. Where selective repurchases are used as a takeover defense, however, either by repurchasing shares from the would-be takeover raider (so-called "greenmail") or as part of a recapitalization designed to impede a takeover bid, the heightened judicial scrutiny applicable to such cases poses more serious problems for the board.[22] *Strassburger v.*

---

[18] 328 N.E.2d 505 (Mass.1975).

[19] Id. at 593 (quoting Cardullo v. Landau, 105 N.E.2d 843, 845 (Mass.1952)).

[20] A proposition also supported by Jones v. H.F. Ahmanson & Co., 460 P.2d 464 (Cal.1969).

[21] See, e.g., Wilkes v. Springside Nursing Home, Inc., 353 N.E.2d 657 (Mass.1976).

[22] See, e.g., Unocal Corp. v. Mesa Petroleum Co., 493 A.2d 946 (Del.1985) (discriminatory self-tender offer); Cheff v. Mathes, 199 A.2d 548 (Del.1964) (greenmail).

Earley,[23] for example, held that a corporation generally may repurchase shares of particular stockholders selectively, without being required to offer to repurchase the shares of all stockholders generally. Where the repurchase was effected for the "primary purpose" of entrenching the incumbent board or managers in control of the corporation, however, the transaction is unlawful even if the price paid was fair.

The other major legal hurdle to redemptions, even as to a repurchase program open to all shareholders, is the risk of insider trading liability on the issuer's part for illegally trading in its own stock.[24] In any repurchase plan, counsel therefore must be careful to ensure that the issuer does not possess any material nonpublic information that could give rise to an insider trading claim. In large companies with diverse information flows, this can obviously be very difficult. Under basic principles of agency law, information known even to a single officer can be attributed to the corporation. The safest times to engage in repurchases therefore are immediately after annual and quarterly disclosure reports are filed with the SEC, as there is less likelihood of undisclosed material information at those times.

§ 13.5 Stock Splits and Dividends

A stock dividend is not really a dividend at all. Instead, a stock dividend is the issuance of additional shares of the corporation to its shareholders at no charge to the shareholders. Note, however, that a distribution of stock of another company would be treated as a distribution of property subject to the dividend statute. Suppose Acme Corporation owned 100,000 shares (representing 51 percent of the equity) of Ajax Corporation. If Acme distributed the Ajax shares it owned to its shareholders, a so-called "spin-off transaction," that distribution would be a dividend subject to the dividend statute of Acme's state of incorporation.

A. Stock Dividends

Suppose that ABC Corp sells 2,000 shares of $5 par value stock at a price of $10 per share. Its balance sheet reads as follows:

Assets   *Liabilities/Shareholder Equity*

Cash $20,000   Liabilities 0
                         Capital $10,000
                         Surplus $10,000

---

[23] 752 A.2d 557 (Del.Ch.2000).

[24] If the issuer repurchase program is deemed to be a self-tender offer, the issuer will also have to comply with the disclosure and procedural requirements of Securities Exchange Act Section 13(e) and the SEC rules thereunder.

If ABC now declares a share dividend of 200 shares, what effect will that transaction on the corporation's balance sheet? DGCL § 173 provides that: "If the dividend is to be paid in shares of the corporation's theretofore unissued capital stock the board of directors shall, by resolution, direct that there be designated as capital in respect of such shares an amount which is not less than the aggregate par value of par value shares being declared as a dividend and, in the case of shares without par value being declared as a dividend, such amount as shall be determined by the board of directors." Accordingly, in ABC's case, the effect of the stock dividend is to transfer $1,000 (200 shares times $5 par value per share) from surplus to capital. It has no other effect on the balance sheet. Because a stock dividend has no significant balance sheet effects, in most states they are not subject to the statutory restrictions on dividends.[25]

B.   Stock Splits

In colloquial speech, the term "stock split" is often used to describe a stock dividend in which the number of shares issued equals or exceeds the number of shares outstanding. In legal capital terms, however, this is a misuse of terminology. A stock dividend is an issuance of authorized but unissued stock to the shareholders and may be effected by the board of directors acting alone. A stock split, in contrast, is effected by amending the articles of incorporation to reduce the par value. Suppose ABC's board wanted to effect a 2:1 split, in which each shareholder will end up owning 2 "new" shares post-split for every one pre-split share. ABC's board would recommend that the shareholders approve an amendment to the articles of incorporation reducing the par value from $5 to $2.50 per share. Each shareholder will then receive two "new" shares of common stock for each "old" share they previously owned. Because a stock split is effected via a reduction in the par value, it has no impact on the corporation's balance sheet. Accordingly, the board need not redesignate surplus "as capital . . . if shares are being distributed by a corporation pursuant to a split-up or division of its stock rather than as payment of a dividend declared payable in stock of the corporation."[26] This is so because the capital is the aggregate par value of all outstanding shares. Here the number of outstanding shares went up by 2 but the par value is ½ its former value, so capital is unchanged.

---

[25] Which is not to say that the board may issue stock dividends will-nilly. In Reiss v. Superior Indus., Inc., 466 So.2d 542 (La.Ct.App.1985), for example, a close corporation issued a share dividend to two living shareholders but not to heirs of a deceased shareholder. The court invalidated the dividend on grounds that it constituted a breach of fiduciary duty.

[26] DGCL § 173.

C. Reverse Stock Splits and Freeze-Outs

An interesting wrinkle on this class of transactions is provided by the so-called "reverse stock split." Consider *Leader v. Hycor, Inc.*,[27] for example, in which the corporation's shareholders approved an amendment to the articles of incorporation changing the par value from one cent to $40 per share. As with a regular stock split, the transaction had no impact on Hycor's balance sheet. Hycor shareholders, however, received one new post-split share for every 4,000 "old" shares they owned pre-split. What happened, you may ask, to shareholders who owned less than 4,000 shares? If you owned 1,000 shares, would you have received a quarter share? Like most states, Massachusetts allows but does not require a corporation to issue fractional shares. Where a corporate transaction would leave some shareholders with fractional shares, the corporation may cash out the holders of such shares by paying them the fair value of their fraction of a share. The effect (and presumably the intent) of Hycor's reverse stock split thus was to squeeze-out the firm's minority shareholders, all of whom owned less than 4,000 shares. Such transactions are thus subject to review under the fiduciary duty standards applicable to freeze-out mergers or close corporation squeeze-outs.[28]

The use of reverse stock splits to squeeze-out minority shareholders is also mitigated somewhat by the fact that such transactions require an amendment to the articles of incorporation. Indeed, under the MBCA a reverse stock split triggers both group voting and appraisal rights.[29]

§ 13.6 Dividends on Preferred Stock

Preferred stock with a dividend preference is entitled to receive its specified dividend before any dividends are paid on the common stock. The dividend preference stated in the articles of incorporation, of course, does not trump the statutory limitations on

---

[27] 479 N.E.2d 173 (Mass.1985).

[28] *Hycor* involved a going private transaction by a Massachusetts corporation. Without deciding whether Hycor should be treated as a close corporation and thus be subjected to the exacting fiduciary duties applied by Massachusetts to such firms, the court concluded that Hycor had met that standard. Eliminating the costs associated with being a public corporation was a legitimate business purpose and that the objecting minority could show no less harmful alternative. Id. at 177–78. See also Goldman v. Union Bank and Trust, 765 P.2d 638 (Colo.Ct.App.1988) (courts reviewing freeze-outs effected by a reverse stock split usually require defendants to show a legitimate business purpose for the transaction); Teschner v. Chicago Title & Trust Co., 322 N.E.2d 54 (Ill.1974) (plaintiff not entitled to relief in connection with a freeze-out effected by reverse stock split where plaintiff failed to show that the transaction was fraudulent, unfair, or had an improper purpose); Lerner v. Lerner, 511 A.2d 501 (Md.1986) (freeze-out by reverse stock split enjoined on fiduciary duty grounds).

[29] See MBCA § 10.04(a)(4) (group voting); MBCA § 13.02(a)(4) (appraisal rights).

payment of dividends. Just as with dividends on the common, dividends on the preferred must pass muster under the relevant statute.

Recall that dividends differ significantly from interest payable on a bond. Payment of interest on debt obligations is not discretionary—failure to pay interest when due is a default. Payment of dividends, in contrast, is discretionary. In order to make preferred stock more attractive to investors, however, issuers generally assume contractual obligations that give the preferred shareholders some assurance that they will in fact receive the stated dividend.

A. Cumulative Dividends

A very common dividend protection is the so-called cumulative dividend. Assume that the issuer's articles of incorporation provide that the preferred stock is entitled to a dividend of $1 in each calendar quarter. If the corporation fails to pay a dividend for a given quarter, the missed dividend "accumulates." This is true even if the corporation could not lawfully pay a dividend for the given quarter. Although the corporation may accumulate missed dividends for an indefinite period, all accumulated dividends on the preferred must be paid before any dividend is paid to the common.

Suppose the issuer has failed to pay any dividends for four quarters. In such a situation, the corporation would have to pay the missed dividends ($4) before it can pay any dividends to the common. Indeed, if the dividend for the current quarter is already due, it will have to pay that dividend, as well, for a total of $5 per share, before paying anything to the common.

Outside venture capital transactions, noncumulative preferred stock is rare. If the articles specify that the dividend is noncumulative, however, a couple of interesting questions arise. First, suppose the issuer had sufficient funds to pay the noncumulative dividend to the preferred but decided not to do so. Instead, the board opted to retain those funds for internal purposes. Do the preferred stockholders have a cause of action against the board? Second, suppose the issuer had sufficient funds to pay a dividend on the noncumulative preferred but lacked funds to pay a dividend on the common. If the board paid a dividend on the former but not the latter, do the common shareholders have a cause of action against the board? The latter question is easy. The business judgment rule would preclude bringing such a claim.

As to the former question, the majority rule is that payment of noncumulative dividends is within the board's discretion. Liability arises only if the board abused its discretion in declining to pay such dividends.[30] If no dividend is declared on noncumulative dividends for a given fiscal year, "the claim for that year is gone and cannot be asserted at a later date."[31] Indeed, while payment of a noncumulative dividend for a given fiscal year is discretionary, once that fiscal year has ended, the directors are "left with no discretion ever to pay any such dividend."[32] Or, as Berle put it, the "popular interpretation" is that "dividends on noncumulative preferred stock, once passed or omitted, are 'dead'; can never be made up."[33]

Suppose, for example, that the articles of incorporation provide for an annual noncumulative dividend of $8 per share of preferred. The issuer's board failed to declare dividends in Years 1 and 2. In Year 3, the board wishes to declare a dividend on both the common and the preferred. A holder of the noncumulative preferred asserts, however, that the issuer owes the preferred $24: $8 for each of Years 1 to 3. The issuer's board replies that it need only pay the $8 dividend for Year 3. Under the majority rule, the board will prevail.

The principal exception to the foregoing is the so-called dividend credit rule followed by New Jersey.[34] This approach interprets a noncumulative dividend provision as precluding accumulation of dividends only in years in which the corporation had insufficient earnings to pay the specified dividend. In the preceding example, if the corporation had sufficient earnings in Years 1 and 2 to pay a noncumulative dividend, but chose to retain those earnings for reinvestment, the preferred would get a credit for the unpaid dividends and the board would indeed have to declare a $24 dividend on the preferred before paying anything to the common.

It is possible to achieve the New Jersey result by contract using a so-called cumulative to the extent earned dividend preference.[35] Where the articles of incorporation do not so provide, however, the New Jersey rule is absurd. The preferred shareholders bought stock that said "non-cumulative." The price they were willing to pay for such stock presumably was discounted to reflect the lack of protection resulting from the absence of a cumulative preference.

---

[30] Guttmann v. Illinois Central Railroad Co., 189 F.2d 927, 928 (2d Cir.1951).

[31] Wabash Railway Co. v. Barclay, 280 U.S. 197, 203 (1930).

[32] *Guttmann*, 189 F.2d at 929.

[33] Adolf Berle, noncumulative Preferred Stock, 23 Colum. L. Rev. 358, 364–65 (1923).

[34] See, e.g., Sanders v. Cuba Railroad Co., 120 A.2d 849 (N.J.1956).

[35] In Kern v. Chicago & Eastern Illinois Railroad Co., 285 N.E.2d 501 (Ill.App.1972), the court considered the meaning of a provision under which the preferred stock's dividends were "cumulative but only to the extent that there are 'net earnings available for dividends.'" Id. at 502. The court rejected plaintiff's claim that undistributed earnings of a wholly owned subsidiary should have been considered in determining whether the parent had net earnings for a given year. Id. at 504.

They made their bed, so they should lie in it. As Judge Frank famously put it, "the preferred stockholders are not—like sailors or idiots or infants—wards of the judiciary. As courts on occasions have quoted or paraphrased ancient poets, it may not be inappropriate to paraphrase a modern poet, and to say that 'a contract is a contract is a contract'."[36]

B. Contingent Voting Rights

Contingent voting rights are the other common protection given preferred stock's dividend preference. In other words, so long as dividends specified by the articles are paid, the preferred will have no voting rights. If a specified number of dividends are missed, however, the preferred is given the right to elect some or all of the members of the board of directors. Four to six missed quarterly dividends seems to be typical. The precise voting rights given the preferred will be specified in the articles of incorporation. Commonly used options include giving the preferred shareholders the right to elect a specified number of directors, giving convertible preferred shares the right to vote on a fully-diluted basis—i.e., casting the number of votes they would have been entitled to cast if they converted into common, and allowing the preferred to vote as a separate class.

§ 13.7 Suits to Compel Declaration of a Dividend

Stockholders have no right to dividends. The decision of whether, when, and how much of a dividend should be paid is reserved to the discretion of the board.[37] Despite this clear and well-accepted principle, one occasionally sees suits brought by shareholders to compel the board to declare a dividend. Such suits rarely succeed, however, because the decision to declare a dividend (or not to do so) is protected by the business judgment rule.[38] If brought, a suit to compel declaration of a dividend typically is regarded as direct rather than derivative.[39]

---

[36] *Guttmann*, 189 F.2d at 930.

[37] See, e.g., Liebman v. Auto Strop Co., 150 N.E. 505, 506 (N.Y.1926) ("It is a fundamental rule relating to the management of corporations that it is within the discretion of the directors to determine when and to what extent a dividend shall be made, subject of course to the qualification that the same shall not encroach on the capital. . . . It is for the directors to say, acting in good faith of course, when and to what extent dividends shall be declared.").

[38] See, e.g., In re Tube Methods, Inc., 73 Bankr. 974 (Bankr.E.D.Pa.1987) (holding that, under Pennsylvania law, the decision to declare a dividend is vested in the discretion of the board and that judicial review of board decisions is subject to the business judgment rule).

[39] Sobel v. Whittier Corp., 95 F.Supp. 643, 645 (D.Mich.1951); Gordon v. Elliman, 119 N.E.2d 331, 334 (N.Y.1954) (stating that since "a corporation has no right to compel itself to pay a dividend, the stockholders' right cannot possibly 'derive' from it"); cf. Stevens v. United States Steel Corp., 59 A. 905, 906

The situation is rather different once the board has declared a dividend. If the board declares a dividend, but fails to pay it, the court will treat the shareholder as having a contractual right to receive the dividend and order the corporation to pay it.[40]

As between shareholders and directors, the allocation of decisionmaking authority to the board makes sense. The decision whether to declare a dividend differs but little from any other board decision. Absent facts indicating that the decision was tainted by a conflict of interest, the policies behind the business judgment rule thus apply in full force to dividend decisions.

Cases involving self-dealing thus seem the most likely scenario in which a suit to compel a dividend will succeed.[41] The Delaware Supreme Court, for example, has noted that structuring a dividend so that it is paid only to a controlling shareholder could involve self-dealing sufficient to set aside the business judgment rule:

> For example, suppose a parent dominates a subsidiary and its board of directors. The subsidiary has outstanding two classes of stock, X and Y. Class X is owned by the parent and Class Y is owned by minority stockholders of the subsidiary. If the subsidiary, at the direction of the parent, declares a dividend on its Class X stock only, this might well be self-dealing by the parent. It would be receiving something from the subsidiary to the exclusion of and detrimental to its minority stockholders. This self-dealing, coupled with the parent's fiduciary duty, would make intrinsic fairness the proper standard by which to evaluate the dividend payments.[42]

Where the minority shareholders get their pro rata share of any dividends, however, there is no self-dealing and the business judgment rule applies.

Self-dealing might also be found where the board suspended regular payment of a dividend for the benefit of a controlling shareholder. In *Gabelli & Co. v. Liggett Group, Inc.*,[43] for example,

---

(N.J.Ch.1905) (stating that a dividend, as a debt owed by the corporation, is owed to stockholders severally as individuals).

[40] State by Parsons v. Standard Oil Co., 74 A.2d 565, 575 (N.J.1950) (stating that declaring a dividend gives rise to a debt in favor of stockholders and that once money has been set aside for the payment of dividends, it is held in trust and can not be reached by other creditors).

[41] In close corporations courts may order payment of a dividend as a remedy for oppression of minority shareholders by the majority. See, e.g., Miller v. Magline, Inc., 256 N.W.2d 761 (Mich.App.1977); Patton v. Nicholas, 279 S.W.2d 848 (Tex.1955); see also Gottfried v. Gottfried, 73 N.Y.S.2d 692 (N.Y.Sup.Ct.1947) (recognizing remedy but declining to grant it on facts); Zidell v. Zidell, 560 P.2d 1086 (Or.1977) (same).

[42] Sinclair Oil Corp. v. Levien, 280 A.2d 717, 722 (Del.1971).

[43] 444 A.2d 261 (Del.Ch.1982), aff'd, 479 A.2d 276 (Del.1984).

Liggett was the subject of a takeover bid by Grand Metropolitan Ltd. ("Grand Met"). Grand Met first acquired roughly 85 percent of Liggett's outstanding stock through a tender offer. Grand Met planned to eliminate the remaining minority shareholders through a reverse triangular merger—Ligget would merge with GM Sub, a wholly-owned subsidiary of Grand Met, with Liggett as the surviving corporation. While the merger was pending, Liggett's board suspended payment of its regular quarterly dividend (62.5 cents per share). The Chancery Court held that the decision to suspend a regularly paid dividend is protected by the business judgment rule. Consequently, "it is settled law in Delaware that the Court of Chancery will not compel payment of a dividend unless the corporation is in the proper business and financial posture to do so, and if the failure to declare the dividend is the result of an 'oppressive or fraudulent abuse of discretion.'" The case at bar, however, involved a freeze-out merger by a controlling shareholder and therefore implicated that shareholder's fiduciary duties. Accordingly, the question was whether the merger price was fair. In other words, did the merger price reflect and include the value of the foregone dividend? If so, no harm—no foul.

An interesting twist on the problem was presented by *Baron v. Allied Artists Pictures Corp.*[44] Allied's articles of incorporation provided that if six or more quarterly dividends were missed the preferred shareholders, voting as a class, would have the right to elect a majority of the board of directors. Allied missed the requisite number of preferred dividends, triggering the preferred shares' contingent voting rights. The idea behind contingent voting rights, of course, is that the preferred shareholders' board representatives will change corporate policy so that the firm can begin paying dividends on the preferred. Once the missed dividends are caught up, the preferred shareholders' representatives step down and control returns to the common. (Classically minded readers will note the parallel to the story of Cincinnatus, the Roman general who left his farm to defeat the Aequi and Volscians and, after victory, went back to his farm.) In Allied's case, however, the board failed to begin paying dividends on the preferred stock. As a result, the preferred retained their right to elect a majority of the board— for a period of ten years.

Plaintiff was a common shareholder who sued, in effect, to compel the board to declare such dividends as would be necessary to return control to directors elected by the common. The Chancery Court rejected plaintiff's claim, holding that the directors have discretion to declare dividends or to refrain from doing so. The

---

[44] 337 A.2d 653 (Del.Ch.1975), appeal dismissed, 365 A.2d 136 (Del.1976).

exercise of that discretion is not unbounded, of course. A board elected by the preferred "does have a fiduciary duty to see that the preferred dividends are brought up to date as soon as possible in keeping with prudent business management." Note, however, that the latter qualification substantially eviscerates the scope of the stated duty. The board need not begin paying dividends on the preferred the moment sufficient funds have become available, so long as there is a good business reason for retaining earnings. Worse yet, the business judgment rule precludes the court from second-guessing the board's decision absent "fraud or gross abuse of discretion." In light of the volatile nature of the motion picture business and the resulting need to retain sufficient reserves against major losses, the court refused to grant relief.

Oddly, everyone seems to have ignored the fact that over half of Allied's preferred stock was owned by a single shareholder—Kalvex, Inc.—who owned almost none of Allied's common stock. Because the preferred voted as a class without benefit of cumulative voting, Kalvex controlled the outcome of board elections, despite owning only 7 percent of Allied's total equity. As a result, there was a substantial interlock between the two companies' boards and management. Allied's president, for example, was also the president of Kalvex. Although Kalvex was mainly a preferred shareholder, it could have (and should have) been treated as Allied's controlling shareholder subject to the attendant fiduciary duties. Under the duty of loyalty applicable to controlling shareholders, the question would be whether Kalvex received a benefit at the expense of and to the exclusion of the other shareholders. If so, Kalvex would have to justify that benefit under the intrinsic fairness standard. Plaintiff would have argued that control of the corporation is itself a benefit, which the preferred shareholders seized to the exclusion of the common, and also pointed to the highly remunerative compensation Kalvex's officers received by virtue of their positions at Allied. Would plaintiff have won? Maybe not, but certainly plaintiff's chances would have been far greater than under the theory actually used.

Chapter 14

CLOSE CORPORATIONS

§ 14.1 Exit Versus Voice

A "close corporation is one in which the stock is held in a few hands, or in a few families, and wherein it is not at all, or only rarely, dealt in by buying or selling."[1] The firm's size thus is not determinative, although most close corporations tend to be small, local businesses. Instead, the hallmarks of the closely held corporation are the small number of shareholders and, most important, the absence of a secondary market in which its stock is traded.

This definition emphasizes a critical difference between the public and close corporation; namely, the absence of a market out. If shareholders of a public corporation are unhappy with the firm's management, they can easily exit via the stock market. Consequently, they can simply sell out and put the unhappy experience behind them. Shareholders of a close corporation, in contrast, have no access to a secondary trading market for their shares and, as a result, may find it very difficult to locate a buyer for their shares. Where exit is precluded, dissatisfied constituencies of an organization must resort to voice; that is, because they cannot escape from the unsatisfactory situation, they must seek to change it through internal governance mechanisms.[2]

Unlike a large public corporation, where collective action problems preclude shareholders from bargaining with one another, the small group of investors in a close corporation permits them to bargain at comparatively low cost. Investors would be foolish to agree to invest in the business, but leave planning the details about the firm until the future. Instead, they should settle the critical questions in advance—before they've invested money in the business.

The small number of shareholders typical of close corporations also vitiates the efficiency rationale for separating ownership and control. To the contrary, shareholders of close corporations are far less likely to be passive investors than is the case with respect to public corporations. (These are exceptions, of course, as many close corporations have "silent partners.") A desire for active involvement

---

[1] Galler v. Galler, 203 N.E.2d 577, 583 (Ill.1964). See also G & N Aircraft, Inc. v. Boehm, 743 N.E.2d 227, 236 n. 2 (Ind.2001) ("A minimum requirement is a lack of a public market for the shares, and most would require a small number of shareholders as well.").

[2] See generally Albert O. Hirschman, Exit, Voice, and Loyalty (1970).

follows directly from the lack of a market out. If the shareholders cannot protect themselves by selling out, they are wise to want an effective voice in how the firm is operated.

Earning a return on one's investment provides yet another reason for shareholders to be actively involved in running the close corporation. Most close corporations do not pay significant dividends. Instead, for tax reasons, the shareholders' principal return on their investment comes in the form of salary and bonuses. Dividends are not deductible by the firm, so they are subject to double taxation, once at the firm level and again when received by the shareholder. In contrast, reasonable salary and bonuses are deductible by the firm, so they are taxed only once (at the shareholder/employee level). Because of these tax consequences and the resulting practice of not paying dividends, a denial of employment to a minority shareholder may deny that shareholder a fair return on his investment.

Finally, unlike the public corporation context, it is often practical for the shareholders to be actively involved in running the store. In many closely held corporations, all shareholders are employees and/or directors of the firm, which means that they are in a much better position to monitor the firm's performance and the performance of other firm employees than their public corporation counterparts.

The difficulty, of course, is that the corporation statutes fail to take this into account. Recall that shareholders have no meaningful management rights. Instead, once they have elected the directors, the firm is run by the board of directors. As we have just seen, however, this approach makes very little sense in the context of a small firm where the managers, directors, and shareholders are likely to be one and the same.

There are a wide variety of techniques by which close corporation shareholders can be given effective control over firm management. Most entail some degree of private ordering. Will courts enforce private contracts that derogate from the statutory allocation of powers and rights? If private ordering fails, what ex post extra-contractual rights do allegedly injured shareholders possess?

A number of states have adopted special statutes for close corporations, commonly modeled on the ABA's Model Close Corporation Supplement. Promoters of a close corporation may opt into coverage by such statutes through an express designation of such status in the articles of incorporation. The regulatory regime for statutory close corporations is substantially more liberal in a variety of ways than is mainstream corporate law.

Nevertheless, these statutes are little used. Courts frequently grant comparable benefits to nonstatutory close corporations, moreover. In *Ramos v. Estrada*,[3] for example, defendants noted that California's close corporation statute authorizes vote pooling agreements but the general corporation statute was silent. Defendants inferred that vote pooling agreements were invalid in close corporations that had not opted into the special statute. The court rejected that argument, upholding vote pooling agreements as valid even in nonstatutory close corporations. Accordingly, separate treatment of those statutes is omitted in this text.

§ 14.2   Private Ordering in Close Corporations

A.   Private Ordering of Voting Rights

Whether a corporation is public or close, the most important thing shareholders do as shareholders is the election of directors. Shareholder voting on such matters as dissolution, mergers, and the like runs a reasonably close second. In the close corporation, with its limited number of shareholders, voting can prove problematic in a variety of ways. If shareholders are evenly divided on some issue, deadlock may ensue.[4] More likely, a majority faction may use its voting power to oppress the minority. The majority might, for example, decline to elect minority representatives to the board of directors. The law provides two contractual solutions to this problem: the voting trust and the vote pooling agreement.

1.   Voting Trusts

A voting trust is an agreement among shareholders under which all of the shares owned by the parties are transferred to a trustee, who becomes the nominal, record owner of the shares. The trustee votes the shares in accordance with the provisions of the trust agreement, if any, and is responsible for distributing any dividends to the beneficial owners of the shares.

At common law, voting trusts originally were suspect. Early courts believed that the power to vote stock was an essential incident of owning shares and that separating voting rights from

---

[3] 10 Cal.Rptr.2d 833 (Cal.App.1992). See also Zion v. Kurtz, 428 N.Y.S.2d 199 (1980) (similar holding under Delaware law).

[4] A creative solution to the deadlock problem was validated in Lehrman v. Cohen, 222 A.2d 800 (Del.1966). The Lehrman and Cohen families were equal partners in a grocery store corporation. The corporation had three classes of stock. One class was owned solely by the Lehrman family and gave them the right to elect two directors. A second class was owned solely by the Cohen family and gave them the right to elect two directors. A third class with very limited economic rights but also the right to elect one director was issued to the corporation's legal counsel, who thus functioned as a tie-breaker between the two families. The Delaware supreme court held that the third class was a valid class of stock and that the agreement did not constitute an illegal voting trust.

ownership therefore violated public policy.[5] This oddly formalistic approach ran counter to the basic corporate law principle allowing separation of ownership and control. Because it impeded private ordering, the policy also was inconsistent with basic principles of freedom of contract. Legislatures uniformly have overruled the common law, adopting statutes authorizing voting trusts.[6] Lingering judicial hostility to voting trusts can be seen in cases invalidating voting trusts for relatively trivial failures to comply with statutory requirements.[7] In recent years, however, courts have been more tolerant of minor deviations from the statute. In *Goldblum v. Boyd*,[8] for example, a shareholder sought to invalidate a voting trust for failure to comply with a statutory requirement that voting trusts be filed with the corporation's office. Because the parties had kept a photocopy of the trust agreement in the office, the court deemed them to have substantially complied with the statutory requirement and upheld the trust. In *Oceanic Exploration Co. v. Grynberg*,[9] the Delaware chancery court invalidated a voting trust for failure to comply with several statutory requirements. The Delaware supreme court reversed, excusing noncompliance with those requirements by recharacterizing the instrument as a vote pooling agreement.

The chief advantage of a voting trust is that it eliminates the possibility of shareholder deadlock, because all shareholders put their shares in the trust and only the trustee votes. The disadvantages are more numerous. Shareholders experience a significant loss of control. Most states limit the duration of a voting trust to ten years, after which time it must be renegotiated.[10] Finally, the voting trust does not fully prevent oppression of the minority. A majority coalition of directors still could use its powers on the board to oppress the minority.

2. Vote Pooling Agreements

Suppose four friends—Alpha, Beta, Charlie, and Delta—form a corporation in which each owns 25% of the voting common shares. They sign a contract pursuant to which each agrees to vote for the others when electing the board of directors, thereby ensuring that

---

[5] See, e.g., Luthy v. Ream, 110 N.E. 373, 375 (Ill.1915); Warren v. Pim, 59 A. 773, 789 (N.J.1904).

[6] Only Massachusetts has not done so. See MBCA § 7.30 cmt. On the other hand, Massachusetts courts have long recognized the validity of voting trusts even without statutory authorization. See, e.g., Colbert v. Hennessey, 217 N.E.2d 914, 920 (Mass.1966).

[7] See, e.g., Christopher v. Richardson, 147 A.2d 375, 376 (Pa.1959) (invalidating a voting trust whose term exceeded the statutory ten year limit).

[8] 341 So.2d 436 (La.App.1976).

[9] 428 A.2d 1 (Del.1981).

[10] See, e.g., MBCA § 7.30.

all will be elected. Would such an agreement be enforceable? In brief, yes. Given that a single majority shareholder validly could decide in advance whom to elect, the courts allow several shareholders to decide together in advance whom to elect.[11]

Such a vote pooling agreement differs from a voting trust in that there is no transfer of legal title to the stock in question. As such, the historic prejudice against voting trusts generally was not extended to vote pooling agreements.[12] A notable exception to this general rule was the Delaware supreme court's decision in *Abercrombie v. Davies*,[13] in which the court recharacterized a vote pooling agreement as a voting trust and held it invalid for failure to comply with the voting trust statute. Consequently, where the substantive effect and purpose of the agreement is "sufficiently close to the substance and purpose of [the voting trust statute] to warrant its being subjected to the restrictions and conditions imposed by that Statute," the court will recharacterize the agreement.[14] In contrast, however, the Delaware supreme court's subsequent decision in *Oceanic Exploration Co. v. Grynberg*[15] recognized the ongoing liberalization of judicial attitudes towards voting trusts and pooling agreements. In that case, the court recharacterized a voting trust as a vote pooling agreement. To be sure, *Oceanic Exploration* did not overrule *Abercrombie*. In *Oceanic Exploration*, however, the court acknowledged that judicial hostility towards private ordering was unsound, which signaled a move towards freedom of contract.

Today, a vote pooling agreement is most likely to be recharacterized as a voting trust where some provision separates the right to vote the shares from the other incidents of stock ownership. Suppose two shareholders holding an equal number of shares enter into a vote pooling agreement. Recognizing the risk of deadlock, they agree to submit any disagreements as to how the shares should be voted to a third-party arbitrator. They further grant the arbitrator an irrevocable proxy to vote the shares, so as to provide a mechanism for enforcing the arbitrator's decisions. Such an agreement resembles the definition of a voting trust implied by DGCL § 218, which applies to written agreements by which the shareholders "transfer capital stock to any person" and vest that person with the right to vote that stock. As with a voting trust, they

---

[11] See, e.g., McQuade v. Stoneham, 189 N.E. 234, 236 (N.Y.1934) (noting the "well settled" rule that shareholders may "combine to elect directors").

[12] See, e.g., Luthy v. Ream, 110 N.E. 373, 376 (Ill.1915) ("the pooling of stock for the purpose of electing directors and officers and controlling the management and business of the corporation is not necessarily illegal").

[13] 130 A.2d 338 (Del.1957).

[14] Lehrman v. Cohen, 222 A.2d 800, 806 (Del.1966).

[15] 428 A.2d 1 (Del.1981).

have divorced the right to vote their shares from the other incidents of stockownership and vested that right in some third party. Such an agreement thus is a likely candidate for recharacterization as a voting trust, at least under the illiberal rules laid out in cases like *Abercrombie*.[16] In light of the hyper-technical approach many courts take to voting trusts, under which minor deviations from the statutory provisions are sufficient grounds for invalidating the trust, a recharacterized agreement is very vulnerable. It would be surprising if the drafter of a vote pooling contrast will have bothered to comply with every statutory requirement for a voting trust.

Vote pooling agreements present a number of significant planning and drafting considerations. Should the agreement attempt to specify how the parties will vote their shares (for example, by stating that Alpha agrees to vote for Beta, Charlie, and Delta as directors)? If the agreement does not specify how the shares should be voted, what mechanisms might be adopted to facilitate achieving consensus on that issue? How can one prevent defection by shareholders party to the agreement? Should courts use specific performance to enforce such agreements?

The classic voting pooling decision remains the Delaware supreme court's opinion in *Ringling Bros.-Barnum & Bailey Combined Shows v. Ringling*.[17] When our story began, the circus was owned by descendants of the eponymous Ringling Brothers. The family had split into three factions. Edith Ringling and Aubrey Ringling Haley each owned 315 of the 1000 outstanding shares. The remaining 370 shares were owned by John Ringling North. In 1941, Edith and Aubrey entered into a vote pooling agreement, apparently codifying an earlier agreement dating from 1934, pursuant to which they sought "to act jointly in all matters relating to their stock ownership." More specifically, the agreement required them to "consult and confer" before voting. If they were unable to agree as to how their shares should be voted, the issues was to be referred to a designated arbitrator, one Karl D. Loos, who was also their lawyer. According to the agreement, Loos' decision was "binding" on the ladies.

The corporation used cumulative voting in the election of directors. If each shareholder voted separately, Aubrey and Edith could each elect two directors, while John could elect three. If properly cumulated, however, Edith's and Aubrey's shares

---

[16] Cf. Galler v. Galler, 203 N.E.2d 577, 586 (Ill.1964) (refusing to recharacterize a vote pooling agreement as a voting trust on grounds that it was "a straight contractual voting control agreement which does not divorce voting rights from stock ownership").

[17] 53 A.2d 441 (Del.1947).

empowered them to elect five of the seven directors. Edith and Aubrey were each entitled to 2205 votes (multiply their 315 shares by the seven vacancies to determine the number of votes). Acting together, they could therefore cast 4410 votes, which could be divided so as to allow 882 votes for each of 5 candidates. (Note that at least one of the five would have to receive votes from both Edith and Aubrey.) John, by virtue of his 370 shares, was entitled to cast 2590 votes, a total that could not be divided so as to give to more than two candidates as many as 882 votes each.

In 1946, however, Aubrey and Edith had a falling out and were unable to agree on the identity of the fifth director to be elected by their block.[18] Edith demanded arbitration by Loos, who directed that Edith should vote her shares as follows: 882 votes for Edith herself, 882 for her son Robert, and 441 for a Mr. Dunn. At the meeting, Edith did so. Loos also directed that Aubrey vote her shares as follows: 882 for Aubrey, 882 for her husband James, and 441 for Dunn. At the meeting, Aubrey was represented by her husband James, who refused to comply with Loos' direction. Instead, James cast 1103 votes for Aubrey and 1102 for himself. John divided his votes across three candidates, casting 864 votes for a Mr. Wood, 863 for a Mr. Griffin, and 863 for himself.

If the votes had been cast as directed by Loos, the now defunct Edith-Aubrey coalition would have elected its usual five directors: Edith, Robert, Aubrey, James, and Dunn. If the votes stood as cast, however, Dunn would not be elected. Instead, John would elect all three of his candidates. Edith sought judicial review of the election under what is now DGCL § 225, which authorizes the chancery court to determine the validity of a director election. The vice chancellor upheld the agreement, finding that where one party refused to comply with the arbitrator's judgment the agreement gave the willing party an irrevocable proxy to vote the recalcitrant party's shares as directed by the arbitrator.[19] The vice chancellor

---

[18] The falling out apparently grew out of intra-family disputes triggered by the aftermath of a disastrous fire in the circus big top. Henry Ringling North & Alden Hatch, The Circus Kings: Our Ringling Family Story (1960).

[19] Why didn't the parties avoid the problem by giving Loos an irrevocable proxy? Several answers suggest themselves. First, they may not have wished to give up that much control. Second, they may have been concerned that including an irrevocable proxy might make it more likely that the agreement would be recharacterized as a voting trust on grounds that such a proxy would separate the right to vote their shares from the other incidents of stock ownership that they retained. Third, the common law strongly disfavors irrevocable proxies. To be deemed irrevocable, a proxy must state that it is irrevocable and be coupled with an interest. See, e.g., Calumet Indus. v. MacClure, 464 F.Supp. 19, 26 (N.D.Ill.1978); Abercrombie v. Davies, 123 A.2d 893, 906 (1956), rev'd on other grounds, 130 A.2d 338 (Del.1957). "The 'interest' necessary in order to support irrevocability may be, for example, security for a loan, title to the stock itself, or, in more recent cases, an employee's interest in the corporation." Calumet Indus., 464 F.Supp. at 26. Common law courts divided as to whether the requisite interest must be one in the shares or merely in the corporation. Compare In re Chilson, 168 A. 82, 86 (Del.Ch.1933)

proposed to enforce this decree by ordering a new election to be held before a special master who would give effect to the agreement. The newly-formed Aubrey-John coalition appealed.[20]

On appeal, the Aubrey-John coalition argued that vote pooling agreements were illegal. The only way for shareholders to precommit to a particular voting scheme, they contended, was through a voting trust that fully complied with the various statutory requirements. The Delaware supreme court squarely rejected that argument, distinguishing voting trusts from vote pooling agreements and upholding the validity of the latter.[21] Although the opinion contains sweeping language with respect to the validity of vote pooling agreements, the court's enthusiasm for contractual enforcement mechanisms was more restrained. *"Reasonable* provisions for cases of failure" to agree "seem unobjectionable," the supreme court opined, which invited other courts to invalidate unreasonable anti-defection provisions. If so, however, courts have declined to accept that invitation.[22]

(requiring "some recognizable property or financial interest in the stock in respect of which the voting power is to be exercised") with Deibler v. Chas. H. Elliott Co., 81 A.2d 557, 561 (Pa.1951) (asserting the "rule in general" to be "that the interest which will support an irrevocable proxy need not be in the stock itself"). Under *Chilson,* which was still good law in Delaware when *Ringling* was decided, any proxy given Loos likely would be deemed revocable. In Haft v. Haft, 671 A.2d 413, 420 (Del.Ch.1995), however, the Delaware chancery court recognized that *Chilson* had been overruled by statute. Today, for example, MBCA § 7.22(d)(5) expressly recognizes that the requisite interest arises in connection with the appointment of a party in connection with a vote pooling agreement. The Delaware code contains no such express provision, but one suspects that Delaware courts would enforce an irrevocable proxy created in connection with such an agreement.

[20] Why did John care? After all, assuming the Haleys were now firmly on his side, he would control the board by a 4–3 margin. The new coalition apparently intended to install John as President. If the board was elected as specified by Loos, the coalition would have had only 4 votes to Edith Ringling's 3 (assuming Dunn would side with Edith). The vote would be 4–3 for John as President, but only by counting John's own vote. Suppose Edith challenged the election on conflict of interest grounds. Assuming John's position as President carried with it a salary or other benefits, his election to that position would implicate the interested director transaction provisions of what is now DGCL § 144. Although § 144(a) allows the board to approve conflicted interest transactions, John's vote could not count for that purpose. Consequently, the vote would split 3–3. To be sure, his appointment likely would have passed muster under § 144(a)(3) on grounds that it was fair to the corporation at the time it was approved, but that approach invited further litigation. Obtaining a fifth vote would avoid that problem, by allowing the board to approve the transaction 4–2 (with John abstaining). (Note that this analysis assumes the current state of the law on director voting and conflicts of interest.)

[21] Ringling Bros.-Barnum & Bailey Combined Shows v. Ringling, 53 A.2d 441, 447 (Del.1947). See also Nixon v. Blackwell, 626 A.2d 1366, 1380 (Del.1993) (positing the validity of "definitive stockholder agreements, and such agreements may provide for elaborate earnings tests, buy-out provisions, voting trusts, or other voting agreements").

[22] In Ramos v. Estrada, 10 Cal.Rptr.2d 833 (Cal.App.1992), for example, the contract provided for a mandatory buyout of the defecting shareholders' stock at the disadvantageous price of cost plus 8 percent annual interest. Despite that rather onerous anti-defection provision, the court exhibited no qualms about upholding the agreement.

Curiously, the court failed to grapple with the most significant objection to the agreement's validity. One of the supposed evils of voting trusts is the potential for "secret, uncontrolled combinations of stockholders" to collectively "acquire control of the corporation to the possible detriment of non-participating shareholders."[23] Hence, presumably, such statutory requirements as the obligation to file the trust agreement with the corporation's principal office.[24] If this concern has merit, is not a vote pooling agreement equally problematic? Creating a "combination" to acquire greater control of the corporation was the very purpose of the Edith-Aubrey agreement. To be sure, in this instance, the agreement was open and notorious. But public notoriety is not demanded by *Ringling* or its progeny. The answer presumably is that the supposed concern lacks merit. After all, if directors favored by a particular group of shareholders keep getting elected at the annual stockholders' meeting, even the densest of investors will eventually figure out that a "combination" has acquired control of the corporation. If we are going to let an individual majority shareholder to control the corporation, as we do, there seems no reason that a group of shareholders should not be allowed to the same through collective action without regard to whether they put their fellow shareholders on notice. If the excluded shareholders feel aggrieved, let them induce one or more of the contracting shareholders to defect or, in appropriate cases, pursue claims for breach of fiduciary duty or dissolution.

Equally curiously, having upheld the agreement, the *Ringling* court failed to provide the obvious remedy. Edith and Aubrey surely intended that, in the event of disagreement, Loos' decision would be binding and the shares voted as he directed. The easiest way for a court to effect that intent would be to order specific performance of the agreement. Many courts have granted specific performance of vote pooling agreements and the MBCA provision validating such agreements expressly authorizes specific performance.[25] In *Ringling*, however, the court apparently felt constrained by the nature of the proceeding. In a review of an election, the court opined, the chancellor may reject votes cast in violation of a vote pooling agreement. As a result, the Haley votes should be rejected and not counted. The effect was that six people were elected— John's three nominees, the two Ringlings, and Dunn. The result seems objectionable on several grounds: It disenfranchised the Haleys. It is almost surely not the outcome the parties intended. It

---

[23] Oceanic Exploration Co. v. Grynberg, 428 A.2d 1, 7 (Del.1981),

[24] DGCL § 218(a).

[25] MBCA § 7.31. For decisions granting specific performance of a vote pooling agreement, see, e.g., Ramos v. Estrada, 10 Cal.Rptr.2d 833 (Cal.App.1992); Weil v. Beresth, 220 A.2d 456 (Conn.1966); Galler v. Galler, 203 N.E.2d 577 (Ill.1964).

elevates a formalistic concern with the nature of the proceeding over the basic principle of freedom of contract. Specific performance seems clearly preferable.

To be sure, specific performance is a relatively rare remedy in contract law. Yet, investments in close corporations are unique. There is no readily available substitute for the investment, which is typical of contracts for which specific performance is awarded (the classic example being real estate contracts). In addition, damages for breach of a shareholder agreement often would be speculative. How can we monetize the injury Edith suffered from the Haleys' defection?

B. Private Ordering re Decisionmaking Authority

A vote pooling agreement—even if it ensures that all shareholders are elected to the board—cannot fully protect minority shareholders from oppression by the majority. A majority of the directors has the power to take such actions as ceasing the payment of dividends, refusing to elect minority shareholders as corporate officers,[26] or terminating a minority shareholder's employment with the corporation. Consequently, shareholders frequently adopt agreements restricting director discretion. Such agreements typically provide that all shareholders shall be appointed as officers. They also commonly set out specific requirements as to salary, dividends, pensions, tenure in office, and the like.

Private ordering affecting the directors' powers runs afoul of the foundational principle that the corporation is "managed by or under the direction of a board of directors."[27] This principle is so strongly ensconced in corporate law that courts originally were quite hostile to shareholder agreements purporting to limit the board's powers.

The classic expression of such hostility is the New York Court of Appeals' decision in *McQuade v. Stoneham*.[28] Charles Stoneham was the majority shareholder of the corporation that owned the New York Giants baseball team. He entered into a shareholders agreement with John McGraw, the team's manager, and Francis McQuade, a New York City magistrate. Under the contract, the three agreed to use their best efforts to elect each other directors and appoint each other as officers at specified salaries. McQuade later fell out of favor with Stoneham, who thereupon engineered McQuade's ouster as officer and director. McQuade sued, seeking

---

[26] In a number of states, the articles of incorporation or the bylaws may authorize election of officers by shareholders. A vote pooling agreement with respect to such election should be valid.

[27] DGCL § 141(a).

[28] 189 N.E. 234 (N.Y.1934).

specific performance of the agreement. The court agreed with Stoneham that the contract was invalid. Directors must exercise their independent business judgment on behalf of all shareholders. If directors agree in advance to limit that judgment, shareholders do not receive the benefit of their independence, and the agreement is therefore void as against public policy.[29]

In *Clark v. Dodge*,[30] the New York Court of Appeals revisited this issue, striking a new balance between freedom of contract and constraining externalities. Clark and Dodge jointly owned two drug companies, with Clark owning 25% of the stock and Dodge owning the remaining 75%. Pursuant to a shareholders agreement, they jointly decided whom to elect as directors and officers of the firms. After a falling out, Dodge used his voting control to oust Clark. When Clark sued, Dodge cited *McQuade* for the proposition that the agreement was void. The court rejected Dodge's argument, holding that *McQuade* was intended to protect minority shareholders not party to the agreement. Where the corporation has no minority shareholders, as was the case here, the prohibition is unnecessary. Absent potential harm "to bona fide purchasers of stock or to creditors or to stockholding minorities," i.e. externalities, there was no justification for invalidating the contract even though it "impinges slightly" on the principle of director primacy.[31]

Is unanimity required? Conversely, does unanimity suffice? The answer in New York seems to be yes to both. On the one hand, a careful analysis of *Clark*, albeit in a dissenting opinion, concluded that:

> In those cases in which the agreement is made by less than all the shareholders, almost any attempt to reduce the authority granted to the board by law will create a significant potential for harm to other shareholders even if the potential for harm to the general public is minimal.

---

[29] The court carefully distinguished the agreement before it from vote pooling agreements. "Stockholders may, of course, combine to elect directors. . . . The power to unite is, however, limited to the election of directors and is not extended to contracts whereby limitations are placed on the power of directors to manage the business of the corporation by the selection of agents at defined salaries." Id. at 236.

[30] 199 N.E. 641 (N.Y.1936).

[31] Id. at 642. See also Adler v. Svingos, 436 N.Y.S.2d 719 (App.Div.1981) (upholding a shareholder agreement effectively giving each shareholder a veto over board decisions); Zion v. Kurtz, 428 N.Y.S.2d 199 (1980) (reaching same result under Delaware law). Agreements that impinge more significantly on the board of directors' powers, however, may still be vulnerable under New York law. See, e.g., Long Park v. Trenton-New Brunswick Theatres Co., 77 N.E.2d 633 (N.Y.1948), in which the court of appeals invalidated a shareholders' agreement purporting to delegate "full authority and power to supervise and direct the operation and management" of the business to one of the shareholders. Distinguishing Clark v. Dodge, 199 N.E. 641 (N.Y.1936), as involving only "a slight impingement" on the board's powers, the *Long Park* court invalidated the agreement on grounds that it violated the statutory assignment of managerial authority to the board.

This is so because the effect of such an agreement is to deprive the other shareholders of the benefits and protections which the law perceives to exist when the corporation is managed by an independent board of directors, free to use its own business judgment in the best interest of the corporation. In *Clark*, the possibility of harm to other shareholders was nonexistent, for in fact there were no other shareholders.[32]

On the other hand, New York Business Corporation Law § 620(b) provides that a shareholder agreement will be valid even if "it improperly restricts the board in its management of the business of the corporation" provided such an agreement was authorized in the articles of incorporation by "all the incorporators or holders of record" and subsequent transferees had notice of the provision. The official comments to § 620 state that subsection (b) "expands the ruling in *Clark*," presumably by authorizing agreements that impinge more than slightly on director discretion. Hence, unanimity is necessary under New York law, but also suffices to validate an agreement that infringes on the powers of the board without regard to the extent of any such infringement.

In *Galler v. Galler*,[33] by way of contrast, the Illinois supreme court answered both questions in the negative. Benjamin and Isadore Galler ran a wholesale drug company. Benjamin and his wife Emma owned 47.5% of the shares; Isadore and his wife Rose owned 47.5%. An employee named Rosenberg owned the remaining 5 percent. Benjamin and Isadore entered into a shareholders agreement, to which Rosenberg was not a party, pursuant to which: (i) the two families would each have two seats on a four-person board of directors, even if one of the brothers died; (ii) the firm would pay specified dividends, subject to minimum-earned-surplus limitations; and (iii) the firm would pay a specified death benefit to the widow of either brother. After Benjamin died, Emma tried to enforce the agreement. When Isadore and his son Aaron refused to comply, Emma sued. (In July 1961, before the case was tried, Isadore and Rose bought Rosenberg's shares.)

The *Galler* court held that a nonunanimous shareholders agreement could be (specifically) enforced where: (1) the corporation is closely held, (2) the minority shareholder does not object, and (3) the terms are reasonable.[34] On the facts before it, the court

---

[32] Triggs v. Triggs, 413 N.Y.S.2d 325, 314 (N.Y.1978) (Gabrielli, J., dissenting).

[33] 203 N.E.2d 577 (Ill.1964).

[34] Illinois law now provides two statutory solutions to the *Galler* problem. Section 7.70 of the Illinois Business Corporation Act of 1983, applicable to all corporations except statutory close corporations, generally authorizes voting agreements among shareholders, without any of the limitations inherent in *Galler*. Section 7.71 even more specifically authorizes unanimous shareholder agreements as

deemed the agreement's terms to be reasonable. The duration of the agreement was limited (to the lifetimes of the parties). The company had no obligation to pay dividends if it lacked sufficient earned surplus. Providing a death benefit for surviving spouses of key employees was a legitimate corporate expenditure and the amount payable under the contract was reasonable in amount. Indeed, the stipend for his widow doubtless constituted an important part of Benjamin's compensation. Such a death benefit (called a salary continuation agreement for tax reasons) is akin to so-called "key man" life insurance. So long as the firm benefits from the executive's services and death benefits help secure those services most cheaply, it is hard to see why such an agreement should not be enforced.

Galler rests explicitly on a conception of the close corporation as a *sui generis* entity having more in common with a partnership than a public corporation: "the shareholders of a close corporation are often also the directors and officers thereof. With substantial shareholding interests abiding in each member of the board of directors, it is often quite impossible to secure, as in the large public-issue corporation, independent board judgment free from personal motivations concerning corporate policy."[35] In embracing freedom of contract within such firms, *Galler* is consistent with the trend in the law governing unincorporated business organizations. Section 103 of the UPA (1997), for example, provides that the partnership agreement trumps contrary provisions of the partnership statute, subject to certain enumerated exceptions relating mainly to fiduciary duties and rights of third parties. Section 1101(b) of Delaware's Limited Liability Company Act goes even further, expressly adopting freedom of contract as the core policy of the act.

---

to matters concerning the management of the corporation, so long as there is no fraud or apparent injury to the public or to creditors. Some claim that § 7.71 was a legislative compromise intended to codify *Galler*. See Donald R. Tracy & Stephen A. Tsoris, Illinois Close Corporation Law: To Elect or Not to Elect, 80 Ill. B.J. 552 (1992). By negative implication, however, § 7.71(b) goes beyond *Galler* to provide that a shareholder agreement is effective as against a shareholder who is not a party to the contract so long as the shareholder had actual knowledge of the agreement at the time he became a shareholder or the agreement is conspicuously noticed on the certificate of incorporation. The principal limitation on shareholder agreements now contemplated by Illinois law is that only statutory close corporations may properly replace the board of directors with direct shareholder governance (see Illinois Business Corporation Act (§ 8.05(a))), although § 7.71(c) provides that an agreement which improperly attempts to do so shall not be grounds for piercing the corporate veil. There do not appear to be any Illinois decisions attempting to reconcile these statutory provisions with *Galler*. For statutory close corporations (which are reportedly quite rare in Illinois), Illinois Business Corporation Act §§ 2A.40 and 2A.45 also broadly authorize unanimous shareholder agreements relating to the management of the corporation, specifically including both agreements that limit director discretion and ones that provide for direct shareholder management.

[35] Galler v. Galler, 203 N.E.2d 577, 584 (Ill.1964).

In contrast, the Model Act's provisions on shareholder agreements are significantly less liberal. Under MBCA § 7.32(b), shareholder agreements must be unanimous and (like voting trusts) are limited to 10 years duration. The agreement's existence must be conspicuously noted on the stock certificates, per § 7.32(c), and any purchaser who takes without notice of the agreement is entitled to rescission. Section 7.32(a) enumerates seven specific provisions an agreement may properly include, including restrictions on the discretionary powers of directors, before concluding with a broad catchall for agreements governing "the exercise of the corporate powers or the management of the business affairs of the corporation or the relationship among the shareholders, the directors and the corporation, or among any of them, and is not contrary to public policy." The drafters acknowledge that this creates uncertainty as to the permissible scope of shareholders agreements, but suggest that "in defining the outer limits, courts should consider whether the variation from the Model Act under consideration is similar to the variations permitted by the first seven subsections."[36] As an example of an agreement falling outside § 7.32(a)'s limits, the drafters cite a contract purporting to eliminate the duty of care and/or loyalty.

C.   Private Ordering re Exit Rights

The absence of a market out for close corporation shareholders presents a number of difficult business planning issues: Should the shareholders be free to sell to an outsider without the consent of their fellow shareholders? If so, should the other shareholders get a right of first refusal? Under what circumstances and upon what terms or conditions should shareholders be able to liquidate their investment?

1.   *Restrictions on Transferability*

In general, one of the great advantages of the corporate form is that shares of stock are freely transferable. Any such transfer has no effect or impact on the corporation, except that there is now a new voter of the transferred shares. In contrast, partnership law is far more restrictive. Absent agreement to the contrary, no one can become a partner without the unanimous consent of all other partners.[37] A partner may assign his interest to another party, but the assignee does not become a partner of the firm and has no rights vis-à-vis the firm other than the right to receive whatever income the assignor partner would have been entitled to.[38] For a

---

[36]   MBCA § 7.32 cmt. 1.

[37]   UPA (1914) § 18(g); UPA (1997) § 401(i).

[38]   UPA (1914) § 25–27; UPA (1997) §§ 502–04.

typical partnership, these rules make sense because the identity of one's fellow partners often matters a great deal. The success or failure of a small business depends largely on the ability of its owners to cooperate.

Because the close corporation resembles an "incorporated partnership," it seems safe to assume that the identity of one's fellow shareholders likewise will often matter in that setting.[39] Again, private ordering comes to the rescue. Close corporation shareholders often include restrictions on share transferability in the articles of incorporation or in a shareholder agreement. These restrictions commonly take the form of either a right of first refusal or, more aggressively, an outright prohibition of transfer without the consent of the other shareholders. A right of first refusal is triggered when a shareholder receives an offer from an outsider. The right gives either the corporation and/or the other shareholders an option to purchase the shares on the same terms and conditions offered by the outsider.[40] For example, if Purchaser offers Shareholder $120,000 for the latter's stock, the right of first refusal gives the corporation and/or other shareholders an option to buy the stock for $120,000.

At common law, some courts viewed such restrictions as a restraint on alienation—indeed, some still do so. In *Ogden v. Culpepper*,[41] for example, a Louisiana court opined: "Restrictions on the transfer of corporate stock are to be strictly construed as they unduly restrict the free flow of commerce." In general, however, most courts uphold transferability restrictions so long as they are "reasonable" and the complaining shareholder took the stock with notice of the restriction.[42] Applying this standard, rights of first refusal have been routinely upheld.[43] In contrast, outright prohibitions of transfer absent consent often have been struck down

---

[39] Cf. Donahue v. Rodd Electrotype Co. of New England, Inc., 328 N.E.2d 505, 512 (Mass.1975) ("Just as in a partnership, the relationship among the stockholders must be one of trust, confidence and absolute loyalty if the enterprise is to succeed.").

[40] An alternative, sometimes referred to as the right of first option, gives the corporation and/or other shareholders the right to purchase the would-be seller's stock on terms and conditions specified in the governing documents.

[41] 474 So.2d 1346, 1350 (La.App.1985).

[42] See, e.g., Allen v. Biltmore Tissue Corp., 161 N.Y.S.2d 418, 422 (1957).

[43] See, e.g., Groves v. Prickett, 420 F.2d 1119 (9th Cir.1970); Allen v. Biltmore Tissue Corp., 161 N.Y.S.2d 418, 422 (1957); In re Estate of Spaziani, 480 N.Y.S.2d 854 (N.Y.Surrogate Ct.1984); In re Mather's Estate, 189 A.2d 586 (Pa.1963); Bruns v. Rennebohm Drug Stores, Inc., 442 N.W.2d 591 (Wis.App.1989). On the other hand, some courts still hold that rights of first refusal are to be strictly construed. See, e.g., Frandsen v. Jensen-Sundquist Agency, Inc., 802 F.2d 941, 946 (7th Cir.1986). In Winter v. Skoglund, 404 N.W.2d 786 (Minn.1987), for example, the court invalidated a right of first refusal on grounds that it had not been signed by all shareholders.

as unreasonable.[44] MBCA § 6.27 authorizes both types of restrictions, with respect to persons on notice of thereof, so long as they are adopted for a reasonable purpose and, with respect to consent requirements, their terms are not manifestly unreasonable.

2. Buyout Agreements

A well-drafted shareholders agreement typically will contain some sort of buyout provision. Such provisions provide a contractual exit for close corporation shareholders, giving them liquidity, while also ensuring that the remaining shareholders have some control over who owns stock in the corporation. The critical "deal points" are three-fold: What events trigger a buyout? Does the buyout create a put (giving the shareholder the right to force a sale), a call (giving the corporation the right to mandate a sale), or both? How are the shares to be valued? Our focus here is on the latter issue.

A right of first refusal is a commonly used solution to these problems. Typically, the would-be seller is obliged notify the corporation and/or his fellow shareholders of the terms of the proposed sale. Some rights of first refusal allow the corporation and/or its shareholders to purchase the would-be seller's stock at book value.[45] Book value is likely to be far less than fair market value, of course, given its focus on historical cost and disregard of going concern values. Because book value thus is almost certain to be much lower than the price an otherwise willing buyer likely would pay, such a provision deters outsiders from bidding. Why should an outsider invest time and effort in making a deal when the other shareholders can almost certainly under-bid the outsider's offer? As a result, such provisions substantially limit shareholder liquidity.[46]

A seemingly more transfer-friendly right of first refusal requires the corporation and/or other shareholders to purchase the would-be seller's stock at the same price offered by the prospective

---

[44] Compare Hill v. Warner, Berman & Spitz, P.A., 484 A.2d 344, 351 (N.J.App.Div.1984) (invalid); Rafe v. Hindin, 288 N.Y.S.2d 662, 665 (App.Div.1968) (same) with Colbert v. Hennessey, 217 N.E.2d 914, 920 (Mass.1966) (valid).

[45] Note that a repurchase of shares by the corporation will be subject to the relevant legal capital statute of the state of incorporation. The well-drafted buyout agreement therefore typically allows the nonselling shareholders to buy the stock in question, in case the corporation lacks sufficient surplus to effect the purchase. See Van Kampen v. Detroit Bank & Trust Co., 199 N.W.2d 470 (Mich.App.1972) (holding that the board of directors acted properly in refusing to buyback shares when the corporation's capital was impaired, even though doing so violated shareholder buyout agreement).

[46] Note that there is no legally "correct" pricing term. Setting the buyout price is a matter of business discretion for the client. See Nichols Construction Corp. v. St. Clair, 708 F.Supp. 768, 771 (M.D.La.1989), aff'd mem., 898 F.2d 150 (5th Cir.1990) (holding that "the mere failure to pay 'fair value' for stock under a stock redemption agreement" does not amount "to fraud or breach of fiduciary duty"); see also Palmer v. Chamberlin, 191 F.2d 532 (5th Cir.1951).

purchaser. One key advantage of such a provision is that it, in effect, creates a market price for the shares, which allows one to avoid messy valuation questions. The price an outsider is willing to pay, however, likely will reflect both a marketability and minority discount. In addition, the outsider still must invest time and resources in deciding what to pay. This is a sunk cost. The right of first refusal means that the outsider likely won't get the shares, however, so the outsider will be unwilling to invest significant sunk costs in accurately pricing the shares. In turn, this means that the outsider will further discount the price for uncertainty. Accordingly, relying on a right of first refusal to create a "market" price is likely to result in a value much lower than the shares' fair value. Finally, such a provision does not fully resolve the liquidity problem, as a shareholder can only get out by finding a willing buyer.

Identifying the transactions that trigger the right of first refusal is a critical drafting issue. Judge Richard Posner's decision in *Frandsen v. Jensen-Sundquist Agency, Inc.*[47] nicely illustrates the key issues. The Jensen family owned 52 percent of the Jensen-Sundquist Agency, Inc. (JSA), which in turn owned a majority of the shares of the First Bank of Grantsburg (FBG). Dennis Frandsen owned 8 percent of JSA. The parties' shareholders agreement contained a right of first refusal pursuant to which the Jensen family was obliged to offer their shares to Frandsen before selling to an outsider. If Frandsen exercised the right of first refusal, he was obliged to pay the same price as that offered by the prospective purchaser. If Frandsen did not exercise his right of first refusal, however, the Jensen family was obliged to offer to buy Frandsen's stock at that price. This is a so-called "take-me-along" or "equal sharing" provision.

First Wisconsin Corp. wanted to buy FBG. If First Wisconsin had directly bought the FBG shares from JSA, no problems would have arisen. The right of first refusal only applied to a sale of the Jensen's family's JSA stock, not to a sale of FBG stock by JSA. For reasons that remain unclear, however, the parties initially structured as a merger in which all of the JSA shareholders would be bought out for cash. Frandsen objected, claiming the merger triggered the right of first refusal and that he was therefore entitled to purchase the Jensen family's JSA shares. The Jensen family and First Wisconsin thereupon restructured the deal so that First Wisconsin would buy the FBG stock directly from JSA. The issue presented was whether the court should construe the right of first refusal clause as being triggered by a merger in which all shareholders would participate. (Although the merger would give

---

[47] 802 F.2d 941 (7th Cir.1986).

Frandsen cash for his shares, he apparently preferred owning FGB to being cashed out.) Judge Posner held that the right of first refusal was not triggered. The clause stated that if the Jensen family "at any time [should] offer to sell their stock" in JSA, they had to give Frandsen a right of first refusal. Because a merger has different legal implications than a sale of stock, and because an experienced businessman like Frandsen should have recognized that distinction and protected himself, the court declined to give the term "offer to sell" an expansive construction encompassing a merger. (Note the similarity to de facto merger doctrine, in that the court is elevating form over substance.[48]) Other courts have likewise tended to give rights of first refusal fairly narrow constructions,[49] thereby putting a premium on careful ex ante negotiation and drafting.

An alternative to the right of first refusal as a solution to the problem of setting the price at which the buyout is to occur is illustrated by the agreement at issue in *Helms v. Duckworth*.[50] The agreement included a buyout provision applicable when one of the two shareholders died. The buyout clause provided: "The price which the surviving stockholder shall pay for the stock of the deceased stockholder shall be at the rate of $10.00 per share; provided, however, that such sale and purchase price may, from time to time, be re-determined and changed in the following manner: During the month of January in any year while this agreement remains in force, the parties of the first and second part shall have the right to increase or decrease the sale and purchase price by an instrument in writing. . . ." What happens if one of the

---

[48] In Seven Springs Farm, Inc. v. Croker, 748 A.2d 740 (Pa.Super.2000), for example, the Pennsylvania court held that a buyout provision in a shareholders agreement did not apply to a cash-out merger. The court found that the merger was structured so as to avoid triggering a right of first refusal contained in the buyout agreement, but the court thought that fact irrelevant to the task of interpreting the contract. The court interpreted the agreement as being limited to acts of a shareholder, such as a sale of stock to a third party, while a merger was deemed a corporate act. In thus elevating form over substance, the court opined: formalities are crucial in corporate law. . . . It has been said of corporate law that it is not so much what is done, but how it is done. Id. at 749. See also Frandsen v. Jensen-Sundquist Agency, Inc., 802 F.2d 941 (7th Cir.1986), in which Posner explained that corporate law "is an area of law where formalities are important, as they are the method by which sophisticated businessmen make their contractual rights definite and limit the authority of the courts to redo their deal." Id. at 947.

[49] See, e.g., Engel v. Teleprompter Corp., 703 F.2d 127 (5th Cir.1983) (under Texas law the merger of subject corporation's wholly owned subsidiary with corporate majority shareholder was not a sale, transfer, assignment, or other disposition of stock of subject corporation within meaning of the right of first refusal); Louisiana Weekly Pub. Co., Inc. v. First Nat'l Bank of Commerce, 483 So.2d 929 (La.1986) (right of first refusal restricting sales of stock not triggered by a gift of stock); Helfand v. Cohen, 487 N.Y.S.2d 836 (App.Div.1985) (right of first refusal limiting sales of stock was not triggered by sale of corporation's sole asset); In re Estate of Spaziani, 480 N.Y.S.2d 854 (Surr.1984) (right of first refusal limiting sales of stock was not triggered by bequest of shares).

[50] 249 F.2d 482 (D.C.Cir.1957).

parties refuses to bargain in good faith, as in fact did happen in *Helms v. Duckworth*? Defendant Duckworth's lawyer made a serious tactical error in allowing Duckworth to sign an affidavit stating that the price had never been renegotiated and, worse yet, that Duckworth never intended to allow a change in the initial price. In light of that testimony, the court declined to enforce the buyout agreement. The court held that Duckworth had a fiduciary duty to bargain in good faith. Duckworth's secret intent not to bargain violated that duty.

It is unclear what a duty to bargain in good faith means in this context. Did Duckworth have a duty to raise the issue, even if the other shareholder did not? A better basis for the result thus is the court's alternative holding that Duckworth had a duty at the time the contract was signed to disclose his intention to refuse to allow an increase in the buyout price. His failure to disclose that intention constituted fraud, which created an independent and sufficient basis for holding the contract unenforceable.

A third approach simply establishes a valuation formula in the buyout agreement. The agreement might provide, for example, that the corporation should be valued at some contractually specified multiple of earnings. Buyout agreements taking this tack tend to use relatively unsophisticated valuation techniques. One rarely sees close corporation buyout agreements using discounted cash flow valuation, for example. In part, this may be attributable to a lack of sophistication on the part of the drafting attorney. Even if the lawyer understands valuation, the clients may not have the financial sophistication necessary to understand the document or to later apply it. Even relatively simple valuation formulas, such as capitalized earnings, moreover, can require forecasts of uncertain future events and lots of subjective judgments. (What multiple shall we select? Will that multiple still be relevant 20 years from now? How do we measure earnings? etc.) One either gets very high ex ante bargaining costs or lots of ex post disputes or both. As in most drafting matters, the lawyer must strike a balance between accuracy and certainty, which arguably ought to tip in favor of certainty.

The need for certainty and predictability may also explain why one rarely sees valuation provisions that require hiring an appraiser. The value appraisers or arbitrators put on the company will depend in large part on the methodology used by the appraiser, which means the drafter either needs to select an appraiser in advance or face grave uncertainty.

A final issue with respect to buyout agreements is the extent to which courts will apply them in settings not contemplated by the agreement. In *In re Pace Photographers, Ltd.*,[51] for example, the parties' shareholder agreement contained a right of first refusal under which sales of stock made during the first five years would be priced at a steep discount to fair value. Three years into the deal one shareholder had a falling out with his fellows and brought an action for involuntary dissolution. Invoking a New York statute under which the corporation could elect to buyout the complaining shareholder's stock in lieu of dissolution, the other shareholders contended that the valuation set by the shareholder agreement should control. Acknowledging that shareholders in theory could contractually set a price to be applied in an involuntary dissolution proceeding, the court held that such an agreement needed to do so explicitly. A valuation provision applicable on its face solely to voluntary sales thus did not control judicial valuation in a dissolution proceeding.

§ 14.3 Fiduciary Duties in Close Corporations

At early common law, shareholders as such owed no fiduciary duties to the corporation or to other shareholders. Consequently, when acting in their capacity as shareholders, the shareholders were free to vote or otherwise to act in their own self interest. We have already observed some erosion of this doctrine in the context of a majority shareholder of a public corporation. *Sinclair Oil*, for example, prohibits controlling shareholders from benefiting themselves at the expense of the minority in connection with ordinary business decisions.[52]

A similar erosion of the common law rule has occurred in the close corporation context. Indeed, the concept of shareholder fiduciary duties is most highly developed in closely held corporations. This is not surprising when one considers the superficial similarities between the close corporation and partnership forms of organization. Recall Judge Cardozo's opinion in *Meinhard*,[53] which exemplifies the strong fiduciary duty concepts courts have created in the partnership setting.

A. The Massachusetts Line of Cases

1. *The Fiduciary Duties of Majority Shareholders*

Massachusetts has been by far the leader in imposing partnership type fiduciary duties on close corporation shareholders, so our discussion will initially focus on a series of cases decided by

---

[51] 530 N.Y.S.2d 67 (1988).

[52] Sinclair Oil Corp. v. Levien, 280 A.2d 717 (Del.1971).

[53] Meinhard v. Salmon, 164 N.E. 545 (N.Y.1928).

its courts. The series began with *Donahue v. Rodd Electrotype*.[54] Harry Rodd, the controlling shareholder of the eponymous Rodd Electrotype corporation, wished to retire. Harry gave some his stock to his sons and daughter. One of his sons, Charles Rodd, was then elected as president of the corporation. Harry then negotiated with Charles, who acted on behalf of the firm, an agreement whereby the corporation would purchase the remainder of Harry's stock. Donahue, a minority shareholder, objected. Donahue requested that the corporation redeem his shares on the same terms as those given Harry, a request the firm refused. Donahue sued, claiming the firm's refusal to accord him an equal right to sell his shares constituted a breach of the controlling group's fiduciary duties (the group now being composed mainly of Harry's children).

In *Donahue*, the Massachusetts supreme judicial court began by describing the close corporation as an incorporated partnership. In the court's view, the shareholders adopted the corporate form to obtain, among other advantages, tax benefits and limited liability. But while its form may be corporate, in substance the firm remains a partnership. Accordingly, the court opined that shareholders of a close corporation owe one another the same fiduciary duties as partners owe to one another. More specifically, the court adopted Judge Cardozo's *Meinhard* formulation, holding that shareholders of a close corporation must deal with one another with the "utmost good faith and loyalty." On the facts before it, the court concluded that the purchase of Harry's shares, coupled with the refusal to buy Donahue's shares, constituted a breach of this duty because it gave Harry—but only Harry—a market for his shares. The court thus held that the majority could not use its control of the firm to, in effect, create a market for their shares, without extending the same opportunity to the minority.

In reaching that result, *Donahue* used language so broad as to imply that the majority must always subordinate their interests to those of the minority. Arguably, a relatively strong set of fiduciary duties is justified in the close corporation setting, because of the risk that the majority shareholder will use its control to oppress the minority shareholder. Even so, it is far from clear that one should go as far as the court did in *Donahue*. In *Wilkes v. Springside Nursing Home*,[55] the Massachusetts supreme judicial court in fact reconsidered and retrenched. Plaintiff Wilkes, one of four shareholders in a close corporation, had been a director and salaried officer of the corporation. Relations between Wilkes and the other shareholders deteriorated to the point that Wilkes gave

---

[54] 328 N.E.2d 505 (Mass.1975).
[55] 353 N.E.2d 657 (Mass.1976).

notice of intent to sell his shares. Wilkes was then stripped of his salary and offices.

The Massachusetts supreme judicial court held that the denial of employment constituted a freezing out of the minority shareholder. Indeed, Wilkes lost both the return on his labor and on his investment in the nursing home. The former he could recoup by finding another job, but the latter he would lose entirely unless the firm repurchased his stock or began paying dividends.

Under *Donahue*, this is an easy case. If the majority must always subordinate its interests to those of the minority, the actions of the majority shareholders in *Wilkes* clearly breached that duty. But while the court did not disavow *Donahue*, it did tweak—and limit—the rule substantially. According to *Wilkes,* there must be a balance between the fiduciary duty of the majority and its right to selfish ownership, which gives the controlling group "some room to maneuver" in setting policy. In most cases, the majority will have made a larger investment, by which it effectively purchased the right to control. Hence, the majority should have a greater voice in setting corporate policy.[56] In addition, the minority shareholders presumably knew a controlling block existed when they bought into the firm. The minority shareholders therefore assumed the risk that some decisions would be adverse to their interests.

Wilkes held that the controlling group must first demonstrate some legitimate business purpose for its action. If such a showing is made, the burden then shifts to the minority shareholder to show that the legitimate purpose could have been achieved through an alternative less harmful to the minority's interest. The court must then attempt to balance the legitimate business purpose against the practicability of the proposed less harmful alternative.

A legitimate business purpose could have been shown on the facts of this case if Wilkes had been negligent in failing to perform his duties or in failing to perform them with due care. Wilkes, however, had been competent and remained willing to perform his tasks. Instead, the shareholders for personal reasons had forced Wilkes out by denying him any return on his investment and then offering to buy his shares at a price they admitted they would not accept.[57]

---

[56] *Wilkes* does not offer controlling shareholders of close corporations anywhere near the level of protection the business judgment rule gives to directors and controlling shareholders of public corporations, however. The initial burden of proof is on the controlling shareholders and, even if they meet that burden, the court will go on to compare their action against alternatives they might have selected. On the other hand, the *Wilkes* formulation does not give minority shareholders as much protection as partners receive under cases like *Meinhard*.

[57] In Brodie v. Jordan, 857 N.E.2d 1076 (Mass. 2006), the court held that the *Wilkes* duty is violated when the controlling shareholder (or shareholders) "act to

Wilkes is subject to criticism from a variety of perspectives. On the facts at bar, the parties had an agreement—or, at least, an oral understanding—pursuant to which all were to be directors and salaried officers. Accordingly, this case could have been decided as a simple breach of contract. It is not at all clear why fiduciary duty concepts even come into the picture.

Assuming the relevance of fiduciary obligation, should partnership-like fiduciary duties be imposed in the close corporation setting? On the one hand, the court rightly notes that close corporations operate much like partnerships, and face the same practical constraints. If so, why is there any difference in the duties? Neither partners nor shareholders in closely held corporations have a ready market for their investments. If partners need stringent legal protection, so too do shareholders; if shareholders need managerial flexibility, so too do partners.

On the other hand, while the partnership analogy is a useful one, we should not overstate it. Investors are heterogeneous and the best approach may be to offer them standard form contracts—off the rack rules—that provide significant choice. Corporate and partnership law differs in many respects. Courts will maximize investor welfare by letting investors choose the form best suited to their business. If investor choice is a virtue, in other words, Massachusetts' decision to harmonize close corporation and partnership law was wrongheaded. A better approach would be to retain a real choice by not imposing higher fiduciary duties on close corporation shareholders. To be sure, in the past, some investors probably preferred partnership rules but felt it necessary to incorporate so as to get the benefit of limited liability. These days, such investors can form a limited liability company, which combines a more-or-less partnership-like governance structure with limited liability. Accordingly, the case for maintaining a clear distinction between partnership and corporate law has become even stronger.

'freeze out' the minority." The court then "defined freeze-outs by way of example," listing such situations as when the defendants "may refuse to declare dividends; they may drain off the corporation's earnings in the form of exorbitant salaries and bonuses to the majority shareholder-officers and perhaps to their relatives, or in the form of high rent by the corporation for property leased from majority shareholders . . . ; they may deprive minority shareholders of corporate offices and of employment by the company; they may cause the corporation to sell its assets at an inadequate price to the majority shareholders. . . ." The court then explained that "[w]hat these examples have in common is that, in each, the majority frustrates the minority's reasonable expectations of benefit from their ownership of shares." Accordingly, it seems that a plaintiff minority shareholder must first demonstrate that he or she has been frozen out before the burden shifts to the defendants to satisfy the three-prong *Wilkes* test.

2.　*The Fiduciary Duties of Minority Shareholders*

Ownership of voting stock is not the only basis on which control may rest. In the close corporation, a shareholder agreement may give minority shareholders considerable power. A Massachusetts appellate court evaluated the implications of *Donahue* and *Wilkes* for such a situation in *Smith v. Atlantic Properties*.[58] Four shareholders bought equal amounts of stock in a real estate venture. A supermajority provision was included in both the articles of incorporation and bylaws, under which no corporate action could be taken without the approval of 80% of the outstanding shares. As such, each shareholder could effectively veto any proposed corporate action. Shareholder Wolfson used his veto power to prevent the corporation from paying dividends. Wolfson claimed he wanted to spend the firm's earnings on maintaining and improving the firm's property, but the other shareholders were unwilling to do so. In fact, Wolfson's reluctance to permit dividends most likely arose out of tax considerations. In the years at issue, the maximum marginal individual tax rate was 90 percent (1954–1963) or 70 percent (after 1963) but the maximum capital gain rate was 25 percent. Wolfson apparently was a high bracket taxpayer, so that payment of dividends would leave him little after taxes. If Atlantic Properties retained its profits, increasing the value of the shares, however, the increased value could be realized by selling the shares and the resulting gain would be taxed at the much lower capital gains rate.

Because the firm was unable to pay dividends over Wolfson's veto, however, another tax issue arose. The accumulated earnings tax penalizes corporations that accumulate excess earnings that are neither paid out to shareholders nor otherwise spent. Due to the deadlock between Wolfson and the other shareholders, the firm was unable either to spend its earnings on improvements or to pay them out as dividends. As a result, the firm eventually incurred the accumulated earnings tax penalty. The other shareholders sued, alleging that Wolfson's use of his veto power constituted a breach of fiduciary duty. The Massachusetts court agreed, holding that minority shareholders, at least where they have a veto power over corporate action, are subject to the same fiduciary duties as those imposed by *Donahue* and *Wilkes*. On the facts before it, the court held that Wolfson's use of his veto power violated those duties because it subjected the corporation to an unnecessary assessment of penalty taxes.

The basic proposition—that a veto power vested in the majority shareholders should be subject to fiduciary analysis—seems

---

[58]　422 N.E.2d 798 (Mass.App.1981).

unobjectionable.[59] On the facts, however, it is inapt. Wolfson no more caused the firm to incur the accumulated earnings tax than did the other three shareholders. To be sure, Atlantic could have avoided the tax by paying dividends, but it could just as well have avoided that tax by reinvesting the money in the firm's real estate. The court implied that Wolfson opposed the dividends because he was in a higher tax bracket than the others. But so what? It was just as selfish for the others to vote for dividends because they were in a lower bracket. In this instance, each of the four shareholders rationally voted his individual self-interest. It was because each side refused to compromise that the firm was liable for the tax penalty. The *Wilkes* line of cases simply has no application where the issue is deadlock, which was the case here.

Nonetheless, Massachusetts cases continue to follow *Wilkes*, albeit not always fatally to the interests of the minority. In *Medical Air Technology Corp. v. Marwan Inv., Inc.,*[60] for example, the court held that a 15% shareholder did not breach its fiduciary duties to its fellow shareholders by voting against a proposed merger. Because the merger agreement required approval by 95% of the outstanding shares, the 15% shareholder's opposition sufficed to scuttle the deal. The majority claimed that the minority shareholder lacked a legitimate business purpose for its negative vote, as required by *Wilkes*, because the minority shareholder was acting in its own self-interest. The minority shareholder had lent substantial sums to the corporation. If the merger failed, the majority alleged, the minority shareholder would be able to foreclose on its loans, seizing corporate assets.

The court rejected the majority's argument that argument that "a minority shareholder may never, under the *Donahue* rule, take its own interest into account in deciding its vote." The court held that "self-interest may be a proper motive for a stockholder's actions, so long as that interest does not result in acts in derogation of the stockholder's fiduciary duty." In this case, the majority had failed to disclose all material facts and the minority shareholder reasonably believed the merger would not solve the company's financial problems. Hence, the court ruled, the minority had a legitimate business purpose for opposing the merger. The case thus does not resolve the question of whether a minority shareholder's

---

[59] Some cases suggest that minority control through a veto provision may not be necessary to impose fiduciary obligations on the minority. See, e.g., A.W. Chesterton Company, Inc. v. Chesterton, 951 F.Supp. 291 (D.Mass.), aff'd, 128 F.3d 1 (1st Cir.1997) (holding that a minority shareholder's proposed sale of his shares to other corporations, which would terminate the corporation's favorable tax status as subchapter S corporation, would constitute a breach of fiduciary duty); see also Zimmerman v. Bogoff, 524 N.E.2d 849 (Mass.1988) (holding that "fiduciary obligations may arise regardless of percentage of share ownership").

[60] 303 F.3d 11 (1st Cir.2002) (applying Massachusetts law in a diversity case).

self-interest standing alone constitutes a legitimate business purpose, although dicta in the opinion implies that it would not.

B. California Law

In *Jones v. H.F. Ahmanson & Co.*,[61] the California supreme court used fiduciary duty concepts to limit the ability of controlling shareholders to create a market for their shares without providing comparable liquidity for the minority. The United Savings and Loan Association of California was a closely held financial institution. The defendants owned about 85 percent of United's shares. Defendants wished to create a public market for their shares, a task that could have been accomplished using any of several methods, most of which would have created a market for all shareholders' stock. Instead of adopting any of those options, however, the defendants set up a holding company, to which they transferred their shares. The holding company then conducted a public offering of its stock, which created a secondary trading market for that stock. The 15 percent of United's stock that was not owned by the holding company was thus left without a viable secondary market. The California supreme court held that when no active trading market for the corporation's shares exists, the controlling shareholders may not use their power over the corporation to promote a marketing scheme that benefits themselves alone to the exclusion and detriment of the minority.

It once seemed likely that *Ahmanson* would become an important precedent, perhaps precluding a wide range of transactions including sales of control blocks at a premium. At least outside California, that has not happened.[62] Even in California, there seems to be something of a trend towards limiting *Ahmanson* to its unique facts and procedural posture.[63] If *Ahmanson* is to remain on the books, it should be so limited. The case was decided on appeal from the trial court's grant of a motion to dismiss. Interpreting the facts most favorably for the plaintiffs, the defendants went out of their way to deprive the minority shareholders of a market for their shares, reduced the dividend in order to deprive the minority shareholders of any economic return,

---

[61] 460 P.2d 464 (Cal.1969).

[62] See Nixon v. Blackwell, 626 A.2d 1366 (Del.1993); Toner v. Baltimore Envelope Co., 498 A.2d 642 (Md.1985); Delahoussaye v. Newhard, 785 S.W.2d 609 (Mo.App.1990).

[63] See, e.g., Miles, Inc. v. Scripps Clinic and Research Foundation, 810 F.Supp. 1091 (S.D.Cal.1993) ("The Jones case did give the narrow circumstance in which a fiduciary duty may be imposed: when a majority shareholder usurps a corporate opportunity from or otherwise harms the minority shareholder."); Kirschner Bros. Oil, Inc. v. Natomas Co., 229 Cal.Rptr. 899 (Cal.App.1986) (noting that Ahmanson's sweeping dicta must be "carefully related" to the facts before a violation can be found; hence, plaintiffs must explain with "specificity what they . . . might have been entitled to that they did not receive").

at least in the short run, and displayed their true objective by offering a low price for the minority shares. In short, this is just a run of the mill squeezeout case. Unfortunately, there is much broader dicta in the opinion—and it is that dicta for which the case is frequently cited.

C. Delaware Law

In *Nixon v. Blackwell*,[64] the Delaware supreme court faced a very common close corporation problem. The founder of a closely held business died, leaving behind a messy estate. Control of the corporation passed to a group of loyal employees, who received all of the voting stock. The founder's family received nonvoting stock, which left them with a significant equity stake in the business but without any control rights. The employee block tried to buyout the family block, which rejected the offer as too low. The corporation paid modest dividends, leaving the minority with virtually no economic return on their shares. Meanwhile, the controlling group of employees adopted an ESOP and took out so-called key man life insurance policies on themselves. Under such policies, in the event one of the shareholders dies, the proceeds go to the corporation, which then uses the proceeds to buy the shares from the dead employee's estate.

The minority sued, alleging a breach of the controlling group's fiduciary duties. The Delaware supreme court used this opportunity to expressly reject any special fiduciary duties applicable only to close corporations. The decision does not leave the minority shareholders without a remedy, however. The court noted that standard corporate law fiduciary duty principles constrain the conduct of both directors and controlling shareholders. Because the ESOP and key man life insurance policies entailed conflicted interest transactions, they were to be reviewed under the entire fairness standard applicable to duty of loyalty claims. On the facts before it, the court deemed that test to be satisfied. ESOPs and key man insurance policies are a normal corporate benefit, but in this case they also were a reasonable way of pursuing the founder's intent that the business continue as an employee-controlled corporation.

The court made something of a production out of its rejection of special fiduciary duties for close corporations. But does it matter? Under *Wilkes*, the majority could have shown a legitimate business purpose for what it did. ESOPs and key man insurance policies provide important benefits to the corporation. How could the minority have shown a less restrictive way of accomplishing these

---

[64] 626 A.2d 1366 (Del.1993).

purposes? Unless we read *Wilkes* to say that the minority has a right to liquidity, plaintiffs probably would have lost even under *Wilkes*.

As a practical matter, it thus is not clear that the Delaware and Massachusetts approaches are all that dissimilar. These cases typically involve situations in which the majority has benefited itself at the minority's expense. In almost all such cases, the majority shareholders are also directors or control the directors. Given the absence of a disinterested decisionmaker and the presence of the majority on both sides of the transaction, Delaware courts would apply the entire fairness standard to most of the cases litigated under the Massachusetts standard. Accordingly, while the doctrine differs, the results may not.

D. Lawyers and Freeze-Outs

Where counsel for the corporation also represents the controlling shareholder, a number of problems arise. First, the communications between the lawyer and the majority shareholder are not privileged. As such, the lawyer may be compelled to testify as to any such communications. Indeed, even before any litigation, the lawyers may have a duty to disclose to the minority shareholders their advice as to corporate matters rendered to the board of directors and/or the controlling shareholder.[65]

Second, a lawyer who represents both the corporation and its controlling shareholder may face personal liability. In *Granewich v. Harding*,[66] a minority shareholder of a close corporation complained that the majority was attempting to freeze him out by removing him as a director and terminating his employment. Counsel for the corporation allegedly assisted the majority shareholders' freeze-out campaign in a variety of ways, including providing legal advice to the majority and drafting fraudulent letters to the plaintiff. The trial court dismissed the case as to the lawyers on grounds that they owed no direct fiduciary duty to the minority shareholder and could not be held vicariously liable for any breach of fiduciary duty by the majority shareholder. The Oregon Supreme Court reversed, holding that lawyers can be held liable for aiding and abetting a breach of fiduciary duty owed by the majority to the minority shareholders. The complaint stated a claim on this basis in two respects. First, the plaintiff alleged that the lawyers themselves had committed tortious acts pursuant to an agreement with the majority shareholder the objectives of which contemplated a breach of the majority shareholder's fiduciary duties to the minority.

---

[65] Evans v. Blesi, 345 N.W.2d 775, 780–81 (Minn.Ct.App.1984).

[66] 985 P.2d 788 (Or.1999).

Second, the lawyers knowingly provided substantial assistance to the majority shareholder.

E.   Private Ordering of Fiduciary Obligation

Partnership and corporate law each provide what amounts to a standard form contract setting out the relationships among the various stakeholders in the organization. One can debate the extent to which the close corporation is a hybrid of the two and, if so, the extent to which such corporations should be subject to default terms closer to those of partnership law than to corporate law. What is not debatable is that one size does not fit all. Rules that work well for some investors will prove a straightjacket for others. The contractarian model contends, of course, that corporate law should consist mostly of defaults that the parties are free to modify as they see fit. Modern partnership law explicitly embraces this freedom of contract approach. UPA (1997) § 103(b)(3), for example, provides that a partnership agreement may not eliminate the duty of loyalty, but may "identify specific types or categories of activities that do not violate the duty of loyalty, if not manifestly unreasonable," or specify a mechanism for approving or ratifying transactions that "otherwise would violate the duty of loyalty." Do we stretch the partnership analogy too far when we urge that corporate law do likewise?

Suppose a businessman hired a key employee and, as part of the employment bargain, caused the corporation to issue stock to that newly hired employee. At the time of hiring, they also enter into a shareholder agreement under which if the employee should "cease to be an employee of the Corporation for any reason," the controlling shareholder has the right to buy the new employee's shares at a specified price. After several years, the controlling shareholder brings his two sons into the business and fires the employee. The businessman then claims his firing of the employee triggered the buyout provision of the shareholder agreement. The employee asserts that, as a shareholder, he has a "fiduciary-rooted protection against being fired." Does the contract trump the fiduciary duties of a controlling shareholder?

On these precise facts, the New York court of appeals, in *Ingle v. Glamore Motor Sales,* expressly rejected the Massachusetts approach: "No duty of loyalty and good faith akin to that between partners, precluding termination except for cause, arises among those operating a business in the corporate form who 'have only the rights, duties and obligations of stockholders' and not those of partners."[67] Despite his shareholder status, Ingle was still an

---

[67] 535 N.E.2d 1311 (N.Y.1989).

employee-at-will with no contractual guarantee of continued employment. When he was fired, he ceased to be an employee, and the divestiture of his shares followed as a logical matter by virtue of the shareholders agreement.

Because the court enforced the buyout provision, *Ingle* arguably stands for the proposition that you can contract around fiduciary duties.[68] Admittedly, *Ingle*'s facts differ from those of *Wilkes* in several respects. In *Wilkes* all the shareholders started out together and formed a new business, while in *Ingle* Glamore was the original owner who brought in Ingle as an employee. Put another way, employment followed from stockownership in *Wilkes*, while stockownership followed from employment in *Ingle*. The partnership analogy thus works a lot better for *Wilkes* than it does for *Ingle*. Yet, courts have not tried to make this sort of fine distinction. Distinguishing close from public corporations can be tricky enough, without adding further refinements to the mix.

Private ordering has also been validated in Massachusetts, albeit less emphatically. On the one hand, *Donahue* itself suggested that fiduciary obligation would not stand in the way of an otherwise valid shareholder agreement providing for, inter alia, a stock repurchase plan.[69] In *Blank v. Chelmsford Ob/Gyn*, the court interpreted this aspect of *Donahue* as standing for the proposition that "questions of good faith and loyalty with respect to rights on termination or stock purchase do not arise when all the stockholders in advance enter into agreements concerning termination of employment and for the purchase of stock of a withdrawing or deceased stockholder."[70] Accordingly, the plaintiff, a minority shareholder of an incorporated medical practice, who was terminated in accordance with the terms an employment agreement and whose shares were redeemed under the terms of a stock repurchase agreement, had no remedy. On the other hand, the Massachusetts courts also have held that the existence of an employment agreement or otherwise valid shareholder agreement does not divest shareholders of the *Donahue*-based fiduciary duty

---

[68] In Gallagher v. Lambert, 549 N.Y.S.2d 945 (1989), the New York court of appeals even more explicitly embraced that proposition. Observing that shareholder "agreements define the scope of the relevant fiduciary duty and supply certainty of obligation to each side," the court further opined that such agreements "should not be undone simply upon an allegation of unfairness." Id. at 947.

[69] Donahue v. Rodd Electrotype Co., 328 N.E.2d 505, 518 n. 24 (Mass.1975).

[70] Blank v. Chelmsford Ob/Gyn, P.C., 649 N.E.2d 1102, 1105 (Mass.1995). Similarly, in Merola v. Exergen Corp., 668 N.E.2d 351 (Mass.1996), the court denied a remedy to a 4.1 percent shareholder who allegedly had been terminated because of a personal conflict with the majority shareholder rather than for any legitimate corporate purpose. The court explained: "Not every discharge of an at-will employee of a close corporation who happens to own stock in the corporation gives rise to a successful breach of fiduciary duty claim. The plaintiff was terminated in accordance with his employment contract and fairly compensated for his stock." Id. at 355.

they owe to one another.[71] The precise degree to which parties have freedom of contract in Massachusetts thus remains somewhat uncertain. Both clarity and efficiency would be promoted if Massachusetts courts clearly held that contract trumps fiduciary obligation.

§ 14.4 Dissolution

As we have seen, close corporations entail significant agency costs, especially the risk of oppression of minority interests by majority shareholders. One way in which corporate law has sought to limit agency costs in this context is through imposition of fiduciary duties going well beyond those imposed in the public corporation context. This method, however, is far from satisfactory as a general solution to the problem. In the first instance, fiduciary duty cases necessarily involve relatively high costs of judicial enforcement. More importantly, it often may be very difficult to construct a remedy for breach of fiduciary duty. To what compensation is someone entitled when they are squeezed out of employment with the close corporation?

As an alternative to suit for breach of fiduciary duty, the disgruntled minority shareholder may seek judicial dissolution of the corporation.[72] All states have provisions under which a shareholder may seek an involuntary dissolution of the corporation.[73] If granted, dissolution leads to a winding up and liquidation of the firm, followed by a distribution of the firm's remaining assets to creditors and then to shareholders.

MBCA § 14.40 is typical of these statutes. It provides four grounds upon which a court may dissolve the corporation at a shareholder's request: (1) Deadlock among the directors. The directors must be evenly divided and therefore unable to make corporate decisions. The shareholders must be unable to resolve the deadlock. The deadlock must threaten irreparable injury to the corporation or prevent the business of the corporation from being

---

[71] See, e.g., King v. Driscoll, 638 N.E.2d 488 (Mass.1994).

[72] Various other grounds for dissolution are created by statute. A corporation that has not issued shares or commenced business may be dissolved by the incorporators or initial board of directors by filing articles of dissolution with the secretary of state. MBCA § 14.01. The board and shareholders may approve a voluntary dissolution. MBCA § 14.02. The secretary of state may commence an involuntary dissolution proceeding if the corporation, for example, fails to pay its franchise taxes. MBCA § 14.20. In this section, we focus solely on judicial proceedings for involuntary dissolution initiated by a shareholder.

[73] In most states dissolution is a matter of statute—there is no common law cause of action for dissolution of the firm. A few states, like New York, preserve a dissolution remedy available in equity. According to In re Kemp & Beatley, Inc., 473 N.E.2d 1173 (N.Y.1984), an equitable decree of dissolution is still available in New York when the directors have committed a palpable breach of the fiduciary duty for which there is no adequate remedy in law, such as a shareholder derivative suit for damages.

conducted to the advantage of the shareholders. Director deadlock seemingly will not justify a dissolution where the firm is still making a profit—it goes to situations in which the deadlock is preventing the firm from functioning at all. (2) Waste of corporate assets. (3) Deadlock among the shareholders. The shareholders must be evenly divided and, because of their division, unable to elect a board of directors for a period covering at least two annual meeting dates. (4) Dissolution is authorized where the directors or controlling shareholders have acted in a manner that is illegal, oppressive or fraudulent. The fourth basis has provided the most fertile ground for creative lawyering.

A. Dissolution on Grounds of Oppression and the Reasonable Expectations Standard

In *In re Kemp & Beatley*, the New York Court of Appeals defined oppression as conduct that substantially defeats a minority shareholder's reasonable expectations.[74] Reasonable expectations, in turn, are those that objectively viewed were reasonable under the circumstances, known (or should have been known) to the majority, and were central to the petitioner's decision to join the venture. Oppression thus is something more than mere disappointment, it must mean that the very reasons for participating have been defeated.

On the facts before it, the court concluded that the minority had in fact been oppressed. The firm in question had a long-standing policy of awarding de facto dividends in the form of bonuses based on stock ownership. This practice was a known incident of stock ownership. If you owned stock, you participated in firm management and were paid salary and profits in the form of bonuses. This policy was changed after the minority shareholders left the firm, so that bonuses were dependent on services rendered to the corporation. This change in policy was deemed an attempt to exclude the minority shareholders from gaining any return on their investment. Note the parallel to the fiduciary duty analysis in cases like *Wilkes v. Springside Nursing Home*.[75] Although *Wilkes* and *Kemp* involved different remedies, they shared an analytical assumption that shareholders of a close corporation can reasonably

---

[74] In re Kemp & Beatley, Inc., 473 N.E.2d 1173 (N.Y.1984). Similarly, in interpreting a North Carolina statute authorizing dissolution where it is "reasonably necessary" for the protection of the "rights or interests" of the complaining shareholder, the North Carolina supreme court held that those rights and interests include the "reasonable expectations" the complaining shareholder has in the corporation. "Only expectations embodied in understandings, express or implied, among the participants should be recognized by the court." Meiselman v. Meiselman, 307 S.E.2d 551, 563 (N.C.1983). But see Kiriakides v. Atlas Food Sys. & Serv., Inc., 541 S.E.2d 257, 264–66 (S.C.2001) (rejecting *Meiselman's* reasonable expectation approach in favor of an "elastic" and "fact-specific" approach to defining oppression).

[75] 353 N.E.2d 657 (Mass.1976).

expect to receive a return on their investment in the form of salary, bonuses, and retirement benefits. By denying these benefits, the majority defeated those reasonable expectations and opened itself to suit.

In *Mueller v. Cedar Shore Resort, Inc.*,[76] Al Mueller formed two corporations. All of his children initially participated in the family businesses. Son Paul Mueller, however, eventually left the business to attend law school. After graduating from law school, Paul repeatedly requested a formal position with the business but Al repeatedly refused. Instead, over time, Paul was informally involved in various aspects of the family business. After various family squabbles over the years, however, Al finally terminated Paul's "employment" with the business. Paul then sued, alleging oppression.

The South Dakota court first held that whether a shareholder has been oppressed is a question of law, which an appellate court reviews de novo. The court then held that although South Dakota's version of the Model Business Corporation Act permits equitable relief when a shareholder has been oppressed, the Act does not define the term "oppression." As a working definition of that term, the court adopted the reasonable expectations standard.

Mueller usefully clarifies many aspects of the reasonable expectations standard. First, the court makes clear that reasonable expectations can include "participation in management of corporate affairs." The reasonable expectations test, however, does not guarantee employment for all shareholders. The minority's expectation of employment must be balanced against the board of directors "ability to exercise its business judgment and runs its business efficiently." Indeed, the court indicated that a form of the business judgment rule insulates director decisions even in this context. Consequently, neither the denial nor the termination of employment was in and of itself an act of oppression.[77] Finally, the court held that the reasonable expectations standard applies only where the shareholder in question actually invested in the firm. Where the shareholder received his shares by gift or inheritance, a lower standard applies under which the controlling shareholders need only behave decently towards the minority. Or, as a similar New York decision put it: "Even if an original participant had had a reasonable expectation of personal employment, after his death the

---

[76] 643 N.W.2d 56 (S.D.2002).

[77] In employment-at-will states, even a wrongful termination of employment is not deemed oppressive standing alone. Mueller v. Cedar Shore Resort, Inc., 643 N.W.2d 56, 65 (S.D.2002); Willis v. Bydalek, 997 S.W.2d 798, 802–03 (Tex.App.1999).

surviving shareholders would not be bound to employ any dolt who happened to inherit his stock."[78]

From a transactional planning perspective, these decisions drive home the absolute necessity of ex ante contracting. Absent an explicit employment contract, a shareholders expectation of continued employment likely will not be deemed "objectively reasonable."[79] Absent an explicit buyout agreement, a shareholder may be denied both dissolution and a return on his investment. The well-counseled client thus will enter a close corporation with both an express contract of employment with provisions sharply limiting the firm's ability to discharge the client, such as by limiting discharge to termination for cause, and a buyout agreement providing reasonable grounds for exit.

B. Buyout in Lieu of Dissolution

Dissolution is an extreme remedy. Many firms will be worth more as going concerns than if they were split up and sold off in pieces. This fact counsels against granting dissolution, which would lower the value of the firm to everyone—both the complaining shareholder and the defendants. In recognition of that fact, MBCA § 14.34 grants the noncomplaining shareholders the right to buyout the complaining shareholders in lieu of dissolution. If the parties are unable to agree on a price, the court will determine the fair value of the shares.[80] The share repurchase option effectively creates a market out for the complaining shareholders by coercing the majority into buying the minority's shares, while also preserving the going concern value of the firm.

In *Alaska Plastics v. Coppock*, the Alaska supreme court concluded that judges have equitable discretion to order a stock buyback in lieu of dissolution even in the absence of express statutory authorization.[81] Three investors originally owned Alaska

---

[78] Gimpel v. Bolstein, 477 N.Y.S.2d 1014, 1019 n.6 (Sup.Ct.1984).

[79] Willis v. Bydalek, 997 S.W.2d 798, 803 (Tex.App.1999).

[80] See, e.g., Brown v. Allied Corrugated Box Co., 154 Cal.Rptr. 170 (Cal.App.1979); In re Gift Pax, Inc., 475 N.Y.S.2d 324 (Sup.Ct.1984), aff'd, 486 N.Y.S.2d 272 (App.Div.1985); Charland v. Country View Golf Club, Inc., 588 A.2d 609 (R.I.1991). In Trahan v. Trahan, 120 Cal.Rptr.2d 814 (Cal.App.2002), the court explained that the objective of the statutory appraisal process in connection with a suit seeking a buyout in lieu of dissolution is to determine the fair value of the shares of the parties seeking dissolution. Fair value in this context is measured by the liquidation value the movants would have received if their dissolution action been allowed to proceed to a successful conclusion. The court further held that the movants were not entitled to have estimated future profits from corporation's existing but uncompleted contracts to provide services included in the valuation, as a result of which the movants ended up with a negative valuation.

[81] 621 P.2d 270 (Alaska 1980). Other courts have concluded that they have equitable power to order an even broader range of alternative remedies, such as compelling the board to declare dividends. See, e.g., In re Kemp & Beatley, Inc., 473 N.E.2d 1173 (N.Y.1984); Baker v. Commercial Body Builders, Inc., 507 P.2d 387 (Or.1973).

Plastics, but one transferred half of his shares (or a 1/6 interest in the firm) to his ex-wife (Muir) in a divorce settlement. The three original owners paid themselves directors' fees, but paid no dividends. Muir eventually sued, alleging various causes of action. The lower court ordered Alaska Plastics to buy Muir's shares at their fair value.

The supreme court reversed and remanded. Alaska corporate law permits shareholders to sue for dissolution and, if a plaintiff meets the requirements for dissolution, Alaska courts have equitable power to order such a buyback in lieu of dissolution. To obtain a decree of dissolution in the first place, however, the plaintiff-shareholder must show oppression or fraud. Because the lower court made no finding of oppression, the supreme court sent the case back for further proceedings.

On remand, Muir prevailed, which seems surprising. To be sure, the directors arguably breached their fiduciary duties to Muir by paying themselves fees, while denying any return to Muir.[82] Her ex-husband, Crowe, moreover, only owned one-sixth of the shares, but received the same "dividend" as the other majority shareholders, who each owned one-third. The majority, moreover, offered her an unacceptable price for her shares. The majority also failed to notify Muir of shareholder meetings. But does all that amount to oppression? What reasonable expectations of Muir, known to and accepted by the majority, had been substantially frustrated? Muir could have sued derivatively to recover the fees improperly paid the majority. Alternatively, she could have sued directly for her share of the de facto dividends. She could have sued her divorce lawyer for getting her into this mess in the first place. It is hard to see how she was oppressed, however, at least under the reasonable expectations standard.

The best way to solve a freeze-out is to avoid it from the start, by negotiating a buyout agreement with the majority shareholders or the corporation. Not all shareholders are so farsighted, however, and when shareholders have negotiated no such agreement, freeze-outs become even less tractable than usual. In such cases, the parties may use corporate dissolution statutes as low-budget alternatives to the buyout agreements they should have negotiated but did not. All of which leads to the interesting question of

---

[82] Embracing the Massachusetts approach as set out in Donahue v. Rodd Electrotype Co., 328 N.E.2d 505 (Mass.1975), the Alaska supreme court indicated that the payment of directors fees and other benefits to the shareholders other than Muir violated her right to "equal treatment." If the other shareholders received disguised dividends (e.g., directors' fees), Muir should receive them as well. Because the other shareholders did not have the right to sell their stock to the firm, however, equal treatment does not require the firm to buy Muir's stock. Alaska Plastics, Inc. v. Coppock, 621 P.2d 270, 276–77 (Alaska 1980).

whether it was appropriate for the Alaska supreme court to create a buyback remedy when the statute didn't provide one?

Serious questions of institutional competence are raised when court engage in interstitial lawmaking of the sort exemplified by Alaska Plastics, but those issues lie far outside our field of inquiry. Instead, our attention must turn to more pragmatic matters. One could argue, for example, that a buyout order is unnecessary given the practical effect of a decree of dissolution. Where dissolution would destroy the firm's going-concern value, the majority likely will prefer to prevent dissolution. The dissolution remedy thus has the virtue of forcing the majority to bargain with the frozen-in minority. Indeed, one would expect the majority to offer to buy the minority's stock—and, according to the leading empirical study, that is exactly what happens.[83]

One might also object to *Alaska Plastics* on the ground that ordering a buyout in lieu of dissolution really is no less drastic than dissolution. The virtue of such an order is that it settles the dispute quickly and forever. Yet, it also has draconian result. By virtue of arguably minor transgressions, the majority was forced to buy out Muir.

A third objection is that liberal dissolution rights allow minority shareholders to hold up the firm or the other shareholders. Because few firms ordinarily hold large amounts of liquid assets, the threat of filing a dissolution proceeding is often powerful. In effect, liberal dissolution coupled with a buyout order in lieu of dissolution gives a powerful gun for minority shareholders to hold to the head of the majority. There is some substantial risk that the minority will use that power to extract a nonpro rata share of corporate benefits.

The latter objection to *Alaska Plastics* leads to the broader question of whether courts and legislatures should create an even more liberal dissolution regime than currently exists, thereby allowing minority shareholders even greater freedom to dissolve the firm over the majority's opposition.[84] A recurrent theme of this text is that firms are essentially contractual in nature. A key insight flowing from our contractarian approach, which we have seen on many occasions, is that the corporation statutes are analogous to off the rack rules or, put another way, standard form contracts that the parties are largely free to adopt or modify as they see fit. As with

---

[83] J.A.C. Hetherington & Michael P. Dooley, Illiquidity and Exploitation: A Proposed Statutory Solution to the Remaining Close Corporation Problem, 63 Va. L. Rev. 1 (1977).

[84] See, e.g., Meiselman v. Meiselman, 307 S.E.2d 551, 560 (N.C.1983) (noting a "trend toward enactment of more liberal grounds under which dissolution will be granted to a complaining shareholder").

any standard form contract, corporate statutes thus serve to reduce bargaining costs.

As we have seen, courts should avoid interpreting the corporation statute in ways that make it more closely resemble the partnership statute and vice-versa. Preserving clear-cut choices between the various standard form contracts by preserving sharply delineated differences between their rules usually should lower bargaining costs. Partnership law provides very liberal dissolution rights.[85] A liberal approach to dissolution is appropriate for the typical partnership—a small firm in which all of the owners have roughly equal economic stakes and are actively involved in firm management on a more or less equal basis. Personal conflict will be highly disruptive to such a firm. At the very least, such conflict adversely affects decisionmaking by interfering with the consensus-building process. At worst, it can have devastating economic consequences, as when the conflict becomes public and drives away customers (as happens all too frequently, especially in service businesses). Consequently, rational partners will prefer liquidity to stability. In hypothetical bargain terminology, liberal dissolution rules will emerge as the majoritarian default because they create de facto liquidity.

In contrast, corporation law is designed for large firms with many owners. Corporation law rests on an assumption that ownership is separated from control and, moreover, that ownership will be essentially passive. Interpersonal relations between the firm's owners are thus irrelevant to the economic viability of the firm, which is a key factor distinguishing the corporation from the partnership, and a strong argument against allowing shareholders to force a dissolution of the corporation. We therefore expect that corporation law would make dissolution considerably more difficult than does partnership law. Consistent with that prediction, MBCA § 14.30 leaves shareholders of a public corporation essentially powerless to dissolve it.

The standard form contracts thus seem well-designed for the firms for which they were designed. But what about the hybrid close corporation? Is this an instance in which we ought to treat the close corporation as an "incorporated partnership" and therefore provide liberal partnership-like dissolution rights? Like partners, investors in close corporations may prefer liquidity to stability, but the standard form contract gives them stability rather than liquidity.

---

[85] Indeed, unless the parties have expressly or implicitly agreed on a definite term for the enterprise, partnerships exist "at will" and may be dissolved without cause at any time. See, e.g., Page v. Page, 359 P.2d 41 (Cal.1961).

There are at least three reasons to reject the argument for liberal dissolution rights, two of which have already been noted. First, liberal dissolution rights allow the minority to hold up the majority and, as such, may frustrate the majority's reasonable expectations. Second, parties who want liberal dissolution rights may bargain for them by insisting on an appropriate buyout agreement before investing. As to close corporations, the default rules of corporate law operate as a penalty default encouraging parties to bargain, while preserving the desirable distinction between partnership and corporation law.

The remaining reason for denying liberal partnership-like dissolution rights in the close corporation context is that such rights will create a significant negative externality. An important function of organization law is to provide affirmative asset partitioning, which refers to the principle that creditors of the firm have prior access to firm assets vis-à-vis both the firm's equity investors and the personal creditors of such investors.[86] Affirmative asset partitioning thus allows the firm to create a pool of assets that serves as a bond for all the firm's contracts. Protecting the firm's going concern value is another significant benefit of affirmative asset partitioning. Creditors of a corporation (close or public) make lending decisions mainly on financial factors such as net assets and cash flows. By virtue of affirmative asset partitioning, creditors of a corporation need not be concerned with such other considerations as the interpersonal relations among equity investors.[87] Under a regime of liberal dissolution rights, however, creditors of the corporation may find the corporation dissolving unexpectedly due to a relatively trivial falling out among the equity investors. Liberal dissolution rights thus undercut the benefits of affirmative asset partitioning, disadvantaging creditors of the corporation, requiring them to monitor factors as to which they lack a comparative advantage, increasing creditor costs, and thus raising the cost of capital.

---

[86] Henry Hansmann & Reinier Kraakman, The Essential Role of Organization Law, 110 Yale L.J. 387 (2000).

[87] Without this protection, the creditors of a bankrupt minority shareholder could force the inefficient liquidation of a firm in order recoup the value of the minority shareholder's ownership in the firm. With the protection provided by affirmative asset partitioning, however, creditors are only able to claim the same rights as the minority shareholder held pre-bankruptcy.

TABLE OF CASES

523

INDEX

535